HISTORY
AND
MYSTERY

THE COMPLETE ESCHATOLOGICAL ENCYCLOPEDIA
OF PROPHECY, APOCALYPTICISM, MYTHOS,
AND WORLDWIDE DYNAMIC THEOLOGY

(REVISED AND EXPANDED EDITION)

VOLUME 4

BERNIE L. CALAWAY

The following is used by permission of the copywriter with appreciation:

Selected titles for the praise sections of Revelation from *Songs of Heaven* by Dr. Robert E. Coleman, published by Fleming H. Revel Co.

A reproduction of "Contrasts Between the Rapture and the Second Coming" from *A Bible Handbook to Revelation* by Mal Couch, published by Kregel Publications.

All Scripture quotations in this publication, unless otherwise identified, are from the Holy Bible, New International Version. Copyright 1973, 1978, 1984, International Bible Society and the Zondervan Corporation.

All prophetic term definitions and explanations of prophetic issues are solely the responsibility of the author and not intended to slight or disparage any other approach.

ISBN: 978-1-64314-637-9 (Paperback)

AuthorsPress
California, USA
www.authorspress.com

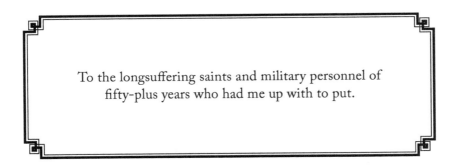

To the longsuffering saints and military personnel of fifty-plus years who had me up with to put.

FOREWORD TO THE ESSAYS AND ENCYCLOPEDIA

ARE YOU AWARE THAT the major task of a prophet is *not* to predict stuff? Has your neighbor used the term "eschaton" and left you puzzled? Having trouble with the details of those multi-horned monsters in the book of Revelation? Don't know how to properly use an athame?

Fret not. The *History and Mystery: The Complete Eschatological Encyclopedia of Prophecy, Apocalypticism, Mythos, and Worldwide Dynamic Theology* has arrived to help you out. And here it is, edited and expanded for another try for illumination. Few of us have the leisure of thumbing through thick Bible dictionaries or clicking on twenty websites, only to find there are no definitions that differentiate the apocalyptic from the eschatological material. (Uh, what *is* apocalyptic and eschatological substance anyway?) Even with that marvel of media, *Wikipedia*, we may end up trying the chase the devil around and around a round-trimmed bush. Nor is it convenient to stop a study here and there along the way wondering what exactly one is reading. To push the idea a bit more, an attempt has been made to introduce Bible names and terms that not only pertain directly or exclusively to prophecy and eschatology but also history, science, the mystery religions, ecclesiology, philosophy, ethics, religious aberrations and cults, anthropology, pagan or foreign religions and many other disciplines. The word reviews are as thorough as possible but back away from tedious. Or, as one reviewer put it, "These aren't definitions; they're explanations." A person can actually *understand* them.

The encyclopedia you plunked down good money for is unique. The first segment of the multi-volume set is a series of some sixty essays relating to prophetic or theological topics that may be a bit "difficult" or begging for a fuller explanation. The information provides a good base from which to start the search for information and understanding and is therefore placed in front. Next door to the explanations come the definitions themselves. Prophetic or esoteric words and phrases are identified and defined. Here is everything from Aaron to Zwingli. But still, more is needed since the interpretation of such a complex subject must delve into myth, religious history, and worldwide concepts of beliefs that are required for a comprehensive perspective. You will find terms not readily available in most standard Bible dictionaries or encyclopedias, either conveniently online or in print.

Surely, there are risks when a solitary person (*i.e.,* without resources from specialized researchers, editors, brains, etc.) attempts to compile a glossary. The words must be carefully chosen and neither too detailed nor too generalized. Edgar Allen Poe once effused: "A definition is that which so describes its object as to distinguish it from all others." By contrast, the philosopher F.C.S. Schiller said, "All words cannot be defined." Somewhere within this annoying juxtaposition somebody has to try for the practical. Within the hubris of theology versus mysticism, that task is even more daunting. All words and every nuance of definition are not included—that's an impossible task. If the subject is too vast to be reasonably explored, only the most common references are listed. But the important terms are present, at least all those I could think up or look up. Biblical and historical figures have been selectively chosen with more expansion in the essays. Both the expositions and the dictionary carry a Christian, perhaps even an evangelical, bias that seems logical and consistent to the purpose of the research and interest to most readers.

Still, the questions keep piling up. What does a kiss have to do with apocalyptic judgment? How did the Moabites help form Hebrew and Christian eschatology? How does Roman Catholic end time doctrine line up with the Baptists? or a Hindu? Why do Branch Davidian types and Islamic terrorists seek suicide in apocalyptic fervor but the general public lends it scant attention? How can a lamb be ferocious and a wolf be a pacifist? Why did the Vikings see the world ending in violence but the ancient pharaohs only heard a gentle whimper? How is magic different from foreordination? And who cares? To hear the Almighty, do we need a God helmet or a prophet's mantle? My Social Security number has three sixes in it. Should I upgrade? Am I a universalist or a pre-millennialist? Who started the odd Quaker apocalyptic movement? Was the wizard Merlin a better prophet than Robin Goodfellow? How come the Mayans got it wrong? Is the UN about ready to tax your unleaded gasoline and your diet sodas? How are prophecies are related to miracles? Puzzles like that can slow your metabolism and keep you up all night.

Nobody knows all the answers, and even fewer of the questions, but we can learn something. Certainly, it's a great help to have a dictionary at hand. As a tip to the user, bear in mind that different translations of the Scripture and other sources may employ alternate words for the same subject. In most cases, the New International Version is the preferred Bible translation used here with scholarly essay for the remaining supply. If that doesn't work, I am confident you're smart enough to find another approach to the solution. Be a valiant, intrepid investigator.

This lexicon edition hits church history (mostly American) and the human condition (both ancient and modern) with more than a gentle tap. Those features are intentional because our living faith today (and certainly beyond today) is the lasting bequeathal of the prophetic thrust. All is not done. Everything relates. Even the pagan and the modernist feed off each other sometimes. Those high-octane technical words are also important because they're the language of the theologians. The extended "*See also*" sections following most of the definitions are sure to aid in further study if desired, as will the consulting bibliography at the end. Also, don't forget to use the "history and mystery of..." section of the lexicon for a sort of mini-index to related or linked subject matter. And you will need assistance to facilitate your research, being aware that aside from the Scripture, world culture and local usage also show multiple terms that may be identical or may differ from our common understanding. Or there may be several meanings. Despite what may be a violation of accepted dictionary alphabetizing, any "s" within parentheses to indicate the plural is ignored when arranging alphabetically. As to all those words that think they should be capitalized—who knows? Most major characters of the Old and New Testaments are identified to enhance clarity and give the "human" touch. Only the most prophetically, historically, and theologically pertinent titles and terms are cited in the encyclopedia, lest the texts become unwieldy. Even so, there are around 10,000 entries throughout the volumes in an effort to be comprehensive. In all charity, however, everything cannot be named. Religion and myth through the ages hold more aspects of every inanimate object and living creature than the human brain can even begin to imagine.

A word of caution may be in order next. Some may feel offended that certain individuals, groups, or institutions are classed within the textbook as "cults," false prophets, or some other seemingly maligned description. If such there be, I see no remedy for it. The work is, after all, written in the Judeo-Christian perspective and that which is deemed outside the lines of that boundary can only be; it is what it is. Certainly, there is no subtle pleasure or ulterior motive associated with the treatment of any term defined or explained. Remember, Christianity itself is (and always has been) hardly immune to negative labeling, worthy of it or not and true or not. Striving for artificial political correctness would inevitably drive both dictionary and essay into the ditch of mediocrity.

One more caveat needs careful explanation. The reader will hardly fail to notice the prominence of dispensational and premillennial theology in both the expositions and the dictionary. The predominance of those themes is almost inevitable. Furthermore, knowledge dealing with dispensationalism and premillennialism is the most complex and detailed structure of modern eschatology and apocalyptic writing whereas other viewpoints are relatively straightforward. According to non-dispensational theories, all apocalyptic description in the Bible is either: (1) symbolic or metaphorical—almost never literal, (2) such language and the apocalyptic style of writing were common in the first century and in post-Babylonian Judaism but is practically unfathomable today, (3) various Bible renditions have mistranslated some of the text, which can therefore, be manipulated according to a favorite interpretation, (4) apocalyptic language, and its sister non-literal genre (poetry), must always be taken in as romantic or esoteric writing—never historically, (5) all apocalyptic scenes and descriptions are whole within themselves and bear little or no relation to similar paradigms, (6) details of dispensational eschatology are being foisted upon the uniformed and youthful generation who are incapable of full comprehension and should thereby be subject to vilification or, at least, refutation, (7) the Bible does not discuss the end of the age anywhere at any time. Any one of the assumptions mentioned can easily "explain" eschatology in such a context for it refers only to a theology of symbolic hope and steadfast perseverance in times of trouble. That essentially makes eschatology practically irrelevant to our times, except in its last remaining function as an encourager to the believer. Premillennial and dispensational thinking, however, requires far more investigation and explanation to expound the doctrine fairly. So then, the emphasis in the word list exceeds the simple "comfort and hope" purposes for the future and develops, not necessarily from the author's hermeneutics, but from sheer necessity.

Finally, (sigh mournfully) something you need may have been omitted, or maybe an error is made somewhere. I regret that (really) but am not to be surprised by it. I'm nearly human so mistakes will crop up. So then, accept my humble apologies beforehand. Kindly try to remember the writing is from the perspective of biblical scholarship, not stupefying theology.

Here's hoping that what is presented will be interesting and helpful. If that happens, I'm one happy old writer dude.

Bernie L. Calaway
Myrtle Beach, SC

CONTENTS

Foreword to the Essays and Encyclopedia v

Encyclopedia of Eschatological and Mystical Terminology

"Q"—quyit..1-12

Ra—Rutherford, Joseph Franklin 13-117

Sabaeanism—Syzygus...118-389

"tabernacle (dwelling) of God is among men, the"—
    Tzotzil religion 390-532

UAP—Uzziah..533-556

Vacation Bible School—vultures to a carcass 558-594

wafer—Wye River Agreement 595-670

Xavier, Francis—xystus 671-673

Yahud—Yule 674-684

Zabur—Zwingli, Ulrich (Huldrych)...........................685-711

Bibliography...713

Encyclopedia of Eschatological
and Mystical Terminology

Q

"Q": the letter Q (taken from the German *Quelle*, meaning "source"), which is often applied in biblical studies to an unrecovered document (and certain oral traditions) said to comprise some of the sayings of Jesus. The material is supposedly the main repository for parts of some or all of the Gospels, especially Mark. *See also* Agrapha; Gospel(s); "L"; *logia;* "M"; Mark as New Testament Gospel; oral tradition; source criticism; unwritten prophecies.

Qabbala: sometimes appearing as Cabala or Kabbalah with numerous alternate spellings. Some call the interpretive process with the rather unsophisticated term "letterism." Qabbala is a method of scriptural interpretation used by some ancient rabbis. At times, the practice even approaches reverence for the procedure itself. Cabala literally means "receiving," as from inspiration. The process is a mystical idea centered on the belief that there are relationships between numbers and words of the same numerical value. Many post-Ezra rabbis believed that the whole of the Torah was delivered to Moses in detail on Mount Sinai, including the verses, words, letters, vowel points, and accents. Therefore, the very words and letters of the Law must hold some magical portent. Some even announced that God Himself spends three hours a day studying the Law. Perhaps none popularized the method more than the Qabbalist known as "Cheiro" (1866–1936). References to medieval mysticism, pseudoscience, and certain coded texts from the 13th century (such as the *Zohar*) are common techniques in the Qabbalist approach. Systematic beliefs are by no means uniform, but some tenets are generally recognized: 1. the process encompasses the complete likeness of the Creator, and such a gift may someday be manifested in the Messiah, 2. the physical world is illusion, 3. the human soul and Creator are already united, but the soul does not recognize its exalted state, 4. only the Creator gives and only the man receives, 5. recruitment to the movement is important and usually accomplished by peer pressure—it must be pushed on the world as a new system of education using mainly women and children to advance the cause since they are said to be the most susceptible to the process, 6. the world will someday be a united and peaceful community, 7. Qabbalism is the inner core of the Torah, and 8. outward demonstrated acts of religion are secondary to deep spiritual enlightenment. The practice is highly esoteric and metaphysical, often using various acrostic techniques. Despite its complex and detailed language, the main idea of Qabbalistic teaching seems to be that God is seeking to heal the universe by collecting the divine fragments of heavenly light now scattered and to present them back to God. In this way, the hidden radiance of goodness can become visible to us. Kabbalism, then, is not a religion nor an organization but a system of thought linked to esoteric Jewish theosophy, science, and mysticism. Parts of the philosophy may be studied logically or allegorically by the use of four major texts: the Bible (particularly the Old Testament), the Book of Creation (*Sepher Yetzidrah*), the Book of Splendor (*Sepher ha Zohar*), and the Apocalypse (the book of Revelation). See *also* Aggadah; Aqiba, Rabbi Joseph ben; Atbash; Berg, Philip; Bible Code; *B'nai Noach;* Cheiro; *Corpus Hermecticum;* cosmic exile; de Leon, Moses; 888; eleven; emanations, doctrine of; 'Emeth; enneagram; Falk, Hayyim Samuel Jacob; *gematria;* Gnosticism, Gnostic(s); Halakha; Husk(s); *isopseplia;* Judaism; Kaduri, Rabbi Yitzchak; logoprosodic analysis; Luria, Isaac; Masseket Hekalot; Mathers table; Merkabah mysticism; metaphysics; *mitzvot;* mystical; mystical interpretation; mysticism, mystics; Newton, Sir Isaac; Noor, noor; *notarikon;* numbers, symbology of; Pardes; primal light; Revelation as New Testament prophecy; *Sefirot;* Sephiroth; Sephirotic Tree; seventy-two; Shemhamforesh; *temoorah;* Zevi, Shabbatai; *Zohar.*

Qabbalistic method. See *gematria;* Qabbala.

Qadesh. See Qetesh.

qere. See kere.

Q'ero Inca. See Inca.

Qetesh: Qadesh or (Kadesh) a Syrian goddess of sacred love and ritual sex, later imported to ancient Egypt who seemed to be the female equivalent of Hathor. The name is used in the Old Testament for a temple prostitute, and some towns and villages employed part of the word to identify their locale and worship preference. *See also* Egyptian pantheon; Levant pantheon; Syria.

qi: or *ch'i,* the vital force of any living entity, according to traditional Chinese folklore. Certain qigong exercises are said to rebuild or rebalance *qi* through controlled movement. *See also Ka;* qigong; soul(s); spirit; *zoe.*

qigong: various synchronized movements and breathing exercises as practiced in China intended to develop meditation and healing. The techniques had been incorporated into the philosophies of Daoism, Confucianism, and Buddhism in their respective countries for many years. A strong advocate and promoter of the program names Li Hongzhi, founder of the Falun Dafa movement in the early 1990s. The Chinese government then declared the practice as heretical whereas before it had supported the process. *See also* Falun Gong; *qi.*

Qoheleth: Hebrew word for "the teacher" or "leader of the assembly" (Ecc. 1:1–2; 12:8–10) who claims to have composed the book of Ecclesiastes. The writer, or "preacher," claims to be the wealthy and wise son of David whom historians almost always name as Solomon. *See also* Ecclesiastes; Jew(s); rabbi; Solomon.

Quadragesima: Latin for "the fortieth," designating the forty days of Lent before Easter. *See also* Jew(s); liturgical year; liturgy, Christian; Quinquagesima; Roman Catholic Church: Sexagesima.

Quadratus: the first known Christian apologist (venerated in both the Eastern and Roman churches), part of an influential intellectual movement beginning in the second century. The purpose of the connection was to promote Christianity and defend the faith against pagan and Jewish criticisms. Eusebius claimed that Quadratus was a disciple of the apostles and that he argued the faith to the Emperor Hadrian in A.D. 125–126. *See also* Eastern Orthodox Church.

Quad scripsi, scripsi: the response of Pontius Pilate when asked by the Jewish leaders to change the plaque over the cross of Jesus. The titulus as approved by the governor read: "Jesus of Nazareth, king of the Jews." The Jewish authorities desired it be changed to read: "this man *claimed* to be king of the Jews." Pilate, likely offended that the Jewish influentials had manipulated him into declaring Jesus' guilt, refused their request and responded with: "What I have written, I have written." *See also* INRI; Pilate, Pontius; titulus.

Quakers. See Society of Friends.

qualia: subjective perception derived from the study of consciousness. It is impossible to objectively measure subjective perception but perhaps something beyond our understanding can be experienced as we contemplate imponderable questions like "how do we perceive the color blue?" or "why does the scent of lavender differ from bergamot?" or "what compels us to feel transported by a snowy field?" A more or less scientific definition of qualia has been put forth as "the transformation of an objective cerebral computation to a subjective experience." Somehow the brain must imbue certain bits of auditory, visual, and olfactory information with emotional meaning. Surely the concept has religious components not fully studied nor contemplated.

qualified universalism. See biblical universalism.

Quantum Entanglement: or sub-atomic consciousness, a theory from theoretical physics that humans do indeed have souls but, according to the concept, that essence may be living sub-atomic elements like atoms, protons, electrons, neutrons, and assorted matter. Sir Roger Penrose, an experimental physicist of Oxford University, has stated that "consciousness may be a function of the universe." The physicist meant that the universe is a thinking being and conscious of its own existence. He also implies that that comic make-up is God Himself. As such, those particle elements contain all the information about us as individuals and do not die when our bodies do, but exist in space until the universe burns itself out trillions of years from now. Our consciousness, then, continues after death and that essence may constitute our very souls.

quantum theory: a.k.a. quantum physics or quantum mechanics, a branch of physics dealing with the actions of the dual "particle-like" and "wave-like" interactions of energy and matter. The mathematical properties of quantum mechanics are complex and abstract but may eventually more fully reveal the physical properties of the atomic particle. The theory inevitably enters into play when discussing creation and evolution. *See also* big bang theory; creationism; evolution; God particle, the; Large Hadron Collider (LHC).

Quarmatians: a sect labeled "those who write in small letters" or "greengrocers" because they are strict vegetarians. Quarmatians are a syncretic branch of Islam, combining elements of Shi'ite and Persian mysticism. Their history tells of rebellion against the Abbasid Caliphate, even to the point of desecrating the holy shrines at Mecca. *See also* Abbasid Caliphate; Alawites; Druze; Islam; Ismailis; sect(s).

quarterly: a printed Sunday school lesson guide used in many Protestant educational programs. The name derives from the adverb "quarterly" (an interval of three months) since the periodicals are normally printed and distributed during that time frame. *See also* religious education; Sunday school(s).

Quartodecimans. See Paschal controversy.

Quartus: a Christian from Corinth who forwarded greetings in Paul's letter to the Roman church (Rom. 16:23).

Quashee: a West Indian black demon who, with proper motivation, bestows certain magical powers on the loogaroos (people, usually elderly women). To earn the gifts, the desirous must render him a quantity of rich warm blood. This is accomplished by shedding one's skin before the occultic silk-cotton tree (*bombax ceiba*), also called the Devil tree or Jumbie tree. The skin must be carefully folded and hidden. After, the devotees are free to fly off in a ball of light to collect the ransom. *See also* demon(s), demonic; mythological beasties, elementals, monsters, and spirit animals.

***Quds* Day:** the last day of Ramadan on the Islamic calendar, a date commonly known for violence against the United States and Israel by Muslim agitators. *See also* Islam; Ramadan; terrorism; terrorist(s).

Queen: a ruling title or specified consort of a king (normally capitalized when preceded by a personal name). The term is not used in Scripture to refer to God (as is King) but can name a pagan female deity or secular ruler. *See also* divine right of kings; King; king(s); King, a; queen(s); queen of heaven; Religious Babylon.

queen(s): usually the wife or consort of a king, or a female ruler in her own status. Apocalyptic language often speaks derogatorily of the position if a symbol of evil is needed (*i.e.*, "the queen of heaven," Queen Jezebel, the whore of Babylon, or other evil females of influence). Athaliah was the wicked queen of Judah. Revelation 18:7 uses the title "queen" in a metaphorical sense to refer to Babylon the Great, the mother of harlots. In other instances, as with Queen Esther, the title is favorable. *See also* Alexandra; Anne, Queen de la Palude; Ashtaroth, Ashtoreth(s); Athaliah; Bathsheba; Belkis; Bernice; Candace; Cassiopeia; Cleopatra of Egypt; Cleopatra of Syria; crown(s); Cush, Cushites; David's wives; Demeter; divine right of kings; Elizabeth I, Queen; Esther as Hebrew heroine; Eriskegal; Glaphyra; Great Prostitute, the; Hamutal; Hecate; Helena; Hera; Herodias; Irene; Jezebel; Kamehameha King, and Emma; King; king(s); king, a; Lamia; Louis VII, King and Queen Eleanor; Makeda; Mary, Queen of Scots; Morrigan; Mystery Babylon the Great the Mother of Prostitutes and Abominations of the Earth; Nitocris; Nubia; Queen; queen of heaven; Queen of Sheba; Queen of the South; Religious Babylon; Semiramis; Sheba; throne(s); Vashti, Queen; whore of Babylon; William and Mary.

Queen James Bible: a tampered Bible rendition (printed 2012) that reinterprets certain passages to make them appear more appealing to homosexual practices. The justification offered was that the edition was to prevent misinterpretations of gay persons and their lifestyles. *See also* Bible translations; LGBTQ.

queen of heaven: 1. a pagan goddess also known as Astarte or Ishtar. She was still being worshiped in Judah, mostly by women, just before the nation's fall to the Babylonians. The idolaters insisted that all was well with those who worshiped the queen of heaven, assuredly a false assumption. She seems to be the model for much of apocalyptic language when female personalities represent evil (*viz.*, Religious Babylon of Revelation 17). The title may also refer to Sumerimus, the queen of Bab-el and mother of Tammuz who helped establish the deeply pagan and occult worship centered in the tower of Babel. 2. sometimes the bright woman of Revelation 12 (representing Israel) is named "the queen of heaven" but that designation is perhaps not the best description. 3. Some view Roman Catholicism's veneration and elevation of

Mary, called the *Regina Coeli*, to be a throwback to the ancient worship of the queen of heaven (Jer. 7:18; 44:17–19, 25). There her cult was made up mostly of fallen Jewish women. The Roman pope, however, has declared that the woman in Revelation 12 is Mary the mother of Jesus. *See also* Ashtoreth(s), Ashtaroth; Bab-el; Babel, tower of; co-redemptrix; Ishtar; Levant pantheon; Marianist; Mariolatry; Mary; Mary Mother of God, Feast of; Nimrod-bar-Cush; Our Lady of the Angels; Queen; queen(s); Roman Catholic Church; Second Eve, the; Semiramis; Sumerian and Babylonian pantheon; Tammuz.

Queen of Sheba: a ruler, possibly from southern Arabia, who came to Jerusalem with rich gifts to meet King Solomon. She desired to experience firsthand his renowned wisdom and fabulous wealth and realistically to probably negotiate a trade agreement (1 Ki. 10:1–13). Christ referred to her as "the Queen of the South" (Mt. 12:42). The Ethiopian Church claims that her name was Makeda, that she and Solomon had a son named Menelik, and that the ark of the covenant made its way to Ethiopia through them. According to the legend, the ark now resides in the church of Maryam Seyon (Mary of Zion) in Aksum. Which country is represented by Sheba, Ethiopia or Arabia, has not been satisfactorily resolved. The point of origin may very well have been Yemen. *See also* Arabia; ark of the covenant; Belkis; Cush, Cushites; Falasha Jews; Haile Selassie; *Kebra Nagast;* Makeda; Menelik, Prince; Nubia; Queen; queen(s); Queen of the South; Sheba; Solomon.

Queen of the South: probably the Queen of Sheba. Jesus declared (Lk. 11:31–32) that someday she will rise up to condemn the generation of Jesus' time because her reverence for the wisdom of Solomon counted for more than the Jewish disregard for the Lord at the time. *See also* Belkis; Cush, Cushites; Makeda; Nubia; Queen; queen(s); Queen of Sheba; Sheba.

Quetzalcoatl: the Mesoamerican deity known as the "Sovereign Plumed Serpent" whom the Mayans and others believed would someday return to earth as a savior type. It is possible that the Aztecs mistook the Spanish conquistadores as the arriving Quetzalcoatl, much to their grief, although this subterfuge is regarded as myth by many historians. The name remains associated with certain aspects of the Mayan doomsday prophecy of December 21, 2012, along with a number of other Mesoamerican and Native American stock. The name was rendered as Quetzalcoatl in Mexico, Gucumatz in Quiche, Amaru in Peru, and known to the Maya as Kulkulcan. Quetzalcoatl-like entities are present in other cultures as well: the enormous plumed serpent god of the Hopi tribe was called Baholinkonga; the Egyptian serpent god was Enuph; the East Indian mystical human-like reptilians were Nagas; the Phoenicians claimed Agathodaimon; and even the Hebrew bronze serpent called Nehushtan bears a resemblance. *See also* Aztecs; Chilam-Balam; conquistador(s); Cortez, Hernando; *Dresden Codex;* eagle and the condor, the; Eagle Bowl; Egyptian pantheon; five stages of earth, the; Inca; Itza-Maya; Katun Prophecies; Maya; Mesoamerica; Montezuma II; mythological beasties, elementals, monsters, and spirit animals; Nagas; Nehushtan; *Popul Unh;* reptilian theory; Sun Stone; Toltecs; "transition of consciousness"; 2012, advocates of; 2012, prophecy of; Votan, Pacal; Xibala; Xolotl.

Quiboloy, Apollo: a Filipino religious leader and false Messiah (b. 1950). He heads the Kingdom of Jesus Christ, The Name Above Every Name, Inc., one of the fastest-growing cults in the world. His mansion is called the "New Jerusalem." Quiboloy's recruitment methods have been questioned as to morality and legality. *See also* cult(s); televangelism, televangelists.

quietism: a theological or worship stance that emphasizes the contemplative over the outwardly expressive display. The term is in direct opposition to emotionalism. Some equate the style with Pietism. *See also* ecstasy; Inner Light; liturgy, Christian; Pietism, Pietists; Society of Friends.

Quimbanda: a Voodoo-type religion common in urban Brazil but also practiced in Argentina, Paraguay, and Uruguay. The rituals and origins are associated with Macumba, Orisha, and Yoruba but practitioners insist they are a separate group, especially since the start of the 21st century. The philosophy and aims of Quimbanda are almost opposite those of its sister cult, Umbanda. Whereas the latter claims to invoke more "white" magic, the Quimbandas are not averse to more sinister endeavors. Worship centers on the promotion of magic through the male spirits (Exus) and the female (Pomba Giras). Orgun is the god of warfare, metal, and justice. *See also* animism; Brujeria; Candomble; Creole (Caribbean) religions; cult(s); Kumina; Macumba; magic, magick; mojo; Obeah; occult, occultic; Orisha; poppets; Rastafarianism; Santeria; shaman, shamanism; Shango; spiritism; Spiritual Baptists; Umbanda; Voodoo; Vodou; Yoruba.

Quimby, Phineas Parkhurst: a mesmerist from Maine (1802–1866) who pioneered the mental healing movement. Quimby eventually fleshed out his beliefs, the doctrines of which emerged later as the New Thought Movement and Christian Science. He specialized in healing under hypnosis but came to believe that the patients cured themselves so hypnosis was unnecessary for treatment. *See also* animal magnetism; Church of Christ, Scientist; Eddy, Mary Baker; faith healing; magnetism; mesmerism; mind science; New Thought Movement.

Quinquagesima: the last Sunday before Lent in many liturgical churches. *See also* Lent; liturgical year; liturgy, Christian; Quadragesima; Roman Catholic Church; Sexagesima.

Quinque Viae: the five ways in which Thomas Aquinas tried to prove God's existence. *See also* Aquinas, Thomas; Five Ways, the; *Summa Theologia;* teleology.

quintessence: 1. the pure or essence of a thing. 2. the fifth and highest element after earth, fire, water, and air. 3. the dark energy of space in the scalar field.

Quirinius: a governor of Syria, a position he likely held twice. It was he who required that a census be taken of the Roman Empire in each of his terms in office, one of which occurred around A.D. 7. An earlier one is mentioned by Luke, and he specifically called it "the first." Citizens were required to journey to their ancestral homes to be enrolled, a fact that figures prominently in the narration of Jesus' birth. Josephus also mentioned the man (which he spelled as Cyrenius) and his taxation mandate. *See also* census; Roman Empire; Syria.

Qumran: site of the communal residence of many of the Essene sect and those like them. Qumran is a mountainous desert region near the Dead Sea about thirteen miles east of Jerusalem. Most scholars agree that the ascetics separated from mainstream Judaism between 171 and 167 B.C. The bulk of the Dead Sea Scrolls was discovered in that area. The communities were considered apocalyptic because of their sense of being centered on the world to come. In the Qumran societies, history is understood to be a battle between the Sons of Light and the Sons of Darkness. A final eschatological clash will come about in which Michael, the Prince of Light, will defeat those led by Belial, the Prince of Darkness. With the aid and spirit of the Qumran warriors and the supernatural intervention of God, the eschatological victory for the Sons of Light is assured. *See also* Angel of Darkness; Angel of Light; communal communities; Copper Scroll; Dead Sea; Dead Sea Scrolls; Essenes; Isaiah Scroll; Manual of Discipline; Renewal, the; Shrine of the Book; Sons of Darkness; Sons of Light; Teacher of Righteousness; *War of the Sons of Light Against the Sons of Darkness;* War Scroll; Wicked Priest; Zadokites.

Quo Vadis **legend, the:** a description in the *Acts of Peter,* a third-century work that records certain unverified words and actions of the apostle Peter during the Neronian persecution. In it, Peter is fleeing Rome, yet again in one of his periodic bouts of cowardice, rather than be murdered with the other Christians in Rome. He meets Jesus going the opposite way, toward the city. Peter asks: *"Quo Vadis, Domine?"* ("Where are you going, Lord?") Jesus replied, "To Rome, to be crucified again." Shamed, Peter turned to retrace his steps back to the capital where he insisted he be crucified upside down as one unworthy to copy his Lord. Most historians agree that Peter and Paul were both martyred in Rome and buried there, but both locations are not firmly established nor are all legends of their deaths reliable.

Qur'an: the Koran, the Muslim holy book supposedly dictated to Mohammed by the angel Gabriel and copied from twelve tables resident eternally in the heavens. The title in translation means "Recitations" or "that which is to be recited." Even with its name which implies speaking, the title holds firm for its written or printed form as well. The *Qur'an* governs Islamic thinking, action, civil law, and theology today as it has from its inception. Islam is mindful of the antiquity of the Old and New Testaments (Jews and Christians are considered "people of the book") but replaced the authority of both with a new version they call the supreme revelation of God. Most Muslims consider the *Qur'an* itself to have a living soul. The text is considered to be perfect in its moving poetic style, causing Islam to harden itself against making sculptures and three-dimensional images. The Arabic script is considered to be supremely lovely in itself. The tome consists of 114 sections, called *suras*, a third of which were written in Mecca and the remainder in Medina. The first division consists of moral and eschatological subjects, and the latter is a series of polemics against other religions and discussions of civil legislation. The Muslim Holy Book is smaller than the Christian Bible but is probably subject to more additions, renditions, commentaries, and interpretations than any other religious study. This information, plus the fact that the *Qur'an* was not written in pure Arabic, makes a uniform understanding or translation extremely difficult. Multiple meanings have blossomed because, unlike early Christianity, Islam had no hierarchy of clergy to set down in canon law what was orthodox or to champion any single interpretation. Many Muslims, perhaps the vast majority, prefer to follow the commentaries and teachings of their imams rather than apply themselves to the original text. Thus, numerous sects and beliefs are rampant in Islamic society. The tome names some twenty-five prophets and hints there may be more. The most prominent are Adam, Noah, Abraham, Moses, David, Jesus, and Mohammed (the last being the greatest). The *Qur'an* saw its first minor recording about seventy years after the death of Mohammed, followed by many additions and editions in the years following. The results are not chronological and many inclusions are downright contradictory. The odd belief that suicide bombers and other extremists, for example, will be rewarded in Paradise with access to seventy-two virgins (*houris*) and other sensual pleasures is not found in the Koran but among some obscurities of its interpretations. *See also* ayat; Baha'i International; book(s); *Dajjal; houris;* Islam; *jihad; Ka'bah;* madrassa(s); Mohammed ibn 'Abdallah; Saracens; Shari'a ; sura(s); *tahrif;* Wahhabism.

quyit: a magic ritual or gesture in ancient China in which magicians traced intersecting vertical and horizontal lines in the air with incense sticks. The process was intended to ward off evil spirits. *See also* gestures; magic, magick.

R

Ra. See Re.

Raamah: (Ramah) an uncertain location but possibly in the Persian Gulf area.

rabbi: the ancient and modern Jewish title for a respected religious teacher or leader. The term originally meant "my master" but subsequently became the designation for ordained clergy or a teacher among the Jews. Jesus was sometimes addressed as "Rabbi" or *Rabboni* (Mt. 23:7; Jn. 1:38; 6:25). The later Jewish schools are said to have designated three ranks of esteemed teachers: *rab* (master) as the lowest, *rabbi* (my master) as the rank between *rab* and *rabban*, and *rabban* (lord, master) as highest. In the Scripture, however, the term carries the basic meaning of "master" or "teacher." Some rabbis are unpaid and begin their training as young as six or seven. *See also* call(ing); chaplain(s); clergy; Jew(s); Judaism; ministry; officiant; man of God; ministry; minister(s); *Qoheleth;* shepherding (pastoral); shepherd/shepherdess.

Rabbath Ammon: present-day Amman, Jordan.

rabboni. See rabbi.

Rabshakeh: a deputy of the Assyrian king Sennacherib, meaning "chief officer," sent to Jerusalem to demand the city's surrender. King Hezekiah, on the advice of Isaiah, refused to hand over the city despite a clever capitulation speech given by Rabshakeh (probably his title—not his name) and the city was saved. Other Assyrian officials include the Tartan, "second in rank," and Rabsaris, "chief eunuch." *See also* Assyria, Assyrians.

Raca: a New Testament term of contempt, used at least once by Jesus (Mt. 5:22). The word closely resembles our expletive for "fool" or a similar message of scorn. *See also* Dame Folly; dog(s); fool, "where angels fear to tread."

Raccolta: from the Italian for "collection," a book of prayers and pious expressions to which the pope has added indulgences to be recited as coin for releasing those in purgatory. The composition started in 1807. *See also* Roman Catholic Church.

Rachel: or Rahel, the beautiful and favored wife of Jacob, a daughter of Laban. As a rival wife to Leah, Rachel was barren until God favored her with two sons, Joseph and Benjamin. *See also* Haran; Jacob; Laban; Leah; Rachel weeping for her children.

Rachel weeping for her children: a prophetic lament foretelling the murder of the innocents. The prophet Jeremiah (Jer. 31:15) represented her (substituting the name for the nation as a whole) as weeping for her children, the descendants of Joseph (the people of Ephraim and Manasseh) who were in captivity. The passage recording Rachel's lamentation is to be considered a type or prophecy for King Herod's execution of the Bethlehem babies and is quoted as such in Matthew 2:17–18. *See also* slaughter of the innocents; Rachel; woman (women).

racism: unwarranted prejudice against a given ethnic group or overly favoring one's own race. *See also ad hominem* argument; American Party; anti-Semitic; ghetto; "hate crimes"; militant domestic organizations; Million Man March; social issues; woke; xenophobia.

Radhasoami Satsang: a religion in the Sant Mat tradition founded in 1861 in Northern India with some Sikh and esoteric Hindu elements. *See also* Sant Mat; sect(s).

radicalized: the result of cultural pressure and propaganda when a person is initiated into radical or extremist Islam. Salafist influence, Wahhabism, peer pressure, and the desire to serve a seemingly self-affirming cause motivate the majority of efforts to solicit fighters. Most recruits are young, from the lower or median low economic group, and are susceptible to religious and political extremist persuasion. *See also Alluha Akbar:* al-Qaeda; al-Shabab; anti-Semitic; Boko Haram; Daesh; Hamas; Hezbollah; Islam; Islamic State in Iraq and Syria (ISIS or ISIL); *jihad*; Muslim Brotherhood; Nusra Front; Palestinian Islamic Jihad (PIJ); Palestinian Liberation Organization (PLO); Salafi; Taliban; terrorism; terrorist(s); Turkistan Islamic Party; Velayat Sinai; Wahhabism.

radical preterism: an extreme branch of preterism. As opposed to moderate preterism, radical preterists (who prefer to be called "full" or "consistent" preterists) believe that all events predicted in the Scripture, including the Second Coming, the resurrection of the dead, and the final judgments, have already taken place. *See also* preterism; moderate preterism.

Radueri'el: the great heavenly angelic scribe and historian in *3 Enoch*. It is he who grants access to God and the heavenly council. Each word from his mouth creates a new angel. *See also* angel(s).

Raelism: a UFO cult, perhaps the largest in the world, originating in France under the former race car driver Claud Vorilhorn in 1974. The organization is doomsday in its agenda and has warned that a massive interplanetary edifice must be constructed in Israel before 2030 lest a nuclear holocaust envelop us all. So far, the Israelis have refused a building permit because a major symbol of the sect is the swastika. Rael (as Vorilhorn calls himself) insists he has actually seen and conversed with the aliens who control our destiny. The cult made international headlines several decades ago by claiming it had cloned a human being. No clones have appeared and no research data were presented to date despite Raelian assurances they are living. *See also* cult(s); Human Enhancement Revolution (HER); panspermia theory; UFO; Vorilhorn, Claud; zero-point energy.

Rafsanjani, Akbar Hashemi: president of Iran from 1989–1997. He was arguably the leader most responsible for promoting the Iranian Revolution Guard Corps (IRGC) to its high political and religious power operative in the country today. The IRGC is now dominant in the private industries, banking, trade, civil engineering, real estate, and education sectors of Iran helping to maintain and promote the nation as a militant Islamic state. Moreover, the force has broad influence in manufacturing, the vital national oil industry, border security, high-tech telecommunications, and, certainly, all forms of the nation's military. Its economy has grown despite international sanctions imposed because of the refusal to abandon the country's nuclear weapons development program. Rafsanjani's successor, Mohammad Khatami (1197–2005) (though critical of his predecessor) has moved the IRGC even further into state security interests, national politics, the intelligence community, and the practice of vote fraud where it thrives to this day. *See also* Islam, Iranian military; terrorist(s).

raghead: a derogatory ethnic and religious slur used primarily for far and near eastern males, usually Muslim. The term is drawn from the turban or keffiyeh worn as a headdress. Other terms for the same class, including Arabs, may be heard as towelhead, sand nigger, camel jockey, oil nigger, Paki, and others. *See also* Islam; slurs, religious.

Ragnarok: according to Norse mythology, the last great battle, or series of battles, between the forces of good and evil under the leadership of the gods, both good and evil. Fierce theomachy is anticipated at the end of the age. The good forces are predicted to be winners but much of the earth will be destroyed in the process. *See also* Asatru; *Edda,* the; Fimbulwinter; Lif and Lifthraser; Loki; Midgard-serpent; *Naglfar;* Norse and Old Germanic pantheon; Surt; wolf.

Rahab: 1. the innkeeper (some alternate readings insert "harlot" since many hostel managers of those days were so occupied) in the city of Jericho who aided the Hebrew spies during the conquest of the Promised Land (Josh. 2:1). She is listed as being in the ancestral line of Jesus. Was she a prophetess as well? Such thinking is reasonable for how else was she to know the identity or intent of the spies in her care? 2. a mythical beast of the sea, or perhaps an amphibian, symbolic of chaos but controlled by the power of God (Job 26:12–13; Ps. 89:10). The beast may be an alternate name for Leviathan. The name means "boisterous one" and holds dragon-like overtones. 3. a tag name for Egypt (Ps. 87:4). At one point, God labeled Egypt as "Rahab the Do-Nothing" (Isa. 30:7) to emphasize that nation's impotence. *See also* animals, birds, and insects, symbology of; Behemoth; dragon; Egypt, Egyptians; Egyptian pantheon; Levant pantheon; Leviathan; mythological beasties, elementals, monsters, and spirit animals; prophetess(es); reptilian theory.

Rahab the Do-Nothing: a derogatory and salacious name for Egypt taken from Isaiah 30:7.

Rahati'el: the angel of the stars and constellations as noted by *3 Enoch.* *See also* angel(s); angels of the heavens; constellations; star(s).

Rahman, Sheikh Omar: the blind Islamic cleric who began plotting with terrorists to "kill Americans wherever you find them; destroy their embassies, sink their ships, shoot down their planes."

Rahman was responsible for conspiracy in the 9/11 attacks and the bombing, or attempted bombings, of several locations in New York, New Jersey, and elsewhere around the world. He was serving a life sentence in United States custody until his death in February of 2017. *See also* Islam; terrorism; terrorist(s).

"Raiders of the Lost Ark": an action-adventure movie from Seven Spielberg released in 1981. The production starred Harrison Ford in the portrayal of Dr. Henry "Indiana" Jones who risks life and limb in search of the legendary ark of the covenant. The Indy character may have been inspired by the real life Dr. Vendyl Jones—a prominent ark of the covenant researcher. If the *v* and *l* are dropped from Vendyl, it yields Endy Jones. *See also* archeology, archeologists; ark of the covenant; eschatology, eschatological; Jones, Vendyl Miller.

Raikes, Robert: an empathetic Anglican layman (1736–1811). He felt compassion for the poorer children of London and set about to educate them and improve their lives. The result became known as "Sunday schools" because the best available time for teaching was Sunday; on the other six days, most of the boys and many girls worked in the factories. Raikes hired women to teach the children (mostly at his own expense), using the Bible as their textbook. Pupils learned to read, received a moral start in life, and had lunch in a safe and clean environment. By 1831, over a million children had benefitted. Raikes's efforts were the basis for the state English school system. *See also* Church of England; religious education; Sunday schools.

Raimarus, Nicholas: (c. 1551–1600) German visionary, mathematician, and astronomer with questionable credentials who penned a rather unique account of the end times scenario published in 1606. He called the work *Chronical, Certain, and Irrefutable Proof, from the Holy Scripture and Fathers, That the World Will Perish and the Last Day Will Come Within 77 Years.*

raiment: a common biblical name for clothing. White raiment almost always is symbolic of purity or righteousness. *See also* linen; robe; white raiment; wool.

rain: natural moisture from the sky. The term has frequent apocalyptic application because rain (often associated with dew as well) is often withheld as a form of divine punishment, a particular talent of Elijah and the two super witnesses of Revelation 11. Or God may choose to "rain down" disaster on unrepentant peoples. Seasonal rains were considered blessings from God because the fields and crops could produce their life-giving beauty and bounty. *See also* hail; latter rain, the; snow.

rainbow: the color spectrum in the atmosphere caused by sunlight refracted on raindrops. The "bow" (a frequent shortened reference to the rainbow) was a sign of the covenant pledge between God and Noah (Gen. 9:8–17). The colors making up the rainbow have been termed the primary colors from which every other color is made. The rainbow symbol is seen again in Revelation 4:3 where one of emerald color encircles the throne of heaven, and again in Revelation 10:1 as part of the dress of a mighty angel. The rainbow sign is a common one when dealing with theophanic descriptions throughout Scripture. *See also* flood; Noahic Covenant; Rainbow Coalition; Rainbow Family; Rainbow Warriors, the; sign(s).

Rainbow Coalition: a collective name for activist groups of some description ranging from environmental issues to so-called "gay rights." More than a few operatives have claimed the name and rainbow symbol, each of which fits the description of any special interest groups formed with differing ethnic, religious, or political agendas seeking to promote various causes or initiatives. As a sample: 1. the International Order of the Rainbow for Girls is a para-Masonic order of young girls, mostly daughters of Freemasons who belong. 2. the Rainbow Bridge (antahkarana) is a New Age movement seeking to build a bridge between man and Lucifer who, they say, is the over-soul. 3. Rainbow/Push (originally The National Rainbow Coalition) is a political activist organization founded by Jesse Jackson. 4. the Rainbow Family is a cult focused on the unity or disunity of world religions. 5. the Rainbow Warriors represent a Hopi prophecy predicted to redeem the earth in future days. 6. the lesbian and gay rights movement has adopted the rainbow as its centralizing trademark. 7. at times, the rainbow symbol has been the choice of certain environmental protection organizations, New Age religion, peace activists, and the sinister work of the Illuminate. Though the detailed meanings of the rainbow colors may vary somewhat, some basic hues of the rainbow flag are fairly common. The design artist of the gay flag, for example, (Gilbert Baker in 1978) disclosed his eight strips should be received as: pink– for sexuality, red– for life, orange– for health, yellow– for sunlight, green– for nature, turquoise– for magic, blue– for serenity, and violet– for spirit. In any case, modern usage of the rainbow differs markedly from the biblical intent of the sign. Noah's rainbow was a pledge from God not to destroy the earth by water again and to motivate the survivors to repopulate the earth. *See also* Blue Star prophecy; civil unions; "clobber passages"; cult(s); Freemasonry; Illuminate; Jackson, Jesse Louis; LGBTQ; New Age religion; peace symbol; religious organizations; rainbow; Rainbow Coalition; Rainbow Family; Rainbow Warriors, the; sign(s); social issues.

Rainbow Family: a United States-based cult following who meet regularly to celebrate the rainbow, which they see as a representative of the division of the world's religions. They look for a messiah-type figure—a "prism"—who will end the divisiveness and unite all religions. From another context, the rainbow is also a symbol of the gay (homosexual) coalition. *See also* cult(s); LGBTQ; rainbow.

Rainbow Warriors, the: a Hopi prophecy that relates how certain children of the future (the "Rainbow Warriors") will rescue the earth by bringing back the animals, trees, and, of course, the rainbow after all have come to ruin. The legend appears in a number of forms, some of which incorporate bits of the Great Purification and Kachina predictions. *See also* Blue Star prophecy; Great Purification, the; Hopi.

raisin cakes, the sacred: a delicacy made from pressed grapes (*cf.* Song of Solomon 2:5 and 2 Samuel 6:1) for the basic ingredient for the cakes. These were distributed from time to time within a worship context (*cf.* Isaiah 16:7 and 1 Chronicles 16:3). Such treats played an important role in the agrarian-oriented Canaanite religions, as demonstrated in Hosea 3:1. *See also* witch cake.

rally: a special gathering familiar to many Protestant denominations staged to promote a particular church activity or group action. Youth rallies are probably the most common. *See also* feasts and special days of Protestantism; religious education.

ram: the male goat, central in Israel for sacrifice, livestock, and other practical uses. *See also* animals, birds, and insects, symbology of;

Azazel; flocks and herds; flying goat; goat; Medo-Persia; ram and the goat, the; two-horned ram; *shofar.*

Rama: or Ramachandra, whom Hinduism reveres as an important deity. He is considered the seventh avatar of the god Vishnu and even rated as the Supreme Being by some sects. Tales of Rama's life are recorded in the *Ramayana,* a popular text in Southern and Southeastern Asia. Perhaps the most popular story involves the kidnapping of Rama's wife Sita by the demon Ravana and the god's extensive efforts to rescue her. A Ramlila festival is held annually in the autumn. There are also trace references to Rama in Jainism and Buddhism. *See also* Hinduism.

Ramadan: an important Muslim religious holiday. Ramadan consists of twenty-eight days of daylight fasting, sexual abstinence, and meditation. The period commemorates the giving of the *Qur'an* to Mohammed by the angel Gabriel. *See also Arkin-al-din; Eid-al-Adha; Eid-al-Fitr;* Islam; Five Pillars of Islam; Islam; *Quds* Day.

Ramah: called Ramathaim-zophim to distinguish it from other locales by the same name, which was the family home of the prophet Samuel and the place of his burial. He headed a school of prophets there as well, but its precise location remains uncertain. Samuel also made the town the center of his circuit route as he traveled about as judge among his people.

ram and the goat, the: Daniel's vision of a ram with two unequal horns and a goat who glided across the ground (probably a rhinoceros) with only one horn (Dan. 8:1–14). The two beasts engage in battle, with the flying goat (Greece) as victor over the ram (Medo-Persia). When the combat was finished, the single-horned beast sprouted four more horns (representing the factions of the Grecian kingdom after the death of Alexander the Great). From these four, sprang another, a little one, representative of Antiochus IV Epiphanes and ultimately the Antichrist. *See also* Alexander the Great; animals, birds, and insects, symbology of; belly and thighs of bronze; Diadochi; flying goat, the; Greece; horn(s); Medo-Persia; ram; two-horned ram, the; winged leopard, the.

Ramathaim-zophim. See Ramah.

Ramayana: a Hindu epic poem that tells of the relationship between Prince Rama and his wife Sita, a popular story among its many readers. Sita was kidnapped by the demon Ravana which the narrative explores but with its companion work, the *Mahabharata,* also comments on moral dilemmas and the value of the Vedic sacrifices, along with the consequences of royal rivalries. *See also Bhagavad Gita;* Hinduism; *Mahabharata.*

Ram Bahadur Bamjan: b. about April 9, 1990, a.k.a. Palden Dorje, the "Buddha Boy," or "Dharma Sangha" from his home in Nepal. Followers of the young guru claim he is the reincarnation of Buddha, though this belief is controversial among his detractors since Buddha presumably has achieved Nirvana and cannot reappear. Bamjan is known for his long periods of meditation from time to time and from place to place across India. Presently, he holds the Guinness World Record for the longest sustained life without water—eighteen days. Observers say he can remain motionless for days without food or drink. *See also* cult(s).

Rambam. See Maimonides, Moses.

Ramses II: Pharaoh of Egypt around 1320 B.C. Some scholars believe he was the Pharaoh of the Exodus, but there are a number of other possibilities for that distinction, some seemingly with a stronger intellectual pedigree. *See also* Amasis; Amenhotep II; Ay; Egypt, Egyptians; Hophra; king(s); Menses; Merneptah; Necho II; pharaoh; Pharaoh of the Exodus; Sesotris; Shabaka; Shishak; So; Tirhakah.

ram's horn. See *shofar.*

Randi, James: *nee* Randall James Hamilton Zwinge (b. 1928), a stage magician and scientific skeptic icon. The naturalized American from Canada has become famous as the premier debunker of the paranormal (a belief he calls "woo-woo") and pseudo-science. He is also an avid atheist and advertises with some pride that he was thrown out of Sunday school as a child. During his career, he offered a million dollar prize to any who could provide any proven evidence of the paranormal, supernatural, or occult power. *See also* atheism, atheist(s); paranormal; magic, magick; thaumaturgy.

Randolph, Paschal Beverly: a significant advocate of Rosicrucianism, rising to the position of Supreme Grandmaster for the Western World. Despite his beginnings in the poorhouse, he founded the *Fraternitas Rosae Crucis* as the true center of the sect in North America. His life was tragic, however, as he committed suicide at age forty-nine, having been accused (no conviction) on trumped-up charges of immorality. The momentum carried on after his death until Rosicrucianism was graded with the most recognized fraternal membership second only to Freemasonry. *See also* Order of the Rosy Cross; Rosicrucianism.

ransom theory of atonement: a.k.a. the ransom to Satan atonement, one of the earliest church doctrines (often called the "patristic" view) that postulates God was able to arrange a sacrifice in Christ as payment to Satan for the redemption of the human soul and to settle just claims that the devil held against mankind. Origen and Augustine were proponents but Anselm opposed. The theory did not endure past thousand years. *See also* atonement; reconciliation; satisfaction theory of atonement; vicarious atonement.

Ranters. See antinomianism.

rantize. See aspersion.

Raphael: an archangel named in pseudepigraphal sources (not Scripture) who is said to rule over the spirits of men. He is also named as a healer, even the one who healed Abraham after his circumcision! The book of *Tobit* depicts him as the angel who presents the prayers of the saints to God. Other stories see him as the one who escorts souls to Sheol (the afterlife) and one legend says he was one of Abraham's three visitors before Sodom, the other two being Michael and Gabriel. Some Christians see him as the angel who stirred the waters in the healing pool at Bethesda. Still another Jewish tradition finds him presenting a book of instructions on how to build an ark, entitled *Sefer Razi'el,* to Noah. *See also* angel(s); archangel(s); liturgical year; *mal'ak; Tobit.*

Raphan, star of: associated with the god Remphan (Rephan), a star deity illicitly worshiped by the exiles in the wilderness (Amos 5:25–27; Acts 7:43). The Amos passage contains a reference to the idol, the details of which seem to derive from the Septuagint. Mention is made of "Sukkuth (Sikkuth) your king," "Kaiwan your idols," "your star-gods," and Molech. "Kaiwan" is a corrupted transliteration of the Akkadian name for Saturn and is likely the god Chiun which Amos condemned (Amos 5:26). Stephen's pre-martyrdom sermon names the worship of such idols as a major failure of his Jewish ancestors (Acts 7:43). *See also* Levant pantheon; Remphan; Saccuth; Stephen of Jerusalem.

Rapp, Father Johann Georg: founder (1757–1847) of the cult known as the Harmonists or the "Rappites." Rapp was a refugee from Germany who fled to America after tumbling into trouble with the Lutheran Church in his home country. He established a colony in Economy, Pennsylvania, when he became convinced that Jesus would appear before his death. The group then moved to Indiana and back again to Harmony, Pennsylvania. On his deathbed, he was reported to have said: "If I did not know that the dear Lord meant I should present you all to him, I should think my last moment's come." Rapp was relieved by his adopted son, Frederich (Reichart) Rapp (1775–1834), and the colonies endured for about 100 years. *See also* New Harmony Society of Equality.

rapture: a term (not found in its Anglicized form in Scripture) of Latin derivation meaning to be "caught up" or "seized." *Harpazo* is the correct form in Greek (used thirteen times in the New Testament) and *rapio* is the Hebrew counterpart. It is therefore a technical word drawn from 1 Thessalonians 4:13–18 and elsewhere that describes believers being carried from earth to heaven in a grand supernatural act of resurrection of the dead in Christ and the instantaneous snatching away of all living believers from the earth. Examples can be found among which Enoch, Elijah, and Jesus are the most recognizable. Some biblicists also name Isaiah, Philip the evangelist, and Paul as possibly having experienced a catching up to heaven or to another location on earth. Obviously, the most dynamic rapture is to occur when the Church, the bride of Christ, is lifted to him. Scripture uses other language to identify the same action (provided the accounts can be proven as genuine rapture events and not the Second Coming or other episode): entering the bridal chamber (Isa. 26:19-21), the rescue (Dan. 12:1–2), the receiving (Jn. 14:3), adoption as sons and redemption of the body (Rom. 8:18–25), the revelation of Jesus Christ (1 Cor. 1:7; 1 Pe. 1:13), the changing (1 Cor. 15:52), the transformation (Phil. 3:20–21), the rescue or deliverance from the wrath to come (1 Th. 1:10), the catching away (1 Th. 4:17), the gathering (2 Th. 2:1), the blessed hope (Titus 2:13), the appearing (Heb. 9:28), and the mercy (Jude 21). Noncanonical writings do not reference a form of rapture either unless *2 Esdras* 6:26 carries an allusion to the act. Few Bible authorities doubt the authenticity of a rapture of some description, but there is disagreement concerning when it occurs. Is it before, during, or after the Tribulation? Each idea is represented in the pre, mid, and post-Tribulation theories. If we look at our models: Enoch was caught up to heaven *before* the great flood—before any tribulation; Elijah was caught up *after* exposing the sin of Israel and defying Queen Jezebel—a time when danger was mostly past; and the two great witnesses of Revelation are to be taken *in the middle* of the Tribulation—during the trouble. Not much help is there as all were whisked away in differing circumstances. There appear to be both similarities and differences between the rapture and the Second Coming expositions, so the concept deserves careful study. The logical tendency is to see rapture as a calling out of the living; resurrection is for the dead. Some millennialists have come to believe the rapture initiates the Tribulation but that season, officially, does not start until the signing of a peace treaty between Israel and the Antichrist. The rapture does, obviously, trigger great world changes and makes conditions ripe for the Antichrist's rise to power during the interval between the two events. Those who posit an early rapture of the Church do so for many reasons. In summary, they see 1) a pattern of divine rescue from God's wrath throughout Scripture (Gen. 6-8; 19), 2) trust in the prophecy of Paul (1 Th. 4:13-19) and the portrayal of the Church in Revelation and, 3) the promise of Jesus to return for his disciples (Jn. 14:1-3). *See also* "any moment rapture"; blessed hope, the; bodily resurrection; "Come up here"; covenant of death; Death; death; *epiphaneia;* eschatology, eschatological; Gabriel; "here, there, or in the air"; imminence; Jurieu, Peter; last trumpet, the; loud command, a; mid-Tribulation, mid-Tribulational; partial rapture theory; post-Tribulation, post-Tribulational; pre-Tribulation, pre-Tribulational; prewrath rapture; "rescue from the coming wrath"; resurrection(s); resurrection, the first; secret rapture; seven years covenant with Israel; shout; spared from the hour of trial; sounds of the rapture; termination dates; translation; trumpet call of the elect; twinkling of an eye; voice of the archangel, the; voice of God; voice out of heaven; voices of Revelation.

Raqia. See heaven.

Raquel: one of the archangels named in pseudepigraphal sources (not Scripture) as one who takes vengeance on the world of luminaries. What such a title was meant to the ancients is ambiguous but probably has to do with angelic opposition to God. *See also* angel(s); archangel(s); liturgical year.

Rashi: Rabbi Shlomo Yitzchaki (1040–1105) or Solomon ben Isaac, the foremost Torah scholar of Medieval France. His commentaries on the Talmud and *Tanakh* are exceptionally comprehensive and clear. *See also* Jew(s); Judaism.

Rashidun Caliphate: the ruling caliphate after the time of Mohammed (A.D. 623) and considered to be the first. It is also known as the patriarchal caliphate and was created in Arabia. *See also* Abbasid Caliphate; Arabia; Ayyubid dynasty; caliph; caliphate; Fatimid Caliphate; Islam; Umayyad Caliphate.

rasophore: lowest ranking monk in the Orthodox monk tradition. *See also* Eastern Orthodox Church; monk(s).

Rasputin, Grigori Efimovitch: a mystic Russian monk of the early 1900s who gained considerable influence with the Romanov czar and czarina, Nicholas II and Alexandra. Rasputin was a member of the radical sect, the Khlysty (People of God), a neo-Gnostic group that practiced flagellation and sexual indulgence as a way to contact the Divine. Rasputin was unkempt in appearance and abjectly immoral in his sexual conquests and excessive appetites. He was a horse whisperer as well and seemed to have extraordinary healing powers, along with other psychic abilities, even reputedly saving the life of the emperor's hemophilic son, much to the wonder of Alexandra. Rasputin's prophetic utterances were significant as well, including his warning that the czar should abstain from Russian involvement in World War I, which would lead to disaster for the nation and the monarchy (which it did). Recent discoveries are said to reveal he that predicted the end of the world on August 23, 2013, "when a fire shall devour all living things, then, the planet will be a quiet grave." He also warned that the Romanov line would vanish if he were assassinated (also true). By 1913, those of the aristocracy and foreign intelligence services had begun attempts to castrate and murder him for fear of his unholy influence at court. Finally, in December of 1916, he was lured into a trap by conspirators led by Prince Felix Yusapov. The monk was fed cakes and wine (which he favored) laced with cyanide, which had no visible effect. He was then shot point-blank in the chest but recovered enough to continue his fight for survival. He was pursued outside and shot twice more, then loaded into a car and dumped into the icy river. Stories persisted that he was still alive for a time even then and finally died from drowning. *See also* Holy Fool(s), the; Khlysty, the; monk(s); priest(s); Russian Orthodoxy.

Ras Shamra Tablets: a.k.a. the Ugaritic Tablets, a cache of administrative, legal, and economic documents written in Akkadian. They were discovered near a Syrian seaport in Ugarit. The real value to biblical researchers, however, is in the collection of cuneiform clay tablets containing a Canaanite mythological text of many of the Mediterranean pantheons. *See also* Levant pantheon.

Rastafarianism: a Jamaican and United States-based religion centered in reverence for Emperor Selassie of Ethiopia (1892–1975) and who regard the country of Prince Ras Tafari (Ethiopia) as heaven. Selassie is believed to be the elect of God and savior of the black race. The Ethiopians are even named in their sacred writing (*Holy Piby* as written in Anguilla) as God's chosen people. Rastafarians believe they are the reincarnation of Old Testament Israel, and most are readily recognized by their peculiar dreadlock hair braids, marijuana use, absence of pork or anything from the grape in the diet, and reggae music. Their Western Wisdom Teachings show that the day of Christ will end the so-called Aryan epoch when the earth will experience a "days of Noah" type of judgment. Those who pass the test may move on as "pioneers" or "sheep" into the next evolution called the ethereal conditions of the "New Galilee." Ultimately, however, all will be saved—a cardinal tenet of universalism. Rastafarianism is the largest of the so-called Creole religions of the Caribbean though they dislike any hint of Vodou in their society nor do they favor being called any form of "Rastafarianism." A key figure who helped popularize the sect worldwide was the famous musician Bob Marley (named in the *Holy Piby* as a prophet). Archibald Dunkey and Joseph Nathaniel Hibbert were early preachers in the movement. The movement is as much a political or social program as a religion. *See also* animism; Brujeria; Candomble;

Creole (Caribbean) religions; cult(s); Haile Selassie; Kumina; Macumba; Menelik, Prince; Obeah; occult, occultic; Orisha; Quimbanda; Santeria; shaman, shamanism; Shango; spiritism; Spiritual Baptists; Umbanda; Voodoo, Voudou; Yoruba.

Ras Tafari, Prince. See Haile Selassie.

rasul: "one who is sent"—a messenger or envoy for Allah to an Islamic community. Mohammed was both a *rasul* and a prophet. *See also* Islam; Islam, prophets of; prophet(s).

rationalism: the assumption of some liberal theologians that prophetic prediction is impossible. Rather, prophecy is a somewhat vivid way of writing history after the event. This interpretive method grew in academic circles after the Reformation and is not likely to substantially diminish. A significant turn occurred in 18th century Protestantism when many theologians abandoned biblical inerrancy and began to view the Bible as merely a historical document. *See also* empiricism; *ex eventu* prophecy; liberalism, liberalist(s).

Rattlesnake Prophecy, the: also known as the Star Constellation Prophecy, one of the apocalyptic predictions offered by the Chickamauga Cherokee issued in 1811–1812 when they were revealed to certain elders in supernatural visions. The revelations are part of the Cherokee Third Great Shaking of the earth phenomenon, the exposition of which mentions several events related to the year 2012. Part of the oracle predicts the return of Quetzalcoatl, the feathered serpent, along with various cosmic alignments involving the planet Venus. The prophecy features a unique concept called "Time/Untime" which seems to contrast the Western method of calendar making or, it may simply be a distinction between the spiritual and the physical. Interpretations involve a description of a snake with fifty-two scales on its mouth, each representing a day on the Cherokee calendar and marking off the "Wheel of Time." *See also* Blue Stone prophecy; Day of Purification; Fifth World, the; Great Shaking, the; Quetzalcoatl; reptilian theory; Venus; Wheel of Time, the.

Rauschenbusch, Walter: the foremost organizer and motivator for the American Protestant movement called the Social Gospel (1861–1918). He launched his campaign in 1886 at Hell's Kitchen, New York, and immediately promoted close ties between the gospel ("good news") outreach and social action on the humanitarian level. *See also* Baptists; Social Gospel; social issues.

raven: coal-black birds kin to the crow but larger, a species that holds its own stark beauty (S. of S. 5:11). Ravens fed Elijah miraculously in his flight to avoid the wrath of Jezebel (1 Ki. 17:4–6). Noah released one from the ark to test the flood levels on earth (Gen. 8:6–7). Scripture names the raven as a metaphor for God's generous and sure provision; He graciously supplies their needs so surely that He will surely deliver ours (Job 38:41; Ps. 147:9; Lk. 12:24). Ravens were also special to the Celts. They were used to warn the god Lugh of approaching danger and even coins were cast with the bird's image on them; the avians were the Celtic symbol of death and battle. Even so, the raven, along with the owl, are sometimes named as symbols of desolation (Isa. 34:11) or punishment (Pro. 30:17) and was numbered among the ritually unclean fowl (Lev. 11:13–19). The croaking of a raven was almost universally seen as a bad omen. *See also* animals, birds, and insects, symbology of; bird; crow; Celtic folklore and religion; Elijah; goose; mythological beasties, elementals, monsters, and spirit animals; names, symbology of; Noah's ark; owl; Paul of Thebes; unclean; zodiac.

Ravidassia: a strongly monotheistic Eastern religion began by the Guru Ravidass in the 14th century. Religious belief centers on the idea that the soul is part of the divine and the purpose of living is to allow us to realize God. Such blessings are not even denied to the "untouchables" sect of Indian society. *See also* sect(s).

razor from beyond the River, a: a reference (Isa. 7:20) to the land beyond the Euphrates, specifically the king of Assyria. God will hire him to shave the hairs of Israel's head, beard, and limbs (a consequence of shame) as punishment for her disobedience. *See also* Assyria, Assyrians

Re: also seen as Ra or Ra-Atum—the Egyptian sun god, perhaps the principal deity of the land. Unlike most of the Egyptian pantheon that featured animal figures for identification, Re was represented by the plain solar disc. At one point in Egyptian history, Pharaoh Akhenaton even decreed a short-lived monotheism of heliolatry. *See also* Amon; Ay; *ba;* Draco; Egypt, Egyptians; Egyptian pantheon; Heliopolis; *ka; maat;* pharaoh; sun worshipers.

reaffiliation: the process encountered when a church member departs one church and aligns with another. The action is not the same as conversion and is not restricted to denomination or location.

Reagan, Ronald: Hollywood actor turned union leader, Democrat turned Republican, governor of California turned the fortieth president of the United States (1911–2004). Born to a church shaped by the influence of the Second Great Awakening, Reagan was perhaps the first national figure outside of fundamentalist circles to openly affirm his belief in apocalyptic theology. His presidential predecessor, Jimmy Carter, had already opened the way for professing Christians in high office and every president since has acknowledged, to one degree or another, a Christian or religious sympathy. As president, Reagan surrounded himself with advisors who shared his eschatological or faith views, Secretary of Defense Caspar Weinberger and Interior Secretary James Watts among them. Reagan was keen to consult the book of Revelation and even Hal Lindsey's *The Late Great Planet Earth*, to help him form national and international policy—a stance that allowed him to risk labeling the Soviet Union as the "evil empire" at one point. "There is sin and evil in the world," he said, "and we're enjoined by Scripture and the Lord Jesus to oppose it with all our might." Reagan, according to most unbiased analysts, is classed as one of the nation's most endearing and effective chief executives. *See also* "zero years" prophecy, the.

Reality Therapy: a psychological approach, along with its sister designation—Integrity Therapy—which utilizes ethics and self-discipline in its approach to cure aberrant behavior and to practice mental hygiene. The basic precept (which is contrary to conventional psychiatric therapy) insists persons take responsibility for their actions both as citizens and individuals. The process was introduced by Dr. William Glasser in the mid-1960s which was the time of its greatest impact. It is perhaps the most Judeo-Christian-based mental and behavioral treatment program ever devised. *See also* ethics; exemplar motif; mental reservation; moral relativism; metathesis; orthopraxy.

realized eschatology. See amillennialism; preterism.

realized millennialism: the belief that we are in the Millennium now, a premier amillennialist concept. *See also* amillennial, amillennialism; idealist eschatology; preterism.

real presence: sometimes named sacramental union or corporal presence, the theological stance of some formalized denominations (principally Lutheran) that the body of Christ is fully manifest in the Eucharist following consecration by a priest either via consubstantiation or transubstantiation. Such a combination, or "union," is in the same theological school of other types of mystical joining (*i.e.,* the personal merger that defines the two natures of Christ—human and divine—or the mystical union that describes Christ's connection with his Church. Such a natural blending can even portray the relationship of the human body and soul. *See also* capernaitic eating; concomitance; consubstantiation; elevation; mystery; mystery of God; mystical union; mysticism, mystics; natural union; sacrament(s); theophagy; transubstantiation; wafer; wine.

Rebecca. See Rebekah.

rebeck: a three-stringed musical instrument of the viola family sporting a pear-shaped body and slender neck. It was a popular instrument in the Middle Ages, including usage in religious orchestral renditions. *See also* musical instrument(s).

Rebekah: or Rebecca in the New Testament. She was the miraculously chosen wife of Isaac and mother to Jacob and Esau and sister to Laban of Haran. In her parental role, Rebekah favored her son Jacob and conspired to assure he was the recipient of Isaac's blessing and birthright even though she had already received the prophecy that Jacob, not Esau, would have preeminence. *See also* Esau; Haran; Isaac; Jacob; Laban; Leah; Rachel.

rebellion: the act of turning from an established belief, leader, or condition. Such a break may be violent or peaceful. In Scripture, sin is frequently referred to as rebellion against God, whether precipitated by human or angel.

rebellion of the angels. See sin (rebellion) of the angels.

rebirthing: a New Age practice consisting of attempts made to revisit the moment of birth of an individual (or births if reincarnation is a factor). The belief is that experiencing this trauma again will rid the soul of bad karma and prevent regression. *See also* afterlife; future life, doctrine of the; metempsychosis; New Age religion; past life regression; reincarnation.

rebuilding the Temple: the concept or anticipation that the Jewish Temple will be rebuilt in Jerusalem at some point in the Tribulation. It is this structure that the Antichrist will defile. *See also* crushing rock that became a mountain; election; elect, the; eschatology, eschatological; kingdom that cannot be shaken, a; kingdom, the; messianic age, the; millennial geography; millennial Sabbath; millennial sacramentalism; millennial Temple; millennial worship; Millennium, millennial; New Covenant, the; New Eden; remnant; restoration of all things; restoration of Israel (the Jews); restoration Temple (and land); rod of iron; Sabbath rest; seven years covenant with Israel; Temple(s); third Temple; times of refreshing; Tribulation Temple.

recant: to retract or regret. In religious circles, the term may describe repentance following heretical or immoral acts. *See also* abjuration; ascesis; conversion; *metanoia;* repent; repentance; rogation; sinner's prayer.

recapitulation approach to Revelation: the idea that the three main sections of the Tribulation (the seals, trumpets, and bowls) related in Revelation consist of a triad of repeats or summaries. The concept is old, having probably originated with Victorinus (d. A.D. 304), but it carries certain exegetical problems. Essentially, the question must be asked: why repeat the same information three times, even if there are different approaches to the same subject? *See also* chronological approach to Revelation; contrapuntal approach to Revelation; progressive/complementary approach to Revelation.

recapitulation theory of atonement: the Christian doctrine, much of which was articulated by Irenaeus, that humanity has been redeemed in Jesus' sacrificial death and resurrection. In essence, Christ has "summed up" all of God's purpose for human destiny in one unselfish act of salvation. *See also* atonement; Irenaeus; reconciliation; redemption; sacrifice; salvation; vicarious atonement.

Rechabites: a tribe of nomadic families, evidently not Hebrew, who were descended from Jonadab. They were known for their simplistic way of life and their fanatic teetotalism. In the days of Jeremiah, the prophet used the Rechabites as an object lesson to shame the unfaithful among his own people. He tempted the

Rechabites to drink wine in the Temple; when they refused (as he knew they would), the people of Judah were rebuked and the Rechabites were blessed by the promise of God that they would "never want a man to stand before me [God] forever" (Jer. 35:19). Legend says that the Rechabites married into the tribe of Levi and became eligible to serve before the Lord as "Rechabite priests." *See also* Jonadab; Kenites.

reconciliation: to return to friendship or to heal mental suffering after a quarrel. As a theological word, reconciliation affirms that the relationship between God and sinful man was "made right" in Christ. Believers have been "reconciled" to the goodness of God by His actions and their move to repentance (Rom. 5:10–11; 2 Cor. 5:19). *See also* absolution; atonement; recapitulation theory of atonement; eternal security; forgiveness; redemption; restoration.

***Reconquista*:** the name given to the fierce struggle to drive the Muslims (the Moors) out of the Iberian Peninsula in the 11th century. Pope Alexander II had given his papal blessing of eternal soul security to all who were killed in the conflict. The campaigns, began by Charles Martel, were finally successful when Granada fell to the Christians in 1492 after a struggle of 780 years. Count Vimara Peres did the same for Portugal in 868. Alfonso VII of Castile led a coalition in 1212 A.D. to produce another victory over the Moors (the battle of Las Novas de Tolosa). All of Spain was finally freed under King Ferdinand and Queen Isabella. The remaining Muslims were forced to convert to Christianity. Those efforts may be properly interpreted as early Crusades. *See also* Crusades; Islam; Martel, Charles; Moors.

Reconstructionism: a relatively modern take on postmillennialism. Adherents believe, and ardently work for, a society of harmony much like a theocratic kingdom. The construct of that kind of government would be largely dependent on the Ten Commandments with all the stipulations and punishments fixed in the Mosaic Law. Such a program would be an ideal platform for the return of Christ—as is advanced by the advocates of the theory—and may even precipitate it. *See also* dominion theology; postmillennial, postmillennialism; Reformed Reconstruction Movement; seven mountains dogma; theonomy; Whitby, Daniel.

record of Ahasuerus. See book(s).

records of the seers. See book(s).

Recreant Church: a contrived name for the church at Laodicea (Rev. 3:14–22) according to dispensational theology. The period indicated is from 1914 to the present, which can be described as a time of spiritual complacency (what Jesus termed "lukewarm"), doctrinal confusion, and loss of influence in the world. There are, nonetheless, some points of accomplishment in today's Church even though the Laodiceans received no compliments from the Lord's examination of them.

rector: an Anglican pastor of a self-supporting congregation or a university head. A rector may also be an incumbent to a parish who is entitled to a tithe. *See also* Church of England; clergy; dean; don; ecclesiastic(s); episcopate; minister(s); pastor(s); priest(s); vestry.

rector motif: also called moral governance, the theological idea that Jesus' death for sin was a statement about the seriousness of sin rather than a penal sacrifice. God, according to the rector motif, provides salvation by executive clemency rather than a demand for legal satisfaction. *See also* atonement; conquest motif; deliverance motif; endurance motif; exchange motif; exemplar motif; salvation; victor motif.

recusant: a Catholic who refuses to attend Mass. Originally, the term referred to those, such as the Jacobites, who refused attendance at Church of England services. *See also* Church of England; Jacobites; Roman Catholic Church.

red. See crimson.

redaction: the process or result of intentionally manipulating or changing the earliest rendition of Scriptures. The practice is fraught with risk since the editor could easily misinterpret the material or insert personal prejudices. A biblical redactor is essentially a document editor (*e.g.* the work of Julius Wellhausen). In a less technical sense, a redactor is but a secretary or copyist. *See also* accideme; alliteration; apostrophe; apothegm; assonance; autograph; Bible; Bible manuscripts; Bible translations; biblical criticism; chiasmus; conflict story; *constructio ad sensum;* context; contextualization;

dittography; double sense fulfillment; doublets; doubling; edification; eisegesis; epanadiplosis; epigrammatic statements; etymology; eisegesis; exegesis; figure of speech; folio; form criticism; gattung; gloss; gnomic sayings; grammatical-historical interpretation; *hapax legomena;* haplography; hermeneutic(s); higher criticism; homographs; homonyms; homophones; *homoteleuton;* hyperbole; idiom; *inclusio;* interpolation; interpretation; inverted nun; irony; isagogics; *itture sopherim;* jot and tittle; kere; *kethib;* "L"; liberalists interpretation; literal interpretation; litotes; loan words; lower criticism; "M"; Masoretic Text; minuscule(s); mystery of God; omission; onomastica; onomatopoeia; palimpsest; papyrus; paradigm; parallelism; parchment; *paroimia; paronomasia;* pericope; personification; Peshitta; pointing; point of view; polyglot; preunderstanding; principles of interpretation; proof texting; pun(s); "Q"; revelation, theological; rhetorical criticism; rhetorical devices; riddle; satire; *scripto continua;* scriptorium; *sebirin;* simile; similitude; source criticism; sources, primary and secondary; special points; strophe; superscription; symbol(s); synecdoche; syntax; synthetic parallelism; text; textual criticism; *tiggune sopherim;* Time Texts; Torah; translation; transposition; trope; type(s); typology; uncial(s); vellum; verbicide; Wellhausen, Julius.

red dragon: Satan, in the imagery presented in Revelation 12. *See also* animals, birds, and insects, symbology of; dragon; reptilian theory; Satan; seed of the serpent; serpent; tail of the dragon.

rede: an Old English word for "law" or "rule." The term has both ecclesiastical and occultic usage. *See also* apodictic law; canon(s) of the church; statute(s); Wiccan Rede.

Redeemed of the Lord, the: a name for sanctified Israel, most likely specified for the millennial era, in which the people of God will rest in salvation and purity (Isa. 62:12). Those Christians whose faith is in the savior Christ are properly pronounced as redeemed as well, but the title is not normally capitalized. *See also* Beulah; City No Longer Deserted; Deserted/Desolate; Hebrews as a people; Hephzibah; Holy People, the; Jerusalem as city; Jew(s); Judaism; name, a new; Sought After.

Redeemer: a name for God Who defends and rescues as described by the afflicted Job (Job 19:25). The name has since become a common expression for the Lord in almost every age—a savior. *See also* King of the Ages; redemption; names (titles) for God; names (titles) for Jesus.

redemption: the theological word expressing the fact that God, in Christ, is ready and capable to "redeem" or purchase sinful humanity through the sacrifice of Jesus (Rom. 3:22–24). The doctrine seems to spring from the ancient Hebrew law requiring the sacrifice of the first male animal from the womb, or its equivalent in money, to claim or sanctify the firstborn of every Jewish household (Ex. 13:15). The basis for such a requirement rests in the last plague of Egypt—the death of the firstborn of the Egyptians, from which the Israelites were spared when the death angel of God "passed over" the homes of the Israelites. Redemption is at the core of Christian theology because of its inscrutability, necessity, and power. It is unlike any explanation for guilt relief present in human history. Realistically, most Christians view the theology of redemption as an event, *viz.*, the crucifixion cross. For better understanding, however, the doctrine may best be considered as a story or process—a history and a mystery of how God has acted from creation and will work in like manner to the Second Coming as He provides deliverance and salvation from start to finish. Stories or records of His actions are favored Bible methods to convey complex truths anyway, just as Jesus chose parables and illustrations rather than dry lectures to explain his teachings. For example, Psalm 105 is an excellent review of Israel's history dealing with rescue and salvation for the nation. God works in time and miraculous feats to pursue eternal goals for His redemptive plans. So then, God has worked long and carefully to secure our freedom from sin with the penultimate event enacted on His Son's cross of sacrifice. Christianity's way out of our moral mess centers on Christ; other religions have formulated differing approaches. The ancient Egyptians used an escape from morality with elaborate funeral ritual, as seen in the *Book of the Dead*. The Greeks sought release from ignorance with knowledge and philosophical speculation. Buddhists yearn for escape from life—Nirvana—into nothingness. The Christian finds forgiveness in moral reality, facing sin and guilt, and accepting both grace and judgment from God. Atonement is a supernatural act of rescue from that which is outside of ourselves.

See also absolution; atonement; eternal security; fall from grace; forgiveness; Passover; perseverance of the saints; prayers of Revelation; recapitulation theory of atonement; Redeemer; restoration; salvation; shrive; sin(s).

Redemptioners: the name by which the first settlers of the colony of Maryland called themselves. *See also* Calvert, Cecilius and George.

redemptive history: the theological concept that all of history is God's method of moving His creation through salvation, redemption, and the sanctification processes—from rescue to perfection.

Redemptorists: an organization of lay brothers and priests of the Roman Catholic Church dedicated to missionary work worldwide. The official name of the faction is the Congregation of the Most Holy Redeemer (CSSA). *See also* Heckler, Isaac Thomas; missions, missionaries; religious organizations; Roman Catholic Church.

red heifer. See ashes of the red heifer.

red horse: the steed of the second horseman of the Apocalypse represented as War (Rev. 6:3–4). *See also* animals, birds, and insects, symbology of; black horse; eschatology, eschatological; four horsemen of the Apocalypse; horse; pale horse; white horse.

redivivus myth. See *Nero redivivus.*

Red Jacket: the Seneca tribal leader named Sagoyewatha (ca. 1758–1830) known by the red uniform tunic he often wore as a gift from a British officer. He was a reluctant supporter of England in the Revolutionary War but publically opposed (yet secretly aided) land concessions to the whites to thwart his rivals, Chiefs Cornplanter and Handsome Lake. Red Jacket kept the tribe loyally in the United States camp during the War of 1812 but spent the remainder of his life opposing white culture, especially Christian missionary work in Indian lands. Despite his stand, he was buried in a Christian cemetery on the reservation.

Red Letter Christians: a non-denominational movement began by Jim Wallis and Tony Campolo. The organization is a reaction to what the authors claim is extreme left or right-wing evangelism, making the contemporary religious model too partisan and politicized. The aim is to return to the pure teachings of Jesus, especially concerning social justice. The unusual name comes from the New Testament translations that employ red ink to highlight the quotes from Jesus. *See also* religious organizations.

Red Sea: the body of water separating Egypt from Arabia, the better translation of which is "Reed Sea" or *Yam Suph* in Hebrew. It was the waterway crossed by the escaping Exodus Israelites and the place where Pharaoh's pursuing army was drowned.

redshift: a phenomenon of astrophysics that describes an event occurring when electromagnetic radiation (such as light) from an object moves away from the observer and increases its wavelength. The shift is toward the "red end" of the visible spectrum. The science has implications for the study of the big bang theory and gravitation. *See also* big bang theory.

Red Shirts: a para-military of post-Civil War Democrats in South Carolina who vowed to keep white Republicans and blacks from voting during Reconstruction. These white supremacists formed numerous "rifle" and "saber" clubs in the state to break up campaign rallies and intimidate black voters. Unlike similar organizations like the Ku Klux Klan, the Red Shirts sported their colors in tunics modeled from those worn by Italian liberator Giuseppe Garibaldi's revolutionists. Restoration of Democratic rule in South Carolina ended the Red Shirts. *See also* American Party; Aryan Nation; Christian Identity Movement (CIM); Covenant, The Sword, and the Arm of the Lord, The (CSA); Fenians; Knights of the Golden Circle; Knights of the White Camellia; Ku Klux Klan; militant domestic organizations; Molly Maguires; Neo-Nazi(s); Patriot Movement, the; terrorism; terrorist(s).

reed: a length of reed stem grown mostly near the Nile. The portion was cut to specified standards (six cubits) if it was to be used as a measuring device. The cut reed tends to be fragile, so much so that if one leans on it like a cane, it may shatter and pierce the hand (2 Ki. 18:21; Isa. 36:6; Ezk. 29:6–7). That was precisely the intent when God referenced Israel's unfortunate habit of appealing to Egypt when in political or military difficulty. *See also* angels of measurement; measuring line; measuring rod, papyrus; plumb line.

Reed Sea. See Red Sea.

refectory: or frater, the room in a monastery, abbey, college, or similar institution where meals are taken. *See also* monastery; monasticism.

refined gold: gold that has been smelted and free of adulteration. The term represents the finest element of purity when speaking of morality and good conduct metaphorically. *See also* deontology; ethics; exemplar motif; gold, frankincense, and myrrh; gold, golden; gold of Ophir; gold of Uphaz; Judeo-Christian ethic; metathesis; moral relativism; normative ethics; orthopraxy; scruples.

refiner and purifier: terms for judgment that depict the harshness among God's methods to make us spiritually pure. The process involves prickly chafing or scrubbing to cleanliness. The prophet Malachi used fire and launderer's soap as illustrations of this rather uncomfortable type of discipline (Mal. 3:2–4).

reflexology: the holistic practice of flexing (massaging) the hands and feet to unblock the body's energy for healing in a different organ. *See also* holistic.

Reformation Day: the annual celebration of the date Martin Luther tacked his "Ninety-Five Theses" to the Whittenberg Chapel door. The recognized day is October 31. The occasion officially marks the start of the Reformation for historical and liturgical purposes. *See also* feasts and special days of Protestantism; liturgical year; Protestant Reformation, the; "Ninety-Five Theses, The"; Reformed churches.

Reformed Christianity. See Church of Jesus Christ of Latter-Day Saints.

Reformed Churches: those religious bodies with a history formed by bolting out from Roman Catholicism in the 16th century. The various branches were influenced by (not necessarily started from) Swiss reformers like John Calvin, Ulrich Zwingli, and others across Europe. The grouping is a large one, but some common theology can be discerned if enough autonomy and autocephalous polity of the local congregation is taken into account. Reformed believers generally mistrust tradition that is not related to Scripture, and they hold carefully to the covenant of grace. They adhere to the certainty of God's sovereignty (an influence of Calvinism) and are strictly Christo-centric. Some use the Westminster Confession of Faith as a doctrinal guide, and most are suspicious of written credo statements with the exception of the Apostles' Creed and certain older catechisms. Specific groups in the Reformed category would include Presbyterians (*e.g.* Associate Reformed, Cumberland, and the Presbyterian Church in America). Most Baptist persuasions, along with Protestant Episcopalians, may be counted, but a substantive listing is difficult because there are over 125 separate Reformed bodies in the world. The Moravian Church in America, the Reformed Church in America (along with one of its later affiliates, the United Church of Christ), and the Evangelical Covenant Church of America should also be included. Beliefs in eschatology are wide-ranged and differ from church to church. Doctrine runs the gamut on questions like the Millennium, the Tribulation, Armageddon, and the rapture. Most Presbyterians are decidedly preterists. Many denominations are amillennial or postmillennial. Considering Baptists alone as an example, apocalyptic belief would range from High Church amillennialism to Two-Seed-in-the-Spirit Pedestrian Baptist dispensationalism. Most eschatological thinking is individualized to a local body but not addressed from a superior ecclesiastical organization. The newly formed Cooperative Baptist Fellowship, to offer a case in point, partners with a broad range of Baptist-style believers without officially questioning any group's stance concerning eschatology or even other doctrinal standards. In general, Reformed Churches hold to the tenets of Ulrich Zwingli and John Calvin, having spread from Switzerland in 1561. Early history saw them in two divisions—Dutch Reformed and German Reformed—but most Arminian, Huguenot, Presbyterian, Baptist, Methodist, Lutheran, and other Protestants from Roman Catholicism can find a fit in their theology and history. Most are deeply interested in evangelism and religious education. *See also* Alsted, Johann Heinrich; Anglicanism; Anabaptists; antistes; Arminian Churches; Baptists; Barth, Karl; Book of Concord; Brunner, Emil Heinrich; Calvinism; Calvin, John; Camping, Harold; Canons of Dort; Chicago-Lambeth Conference; Christian Church (denomination); church bodies in America (typed); Churches of Christ; Church of England; Church of God;

Church of the Nazarene; Church of the United Brethren; classis; Cocceius, Johannes; Concords of Dort; confession(s) of faith; Congregationalists; consistory; Cotton, John; denomination(s), denominationalism; Disciples of Christ; Evangelical Covenant Church in America; Evangelical Free Church in America; 1 and 2 Helvetic Confessions; Five-Point Calvinism; Free Church(s); Frelinghuysen, Theodorus; *Geneva Psalter;* Great Awakenings, the; Hampton Court Conference; Heidelberg Catechism; Helvetic Consensus; Huguenots; Inner Light Churches; *Institutes of the Christian Religion;* Knox, John; Lutheran Church; mainline Protestantism; Methodists; Moravian Church; normative principle; open theism; *ordo salutis;* Oxford martyrs; Peale, Norman Vincent; Pentecostalism; predestination; Presbyterians; preterism; progressive revelation; Protestant Episcopal Church; Protestantism, Protestants; Protestant Reformation, the; Puritanism, Puritan(s); Raikes, Robert; Reformed Church in America; Reformation Day; Remonstrants; *Remonstrants,* the; Restoration Movement in America; River Brethren; Saybrook Platform; Salvation Army; Savoy Confession; Schaff, Philip; Schleiermacher, Friedrich Daniel Ernst; Schwarzenau Brethren; Schwenkfelder, Caspar von Ossig; Separatists; *sola Christo, sola fide; sola gratia, sola Scriptura;* sodality; *soli Deo gloria;* supralapsarianism; Taylor, Graham; Thirty-Nine Articles, the; total depravity; Tractarianism; TULIP; United Churches; United Church of Christ; Waldenses; Weems, Mason Locke; Wesleyan Church; Westminster Confession; William an d Mary; Wolsey, Thomas; Zwingli, Ulrich (Huldrych).

Reformed Church in America: a Protestant denomination springing from the tenets of Ulrich Zwingli and John Calvin. The fellowship in America began in 1628 as a plant of Dutch Reformed colonists from Europe with the first congregation established in New Amsterdam, New York, under the pastoral leadership of Jonas Michaelius. In 1754 they set up Queens College (now Rutgers) and have grown to about 224,000 but membership has been steadily declining for several years. *See also* church bodies in America (typed); denomination(s), denominationalism; Reformed Churches.

Reformed Era: a contrived name for dispensational theology's reference to the church at Philadelphia (Rev. 3:7–13). The time indicated is about 1548–1914 when the Church was experiencing growth, missionary outreach, improved morality, expanded lay application, congregational hymn singing, and solid doctrine. *See also* dispensation(s); dispensational theology; Philadelphia.

Reformed Reformation Movement: a.k.a. Reformation Reformed Movement, Reformed Truth Movement, and other names. Reformed Reformation is a somewhat modern theological outlook that perceives today's Church as perched on the edge of a new awakening that will be nothing short of releasing worldwide conditions to precipitate Christ's Second Coming in the 21st century. To that end, the doctrines of the movement resemble postmillennialism or dominion theology. However, there are no particular end time theories that adequately cover the program of the sect. Among the main leaders are C. Peter Wagner and Bill Hamon (with others), who claim to have created a global network of new kingdom enthusiasts ready to transform the present-day Church. The principles of the Reformed Reformation center on the idea that church history marks out a pattern of moral and theological gains and losses, which will only be terminated when world conditions are fully implemented according to Christ's will for his Church. There have been a total of three periods of Restorations in the body of Christ, interrupted by years of falling away. The first demonstration occurred 4 B.C.–A.D. 313—from the birth of Jesus to the church's fall into the Dark Ages under a corrupt Roman Catholic system. The Church was then established by the Holy Spirit and given its needed tools for success. Much was lost in the interval until the Protestant Reformation era, dated from October 31, 1517, to the year 2007. Progress was helped along by the *restoration* of the prophetic gifts periodically lost along the way. In 500 years, the Church moved forward again, aided by renewals of the faith such as the Protestant revolt of the 1500s, the evangelical movements of the 1600s, the holiness movement of 1700s, the faith healing emphases of the 1800s, the Pentecostal explosion of 1900s, the charismatic movement in 1950, the prophetic-apostolic movement in 1980 (re-establishment of the offices of prophet and apostle), and the start of the "saints movement" (legions of mainstream Christians hard at work in the marketplace perfecting the Church) in 2007. So, then, the third great Restoration began in 2008, according to

Acts 3:21, and conditions are now right on the planet to allow the release of Christ from heaven to claim his Church on earth. The movement is now so organized that it is generating its own theological language to facilitate its actions. Strange terminology (to most of us) has appeared with the advent of Kingdom Enforcers, Church Reformation for City Transformation, Seven-Mountain Ministers, Kingdom Demonstration for World Transformation, Elijah Revolutionaries, Davidic Company, Joshua Generation, Transformers, Omega-Transition Generation, Christian International Ministers, etc. For the consummation of the kingdom of God, only a few more prophetic Scriptures are yet to be fulfilled. The list following is retrieved from Bill Hamon's compilation: (1) Christ's Church must fully preach and demonstrate the gospel (Mt. 24:14), (2) all biblical truths must be restored (Acts 3:21), (3) whereas the Second Reformation fulfilled the first four of six doctrines of Christ, the Third must complete the remaining two (Heb. 6:1–2), (4) God must raise up strong kingdom influences like the prophets of old (Dan. 7:14, 18, 22, 27), (5) the Third Reformation saints and fivefold ministers must disciple the nations (Mt. 28:18–19), (6) the Third Reformation must reap a great harvest of souls to complete the magic number for the kingdom's capacity (Rev. 6:11; Ps. 139:16; Eph. 3:10–11, 21), (7) the new prophets and apostles must receive the revelations of the final mysteries of God (Rev. 10:7; Eph. 3:3–5), (8) five-fold-ascension-gift ministers must equip the saints of today and do the greater work of Christ (Eph. 4:11–16), (9) God's true prophets must start ministering their mandate to exercise authority over the nations (Jer. 1:5, 10; Rev. 11:3–6), (10) Third Reformation saints must pray the Lord's Prayer until the kingdom of heaven is here on earth in reality, as well as figuratively (Mt. 6:10), (11) continue to present the Church commission until every country of the world is either a sheep nation or a goat nation (Mt. 25:31–34), (12) usher the time when Christ will make his enemies his footstool (Heb. 1:13; Ps. 110: 1), (13) the redemption of the physical body to a new one (Rom. 8:18–23; Eph. 1:13–14; Phil. 3:21), (14) the saints of the Most High must possess the kingdom of God (Rev. 5:10; 11:15; Dan. 7:14, 18, 22, 27), (15) the Saints of God must assume authority to execute heavenly judgments (Ps. 49:6–9; 1 Cor. 6:2–3; Rev. 2:26–27; *et al.*), (16) after the full Restoration, all must be consummated according to the plan of God (Eph. 1:10; Acts 3:21–25). By the movement's own evaluation: "The thought of the Church influencing the nations of the world, executing the judgments of God, and supernaturally demonstrating the Kingdom of God until they become Christian nations is beyond the comprehension of the natural mind." Nevertheless, the advocates say it will happen. Perhaps because of the complexity of its basic doctrines (along with its overt institutional optimism) the movement appears to be gaining little attention in the contemporary world. *See also* dominion theology; 888; postmillennial, postmillennialism; reconstruction; sect(s); seven-mountain dogma.

Refreshment Sunday. See Laetare Sunday.

regalism: the principle that royalty has supreme power in government, politics, and diplomacy, especially when referencing the church. *See also* disestablishmentarianism; caesaropapacy; collegialism; civil religion; divine right of kings; Establishment Clause and Free Exercise Clause; Mandate of Heaven; state church.

regathering of Israel. See restoration of Israel (the Jews).

regeneration: a theological word asserting that sinful persons can be "reborn" in forgiveness by the sacrificial act of Christ. God can renew the spiritual condition of the sinner and provide a new life. *See also* accept Christ, to; altar call; "asking Jesus into my heart"; birth from above; blood of Christ; blood of the Lamb; born again; conversion; firstfruits of the resurrection; firstfruits of the Spirit; "plead the blood"; profession of faith; salvation; "saved"; turn your life [heart] over to Jesus; "walking the aisle; "washed in the blood."

Regina the Seeress: an early 20th century prophetess who predicted that the earth would be destroyed by epidemics, famines, and poison. Survivors will eventually emerge from their caves to start civilization again. By way of interest, an Internet search of the name "Regina" will surface numerous links of prophetic sites as if it were a sort of code or cryptogram for eccentric foretellers. *See also* prophetess(es); psychic(s).

regula: the rules of monastic living based on poverty, chastity, and obedience. *See also* mendicant(s); monasticism; orders.

regulative principles of worship: an approach to public worship that only allows expression of what God commands as recorded in the Bible. If a practice is not promoted in Scripture, it is not to be employed. *See also* dialogical principle of worship; elements of worship; form of worship; liturgy; normative principles of worship; worship.

Rehoboam: king of the unified kingdom of Israel inherited from his father, Solomon. This situation quickly changed, however, when Rehoboam dismissed the counsel of his mature elders and heeded the advice of his radical young friends instead. The recommendation of the inexperienced youths was that the new king should act harshly toward the ten northern tribes who were eager to loosen the grip of Solomon's iron rule and heavy taxation. Such an attitude could only bifurcate the nation, which indeed happened within days of the start of Rehoboam's reign (931–913 B.C.). Now the nation was split into the Northern Kingdom of ten tribes called Israel and the Southern Kingdom of Judah. The union of North and South had endured a mere seventy-three years. Rehoboam was unable to heal the breach, and only the tribes of Judah and Benjamin remained loyal to the line of David. *See also* king(s); kings of Israel and Judah; kings of Israel and Judah in foreign relations.

reign (in heaven): God's sovereignty as precipitated from heaven. There, in interaction with the Trinity, God may direct His providence both in the now and in eternity. *See also* heaven.

reign (on earth): the rule of Christ and his saints on the earth, usually considered in light of the Millennium. There (Rev. 22:4), the residents are marked as belonging to God and the Lamb and are offered ruling authority with the divine forever. Over whom do they reign, however? each other? those in the lake of fire? over themselves? Those ideas seem nonsensical, so perhaps the reign covers the universe and that which is beyond knowable reality. Part of knowing faith is the never-ceasing thirst for learning and spiritual discipline.

Reiki: from the Japanese language meaning "ghost energy," an occultic style of massage therapy. The practice may be the same as Therapeutic Touch but using one's Reiki spirit guides to spiritual understanding. *See also* occult, occultic; psychic healing; spirit guide(s).

reincarnation: the belief, considered fallacious by standard Christian doctrine, that life is renewed periodically by new birth in a different form and age. Reincarnation may be into human or animal form and, as generally interpreted, may be progressive to a higher plane of living or regression to a lower one. The concept is also known as transmigration of the soul, metempsychosis, or palingenesis, particularly as it is developed in Hinduism. *See also* afterlife; born again; Buddhism; future life, doctrine of the; Hinduism; Ifa; metempsychosis; Nietzsche, Friedrich; past life regression; rebirthing; soulmate; Wheel of Time, the.

rejoicing: the emotion or expression of joyfulness or praise. The Scriptures, including a particular emphasis in apocalyptic language, are filled with instances of thanksgiving and praise to God for His blessings and actions. Perhaps the best expression of rejoicing is found in the letter to the Philippians, especially Philippians 4:4 and certain portions of Revelation. The prophets were not necessarily adverse to joviality but, for the most part, are perceived as austere in their demeanor, a condition no doubt brought on by their difficult calling and dangerous existence. They did, nevertheless, celebrate God's bounty with blessing and praise and encouraged others to do so.

relative deprivation: the psychological perception that some individuals or groups lack what others may have, especially if that feeling fosters a sense of injustice. Such a circumstance may suggest that certain sects, for example, can compensate people for what the mainstream churches have neglected for them. The theory may also explain why some religious institutions are excessively morally strict or exclusive in their membership. *See also* sociology of religion.

relativism: the proposition that absolute truth does not exist. Rather, every moral or theological issue must be considered with extenuating circumstances in mind. The concept wreaked havoc with established Christian doctrine, which asserts that God is unchangeable and His laws are not flawed nor His purpose false. The antonym for relativism is absolutism. Theologically speaking, relativism is a philosophical concept that every belief or practice has its own merits when viewed with all others. Ideals such as truth, morality, knowledge, and the like cannot exist alone but must be studied and practiced in context with the prevailing culture, society, or history where it is utilized; so then, every so-called truth is not unconditional but is defined by what existentialism says it might be. Many denominations, cults, sects, and secret societies operate on this philosophical basis, not the least of whom are the Jesuits. *See also* absolutism; cultural relativism; culture wars; metathesis; moral relativism; normative ethics; orthopraxy; PC; philosophy of religion; postmodernism; Reality Therapy; scruples; secular humanism; social issues; Society of Jesus; sociology of religion.

relic(s): any object that is declared to have holy or magical qualities. Most religions, with the general exception of Protestantism, possess any number of them. The Roman Catholic Church cherished the veneration of relics from about A.D. 451 to 1050. The Eastern branch was also keen to have them, and their venerated icons held some of the same magical properties. No new church could truly be established without one; at least a splinter of the true cross, nails from the cross, bones or body parts of Jesus or of a saint, articles of clothing or footwear, a thorn from the crown of thorns, an object from the last supper, or some other sacred object were a source of power and prestige. Authentic religious relics are rare, if they exist at all, so most displayed in the past and present are fake, or of dubious authenticity at best. Still, the Roman Catholic Church ranks them numbered as first, second, and third according to their importance and sources and they are utilized in Eastern Orthodoxy. Genuine relics, even if in continuation, by no means prove they have esoteric spiritual or magical properties. The objects can easily ease into the minds of some devotees as objects of reverence or even idols. Nevertheless, the Roman Catholic Church has created a holy day for them. *See also* Aaron's rod that budded; amulet(s); ankh; ark of the covenant; Ark, the synagogue; ashes of the red heifer; astrolabe; athame; bagua; beast, image of the; Belial; bells on the horses; *besom;* black mirror; black stones; Bondi Tree; bone(s); Bread of the Presence; breastplate of the high priest; Bridget's Cross; bronze serpent; Celtic wheel; chains of Saint Peter; charm(s); Chintamani Stone; Christingle; Coronation Stone; crosier; Crosier of Saint Patrick; cross; crown(s); crucifix; crystal skulls; Eagle Bowl; Eastern Orthodox Church; Ebenezer; Elijah's chair; Emerald Tablet of

Hermes, the; enneagram; ephod; Foundation Stone; furniture and furnishings of the modern church; furniture and furnishings of the tabernacle, temples, and modern synagogue; God helmet, the; golden plates; golden rose; golden stool; gargoyle(s); gris-gris; Helm of Awe; Holy Blood, the; Holy Grail; holy nails, various; Holy Rood; horoscope(s); hyssop; icon, iconography; *icthus;* Januarius (San Gennaro); Jesus junk; juju; juniper; lamp, lampstand(s); liturgical year; magic square; mala beads; mandala; Mandylion, the Holy; manna; Menorah; mercy seat; monstrance; Nehushtan; oil of anointing; oil of saints; ouija board; Palladium; pentagram; Pieta; powder of projection; Prepuce, the Holy; Procession of the Holy Blood; purdah; raisin cakes, the sacred; reliquary; robe of Christ; Roman Catholic Church; rosary; rune(s); *Sacra Cintola;* sacred bowls; sacred drink; Sanctus bell; *Sacra Cintola;* sandals of Jesus; *Santa Camisa; Santa Cruz;* sash; *shofar;* shrine(s); Shroud of Turin; signet ring; Spear of Destiny; spoons, apostle; stations of the cross; Sudarium of Oviedo; Sun Stone; tabot; talisman(s); tarot; Temple utensils; threshold, not stepping on the; titulus; token; totemism; unknown god, an; Urim and Thummin; veil of Veronica; votive; wafer; wanga; white stones; witch cake.

religion: the ritualistic practice of worship or faith expression—any action done regularly (*religiously*) as a routine. Religion as worship or a lifestyle is considered the cultus of one's beliefs. Not only is religion central to individual faith and practice, but it is also an essential ingredient for nations. No political entity has ever succeeded without a form of religion to give it inspiration and form. Even so, the future destructive Antichrist will attempt it when he destroys Religious Babylon from his kingdom. It should be noted that religion is not the same as faith but both are essential to produce a positive effect in the believer. It has been said that religion without faith (trusting what we cannot prove) is scarcely religion at all. A proven proverb declares, "religion is for those who fear hell, while spirituality is for those who'd been there." Religion may, and does, take many forms worldwide. Of the 7.9 billion people alive today, some 4.7 billion worship some god other than Jesus Christ including Buddhism, Hinduism, Islam, African rituals, Chinese folk expressions, Eastern mysticism, Native American traditions, and Australian aboriginal practices.

Some find expressions in Baha'i, Shinto, Sikhism, Taoism, Wicca, or Zoroastrianism. Another 330 million make up idols or reserve adoration for the self. Humans are irrepressibly religious in one or more of its many expressions while those not counted appear to rest their faith in nothing. *See also* faith; liturgical year; liturgy, Christian; liturgy, Jewish; Religious Babylon; religiosity; sociology of religion; worship.

religiosity: the degree to which a person may be deemed "religious" or "spiritual." Sociologists, and some other specialists, are interested in such data and test for its influence in society. The process, even so, is predictably subjective to some extent by its very nature of observation. *See also* devout; moralistic therapeutic deism; religion; religious capital; sociology of religion; Stark effect.

religious abuse. See church abuse.

Religious Babylon: the derived name for the corrupted ecclesiology of Babylon the Great as chiefly described in Revelation 17. Mystery Babylon is an alternate name for the same entity. *See also* Babylon the Great; cup of adulteries; eschatology, eschatological; False Church; filth of her adulteries; "glorified herself"; Great Prostitute, the; Mystery Babylon the Great the Mother of Prostitutes and of the Abominations of the Earth; religion; Secular Babylon; whore of Babylon; wine of her adulteries.

religious capital: the loyal affiliation to a religion, creed, or faith culture. The amount of time, money, and talent invested in one's faith increases loyalty to the group and investment of devotion. *See also* religiosity; sociology of religion.

religious education: the processes by which religion and faith principles are taught to children and adults. Roman Catholicism relies heavily on the catechism, but Protestants usually take another view of the taxonomy of "Sunday school," group Bible studies, and other methods of teaching and learning. Most educators favor a six-step program in its indoctrination to faith development: approach, style, strategy, method, technique, and "step" (inculcation), all with a vertical (God to man and man to God) paradigm included. Subjects may be approached from a short list of perspectives: 1. the historical, 2. the psychological, 3. the sociological, 4. the logical, or 5. the structural. The understanding is that a planned and dynamic approach overcomes the deficiencies of pedagogy. The philosophy of religious education is at the heart of the effort. Is religion rational or non-rational? Is it cognitive or expressive? Is it science or art? No method is completely satisfactory but ever fascinating. Sunday schools for all ages abound, often taught by laypersons. Theological seminaries and Bible colleges are available for clergy training on an advanced level. In early America, almost all institutions of higher learning were private and church sponsored. The first was Harvard, established in 1636 by the Puritans for the training of young clergy for missionary action on the Massachusetts frontier. Then came William and Mary in Virginia (1693) by the Anglicans and Yale (1701) by Congregationalists in Connecticut. After the Great Awakening, several universities arose, including the College of New Jersey (later Princeton in 1746) from the Presbyterians, King's College (Columbia University in 1759) by Anglicans, the College of Rhode Island (Brown University in 1764) from Baptists, and Queen's College in New Jersey (Rutgers in 1766) by the Dutch Reformed. In 1769 came Dartmouth in New Hampshire, founded by Congregationalists to educate both white and Indian preachers. In the modern era, almost all vestiges for any religious base have eroded and given way to secularism, with the exception of privately endowed colleges and universities still somewhat affiliated with interested denominations. Colleges for women were later in development but now offer quality education. By the end of World War II, coeducation was about 93 percent nationwide. Notable pioneer female schools included Elizabeth Female Academy in Mississippi (1819), Troy Female Seminary (1821), Mount Holyoke College (1836), Vassar (1861), Wellesley (1870), Smith College (1871), Bryn Mawr (1880), Newcomb (1826), Barnard (1889), Pembroke (1891), and Radcliff (1894). One hundred and six of the first 108 colleges in America were founded in Christianity; college presidents were almost always clergymen until 1900. Without doubt, education in Colonial America, both public and religious, was a founding principle that set the nation on the road to greatness. *See also* Abode of Learning; Assemblies of the Wise; Assemblies of Wisdom; auxiliary ministries; Bible baseball; Bible of the poor; Bible societies; Bray, Thomas; Campus Crusade for Christ; catechism; Chafer, Lewis Sperry; Chautauqua Movement, the; confession(s) of faith; cursillo;

Dallas Theological Seminary; Davis, Samuel; didactic method; didactic theology; Didascalia; disputation; Dunster, Henry; Dwight, Timothy; edification; episcopate; *episcopos;* family altar; Finney, Charles Grandison; gaon; Gideons International; Glover, Jose; Harvard, John; Hughes, John Joseph; InterVarsity Christian Fellowship; madrassa(s); magisterium; Marsh, Jedidiah; Mather, Increase; McCosh, James; Moody, Dwight L.; mystagogy; Navigators; Niagara Bible Conferences; "Old Deluder Satan Law"; palanca; parochial school(s); Payne, J. Barton; Pentecost, J. Dwight; quarterly; Raikes, Robert; rally; retreat; Rite of Christian Initiative of Adults (RCIA); scholasticism; secular institutes; seminaries, theological; shepherding (discipleship); Sunday school(s); sword drill; synagogue; tract(s); systematic theology; Union College; Vincent, John Heyl; Wahhabism; Walvoord, John; Wheelock, Eleazar; Wise, Isaac Mayer; Young Men's and Young Women's Hebrew Associations; Young Men's Christian Association; Young Women's Christian Association; youth religious organizations.

Religious Left, the: a disparate group made up primarily of progressive clergy, activists, and academics which has experienced a resurgence of sorts since the election of President Donald Trump in 2017. The unofficial membership can be considered the left, or "liberal," side of the more readily recognized Religious Right in the United States and interested in community aspects of topics like immigration, gun control, social welfare, health care, and the like in the public square. There has long been a so-called Religious Left in the country active in such issues as slavery, civil rights, protests against the Viet Nam war, and other high-profile national affairs but seems to be presently experiencing a more robust (and some would say spiteful) influence in the political arena. *See also* Christian Coalition; liberalism, liberalist(s); Moral Majority; public square; Religious Right, the; social issues.

religious organizations: structured religious cooperatives that, in some way or another, seek to promote the sponsoring faith group or its goals. The organization may be public or private or non-profit or for-profit but is always faith-based. Any given association may support scripture societies, humanitarian aid, missions, education, public health, political issues, evangelism, counseling services, disaster relief, sports, trade or labor unions, finances, charitable work, youth activities, information dissemination, morality, philosophy, ecumenism, or almost any other creditable cause imaginable. Churches, mosques, synagogues, chapels, religious fraternities, monasteries, abbeys, priories, friaries, pious orders and societies, temples, and the like are religious organizations within themselves. *See also* Abode of Learning; American Bible Society; American Society for the Promotion of Temperance; Anthroposophical Society; Anti-Saloon League; Assemblies of the Wise; Assemblies of Wisdom; Association for Research and Enlightenment; Assumptionist Orders; *Ateret Cohanim;* Augustinian Order; Barnabites; Benedict, Order of; Bible societies; Black Canons; *B'nai B'rith;* Campus Crusade for Christ; canon(s) of the church; Capuchin Order; cardinal(s); Carmelites; Carthusians; Catholic Women's League (CWL); Celestines; Center for Research on the New World Order (NWO); Chautauqua Movement, the; Christian Coalition; church; Christian Identity Movement (CIM); Cistercians; Clapham sect; communal communities; conclave; confraternities; Congregation for the Propagation of the Doctrine of the Faith; consistory; Consistory, the; convent; conventicle; councils, church; Council on American-Islamic Relations; Counter Cult Movement; Creativity Movement; Cult Awareness Network; *Curia;* Dallas Theological Seminary; Dionysian Artificers; discalced; docastry; Dominicans; Dragonnades; endorsing agency; Evangelical Alliance; faith-based initiative(s); Focolare Movement; fold; Franciscans; Francis de Sales; Freedom from Religion Foundation; full gospel; Gideons International; Herodians; *Hojjatieh;* Holy Club, the; Holy Name Society; house of prayer; hub(s); infirmieri; Interchurch World Movement; International Fellowship of Christians and Jews; InterVarsity Christian Fellowship; Invisible College; "invisible institution, the"; knighted orders; Knights of Columbus; Legion of Christ; Lily Dale Assembly; Manifest Sons of God; Minim; mission; missions, missionaries; monasticism; Moral Majority; Moral Rearmament Movement; mosque; National Council of Churches; Navigators; *Neturei Karta;* Niagra Bible Conferences; oblate; offering; *Opus Dei;* Opus Santorum Angelorum; orders; Papal Bodyguard, Swiss; Parliament of the World's Religions; parochial school(s); Paulist Fathers; Pharisees; Poor Clare Sisters; Premonstratensian

Order; priory; Promise Keepers; prophetic associations; Rainbow Coalition; Redemptorists; Red Letter Christians; Rite of Christian Instruction of Adults (RCIA); sacellum; Sadducees; Sanhedrin; scribe(s); secular institutes; seminaries, theological; Servite Order; settlement houses; Shi'ite Islam; Shrine of the Book; shul; Sicarii; Society for the Promulgation of the Gospel in Foreign Parts; Society for the Promulgation of the Gospel in New England; Society of Christian Socialists; Society of Jesus; Society of Saint Vincent de Paul (SVP); sodality; Solomon's Temple; sons (school) of the prophets; Student Volunteer Movement; Sunday School(s); Sunni Islam; synagogue; Synagogue of the Freedmen; Temple(s); temple(s); Temple Institute; Temple Mount and Land of Israel Faithful Movement; tertiary; trade guilds; Trappist Order; Tubingen School; 24/7 Prayer Movement; Union College; Vacation Bible School; Voluntary Human Extinction Movement; Waqf; Watch Tower Bible and Tract Society (WBTS); Witenagemot; Woman's Christian Temperance Union; World Church of Peace; World Pantheist Movement; Young Men's and Young Women's Hebrew Associations; Young Men's Christian Association (WMCA); Young Women's Christian Association (YWCA); youth religious organizations; Zealots.

Religious Right, the: a general term, pushed mostly by the media, to name those religious/political groups who operate to the more conservative moral and political stance. The most recognizable organizations in the United States on the list would likely include the American Family Association, Christian Coalition, Concerned Women for America, the Family Research Council, and Focus on the Family. Themes of debate mostly center on cultural and religious issues, such as abortion, homosexuality, same-sex marriage, prayer in public schools, physician-assisted suicide, etc. *See also* Christian Coalition; Moral Majority; public square; Religious Left, the; social issues.

Religious Science: a spiritual, metaphysical, and philosophical movement began in 1927 by Ernest Holmes (1887–1960). It was patterned, as were many in that era, after the blooming New Thought Movement and should probably not be classed as an organized church. *See also* Akashic Records; Divine Science, Church of; mind science; New Thought Movement; sect(s).

religism: the belief that one particular faith is superior to another. The term can also signify a distinct fear or hatred of persons of different faiths. *See also* social issues; xenophobia.

reliquary: a *reliquiae,* a shrine or casket to hold the remains of saints venerated as relics. The term means "remains." *See also* furniture and furnishings of the modern church; ossuary; relic(s).

remnant: a remainder, a select group (either Jews or Gentiles) who survive the punishing judgments of God. According to some premillennialists, dispensationalists, and some other viewpoints, those few among the Jews who will acknowledge their Messiah, Jesus, during or after the Tribulation are collectively known as the remnant of Israel. Some estimates claim that only one-tenth of the surviving Tribulation Jews will enter the Millennium, but how this number is determined remains unclear. The prophet Zechariah may be the best predictor of such national repentance (Zech. 12:10–14) who predicts the survivors will be one-third of the population. This preserved minority will be among the seed population for the Millennium and will be principal worship leaders there. The Jews also use the term in basically the same context as a surviving group (*i.e.,* Ezra 9:8). Examples may be found as early as Genesis where Joseph and his brothers were considered remnants saved from famine in the land (Gen. 45: 7). The eighth century prophets (Amos, Hosea, Micah, and early Isaiah) had scant hope for national survival—they could only promise a few survivors as God spelled out His intent for the people of that day. The prophet Habakkuk came to realize that although his nation was certainly to be conquered by Babylon, he could state: "We will not die." Since individual Jews did indeed die in the invasion, he surely meant they would not perish as a people (Hab. 1:12). Hope grew later as the Jews began to ponder those preserved as "a remnant will return" (Isa. 10:21). Such was a proven truth since the returning Jews from the Babylonian Captivity were also called a remnant (Ez. 9:8). The day of Israel's final salvation will have a future occurrence, but when? We do not know exactly at what time that event will transpire but we do know when it began: at the point when the nation rejected her Messiah Jesus (her "offense" as the Gospels call it) and the Lord's subsequent crucifixion. That affliction will end in the days of Tribulation when the race, or its remnant, will seek the Lord's face in repentance and humiliation. It is then the repentant Jews will come to believe *Yeshua Hamashiach*—Jesus is Messiah. Numbers of aware people are finding that deliverance even in our day. Some would insist that the great date of national repentance lies 2000 years beyond the crucifixion or 4000 years from the creation of Adam. The numbers are derived by calling a scriptural "day" as equivalent to 1000 years. Thus, after two days (2000 years) following the cross or four days (4000 years) from Adam's appearance Israel will be saved. So then, after six days (6000 years) Israel will be regathered to be followed by the final day (1000 years) of the Millennium. They are saying God worked 6000 years to restore the ruined creation and rested on the seventh, so He must work another 6000 to restore the subsequent recreation after Christ's rejection to be followed by another 1000 in the Millennium. But let us not tumble headlong into the highly questionable literalist interpretation of 2 Peter 3:8 which bases their assumptions. "With the Lord a day is like a thousand years, and a thousand years are like a day." The reference is to God's unhampered use of time, not its measurement. Counting the days and years after creation, then counting the days and years before the end, is impossible. And how do they know God will use 6000 years of the second half of the formula simply because He did in the first? The straightforward consideration is that Christ will complete his work of redemption when the Father's time is set for it. Israel will be saved in her proper time, as will all redeemed non-Jews. *See also* Abraham's seed; Azal; angelic miracles; blindness of Israel; Bozrah; crushing rock that became a mountain; curses of Isaiah; Edom, Moab, and Ammon; election; elect, the; eschatology, eschatological; Jewish persecution; Joktheel; kingdom that cannot be shaken, a; kingdom, the; messianic age, the; millennial geography; millennial Sabbath, millennial sacramentalism; millennial Temple; Millennium, millennial; Mount Paran; New Covenant, the; New Eden; "one new man"; Pella; Petra; rebuilding the Temple; restoration of all things; restoration of Israel (the Jews); restoration Temple (and land); rod of iron; Sabbath rest; Sabbatical millennialism; second Exodus; seed of Israel; Seed, the; Sele; septa-millennial; Shear-Jashub; "six-day theory, the"; spiritual Israel; Temple(s); time of Jacob's trouble; times of refreshing; Ussher, James; witnesses, great cloud of.

Remonstrants: Dutch Protestants and followers of Jacobus Arminius. The name trends from five "Remonstrants" presented to the state, naming their points of differences with Calvinism. The five make up the major tenets of Arminianism: 1. predestination is conditional—not absolute, 2. atonement is universal in intent, 3. man cannot exercise a saving faith alone, 4. the grace of God is necessary, but it is not irresistible to the human spirit, 5. believers can resist sin but can fall from grace. *See* also Arminian Church; Arminianism; Arminius, Jacobus; Calvinism; Canons of Dort; conditional election; election; eternal security; fall from grace; free will; "once saved, always saved"; perseverance of the saints; predestination; *Remonstrants, the*; Synod of Dort; total depravity; TULIP.

***Remonstrants*, the:** a series of influential articles expressing the truths of Arminianism. The chief framer was named to be John Uytenbogaert, chaplain to the German prince, Maurice. The publications were bolstered by a single Christian writer known simply as Koornheert, along with Arminius himself (oddly enough, he had been engaged to refute Koornheert), and Hugo Grotius. A *Counter-Remonstrant* predictably followed to criticize the first. *See also* Arminius, Jacobus; Arminianism; Canons of Dort; confession(s) of faith; Grotius, Hugo; Remonstrants; Synod of Dort.

remote viewing: the pseudoscientific practice of "sensing with the mind"—an attempt to visualize unseen and distant objects. Practitioners have used extrasensory perception (ESP) and millions have been spent on research of the idea but no evidence has emerged that any experiment has been successful. The concept is similar to clairvoyance. *See also* anthropomancy; anthroposophy; apotropaic magic; Ariosophy; astral projection; astrology, astrologers; audition; augury; automatic writing; bagua; belomancy; bibliomancy; black arts; cartomancy; chiromancy; clairaudience; clairsentience; clairvoyance; cleromancy; cone of power; conjure; cryptesthesia; crystallomancy; curious acts; divination; dream(s); dreams and visions; ecstasy; enchantment; enneagram; evil eye; extrasensory perception (ESP); foreknowledge; foretelling; geomancy; grimoire; hepatoscopy; Hermetic wisdom; Hermetic writings; hex; hierscopy; horoscope(s); hydromancy; Ifa; incantation; labyrinth walk; lecanomancy; locution; magic arts; magic, magick; magic square; magnetism; *mana*; mantic wisdom; mantra; monition; necromancy; New Age religion; numbers, symbology of; occult, occultic; omen; oneiromancy; oracle(s); otherworldly journeys; ouija board; out-of-body experiences (OBEs); paranormal; peace pole(s); pentagram; portent; precognition; prediction; prefiguration; premonition; prodigy; prophecy, general; psi; psychic healing; psychic reading; psychomancy; psychometry; pyramidology; remote viewing; retrocognition; revelation; prophecy, general; rhabdomancy; scrying; séance; secret wisdom; sorcery, sorceries; spell; spell names; spiritism; stigmata; superstition; tarot; telegnosis; telepathy; telesthesia; theugry; third eye, the; totemism; vision quest; visions; visualization; Voodoo; Voudou; witchcraft; *ya sang*; yoga; Zen; *zos kia* cultus.

Remphan: or Rephan, an astral deity worshiped by the Israelites during part of their wilderness wanderings (Acts 7:43). The name is derived from the Septuagint rendering of "Raiphan" found in Amos 5:26. The idol is likely related to Chiun (Saturn). *See also* Levant pantheon; Raphan, star of; Saccuth.

Remuel: one of the archangels named in pseudepigraphal writings (not part of the Scripture) who is said to be in charge of those who rise (the resurrected?). *See also* angel(s); archangel(s); liturgical year.

Renaissance: a new way of thinking and a fresh approach to the world that arose with Europe's emergence from the Middle Ages and the innovation of humanistic thinking, an age of "enlightenment." The new scholars had merely rediscovered the Greek and Roman classics, especially Plato, and called it a "rebirth." The term "Renaissance" comes from the Italian word *renascita*— rebirth or renewal—which 19th century thinkers named by its French form, *Renaissance. See also* age of reason; arabesque; Bacon, Roger; Erasmus, Desiderius; Haran; humanism; Newton, Sir Isaac; scholasticism.

rending of garments: a sign of distress or mourning for practicing Jews. The action was both dramatic and sacrificial because clothing was precious and expensive. In a funeral setting, the practice of tearing or cutting one's clothes is called *keriah*. On such occasions, the clothing may be repaired after seven days, except for the death of parents—in such instances, the dress is never restored. The Talmud names at least ten accidents or circumstances for which the Jews ought to rend their garments, something many of the prophets did on a regular basis. The people were prone to tear their clothes when: a sage dies; in the presence of death; the demise of one's Torah tutor, a patriarch, or a judge; upon seeing the sacred scrolls burnt; seeing Jerusalem or Judah desecrated; upon contemplating the destroyed Temple site; upon perceiving blasphemy against God; for repentance; at the rejection of God's plan for His people; or as an expression of rage. The high priest at the trial of Jesus rent his uniform (Mk. 14:63) in anger. Ecclesiastes (Ecc. 3:7) asserts that there is "a time to tear and a time to mend" in the pursuit of normal living. There is a superseding condition, however, that trumps even the act of tearing of one's garments, namely, when we are to express our feeling in true passion),—to "rend your hearts and not your garments" (Joel 2:13). *See also* gestures; tear.

Renewal, the: an eschatological doctrine of the Essenes wherein the two spirits of man—the evil and the good—will be resolved to righteousness for eternity. *See also* Angel of Darkness; Angel of Light; Copper Scroll; Dead Sea Scrolls; eschatology, eschatological; Essenes; Isaiah Scroll; Manual of Discipline; Qumran; Sons of Darkness; Sons of Light; Teacher of Righteousness; *War of the Sons of Light Against the Sons of Darkness;* War Scroll; Wicked Priest.

Reorganized Church of Jesus Christ of Latter-Day Saints. See Community of Christ (Mormon).

Repairer of Broken Walls: a name expounded by the prophet Isaiah to bless those faithful to God who would desire to live for Him in repentance, righteousness, and selflessness (Isa. 58:12). *See also* Restorer of Streets with Dwellings.

repeated fulfillment: a prophecy that may have more than one occasion of achievement or sense of accomplishment. For example, when Jesus healed Peter's mother-in-law, Matthew interpreted the act (Mt. 8:14–17) to be a fulfillment of Isaiah's prediction (Isa. 53:4) that states, "He took up our infirmities and carried our sorrows." However, Jesus' healing acts did not end at that point as there were, and will be, many more. *See also* double sense fulfillment; multiple fulfillment; prophecy types.

repent: the attitude and act of contrition that leads to seeking forgiveness for wrongdoing, either to God or another person. Sorrow for sin can lead to an active redress and fresh beginning in relationships and a cleansing of conscience so is commendable for adherents to most religious expression. *See also* abjuration; ascesis; harmartiology; *metanoia;* penance; recant; repentance; rogation; salvation; sin(s).

repentance: a turning about of one's life from sin or immorality to an attempt to live a more altruistic and faithful life. The concept is essential to Christianity because it is a prerequisite for receiving the forgiveness of Christ. The Greek term is *metaneo,* meaning "to change one's mind." Moreover, it should be kept in mind that even the act of repentance is not possible in our own strength; it is precipitated by the pulling attraction of God in the Holy Spirit, who makes it attractive and possible to find salvation. It should be noted as well that repentance to perfection is neither possible nor required. Jesus himself declared the sinner guiltless. Without repentance or a desire for it in confession, however, the future fate of any person's life would be dismal and fatalistic. The concept is an appeal to righteousness, occurring numerous times in Scripture, including a large amount of apocalyptic literature (*e.g.,* Revelation 2:16 and many other Bible references). Its occurrence in Revelation alone is so frequent as to be termed a leitmotif. All the seven churches (Rev. 2–3) received the admonition to repent except Philadelphia. *See also* abjuration; ascesis; harmartiology; *metanoia;* penance; recant; repent; rogation; salvation; sin(s).

Rephaim. See Bashan; giant(s); Og; Valley of the Rephaim.

rephaim. See *nephesh; Sheol.*

Rephan. See Raphan, star of; Remphan.

replacement theology: the theological stance (a cardinal principle of amillennialism) that asserts the Jews and their religion are no longer players in the grand scheme of God's providence. Supercessionists (as they are sometimes called) insist that the Church, as the New Israel, has taken over the former prerogatives of Judaism, along with their covenants and future as a nation. Dispensationalists, by contrast, are strong adversaries of replacement theology and leave ample room for the future restoration of Israel in some form and numbers. *See* *also* dominion theology; eschatology, eschatological; New Israel, the; Reconstructionism; restoration of Israel (the Jews); seven mountains dogma; theonomy; Whitby, Daniel.

representative polity: the form of church organization that governs itself with representative groups such as deacons, boards, or elders. These are normally selected by the congregation, not higher authority, in the mode of Presbyterians and Reformed Churches. *See also* acephali; autocephalous; church, administration of the early; church models; conciliarism; congregational polity; connectional polity; ecclesiology; episcopate; faith and order; Free Church(es); hierarchical polity; magisterium; plebania; polity; prelacy; presbytery; rite; ritual; shepherding (cultic); shepherding (discipleship); shepherding (pastoral); sobornost.

reprobate: counterfeit, impure (Jer. 6:30), abominable, disobedient, and contrary to every good work (Tit. 1:16). Any person indulging in such conduct may be labeled a reprobate. *See also* reprobation; social issues.

reprobation: God's decision to choose certain people for damnation. Perhaps that dogma may be the most controversial of John Calvin's doctrinal statements, especially as it applies to so-called "double predestination." Reprobation refers to eternal damnation and to the punishment itself. In more contemporary language, reprobation is reprehensible behavior. *See also* Calvinism; determinism; predestination; reprobate; social issues; TULIP.

reptilian theory: contemporary occultic nomenclature for the many serpentine-like gods and goddesses that make up our bloodline far back to pagan concepts of creation. We find the saurian depiction in paganism, science fiction, UFOlogy, conspiracy theories about the Illuminati, and other subjects often labeled as humanoid reptilian, snake creatures, homo saurus, lizard people, or other creepy terms. Even the book of Genesis describes the great tempter of Adam and Eve as a serpent. Native American Hopi speak of a reptilian race living underground called the *Sheti* or "Snake Brothers." Pre-Columbian myth mentions a primordial Eve named Bachue who could transform herself into a great snake called "The Serpent of Heaven." The first legendary king of Athens, Cecrops, was half man and half snake. In Grecian mythology, the Titans owned snake servants and their lower extremities are said to resemble serpentine bodies. In Indian legend and scriptures, the Negas are snake people living underground but in contact with people above. A Sanskrit term for snake/serpent beings called the Sarpa are another race. Some Asian countries hold legends of the Long (Yong in Korean and Ryu in Japanese) who dwell in the astral plane; they are more commonly recognized as dragons. The Japanese also recount a legendary race of humanoid reptilians called the Kappa. In the Middle East they are jinn; in Africa they are Dogon (claimed to be descended from the god Amma, an alien from the star Sirius B). The ancient Egyptian god Sobek is a man with a crocodile head. Why are such entities often described in terms that are reptilian or "snake-like" in appearance and behavior and not some other animal? Some neuroscientists and others assert the primeval human brain evolved from a reptilian complex in three layers. The first, the reptilian or complex-R was but fundamentally brutal and protective. The second, the limbic system, generated emotions. The third, the neocortex, was essentially reptilian but ruled by imagination and automatic motor functions. But who can state with certainty that that theory, or any other, influenced primitive man and his religion? How are we to know what has crept into our ancestry and cultures from the deep past? Even if we joined the sect of The Ancient Egyptian Order of the Serpent we would likely learn little more. *See also* Aion; Anunnaki; Apophis; Asclepius; Ayida Wedo; *Bel and the Dragon;* bugbears; Cainites; chimera; Chronos; crocodile; Dogon Nommos; Draco; dragon; *Edda,* the; Egyptian pantheon; *elohim;* Gadreel; Guardians; Hopi; Hydra; kundalini; Lamia; Leviathan; lizard(s); Loki; Medusa; mushrishu; mythological beasties, elementals, monsters, and spirit animals; Naasseni, Napier; Nagas; Nehushtan; Nuwa and Fuxi; Ogdoad; Ophites; ouroboros; Peratae; *Popul Unh;* Python, python; Quetzalcoatl; Rahab; Rattlesnake Prophecy, the; red dragon; Satan; serpent; serpent seed doctrine, the; Sethianism; seven-headed cobra; snake handling; *vouivre.*

reputation: the general recognition of one's character and good name. Often enough, the classification is accurate but can be unjust as well. Most of the prophets were not immune to the latter type of slandering. In Scripture, certain groups carried a "bad" reputation, such as the Corinthians (2 Cor. 6:1; 13:2–3), the Cretans (Tit. 1:12), and the Nazarenes (Jn. 1:46).

Requiem: a ritualized remembrance of one departed or memorial mass, often within the context of a funeral. Many classical music compositions have been written and performed for such an environment. There is even a biblical requiem of sorts found in Zechariah 1:15–16 which laments the end of the world. *See also* burial; chant, death; *Dies Irae;* dirge; exequy; funeral; jeremiad; *kinah;* kontakion; lament; liturgical year; liturgy, Christian; Mass; memorial(s); music; obit; obsequy; Pannychis; requiescat; Roman Catholic Church; sacred music; threnody; treasury of merits; vigil.

requiescat: in Latin, *requiescat in pace* ("to rest"), a short prayer or epitaph for the souls of the dead. The ritual is familiar to Roman Catholic practice and early Christianity but has a sort of equivalency in Judaism with a meaning of "come and rest in peace." There is even a similar or nascent reference in Isaiah 57:2. Most are more familiar with the words when seen as R.I.P. (rest in peace) found on many tombstones. *See also* chant; death; dirge; exequy; funeral; jeremiad; *kinah;* kontakion; lament; liturgical year; liturgy, Christian; liturgy, Jewish; obit; obsequy; Pannychis; Requiem; Roman Catholic Church; threnody; vigil.

rescript: an official answer from a pope or emperor to any religious inquiry posed.

"rescue from the coming wrath": a phrase from Paul (1 Th. 1:8–10) that could have allusion to the exemption of Christians from the approaching Tribulation. Though not entirely clear, the immediate context of the words speaks of Christ coming from heaven for a rescue from some catastrophe. The larger context of the letter also fits because much of the subject matter in both epistles to the Thessalonians concerns Second Coming themes. If the reference *is* to sparing believers in the rapture, it can join with Revelation 3:10 and other paradigms that seem to support the Church exclusion theory. In any case, the comforting words indisputably assure eternal security for all who avail of the saving faith of Christ in adversity or not. *See also* judgment(s); rapture; wrath, the coming.

rescuers of the Church: a sort of manufactured name for a series of individuals, both real and imagined, who were potential or hoped-for persons or institutions who might save the Church of Christ from utter failure and dissolution. Among them should be listed: 1. Prester John, 2. the Tiburtine Sibyl, or the Sibyl of Tivoli, a seeress who was summoned to the court of Trajan in the early second century to interpret a dream that had miraculously disturbed 100 Senators in a single night. She reported an elaborate prophecy foretelling of the appearance of a young man, "tall and handsome, well put together in all his parts" who will call the Jews and pagans to baptism and unite the Eastern and Western factions of the Roman Church, 3. the Last World Emperor who was destined to save the world of religion (who may have been the youth predicted by the Tiburtine Sibyl), 4. Pastor Angelicus, or the "Angelic Pope," a wholly benign figure who is destined to replace the venal characters of the papacy, 5. any number of personalities or their organizations throughout history who considered themselves, or others did, as saviors of Christianity. What goes too often unrealized is that Christ, not humans, is solely capable of sustaining the Church, even from the ravages of the gates of hell. *See also* church decline; church models; Francis of Assisi; Prester John; "Prophecy of the Popes"; Sibyl of Tivoli, the; World Teacher, the.

reservation of the sacrament: the practice in liturgical churches of preserving some of the sanctified Eucharist for those who are ill, infirm, or otherwise indisposed or absent from church attendance for a "weighty cause." *See also* fermentum; sacrament(s).

Resheph: or Reshef, a Canaanite fertility deity. He may be referenced in the theology of Habakkuk 3:5 with the words "a plague followed close behind" since Resheph was a god of pestilence in some accounts. His children are said to "fly up" like sparks (see Job 3:8) to pester mankind. *See also* Levant pantheon; mythological beasties, elementals, monsters, and spirit animals.

responsive reading: one or more paradigms arranged and annotated to be read alternately between a worship leader and the congregation. Often they are to be found in church hymnals and may consist of Scripture portions or devotional material. *See also* antiphon; cathisma; hymnal; liturgical year; liturgy, Christian; liturgy, Jewish; music; responsory.

responsory: or responsorial, a set of responses for worship that are sung or spoken after a liturgical reading. *See also* liturgical year; liturgy, Christian; music; responsive reading.

restorationism: 1. a tenet of the doctrine of redemption and the theory of preservation. If one "falls from grace" in her Christian pilgrimage, can she be restored to God's favor? Is it possible to lose favor with God in the first instance? If yes, restoration would be desirable and necessary; it not, the concept of restorationism is moot. 2. the belief that the true Christian Church died in the second century and was not replaced until resurrected and corrected by Joseph Smith with Mormonism. The name "Restorationists" was then sometimes applied to Mormonism and Jehovah's Witnesses as well. 3. the belief or conviction that the present church system must be replaced with the early church as the true model. The movement is of concern because the advocates favor a *restoration* for the modern church and not merely a *reformation* of it. *See also* Church of Jesus Christ of Latter-Day Saints, the; eternal security; fall from grace; redemption; perseverance of the saints; restoration of all things; restore everything, to.

Restoration Movement in America: a religious trend in the United States that produced many of the elements of the Great Awakenings. The frontier-style of preaching with "camp meetings" numbering hundreds or thousands in attendance over days were prominent evangelical tools. New denominations were formed, with the most gains going to the many forms of Baptists, the Methodists, and the evangelical wing of Presbyterianism. New denominations like the Christian Church and Disciples of Christ sprang up. The new converts preferred emotionalism, an expression of a personal conversion experience, and a non-creedal approach to theology (aside from the Bible alone) over the staid rituals of the older churches. *See also* Afro-American theology; apocalyptic fervor; Baccus, Isaac; Baptists; Campbell, Alexander; camp meeting(s); Cartwright, Peter; Chauncy, Charles; Christian Church (denomination); Churches of Christ; Davenport, James; Davis, Samuel; Disciples of Christ; Edwards, Jonathan; Frelinghuysen, Theodosius; Great Awakenings, the; McGready, James; Methodists; Presbyterians; Occom, Samson; "sawdust trail, the"; revivalism; Stone, Barton W.; Wesley, Charles and John; Whitefield, George.

restoration of all things: a reference to the Millennium (Acts 3:21), a return to an Eden-like environment. *See also* age of redemption; crushing rock that became a mountain; election; elect, the;

eschatology, eschatological; Ezekiel's vision of the new Temple and new land; Ezekiel's vision of the restored theocracy; Ezekiel's vision of the valley of dry bones; kingdom that cannot be shaken, a; kingdom, the; messianic age, the; millennial geography; millennial Sabbath; millennial sacramentalism; millennial Temple; millennial worship; Millennium, millennial; New Covenant, the; New Eden; rebuilding the Temple; *palengenesia;* rebuilding the Temple; remnant; restoration of Israel (the Jews); restoration Temple (and land); restore everything, to; rod of iron; Sabbath rest; Temple(s); third Temple; times of refreshing.

restoration of Israel (the Jews): the prophecy that Israel is destined to be fully regathered and occupy the land of Palestine in peace. The process may have already commenced with the return from Babylonian Exile under Zerubbabel. It is estimated that only about 50,000 exiles elected to return to Judea at that time (Josephus set the number at 42,462). Isaiah predicted the return 140 years before it happened. Next, the nation of Israel was formed in 1948 and has continued to exist despite heavy and unrelenting opposition. Certainly, it will be accomplished to completion in the Millennium where Jews in that time and place will perform as worship leaders for the world (according to most dispensational and conservative theology). They will endure in the latter days despite the final efforts by the Antichrist to overthrow them and the attack of Gog and Magog. Those who believe otherwise (asserting that Israel has forfeited her historic eschatological destiny) are labeled as advocates of replacement theology. *See also* age of redemption; crushing rock that became a mountain; Cyrus the Great (Cyrus II); election; elect, the; eschatology, eschatological; Ezekiel's pledge to the Jewish remnant; Ezekiel's vision of the new Temple and new land; Ezekiel's vision of the restored theocracy; Ezekiel's vision of the valley of dry bones; Judaism; land for peace; Law of Return; messianic age, the; Middle East peace initiatives; millennial geography; millennial Sabbath; millennial sacramentalism; millennial Temple; millennial worship; Millennium, millennial; New Covenant, the; New Eden; "next year in Jerusalem"; rebuilding the Temple; remnant; replacement theology; restoration of all things; restoration Temple (and land); rod of iron; Sabbath rest; second Exodus; super-sign, the; Temple(s); third Temple; times of refreshing.

restoration Temple (and land): the promised replacement of the land and Temple of Jerusalem predicted for the Millennium. Ezekiel chapter 40 and several sections following are the most detailed description of the millennial Holy Land. Among the items delineated are: a new Temple area and new Temple, new Temple gates on the east, north, south, and west (three gates for the city in each wall), Inner and Outer Courts, rooms for the priests, areas for sacrificial preparations, and a replacement altar. Additionally, the proposed layout of the land and boundaries of the new Israel is described, along with the tribes who will dwell in each area. Separate plots are set aside for the ruling prince (David?), and there is a special section for the ministering priests and Levites. Revised rituals, at least one sacrificial ceremony, and certain festivals are to be prescribed. A special river will flow from the Temple itself to the Dead Sea, which will become freshwater. The most important consideration of the prophet's description may be that the glory of the Lord has returned to His Temple. The final words in Ezekiel declare the new name for Israel at that time: THE LORD IS THERE. *See also* crushing rock that became a mountain; election; elect, the; eschatology, eschatological; Ezekiel's vision of the new Temple and new land; Ezekiel's vision of the restored theocracy; Ezekiel's vision of the valley of dry bones; messianic age, the; millennial geography; millennial Sabbath; millennial sacramentalism; millennial Temple; millennial worship; Millennium, millennial; New Covenant, the; New Eden; rebuilding the Temple; remnant; restoration of all things; restoration of Israel (the Jews); rod or iron; Sabbath rest; Temple(s); third Temple; times of refreshing.

Restored Church of God. See Worldwide Church of God.

restore everything, to: the descriptive phrase used by the apostle Peter pointing to the Second Coming of Christ, a promise he insisted was made from God through the holy prophets (Acts 3:21). *See also* eschatology, eschatological; restorationism; restoration of all things.

Restorer of Streets with Dwellings: a name expounded by the prophet Isaiah to bless those faithful to God who would desire to live for Him in repentance, righteousness, and selflessness (Isa. 58:12). *See also* Repairer of Broken Walls.

restrainer, the: the agent of this age who is active in controlling evil lest it overwhelm the world and the people of the world. As such, that agent can also hinder the Antichrist either in his rise to power or his actions in the Tribulation. Paul spoke of the restrainer (2 Th. 2:6–7) whom he seemed to imply is the Holy Spirit. Some assert that the restrainer is the Church, civil government, or some other benevolent human entity. Many of the early church viewed the restrainer as the Roman Empire. As long as Rome stood, the ten-kingdom confederation dreaded in Revelation of the last days was forestalled. Some even claim the restrainer is the archangel Michael, probably from notes in Jude 9 and Revelation 12. The pronouncement that the restrainer is Michael simply does not "fit" as we tend to think of the restrainer as active now, in the future, and in all ages and locales—not just in the Tribulation. Others have proposed that the restrainer is the Jews or the gospel. Perhaps the restrainer can be the promise of the rapture event itself since the Antichrist cannot appear until the Church is removed? There may be truthful elements in such thinking inasmuch as the Spirit of God may be active in those institutions. The true and effective restrainer, however, is surely the Holy Spirit himself. *See also* Antichrist; Holy Spirit; katechon; names (titles) for the Holy Spirit; spirit of prophecy; spirit of truth.

resurrection(s): rising from the dead, *anastasis* in Greek. Resurrection is not as rare in Scripture as some believe but is a cardinal principle of eschatology. There are at least twelve narratives of people being resurrected, all demonstrating Christ's power to do so again at the end of the age. References in the New Testament are so frequent that the theme may be called a motif; the Old Testament, however, is not without its descriptions of resurrection as well (*i.e.,* Isaiah 26:19). The word appears forty-two times in the New Testament alone. Both the righteous and the unrighteous will experience resurrection at some point in the scheme of God's eschatological plan. Samples of resurrections include: the widow's son from Zarephath by Elijah (1 Ki. 17:22), the son of the Shunammite woman by Elisha (2 Ki. 4:32–35), an individual raised when he touched the bones of Elisha (2 Ki. 13:20–21), Jairus's daughter by Jesus (Lk. 8:52–56), the son of the widow of Nain by Jesus (Lk. 7:14–15), Lazarus of Bethany by Jesus (Jn. 11), certain righteous ones in Jerusalem at the time of Jesus' death by the Holy Spirit (Mt. 27:50–53), Dorcas by Peter (Acts 9:40), and Eutychus by Paul (Acts 20:9–12). The most significant resurrection, certainly, was that of Jesus himself who arose from the tomb in prophetic completion and saving triumph. *See also anastasis;* ascension; blessed hope, the; bodily resurrection; body; Death; death; Easter; firstborn from the dead; Firstfruits; firstfruits of the resurrection; firstfruits of the Spirit; glorification; glorified body (bodies); great white throne judgment; immortality; judgment of the Old Testament saints; judgment of the Tribulation martyrs; judgment of the Tribulation saints; miracles of Jesus with eschatological emphasis; multitudes that sleep in the dust of the earth; myths universally depicted in the Bible; ostrich eggs; rapture; resurrection and the life, the; "resurrection gods"; resurrection(s) in Daniel; resurrection(s) in Ezekiel; resurrection of Jesus; resurrection, the first; resurrection, the general; resurrection, the second; sign of Jonah; spiritual body; terrestrial body.

resurrection and the life, the: Jesus' description of himself addressed to his friend Martha (Jn. 11:25). The declaration places the Lord in control of this bodily life and the next resurrected form. *See also* firstborn from the dead; firstfruits of the resurrection; firstfruits of the Spirit; judgment of the Old Testament saints; judgment of the Tribulation martyrs; judgment of the Tribulation saints; names (titles) for Jesus; resurrection(s); resurrection of Jesus; resurrection, the first.

"resurrection gods": Those pagan mythological gods who are ascribed to be "born again" in the usual "death—sojourn in the underworld—resurrection" theme of many ancient religions. The most commonly listed are Attis, Adonis, Asclepius, Baal, Dionysus, Mithras, Orpheus, Osiris, and Tammuz. Some scholars include the hero Gilgamesh among the reborn gods, but his history does not quite fit the pattern. *See also* Attis; Adonis; Asclepius; Aslan; Baal; Demeter; Dionysus the god; Eriskegal; fertility gods; fertility rites; Gilgamesh; Hadadrimmon; Hades; Harry Potter; Hecate; Hel; Helheim; Mithras; nature cult(s); Nergal; orgies; Orpheus; Osiris; pagan, paganism; pagan practice; Persephone; Pluto; resurrection(s); Tammuz; underworld.

resurrection(s) in Daniel: those saints named in Daniel 12:1–3 whom the mighty angel promised would arise on the last day. They are named as: 1. "your people" (Jews) [and/or] everyone whose name is written in the book [of life], 2. multitudes who sleep in the dust of the earth who will awake—some to everlasting life and some to eternal doom, 3. those who are wise who will shine like the brightness of heaven, and 4. those who lead many to righteousness who are bright like stars. *See also* Daniel's vision of end time; multitudes that sleep in the dust of the earth; resurrection(s); resurrection(s) in Ezekiel.

resurrection(s) in Ezekiel: descriptions of the prophet Ezekiel as to the process of resurrection from the dead. Ezekiel's account of revivification is in oracular form by which the dead are depicted as a vast collection of dead and dry bones. As the spirit of God explained by the prophet's preaching is manifest, the bones begin to take on human form until the final breath of God revives them fully. *See also* Ezekiel's vision of the valley of dry bones; resurrection(s); resurrection(s) in Daniel.

resurrection of Jesus: the coming to life of Jesus after three days in the tomb. He is called the "firstfruits" of resurrection, as modeled by the saints who arose in Jerusalem at the crucifixion (Mt. 27:50–53), since he was the first to set the pattern of permanent life after death. *See also* angelic miracles; bodily resurrection; Bright Monday; Bright Sunday; Easter; Evangelical Alliance; firstborn from the dead; Firstfruits; firstfruits of the resurrection; firstfruits of the Spirit; Nicene Creed; Paschal; Paschal greeting; resurrection(s); resurrection and the life, the; resurrection, the first; sign of Jonah.

resurrection, the first: New Testament reference to the coming to life of believers after which they will never again die, including the bringing to life of all the martyred and faithful saints of the Tribulation (Rev. 20:4–6). The qualifier "first" does not mean this action is the first-ever chronological resurrection since others have already taken place. Those recorded in the Old Testament, those occurring during Jesus' ministry and the resurrection of Jesus himself, those of the New Testament era, plus those recorded in Revelation before chapter 20 are to be counted as inclusive in the *first* resurrection, all of which have already transpired.

Furthermore, if the doctrine of the rapture holds true, many more resurrections will have already taken place before this one referenced in Revelation 20. Rather, it is *first* (considered collectively) in the sense that it precedes the terrifying *second* resurrection of the great white throne (Rev. 20:11–15) which is also called "the second death." It should be remembered that any number of resurrections have occurred throughout the Bible. We can note those in the Old Testament (*i.e.*, 2 Kings 13:20–21 and others). Certain New Testament resurrections are also noted: Lazarus (Jn. 11) and certain saints who walked the streets of Jerusalem at the time of Jesus' crucifixion (Mt. 27:50–53), a group included in what the writers called "firstfruits" of the living. These, however, are not technically included in "the first resurrection" because presumably they all died again. With the resurrection of Christ, however, we can see the genuine first coming to life for all of eternity (Mt. 28:1–10). This will be followed by the rapture of the Church (1 Th. 4:13–18), the two witnesses (Rev. 11), the Tribulation martyrs (Rev. 7:9–17), the Old Testament saints (Isa. 26:19), the Old Testament righteous (Ps. 16:9–10, 17:15, 49:15, 73:23–28; Job 14:13–17, 17:25–27; Dan. 12:2–3). Finally and lastly, the resurrection before the great white throne of judgment is due. The fact that there are distinctions between the first and second resurrections constitutes a surprise for some people. The same was true for the favored disciples in Mark 9:10. These three understood perfectly what resurrection *of* the dead meant, for this was a commonly accepted Jewish doctrine (except among the Sadducees). But the resurrection *from* [out of] the dead was a new teaching and has provided the separation point between the resurrection of the justified and that of the wicked. The conclusion then is that the "first" resurrection is inclusive for all, except those before the great white throne. Those awakenings of the righteous can be taken together because they involve believers only and are destined for eternal bliss, whereas those judged before the great white throne are forever condemned. The Scripture also declares that the second death has no claim on the saved. *See also* bodily resurrection; death, the first; death, the second; firstfruits of the resurrection; firstfruits of the Spirit; great white throne judgment; judgment of the Old Testament saints; judgment of the Tribulation martyrs; judgment of the Tribulation saints; rapture;

resurrection(s); resurrection and the life, the; resurrection of Jesus; resurrection, the general; resurrection, the second; sign of Jonah.

resurrection, the general: coming to life of all persons, some to eternal reward for believers and eternal condemnation for others. The general resurrection seems to be a generic name for all types of resurrections that have been or will be experienced, with particular reference to which group is being considered. *See also* resurrection(s); resurrection(s) in Daniel; resurrection(s) in Ezekiel; resurrection of Jesus; resurrection, the first; resurrection the second; sign of Jonah.

resurrection, the second: also called "the second death." The second resurrection is essentially the procedure and results of the great white throne judgment described in Revelation 20:11–15—for those without salvation. The event is in direct contrast to "the first resurrection," which includes all phases of the resurrections of the righteous. Whereas the first resurrection (in all its phases) benefits believers, the second is reserved only for the unrighteous who are to be judged before God's great white throne. *See also* death, the second; great white throne judgment; resurrection(s); resurrection, the first; resurrection, the general; sign of Jonah.

retreat: the rather common religious practice of secluding oneself or with like-minded others for a period of uninterrupted study or meditation. The withdrawal can be refreshing to the spirit, educational, or inspirational and practiced by any age group of believers. Some retreats are led by qualified facilitators and others are solitary. *See also* cursillo; religious education.

retrocognition: the psychic ability to recall past events even though the physical senses do not become active in the process; it is a mind regression technique alone. Such ability has never been proven. *See also* anthropomancy; anthroposophy; apotropaic magic; Ariosophy; astral projection; astrology, astrologers; audition; augury; automatic writing; bagua; belomancy; bibliomancy; black arts; cartomancy; chiromancy; clairaudience; clairsentience; clairvoyance; cleromancy; cone of power; conjure; cryptesthesia; crystallomancy; curious acts; divination; dream(s); dreams and visions; ecstasy; enchantment; enneagram; evil eye; extrasensory perception (ESP); foreknowledge; foretelling; geomancy; grimoire; hepatoscopy; Hermetic wisdom; Hermetic writings; hex; hierscopy; horoscope(s); hydromancy; Ifa; incantation; labyrinth walk; lecanomancy; locution; magic arts; magic, magick; magic square; magnetism; *mana*; mantic wisdom; mantra; monition; necromancy; New Age religion; numbers, symbology of; occult, occultic; omen; oneiromancy; oracle(s); otherworldly journeys; ouija board; out-of-body experiences (OBEs); paranormal; peace pole(s); pentagram; portent; precognition; prediction; prefiguration; premonition; prodigy; prophecy, general; psi; psychic healing; psychic reading; psychomancy; psychometry; pyramidology; remote viewing; revelation; prophecy, general; rhabdomancy; scrying; séance; secret wisdom; sorcery, sorceries; spell; spell names; spiritism; stigmata; superstition; tarot; telegnosis; telepathy; telesthesia; theugry; third eye, the; totemism; vision quest; visions; visualization; Voodoo; Voudou; witchcraft; *ya sang*; yoga; Zen; *zos kia* cultus.

retrogression: the Buddhist belief that one can be born to a lower realm after reincarnation. *See also* Buddhism.

Reuben: one of the twelve tribes of Israel descended from the patriarch Jacob and his wife Leah. Although firstborn, Reuben did not receive a sterling blessing from Jacob in Genesis 49:3–4 because he had dishonored his family and all of Israel by sleeping with his father's concubine, Bilhah. The tribe is listed among the 144,000 servants of Revelation 7:5. *See also* lost tribes, the ten; tribes of Israel, the; twelve tribes.

Reuel. See Jethro.

revealer of mysteries: a designation for God as the deity Who could genuinely interpret dreams and omens issued to both Daniel and King Nebuchadnezzar (Dan. 2:29, 47). *See also* Daniel as Old Testament prophecy; God of gods; Lord of kings; names (titles) for God.

Revelation as New Testament prophecy: the last book in the Bible, alternately called the Apocalypse, and the one most heavily laced with apocalypticism. Also, it may be the most thoroughly Jewish book in the New Testament in that it draws much of its symbolism and imagery from the Old Testament and Jewish apocalyptic literature of the interbiblical period. In fact, the entire writing (technically a letter) is described as a prophetic narrative with references to history past, present, and future. It gives the most detailed explanations of the Tribulation, heaven, the Millennium, and many other eschatological matters than anywhere else in Scripture, with the possible exception of Daniel. The language of Revelation is decidedly Old Testament in style, speaking not in the manner of Paul but like the Old Testament prophets, especially Isaiah, Ezekiel, and Daniel. It is correct to state that Revelation is a prophecy, an apocalypse, and an eschatological letter—God's afflatus for our times and those of the future. A more ostentatious title in some Bible versions reads "The Revelation of Saint John the Divine," which may be somewhat misleading; John was not divine and was neither a saint (in the ecclesiastical sense, nor an instigator of Revelation.) Rather, he was the receptor, redactor, and recorder of the vision from Christ and the heavens. The authorship of the prophecy is debated—at least one is saying it was written by John the Baptist or his disciples, a theory of complete nonsense. The date of writing is also disputed, with some placing it during the reign of Nero and others under Domitian. Few writings, of any genre, have generated more harsh skepticism and utterly blind faith since its creation. Some, both laypersons and theologians, evaluate it with supreme importance and nigh-depthless insight; others, again readers of all persuasions, see it has the headquarters of religious zealots, crackpots, code breakers, and the clinically insane. Fewer than 200 manuscripts of Revelation have been found in the original Greek whereas over 2000 of the Gospels are at hand from antiquity. Linguists say the Greek grammar used by the author is not particularly high-quality. The subject matter is decidedly futuristic, unless such a bias turns radically backward and is viewed as strictly preterist. Some see it as radically violent and counter-culture; others insist it is the epitome of justice and order in the universe. Certainly, what is absent from its pages is just as telling as what is present. There is no mention of the life and times of Jesus Christ, for example, nor is there reference to his sublime moral teachings or any in-depth theological discussion. Yet, the core theme of Revelation is Jesus himself. On the other hand, none doubt that Revelation is the primary source for our understanding of all things eschatological and apocalyptic. A Google search on your personal computer will garner more than 1.6 million "hits." *See also* Apocalypse, the; classes of humanity in the Apocalypse; dream(s); five sins of Revelation; Gregory of Nazianzus; John as apostle; letter(s); plagues of Egypt, plagues of Revelation; praise paradigms of Revelation, the; Qabbala; Revelation, content of; Saumur; vision(s).

Revelation, content of: in general, all the substance of the book of Revelation. There is no standard agreement on how all the theology, literary structure, and message of the book are to be analyzed or understood, but few doubt its profundity and drama. *See also* Apocalypse, the; dream(s); five sins of Revelation; Grand Guignol; plagues of Egypt, plagues of Revelation; praise paradigms of Revelation, the; prayers of Revelation; Revelation as New Testament prophecy; vision(s).

revelation, general: the concept that God's person, glory, and attributes are capable of revelation in nature, conscience, history, or any accepted order, sometimes referred to as "natural" revelation. He has provided both creation and conscience to every person and every generation as a testimony to His authority, the neglect of which leads to darkness, defiance, and ignorance. Therefore, there is no excuse not to worship Him. *See also* means of grace; monition; revelation, theological.

revelation, theological: often called "divine revelation," a theological technical term with reference to the methods and means by which God announces and educates the world and humanity about Himself (Hab. 2:3). God makes His will and essence known to us via prayer, Bible study, interaction with fellow believers, worship, the evangelism of the Holy Spirit, dreams, visions, ecstasy, intuition, and many other resources. A revelation or pronouncement may occur spontaneously in the briefest moment or develop piecemeal over long periods of time and experience. The process is ongoing, progressive, and will continue into eternity long after the eschaton. The wisdom writing called *The Wisdom of Solomon* expounds on what revelation implies for our understanding of God and His works. The writer said that God reveals Himself as he wills by instructing us in the structure of the world, the operation of the elements, the passage of time, the changing of the seasons, the study of the heavens, the study of the biology of Earth, and even the study of psychology. From these disciplines we learn not only about our environment but also about God Himself. Two types of revelation may be unique: God is said to have spoken to Moses "face-to-face" which declares some rare intimacy (Deut. 34:10), and the apostle Paul alludes to "a man" [undoubtedly himself] who ascended to the highest heaven to experience disclosures that he could in no way explain. *See also* allegorical interpretation; analogical interpretation; biblical criticism; concursive inspiration; Draper, John Williams; dream(s); Fourfold Interpretation; grammatical-historical interpretation; hermeneutic(s); idealism; illumination; inspiration; liberalists interpretation; literal interpretation; manifestation of the Spirit; means of grace; Pardes; plenary inspiration; principles of interpretation; progressive revelation; proleptic revelation; revelation, general; rhetorical criticism; source criticism; text; textual criticism; theophany; threefold sense of interpretation; translation; transmission history; vision(s); Word of God.

Revels, Hiram Rhoades: first black person elected to the United States Senate (1877–1901), serving in Washington, D.C., from 1870–1871. Revels was a minister in the African Methodist Church and helped organize the first two black regiments in Maryland to fight in the Civil War. He also served as chaplain to another army group at Vicksburg. *See also* African Methodist Episcopal Church; Afro-American theology; clergy patriots.

Reverend: an honorary title for most Christian preachers but less common in other faiths. The base meaning is intended to render respect to the one addressed because of his or her peculiar calling. *See also* calling; clergy; ecclesiastic(s); episcopate; man of God; parson(s); pastor(s); preacher(s); priest(s).

revitalization movement: a religiopolitical experiment using magical practice that seeks to relieve deprivation or cast off an oppressor. Examples from the religious scene include the ghost dance exercise, cargo cults, and totemism. *See also* cargo cult(s); ghost dance cult; Huna; John Frum religion; magic arts; magic, magick; *mana;* Moai; Modekngei; New Age religion; totemism.

revivalism: a form of evangelical preaching featuring ecstatic renewal beginning with the First Great Awakening series in colonial New England. The first was in the 1740s that led not only to the American Revolution but also to more spiritual awakenings well into the 19th century. Later, after the Civil War, mass meetings (often under traveling tents or crude "brush arbor" shelters) and an emphasis on public response to the gospel appeal sprang up again, but this time on the Western frontier. Many frontier revivals of this Second Great Awakening were fiery in content, lasted for extended periods of time, and were frequently scenes of fervent display. The mass gatherings were called "camp meetings" because the attendees assembled via carriage and wagon and often stayed for days. The assemblies were as much social as religious. Emotional expression was commonplace, everything from speaking in tongues to shaking and even barking, with plenty of lusty gospel hymn singing. These overt displays were called "exercises." The revival process is still practiced today to some extent. The state of revivalism is an expression of change from spiritual morbidity to energy and rededication. The reform is marked by an awareness of truth, a conviction of personal and corporate sin, and a revitalization of faith within believers. Revival can only begin in churches or among people where faith is present because nothing that has never known life can be revived. It can, however, spread to the unredeemed masses when carried outward by the missionary spirit. Naturally, the Hebrew prophets, one and all, were vitally concerned with the revival of their nation as the only possible avenue to safety and well-being in Yahweh. *See also* apocalyptic fervor; Asbury, Francis; Azusa Street Revivals; Backus, Isaac; Bakker, Jim and Tammy; baptism of the Holy Spirit; Beecher, Lyman; Blackstone, William Eugene; Branham, William Morrison; Brownsville Assembly; Campbell, Alexander; camp meeting(s); Cane Ridge camp meeting; Cartwright, Peter; charisms; Christian Church; circuit riders; Conway, Russell; Davenport, James; Davis, Samuel; Dow, Lorenzo; Dwight, Timothy; Eliot, John; *Elmer Gantry;* evangelist(s), evangelism; faith healing; Finley, James B.; Finney, Charles Grandison; Frelinghuysen, Theodorus; glossolalia; Graham, William Franklin (Billy); Great Awakenings, the; Hinn, Benny; holy laughter; "in the Spirit"; Jesus Movement; Kuhlman, Catherine; latter rain, the; liturgy, Christian; Mather, Increase; Mather, Cotton; McGready, James; McPherson, Aimee Semple; Moody, Dwight L.; Nee, Watchman; New Side, Old Side; Occom, Samson; Restoration Movement in America; Roberts, Granville Oral; "saved"; "sawdust trail, the"; Sheen,

Fulton J.; Smith, Rodney "Gypsy"; Stoddard, Solomon; Stone, Barton W.; Sunday, Billy; Swaggart, Jimmy Lee; Taylor, Edward Thompson; televangelist(s), televangelists; Tennent, Gilbert; William, Tennent; theolepsy; tongues; "Toronto Blessing, the"; Van Impe, Jack; "walking the aisle"; Weld, Theodore Dwight; Wheelock, Eleazar; Whitefield, George; Wesley, Charles and John; Wilkinson, Jemima; Woodworth-Etta, Maria.

Revived Roman Empire: a contemporary reference to the soon-coming government of the Antichrist. The new world government is said to resemble the old Roman Empire, which was dictatorial and harsh in its treatment of Christians and Jews. Such a political structure will be the political power base for the Antichrist. Recent scholarship has begun to question whether a Roman-type government is really to be the one in place and has posited the new end times government will be Muslim instead. But the conservatives still insist it is the new Rome. One pundit remarked, "Two hundred years of history verify that apocalyptic Babylon is Rome. It is either pagan Rome, papal Rome, or a future "revived" Rome—but it is Rome." *See also* Antichrist as a Muslim; eschatology, eschatology; New World Order, the (NWO); Roman Empire; Rome; universal church.

reward(s): compensations for good and effective effort. The Scripture is filled with examples of rewards for the faithful, including a great number promised in apocalyptic literature. Faith and belief have inherent emotional and spiritual rewards (both here and in the hereafter), along with any that may come in physical form. Descriptions of heavenly rewards often cite "crowns" as granted (or denied) before the judgment seat of Christ. *See also bema*; crowns; judgment seat of Christ; reward(s) in heaven; welcome, a rich.

reward(s) in heaven: the anticipated eternal blessings welcomed by all believers. Each reward is from God and eternal. "Rewards" entail more than the anticipated pleasures of the Millennium and heaven, however. Descriptions of heavenly rewards often cite "crowns" as granted (or denied) before the judgment seat of Christ. Our status in heaven is sure to involve meaningful work, joyful service, important rulership, and sincere but happy praise to the Godhead. *See also bema;* crown(s); crown of glory; crown of incorruption; crown of life; crown of rejoicing; crown of righteousness; judgment seat of Christ; reward(s); robe, crown, and throne; welcome, a rich.

Rezin: a king of Syria with his capital at Damascus. Though subject to Assyria, he allied with Pekah, king of Israel, in an effort to capture Jerusalem. The attack failed because the prophet Isaiah had issued his great proclamation regarding the matter, which is reproduced in Isaiah 7:1–9:12. The king of Judah, at that time Ahaz, bribed the Assyrian king to aid him. Damascus was eventually overcome by Tiglath-pileser, the people deported and Rezin killed. *See also* king(s); Syria.

Rezon: an enemy of Solomon raised up by God as partial fulfillment of the prophecy that the united kingdom of Israel would be troubled because of the king's indulgence of foreign gods (1 Ki. 11:23–25). Rezon was, at the start, the leader of a rebel band harassing Solomon's rule. Later he became a leader in Damascus and was a continual source of trouble to the kingdom of the Jews. *See also* Syria.

rhabdomancy: divination by use of rods or sticks (dowsing) or by drawing straws. *See also* anthropomancy; anthroposophy; apotropaic magic; Ariosophy; astral projection; astrolabe; astrology, astrologers; athame; audition; augury; automatic writing; bagua; belomancy; *besom;* bibliomancy; black arts; black mirror; blood moon(s); cartomancy; chaos magic; chiromancy; clairaudience; clairsentience; clairvoyance; cleromancy; cone of power; conjure; cryptesthesia; crystallomancy; crystal skulls; curious acts; divination; divining stick; dream(s); dreams and visions; ecstasy; enchantment; enneagram; evil eye; extrasensory perception (ESP); foreknowledge; foretelling; geomancy; grimoire; gris-gris; hepatoscopy; Hermetic wisdom; Hermetic writings; hex; hierscopy; horoscope(s); hydromancy; Ifa; incantation; labyrinth walk; lecanomancy; literomancy; locution; magic arts; magic, magick; magic square; magnetism; *mana;* mantic wisdom; mantra; monition; necromancy; New Age religion; numbers, symbology of; occult, occultic; omen; oneiromancy; oracle(s); otherworldly journeys; ouija board; out-of-body experiences (OBEs); paranormal; past life regression; peace pole(s); pentagram; philosopher's stone;

portent; precognition; prediction; prefiguration; premonition; prodigy; prophecy, general; psi; psychic(s); psychic healing; psychic reading; psychomancy; psychometry; pyramidology; rebirthing; reincarnation; remote viewing; revelation; prophecy, general; scrying; séance; secret wisdom; sorcery, sorceries; spell; spell names; spiritism; stigmata; supernatural; superstition; tarot; telegnosis; telepathy; telesthesia; theugry; third eye, the; totemism; vision(s); vision quest; visualization; Voodoo; Voudou; wanga; warlock(s); water witch; Web-Bot; witchcraft; *ya sang*; yoga; Zen; zodiac; *zos kia* cultus.

rhema: a Greek term for any word having a definite meaning. A *rhema* is a spoken word or "something said." To be more specific, *rhema* is in place to distinguish a "word" from its sister term *logos*. The former is a broad expression with a more general application as verbiage spoken whereas *logos* is a universal idiom for the whole of the Christ message. A *rhema* moment may come, for instance, while reading the Bible but the "Word of God" itself lies behind its revelation. In Romans 10:8, Paul used the term in place of the expected *logos* and the ancient Greek philosophers were fond of it as well. *See also* Logos; *logos*.

rhetorical criticism: the process of identifying persuasive structures and strategies in order to reach the essence of its metaphoric objective or the original intent of the author. *See also* accideme; allegorical interpretation; alliteration; analogical interpretation; apostrophe; apothegm; assonance; autograph; Bible; Bible manuscripts; Bible translations; biblical criticism; chiasmus; conflict story; *constructio ad sensum;* context; contextualization; dittography; double sense fulfillment; doublets; doubling; edification; eisegesis; epanadiplosis; epigrammatic statements; etymology; exegesis; figure of speech; folio; form criticism; Fourfold Interpretation; gattung; gloss; gnomic sayings; grammatical-historical interpretation; *hapax legomena;* haplography; hermeneutic(s); higher criticism; homographs; homonyms; homophones; *homoteleuton;* hyperbole; idiom; *inclusio;* interpolation; interpretation; inverted nun; irony; isagogics; *itture sopherim;* jot and tittle; kere; *kethib;* "L"; liberalists interpretation; literal interpretation; litotes; loan words; lower criticism; "M"; Masoretic Text; minuscule(s); mystery of God; omission; onomastica; onomatopoeia; palimpsest; papyrus;

paradigm; parallelism; parchment; *paroimia; paronomasia;* pericope; personification; Peshitta; pointing; point of view; polyglot; principles of interpretation; proof texting; pun(s); "Q"; redaction; revelation, theological; rhetorical devices; riddle; satire; *scripto continua;* scriptorium; *sebirin;* simile; similitude; source criticism; sources, primary and secondary; special points; strophe; superscription; symbol(s); synecdoche; syntax; synthetic parallelism; text; textual criticism; threefold sense of interpretation; *tiggune sopherim;* Time Texts; Torah; translation; transmission history; transposition; trope; type(s); typology; uncial(s); vellum; verbicide.

rhetorical devices: figures of speech used primarily in literature, such as similes, fables, metaphors, etc. Over 200 rhetorical devices have been identified in use within the Scriptures. By way of biblical interpretation, no system (including the literal) can legitimately deny the existence of such study aids, and they are particularly important to prophetic understanding. By the same reasoning, such literary forms should not be forced into play when they are not clearly present in the text. *See also* accideme; alliteration; apostrophe; apothegm; assonance; autograph; Bible; Bible manuscripts; Bible translations; biblical criticism; chiasmus; conflict story; *constructio ad sensum;* context; contextualization; dittography; double sense fulfillment; doublets; doubling; edification; eisegesis; epanadiplosis; epigrammatic statements; etymology; exegesis; figure of speech; folio; form criticism; gattung; gloss; gnomic sayings; grammatical-historical interpretation; *hapax legomena;* haplography; hermeneutic(s); higher criticism; homographs; homonyms; homophones; *homoteleuton;* hyperbole; idiom; *inclusio;* interpolation; interpretation; inverted nun; irony; isagogics; *itture sopherim;* jot and tittle; kere; *kethib;* "L"; liberalists interpretation; literal interpretation; litotes; loan words; lower criticism; "M"; Masoretic Text; minuscule(s); mystery of God; omission; onomastica; onomatopoeia; palimpsest; papyrus; paradigm; parallelism; parchment; *paroimia; paronomasia;* pericope; personification; Peshitta; pointing; point of view; polyglot; principles of interpretation; proof texting; pun(s); "Q"; redaction; revelation, theological; rhetorical criticism; riddle; satire; *scripto continua;* scriptorium; *sebirin;* simile; similitude; source criticism; sources, primary and secondary; special points;

strophe; superscription; symbol(s); synecdoche; syntax; synthetic parallelism; text; textual criticism; *tiggune sopherim;* Time Texts; Torah; translation; transposition; trope; type(s); typology; uncial(s); vellum; verbicide.

Rhoda: a servant girl in the home of Mary, the mother of Mark. When Peter was miraculously released from prison, he made his way to that home and knocked for entrance. Rhoda responded but was so astonished that she neglected to open the door for him (Acts 12:12–14).

rib(s): the bony cage-like structure surrounding the torso. The term sometimes refers to life since Eve was made of a rib of Adam (Gen. 2:21), or as protection (as the ribs protect the heart and lungs. *See also* bone(s).

Ribaut, Jean: French Huguenot explorer (1520–1565) who established France's first colony in the New World. The settlement was called "Charlesfort" (after Charles IX) and set at Port Royal, South Carolina (then part of the Florida territory), in 1562. Ribaut fell victim to the Protestant-Catholic conflicts on both sides of the Atlantic, causing Charlesfort to fail in his absence. The colony was replaced by Fort Caroline under Rene Gaulaine de Laudonniere, and Ribaut was ordered to resupply the settlers. His fleet and all supplies were lost to a storm at sea and Spanish raids and his expedition was captured. The prisoners confessed to being "Lutherans," causing the Spaniards to hack them all to death. Subsequently, Fort Caroline also fell. *See also* de Laudonniere, Rene Gaulaine; Huguenots.

Riblah: a place on the northern border of Israel (Num. 34:11) where Pharaoh Necho imprisoned King Jehoahaz of Judah after deposing him (2 Ki. 23:33) and where Nebuchadnezzar camped during the siege of Jerusalem (2 Ki. 25:6). It was also the locale where King Zedekiah was captured by the Babylonians, saw his sons executed, was blinded, and from where he was finally escorted into exile (Jer. 52:7–11).

Ricci, Matteo: a Jesuit missionary (1552–1610), as well as a mathematician, scientist, and linguist. His chosen field of work was China, where he tried to convert the emperor and his huge land area of population. *See also* clergy scientists; missions, missionaries. *See also* clergy scientists; missions, missionaries; Roman Catholic Church; Society of Jesus.

Rice Christians: those who convert to Christianity merely for the material gains it accrues. In the case of many missionary experiences, large numbers in Asian countries and elsewhere will convert for free food and other benefits. *See also* Christianese; missions, missionaries; slurs, religious; "souper."

Richard the Lionheart: Richard I, king of England and many of its dominions (1157–1199). He was the son of Henry II and Eleanor of Aquitaine who bolted early and prominently into national leadership. He was active in the third Crusade pitted against the formidable Saladin. His army failed to reclaim Jerusalem and he was even captured, requiring his repatriation by ransom. Oddly, Richard spent only about six months of his reign in England and spoke only French, not Anglo-Saxon English. *See also* Crusades; king(s); Saladin.

riddle: a piece of writing or speech that is intended to puzzle or obfuscate (*e.g.,* Psalm 49:4). The paradox of the number 666 (Rev. 13:8), the handwriting on the wall (Dan. 5), and Samson's playful riddle proposed to the Philistines (Jud. 14:8–20) may be among the very few examples of the technique in use in the Bible. The prologue to the book of Proverbs states that one of the reasons for its writing was for understanding the riddles of the wise (Pro. 1:1–6). Proverbs 25:2 appears to record a sort of paean to the art form. A fine example of riddling is found in *2 Esdras:* "Come then…, weigh me a pound of fire, measure me a bushel of wind, or call back a day that has passed." That writing model is similar to Job 38:16–18 and both express irony. *See also* "Book of Thunder"; cedar of Lebanon and a thistle, parable of the; Daniel's decipher of the hand writing on the wall; dark sayings; deep secrets, so-called; fable of the thorn(s); hand writing on the wall, vision of the; irony; *Mene, Mene, Tekel, Parsin* (or *Uparsin*); mystery; Newton's Riddle; Oedipus; parable(s); Pythagorean Theorem; *Selah*; 666; Sphinx, sphinx(es); thistle and the cedar, fable of the; trees and the thornbush, fable of the.

rider on the white horse: 1. Jesus Christ as victorious Lord at the Second Coming (Rev. 19:11). His white steed represents victory. John characterized the rider with nine names: "Faithful and True" (Rev. 19:11), he who "judges and makes war" in his justice (Rev. 19:11), the one with eyes that are "like blazing fire" (Rev. 19:12), wearing "many crowns" (Rev.19:12), one who carries the name that no one but he himself knows (Rev. 19:12), one dressed in a robe dipped in blood (Rev. 19:13), and whose name is the "Word of God" (Rev. 19:13). The armies of heaven accompany him. Each title offers some vital clue as to the mission and power of the returning Christ. 2. the rider on the white horse of the first seal (Rev. 6:1–2) who is usually considered to be the Antichrist (although some theologians name him as Jesus himself). The two images described above are not to be confused and always viewed distinctively. Both good and evil can alternate as temporary victors in the world's daily struggles, but only the righteous in Christ will ultimately triumph. *See also* animals, birds, and insects, symbology of; eschatology, eschatological; four horsemen of the apocalypse; names (titles) for Jesus; Second Coming; white horse.

Ridley, Nicholas: a prominent Church of England dissenter (1500–1555) who believed the Roman pope to be the Antichrist, a common assertion among the Reformers. Ridley was chaplain to King Henry VIII and many name him the founder of the Protestant church in England. He was bishop of London when he fell victim to the purge of "Bloody Mary" in 1555. He was burned at the stake as one of the so-called Oxford martyrs, which also included Thomas Cranmer and Hugh Latimer. Ridley burned slowly as the wood was too green, causing him great pain in the lower extremities but not hastening death. His prayer was quoted as: "Oh, heavenly Father, I give unto thee most hearty thanks that thou has called me to be a professor of thee, even unto death. I beseech thee, Lord God, have mercy on this realm of England, and deliver it from all her enemies." *See also* Church of England; Cranmer, Thomas; Latimer, Hugh; martyr(s); Mary, Queen of Scots; Oxford martyrs.

righteous Branch, a: a title from the prophet Jeremiah (Jer. 23:5; 33:15). The reference is to the coming Messiah, descended in David's line, who will save Israel and Judah; "The Lord Our Righteousness" is an equivalent description. *See also* Lord our Righteousness, the; names (titles) for Jesus.

"righteous Gentiles": a common name spoken by Jews when referring to any non-Jew of any nationality who has or is willing to aid the Hebrew people. "Righteous among the nations" is an equivalent expression. The title is an honorable one and rendered to any who support Israel with love, protection, finances, encouragement, or friendship. Recent construction in Jerusalem plays tribute to these heroes (Oskar Schindler, Corrie ten Boom, and hundreds of others) which was funded by donations and called the Friends of Zion center. *See also* Gentile(s); Jerusalem, landmarks of; Judaism.

righteous God, my: David's name for God to Whom he appealed in Psalm 4:1. *See also* Daniel as Old Testament prophecy; Lord our Righteousness, the; names (titles) for God; Righteous One.

righteousness: a prolific biblical term to denote purity, sanctity, goodness, or obedience to God. God is also called righteous, but in a far more expressive and complete way than our own attitudes and behaviors. It is God's righteousness that allows any measure of our own. The word may be somewhat complex since we are prone to speak of God as *having* righteousness but that He *makes* people righteous. Picturing the term in Chinese characters may help; there, *righteousness* is depicted as a combination with the top word as "lamb" and the bottom as the idiom for "me." Thus, the lamb is above, or covers, the person. In apocalyptic language, righteousness is usually symbolized by white raiment. *See also* linen; white raiment.

Righteous One: a name for God as encountered in Acts 7:52 and 1 John 2:1. *See also* names (titles) for God; Righteous God, my.

rightful sovereign, the: a reference noted in Ezekiel 21:27, written in the NIV as "the one to whom it rightfully belongs." The prophecy is debated as to whether it indicates the Messiah, King Jehoiachin of Judah, or both. The phrase is eerily akin to Genesis 49:10, which states: "until he comes to whom it belongs." *See also* names (titles) for Jesus; Shiloh; "until he comes."

right hand of Christian fellowship, the: the simple act of a handshake but rendered in the name of comradeship in the family of God. The gesture seems to have replaced what the ancients called the "holy kiss." *See also* Christianese; gestures; hand(s); holy kiss; liturgical year; passing the peace; peace; right hand, the.

right hand of the Most High: God's "hand" of power and judgment so important to many of the prophets. *Third Enoch* shows Yahweh with the right hand held behind His back lest He punish Israel before they repent. This inaction or prolonged delay of discipline may be ending, if we understand *3 Enoch* correctly, as God tires of waiting and is bringing Israel back from the nations in their unbelief. *See also* right hand, the; session of Christ.

right hand, the: an important apocalyptic device for denoting honor, fellowship, strength, or blessing, which is traditionally done with the right hand. The power of the symbol remains whether it is a human hand or God's that is offered. The right side of the body, or any place opposite the left, is the place of honor (*e.g.,* Christ being "seated at the right hand of the Father)." When an angel in Daniel or the Lamb in Revelation desire to refresh or aid the prophets, the right hand is placed on the head or shoulder. Revelation 1:20 shows Christ upholding the seven stars of the seven churches with his right hand. Not only is the right hand of God relevant, but one's own right side can suggest safety from Him (*e.g.,* Psalm 121:5). Even today, the right hand is standard for honors bestowed (*i.e.,* handshakes, military salutes, etc.). *See also* hand(s); hand of [God] the Lord; right hand of Christian fellowship, the; right hand of the Most High; session of Christ.

Rig-Vita. See *Vedas.*

Rimmon: the chief god of Damascus whose name means "to roar" or "to thunder." He was worshiped by the kings of Syria (2 Ki. 5:18), as did the Syrian official, Naaman. When Naaman was cured of his leprosy by bathing in the Jordan River (as directed by the prophet Elisha), he changed his loyalty to Yahweh and worshiped the Lord in secret. Some linguists suggest the term is an alternate name for Mount Hermon. In folklore and the occult, for some reason, Rimmon is the devil's ambassador to Russia. *See also* Levant pantheon; Mount Harmon; Naaman.

ring composition. See *inclusio.*

Ripley, George: Unitarian minister, utopian Socialist, transcendentalist, author, and literary critic (1802–1880). Ripley was the founder of Brook Farm, perhaps the most noted communal colony of the time. He and his wife Sophia kept the operation going until 1847 despite harsh criticism and dissatisfaction among the members. He then devoted his life and career to transcendentalist ideals and writing and became the champion of radical writings like

The Scarlet Letter by Nathaniel Hawthorne and Charles Darwin's *Origin of the Species*. Ripley's most enduring work is the 16-volume *New American Cyclopedia*, which he co-authored with Charles A. Dana from 1858–1863. *See also* Brook Farm; communal communities; transcendentalism; Unitarian Universalists.

rising sun, the. See Morning Star, the.

rite: sacred ordered procedures or observances in service or worship. The order and actions of the rite are usually empowered or directed by habit, tradition, or institutional expectations. *See also* church; ecclesiology; faith and order; habit; liturgical year; liturgy, Christian; liturgy, Jewish; polity; ritual; worship.

Rite of Christian Initiative of Adults (RCIA): a year-long process of training and preparation for an adult to affiliate with the Roman Catholic Church. *See also* religious education; religious organizations; Roman Catholic Church.

rite of passage: ritual or mental discipline, common in many cultures, usually involving young persons on the edge of adulthood. To prove one's worth to accept the responsibilities and challenges of maturity, initiates are expected to undergo a physical or mental test of fitness or ordeal of some description acceptable to themselves, their community, or their god. Many rites of passage are stressful and even dangerous but, if successful, help the candidate assume courage and acceptance. *See also* ordeal(s); test(ing); vision quest.

ritual: the cultus or prescribed performance of worship—an action performed religiously (*i.e.,* consistently). *See also* church; cult(s); ecclesiology; faith and order; gestures; habit; liturgical year; liturgy, Christian; liturgy, Jewish; rite; polity; ritual defilement; worship.

ritual abuse: psychological, physical, sexual, or spiritual maltreatment in the so-called religious process of some dangerous cults and religions. Injuries and deaths have occurred in botched exorcisms, frenetic ceremony, and the like. About one death each year is accounted for from such proceedings, but likely there are others unreported. *See also* Catholic Church abuse scandal; church abuse; church discipline; churching; cult(s); delict; papal revenue; ritual defilement; sacrilege; shepherding (cultic).

ritual defilement: in Hebrew *tumas ohel,* an error or misrepresentation of the worship ritual, either by accident or intent. Most ancient religions, including Judaism, considered ritual error to be a serious taboo, and some even call it "ritual abuse." Those who disregarded standard attitude, dress, or prescribed prohibitions were also classed as being ritually defiled, the *tima* in Hebrew. To illustrate, a woman who entered the Temple at an importune time in her parturition or menstrual cycle, a man who prepared for battle after sexual relations, a priest about to minister in unclean linen, or a leper amid polite society were considered to be in ritual defilements. The condition was determined to be sin, whereby temporary or permanent disbarment from the worshiping or social community could be imposed. In Hebrew stipulation, there were four types of ritual defilement in the body: discharge of semen (male), menstruation (female), contact with a dead animal or human corpse, and leprosy. A ritual error was a procedural mistake by a priest. Ceremonial purity was obtained or restored by the actions of the high priest once a year on the Day of Atonement when he sprinkled blood in the Holy of Holies to obtain forgiveness for the sanctuary and the nation. Foreign and unclean items were taboo, including imported religions like Hellenism and all pagan philosophies. Certain animals were unsuitable for sacrifice. Genealogy of the priest was important because only qualified men from the tribe of Levi were admissible. Ritual purity also extended or was intended to include all social and business exchanges among the people. *See also* blasphemy; boil(s); curse(s); desecrate; leaven; leprosy; "monthly uncleanliness"; moral uncleanliness; Nazirite(s); priest(s); profane; ritual; ritual abuse; sacrilege; shepherding (cultic); sin(s); sore(s); trespass; unclean; unclean animals, Peter's vision of the; wildfire; yeast.

Rituale Romanum: for many centuries the manual for religious rituals of the Roman Catholic Church. Among other features, it contained definitions of demon possession and exorcism procedures. Oddly, many of these supposed symptoms of possession were what the earliest Christians called "gifts of the Spirit," thus condemning the very spiritual gifts that would be useful in expelling evil ones. *See also* demon possession; liturgical year; liturgy, Christian; Roman Catholic Church.

ritual purity. See ritual defilement.

River Brethren: an American offspring of German Baptists and Mennonites from Switzerland starting among the German colonizers in Pennsylvania in 1770. Since they were located along the Susquehanna River they earned the name River Brethren. The group was led by Jacob and John Engle and practiced triune baptism. The movement resisted affiliation with either the Mennonites, the United Brethren, or the Dunkers, all of whom they bear a resemblance. *See also* church bodies in America (typed).

river of fire: the description of the fiery stream issuing from the throne of God in Daniel 7:10. It may be the source of destruction for the ogre with the little horn since subsequent verses indicate such a fate for that monster. *See also* river of the water of life, the; rivers of fire.

river of life, the. See river of the water of life, the.

river of the water of life, the: a feature of the New Jerusalem (Rev. 22:1–2) that is viewed as a source of blessing for the redeemed world. It is pictured as flowing from the throne of God and the Lamb and rushing through the center of the city. On each bank of the river, the tree (trees?) of life is growing, granting healing to the nations. The description in Revelation is unclear as to whether the replacement tree of life is a single growth on the riverbank with overlapping branches or a series of them along the waterway. According to Ezekiel, the river will continue into the restored earth to serve as a way of transport, beauty, and blessing in the new era far into the deserts and neighboring lands. Ezekiel 47:1–12 envisions this flow of precious water in his prophecy of the forthcoming new Temple. Probably, the rivers mentioned in Ezekiel, Daniel, and Revelation are somehow related as to description and intent. *See also* eschatology, eschatological; New Jerusalem; river of fire; water of life.

rivers of fire: the description (in *3 Enoch*) of seven huge fiery rivers that flow about the heavens, only to descend on the heads of those punished in Gehenna. *See also* river of fire.

"river, the": a long-standing reference to the exotic feeling of Pentecostalism or revivalist ecstasy. The term originally developed around the experience of baptism in a flowing stream, then static pools, and finally baptismal tanks or fonts. The expression referred to the metaphorical flow or wave action of emotion often experienced by the believer caught up in the rapture of the moment. *See also* Azusa Street revival; baptism of the Holy Spirit; Brownsville Assembly; charismatic movement; Christ within; ecstasy; glossolalia; Pentecostalism; revivalism; theolepsy; "Toronto Blessing, the"; xenoglossy.

Rizpah: a concubine of King Saul even though a foreigner. She was the mother of two sons by Saul. This pair, along with five sons of Merab, eldest daughter of Saul, was given up by David to the Gibeonites to be executed in retribution for Saul's betrayal of the city. The slain were left unburied, necessitating that Rizpah watch over the bodies for weeks (2 Sam. 21:7–12), protecting them from the elements and wild birds and beasts. When David heard of her devotion, he collected the bones of the young men, along with those of Saul and Jonathan, and had them honorably entombed. David's action to avenge the Gibeonites ended a three-year drought brought upon Israel because of Saul's injustice. *See also* Armoni; Mephibosheth.

robe: traditional dress of the Hebrews and other Orientals, including the special priestly uniform. In Revelation 1:13, Jesus is wearing a long robe with a sash to denote his priestly and kingly authority. *See also* raiment; robe of Christ.

robe, crown, and throne: the three eternal rewards for the righteous according to *The Ascension of Isaiah*. The idea fits nicely with general public knowledge of rewards in the afterlife. *See also* bema; crown(s); judgment seat of Christ; reward(s) in heaven; welcome, a rich.

robe of Christ: the seamless outer garment worn by Jesus at his crucifixion. Because of its value as a whole piece, the Roman soldiers gambled for its possession. Today, a number of Roman Catholic and Greek Orthodox facilities claim they possess it as a relic. The existence of such a relic is highly questionable, as all of them are, due to the long span of time it would be expected to survive. Furthermore, Jesus was likely crucified unclothed to amplify his shame in the presence of the onlookers and the winner of the garment would have eventually disposed of it. *See also* relic(s); robe.

Roberts, Granville Oral: charismatic faith healer, revivalist, and televangelist (1918–2009), probably second only to Billy Graham in evangelistic campaigning success. Roberts claimed to be of Choctaw Cherokee heritage from Oklahoma and was ordained in both the Pentecostal Holiness and United Methodist churches. He founded the Oral Roberts Evangelistic Association and Oral Roberts University in Tulsa, along with a leading medical research center. His ministry can be characterized as proto-prosperity gospel and heavily emphasized on-hands and distance healing via radio, a message that seemed to appeal especially to the poor and minorities. Listeners could request prayer and receive a "prayer cloth" guaranteed to be prayed over by Roberts himself. He even claimed to have raised the dead on occasion. His fund-raising was phenomenal; in 1987 he announced that God told him to raise eight million dollars by the end of the year or He would "call him home." Many interpreted this statement to be a threat of suicide so, despite a shortened deadline, he ended with nine point one million. Roberts called his approach to ministry "seed faith" and continually insisted "God heals, I don't." Family life was not gentle but he did accumulate considerable personal wealth before his death even though his financial dealings were suspect on some levels. *See also* Bakker, Jim and Tammy; Camping, Harold; Christianese; *Elmer Gantry;* eschatology, eschatological; evangelist(s); evangelism; faith healing; "falling into sin"; Falwell, Jerry; Graham, William Franklin (Billy); Hinn, Benny; Kuhlman, Kathryn; McPherson, Aimee Semple; prosperity religion(s); revivalism; Roberts, Granville Oral; Robertson, Marion Gordon "Pat"; Sheen, Fulton J.; Swaggart, Jimmy Lee; televangelism, televangelists; Van Impe, Jack.

Robertson, Marion Gordon "Pat": evangelist, pastor, political activist, and erstwhile prophet. He hinted broadly that the end of the age would occur in the 1980s and has progressively gained a reputation, deserved or not, as one prone to make inappropriate racial, political, or other unsubstantiated remarks at inopportune times. To quote from his *700 Club* TV telecast in May of 1980: "I guarantee you, by the end of 1982, there is going to be a judgment on the world." The next date he set for the world's destruction was supposed to be on April 29, 2007. Robertson claims to be privy to at least one future presidential election but has declined to reveal the divine secret publically. At one point, Robertson announced that God had chosen him "to usher in the coming of My Son." Failing that, he declared himself a Republican candidate for president in 1988. As an unprejudiced evaluation and unintended character assassination, Robertson comes across as a sometimes confused preacher seemingly inconsistent in his worldview of prophecy. Robertson's designation as a modern-day prophet is probably a minority view. *See also* Baptists; *New World Order, The*; Religious Right, the; revivalism; televangelism, televangelist(s).

Robert the devil: the subject of a medieval romance, possibly originating with a pair of Roberts (Robert of Bingen and an obscure martyr named Robustian) who, for some reason, became associated with evil times. (Or we could be speaking of the legendary founders of Rome, Romulus and Remus.) In any case, Robert the devil became the incarnation of such fears, according to his legend and stories, and was blamed for almost all calamities and the very scourge of humanity—arson, rape, natural disasters, torturing of pilgrims, and he even beheaded the knights he had bested in tournaments. Robert was said to be the child of a barren woman who seduced the devil to impregnate her. As payment, the soul of her child would be required. Catholic Rogation Days were partly inaugurated to counter the danger. *See also* Rogation Days; Satan.

Robigus: or Robigo, the Roman agricultural god of frost responsible for keeping blight and crop failure away from the grain and assuring a good harvest. His celebration consisted of sacrificing a dog as part of the ritual. The Roman Catholic holy day on April 25 replaced the celebration with the procession of the Greater Litanies. *See also* Greater Litanies; Rogation Days; mythological beasties, elementals, monsters, and spirit animals; Olympian pantheon.

Robin Goodfellow: also called "Puck" or "Hob" in English folklore. Robin was a long-lived mischievous nature sprite fond of practical jokes and minor but annoying tricks to disturb human life. He is modeled in Shakespeare's *A Midsummer's Night Dream*. *See also* attending spirit(s); banshee; bogle; brownies; bugbears; Celtic folklore and religion; clurichauns; daemons; disa; dryad(s); elemental(s); fairy, fairies; Furies; ghost(s); ghoul; gnome(s);

Green Man, the; hobgoblins; homunculus; household deities; huldufolk; Lares; leprechaun(s); Loa Loas; Manes; mythological beasties, elementals, monsters, and spirit animals; nereid; nisse; nymph(s); nyx; Oniropompi; Orisha; Oya; para; paredri; penates; satyr; Seelie Court, Unseelie Court; selkie; Sidhe; sirens; spiritual warfare; sprite(s); sylph(s); teraphim; territorial spirits; Trickster; Tuatha de Danann; tutelary; undine; wight(s).

Robinson, John A. T.: a New Testament scholar and bishop of the Church of England (1919–1983) known as "Mr. Liberal." His book, *Honest to God,* was widely loved, or hated, while it attempted to "update" Christian theology (sometimes called "secular theology"). Robinson believed in universal salvation and insisted the New Testament was written quite earlier than most acknowledged. He also criticized his colleagues for sloppy exegesis and unoriginal thinking, even to the point of defending the book, *Lady Chatterley's Lover,* from censorship which he admonished as one every Christian should read. *See also* Church of England; Death of God theology.

Robinson, Morgan: an American author who wrote a book in 1897 that he claimed would be a precursor to the *Titanic* disaster. Details of the book are quite similar to those of the actual shipwreck, except that his vessel was called the *Titan.* At least eighteen others are said to have made similar predictions in the years leading up to that famous maritime disaster.

rock(s): hardened sand natural to the earth such as boulders or stones—material useful in building, weaponry, durable writing, ornamentation, an altar, making a shadow for shade in the heat, and other purposes. Metaphorical uses include symbolism for protection, security, refuge, strength, durability, or a solid foundation. Jesus based the rock-like faith of Simon Peter (his name means "rock") as the foundation of his kingdom (Mt. 16:18), or the disciples of Christ being *petros,* "little rocks." In that sense, which is the true sense, the Roman Catholic tenet that papal succession is based on Peter's apostleship is not strong. God is spoken of in the Old Testament as a Rock—a refuge, fortress, and the basis of salvation (Ps. 118:22). Peter and Paul recited Jesus Christ as the cornerstone of the Church (Rom. 9:33; 1 Pe. 2:6–8). Paul named the Messiah as the spiritual rock that aided the Egyptian exiles (1 Cor.10:4). In another sense, Christ is presented as a stumbling stone to the Jews (Rom. 9:32; 1 Cor. 1:21–23). To the unbeliever, Christ the rock is a stone of judgment (Mt. 21:44). The term is frequently a symbol of durability, strength, or obstinacy, or it can serve as a metaphor for a crushing blow, like someone being smashed by falling rock or a slingstone. *See also* apostolic succession; cornerstone (capstone); crushing rock that became a mountain; "fall on us"; living stones; Peter as apostle; Rock (my, the); sacred stones; stone(s).

rock cut out but not by human hands. See crushing rock that became a mountain.

Rock (my, the): a name for God used by the prophet Habakkuk (Hab. 1:12), and in Psalm 18:2, 6; 92:15, Isaiah 44:8, Deuteronomy 32:4, *et al.* Paul used the name (not capitalized) to describe Christ as the source of spiritual sustenance for the Exodus Hebrews (1 Cor. 10:4). David's praise song in 2 Samuel 22:47 and other references uses the title "Rock" to emphasize God's unwavering strength and power. The Rock is also a type for Christ, identified from the water gushing from the rock at Horeb (Num. 20:6–12; 1 Cor. 10:3–4). It is he who provides the "water" of eternal life (Jn. 4:10). Such a rock is also associated with "a stone cut out without hands" drawn from Nebuchadnezzar's dream (Dan. 2:34-35) that became a great mountain. Jesus once compared the believer's faith, based on Peter's confession, as a rock on which he could build his Church (Rom. 9:33). *See also* crushing rock that became a mountain; names (titles) for God; Peter as apostle; rock(s); Rock of Israel.

Rock of Israel: a name for Mount Zion named by the Lord Himself (Jer. 30:29). *See also* Mount Zion; Rock (my, the).

Rock of Truth: a legend contained in the *Apocalypse of Adam*, a Gnostic text from the Nag Hammadi library. The story tells the reader that Adam ordered his son Seth to record all of his and Eve's adventures in the Garden of Eden. This narrative contains prophecy about the coming ages, the coming of a savior (who is Seth himself), and some other secrets, all of which are to be written on stone and hidden. The collection is called the "hidden knowledge of Adam." Seth duly recorded the information and hid it on a holy mountain cared for by a guardian called "O Dreadful One." *See also* Cave of Treasures; Seth.

rod: a stick of some length used to strike, whether the intent is to discipline, punish, defend, or attack. It was the favored weapon of the shepherd who used it to protect his sheep against wild beasts or thieves. A rod and a staff were usually carried by the shepherd, as beautifully portrayed in Psalm 23. And, in Isaiah 11:4, the cudgel becomes a metaphor for the faithfulness of the Messiah to be evident in the Millennium. To be beaten with rods was a severe punishment, something experienced by Paul and a number of his companions. Jewish law strictly regulated the number of blows that could be administered. The book of Micah (Mic. 6:9) contains the enigmatic phrase, "Heed the rod and the One who appointed it." This saying has been emended and reworked many times but still holds some of its mystery qualities. Basically, however, we may see the expression as an admonition to the people to be wise and listen to the message of warning, as well as to God as the One who issued it lest the rod of punishment descend. *See also* canon of the Scriptures; cross; flagrum; measuring rod; rod of iron; staff; whip.

rod of iron: the eschatological description of the method of rule to be practiced by Christ in the Millennium. Some who eschew the Millennium concept, however, view the iron rod of rule as a weapon for the Second Coming and not the peaceable kingdom. The intent, nevertheless, is to project Christ as the undisputed ruler who enforces morality and good government by his unbending will and enforced righteousness—a genuine theocracy. Such a process will guarantee a trouble-free society living in peace and harmony in all of earth's endeavors. How people will react to this required goodness, however, is foreseen in the Gog and Magog rebellion at the end of the Millennium. Then, when much of the earth's population had been chafing under the rules, the protesters will rise up in a final rebellion under Satan's instigation. Christ is said to rule with an iron scepter to convey the idea that his governorship will be strict, moralistic, unyielding to sin, and reverential throughout the millennial population. To be beaten with wooden rods is painful, but to experience such punishment with iron would be nigh unbearable. Perhaps the firm rule of Christ then is intended to prove that even under ideal circumstances, people will squirm under the authority and lean toward rebellion. Only a changed heart, not a changed environment, will push humanity to righteousness. *See* *also* crushing rock that became a mountain; election; elect, the; eschatology, eschatological; he who rules with an iron scepter; kingdom that cannot be shaken, a; kingdom, the; messianic age, the; mighty hand and outstretched arm, a; millennial geography; millennial Sabbath; millennial sacramentalism; millennial Temple; millennial worship; Millennium, millennial; New Covenant, the; New Eden; rebuilding the Temple; remnant; rod; restoration of all things; restoration of Israel (the Jews); restoration Temple (and land); Sabbath rest; scepter; staff; Temple(s); third Temple; times of refreshing.

Roeh: an Old Testament name for a prophet. The term is used eleven times and stresses the ability as a "seer." *See also Chozeh;* interpreter; *Kohen; Lewi;* man of God; man of the Spirit; messenger of Yahweh; *Nabhi';* prophet(s); prophetess(es); servant of Yahweh; servants, my; *Shamar;* watchman.

Roerich, Nicholas K.: *nee* Nicholi Rerikh (1874–1947), a Russian painter, philosopher, writer, scientist, public figure, and world traveler. He spent several years in Tibet studying and recording the theology of the Tibetan monks and their faith, including their eschatology. He was a disciple of Madame Blavatsky's Theosophy but flavored with heavy doses of themes centered in the occult. Roerich was a resident of the United States since 1920 and was reputedly a close confidant of Vice President Henry Wallace and known to Franklin Roosevelt. *See also* Chintamani Stone; cult(s); Holy Grail; philosophy of religion; Shambhala legends.

Roganists: a religious sect appearing in the fourth century that opposed punishment for those who refused to conform to the prescribed rules of righteousness imposed at the time by Roman Catholic or other ecclesiastical authority. *See also* Roman Catholic Church; sect(s).

rogation: asking for supplication, especially in a confessional or when contesting personal spiritual upheaval. *See also* abjuration; ascesis; *metanoia;* penance; recant; repent; repentance; Rogation Days.

Rogation Days: a time of prayer and fasting opportunity in the Western Church rites. The occasion may be celebrated with processions, reciting the litany of the saints, and appropriate abstinence and prayers. April 25 is considered a major observance; Mondays and Wednesdays on days preceding Ascension Day are rated minor. The Rogations, then, form a festive period of three days—Monday, Tuesday, and Wednesday—immediately before the Thursday feast of the Ascension; the exact days fall between April 28 and June 1. The time coincided with the "red moon" or "blood moon" so feared by the ancients. The holiday was intended to end or mitigate misfortune and disaster, especially from such as the terrifying Robert the devil. Pope Leo II (in A.D. 816) made the festival obligatory for all of Roman Catholicism. "Rogation" is derived from the Latin *rogare* for "ash." Its origin, like so many Roman Catholic emphases, seems to have sprung from the Roman ritual of sacrificing a dog (the *Robigilia)* for the god Robigus, who was responsible for keeping the wheat harvest free from disease. *See also* blood moon(s); Ember Days; liturgical year; liturgy, Christian; feasts and special days of high liturgy faiths; Menologion; Robert the devil; Robigus; rogation; Roman Catholic Church.

Ro-Hun **therapy:** the Eastern practice of balancing energy fields in the body to promote good health or enact a cure. *See also* psychic healing.

roll. See scroll.

Roma: 1. the Roman goddess worshiped extensively at Smyrna (Rev. 2:8–11). She held sway in a major temple in Rome as well and personified the city and, in a broader sense, the empire itself. 2. today, the name identifies the Gypsies (the Romani) in their nomadic lifestyles worldwide. They are only recently a targeted group for evangelistic outreach in today's missionary emphasis. The Roma, traveling nomads of several countries, are known by different names but are an old and distinct culture. Evidence is they started in northwest India between A.D. 224 and 642. By the fifth century, they had migrated to Western Europe and America, almost always persecuted as homeless and untrustworthy people. Religious beliefs vary somewhat in the several tribes but the basics are fairly standard. The doctrines can be presented as: (1) a belief in Del (God), (2) a belief in being (Satan), (3) belief in bibaxt (bad luck), (4) belief in mulo (spirits or ghosts), (5) belief in the power of amulets, charms, etc., and (6) belief in the powers of healing rituals and curses. Each gypsy has three names—a secret one known only to his or her mother, a baptismal name (a ritual usually performed in running water) by which he or she is known, and a third if the person becomes a Christian and is rebaptized. Women are considered impure (especially below the waist) so even male and female clothing is laundered separately. The familiar role as fortune-tellers is performed only for non-gypsies, never their own. *See also* Olympian pantheon; Porajmos; Rome; Smith, Rodney "Gypsy."

Roman Catholic Church: the largest Christian denomination (if counted with those received in infant baptism and all aspects of the institution). The religion is prone to call itself the "Holy Mother Church." In America, white Catholics number about 13 percent of the population with another 8 percent Hispanic and yet another 2 percent from other non-white. Eschatologically, the church has adopted the allegorical approach to apocalyptic theology of the type espoused by Augustine. An odd twist in the Second Coming theology of the church does recognize a Golden Age of a thousand years (a Millennium) but posits that it will be followed by a period of rule by the Antichrist. Following that, the age will culminate in a final battle, the last judgment, and the end of the world. So far, the Roman Church has refused to pronounce on any prophecy revealed after the compilation of the Bible, although those visions and revelations are commonly speculated upon and discussed at the highest levels. But no conclusions as to accuracy or authentication of any modern prediction or prophecy have come forth. The patriarchate of Rome slowly rose to prominence from about A.D. 300 in a deliberate strategy of many of her popes to gain ascendency overall others—those of Constantinople, Alexandria, Antioch, and Jerusalem. Alexandria was wrecked by Islam, Jerusalem was neglected, and Antioch faded from apathy or lack of strong leadership after the fall of the Syrian (Antiochian) scholars. Only Constantinople remained as a contender, but that church was troubled by Islam as well and could not resist its preoccupation with bickering and divisive theological debate within itself. Through the natural prestige of Rome as the center of the old Roman Empire, through trickery, and the arbitrary chance of history, Latin Christianity emerged as a clear winner after A.D. 1300. The literature of their beloved poet Virgil and other mindsets and nostalgia for faded Roman glory would not allow the church fathers to truly believe that the

Roman Empire was dead. It was a puzzle to them why God would allow the sack of Rome by barbarians in 410. Was not the Roman Empire of the fourth century the model for God's kingdom on earth? Why was it now fallen to chaos and futility? By far, however, the strongest appeal to supremacy at Rome was her constant insistence that the Church was laid on the foundation of Peter's apostleship. It is interesting that even though both Peter and Paul were killed in Rome, the Church adopted Peter and ignored Paul. Rome's claim to the legacy of Peter is weak in any case, but it was the main impetus to push the Western Church to the top. The Roman liturgy was said in Latin until recent Vatican pronouncements allow worship services in the vernacular. Internal disputes, historical and modern scandals, internecine persecutions throughout its history, and the Protestant Reformation have all but disassembled the Roman claim to preeminence, but the misapprehension remains by force of legend. How is Roman Catholic dogma formed? The ideal process was put forward by Vincent, a monk on the island of Lerins off the coast of southern France (fifth century). It was he who set out the formula: *quod ubique, quod semper, quod ab omnibus creditum est,* "what is believed everywhere in the Church, always, and by everyone." The principle is a favorite quotation by many Catholics but obviously naive. Quickly enough, any issue will prove that it is difficult indeed to enjoy a doctrine always believed by everybody everywhere. Even so, the formed traditions of the Roman faith have grown to regularly supplant even the Bible as church authority. The final break with Eastern Christianity occurred in 1054. *See also* abbess; abbey; abbot; Abelard, Peter; abjuration; ablegate; absolution; acolyte; Act Concerning Religion; Act of Contrition; adelphopoiesis; *ad limina;* Adso; Advent; *Adversus Judaeos;* advocate; advowson; agapetae; aggiomamento; *Agnus Dei;* Agobard; Albertus Magus; Aldebert; Alexander of Alexandria; Alighieri, Dante; Allouez, Claude Jean; altarage; Amaury, Arnauld; Ambrose; Ambrosian Rite; Anamnesis; anaphora; anathema; anaphora; ancress; Angelus*; anima sola;* Anne, Queen de la Palude; annulment; Annunciation, Feast of the; Anomoeans; ante-Nicene fathers; antipope(s); Antony; apocrisiarius; Apollinarius, Apollinarianism; Apollonarius of Hierapolis; Apollonia; apostolic succession; Aquinas, Thomas; archbishop(s); archdeacon(s); Archelaus; Aristo of Pella; Arius; artificial conception; Arnobius; Arius; Arnobius; Ash Wednesday; Assumptionist Order of Augustinians; Assumptionist Orders; Assumption of Mary; Assumption of Mary, Feast of the; *Atlia Vendita;* Augsburg Interim; Augustine, Aurelius; Augustine of Canterbury; Augustinian Order; *auto-da-fe; Ave Maria;* Avignon papacy; Babylonian Captivity of the Church; Bacon, Roger; Baldwin I; Baldwin IV; Baldwin V; ban(s); baptism of desire; baptism regeneration; Barnabites; Basilica(s); beadsman; beatification; Beatus; Becket, Thomas; Bede, the Venerable; Beguines; bell, book, and candle; *Benedicite Omnia Opera;* Benedict of Nursia; Benedict, Order of; Benedict, Rule of; Benedict XVI, Pope; benefice; Bernard of Clairvaux; Berrigan, Daniel and Philip; binding and loosing; bishop(s); Black Canons; Black Madonnas; Boniface; Bosco, John (Giovanni); Brendan of Clonfert; Breviary; Bridget of Kildare; Bridget of Sweden; Bridget's Cross; brother(s); Brownson, Orestes Augustus; Bruno, Gordano; bull; bursary; Cabrini, Francis Xavier; Cadac-Andreas; Cadaver Synod, the; Caesarius of Heisterbach; Caius; calefactory; calendar (Gregorian); camerlengo; Candlemas; canonical hours; canonical penance; canon(s) of the church; canons minor; canons regular; Canute the Great, King; capuchin; Capuchin Order; cardinal(s); Carmelites; Carol, John; carrodian; Carthusians; cartulary; castrato; casuistry; catechumen; catechism; cathedral(s); *cathedraticum;* Catherine of Siena; Catholic Church abuse scandal; Catholic Women's League (CWL); Cecilia; Celestine V, Pope; Celestines; celibacy; cell; cenobium; centering prayer; chamberlain; chancellor; chancery; chant; chantry; Charles I, King; Charles II, King; Christmas; Christ the King, Feast day of; church bodies in America (typed); Church Triumphant, Church Militant; cimelia; circatore; Circumcision, Feast of the; Cistercians; Clement of Alexandria; Clement of Rome; Clement V, Pope; clergy; cloister; close; Clovis; Cluny; coadjutor; Code of Canon Law; Colet, John; Collect; colors, liturgical; commination; Columbanus; Columbus, Christopher; commination; Commodianus; common readings; communion of the saints; *Compactata;* compurgation; conclave; concordant(s); Concordant of Collaboration; condign merit; confession; confessor(s); Confirmation; Confiteor; confraternities; Congregation for the Propagation of the Doctrine of the Faith; congruent merit; consistory; convectile acts; convent; Conventionals; *conversae;* convolution of Aries; Copernicus,

Nicolaus; Coracion; co-redemptrix; Corpus Christi, Feast of; Coughlin, Charles E.; Council of Carthage; Council of Chalcedon; Council of Constance; Council of Hippo; Council of Laodicea; Council of Trent (Roman Catholic); Council on American-Islamic Relations; councils, church; Councils of Constantinople; Councils of Ephesus; Councils of Nicaea; Counter-Reformation; Crassus, Peter; Credo; Creeping Jesus; crosier; Crosier of Saint Patrick; Cross, Feasts of the; crossfigill; crucifix; Crusades; Culleton, R. Gerald; cure; *Curia;* cursillo; Cusa, Nicholas; Cyprian; Cyril of Alexandria; da Casale, Umbertino; Damasus I, Pope; Damian, Peter; datary; Day of Pardon; Day of the Dead; deacon(s), deaconess(es); dean; de Chardin, Teilhard Pierre; de Cisneros, Francisco Ximenes; decretal(s); Decretum; de Escalante, Silvestre Velez and Dominquez, Francisco Atanasio; defrocking; de las Casas, Bartolome; delict; de Molay, Jacques; *Deo gratias;* de Payens, Hughes; Descartes, Rene; desert mystics; De Smet, Pierre Jean; Desmond Rebellions; deuterocanonical books; devil's advocate; de Wyon (Wion), Arnold; dicastry; diet; Diet of Worms; di Gattinara, Cardinal Mercurino; diocese; Dionysius of Rome; discalced; dispensation(s); divine filiation; Doctors of the Church; Dominic; Dominicans; *Donation of Constantine;* "Donation of Pippin"; Donatism; Douay-Rheims Bible; Dragonnades; *dulia;* duomo; du Puy, Raymond; Durer, Albrecht; Easter; Eastern Orthodox Church; Ecumenical Council of A.D. 999; *ego te absolvo;* elevation; Ember Days; embolism; Emmerich, Anna Katherine; encyclical(s); endorsing agency; England, John; epiclesis; Epiphany; Epiphany, Feast of the; Erigena, John Scotus; Eucharist; *ex cathedra;* excommunication; *ex sufflatio; extra ecclesiam nulla salus;* Father; Fatima, Our Lady of; Fat Tuesday; Feast of Fools; feasts and special days of high liturgy faiths; Felix of Nola; ferial day; Ferrer, Vincent; Final Conclave, the; Firmilian; flying bishops; four crowned martyrs; four marks of the Church, the; fraction; Franciscans; Francis de Sales; Francis of Assisi; Francis, Pope; Francis Xavier; Friade, Johannes; friar(s); Friars of Saint Anthony; furniture and furnishings of the modern church; Gaius; Galgani, Gemma; Galilei, Galileo; Garabandal visions; general and particular judgments; genuflection; Gertrude; gestures; Gibbons, Cardinal James; Giles the Hermit; Gobbi, Stefano; Godfrey of Bouillon; Golden Age; golden rose; Good

Friday; Gradual; Great Apostasy, the; Greater Litanies; Great Schism, the; Gregorian reform; Gregory of Tours; Gregory Thaumaturgus; Gregory I, Pope; Gregory XIII, Pope; Guadalupe, Our Lady of; Guardian Angels, Feast of the; guimpe; habit; Hallowmas; Heckler, Isaac Thomas; Hegesippus; hegumene; Helena; Hermas; High Church, Low Church; High Holy Days; Hilary of Poitiers; Hildegard of Bingen; Hippolyte; history and mystery of developing civilization religions; history and mystery of distinctive religious places and constructs; history and mystery of Eastern Orthodoxy; history and mystery of eschatology and apocalypticism; history and mystery of false Messiahs; history and mystery of false prophets, history and mystery of false teachers; history and mystery of Islam; history and mystery of Judaism; history and mystery of modern civilization religions; history and mystery of nonspecific religious persons and vocations; history and mystery of Protestant Christianity; history and mystery of religious documents and sacred writing; history and mystery of religiously significant persons and peoples; history and mystery of religious or sacred objects and relics; history and mystery of the New Testament; history and mystery of the Old Testament; history and mystery of theological words and phrases; history and mystery of the world's religions, denominations, and sects; history of the Church; history of the Old Testament ages; hocus-pocus; holy convocation; Holy Days of Obligation; Holy Family of Our Lord, Feast of the; Holy Innocents, Feast of the; Holy Name of Jesus, Feast of the; Holy Name Society; Holy Rood; Holy Saturday; holy water; Holy Years; Holzhauser, Venerable Bartholomew; home stoup; homily; *Horae Apocalypticae;* House of Loreta; Hughes, John Joseph; Ignatius of Antioch; Ignatius of Loyola; IHS; immaculate conception; Immaculate Conception, Feast of the; impediment; imprimatur; *Index of Forbidden Books;* inerrancy; infirmieri; Innocent III, Pope; Innocent VIII, Pope; Inquisition, the; *Inquisitor's Manual, The;* interdict; interregnum; interstices; Investiture Controversy; invination; Ireland, John; Irenaeus; Isadore of Seville; Janenism; Januarius (San Gennaro); Jerome; "Jesus Prayer, the"; Joan of Arc; Jogues, Isaac; John of Rupescissa; John of the Cross; John of Toledo; John XXIII, Pope; Joint Catholic-Orthodox Declaration of 1965; Jubilate; Justin Martyr; Kennedy, John F.; keys to death and Hades; keys of the kingdom; knighted orders; Knights of

Columbus; Lactantius; Lacunza, Emmanuel; laicisation; Lalemant, Gabriel; La Salette, vision of; Lateran Councils; Lateran Treaty; *latria; lavabo;* lectionary; Legion of Christ; Lent; Leo I, Pope; Leo IX, Pope; Leo X, Pope; le Royer, Jeanne; Lesson; liberation theology; limbo; *Limbus Puerorum;* litany; Lombard, Peter; Lourdes, Our Lady of; low mass, high mass; Loyola, Ignatius; Lucian; Lucian's recession of the Septuagint; magisterium; *Magnificat;* Malachy; *Malleus Malefiracum;* manciple; Marianist; Mariolatry; Maronite Church; Marquette, Jacques; Martin, bishop of Tours; Mary; Mary Mother of God, Feast of; Mary, Queen of Scots; Mass; Mass of Saint Secaire; Mathew, Theobald; Maundy Thursday; Medjugorje; Melito; mendicant(s); mensa; mental reservation; Merton, Thomas; Methodius of Olympus; metropolitan; Michaelmas, Feast of; Minim; misericorde; missal; Molinism; monastery; monasticism; monastic vows; monk(s); monsignor; monstrance; More, Thomas; Most Holy Redeemer, Feast of the; motet; Motherly Sunday; mother superior; Mount of the Jesuits; movable feast(s); mozetta; mystagogy; Mysteries; mysteries of Catholicism, the fifteen; mystery; na Prous Boneta; Nepos; Newman, John Henry; Nicolaitans; Nicholas of Fluh; *nihil obstat;* North American Martyrs, Feast of the; Northern Crusades; Novatian, Novatians; novena; novitiate; nun(s); *Nunc Dimittis;* nuncio; Oahspe Bible; "O" Antiphons; obit; oblate; oblation; Odo; offering; Old Catholic Church; Olivi, Peter John; One, Holy, Catholic, and Apostolic Church; *Opus Dei;* Opus Sanctorum Angelorum; orarium; orders; Ordinal; ordinary; ordinary time; *Ordo;* Oremus; Origen; Our Lady of the Angels; Pachomius; palanca; paleo-orthodoxy; pallium; Pamphilus; Pantaenus; papacy; Papal Bodyguard, Swiss; papal revenue; papal states; Papias; parish; parochial; parochial school(s); particular judgment; patriarch(s); patriarchate(s); Patrick; Paulist Fathers; Paul of Samosata; Peace of Augsburg; Peace of Westphalia; Peasants' Revolt; Pelagius; penance; penitential; pentarchy; Perpetua and Felicity; Peter the Hermit; Petrus Romanus; Philo of Alexandria; Photian Schism, the; Pius V, Pope; Pole, Cardinal Reginald; Polycarp; Polycrates; *Pontifex Maximus;* Pontifical Council; Poor Clare Sisters; pope; Pope Grimoire, the; Pope Joan; "popery"; Porete, Marguerite; pornocracy; postulant; postulator; poustinia; *poverello;* prayer(s) for the dead; prebend; precentor; precessional; prefect(s);

prelate(s); Premonstratensian Order; Prepuce, the Holy; Presentation of the Blessed Virgin Mary; priest(s); primate; *primus inter pares;* p*rinceps; principis;* prior, prioress; priory; processional; proper readings; Propers; "Prophecy of the Popes"; provost; "Pseudo-Isidorian Credentials"; purgatory; Quadragesima; queen of heaven; Quinquagesima; Raccolta; Reconquista; recusant; Redemptorist; refectory; *relaxado en persona;* relic(s); Requiem; rescript; Ricci, Matteo; Rite of Christian Initiative of Adults (RCIA); *Rituale Romanum;* Rock (my, the); Roganists; Rogation Days; Roman Phalanx; Rome; rosary; rubric; Sabellius; Sabellianism; sacerdotalism; sacrament(s); Sacred Heart, Feast of the; sacring; sacrist; saint(s); Saint Bartholomew's Day massacre; Saint Vitus' dance; salvation; samarra; *Sanctus*; Sanctus bell; Sarum Rite; Savonarola, Girolamo; scapular; Schillebeeckx, Edward; Schism of Nepos; Schism, the Great; Schmalkaldic War; Second Eve, the; secular institutes; Sedevacantists; see; sempect; sentences; Septuagesima; Serra, Junipero; Servite Order; Seton, Elizabeth Ann; seven deadly sins; seven psalms, the; Shay, John Dawson Gilmary; Sheen, Fulton J.; shrine(s); Shroud of Turin; *sigillum*; sign of the cross; Simeon Stylites; sister(s); Society of Jesus; Society of Saint Vincent de Paul (SVP); sodality; Solemnity of the Sacred Heart; Spear of Destiny; species; Spellman, Cardinal Francis Joseph; Spirituals; Spirituals of the Franciscan Order; spoons, apostle; state church; stations of the cross; statuary; Steno, Nicholas; stigmata; suffragan; *Summa Theologica;* supererogation; *Syllabus of Errors; Synaxis;* synod; Synod of Whitby; Tatian; Telemachus; temporal punishment; Teresa of Avila; Teresa of Calcutta; tertiary; Tertullian; Tetzel, Johann; Therapeutae; Thirty Years' War; Thomas a' Kempis; three days of darkness; titular sees; Tolkien, J. R. R.; tonsure; Torquemada; tract(s); traditionalism; tradition (Eastern Orthodox and Roman Catholic); "trafficking in Masses"; Transfiguration, Feast of the; Transformation, Feast of the; translation; transubstantiation; Trappist Order; treasury of merits; Tribunal; Tridentine; Tridentine Mass; triduum; Trinity Sunday; triple crown; *triregnum;* Triumph of the Cross, Feast of the; troparion; Truce of God; Tyconius; Typicon; ultramontanism; *Unam Sanctum;* unction; Uniat Church; Union of Brest; Urban II, Pope; Ursula; Ussher, James; Valentine; Vatican I and Vatican II; Vatican Secret Archives; Vatican, the; veil of Veronica; veneration of the saints; Veronica; verse; versicle; *Via Dolorosa; viaticum;* vicar-general; vicar of Christ; vice god; Victorinus; virgins' house; visitation; Visitation, Canonical; Vulgate; warden; Wars of Religion; Wenceslaus I, King; Werdin, Otranto Abbot; White Mountain, battle of; William of Ockham; wimple; woman clothed in (with) the sun, the; Wycliffe, John; Xavier, Francis; XPTO; zucchetto.

Roman collar. See clerical collar.

Roman Empire: the vast and wealthy conquered territory (until its fall) of ancient Rome. At its height, Roman territory stretched from Italy to as far east as Iraq, west and south over Spain, Egypt, and Africa, and north to Britain, France, and Germany. Croatia, Serbia, Turkey, Greece, Syria, and Israel were absorbed. The Roman Empire can be said to have begun in about 27 B.C. and ended its early period in A.D. 284. Some historians count a longer survival, from 31 B.C. to A.D. 476. In the end, some ten barbaric Germanic tribes (of which three no longer exist) subdued Rome. When listed, it may be prudent to be aware that Western Europe is the only area that has had ten tribes in its history and may have a connection to the ten-horns vision of Daniel 7: 7–8. The groupings consist of: Alemannia (Germany), Anglo-Saxon (England), Burgundians (Switzerland), Franks (France), Heruli (eliminated), Lombards (Italy), Ostrogoths (eliminated), Suevi (Portugal), Vandals (eliminated), and Visigoths (Spain). The victory was easy because, as almost all historians agree, Rome was essentially already dead. She had self-administered the humanistic poisons of immorality, materialism, violence, and injustice and corrupted the body from within. For much of its existence, the government and citizenry of the empire were hostile to Jews and Christians. *See also* Aelia Capitolina; Africanus, Scipio; Africanus, Sextus Julius; anti-Semitic; Antonio Fortress; Apollonius of Tyana; Asia Minor; Augustus; "barracks emperors"; basilica(s); *bema;* Cabrius; Caesar cult; Caius; calendar (Julian); Caligula; Cappadocia; Carthage; Cathars; Celsus; centurion(s); Christianity in the Roman Empire; Cicero; Claudius; Claudius Lysias; Cleopatra of Egypt; consistory; Constantine I; Constantinople as city; Colosseum, the Roman; consistory; Constantinople as city; Cornelius; Crassus, Peter; Crusades; curses of Daniel; daemons; Daniel's interpretation of

Nebuchadnezzar's tree dream; Daniel's vision of the destroying monster; decapitation; Diocletian; Domitian; eagle(s); Edessa; Edict of Milan; Edict of Toleration; emperor worship; Ephesus; ethnarch; feet and toes of iron and clay; Felix; Felix of Rome; Festus, Porcius; Florus; Galerius; Gallio; Glaphyra; Goths; Gratian; Hadrian; Heruli; Herod Agrippa I; Herod Agrippa II; Herod Antipas; Herod Antipater I; Herod Antipater II; Herod Archelaus; Herodian dynasty; Herod Philip I; Herod Philip II; Herod the Great; Heruli; Holy Roman Empire; household deities; Imperial Regiment, the; Italian Regiment, the; Jewish War; Judea capta; Julian the Apostate; Julius; Justinian I; Kittim (Chittim); Labarum; Lares; Law of the Twelve Tablets; legion; legs of iron; Lombards; Longinus; Lucius; Lupercalia; Lysanias; Macedonia; Magnesia; Manes; Marcus; *Mare Nostrum;* Mark Minucius Felix; Mithraism; Nero; *Nero Redivivus;* New World Order, the (NWO); Numa Pompilius; numen; Olympian pantheon; Oniropompi; Ostrogoths; Palestine; Parthians; Patronius; *pax Romana, via Romana, lex Romana;* para; paredri; penates; Pergamum; Petrus Romanus; Pilate, Pontius; planets as gods, the; Pliny the Younger; Plutarch; Polyhistor, Alexander Cornelius; Pompey; Popilius Leanas; Pontifex Maximus; Porcius; Praetorian Guard; Praetorium; prefect(s); procurator(s); Publius; *pax Romana, via Romana, lex Romana;* Pompey; Publius; Quirinius; Revived Roman Empire; Roma; Roman Augustus the Little; Romans as nationality; Rome; rosary; Satan's throne; Saturnalia; Sebastenians; Sebasterion; Seneca, Lucius Annaeus; Septimus Severus; Sergius and Bacchus; Sergius Paulus; Sibyl(s); stratified man, dream of the; Syria-Palestine; Tacitus; ten horns; ten kings (kingdoms) of Revelation; ten-nation confederacy; Tertullus; tetrarch; Theodosius I; Tiberius Caesar; titulus; Titus; Trajan; tribune; twelve eagles prediction; Valerian; Vandals; Vespasian; Virgil; Zeus.

Roman Phalanx: a Satanic cult said to be entrenched in the Vatican according to some conspiracy theorists. *See also Atlia Vendita;* conspiracy theories; cult(s); Roman Catholic Church; secret societies.

"Roman Road, the": or sometimes termed "the Roman Road to Salvation" or "the Romans Road to Heaven." The publication or methodology is a selection of Bible references from the book of Romans that present the plan of salvation in tract form. The printing (which can be memorized) is popular among active evangelists to promote their witnessing efforts because it is accessible, user-friendly, and interactive. The markers of the Roman Road are listed in order as: Romans 3:23, 3:10, 5:12, 6:23, 5:8, 10:9-10, 10:13, and 10:17. The verses illumine the six vital steps to redemption for individuals: 1) everyone needs salvation, 2) Jesus died for our salvation, 3) salvation is a gift, 4) we are saved by grace, and 6) God saves all who call upon Him. Despite its appeal, the drawback of the method is that it is based on scriptural content that not everyone accepts. *See also* Christianese; evangelist(s), evangelism; plan of salvation; tract(s); witness(es).

Romans as nationality: citizens of the Roman Empire either born or naturalized. Thinking during the Middle Ages asserted that the Romans were descended from the surviving Trojans following their war with the Greeks. Most Romans were pagan idol worshipers, but many in all social classes became Christians in the first and second centuries. Many Romans believed that the end of the empire, and thus the end of the world, would be 634 B.C.—that is, 120 years after Rome's founding. The legend sprang from the myth of twelve eagles that provided the knowledge to Romulus. Others hypothesized that one eagle equals ten years. *See also* eagle(s); Roman Empire; Rome; twelve eagles prediction.

Romans as New Testament epistle: Paul's letter to the Christians in Rome. There is substantial eschatological data contained in Romans, including explanations of "the times of the Gentiles" and the most extensive discussion of Jewish failures and eventual triumphs. *See also* Paul as apostle.

Romanticism: in a theological stance, a new era of Christianity emerging in the 19th century to emphasize emotion over the intellect in search of a more personal religious experience. The movement was headed by the German theologian Friedrich Schleiermacher who thought he was saving the church from the loss of popular support. Rationalization and dependence on reason and the senses had become "dry" and, to some extent, uninspiring to many. A radical change in how religion and science, or faith and reason, could coexist was needed. The response was a cultural and religious movement paying more attention to feelings and emotions in a time when objects and ideas were being viewed for their scientific credibility only. *See also* Schleiermacher, Friedrich.

Rome: the center of the Roman Empire. Often, in Revelation particularly, Rome is the pattern or model for the evil empire prevalent on the earth during the Tribulation. In about 634 B.C., apocalyptic thinking gripped the Romans who feared that their city would be destroyed in the 120th year of its founding. The prophecy sprang from a myth that twelve eagles had revealed a mystical number to Romulus that would correspond to the end of the empire. Some early Roman thinkers came to believe that each eagle established or represented ten years. Later, in A.D. 247, Rome celebrated its one-thousandth anniversary and launched severe persecution against Christians, some of whom undoubtedly saw the time as the end of days. *See also* eagle(s); Golden Bough, the; Kittim (Chittim); Lupercalia; New World Order, the (NWO); revived Roman Empire; Roma; Roman Empire; Romans as nationality; twelve eagles prediction.

Romney, Mitt: the second, and only serious, Mormon contender to seek election as president of the United States (2012 election). Joseph Smith was a minor candidate in 1844 but never gained momentum in his campaign. Romney lost the election but did break the political barrier to non-Christian or non-affiliated candidates for higher office. *See also* Church of Jesus Christ of Latter-Day Saints, the.

Romulus Augustus the Little: last of the Roman emperors (A.D. 476) who is perhaps projected in the prophecy of Numbers 24:23–24, a passage that many claim surveys the inevitable failing history of Rome. *See also* Roman Empire.

rood: an archaic old English derivative for a cross, sometimes called the Triumphal Cross. More commonly, the representation is a life-sized crucifix erected in the church chancel and sometimes erected on the rood screen, the partition that separates the choir from the audience. *See also* cross; crucifix; "Dream of the Rood, The."

room(s). See mansion(s).

rooster: male poultry, a cock. Peter's denial of his Lord, as predicted by Christ, was announced by the crowing of the rooster. Jesus' prophecy stated that Peter would deny him three times before the rooster sounded the following day (Mk. 14:72; Mt. 26:31–35; Lk.

22:54–62; Jn. 18:15–27). The ancients could reasonably reckon time by the cockcrow, as some moderns may. Some religions consider the fowl to be sacred and numerous animalistic religions sacrifice the breed on many occasions. *See also* animals, birds, and insects, symbology of; hen; Peter as apostle; Peter's denials.

root: the underground resource of nourishment for plants and trees. Rarely, the name (may appear as "stock") represents Israel as a nation (Isa. 60:21) or a lead to identifying the Messiah. *See also* flora, fruit, and grain, symbology of; names (titles) for Jesus; Root and Offspring of David; Root of Jesse; root out of dry ground.

Root and Offspring of David: a title for Jesus as one in the lineage of Judah and David (Rev. 22:16). *See also* Branch from (of) Jesse, the; Branch of the Lord; names (titles) for Jesus; root; Root of Jesse; root out of dry ground; Tree of Jesse.

Root of David. See Root and Offspring of David.

Root of Jesse: a title for the identified with the father of David, Jesse, thus bearing the same connotation as "Root and Offspring of David"— the Messiah (Isa. 11:10). *See also* Branch from (of) Jesse, the; Branch of the Lord; names (titles) for Jesus; root; Root and Offspring of David; root out of dry ground; Tree of Jesse.

root out of dry ground: Isaiah's description of the Messiah in reference to his humiliation, humble background, and lowly birth (Isa. 53:2). The words are a prefigurement of Jesus at the time of his First Advent, being described as "a tender plant, and as a root (shoot) out of dry ground." *See also* names (titles) for Jesus; root; Root and Offspring of David; Root of Jesse.

rosary: a string of beads, usually associated with Roman Catholic devotion, that is manipulated by hand while speaking the prescribed formula: ten "Hail Marys" to one "Our Father." The article is also called "prayer beads." Catholics claim that the process is a meditative aid, but Protestants consider it meaningless ritual and babble. Other cultures use beads, including Hindus, Buddhists, Bahai, Orthodox, Anglicans, and some New Age practitioners, but most are considered stress relievers more than talismans. *See also Ave Maria;* centering prayer; chaplet; gestures; liturgical year; liturgy, Christian; mysteries of Catholicism, the fifteen; mala beads; Mariolatry; Roman Catholic Church.

rose: a woody perennial flower of the genus Rosa with more than 100 species in cultivation. When associated with religion, the rose is an age-old symbol of the Sun and representative of divine illumination. It may also be identified with female sexuality or virginity (and thus allied with the Virgin Mary). *See also* columbine; crocus; flora, fruit, and grain, symbology of; flower(s); flowers of red and white; Gaudete Sunday; golden rose; hyssop; Laetare; lilies; lotus; Mary; papyrus; virgin.

Rosenkreuz, Christian: a.k.a. Christian Rosy Cross, a pseudonym for the founder of the Order of the Rosy Cross (Rosicrucians) possibly in the early 1300s. Rosenkreuz was said to be an accomplished alchemist and occultist with connections to Eastern religions and Zoroastrianism. The prominent work attached to the name, legitimate or not, is titled *Fama Fraternitatis, des Loblichen Ordens des Rosenkreutzes* or The Rosicrucian Manifestos. He is reputed to have lived 106 years, then his uncorrupted body was discovered some 120 years after his death. Whether he was an actual person or not is in dispute but his legend is certainly well established. Claims are made that he was John the apostle or Lazarus of the Gospels from a previous life and that his tomb lies secure in the center of the earth. *See also* alchemy; Brethren of the Light, The; Brotherhood of the Union; Bruno, Giordano; Lewis, Henry Spencer; Lippard, George; *Order* of the Rosy Cross; Randolph, Paschal Beverly; Rosicrucianism; Rosicrucian Manifestos; *Sancti Spiritus.*

Rosenthal, Marvin: a contemporary exponent of the prewrath exposition of the Tribulation scenario. Rosenthal is a Christian Jew (*i.e.,* a "Messianic Jew") and a Baptist who avidly favored the pre-Tribulation view until he switched allegiance to the prewrath theories in 1990. He thereby lost much of his following but remains an effective writer and lecturer today. *See also* Jew(s); prewrath rapture.

Rosenzweig, Franz: Jewish theologian (1886–1929). He taught his brand of Judaism through an emphasis on creationism, revelation, redemption, and relational covenants between man and his God. *See also* Jew(s).

Rose Sunday. See Gaudete Sunday; Laetare Sunday.

Rosetta Stone: an inscribed basalt slab from the Nile River near the settlement of Rosetta. It was uncovered by French workers in 1799 and found to have lines written in hieroglyphic, demotic, and Greek letters. It was eventually translated by Jean Francois Champollion in 1822 to become one of the most important language aids in history.

Rosh Hashanah: the Jewish New Year. The special day marking the beginning of the Jewish new year is closely associated with the sounding of the *shofar* or ram's horn. The roar of the trumpet consists of three particular sounds emitted in sequence: 1) the *Tekiah*– one long blast, 2) the *Shevarim*– three short blasts, and 3) the *Teruah*– nine short blasts. The priests were required to closely observe the moon phases so the exact time could be determined and announced. *See also* Atonement, Day of; book of life; Days of Awe; feasts and special days of Judaism; High Holy Days; Judaism; *shofar;* ten days of awe; Trumpets, Feast of.

Rosh Hodesh: the exact date and time of the New Moon, a major time marker in Judaism. It is the responsibility of the Sanhedrin to calculate the precise appearance of the New Moon. *See also* Judaism; New Moon(s).

Rosh, Prince of: the Hebrew title for a chief prince or leader. The term is disputed when reading Ezekiel 38:2–3 where the name appears. If the King James Version of the Bible is used, the expression there is "chief prince of Meshech and Tubal"; if the Revised Standard Version is employed, the translation is "prince of Rosh, Meshech, and Tubal." So then, Rosh is either a leader of a people or a specific region constituting much of the Gog and Magog scenario. *See also* Beth Togarmah; Cush, Cushites; Gog and (of) Magog; Gomer; Meshach; Persia, Persians; Put; Russia; Tubal.

Rosicrucianism: an active secret society supposedly founded in the late medieval period by Christian Rosenkreuz. The symbol of the sect was a rose cross with its many embellishments, a logo, and philosophy subsequently taken up by any number of Rosy Cross organizations. The Rosicrucians, according to many scholars, appeared to have influenced mysticism through Lutheranism, Freemasonry, and even the writer Dante Alighieri.

See also alchemy; Andreae, Johann Valentinus; Bacon, Sir Francis; Brethren of the Light, The; Brotherhood of the Union; Dee, John; Freemasonry; John XXIII, Pope; Lewis, Harvey Spencer; Lippard, George; Order of the Rosy Cross; Randolph, Paschal Beverly; Rosenkreuz, Christian; Rosicrucian Manifestos; *Sancti Spiritus;* sect(s).

Rosicrucian Manifestos: a trilogy of Rosicrucian philosophy named the *Fama Fraternitatis* (1614), the *Confessio Fraternitatis* (1615), and the *Chymische Hockezeit* or *The Chymical Wedding of Christian Rosenkreuz* (1616 or 1617). The works are said to contain the story of Christian Rosenkreuz himself written as a religious manifesto and allegorical fable. The latter is said to have been penned by Johan Valentinus Andreae (1586–1654), the *Fama* by the Italian Trajano Boccalini, and the *Confessio* by John Dee. Each publication after the first promoted Rosicrucianism to a high degree. Here are descriptions of the society's strange and diverse ceremonies including a reference to the resurrection from the dead. *See also* alchemy; Andreae, John Valentinus; Brethren of the Light, The; Brotherhood of the Union; Dee, John; Lewis, Henry Spencer; Lippard, George; Order of the Rosy Cross; Randolph, Paschal Beverly; Rosenkreuz, Christian; Rosicrucianism; *Sancti Spiritus.*

Round Table: the fabulous round table of Arthurian legend allowing the congregation of King Arthur's knights. The shape was intentional so that jealousies of rank could be avoided. Even so, it was reputed to be foldable or otherwise transportable and held one empty seat reserved for the knight who would retrieve the Holy Grail. Some versions say the table was created by a master carpenter of the day but others claim Merlin the magician as a craftsman. The artifact came to represent the chivalric order. *See also* Arthur, King; Celtic folklore and religion; Holy Grail; Merlin.

Rowling, J. K.: (pronounced *Rolling*), British author of the controversial but phenomenal fantasy series detailing the adventures of three young wizards, chief of whom is Harry Potter. Rowling's first publication was *Harry Potter and the Philosopher's stone* (appearing in America as *the Sorcerer's Stone*) in 1996. There followed six more in the serial: *Harry Potter and the Chamber of Secrets, Harry Potter and the Prisoner of Azkaban, Harry Potter and the Goblet of*

Fire, Harry Potter and the Order of the Phoenix, Harry Potter and the Half-Blood Prince, and the last, *Harry Potter and the Deathly Hallows.* The latter sold eleven million copies in twenty-four hours in three markets. Rowling replaced E. B. White (*Charlotte's Web,* 1982) as the best-selling children's writer, then ousted John Grisham (1982) as the most popular author ever. Rowling's life was in a state of disrepair when the character of Harry Potter popped fully grown in her mind. Controversy swirled about her and her writing since it involved a sort of glorification of witchcraft and sorcery, yet at the same moment, it revealed some undisguised attachment to ancient mythos and the life of Jesus. Rowling has written other works of a differing genre but has become almost unique in her role because she allowed her characters to "grow up" with their telling. Rowling herself claims she is a Christian but has been ambivalent about her faith in certain instances. *See also* Harry Potter; "resurrection gods."

Royall, Anne: *nee* Anne Newport (1769–1854), indefatigable newspaperwoman and travel writer. After her husband's (Virginia farmer William Royall) inheritance was denied to her, she began writing travel sketches amid desperate financial circumstances. Eventually, she had produced ten volumes of firsthand descriptions of almost every sizable American city, along with some 2,000 personality profiles. Royall also edited two small Washington newspapers, the *Paul Pry* and *The Huntress,* in which she lambasted corruption in the government. She was an ardent supporter of Freemasonry and campaigned strongly against evangelical Christianity. The latter activities earned her the derisive nicknames "Goddess Anne Royall" and a "common scold." *See also* Freemasonry.

Royal Art, the. See alchemy.

Royal Law, the: an abbreviated version of the Ten Commandments and other moral regulations of God intended to present the most important (Jas. 2:8)—"the perfect law of liberty" (Jas. 1:25). The royal law honors the two general emphases of the Ten Commandments—the divine and the personal. As quoted by Jesus, the summation reads: "Love the Lord your God with all your heart and with all your soul and with all your mind and with all your strength" and "Love your neighbor as yourself"

(Mk. 12:30–31). Both injunctions are heavily recorded in the Old Testament and the teachings of Jesus. Sometimes modern understanding of the royal law expresses it as the so-called Golden Rule: "Treat others as you would like to be treated." *See also* Golden Rule, the; greatest commandment, the; love; neighbor.

royal priesthood. See chosen people.

royal psalm: a poem extolling a king, either a mortal one or God Himself. The book of Psalms in the Old Testament presents some poems of that structure. *See also* creation psalm; enthronement psalm; historical psalm; imprecatory psalm; messianic psalm; penitential psalm; psalm; psalm of judgment; psalm of lament; Psalms as Old Testament book; supplication psalm; thanksgiving psalm; wisdom psalm; worship psalm.

Royce, Josiah: a metaphysical philosopher (1855–1916) who argued that human minds are part of an "Absolute," and each person is obligated to contribute to the human good. Such thinking countered the stern pragmatism of men like William James. Royce's main literary treatises were *The Religious Aspect of Philosophy* (1855) and *The World and the Individual* (1901). He never embraced organized religion despite a strong Protestant upbringing and admired other communities of faith, especially Buddhism. *See also* James, William; metaphysics; philosophy of religion.

ruach: the Hebrew word for "breath." The term is often associated with the actions of the Holy Spirit. It is the term used when Genesis speaks of the "breath of God" entering Adam, making him a living soul. The word also describes the Holy Spirit's action of "hovering," "brooding," or "breathing" over creation (Gen. 1:2). *See also* breath; Holy Spirit; insufflation; names (titles) for the Holy Spirit; *nephesh; pneuma;* spirit; wind(s); *Zohar.*

rubric: instructions on how to conduct a service of worship, especially in the Latin rite. The guide is usually printed in red for the Latin *ruber,* meaning "red." *See also* Breviary; liturgical year; liturgy, Christian; *Ordo;* Sarum Rite.

Ruby Ridge: site in northern Idaho of the August 1992 shootout between federal agents and an Idaho white supremacist named Randy Weaver and those barricaded with him. The incident sparked renewed activity by several militia/patriot movements, particularly in the western United States. Weaver was to be served with a warrant for federal firearms violations, but a gun battle ensued. During the eleven days of government siege, Weaver's wife, teenage son, a federal marshal, and the teen's pet dog were killed. Weaver surrendered and was convicted of failure to appear but declared not guilty for the firearms charge or the death of the federal agent. Weaver's belief system was heavily apocalyptic.

Rudra: a destructive manifestation of the Hindu deity Shiva, who periodically dissolves the world only to see it created anew. *See also* deva(s), devi(s); Hinduism; Kali; mythological beasties, elementals, monsters, and spirit animals; reincarnation; Shiva; *yugas*.

Rufus: 1. one "chosen of the Lord" to whom Paul forwarded greetings in Rome, along with his mother. Paul said that Rufus's mother was like a mother to him also (Rom. 16:13). 2. a son of Simon of Cyrene. Simon was compelled to carry the cross of Christ (Mk. 15:21) part of the way to Golgotha. The two men may be the same. *See also* Alexander the son of Simon.

Rule for the Final War. See War Scroll.

rule of iron. See rod of iron.

rule of faith: the *regula fidei*, originally a summary of Christian doctrine suitable for teaching to catechumens and to children before baptism or first communion. The practice developed into a theological controversy as to who or what, exactly, is the source and standard of belief? Roman Catholic theologians insist faith and church tradition are equally authoritative. Greek Orthodoxy is the same except it does not accept papal infallibility and recognizes only the early church councils in their pronouncements. The Reformers favored justification alone as a faith presupposition. Calvinism, however, claimed nothing as a basic truth that was not allowed in Scripture. For Lutherans, all is acceptable that does not contradict Scripture. Quaker-type acceptance lies with the soul-felt promptings of the Holy Spirit as authentic. Protestantism in general calls for Spirit-interpreted Scripture as basic for faith structure. *See also* confession(s) of faith; Credo; creed(s); deposit of faith; faith; faith and order; *fideo qua* and *fide quae creditur;* magisterium; *sola Christo, sola fide, sola gratia, sola Scriptura.*

Rule of the Community. See Manual of Discipline.

Ruler: Paul's name for God (1Tim. 6:13–16), which he modified as "God, the blessed and only Ruler, the King of kings and Lord of lords." *See also* King; kingdom; King of kings; King of the nations; names (titles) for God; Lord of lords.

ruler of God's creation: Christ's description of himself to the church at Laodicea (Rev. 3:14). *See also* kingdom; names (titles) for Jesus.

ruler of the kingdom of the air: a reference to Satan expressed by Paul (Eph. 2:2). His commentary noted that the believers of Ephesus (and by implication all the faithful) were formerly followers of Satan and the ways of this world while they were still in their sins. Such a deplorable condition made us objects of God's wrath. Christ, however, has now removed that threat because of his great sacrificial love for us. *See also* accuser of our brothers; angel of light; Anointed Cherub; Baal-zebub; Beelzeboul; Beelzebub; Belial; Cupay; Day Star; dragon; Evil One, the; father of lies; Ghede; goat; god of this age, the; god of this world, the; guardian Cherub; Hahgwehdaetgah; Iblis; *Kategor;* kingdom of the air; kingdom of this world; king of Babylon; king of Tyre; Light-Bringer; lion; Lucifer; Mastema; Morning Star, the; prince of Greece; prince of Persia; prince of demons; prince of the power of the air; prince of this world; red dragon; ruler of the kingdom of the air; Sammael; Sanat Kumar; Satan; seed of the serpent; serpent; Shaytan; son of the morning, son of the dawn.

ruler of the kings of the earth: a reference to Jesus as sovereign ruler of the world (Rev. 1:5). *See also* faithful witness, the; firstborn from the dead; kingdom; names (titles) for Jesus.

ruler (prince) who will (is to) come, the: the title reserved for a wicked prince or disruptive ruler of the Jewish people (Dan. 9:26) who is to arrive in the latter days to harass God's chosen. This person is most often named the Antichrist. Because this title immediately follows a similar one in the Daniel verse immediately before (verse 25), the two are often confused. *See also* coming prince (ruler) the; god of this age, the; eschatology, eschatological; kingdom.

ruler, the. See coming prince (ruler) the.

rulers (powers) of darkness. See authorities.

rulers, the (spiritual). See authorities.

rumspringa: the surprising (some would say astonishing) procedure of many Amish communities which permit the youth in the faith to test their principles and morals by participating in an alternate lifestyle experiment in the modern world. Teens at sixteen are allowed, even encouraged, to partake of formerly forbidden actions. For some, the experience may be the extravagance of wearing strange clothing, attending a theater, visiting a bar, or even indiscriminate sex, wild parties, or other indulgent behavior. Most young people return to the traditional faith following the trial. *See also* Amish; shunning.

rune(s): characters of an alphabet used by the ancient peoples of Scandinavia. In certain primitive beliefs, especially among the Norse, runes could have miraculous or prophetic and apocalyptic powers. The very name "rune" means *secret*, but the Norse used *reginnkunnar*—"born of the gods"—to emphasize their power. Rune artifacts were in existence before the 11th century and believed by the Norsemen to be the sacred invention of Odin, chief of the gods. Most commonly they were in use in Denmark, Sweden, and Norway, but some have been discovered in Germany, Spain, France, and England. Some claim they have found examples even in North America. The rune characters are the basis of the Teutonic alphabet and are decipherable today. *See also* alphabet; Ariosophy; Armanenschafft; Asa; Asatru; Asgard; disa; *Edda,* the; element(s); Norse and Old Germanic pantheon; Odin; Ragnarok; skald(s); Vikings; Valupsa; Wotanism; Yggdrasil.

Russell, Bertrand: fully named as Bertrand Arthur William Russell, renowned mathematician and philosopher (May 18, 1872–February 2, 1970). He was a severe critic of Christianity, especially of some of Jesus' pronouncements in the Olivet Discourse. His book explaining his negative stance is entitled aptly enough, *Why I Am Not a Christian. See also* apatheist; areligious; antitheism; atheism, atheists; meta-atheist; philosophy of religion; scoffers.

Russell, Charles Taze: the first organizer of the Jehovah's Witnesses movement. He began his work in 1872 in Pittsburgh, Pennsylvania, and continued until he died in 1942. The sect achieved unprecedented growth and control during his period of leadership. He was succeeded by Judge J. F. Rutherford, another effective leader. *See also* Jehovah's Witnesses; Rutherford, Joseph Franklin; sect(s); Watch Tower Bible and Tract Society (WTBTS).

Russia: the nation formerly known as the Union of Soviet Socialist Republics (USSR) but known by "Russia" both before and after Soviet domination. Some believe (especially radical apocalypticists) that Russia will be the chief head of the Gog and Magog invaders at the end of the age. Their conclusions are mostly drawn from the rather tenuous idea that "Moscow" and "Tobolsk" are homonyms for "Meshech" and "Tubal." *See also* Gog and (of) Magog; Meshach; Rosh, Prince of; Russian Orthodoxy; Yaroslav Statute.

Russian Orthodoxy: the Muscovite version of Eastern (Greek) Orthodoxy that moved north from Constantinople. The church in Russian did indeed owe its birth to the East, but it quickly developed its own style and view of independence. Church oversight was set with the Tsar (a title meaning "emperor," which harkens back to "Caesar" in the West). The Russian experiment was called "the third Rome," after Rome and Constantinople. The first was considered collapsed to the Barbarians and the second to Islam. To quote a Russian monk named Filofei: "Two Romes have fallen and the third stands. A fourth will not be." Religion in Russia in the 15th century was radically shaped by apocalypticism. It was generally believed that the world would end after the seventh millennium since creation (to their reckoning). No one thought to produce any calendars after the year 1492. Even Russian architecture reflected the signs of the times; the iconic "onion" domes in her cities were meant to anticipate the New Jerusalem. *See also* archiereus; donkey walk; Eastern Orthodox Church; Feast of Fools; Filippovich, Daniel; Holy Fool(s), the; Holy Rus; Ivan IV the Terrible; *Merilo Pravedoyne;* monasticism; monasticism, degrees of Eastern Orthodox; Northern Crusades; Rasputin, Grigori Efimovitch; Sergianism; starets; Stephen of Perm; synaxarium; Vladimir the Great; Yaroslav Statute.

Ruth as Old Testament book: a romantic/historical book of the Old Testament. It contains no apocalyptic material unless one recognizes that the two principal characters, Ruth and Boaz, are in the direct line of descension for Jesus. *See also* Boaz; Hagiographa; kinsman-redeemer; Naomi; Ruth as Old Testament heroine.

Ruth as Old Testament heroine: a Moabitess, the daughter-in-law of Naomi and wife of Boaz. Her name means "friend." She gave birth to Obed, who fathered Jesse, the father of David. Thus, she and Boaz were in the direct line of descent of Judah and Jesus. Boaz was the son of Rahab, whom many consider a prostitute in Jericho at the time of the Israelite invasion of Canaan. Thus, two successive generations featured Gentiles in the line of King David and Jesus. God may skip tradition if His chosen (in this case the Jews) are particularly unfaithful. They certainly were unheeding during the time of both Rahab and the period of the judges. *See also* Boaz; kinsman-redeemer; Naomi; Orpah; Ruth as Old Testament book.

Ruthenians. See Uniat Church.

Rutherford, Joseph Franklin: the successor to the leadership of the Jehovah's Witnesses sect after Charles Taze Russell. He advanced the movement tremendously for a quarter of a century. Under his direction, the sect managed to survive several failed Second Coming predictions of the past and continued to prosper. *See also* Jehovah's Witnesses; *Millions Now Living Will Never Die;* Russell, Charles Taze; sect(s); Watch Tower Bible and Tract Society (WTBTS).

S

Sabaeanism: a people in the land of the Hurranites who worshiped the sun, moon, and planets and built temples specifically for that purpose. Furthermore, they viewed the northern sky, particularly the Pole Star, as the abode of the Primal Cause (perhaps God Himself) and celebrated that belief every year in a festival called the Mystery of the North. This attraction to the Pole Star was shared by many ancient kingdoms including the Ismaili, Brethren of Purity, the Mandaeans of Iraq and Iran, and the angel-worshiping Yezidi. *See also* Horites; Ismaili; Mandaeanism; Pole Star(s); planets as gods, the; Yezidi.

Sabaoth Adonai: the God of thunder who rules, raises the dead, and dissolves fate, according to the *Sibylline Oracles*. In Hebrew, the title usually appears as *Adonai Sabaoth*, "the Lord of hosts," some 211 times in the Bible. *See also* Adonai; El; Elohim; I AM WHO I AM; Jah; Jehovah; Jesus Christ; Name of the Lord, the; names (titles) for God; Name, your; Yahweh.

Sabbat: Wiccan celebration normally performed on eight separate occasions. The two solstices and the two equinoxes are minor Sabbats or esbats. Between each solstice and equinox are four major Sabbats—Samhain (October 31), Imbolc (February 2), Beltane (May 1), and Lammas (August 1). *See also* Beltane; Beltane's Eve; *Book of Shadows;* coven(s); "drawing down the moon"; elementals; esbat; Imbolc; Lammas; Litha; Lughnasadh; Mabon; Magickal Circle, The; Midsummer Day; Ostara; Samhain; thoughtform; Walpurgis Night; wheel of the year; Wicca; witch(es); witchcraft; Yule.

Sabbatarianism: the conviction that the law of Moses should be active in religion or society (or both) today as it was in ancient Israel. The belief is legalism at its base and denies salvation by grace, two standards of the Church today. Saturday Sabbath is certainly included in the dogma. *See also* legalism; Pharisaism; Reconstructionism; Sacred Name movement; Yahweh.

Sabbath: the day associated with several Jewish festivals but usually referring to the seventh day of the week. (Christians prefer the term "Sunday" and name it the *first* day of the week.) The Sabbath is the Jewish day of rest and worship as commanded by God that commences at sundown on Friday. The sacredness of the day is considered no less than God's blessing of time itself. The word means "to cease" or "to desist" from the Hebrew s*habbat.* In near defiance of the meaning, however, the Jews were enjoined to resist mere empty idleness. The benefit of the Sabbath was not only to physically relax but also to "learn the customs and sacred rites of Judaism, as well as to meditate upon the Law of Moses." As to worship on the day, services are held on Friday afternoon or night (*minchah),* the morning greeting of the Sabbath (*kabbalat Shabbat),* and the evening *(maariv).* Exodus 20:8 enjoins all to *remember* the Sabbath, and Deuteronomy 5:12 admonish us to *observe* it; both are important. The holy day is derived from God's ending of creation at which time He declared His work to be good and "rested" on the seventh "day" (Gen. 2:2). The name may have derived from the Babylonian creation of the seven-day week, the last of which was called *Sabattu.* Although God has no need to physically "rest," the day is sacred because humans do need refreshment not only for bodily recuperation but spiritual renewal as well. At points in their history, the Jews have held a near superstitious conviction about ceasing activity on the Sabbath, sometimes to the point of not defending themselves when attacked. Jesus had little patience with the inflexible Pharisaical admonitions about it (Mk. 2:27), insisting that the Sabbath was made for man and not man for the Sabbath. Such faulty theology was precisely the reason they lost the Temple to the Roman general Pompey in 63 B.C. and partly the reason they suffered so under the Seleucids, because they would not defend themselves on the Sabbath. The day has pointed eschatological ramifications also. Jesus warned that the endangered Jews' flight from Jerusalem in the last days would be more hindered if it occurred on a Sabbath (Mt. 24:20). *See also* feasts and special days of Judaism; Judaism; liturgy, Jewish; Lord of the Sabbath; Sabbatarianism; Sabbath day's journey; Sabbath rest; Sabbatical millennialism; Sabbatical year; seventh day; Shabbat angels; Sunday.

Sabbath day's journey: the extent to which a practicing Jew could walk on the Sabbath without violating the Pharisaic injunction against "working" on that day. The length of a Sabbath's walk was about 1,000 steps. *See also* Judaism; Sabbath.

Sabbath rest: a reference from Hebrews 4 that seems to describe the Christian's take on the Jewish Sabbath of rest, which the Israelites never fully attained after their Exodus wanderings. Although the former slaves managed to subdue and settle much of the Promised Land, they could not conquer it all; neither could they find ultimate fulfillment or satisfaction in their relationship to Yahweh or cooperation among themselves in the land. Furthermore, there seems to be an additional reference to God's "rest" on the Sabbath day after creation centering on completeness and excellence. It is safe to construe that the Church (as God's inter-advent body), along with the Jewish remnant, will attain heaven's perfection as the gospel is heeded and practiced through what will be known as the ultimate Sabbath rest—the Millennium. *See also* crushing rock that became a mountain; election; elect, the; eschatology, eschatological; kingdom that cannot be shaken, a; kingdom, the; messianic age, the; millennial geography; millennial Sabbath; millennial sacramentalism; millennial Temple; millennial worship; Millennium, millennial; New Covenant, the; New Eden; rebuilding the Temple; remnant; restoration of all things; restoration of Israel (the Jews); restoration Temple (and land); rod of iron; Sabbath; Shiloh; Sunday; Temple(s); third Temple; times of refreshing.

Sabbatical age. See Millennium.

Sabbatical millennialism: the belief that after six million "days" in the year 6000, the Millennium of peace will begin. The theory draws much of its support, which is minimal at best, by the use of Bishop Ussher's (early 17th century) discredited dating methods that counts one "day" as a thousand years. *See also* calendar (Julian); eschatology, eschatological; Hippolytus; Irenaeus; Lactantius; Sabbath; septa-millennial; "six-day theory, the"; Ussher, James.

Sabbatical year: the *Shemitah,* meaning "the remission," "the release," or "the letting year." By command of God (Lev. 25:2–4), the Israelites were to give respite to the land and its people every seven years. No agriculture was to be practiced, but the poor could benefit from the wild produce left in the fields. Debts were to be forgiven so such a "rest" could help the general populace as well. Most considered it a harsh rule since it impacted labor and management relations, banking, consumerism, and trade;

they rebelled against its demands almost every time it hit the calendar, much to the eventual denigration of the nation. The law that was intended as a blessing turned out to be a curse for, in the days of Jeremiah, the Babylonians swept Judah into captivity for seventy years, the total number of Sabbath years not honored. *See also* Babylonian Captivity; feasts and special days of Judaism; Jubilee Year; Judaism; Sabbath.

Sabbatic River: a watercourse that ran between Arcea and Raphnea in Palestine as described by Josephus and other ancient historians. Its flow was unique in that the fountains that fed it were active for six days, only to cease on the seventh. Thus, the waterway ran swiftly for six days but was dry on the seventh—and thereby received its name. Such a remarkable natural wonder could easily accrue prophetic or superstitious lore.

Sabeans. See Seba, Sabeans.

Sabellius: a third-century priest of Rome, the originator of Sabellianism which affirms that the Son and the Holy Spirit were truly God. He and his followers reconciled the problem as to whether God is one or three by maintaining that Father, Son, and Holy Spirit are but three modes of the one true God's being. *See also* Roman Catholic Church; Sabellianism.

Sabellianism: a type of early modalism that defines the Godhead as forms or examples of the one God. There are no separate persons in Jesus or the Holy Spirit; they are but manifestations of God. The doctrine is essentially the same as modalism but named for a minor church official of the early church who promoted it (Sabellius). *See also* Adoptionism; appropriation; Anomoeans; Arianism; Arius; complementarian view of the Trinity; Councils of Ephesus; diphysitism; Donatism; dualism; Dynamic Monarchianism; dynamism; dyophysitism; eternal subordination of the Son; "four fences of Chalcedon"; *homoiousios; homoousios;* hypostatic union; Immanuel; incarnation; *kenosis;* kenotic view of Christ; miaphysitism; modalism; Monarchianism; monoenergism; Monarchianism; monophysitism; Nestorianism; Nestorius; Nicene Creed; *ousia;* patripassianism; Pelagianism; Pelagius; *perichoresis;* pre-incarnate; psilanthropism; Sabellius; Socianism, Socinians; subordinationism; theanthroposophy; *Theophorus*; Trinity; two natures, doctrine of the; unipersonality.

Sabians: a non-Muslim sect noted in the Qur'an, along with Jews, Christians, and Zoroastrians, worthy of being recognized as religious. Who they really were as a people has not been determined. *See also* Islam; people of the book; Zoroaster, Zoroastrianism.

Sabra: the unofficial nickname of native-born Israelis implying toughness and resiliency, like the hardy plant growing in the region. *See also* Israel; Jew(s); "never again"; sabra.

sabra: a prickly, sturdy plant of the cacti family growing in semi-arid regions, including Israel. *See also* flora, fruit, and grain, symbology of; Sabra; thorn(s), thornbush(es).

Saccuth: or Sakkuth/Siccuth, a Mesopotamian god referred to as "an abominable thing," or the star god in Amos 5:26, related to Kaiwan. The idol is of Sumerian origin bearing the original meaning of "tabernacle." The Hebrews deliberately punned or mispronounced the name to render it "a detestable thing." *See also* Judaism; Raphan, star of; Remphan; Sumerian and Babylonian pantheon; Sumer, Sumerian(s).

sacellum: an alternate but less-used word for a church building but originally referring to a Roman shrine. *See also* adytum; bethel; cella; cathedral(s); chantry; chapel; church; fane; fold; katholikon; kirk; mission; religious organizations; shrine(s); temple(s).

sacerdotalism: a term meaning "priestism" in which the idea is prevalent that only ordained priests or other clergy may manage the sacraments and perform certain other pastoral duties. The process is most clearly seen in Roman Catholicism, especially since that Church introduced "mysterious" or "magical" elements into the sacraments, which only a priest may fathom or administer. Only he can call forth the grace from the rituals necessary for blessing. Even reading the Bible by laypersons is discouraged by some in leadership. *See also* Council of Trent (Roman Catholic); Nicolaitans; priest(s); Roman Catholic Church.

sackcloth and ashes: rough clothing sprinkled with ashes (or sitting amid ash and dirt) symbolizing sorrow, anguish, despair, or even repentance. The two super witnesses of Revelation 11 are presented as clothed in sackcloth because of their despondency over the evil of the Tribulation era and because their message is not a pleasant one for the disobedient. *See also* "ashes to ashes"; dust.

Sacra Cintola: called the "sacred belt," a relic now housed at the Church of Saint Stephen in Prato, Italy. The artifact is said to have been left to the apostle Thomas by Mary the mother of Jesus as she ascended to heaven from the Mount of Olives; it was intended to be proof of Thomas's witnessing of that event. In 1312, a man named Museiattion tried to steal the article but was prevented by a fog generated by the belt itself. *See also* belt; relic(s).

sacrament(s): a church practice, usually restricted to the "High Church" or liturgical persuasions, described as a visible sign instituted by Christ to bestow grace on the worshiper. The Roman Catholic Church identifies seven sacraments: 1. Baptism is the initiatory rite, including pedobaptism, which confers forgiveness for all sin springing from the Fall of Adam and Eve (*i.e.,* Original Sin). 2. Confirmation claims to impart the Holy Spirit and can be administered only by a bishop (in the Western world). It is intended to induct the child into the duties and responsibilities of church life following prolonged study and catechism. 3. Penance provides forgiveness of sins committed after baptism, usually practiced by auricular confession to a priest who requires "satisfaction" from the penitent and offers absolution. 4. The Mass, or celebration of the Lord's Supper (the Eucharist), is presented as the unbloody sacrifice of the body and blood of Jesus. Grace is bestowed through the bread and wine since both Christ's soul and divinity are inherent in the elements. The Mass is the central feature of the Roman Catholic worship ritual as it is in Eastern Orthodoxy. 5. Extreme Unction, also called the "last rites" or the *viaticum*, is the last anointing before death, thus granting a full or plenary indulgence, which does not become effective until the time of one's demise. 6. Matrimony is the union of man and woman in marriage. 7. The sacrament of holy orders is reserved for those entering upon official service in the Roman Catholic Church, particularly that of priest. It sets apart those individuals and qualifies them for the tasks they have chosen. The Roman Catholic Church has long held that the efficacy of the sacraments does not depend on the purity of the priest who performs the ritual, so long as he says the right words. Article XXVI of the Thirty-nine Articles of Anglicanism says essentially the same but other persuasions see problems with such a stance. Protestant sacraments include the Lord's Supper and baptism only. Most conservative denominations prefer the term "ordinance" or some other less precise title in place of "sacrament," for they do not subscribe to the idea that those acts confer soterological grace in any dimension except symbolic. It is presumed that no sacral practices now extant will be needed in the Millennium, except those delineated by Ezekiel as programmed for the New Jerusalem. *See also* Anaphora; anointing; *Arcanum,* the; baptism; baptism regeneration; concomitance; confession; Confirmation; consubstantiation; Council of Trent (Roman Catholic); element(s); elevation; epiccesis; Eucharist; *ex opere operantis* and *ex opere operanto;* Ezekiel's vision of the restored theocracy; fraction; grace; indulgence(s); invination; liturgical year; liturgy, Christian; Lord's Supper; Mass; matrimony; means of grace; mystery; ordinance(s); ordination; Original Sin; penance; real presence; reservation of the sacrament; Roman Catholic Church; sacerdotalism; sacrifice; salvation; Thirty-nine Articles, the; transubstantiation; unction; *viaticum;* wafer; wine.

sacramental union. See real presence.

sacred bowls: special utensils of the altar used to hold the needed concoctions of tabernacle and Temple worship. The prophet Zechariah said that any bowl, even one of domestic use, will be sacred to the Lord in the Millennium (Zech. 14:20). If consecrated bowls were used to preserve material for ritualistic use, they would certainly be classed as sacred in the new order. *See also* bells of the horses; cooking pot(s); furniture and furnishings of the tabernacle, temples, and modern synagogue; Holy to the Lord; pot(s).

sacred drink: a beverage, usually wine or its substitute, imbibed as part of a worship ritual. Pagan, Jewish, and Christian worship may involve some sort of consumed drink representing life or as a memorial. The act is not to quench thirst but to honor the spirit of what it represents. In some Catholic persuasions, wine is denied to the participant because the bread is said to contain all the grace that is needed for the individual. Some pagan rituals used alcoholic or hallucinogenic drugs to induce a trance or invocation. *See also haoma;* intoxication; libation; Lord's Supper; sacred meals; wine.

Sacred Harp: a singing tradition favored in the antebellum South but originating in New England. The name is taken from the style's basic song book called *The Sacred Harp* (first published 1844) consisting of a text with shaped notes representing the sounds of *do, re, mi, fa, sol,* etc. Singers positioned themselves in a square with the tenors, altos, basses, and trebles on each side. The conductor stood in the center to signal the tune with his hand; pitch was provided by a single singer designated for the job. Sacred Harp seemed to aid choirs, congregations, and choral groups with little or no musical training. *See also* liturgy, Christian; music; sacred music.

Sacred Heart, Feast of the: the High Church liturgical emphasis and dedication to the sacred heart of Jesus. Devotion to the loving heart of Christ dates early in the church as far back as the 11th century and celebrated today ten days after Pentecost. *See also* feasts and special days of high liturgy faiths; liturgical year; Roman Catholic Church.

sacred meals: food used in ritual or a worship environment as part of the prescribed procedure. Few religions offer no provision for consumption in some manner, either periodically or regularly. Communion with bread is almost universally offered as one element of observance; sometimes "love feast(s)" or public fellowship meals are also consumed but are not properly labeled "sacred." *See also* Eucharist; food sacrificed (offered) to idols; Lord's Supper; love feast(s); manna; sacred drink.

sacred music: also religious music, that mix of art and sound perceived as set apart or exclusive to the Church in liturgy or worship. In generalized thinking, sacred music immediately brings to mind classical renditions with orchestra and perhaps a choir. All other styles are, then, classified as secular. *See also* canticles; chant; liturgy; music; plainsong; Requiem; Sacred Harp; spirituals; theody.

Sacred Name movement: a relatively modern notion that God must be addressed in a divine title from the Old Testament—Yahweh or an equivalent. Yahwehism is an alternate name for the doctrine. Salvation depends on this observance. Most Sacred Name organizations also practice Sabbatarianism as a way of life and worship. *See also* Sabbatarianism; Yahweh.

125

sacred prostitution: sexual action centered in worship practice, almost exclusively seen in pagan practice and anti-social cults. Ancient cultures and primitive religions were heavily involved with religious prostitution, utilizing both male and female courtesans. *See also* demimondaines; dog(s); fertility rites; Great Rite, the; pagan, paganism; pagan practice; phallic worship; prostitute, prostitution; Shapash.

sacred stones: designations for places with stone arrangements used in idol worship (*i.e.,* Hosea 10:2) and sacrificial platforms or holy memorials for the ancient Hebrews. Israelite altars were invariably constructed of unhewn stones. Occasionally, a heap of stones was suitable for Jewish orthodoxy if it was a marker or commemorative (*cf.* Joshua 22). The stone called Ebenezer is one example. Other such monuments were set up including Joshua's stone at Gilgal (Josh. 4:20), Moses' covenantal memorial (Ex. 24:4-8), Jacob's stone of witness (Gen. 31:43-53), and the memorial of the Eastern tribes called "a witness between us that the Lord is God" (Josh. 22:9-34). Following the battle with the Amalekites, Moses erected a stone monument to commemorate the victory when he was required to hold aloft the rod of the Lord (assisted by Aaron and Hur) as Joshua battled the Amalekites (Ex. 17:15–16). In this instance, and at other times, the memorial was called a "banner." It is quite likely that the sacred stones referenced in Hosea 3:4–5 name the Urim and Thummin. *See also* altar; banner(s); Beth Aven; Bethel; black stones; Boaz and Jachin; breastplate of the high priest; Caelum Moor; Ebenezer; Emerald Tablet of Hermes, the; ephod; gem(s); Georgia Guidestones; Gilgal Refa'im; *Gobekli Tepe;* Judaculla Rock; lot(s); *masseboths;* megaliths; miter; Moai; onyx; oracle; pillar(s); Pillars of Mina, the Sacred; pillars of the Temple; rock(s); sapphire; Sphinx, sphinx(es); stele; stone(s); stone circles; Stonehenge; Urim and Thummin; white stones.

sacred wounds, five: a reference from the Middle Ages that prompted meditation on the five wounds of Jesus on the cross: hands, feet, and side. For some reason, the piercing of the head with a crown of thorns was not mentioned. *See also* crucifixion; *Eloi, Eloi, lama sabachthani?;* liturgical year; seven words from the cross, the.

sacrifice: the act of offering up appeasement or tribute to the gods (paganism) or to God (theism). Blood sacrifice was crucial to

Old Testament worship and to almost all the ancients as it was the means by which the people obtained temporary forgiveness and the favor of God. For Israel, the sacrifices were part of the law but the performance of them did not grant salvation; yet a person could respond to them so as to effect clemency at the time if not for eternity. The practice was consistent, highly ritualized, and prolific. At the dedication of Solomon's Temple, for example, the ceremony extended to seven days and a festival after for seven more. Some 22,000 head of cattle were slaughtered plus 120,000 sheep and goats. A large and expensive offering was called a hecatomb. In Israelite ritual, acceptable sacrificial animals were demanded, carefully chosen for their species and physical perfection. Some aviary fowl were allowed, particularly of the Columbiformes order. Most of the bovine, ovine, caprine, and hircine classes were suitable, excluding the porcine. The ritualistic act of killing an animal in and of itself was considered an inadequate practice if true belief and repentance were not present with the presenter. Prayer at that time was essential as well, a vital element of the formal practice. Such thinking gave reference to alternate terms for the offering with such identifiers as "the sacrifice of prayer," the "sacrifice of praise," the "sacrifice of thanksgiving," and the like. There are five major sacrifices specified by God that were an obligation from Yahweh for the Israelites, all found in Leviticus 1–5. The Burnt offering, the Grain offering, and the Peace offering were voluntary and bonded the giver in fellowship with his Lord. The Sin offering and Trespass (or Guilt) offering were for sin and the only Old Testament manner of achieving God's forgiveness. A *minchah* was a small grain offering that was partially burned on the bronze altar and the rest eaten by the priests. The *olah* was also a burnt offering immolated on the altar fire that was never extinguished; it was not consumed by any party. The smoke of the three freewill offerings was said to be a sweet savor to the Lord but the two sin offerings were a stench in God's nostrils. Not only animals were used, but bread and money were acceptable for certain occasions. Sacrifice for the Christian is not accomplished by the ritual of animal bloodletting but by the expiational act of Christ's death on the cross, which stands as the believer's substitutionary atonement. An excellent commentary on this type of sacrifice is recorded in Hebrews 10:1–18. Many assume the practice of blood sacrifice began with Moses. Actually, God performed the first Himself (Gen. 3:21) when He killed an animal in the garden of Eden to cover the nakedness of Adam and Eve. It was followed by Cain and Abel (Gen. 4:4) with disastrous results, then Noah (Gen. 8:20) and Abraham, Isaac, and Jacob. All the firstborn of Egypt were also taken due to Pharaoh's stubborn attitude (Ex. 11). All involved death of the innocent and the shedding of blood. Some prophetic indications suggest that the Jews (and perhaps some Gentiles also) will again practice some description of sacrificial rite in the Millennium, but the extent and exact purpose of this action is not entirely clear. It should be remembered that "sacrifice" in most religions may constitute ritual worship or material offerings (such as money) with no reference to bloodletting. *See also* animals, birds, and insects, symbology of; atonement; blood; blood of Christ; blood of the Lamb; consecrate; evenings and mornings, prophecy of the; fat, fatness; hecatomb; Holocaust, holocaust; liturgy, Jewish; libation; millennial sacramentalism; millennial worship; morning and evening sacrifices; oblation; offering; perfumes, ointments, and spices; recapitulation theory of atonement; sacrifice, the daily; salt; salvation; tabernacle, the; 2,300 evenings and mornings; woman with a jar of ointment.

sacrifice, the daily: a normal ritual of worship (called the perpetual sacrifice) for the Hebrews, particularly or even exclusively in the Temple and tabernacle. The practice was central to Israel's worship and national interests no matter where or when the oblations were enacted. Daniel (Dan. 6:10) habitually prayed facing Jerusalem three times per day at the accepted time of offerings, even though he was in exile and Jerusalem was 500 miles away to the west. Disruption or impropriety in the sacrificial routine was considered a serious breach of the heart and spirit of Judaism (Dan. 8:11; 9:27; 11:31). *See also* evenings and mornings, prophecy of the; feasts and special days of Judaism; Judaism; liturgy, Jewish; morning and evening sacrifices; sacrifice; 2,300 evenings and mornings.

sacrilege: a violation or misuse of sacred objects, places, persons, or some ritual taboo. *See also* blasphemy; curse(s); desecrate; profane; ritual abuse; ritual defilement; trespass; unclean.

sacring: the moment of consecration in High Church Eucharistic liturgy described as the instant the bread and wine of Mass become the flesh and blood of Jesus via divine intervention (transubstantiation). *See also* Anaphora; concomitance; consubstantiation; elevation; epiclesis; Eucharist; liturgical year; liturgy, Christian; Roman Catholic Church; sacrament(s); transubstantiation; wafer; wine.

sacrist: a monastic official in charge of the library, vestments, vessels, and building maintenance—those duties related to the sacristy. *See also* furniture and furnishings of the modern church; monasticism; sacristan.

sacristan: a church official in charge of the care and use of the sacristy, a church, and its contents. *See also* acolyte; furniture and furnishings of the modern church; sacrist; sceuophyax.

Sadducees: a religious party of the Jews in existence since before the Hasmonean dynasty in Judah. They were closely tied to the Temple and its function and held great financial and ritualistic significance in that arena. Often they are paired with the Pharisees but were far removed from Pharisaic beliefs and were fewer in population (they numbered about 3,000 at the time of Jesus). Sadducees were considerably less stringent in the interpretation of the Law of Moses and recognized only the written Law, the Pentateuch, as binding for Judaism. Eschatologically, Sadducees held no belief in angels, resurrection of the dead, or life after death. Both Pharisees and Sadducees were harshly condemned by John the Baptist and Jesus for their haughty spirits and misapplication of God's law and debasement of His Temple. Josephus said they were even vindictive and rude to others in their own sect. *See also* Aram, Arameans; Essenes; Hellenism, Hellenization; Herodians; Karaites; Pharisees; religious organizations; Samaritan(s); scribe(s); sect(s); Zadokites; Zealots.

Safavid: the dynasty of Persia (1502–1736) that imposed Shi'ite Islam in Iran rather than Sunni as the state religion. *See also* Islam; Shi'ite Islam; Sunni Islam.

Sa-go: a Korean prophet operating about the time of Nostradamus who predicted a Korean Messiah figure for his nation. His major writing was entitled *Gyeokamyurok*, a book of poetic prophecies and teaching related to his mission.

saint(s): originally, people of the early church who were assured of heaven because they would not deny the faith (most of them martyrs). Later, the term expanded in its use. 1. a select group of ultra-righteous individuals who successfully undergo the process of beatification by the Roman Catholic Church, Anglican, or Eastern Church and achieve superior status for their alleged miracles and good works. This procedure has no scriptural basis. All saints of this classification rate special feast days on the liturgical calendar. 2. the righteous of the Old Testament who accrued to salvation by the virtuous recognition of God and/or the retroactive effect of Christ's act of justification of the cross as anticipated by ritual sacrifice. The phrase "Abram believed God, and it was credited to him as righteousness" (Gen. 15:6; Rom. 4:3, 22), along with the employment of the term in Daniel (*e.g.,* chapter 7), most likely fits this usage. 3. Christians who are numbered in the body of Christ and are certified believers. 4. those who will be redeemed in the Tribulation era—most likely not coterminous with the Christian Church at that time—a prime belief of dispensationalists. They are to constitute a vast population, most of whom will be martyred before the Second Coming. The Tribulation saints are to receive their own distinct judgment at the end of the seven years. This final human grouping, and the present Christian population, hold the most interest for eschatology. 5. the holy angels on more rare occasions. The context of the writing wherein the word "saint" is used is often the easiest, or perhaps the only method to determine its exact reference. *See also* beatification; cephalophore; child, children; Christianity; Church of England; Eastern Orthodox Church; classes of humanity in the Apocalypse; elect, the; Hallowmas; judgment of the Old Testament saints; judgment of the Tribulation saints; liturgical year; martyr(s); martyrdom; Menologion; patron saint; postulator; Rogation Days; Roman Catholic Church; saints of the Most High; saints, the host of the; supererogation; theosis; treasury of merits; veneration of the saints.

Saint Anthony's fire: a wasting disease that raged in epidemic in 1089 and 1094 in central Germany. The malady is a fungal infection causing burning in the limbs, gangrene, and ultimately death. The infestation caused 8,000 deaths in twelve weeks and was considered a punishment from God at the time.

Saint Bartholomew's Day massacre: the slaughter of thousands of Huguenots, one of the most vicious the shrewdness of the Roman Catholic and Bourbon establishment could contrive. Pope Pius urged their extermination beginning in 1559, headed by the vindictive Jesuits. Catherine de Medici, mother of the king, instigated the famous Saint Bartholomew's massacre in willing response to the papacy's desires and on the night of August 24, 1572, seventy thousand Huguenots were slaughtered. Thereafter, the Huguenots defended themselves but continued to be condemned. France lost perhaps a fourth of her best citizens because of the deaths and extraditions of the Huguenots. *See also* Camisards; Edict of Nantes; Huguenots; Isaac; La Peyrere, Roman Catholic Church.

Saint Catherine's Monastery: ancient Greek Orthodox monastery, also known as Santa Katarina, at the foot of Mount Sinai. The refuge was reputedly named for Catherine of Alexandria, a Christian martyr sentenced to die on the wheel. She survived the ordeal which only led to her beheading. Legend says her body was transported by angels to Mount Sinai. It was here that Konstantin von Tischendorf discovered the fourth century *Codex Sinaiticus* (plus fragments), some of the oldest known documents and most complete copies of the Scripture ever discovered. *See also* Bible manuscripts; Eastern Orthodox Church; martyrdom; monastery; Mount Sinai; Sinai.

Saint Germain, Comte de: (1712?–1784) a gentleman of ambiguity who carried the reputation as "the man who never dies" since he was said to be at least 500 years of age (or immortal) and was even reputed to have been an advisor to Jesus. Germain arose from obscure background to become an accomplished wit, courtier, musician, alchemist, and linguist of the 18th century. He was wealthy, handsome, and charming, which only contributed to his mystique and charlatan proclivity. Called "the wandering Jew" (also known as Master Rakoczi), he could appear and disappear anywhere and in any age. He was said to possess the exotic elixir of life and once prophesied the French Revolution. Germain was likely a Rosicrucian and carried about him an air of mystery irresistible to many. Saint Germain remains, even today, a center of New Age and occultic interest. Most intriguingly, Germain is said by some to be none other than the reincarnated Sir Francis

Bacon, who faked his death and traveled to the Orient to become an Ascended Master. *See also* Bacon, Sir Francis; New Age religion; occult, occultic.

saints of the Most High: in early theology, considered to be the people of God who are destined to be victorious over the beasts of the earth (the opposing kingdoms) and are to receive the kingdom of God and possess it forever (Dan. 7:18). Recently, this interpretation has been challenged to suggest that the saints of the Most High may actually be angelic beings. The context of the Daniel pericope seems to favor the latter definition, but there is room for disagreement. *See also* angel(s); saint(s); saints, the host of the.

Saint Vitus' dance: a wasting nervous disorder (officially related to Sydenham chorea, rheumatic fever, or epilipsy) in which the victim exhibits violent shaking of the body and limbs, paralysis, fever, lameness, and similar symptoms. To the ancients, the disease seemed to resemble dancing so it was named for Saint Vitus (a.k.a. Guy, c. 290–c. 303). Vitus was a legendary martyr venerated by the Roman Catholic and Easter Orthodox Churches. He was credited with many miracles but was tortured and killed sometime between the age of seven and thirteen because he would not renounce Christianity. Reportedly, he was boiled in a cauldron of tar and molten lead but was unharmed until he was finally put to death under the Diocletian persecution. His cult status grew until his life was celebrated all over Europe as the patron saint of neurological diseases (Saint Vitus dance), dancers, and entertainers in general. His reputation was also said to protect against lighting strikes, animal attacks, and oversleeping. *See also* Eastern Orthodox Church, Roman Catholic Church, martyrdom.

saints, the host of the: also, host of the armies (Dan. 8:12). The group being described in the Daniel paradigm represents those faithful who are overcome by the little horn that became great [Antiochus Epiphanes and Antichrist]. *See also* saint(s); saints of the Most High.

Sakla: a derisive name applied by the Gnostics to identify the Demiurge, the evil God of creation in the Old Testament. *See also* Demiurge; Gnosticism, Gnostic(s).

Saladin: (b. Salah al-Din Yusuf ibn Ayyub in A.D. 1169) perhaps the greatest Muslim (Saracen) warrior of all time who was active in the 12th century. His capture of Jerusalem in 1187 launched the third Crusade. Interestingly, he was born in the small village of Tikrit in Iraq, the same hometown of Saddam Hussein. *See also* Ayyubid dynasty; Crusades; Horns of Hattin; Islam; knighted orders; Outremer; Richard the Lionheart; Saracens.

Salafi: a Muslim term meaning "radical." The word is formed from an Arabic combination for *ancestor* and *submission* (Islam) and rests as the entire base for the Islamic religion and for Shari'a Law— the Islamic legal system supposedly based on the *Qur'an*. Much of its support comes from radical Islamic clergy that produces, legitimizes, and defends it and the concept is the prime mover for *jihadist* Islam. Ninety-nine percent of all suicide bombers are Salafist Muslims and the doctrine is the purest form of radical religion. *See also Alluha Akbar; al-Qaeda; al-Shabab;* anti-Semitic; Boko Haram; Daesh; Fatah; Hamas; Hezbollah; Islam; Islamic State in Iraq and Syria (ISIS or ISIL); *jihad;* Muslim Brotherhood; Nusra Front; Palestinian Islamic Jihad (PIJ); Palestinian Liberation Organization (PLO); radicalized; Taliban; terrorism; terrorist(s); Turkistan Islamic Party; Velayat Sinai; Wahhabism.

Salathiel: another name for Ezra the scribe, used most often in the pseudepigraphal writings. *See also* Ezra as scribe.

Salem. See Jerusalem as city.

Salem witch trials: an episode of mass hysteria involving witch allegation, trials, and punishments in the Puritan settlements in and around Salem, Massachusetts, from February 1992 to May 1693. A number of teen and preteen girls suddenly began to experience erratic behavior (either partly real or self-induced) and subsequently accused a number of their neighbors of practicing witchcraft to their harm. Among the most prominent instigators were Mary Walcott, Ann Putnam, and Mercy Lewis. Over 200 men and women were indicted, summarily tried, and condemned. Nineteen were hanged, one was pressed to death with heavy stones, and others died in primitive prisons before the paranoia ran its course. *See also* Burning Times; church abuse; persecution(s); Puritanism, Puritans; Stoughton, William; Wicca; witch(es); witch cake; witchcraft.

Salette, Our Lady of. See La Salette, vision of.

Salome: 1. daughter of Herodias, the scandalous wife of Herod the tetrarch but the stepdaughter of the king (born A.D. 14 and died sometime between A.D. 62 and 71). Salome danced before Herod on his birthday, and, as a reward for her skill and seductive beauty, she requested the head of John the Baptist on a platter. The act was at the instigation of her vindictive mother (Mk. 6:17–28) who felt slighted by John's condemnation of her behavior. Salome's name is not mentioned in the Gospels, but we know more of her from historical sources. 2. the wife of Zebedee and the mother of James and John (Mt. 27:56). On one occasion she was rebuked by Jesus for asking that her two sons be granted precedence in Christ's kingdom to come (Mt. 20:20–23) which she assumed to be earthly. She was present at the crucifixion and one of the women to visit the tomb on resurrection morning (Mk. 16:1). 3. the elder sister of Herod the Great (noted as Salome I in some histories who died in A.D. 10). She was a subversive and jealous schemer who seemed quite capable of manipulating the king. It was she who caused the death of Herod's beloved second wife, Mariamne, and Herod's two favored sons, Alexander and Aristobulus, by treachery and false rumor in the ears of the king. 4. a daughter of Herod the Great by his wife Elpis. *See also* dance; Herodias.

salt: a condiment or element of great importance in Israel and to all the ancient peoples. Salt was used for flavoring, preservation of food, and healing, as well as an ingredient for the cereal offerings and a number of the burnt offerings. It was also mixed with some recipes for incense and sacrifice. Roman soldiers received part of their pay in salt, the *salarium argentum* (salt money), thus giving rise to our word "salary." The Greeks used it as a medium of exchange for slaves, thus the phrase "not worth his salt." The odd expression "covenant of salt," so crucial in Bible lore, likely refers to the eating of food as part of the treaty-making protocol of ancient times. Some cultures rubbed newborn infants with it, perhaps conveying some medicinal or religious significance. The ground of conquered cities was sometimes strewn with salt to prevent its resurgence. The Dead Sea is heavily concentrated with it, up to 350 parts per thousand. Jesus' statement, "Every one shall be salted with fire" (Mk. 9:49) definitely carries an eschatological connotation. Along those lines, Lot's wife was changed into a pillar of salt for disobeying the angels' command not to look back upon burning Sodom (Gen. 19:26). Of interest, there are no fewer than thirty-two references to the mineral in the Bible. Jesus enjoined his followers to retain the properties of salt as illustrative of the nobility of the Christian life (Mt. 5:13; Mk. 9:50; Lk. 14:34–35). Paul did the same when discussing pure speech (Col. 4:6) as did James (Jas. 3:12). The source of the metaphors is likely the impure ingredient dug from the brine pits of the Dead Sea that could lose its effectiveness through exposure or mixture with gypsum. Salt is often paired with the word "light" to further exemplify the need for responsible living as a believer. In a more esoteric sense salt, as a crystalline substance, is believed by some to hold etheric magnetism. Consequently, soaking in a bath of consecrated salt water can be a remedy for a psychic attack. Or, if you are feeling unsafe, throw some salt over your left shoulder for luck. *See also* bread; charm(s); covenant of salt; eschatology, eschatological; hospitality; incense; light; liturgy, Jewish; perfumes, ointments, and spices; sacrifice; salt and light.

salt and light: the two singular objects chosen by Christ as metaphors for the strived-for perfection and purpose of the Christian life (Mt. 5:13; Jn. 12:35). Salt was undoubtedly selected for its many useful qualities—to preserve and spice food, as medicine and in ritual and sacrifice, and as a sign of judgment (Mk. 9:49). The compound is worthless when its flavor is lost. Light's properties are obvious: illumination for sight, vision, purity, or transparency, and to chase away its metaphorical enemy—darkness. *See also* illumination; light; Lux; salt.

saltire: an x-shaped cross. *See also* cross; crucifixion; Holy Rood.

Salt Sea. See Dead Sea.

Salvation: a millennial name for the walls of Jerusalem or the heavenly New Jerusalem in a poetic sense (Isa. 60:18). *See also* eschatology, eschatological; New Jerusalem; Praise.

salvation: a saving or rescue. Salvation is a premier theological term in Scripture, and especially eschatology and prophecy, for it encompasses the ideal of sanctity with God, the avoidance of Hades, and the forgiveness of sin. The Old Testament centers on bloody sacrifice as essential to forestall the wrath of God on His people, and the New Testament core of salvation is in Christ and his sacrifice at Calvary. Salvation in the Roman Catholic, Eastern Orthodox, and related liturgical Churches is a complicated and rather uncertain process. A state of grace is obtained through baptism and good works according to the good offices of the Church which is its only source as God's representative on earth. The steps to divine acceptance evolve and interact through actual grace (supernatural merit for the sinner), personal faith, good works, baptism, application in the sacraments, penance, indulgences of prayer and intercession, and keeping the Commandments. Salvation is initiated by baptism and sustained through good works. If lost, it is regained by penance which only a priest may grant and if God favors. Even heaven itself may be delayed for further penance in purgatory and acceptance depends on one's sins, their severity, and the tolerance of God. Salvation in general Protestantism, however, is much simpler and more readily assured. There, especially as described by Reformed theology, faith produces *regeneration*, an enabling act performed by God Himself through the sacrifice of Jesus Christ since we as sinful humans are unable to produce it ourselves. Regeneration is followed by *justification*, whereby God declares believers to be righteous in His sight, based only on the merit of Christ that is imputed to them by faith alone. *Adoption* is pronounced wherein believers are received into God's family, making them joint-heirs with Christ. Until death, believers continue to be purified (*sanctification*), the daily process of being more and more enabled to die to sin and live to righteousness. Lastly comes *glorification* when believers are welcomed at death to heaven and eternal fellowship with the divine in resurrected bodies. In both instances and to varying degrees, a doctrine of salvation emphasizes both the responsibility of mankind and the sovereignty of God. The peculiar wording of Hebrews 2:3 may be an exception to the standard definition of salvation if it carries a heavy lifting of eschatology. The verse speaks of "so great a salvation" as if it somehow differs from the special deliverance we presently enjoy from Christ. It may be, instead, a *future* redemption relating to the Christian's rewards of co-rulership and inheritance in the kingdom of the heavens. *See also* adoption; antinomianism; atonement; autosoterism; baptism; baptismal regeneration; conquest motif; covenant theology; covenant of grace; covenant of redemption; covenant of works; deliverance motif; Eastern Orthodox Church; endurance motif; exchange motif; *extra ecclesiam nulla solus;* fall from grace; glorification; grace; heaven; hell; instrumental clause; justification; legalism; means of grace; monergism; Noah's ark; "once saved, always saved"; open theism; *ordo salutis;* papal revenue; penance; perseverance of the saints; predestination; profession of faith; purgatory; Protestantism, Protestants; recapitulation theory of atonement; rector motif; redemption; regeneration; repent, repentance; Roman Catholic Church; sacrament(s); sacrifice; sanctification; satisfaction theory of atonement; "saved"; sin(s); solifidianism; soteriology; synergism; Ten Commandments, the; theology; victor motif; works, salvation by.

Salvation Army: a Protestant denomination formed in England but also active worldwide. The organization was the inspiration of William Booth, whose concern for the downtrodden was paramount to the group's formation. The administrative structure copies the military, complete to martial-style bands, uniforms, discipline, rank, and method of operation. The organization was created and guided by its first leader, General William Booth, on the cusp of the 19th and 20th centuries. The first affiliate in the United States was started by sixteen-year-old Eliza Shirley and her parents in Philadelphia. Still today, the red kettle for donations is a familiar sight at Christmas. *See also* Booth, Evangeline Cory; Booth, General William; church bodies in America (typed); denomination(s), denominationalism; promoted to glory; Smith, Rodney "Gypsy"; social issues.

salve for the eyes: an admonition from Christ to the church at Laodicea (Rev. 3:18). The members there were urged to conduct themselves properly and to put medicine in their eyes so they could more clearly see the will of Christ for themselves and their fellowship. *See also* balm of Gilead; flora, fruit, and grain, symbology of; Laodicea; perfumes, ointments, and spices.

salvific pluralism: the belief that salvation is found in any religion, regardless of doctrinal practice.

Samaria: 1. the ancient capital of the Northern Kingdom of Israel after Omri moved it from Tirzah. The name was derived from the previous owner, one Shemer, with a meaning of "watchtower." The choice was an excellent one because the city stood on a single plateau, guarded the vital north-south trade route, and had walls of 100 feet in height. It once withstood an Assyrian siege for more than fourteen months (2 Ki. 17:5). Often, the name "Samaria" was used as a designation for the entire nation—the "land of Samaria." After it fell to the Assyrians under Tiglath-pileser III, the name "Samaritan" became synonymous with failure and a term of derision by the pure-bred Jews who were their neighbors. In Roman times, the place was called Sebaste. 2. the central province of Palestine during the Roman occupation. Readers may find the area referenced as Samaria, Transjordan, the Golan Heights, or part of the West Bank, depending on the historical context of the writing. 3. one of the two idolatrous worship centers established by Jeroboam. *See also* division of Israel; forest of the south; Galilee; Gilead; Idumea, Idumean(s); Israel; Judah; Judea; Kinneret; Palestine; provinces of Palestine; Samaria and Sodom; Samaritan(s); Syria and Samaria; Tirza; Transjordan; West Bank.

Samaria and Sodom: Samaria and Sodom were called the "sisters of Judah," even though long ago judged for their sins (Ezk. 16:46). Judah's idolatry and immorality before the exile (which Ezekiel termed prostitution) were declared to be even more unsavory than those sins of Samaria and Sodom before her. *See also* Samaria; Sodom.

Samaritan(s): those mixed populations left in former Israel after Assyria conquered the land and dispersed much of the population. Now called Samaritans, the hybrid race was despised by the Jews, a feeling that was near its apex during the ministry of Jesus. Of particular annoyance, the Samaritans at times were prone to claim relation to the Jews when that act favored them, but denied their association to the Hebrew race when the circumstances were reversed. Samaritans recognized only the Pentateuch as the legitimate Word of God and insisted that Mount Gerizim, not Mount Zion in Jerusalem, was the true place of worship. They erected their own temple, which they even named *Jupiter Hellenius* for a time, to avoid persecution from Antiochus Epiphanes. Jesus encountered one of their number at the well of Sychar (Jn. 4:4–26). Another is noted as the model of compassion in Jesus' famous parable called "the good Samaritan" (Lk. 10:25–37). In opposition to local feelings, Jesus loved Samaritans and healed a leper of that race (Lk. 17:11–19). He chastised James and John when they wanted to call down fire on an inhospitable Samaritan village (Lk. 9:51–56). A number of these people, along with certain allies around them, were a hindrance to the rebuilding of the Temple following the end of the Babylonian Captivity. Josephus called this group Cutheans. The Samaritans were the objects of evangelism for the early church in obedience to the Great Commission. The race was practically obliterated by the Romans who also destroyed many of their sacred writings. A small minority of native Samaritans still exists today. Today, the news media has tagged the area as the West Bank; much of Judah is now Palestinian territory. *See also* anti-Semitic; Aram, Arameans; Dositheos the Samaritan; Essenes; Hellenism, Hellenization; Herodians; Marka; parable(s); parables of the New Testament; Pharisees; Sadducees; Samaria; Samaritan Pentateuch; scribe(s); *Taheb;* woman at the well; Zealots.

Samaritan Pentateuch: the scriptures of the Samaritans that consist solely of the first five books of Moses. There are minor deviations, mostly grammatical, in the Samaritan Pentateuch when compared with the Jewish, and most of the wording there follows the LXX. *See also* Bible; Pentateuch; Samaritan(s).

Samaritan woman. See woman at the well.

Samarra: a city in Iraq that Sunni Muslims believe will be the birthplace of the *Mahdi*, the Islamic messiah. *See also* Islam; Karbala.

samarra: a flame-decorated cassock or smock worn by those condemned by the Inquisition. *See also* Inquisition.

Sameas: a unique prophet reviewed by Josephus and other ancient historians. He was active as a member of the Jewish Sanhedrin in Jerusalem during the biblically silent years near the close of the Hasmonean era. Other writers, besides Josephus, called him Simeon the son of Shebach, but he is not mentioned in the Scripture. At one time, the Sanhedrin subpoenaed Herod the Great (early in his career in Judea) to appear before them to be accused of murder. Immediately, King/Priest Hyrcanus II and all the legislative body were awed and intimidated, unwilling to pronounce judgment though they could clearly see Herod's guilt. Only Sameas, among the seventy-two members, was bold enough to speak. He condemned not Herod but his peers for their cowardice and hesitancy. Prophetically, he was moved to announce they would suffer greatly under Herod's coming rule, along with Hyrcanus and all his countrymen. Indeed, when Herod assumed power over the Jews, he slaughtered every member of the Sanhedrin who had dared indict him, along with Hyrcanus, and launched a vicious reign over the people. Sameas was preserved, however, because Herod honored the man's boldness and left-handed political support. *See also* Jew(s); prophet(s).

Samhain: an ancient Gaelic festival marking the end of the harvest season and the start of winter—about halfway between the autumn equinox and winter solstice (lit. "summerend"). It was one of four main observances that included Beltane, Imbolc, and Lughnasadh. Spirits and fairies were said to sneak into our world and dead ancestors could leak through the gates of the afterlife in the Otherworld. All would have to be placated with food and treats lest bad luck plague the living throughout the winter. Mummers and costume-wearers (likely imitating the fairies) went door-to-door to beg for food. The events were saturated with fire, fruits, bonfires, divination, and death. Eventually, it was considered prudent to send children instead because they had less sin and not so likely to be ensnared by the evil spirits. If they were, they could more easily find heaven than sin-laden adults. The Catholic Church bound the festivals into All Hallows' Eve and its related holidays. Wiccans still consider it an important celebration. *See also* Beltane; Beltane's Eve; bugbears; Celtic folklore and religion; Druidism; Hallowmas; Halloween; Imbolc; Lammas; Litha; Lughnasadh; Mabon; New Age religion; Ostara; Otherworld; Sabbat; Tuatha de Danann; Walpurgis Night; wheel of the year; Wicca; Yule.

Samkhya: the philosophy that bases yoga and other mind-cleansing techniques. One of the oldest schools of Indian reasoning, Samkhya requires an absolute dualism between *prakriti* (matter) and *purusha* (pure consciousness). The mind is actually a refined form of matter. A person, then, is parts of the physical body, a worldly self, and a pure and eternal self. Rather than worship a god, the ideal is to release the self to enjoy the clean spiritual nature. *See also* yoga.

Sammael: Satan, as named in *The Ascension of Isaiah*. It was he, according to the pseudepigraphon, who caused the prophet Isaiah to be sawn in half by King Manasseh and precipitated the crucifixion of Christ. It is also possible to name Sammael as a high-ranking demon, according to some speculations, and is named as the Prince of Rome and husband to the harridan Lilith. *See also* accuser of our brothers; Abaddon; Abezi-Thibod; Adramelech; Anammelech; Anointed Cherub; Apollyon; Apophis; Asmodaeus; Azazel; Azrael; Baal-zebub; Baphomet; Beelzeboul; Beelzebub; Belial; Cupay; Day Star; Dibbuk; demon(s), demonic; demonology; devils; Dubbi'el; dragon; Evil One, the; Gadreel; Ghede; goat; god of this age, the; guardian Cherub; Hahgwehdaetgah; Iblis; *Kategor;* Legion; Light-Bringer; lion; Lilith; Lucifer; Mastema; Morning Star, the; Pazuzu; prince of demons; prince of the power of the air; prince of this world; red dragon; Sanat Kumar; Satan; seed of the serpent; serpent; Shaytan; Sceva; son of the morning, son of the dawn; Typhon.

Samothrace: a small island off the coast of Thrace in Greece with high mountains inland but no suitable harbor. The land lay in the much-traveled sea lane of the Hellespont (Dardanelles) and was, therefore, a well-known landmark for sea travelers. The place was home to a pre-Greek cult called the Cabiri who were reverenced as the protectors of sailors. They also performed a periodic drama at the location celebrating the marriage of the Great Mother. Paul visited there at least twice. *See also* cult(s); *Magna Mata;* mystery cult(s).

Samson: an Israelite judge (Jud. 13:1–16:31) from the tribe of Dan. He was a Nazirite and

endowed with great physical strength supposedly drawn from his long hair. Samson's feats of physical prowess are legendary: he killed a lion bare-handed, slew thirty men to confiscate their clothes, captured 300 foxes to which he tied torches and scorched the Philistine crops, slew 1,000 Philistines with the jawbone of an ass, and blatantly lifted the gates of a city and carried them uphill. His moral character, however, was less than exemplary. His dalliances with women, particularly the Philistine princess Delilah, were his downfall despite many heroic achievements for his people. Samson participated in many adventures and victories against the emerging Philistine threat only to be ensnared by the wiles of Delilah, shorn of his locks, captured, blinded, and set to slave work in a grinding mill. In the end, however, he managed to pull down the temple of Dagon where he was being exhibited for sport and ridicule by his captors. His sacrifice caused the loss of over 3,000 Philistine lives and his own. Samson's leadership extended to twenty years. Despite his failures, Samson is listed as one of the heroes of the faith in Hebrews 11:32. He was likely the last of the judges (as twelfth in the line) and ruled twenty years. *See also* Dagon; Delilah; judge(s); Judges as Old Testament book; Manoah; Nazirites(s); Philistia, Philistines.

Samuel: prophet of pre-monarchial times and later, around 1235–1020 B.C. The word means "name of God." Samuel is the spokesman for considerable eschatological material, particularly as it pertains to the Davidic Covenant. From birth, he was destined to be a priest and a Nazirite prophet because his mother Hannah had pledged the child to the service of God if she would be allowed to conceive the baby despite the barrenness of her womb. The young boy received his training under Eli at the tabernacle, then located at Shiloh. It was there that he received the Lord's call in the depth of night. At that time, conditions were chaotic in the land. The settlement was hardly unified enough to be called a "nation" and had barely recovered from the near anarchy of the period of the judges. In fact, 1 Samuel 7:6 called him a "judge," so we may consider him a transition figure from the time of the judges to the beginning of the Hebrew monarchy. Enemies were all around—in Syria, Moab, Canaan, Midian, Ammon, and Philistia. Samuel became a remarkable prophet, priest, and king-maker after the death of Eli and his sons. Few Bible characters have acted with such probity in both his private and public affairs. As a spiritual leader, he carefully tried to move the population along toward a monarchy, even though he was personally opposed to having any king but God. *See also* 1 and 2 Samuel; Hannah; judge(s); Nazirite(s); prophet(s).

Sanamahism: a 2,000-year-old religion based mainly in Southeastern India. The sect has experienced a revival of sorts of late and remains in conflict with its rival Hinduism. Sanamahism is unique among Indian religions as it holds a form of the doctrine of the Trinity. *See also* Hinduism; sect(s).

Sananda: the galactic name for Jesus Christ coined by certain Ascended Masters. Cosmic consciousness advocates claim the name is the soul known as Jesus when he was on earth but insist he is now on the home planet Parutia where he helps Father. *See also* Ascended Masters; Awakening; cosmic consciousness; names (titles) for Jesus; Parutia.

Sanat Kumar: a New Age name equivalent or nearly equivalent to Satan or a satanic figure. *See also* accuser of our brothers; Abaddon; Abezi-Thibod; Adramelech; Anammelech; Anointed Cherub; Apollyon; Apophis; Asmodaeus; Azazel; Baal-zebub; Baphomet; Beelzeboul; Beelzebub; Belial; Cupay; Day Star; Dibbuk; Dubbi'el; demon(s), demonic; dragon; Evil One, the; Gadreel; Ghede; goat; god of this age, the; guardian Cherub; Hahgwehdaetgah; Iblis; *Kategor;* Legion; Light-Bringer; Lilith; lion; Lucifer; Mastema; Morning Star, the; Pazuzu; prince of demons; prince of the power of the air; prince of this world; red dragon; Sanat Kumar; Satan; seed of the serpent; serpent; Shaytan; Sceva; son of the morning, son of the dawn.

Sanballat: a Samaritan of some influence (Neh. 2:10) living in postexilic Jerusalem. Scriptural history calls him a Horonite, and he was likely a governor of Samaria at that time. Sanballat tried desperately and repeatedly to stop Nehemiah's building program and proved to be a persistent obstacle to the reconstruction plans of the returning Jews. Reportedly, he was the father-in-law of one Manasseh, a co-priest of Jerusalem who was married to a non-Jew, whom he appointed to be the high priest of the new Samaritan temple on Mount Gerizim. *See also* Gesham; Tobiah.

sanctification: a theological word describing how redeemed humanity is "set aside" or made holy by the cleansing act of Christ. It is the last stage of redemption in Christ, making perfect the completeness of salvation. *See also* ban(s); consecrate; glorification; henosis; holiness; holiness movement; holy; holy and true; Holy Club, the; Palamism; perfectionism; salvation; sanctuary; second work of grace; theosis.

sanctimonious: an attitude of moral superiority. Dismissing the first impression of meaning, "sanctimonious" does not equate to sanctity or holiness but the opposite. The more common expression is heard as "holier-than-thou." *See also* hypocrisy.

Sancti Spiritus: "Edifice of the Holt Spirit," the secret headquarters of the early Rosicrucian Society. Members centered there vowed to keep their secrets for 100 years in order to preserve continuity. Associates communicated by gestures and symbols related to the Rosy Cross. *See also* Brethren of Light, The; Brotherhood of the Union; Order of the Rosy Cross; Rosenkreuz, Christian; Rosicrucians; Rosicrucian Manifestos.

sanctuary: a designated place of peace, safety, or holiness. The assembly or audience areas of church and chapel buildings are often called "sanctuaries." *See also* church; *dhimmi* status; sanctification.

***Sanctus,* the:** one of the earliest musical worship songs or chants that may be as old as second century Christianity. It is a Syrian composition appropriate for special church ceremonies like baptism, ordination, holy days, etc. Part of the text reads: "Your majesty, O Lord, a thousand thousand heavenly beings worship, and myriad myriads of angels, hosts of spiritual beings, ministers of fire and spirit with cherubim and holy seraphim, glorify your name, crying out and glorifying, 'Holy, holy, holy, God Almighty, Heaven and earth are full of your glories.'" The term means "holy" and usually presented just prior to the Eucharist and after the preface of Thanksgiving in the formal liturgies. The core of the music likely springs from Isaiah 6:3, Psalm 118:26, and Mark 11:9–11. *See also* Anaphora; liturgical year; liturgy, Christian; music; Roman Catholic Church; Sanctus bell; Trisagion, the.

Sanctus bell: the jingle of a bell to announce the nearness of the Eucharist, normally as the host is elevated by the priest. *See also* bell(s); furniture and furnishings of the modern church; liturgical year; Roman Catholic Church; *Sanctus,* the.

sand: granulated deposits of the Earth in the fields or beach. The name is a frequent metaphor for a large or even infinite number. God promised Abraham that his progeny would be as numerous as the sands of the seashore. *See also* dust;stars.

sandal(s): a crude open-surfaced shoe—common footwear for the ancients. It was at times used to verify contracts or pledges in the Hebrew culture (Ruth 4:8). *See also* discalced; sandals of Jesus; shoe(s).

Sandalforn: or Sandalphon, the name of a legendary angel said to sweep in with a host of Seraphim when dispelled on a mission from God. Jewish myth names him as the ascended Elijah who became the angel Sandalforn. One powerful Jewish legend says he collects the prayers of the Jews, weaves them into crowns, then floats them to wherever God is. The poet Henry Wadsworth Longfellow writes of one whom he called "Sandalphon, the angel of glory, the angel of prayer." *See also* angel(s); Elijah; Ishim.

sandals of Jesus: the footwear of Jesus, now claimed to be a relic in any number of Roman Catholic or Eastern Orthodox churches. In one circumstance, Pope Zachery (A.D. 741–752) or Stephen II (752–757) is believed to have donated them to the Benedictine Abbey of Prum. *See also* relic(s); sandal(s).

Sandemanianism: a religious sect formed from Scottish Presbyterianism in 1730 by John Glas (1695–1773). Called the "Glasites," the members observed most of the *Book of Common Prayer* but practiced Communion weekly, and exercised regular foot-washing and other less active rites. The movement spread rapidly under the leadership of Glas's son-in-law, Robert Sandleman, and afterward were more often named Sandlemans. The group was condemned by orthodox Presbyterianism. *See also* Presbyterians; sect(s).

Sanger, Margaret Higgins: or Margaret Sanger Slee (1879–1966), American sex educator, nurse, and birth control advocate. Sanger was a stringent advocate for both preventing and terminating unwanted pregnancies and vigorously promoted family planning and abortion (later in her career). She was also stridently anti-religious but insisted her primary motives were to present contraceptive education to disadvantaged women while further helping them and others with unwanted pregnancies. Anti-abortion critics could, and did, easily accuse her of infanticide. Sanger's basic premise, however, was likely eugenics—the limitation and selection of the human population. Sanger's foundational sex education organization, the American Birth Control League (1921), evolved into the Planned Parenthood Federation of America. *See also* abortion; contraception; eugenics; infanticide.

Sangha: one of the three jewels of Buddhism. The name refers to the community of monks or nuns or to those who have obtained some measure of enlightenment. *See also* Buddhism; Darma; monk(s); Three Jewels of Buddhism, the.

Sangoma(s): a respected clique of South African native women who are experienced in almost all kinds of witchcraft, divination, and shamanism in the land. They, in essence, are the *de facto* leaders of the clans. *See also* Dee, John; hierophant; medium; meonenim; Mugyo; mystagogue; shaman, shamanism; spirit guide(s); witch(es); witchcraft.

Sangrael: the blood of Christ, especially as it is sought by Grail hunters throughout history. *See also Holy Blood, Holy Grail.*

Sanhedrin: or Sanhedrim, the ruling council of the Jews considered the highest government assembly, both civil and religious, in its constitution. The name is derived from the Greek *synedrion,* meaning "council" or "place of meeting." Likely, there were two Sanhedrins at some points in Jewish history—one civil or secular and the other religious—but finally formed as one body. The members or elders in the body, numbering seventy, seventy-one, or seventy-two, had considerable influence during the time of Jesus but could not be authoritative over Roman law, especially in declaring the death penalty. A smaller assembly for minor cases consisted of twenty-three members. The Sanhedrin is the only body authorized to determine the precise location of the Temple, to reinstitute the ancient rituals, and to oversee the myriad of details relating to the preparation and function of Temple practice. The body has been defunct for many years but has since been reorganized on January 30, 2005, for the first time since A.D. 425. The new seventy-one member council was led by Rabbi Yeshi Ba'avad and held its first meeting in the city of Tiberius. Rabbi Adin Steinsaltz is the Sanhedrin president and Rabbi Yoel Swartz is vice-chairman and head of the court. Some prophecies seem to indicate that the Sanhedrin will be strong enough, even in a secular state like Israel, to reinstitute the strict religious laws of Judaism in the last days. Sanhedrin means "assembly." *See also* Gazith; Great Sanhedrin; Judaism; Knesset; religious organization; seventy.

sankirtana: a religious chant or mantra repeated over and over to draw petitioners closer to the goal of their prayers or the god of their worship. *See also* chant; mantra.

Santa Camisa: a tunic said to have been worn by Mary as she birthed the baby Jesus. The relic was given to the cathedral at Chartres by Charles the Bald (grandson of Charlemagne) in A.D. 876.

The miraculous power of the artifact is said to have saved itself and the serving priests during a fire in the 12th century. *See also* relic(s).

Santa Cruz: the Holy Cross supposedly rescued by Empress Helena of the Byzantine Empire. The event is celebrated religiously in the Philippines in the festival of *Santacruzan*, sometimes with live crucifixions. *See also* relic(s).

Santayana, George: philosopher, poet, and critic (1863–1952). Santayana was born in Madrid but had been in America since age eight. He taught at Harvard with other notable philosophers like William James, Josiah Royce, and George H. Palmer. Santayana was known for his voluminous philosophical works including his memoirs, *The Last Puritan,* and volumes of work in his chosen field like *Life or Reason* (1906), *The Realms of Being* (1927–1940), and his autobiography, *Persons and Places* (1944–1953). He was a lifelong skeptic in religious matters but authored what is considered "the most devout book written by a non-believer," his *Idea of Christ in the Gospels.* Santayana is credited with the famous quote: "Those who cannot remember the past are compelled to repeat it." He died in Rome during World War II in the company of the Blue Nuns religious order who had sheltered him during the conflict. *See also* philosophy of religion.

Santeria: also called Lukumi, a syncretistic religion, located mostly in the Caribbean and parts of North and South America that features elements of the old paganism of Western Africa and Roman Catholicism. The original emigrants were displaced Yoruba people sold to Cuban landlords where they practiced the worship of one god (Olorun or Olodumare) with a pantheon of spirits known as Orishas. "Santeria" means "the saint's image" from Roman Catholic influence. Alternate names for the sect include *Regla de Ocha, La Regla Lucumi,* and *Lukumi.* Ritual practice centers on trance-induced dance and animal sacrifice (usually chickens) led by a priesthood of both men and women. Its main origins were in Spanish Cuba and, among its cousins Voodoo and Candomble, is perhaps closest to Catholicism. In worship, hymns are replaced by drumming and chanting with the aim of inducing a trance-like state. *See also anima sola;* animism; Brujeria; Candomble; Creole (Caribbean) religions;

cult(s); Kumina; Macumba; magic, magick; Obeah; occult, occultic; Orisha; Quimbanda; Rastafarianism; santero; shaman, shamanism; Shango; spiritism; Spiritual Baptists; Umbanda; Voodoo, Voudou; Yoruba.

santero: a priest of the Santeria religion. *See also* Creole (Caribbean) religions; Santeria.

Sant Mat: a spiritual way of life practiced mostly in two forms in the Indian subcontinent. The philosophy of life reaches for trust, respect, and love to be expressed in our humanity. The practice has become the basis of a religion begun by spiritual master Sant Baljit Singh but having a succession of leaders. The religious style and promotion seek to counter or oppose the Hindu and Islam caste system and claims that God is within every person. *See also* Radhasoami Satsang; sect(s).

Sapiential books. See Hagiographa.

Sapphira. See Ananias and Sapphira.

sapphire: a semi-precious mineral that can be mined or found loose in colors ranging from crystal clear to black; the most common hue is blue. The seventy elders saw its manifestation on Mount Sinai (probably in its colorless form) as the pavement before God's throne (Ex. 24), and it is numbered among the foundation stones of the New Jerusalem. Ezekiel (Ezk. 10:1) revealed it as shaping God's throne. *See also lapis lazuli;* New Jerusalem; sapphire (emerald) throne; sea of glass; throne(s); throne in heaven with someone sitting on it, a.

sapphire (emerald) throne: certain depictions describing the throne of God. Ezekiel 10:1 explains the seat of the divine as a sapphire (*lapis lazuli*) hovering in the expanse over the heads of the supporting Cherubim. Revelation 4:3 describes God's throne as a bow of green (emerald) surrounding His presence. Moses, Aaron, Abihu, Nadab, and the seventy elders witnessed a pavement under God's stance on Mount Sinai resembling sapphire (Ex. 24). Less reliable sources claim that the sapphire is part of the crown of the chief Seraphim. *See also* breastplate of the high priest; ephod; foundation of New Jerusalem; gem(s); *lapis lazuli;* New Jerusalem; onyx; sapphire; sea of glass; stones, fiery; throne(s); throne in heaven with someone sitting on it, a; Urim and Thummin.

Saquasohuh. See Blue Star prophecy.

Saracens: 1. members of the nomadic tribes on the Syrian border of the Roman Empire. They were not Arabs nor were they organized into a monolithic people. Nevertheless, they carved out territory for themselves in both Africa and Europe. They did unite under Saladin after their defeat in the First Crusade at Jerusalem. 2. increasingly the name began to identify an Arab in localized usage during the Middle Ages. 3. in late usage, any Muslim, including Turks, especially denoting that religion's devotees during the Crusades as a branch of Islam. Those who settled in Spain, southern France, Sicily, and Malta were called Moors. Gradually, the name Saracens came to identify Muslims of any description. 4. fantasy figures (usually not capitalized) of fairies and revenants, beings from the Otherworld marked by his or her inclusion in the dark world of ghosts. *See also* bugbears; ghosts; Islam; Otherworld; Ottoman Turks; Saladin; Seljuk Turks.

Sarah: formerly Sarai. Sarah was the wife of Abraham and co-equal recipient of the prophecies and blessings of her husband. Sarah was childless until the age of about eighty-nine, at which time God promised her a son. Her hesitancy to accept the promise of descendants caused her to offer her maid, Hagar, as a secondary wife. Hagar gave birth to Ishmael. When God's prophecy was fulfilled, Sarah gave birth to Isaac, the son of promise. Sarah means "princess." *See also* Hagar; Hagar and Sarah; names, symbology of.

Sarai. See Sarah.

Saraquel: one of the archangels named in pseudepigraphal writings (not Scripture) who is said to superintend the spirits. The Coptic Christians call him Sarathiel and the seven or eight other archangels named appear in a wide spectrum of faith traditions and traditions. *See also* angel(s); archangel(s); liturgical year.

Sarathiel: an angel recognized by the Eastern Orthodox Church as one of the seven great archangels of God's heavenly court. *See also* angel(s); archangel(s); Saraquel; liturgical year.

sarcophagus, sarcophagi: ancient burial vaults made from heavy materials like stone, marble, or pottery. Most were expensive and available only to royal or wealthy v.i.p.s. In essence, the molds were fancy and expensive coffins. *See also* "ashes to ashes"; bone orchard; bier; charnel ground; catacombs; catafalque; cemetery; death; funeral; grave; graveyard; martyrium.

Sardis: the fifth of the seven churches addressed in Revelation (Rev. 3:1–6). The assembly was criticized by Christ for its dead spirituality. The congregation seemed to be characterized by complacency and ambivalence to confront difficult spiritual and moral issues. They seemed to be "whistling through the graveyard" of their ineffective calling. Let's call them the walking dead of church history. Like their city of Sardis itself, stark white in the sunshine, they looked good on the outside from a distance but inside were full of corruption. Dispensationalists call the church era it represents the Violent Church (1328–1648). Some few in the congregation, however, were complimented for their purity and fidelity. The city of Sardis was a wealthy and prominent settlement dating from the Bronze Age. Its most prominent feature was probably the huge area of burial mounds called "the place of a thousand hills." The citizens were into the wool-dyeing industry and specialized in white garment making. The site was a naturally defensive position but was nevertheless conquered by Cyrus, the Ionians, the Persians, Alexander, and Antiochus the Great. Artemis and Zeus were worshiped there prolifically. *See also* church; dispensation(s); dispensational theology; seven churches of Asia Minor, the; Violent Age.

Sargon II: king of Assyria (ruled 722–705 B.C.), a son of Tiglath-pileser III and younger brother of Shalmaneser V. He ascended to the throne as successor to his sibling by violent takeover, in 722 B.C., the year Samaria fell to the Assyrians. Thus, it is unclear which monarch, Shalmaneser or Sargon, was the actual conqueror. Sargon, however, claimed the credit (Isa. 20:1). He was responsible for the major deportations that sent settlers from Israel to foreign lands and the simultaneous import of aliens to Samaria. Such migrations of the races were intended to be a deterrent to rebellion. *See also* Assyria, Assyrians; king(s); Shalmaneser; Sumer; Tiglath-pileser III.

Sargon of Akkad: ruler of the empire that came to be known as Assyria 2334–2279 B.C. He attained the position by conquering Sumer, the oldest civilization in Mesopotamia. His fierce warriors, known as the Akkadians or the Amorites governed by the Code of Hammurabi, set the precedent for the cruel and oppressive occupation that became the trademark of ancient Assyria. The Assyrians were in turn conquered by the Medes (Persians) and Scythians (Bactrians). This Assyrian individual is of particular interest to Bible students in that his infancy narrative almost parallels that of Moses in that his life was saved by floating him in a basket. He survived to become Sargon I whereas Moses became a prince of Egypt. *See also* Assyria, Assyrians; king(s); Moses; Sumer.

Sartre, Jean-Paul: *nee* Jean-Paul Charles Aymard Sartre (1905–1980), French philosopher, novelist, playwright, political activist, and literary critic. Sartre was an exponent of existentialism and supporter of Marxism and seemed to carry a sort of bitterness of spirit about him. Sartre was awarded the Nobel Prize for Literature in 1964 but refused to accept it; he did later ask for the $53,000.00 reward but was refused. From Sartre's philosophy sprang the "hippie" movement of the 1960s and some of the most anti-Christian and anti-democratic ideas of the 20th century. Others in the existentialism vein included Albert Camus, Martin Heidegger, and Karl Jaspers. *See also* existentialism; Marx, Karl; philosophy of religion.

Sarum Rite: a.k.a. the "Salisbury use," the Roman Catholic method of Mass celebration in the United Kingdom from the 11th century. The rite was established by Osmund, bishop of Salisbury and Richard Poore but abandoned after the 16th century. The ritual is elaborate but periodic attempts to revive the form have been unsuccessful. *See also* liturgical year; Mass; Roman Catholic Church; rubric.

sash: a clothing accessory normally worn across the chest or around the waist and usually reserved for royalty or the priesthood. The article often symbolizes sovereignty or serves a priestly function, as in Revelation 1:13, where Jesus wears a golden sash. The seven angels of the bowls also wear them in Revelation 15:6. *See also* belt; girdle.

Sassanid Empire: a people emerging from the area of modern Iran (Persia) in the third century as a rival to the Eastern Christian Empire. They successfully revolted from their oppressors, the Parthians, and became a significant force during this time when the early church was also rising. As accomplished warriors, they even managed to take the emperor Valerian captive after a battle with the Romans. The Sassanids were devoted Zoroastrians, even resorting to open warfare with the Muslims and Christians from time to time in the zeal of their religion. *See also* Zoroaster, Zoroastrianism.

Satan: also known as "the serpent," "Lucifer," "the devil," and other names such as: "ruler of this world" (Jn. 12:31; 14:30), "god of this world" (2 Cor. 4:4), an "angel of light" (2 Cor. 11:14), the "ruler of the kingdom of the air" (Eph. 2:2), and a "roaring lion, looking for someone to devour" (1 Pe. 5:8). He also carries titles including "the accuser of our brothers (Rev. 12:10), "our adversary" (1 Pe. 5:8), "Beelzebub" (Mt. 12:24), "our enemy" (Mt. 13:39), "the evil one" (1 Jn. 5:19), "father of lies" (Jn. 8:44), "murderer" (Jn. 8:44), "ruler of this world" (Jn. 12:31; 14:30; 16:11), "the tempter" (Mt. 4:3), and "a serpent" (Gen. 3:1; Rev. 12:9). Other names have been used at times: accuser of the brothers, adversary, Beelzebub, Belial (Beliar), Cupay, Day Star, evil one, god of this age, "god of this world," Iblis (Islam), *Kategor;* Lucifer, Old Nick, "power of darkness," power (prince) of the air, son of the dawn, liar and the father of lies, Shaytan, the serpent, Ghede, god of this age, and the ancient title Satanel (Satanail). Those descriptions may vary somewhat due to different Bible translations but the intent is surely to convey the fact that he has great power. In both early and modern theology, the emphasis upon the devil as an active agent in the world has been noted as a necessary ingredient of Christian doctrine. The term *Satan* (from the Hebrew word *Hassatan)* means "accuser," "slanderer," or "adversary," which identifies him as the great opposer of God and the people of God. In the Pseudepigrapha he is Satanal. The Old Testament has little to say about him as the Hebrews were reluctant to set up any rival to God. In early Judaism, the Satan figure is more in the form of a divine counselor or public prosecutor in the court of Yahweh and only later became the great conspirator and enemy of God and all goodness. Jesus, however, spoke freely of him, calling him "a liar and the father of lies" (Jn. 8:44). Supposedly the leader of a host of rebellious and fallen angels, Satan has dedicated his career to thwarting God and destroying believers, even attempting to overthrow the sovereignty of the

Father and to annihilate Jesus. Many theologians understand Ezekiel 28 and Isaiah 14 to be disguised accounts of Satan's fall from grace. He is quite active in apocalyptic literature, especially the book of Revelation where he is pictured as a fierce dragon and sponsor of the beasts from the sea and land. Nor is Satan lacking in legendary nicknames. Among others, he has been tagged Old Nick (from the German *nickel,* meaning "goblin,") Old Scratch, an American folklore label derived from the Scandinavian *skratta* ("goblin" again), the Deuce for the saying "the devil you say" which carries a meaning of "rotten luck," or Auld Hornie and Clootie (used by Robert Burns). His destiny is to be defeated at the return of Christ and imprisoned in the Abyss, then eventually eternally condemned to the lake of fire. "The God of peace will soon crush Satan under your feet" (Rom. 16:20). Many people mistakenly believe he is, or will be, the ruler of hell but nothing could be further from the truth. He will, instead, endure the punishments prescribed for every defier of God. Believers are in constant danger from the deceiver and would be overwhelmed but for the protection of Christ and the restraining and protective influence of the Holy Spirit. *See also* Abaddon; Abdiel; Abezi-Thibod; accuser of our brothers; Adramelech; Anammelech; angel of light; Anointed Cherub; Apollyon; Apophis; Asmodaeus; Azazel; Azrael; Baal-zebub; Baphomet; Beelzeboul; Beelzebub; Behemoth; Belial; binding of Satan; *Book of the Dead;* Brotherhood of Satan; Church of Satan; Council of Nine; Cupay; Day Star; demon(s), demonic; devils; diadem; Dibbuk; dragon; Dubbi'el; Evil One, the; father of lies; Gadreel; Ghede; goat; god of this age, the; god of this world; guardian Cherub; Hahgwehdaetgah; Iblis; *Kategor;* kingdom of the air; kingdom of this world; king of Babylon; king of Tyre; Legion; Leviathan; Light-Bringer; Lilith; lion; loosing of Satan; Lucifer; Luciferans; mark of the devil; Mastema; Morning Star, the; names, symbology of; Pazuzu; pentagram; power of darkness; prince of demons; prince of the power of the air; prince of this world; Rahab; red dragon; Robert the devil; ruler of the kingdom of the air; prince of this world; Sammael; Sanat Kumar; Satanic Bible; satanic salute; Satanism; Satan's so-called deep secrets; seed of the serpent; serpent; Seth; seven-headed beast; Shaytan; son of the morning, son of the dawn; Typhon; Venus; war in heaven; where Satan has his throne.

Satan, binding of. See binding of Satan.

Satanic Bible: the sourcebook of quasi-organized Satanism composed by Anton La Vey. Some apocalypticists believe that the text will be a major primer for the end time as society grows more and more depraved. *See also* Church of Satan; La Vey, Anton Szandor; occult, occultic; Satan; Satanism.

satanic salute: a gesture made by Satanists by extending the small and index fingers with the thumb underneath. The shape represents the head of a goat; some insist that the gesture signifies the devil but that assumption is technically suspect. *See also* Baphomet; gestures; Satan; Satanism.

satanic school: a literary designation, though never organized nor official, in operation around the early 1800s wherein noted authors of the period heaped abuse on Christianity and its morals. The movement consisted of writers like Lord Byron, Percy Bysshe Shelley, George Sand, Victor Hugo, John Keats, and others—especially the poets. The label "satanic school" was coined by the English poet laureate of the time, Robert Southey (1774–1843), who labeled such writers, especially Byron, as users of "monstrous combinations of horrors and mockery, lewdness and impiety…" and "immoral writers, men of diseased hearts and depraved imaginations."

Satanism: the worship of Satan practiced either privately or in organized groups and churches. Technically, there are two forms of the religion; Theistic Satanism sees the devil as a real being whereas Atheistic Satanism views him as a symbol of unworthy traits in humankind. A prominent feature of such ritual involves the parody of the Catholic ritual or Protestant Communion called the Black Mass, or Black Sabbath. The conduct of Satanic worship has been variously described, some extremes of which profess the worship of the head of a donkey, infant and animal sacrifice, and even cannibalism. Perhaps the expression with the most notoriety was organized by Anton Szandor La Vey as the Church of Satan in 1966. In the year 2014, the New York-based Satanic Temple in Oklahoma City unveiled plans for a monument to Satan on the grounds of the state's Capitol (adjacent to the Ten Commandments memorial), and others in Boston held a Black Mass near Harvard. The practice in its formality is said to date from about A.D. 200 according to apologist Marcus Minucius Felix. In a more philosophic take on Satanism reduced to its essence, the concept can be described as—rather than the exclusive worship of some strange creature depicted as a goat or Baphomet—the deification of self. It is an ego illusion that almost every religious tradition deems the "real enemy" of the age. It is the realization of every theological, cultural, economic, and political deviation that allows the human to do as he or she pleases without recrimination. That excess of unbridled freedom is the core belief of the chief Satanist of history, Aleister Crowley, and the means of its existence today in the wider population. *See also Astrum Argentum;* Baphomet; Brotherhood of Satan; Church of Satan; Crowley, Aleister; Hellfire Club; La Vey, Anton Szandor; Luciferans; Mass of Saint Secaire; occult, occultic; pentagram; Satan; Satanic Bible; satanic salute; sect(s); seed of the serpent; Walpurgis Night; Warnke, Alfred "Mike"; Wicca.

Satan's so-called deep secrets: a reference from Christ in Revelation 2:24 addressed to the church at Thyatira. The Lord is commending the members for their resistance to the secretive and destructive teaching of the Jezebel and other false doctrines, such as that of the Nicolaitans or the Gnostics. "Satan's so-called deep secrets" is a phrase intended to implicate the evil one in all systems of the occult and false doctrine. *See also* apostasy; deep secrets, so-called; fable(s); godless myths; heresy; heretic; heterodoxy; miscreance; old wives' tales; Satan; turned to fables (myths); unsound doctrine.

Satan's throne: possibly a Christian view of the famous statue of Zeus in Pergamum which most citizens of the time regarded as the prize of their city. It was dedicated to Augustus and Roma. Another, in nearby Ephesus, depicted Emperor Titus commissioned by his brother Domitian who followed him. Also close by stood the Sebasterion in the city of Aphrodisias (named for Aphrodite). This temple could have also qualified as Satan's throne, a structure three stories in height and called the "temple of the holy ones." There were hundreds more scattered about the vast Roman Empire. *See also* Aphrodite; Domitian; Ephesus; Pergamum; Roman Empire; Sebasterion; temple(s); Titus; Venus; where Satan has his throne; Zeus.

Sathya Sai Baba: Indian guru and philanthropist (1926–2011) who gained a rather extensive following because of his alleged resurrections or reincarnations, clairvoyance, bilocation ability, omnipotence, and omniscience. Reputedly, he could produce great heaps of ashes or eject objects like golden eggs or watches from his mouth which he presented as favors to his followers. He was also known to be a healer, mind-reader, and capable of precognition. Such talents were ascribed to him by devotees as miracles but, to others, they were mere conjuring. He founded a religious and charitable association called the Sathya Sai Organization before his death. Most named him an avatar. *See also* cult(s).

satire: the use of irony, sarcasm, ridicule, etc., to expose or denounce. In literature, satire is a composition of poetry or prose that scorns a type of folly or similar category of abuse in writing or cultural mores. In Scripture, Isaiah 44:9–20 may be considered satirical. *See also* accideme; alliteration; apostrophe; apothegm; assonance; autograph; Bible; Bible manuscripts; Bible translations; biblical criticism; chiasmus; conflict story; *constructio ad sensum;* context; contextualization; dittography; double sense fulfillment; doublets; doubling; edification; eisegesis; epanadiplosis; epigrammatic statements; etymology; exegesis; figure of speech; folio; form criticism; gattung; gloss; gnomic sayings; grammatical-historical interpretation; *hapax legomena;* haplography; hermeneutic(s); higher criticism; homographs; homonyms; homophones; *homoteleuton;* hyperbole; idiom; *inclusio;* interpolation; interpretation; inverted nun; irony; isagogics; *itture sopherim;* jot and tittle; kere; *kethib;* "L"; liberalists interpretation; literal interpretation; litotes; loan words; lower criticism; "M"; Masoretic Text; minuscule(s); mystery of God; omission; onomastica; onomatopoeia; palimpsest; papyrus; paradigm; parallelism; parchment; *paroimia; paronomasia;* pericope; personification; Peshitta; pointing; point of view; polyglot; principles of interpretation; proof texting; pun(s); "Q"; redaction; revelation, theological; rhetorical criticism; rhetorical devices; riddle; *scripto continua;* scriptorium; *sebirin;* simile; similitude; source criticism; sources, primary and secondary; special points; strophe; superscription; symbol(s); synecdoche; syntax; synthetic parallelism; text; textual criticism; *tiggune sopherim;* Time Texts; Torah; translation; transposition; trope; type(s); typology; uncial(s); vellum; verbicide.

satisfaction motif. See exchange motif.

satisfaction theory of atonement: also called the commercial theory, a theology of salvation that emphasizes the fact that Christ died to satisfy a principle of the nature of God. We, as natural sinners, have violated God's honor. As cause to effect, we are now obligated to restore what we have taken; but restoration is inadequate to the crime so we must supply additional compensation as well. A secular judge, in such an instance, might stipulate that a thief not only restore stolen goods to the rightful owner but add a penalty of punitive damage also. Humans are incapable of either satisfaction or compensation for we have not the resources for it. Christ's atonement, then, provides the means. As a result, God and man benefit but Satan does not. *See also* atonement; exchange motif; ransom theory of atonement; reconciliation; salvation; vicarious atonement.

satrap(s): a high official or managerial office originated by King Darius of Persia (Dan. 6:1). The king appointed 120 satraps ("lieutenants") to be sub-rulers of great authority throughout the kingdom of Medo-Persia with three administrators over them. Daniel was likely one of the high-ranking administrators. *See also* prefect(s); procurator(s).

Saturday's child: a proverb of Greece that implies a child born on a Saturday will have special psychic powers and can see ghosts and vampires. Most would consider the bestowal a dubious gift.

Saturn: the sixth planet in distance from the sun readily recognized by its characteristic rings. In mythology, the Romans worshiped Saturn as the god of agriculture and harvest celebrated annually in the riotous festival of Saturnalia. He had a temple in the Roman Forum, which contained the Royal Treasury. From the name we get the weekday designation Saturday. In Greek lore, he was called Chronos. The planet Saturn may also have significance to the Jews as it represented their city of Jerusalem (called *Udi idim* by the Babylonian astrologers). If true, then it may have had some influence in the calculations of the Magi to determine the date of Jesus' birth and even the Canaanites. *See also* Levant pantheon; Olympian pantheon; planets as gods, the; Raphan, star of; Saturnalia.

Saturnalia: the Roman festival celebrating the return of the sun from its winter solstice, known to the Latins as *Natalis solis invicti,* the Feast of the Invincible Sun. Celebrations were held for seven days starting on December 17 in honor of the god Saturn, invariably a week of wild and uncontrolled display. In consideration of this situation (which saw significant Christian application), the Roman Church simply embraced the holiday and called it Christmas, the day of Christ's birth. The Eastern Church, however, already in dispute with the authority at Rome, chose to celebrate Christmas on January 6 as both the birth and baptism date of Jesus. *See also* Christmas; Feast of Fools; Helios; Lord's Day, the; *Mardi Gras;* Rome; Saturn; Sol; sun; sun worshipers.

Saturnius: an early Gnostic (ca. A.D. 100–120) who thought of himself as a creator angel. He taught that Jesus did not have a physical body, that Christ came to destroy the God of the Jews, and that sex, marriage, and procreation were evil; he demanded all his followers practice vegetarianism and asceticism as well. Possibly, he was the third disciple of Simon Magus after Menander. *See also* Gnosticism, Gnostic(s); Menander; Simon Magus.

satyagaha: a method of non-violent protest pioneered by Mahatma Gandhi and utilized effectively by Martin Luther King Jr. *See also ahimsa;* Gandhi, Mahatma Kramchad; King, Martin Luther, Jr.

satyr: in Hebrew *sa'ir,* a term that describes wild animals or demons said to dance among the ruins of Babylon (Isa. 13:21 and referenced in Rev. 18:2). In earlier texts (Lev. 17:7; 2 Chr. 11:5-17), the word names an idol. Ancient myth recognizes the satyr as a lecherous goat being. Some apocryphal writings name the satyr as the fallen angels of Genesis 6 who produced the dreadful Nephilim. *See also* attending spirits; banshee; Baphomet; bogle; brownies; bugbears; chimera; clurichauns; daemons; deceiving spirits; demon, demonic; devils; disa; dryad(s); elemental(s); fairy, fairies; Furies; ghost(s); ghoul; gnome(s); Green Man, the; hobgoblins; homunculus; Horned God; household deities; huldafolk; Lares; leprechaun(s); Loa Loas; Menes; mythological beasties, elementals, monsters, and spirit animals; Nephilim; nereid; nymph(s); nyx; Oniropompi; Orisha; Oya; Olympian pantheon; Pan; para; paredri; penates; prefect(s); Robin Goodfellow; Seelie

Court, Unseelie Court; selkie; Sidhe; sirens; spiritual warfare; sprite(s); sylph(s); teraphim; territorial spirits; Trickster; Tuatha de Danann; tutelary; undine; wight(s).

Saul: 1. the first king of Israel who eventually committed suicide in desperation rather than be slain in battle by the Philistines. The monarchial record pictures him (despite some early good distinctions) as too often disobedient, vindictive, moody, and selfish. Early in life, he is mentioned as having been an occasional member of the sons of the prophets. 2. the early name for Paul the Apostle before and shortly after his conversion. He is identified by that name as being among the five prophets and teachers dispatched to the church at Antioch. After, he became the most prolific missionary and church starter in the Roman world. *See also* Barnabas; kings of Israel and Judah; kings of Israel and Judah in foreign relations; king(s); Lucius; Manean; Simeon; sons (school) of the prophets; Paul as apostle.

Saumur: a center for Protestant activism in western France around A.D. 1596. In that year, a synod in the city issued a decree that prohibited utterance of any comment relating to the book of Revelation without formal approval from church authority. *See also* Revelation as New Testament prophecy.

"saved": a common expression for the state of grace obtained through personal repentance and acceptance of the redemptive power of Christ. All who come to Christ in confession, repentance, and belief are never denied salvation. As to whom will be eligible for salvation in the terrible days of Tribulation, however, the theological responses are more controversial. Opinions range from: 1) no one will be saved as the Great Tribulation is God's punishing wrath on the world (a barely supported supposition), 2) only Jews will be saved since the Church is raptured away or those left behind have forfeited their right to repentance, 3) only those who are kind to the persecuted Jews will enter the kingdom of God, 4) only those who have previously heard the gospel of Christ prior to the rapture or Tribulation are qualified, 5) only those who resist the mark of the beast will be spared, 6) walking the aisle, an evangelical expression to describe the act of presenting oneself publically after accepting Christ's forgiveness of sin and his salvation. The penitent literally "walks the aisle" of a church or similar worship gathering, usually in response to the worship leader's invitation to do so. *See also* accept Christ, to; altar call; "asking Jesus into my heart"; blood of Christ; blood of the Lamb; birth from above; born again; Christianese; confession(s) of faith; conversion; "plead the blood"; profession of faith; regeneration; salvation; turn your life [heart] over to Jesus; "walking the aisle"; "washed in the blood."

Savonarola, Girolamo: an Italian Dominican (A.D. 1452–1498) known for his personal austerity and stern preaching. Savonarola was gaunt in appearance and awe-inspiring in his preaching, voicing sermons that invariably condemned the corrupt papacy, greedy merchants and administrators of the Medici aristocracy, and the gaudiness of the cities around him. Most themes in his language invariably centered on doom, pestilence, and divine wrath. Savonarola's messages were inspired by his obsession with the Last Days (including a prediction of the Second Coming date), his visions, and his announced direct communications with God. He insisted over and over that the Roman Church would be scourged, then renewed, and that the time of recompense was at hand. As was true for many prophets before him, Savonarola was executed by being burned at the stake in 1498. Savonarola was fully aware of the dangers he faced and sometimes thought of abandoning his crusade. His last sermon before death reveals his anguish: "But whenever I went up into the pulpit again, I was unable to contain myself. To speak the Lord's words has been for me a burning fire within my bones and my heart. It was unbearable. I could not speak. I was on fire. I was alight with the spirit of the Lord." As a prophetic voice, he managed to reform much of Italian society and probably precipitated the downfall of the Medici family. It is not out of line to say that he was a "modern-day" prophet in the true sense of the prophetic tradition. An apocalyptic cult called the *Piagnoni* grew after Savonarola's death, designed to perpetuate his memory. Among the classics published by the group was a tome called *Apocalypsis Nova*—"New Account of the Last Days"—in 1502. It predicted the coming of an angelic pastor or pope to save the world, which was then to be ruled by spiritual men. Everyone who was anybody wanted to be that savior type—and some who manage to find and read the *Nova* still do. *See also* "bonfire of the vanities"; cult(s); *Piagnoni;* Roman Catholic Church; Utopia.

Savoy Confession: a Puritan document drawn up mainly by John Owen during Oliver Cromwell's time. The writing speaks of the Antichrist, the calling of the Jews, and the triumph of the Church, among other eschatological topics. *See also* confession(s) of faith; Credo; creed(s); Puritanism, Puritans.

"sawdust trail, the": the colloquial term for actions by the evangelists and audiences of the great revivalist experiments in America around the post-Civil War era. The term springs from the habit of sprinkling sawdust in the aisles of any structure or tent of meeting where services were being conducted. The action gave some definition to the plain surroundings and controlled the dust to some degree. Preachers called their vocation "hitting the sawdust trail" while converts walking forward in contrition were "walking the sawdust trail." *See also* apocalyptic fervor; camp meeting(s); circuit riders; evangelist(s), evangelism; Great Awakenings, the; Restoration Movement in America; revivalism; "walking the aisle."

Saybrook Platform: a.k.a. the Cambridge Platform, a declaration which emerged as a sort of constitution for the early Congregationalist Church in New England. The document was adopted in 1648 at Cambridge, Massachusetts, and served as a mixed civil and religious base for the Half-Way Covenant and Great Awakenings. *See also* confession(s) of faith; Congregationalists; Credo; creed(s); Great Awakenings.

SBNR. See "spiritual but not religious."

scales of balance. See balance scales.

Scallion, Gordon-Michael: one of the more media-savvy psychics, perhaps gaining more notoriety than others of the modern age. He claimed visions of the end time, many of which were inducted by altered states of consciousness (ASC). His website offers "future maps" to aid the end-days-minded geographer and planner. Often he is referred to merely as GMS. *See also* physic(s).

scapegoat: some person, animal, or thing on which blame or a curse is placed upon to allay or shift responsibility for wrongdoing. *See also* Azazel; names, symbology of.

scepter: a small rod symbolizing the reign of a monarch and resembling a "swagger stick" for a military officer. Symbolism uses the term to denote the rule of righteous kings (like David who will never see the ruling scepter depart from his line). Alternately, a scepter could describe a failure of rule (as in Ezekiel 19:14). Christ's millennial scepter is described as a rod of iron. *See also* king(s); queen(s); rod of iron; throne(s).

scapular: an important article of dress for most monastics and some priests. The item drapes over one's shoulders, both in front and behind, often reaching to the knees or longer. There is an opening for the head much like a poncho and, for some styles, the front may be of two cloth panels. Monastic scapulars worn by monks and nuns are somewhat longer than the devotional ones favored by those not members of an order. *See also* furniture and furnishings of the modern church; Roman Catholic Church.

sceuophyax: a sacristan of the Eastern Orthodox Church. *See also* Eastern Orthodox Church.

Sceva: a Jewish chief priest in Ephesus, the father of seven sons who practiced a sort of unsanctioned exorcism of demon-possessed persons. These young men were habitually driving out evil spirits (supposedly) by invoking "the name of Jesus whom Paul preaches" (Acts 19:13–16). Their practice came to a violent end when a certain spirit answered them, "Jesus I know and Paul I know about, but who are you?" Then the possessed man attacked the seven and injured them all. *See also* Abaddon; Abezi-Thibod; Apollyon; Asmodaeus; Azazel; demon(s), demonic; demon possession; Dibbuk; Dubbi'el; Gadreel; Jannes and Jambres; Legion; Lilith; Sammael; slave girl of Philippi; soothsayer(s); Syrophoenician woman; *Tobit;* woman of Canaan.

Schafer, Paul: or Paul Schneider, founder (1921–2010) of the notorious cult known as "Villa Baviera." Schafer was a former Nazi who moved his German immigrant followers to the south of Chile in 1961 where the place finally became known as one of the century's most disreputable religious groups ever founded. There is little dispute that the place has harbored escaped Nazis and sponsored many other serious criminal activities, including child abuse and torture of prisoners. *See also* cult(s); Villa Baviera.

Schaff, Philip: church historian, Bible scholar, and a champion of church union (1819–1893). Schaff was Swiss-born but was educated in Germany before coming to America in 1844. He authored numerous works of importance, but his *Principle of Protestantism* boldly predicts that Catholics and Protestants will join to form a new evangelical catholic church, a scenario most would say is impossible. Schaff rejected revivalism in favor of adherence to church doctrine, a movement he called "Mercersburg Theology." *See also* ecumenism; National Council of Churches; Parliament of the World's Religions; World Council of Churches.

Schechter, Solomon: a Jewish theologian and Talmudist (1850–1915). In 1913 Schechter founded the United Synagogue of America, which became a mainstay for conservative Judaism in America. He was Rumanian-born but immigrated to the United Kingdom and was active in America. It was Schechter who led the study of the Genizah Fragment cache at Cairo, some 50,000 manuscripts, including some lost portions of the Hebrew text of *Ecclesiasticus*. Schechter was an author of histories and the first editor of the *Jewish Encyclopedia*. *See also* Genizah Fragments; Jew(s).

Schillebeeckx, Edward: a Belgian Roman Catholic theologian from the time of the First World War (1914–2009). His theology seemed to spring from Catholic tradition and our present world of experience, which earned him a rather forward-looking clientele. *See also* Roman Catholic Church.

schism: a rending, as of a garment, or a sharp difference of opinion as discussed in 1 Corinthians 12:21–26 and John 7:40–43. The idea brings to mind a break or deliberate disruption in the unity of doctrine or ecclesiology. The modern concept is commonly known as a "church split." When church bodies unite, the term used is "merger." *See also* merger; Photian Schism, the; Great Schism, the.

Schism of Nepos: a pejorative name applied to the historic controversy centered on Nepos, the celebrated African bishop of the third-century (around A.D. 255). First and second century eschatology seemed attractive to Christians but was strongly subdued by the Roman Catholic Church after the third. A strong supporter of millennialism and literalism, Nepos was opposed by another noted early church father, Dionysius. The two debated the issue and each produced books on their separate perspectives. Nepos submitted the *Book of Nepos* and Dionysius's work was *On the Promises*. Those opposed to the millennial outlook concerning the 1,000-year reign of Christ quickly prevailed, mainly because the work of Nepos was lost. Catholic authorities, even today, claim that millennialism was a creation of the Gnostic Cerinthus. Some conservative biblicists claim it as the time the early church abandoned premillennialism and adopted amillennialism. *See also* Dionysius; Nepos; millennialism.

Schism, the Great: See Great Schism, the.

Schleiermacher, Friedrich Daniel Ernst: eighteenth century German philosopher and university professor who firmly believed (after much personal struggle) that emotion and feeling are senior partners of reason. God could be sought by anyone who was contemplative—and thereby find the fruit of revelation. In university matters, he knew that theology could no longer hold its honored place as the chief discipline in the period of the Enlightenment. He was called the "father of liberal theology" in many circles. Still, he held out a dual purpose for its inclusion as pastoral care with the possibility for research analysis like that of science. *See also* philosophy of religion; Romanticism.

Schmalkaldic League. See Schmalkaldic War.

Schmalkaldic War: a conflict between Roman Catholicism under Pope Paul III and the Protestant princes of Germany who had formed themselves into the Schmalkaldic League. The war erupted in 1546 and within a year the Protestants had been utterly defeated. Jealousy between Emperor Charles and the pope prevented the immediate destruction of the Protestants, however, and the conflict was rejoined, with the Protestants regaining all they had lost. The war was ended with the Peace of Augsburg in 1555. *See also* Augsburg Interim; Holy War; Peace of Augsburg; Protestant Reformation, the; Roman Catholic Church; Smalcald Articles.

Schneerson, Menachem Mendel: a Jewish false Messiah (1902–1994) and Hasidic Jew whose given name was Rabbi Menachem Mendel Schneerson von Lubavfitch. He was a prime mover in educational circles and radical Judaism, so much so that he set the end time date on September 9, 1981. Schneerson may be remembered as the rabbi who invented the generic system of taking a Jewish year and transferring the numbers back to Hebrew letters to see if words or an acrostic would appear. He was posthumously awarded the Congressional Gold Medal in 1994 and some still consider him the Messiah of our age. *See also* Jew(s).

schola. See choir.

scholasticism: the discipline of research and study to obtain knowledge. Biblical scholars and their writings are vital to our understanding of Scripture. Theologians like Peter Abelard and Peter Lombard in the 12th century and Thomas Aquinas in the 13th became the dominant medieval thought and obscured many cherished biblical doctrines. It should be noted, however, that scholasticism during the Renaissance held a slightly different meaning. To the 12th century intelligentsia, "scholarship" was education by building up knowledge through discussion and debate predominately at the university level. The system allowed Martin Luther to tack his "Ninety-Five Theses" to the door of his university chapel as a normal procedure. The subjects of his proposed debates, or so it seems, went beyond the normally open and liberal approach to knowledge from the elite of the Renaissance. To question the Roman Catholic hierarchy was risky business indeed. *See also* Aquinas, Thomas; Christoplatonism; humanism; Lombard, Peter; religious education; Renaissance.

School of Alexandria: center of scholastic learning in philosophy, literature, science, and religion of ancient Alexandria in Egypt. Most famous rabbis and church leaders in the prime of the school's existence were noted for their attempts to combine Greek philosophy with Jewish and Christian doctrine. Most favored the allegorical methods of scriptural interpretation. Philo may be the premier Jewish allegorist followed by, around the second century, church fathers like Pantaenus, Clement of Alexandria, and Origen. Augustine, too, reflected many allegorist tendencies and is credited as the founder of amillennialism. Much of the school's objection to millennialism sprang from their idea that the doctrine was materialistic, especially in Revelation's description of the New Jerusalem. As such, it was said to be too sensual and appealed to the baser instincts instead of the higher "spiritualism" to which all Christians should strive. *See* *also* Alexandria as city; allegorical interpretation; amillennialism; idealism; Pantaenus; patriarchate(s); pentarchy; philosophy of the Greeks; School of Antioch.

School of Antioch: a center of philosophical and religious learning founded by Lucian (died A.D. 312) located at Antioch of Syria. Many noted church fathers numbered among its alumni, including Theodore of Mopsuestia, Chrysostom, and Theodoret. In contrast, even in opposition, to the Alexandrian promotions of allegorism as the premier tool of scriptural interpretation, the Antiochian scholars were staunch literalists. Their influence faded in the fourth and fifth centuries due to internal theological disputes and left the Alexandrians as virtual victors of the academic field. *See also* Antioch as city; literal interpretation; Lucian; patriarchate(s); pentarchy; School of Alexandria; Syria.

schools of the prophets. See sons (school) of the prophets.

Schopenhauer, Arthur: German philosopher (1788–1860), a nontheist who believed that the world is nothing but blind will, a never-ending struggle going nowhere. Heavily influenced by Buddhism, he maintained that humans can only escape or find respite in the cessation of desire. Schopenhauer can be called the greatest exponent of the pessimistic philosophy. *See also* pessimism; philosophy of religion.

Schwarzenau Brethren: or German Baptist Brethren. The group consisted of radical Pietists of seventeenth and 18th century America who fervently wished for the return of Christ. The movement started in Germany under Alexander Mack (1679–1735) growing out of the Reformed Lutheran tradition. The American version rejected Lutheranism as too liberal but embraced radical pietism and Anabaptist markings. *See also* church bodies in America (typed); sect(s).

Schwenkfelder, Caspar von Ossig: leader of the (then unaligned) religious group known as Schwenkfelders (1489–1561). He was a contemporary of Martin Luther who called him "that poor simpleton" who was possessed of the devil. Schwenkfelder graciously declined to retaliate so as to retain his humble and forgiving nature. His leadership tried to navigate the believers in a position somewhere between the Reformation doctrines of Luther, Calvin, and Zwingli and the more radical

Anabaptists even though he was raised in a Catholic home. *See also* Schwenkfelders.

Schwenkfelders: a small American communion with roots in the 16th century Protestant Reformation but organized as a church only in the twentieth century. The original devotees were led by Caspar von Ossig Schwenkfelder who sought "Reformation of the Middle Way," a centrist position between radical Anabaptists and the reforms of Luther, Calvin, and Zwingli. The adherents are Germans and claim the legend that the devil was once taking a group of them to hell when his bag broke over Harpersdorf. As persecution grew, several migrations to America landed most of them near Philadelphia. Local churches (of which there are few) are decidedly autonomous, depend upon the Inner Light of the Holy Spirit, believe that Jesus' divinity is progressive, and have liberal beliefs regarding baptism and the Lord's Supper. *See also* church bodies in America (typed); denomination(s), denominationalism; Pennsylvania Dutch; Schwenkfelder, Caspar von Ossig; sect(s).

Scientology, Church of: an apocalyptic cult and multi-million-dollar investment scheme started by L. Ron Hubbard. The system can also be identified by other titles known to the public as Narconon, Criminon, Way to Happiness Foundation, WISE, Hubbard College of Administration, and Applied Scholastics. The system is based on Hubbard's system called "Dianetics," which requires complicated (and expensive) counseling techniques and discipline. According to Scientology, people are immortal beings who have forgotten their true nature. It can be regained by "auditing," a rehabilitation and self-help program. The spirits of persons are called "thetans," a cosmic source or reincarnate race who once lived on outer planets but created our world as an amusement for themselves. A thetan has an immortal spirit and great power but remains unknown to the unenlightened. One can even be elevated to an "operating thetan" with control over matter, energy, space, and time if devotion is applied to the "bridge to total freedom." One must work with a personal auditor against "engrams" (negative experience units) to find a state of "clear." The organization seeks to operate as a religion but is essentially a for-profit business with depleted ethics. Scientology officials have often been involved in the judicial system, either as accused criminals or lobbyists, to force the government to recognize them as a church. Celebrities (Patty Hurst, John Travolta, Tom Cruise, Goldie Hawn, *et al.*) seem drawn to it and are definitely coddled by the leadership to benefit from the inevitable publicity and exorbitant fees. *See also* cult(s); Hubbard, L. Ron; Free Zone.

scoffers: those who doubt and ridicule the teachings of Christ and sound Christian doctrine. Peter warned (2 Pe. 3:3) that the world can expect a dramatic upsurge in the number and influence of scoffers as the end of the age draws near, as did Jude (Jude 18). Scoffers, both ancient and modern, are a prime reason the word of the prophets, and religion and prophecy in general, is often ridiculed and rejected. *See also* agnosticism, agnostic(s); antitheism; apatheist; areligious; atheism, atheist(s); atheism, the new; Brights, the; Freedom from Religion Foundation; meta-atheist.

Scofield, C. I.: the most dynamic exponent of dispensationalism in America (1843–1921). He was best-known by his initials, which stood for Cyrus Ignatius. Scofield was a lawyer, ex-soldier in the Civil War, and a Congregational minister without credentials. His refinements of dispensational theology, first advocated by John Nelson Darby in England, moved the doctrines far afield in the United States. He was the author of *The Scofield Reference Bible*, which is the King James Version with interlineal notes scattered prolifically throughout. *See also* Darby, John Nelson; dispensational theology; Edwards, Morgan; Irving, Edward; Jurieu, Peter; Lacunza, Emmanuel; MacDonald, Margaret; Niagara Bible Conferences; *Scofield Reference Bible, The.*

***Scofield Reference Bible,* the:** the King James Version of the Bible infused with prolific interlineal notes by C. I. Scofield. The publication, in its several editions, proved popular in America and is the undisputed sourcebook for much of dispensational theology. Often enough, readers could not, or did not, distinguish clearly between the true Word and Scofield's notes, thus causing some misunderstandings or suspicions of the doctrine presented. *See also* dispensational theology; Scofield, C. I.

Scopes Trial: the court trial of John Scopes (held in 1925), a high school teacher in Dayton, Tennessee, who was accused of teaching Darwin's theory of evolution in violation of state law. William

Jennings Bryan was an advisory prosecutor with Clarence Darrow for the defense. The procedure underscored the deep conflict between science and religion but Bryan, foolishly allowing himself to be called as an expert witness, came across as inept. The populists called the process "the monkey trial" and gained nationwide attention. Scopes was convicted but the damage to the fundamentalists' image was telling. Scopes was fined a mere $100.00 and the case was overturned on a technicality. William Jennings Bryan died a mere five days later, on June 5, 1925, no doubt in humiliation. *See also* chaos magic; cosmogony; cosmology; *creatio ex nihilo;* creation; creationism; creation science; Creator; evolution; evolution, theistic; fundamentalism, fundamentalists; *Fundamentals, The*; intelligent design; involution; naturalism; Omphalos Hypothesis; progressive creationism; "six-day theory, the"; Young-Earth Creationist Movement.

scorpion: a stinging arachnid capable of inflicting great pain when provoked. The fifth seal of Revelation (Rev. 9:1–12) describes demonic-like hordes resembling locusts that erupt from the Abyss. These are allowed to attack the population of Tribulation earth with the ferociousness of scorpions, including tails for stinging, which torment people for five months. The leader of the horde is named Abaddon or Apollyon. Scorpions may symbolize punishment or torment in other biblical texts as well, including Deuteronomy, 1 Kings, 2 Chronicles, Ezekiel, and Luke. *See also* Abaddon; animals, birds, and insects, symbology of; Apollyon.

Scott, Michael: Scottish mathematician and philosopher serving at the court of Frederick II of Sicily (1175–c. 1232). He was considered a master of the occult sciences in the Middle Ages. Dante places him in the lower depths of hell in his *Inferno XX* as one who "truly knew every trick of the magical arts." *See also* magic, magick; occult, occultic; philosophy of religion.

scribe(s): a person of letters who is proficient at copying or composing in the alphabet of his culture whom the Jews called *sopherim*. More specifically in the New Testament, the scribes were a Jewish religious and scholarly sect who began to take on great prominence during and after the Babylonian Exile. They held significant influence because they were literate and because they came to be known not only as copiers of the Law of Moses but also experts of its interpretation. They were ceremonially strict, much like the Pharisees with whom they are often paired. Again, like the Pharisees, they favored the oral traditions of the rabbis as much or more than the written Word of God, and many held both offices. Most were prideful of their position, greedy, and punctilious (Jer. 8:8), but a few were worthy (Mt. 8:19); Nicodemus may have been a scribe as well as a Pharisee. Jesus did not dispute their expertise as teachers but did renounce them for their poor example to the people and haughty behavior before God. Some angelic-type beings in apocalyptic dreams and visions are also called scribes but are identified by their purpose to the revelation. *See also* Aram, Arameans; Essenes; Ezra the scribe; Hellenism, Hellenization; Herodians; Karaites; Masoretic Text; Pharisees; pride; Sadducees; Samaritan(s); sect(s); Zealots.

scribe clothed in linen. See Daniel's vision from the revealing angel; Ezekiel's report of the scribe clothed in linen.

scripto continua: a copyist mistake occurring when joining or dividing words. As far as is known, there are none in Scripture. A professional typesetter or computer programmer might think of *scripto continua* as the uninterrupted flow of words to the end of the line without a forced break within the sequence. *See also* accideme; alliteration; apostrophe; apothegm; assonance; autograph; Bible; Bible manuscripts; Bible translations; biblical criticism; chiasmus; conflict story; *constructio ad sensum;* context; contextualization; dittography; double sense fulfillment; doublets; doubling; edification; eisegesis; epanadiplosis; epigrammatic statements; etymology; exegesis; figure of speech; folio; form criticism; gattung; gloss; gnomic sayings; grammatical-historical interpretation; *hapax legomena;* haplography; hermeneutic(s); higher criticism; homographs; homonyms; homophones; *homoteleuton;* hyperbole; idiom; *inclusio;* interpolation; interpretation; inverted nun; irony; isagogics; *itture sopherim;* jot and tittle; kere; *kethib;* "L"; liberalists interpretation; literal interpretation; litotes; loan words; lower criticism; "M"; Masoretic Text; minuscule(s); mystery of God; omission; onomastica; onomatopoeia; palimpsest; papyrus; paradigm; parallelism; parchment; *paroimia; paronomasia;* pericope; personification; Peshitta; pointing; point of view; polyglot; principles of interpretation; proof texting; pun(s); "Q";

redaction; revelation, theological; rhetorical criticism; rhetorical devices; riddle; satire; scriptorium; *sebirin;* simile; similitude; source criticism; sources, primary and secondary; special points; strophe; superscription; symbol(s); synecdoche; syntax; synthetic parallelism; text; textual criticism; *tiggune sopherim;* Time Texts; Torah; translation; transposition; trope; type(s); typology; uncial(s); vellum; verbicide.

scriptorium: a room or space, perhaps a library, in which biblical scrolls and other documents are examined and copied. A scriptorium was discovered at Qumran and determined to be of great significance to the operations of the Essenes and other Dead Sea area copyists. Library space was critical to the many monk copyists and artists who preserved much of the ancient learning during the darkened Middle Ages. See also Dead Sea Scrolls; Essenes; lower criticism.

scroll(s): an ancient compilation of writing produced on parchment or another material wound around two sticks, one at each end. The material was normally made of papyrus and extended to about forty feet in length. In apocalyptic language, a scroll is often a vehicle to promote some eschatological expression (*i.e.,* Revelation 5–6 and 10). *See also* edible scrolls, the; little scroll, the; Megillot; scroll of Babylon's doom; scroll of remembrance; seven-sealed scroll, the.

scroll of Babylon's doom: a written prophecy entrusted to the high priest Seraiah, who was to carry the document into exile in Babylon and read it aloud to the people. After reading, the scroll was to be weighted and thrown into the Euphrates. The message attested to Babylon's eventual certain downfall and destruction (Jer. 51:59–64). *See also* scroll(s); Seraiah.

scroll of remembrance: a public recording of those persons who are faithful and righteous to the Lord (Mal. 3:16). The record seems to be the Old Testament equivalent of the Lamb's book of life in the New Testament since the document can take on an eschatological significance when used figuratively. *See also* book(s); book of life; Lamb's book of life; scroll(s).

scruples: a code of conduct that generates a finely tuned sense of conscience or a keen desire to "keep the rules." Usually, scrupulous people are overly sensitive to rigid behavior resulting in unfounded apprehension for what they fear is sinful but is not. Fastidious observation of religious laws is common. Let it be said, however, that people who favor at least the basic scruples of behavior may very well be the backbone of a moral society. *See also* cardinal virtues; conscience; deontology; ethics; exemplar motif; Judeo-Christian ethic; metathesis; moral relativism; normative ethics; orthopraxy; refined gold; social issues; way to heaven.

scrying: "seeing" or "peeping." Scrying involves staring into a translucent object with the objective of divination. Gazing into a crystal ball is a common fortune-telling technique and such distance viewing has been in practice through the ages. *See also* crystallomancy; divination; New Age religion; theurgy; Urim and Thummin.

Scythians: or Bactrians, barbarian hordes who once swept down on the Fertile Crescent around 628–626 B.C. Their point of origin may have been the northern steppes of the Black Sea and the Caucasus. The invasion must have been a shock to Israel and a cause or reason for Judah's effort of reformation under King Josiah; it may also be the background occasion for the writing of the book of Zephaniah (Zeph. 1:1–13; Jer. 6:22–26). In the Old Testament, the Scythians are referred to as the Ashkenazi, or Ashkenaz (Gen. 10:3; 1 Chr. 1:6; Jer. 51:27) and may bear some relation to the descendants of Gomer. They are also mentioned in Colossians 3:11 by which it is assumed some of them still existed. Most experts consider them to be the early inhabitants of the "stan" countries—Kazakhstan, Kyrgyzstan, Uzbekistan, Turkmenistan, Tajikistan, and possibly Afghanistan. The race seems to have developed into a type for all barbarians in general. *See also* Ashkenaz, Ashkenazi; barbarian(s); Gog and (of) Magog; Sephardim.

sea(s): 1. oceans or large bodies of salt water. In apocalyptic language, seas often represent multitudes, masses of humanity, or the restless confusion of society picturing the restless waves of the ocean. One of David's poems calls such awesome waters the "great deep" (Ps. 36:6). And, depending on the context, the sea may also identify a reservoir of evil out of which come horrible things (as in Daniel 7 and Revelation 13). For this reason, perhaps, there is no sea on the renewed earth at the end of the age (Rev. 21:1). Mythology taught that the sea and dragons were gods and that the turbulent waters teemed with demonic forces and monsters. The Israelites were not typically venturesome sailors. The sea may also be a barrier over which one must not pass; in that sense, the sea of glass before God's throne may represent His unapproachable holiness (Ex. 24:9–11; Rev. 4:6). 2. the great laver in Solomon's Temple was also called a "sea," perhaps because it held so much water. *See also* Behemoth; dragon(s); Leviathan; molten sea, the; Rahab; sea of glass; sea was no more; water(s).

Seabury, Samuel: an Anglican priest (1729–1796) who sought ordination in England so he could become a legitimate bishop of the Anglican colonies of the New World. No one would perform the ordination because Seabury refused to swear allegiance to the Crown. He was eventually consecrated by three Scottish bishops, and the English Church relaxed its policy of bishop qualifications for those destined for America. *See also* Anglicans; African Methodist Episcopal Church; clergy patriots; nonjurors; Protestant Episcopal Church.

sea kings: those princes or nations that engaged in expansive trade by sea with Tyre, according to their biblical descriptions.

seal(s): a fastener to a document (*chotam* in Hebrew), often using wax, into which is stamped the signet of the writer to assure no tampering with the contents could occur before it reached its authorized recipient. The book of Daniel is declared to be sealed and is only now being fully opened. Some go so far as to declare the sealed scroll held by the Lamb in Revelation 6 is actually the book of Daniel. A seal could bear witness to the identity and ownership of the sender and was not to be opened except by the one to whom it was addressed with the authority to do so. An analogy to the process is found in Job 38:14. In Revelation, the first series of woes consists of seven seals affixed to a scroll that are broken one-by-one by the Lamb. It is no surprise that the book of Revelation, a book of revealing in essence, supplies nearly one-third of its content in the breaking of seals. Jesus Christ is the only worthy one authorized by his status and righteousness to crack them. Each issue of the snapped seals unleashes some portion of God's wrath on Tribulation earth. They consist of the following: the four horsemen of the apocalypse, a view of the souls under the altar, an Armageddon-like experience, and a final seal that merely evolves into the first of the seven trumpets. One interpretation, perhaps a rather sound one, sees the sixth seal as a direct response to the plea of the slain souls under the altar for justice and a recounting of the final Armageddon battle. The follow-on trumpets and bowls sequences are parallel but complementary visions also leading to the end. *See also* bowl(s); bull; *bulla;* eschatology, eschatological; four horsemen of the Apocalypse; letter(s); mark of Cain; Olivet Discourse, the; 144,000, the; sealed words of Daniel; seal of God; seal of Zion; signet ring; *sigillum;* Spirit of glory and of God; thunder revelations; Tribulation; trumpet(s).

sealed words of Daniel: God's instructions to Daniel (Dan. 12:4) to "seal up" (secure or segregate in secrecy) his prophecy until the time of the end. It is reasonable to assume that Revelation and subsequent eschatological insights are the progressive "unsealing" or revealing of those oracles, along with other mysteries of God. *See also* Daniel as Old Testament prophecy; seal(s); seal up vision and prophecy.

seal of God: a mark of the living God by which divine protection is experienced in Revelation 7:1–8. What the seal might be precisely, is a matter of conjecture; neither is there certainty if the seal is visible or concealed. In other references of the New Testament, the seal of God is the protection and affiliation of the Holy Spirit with the believer, so perhaps the Revelation 7 action is the same. Some speculate that the sealing is baptism, although baptism is not mentioned in Revelation. Another similar sealing occurred in one of Ezekiel's visions (Ezk. 9:3–4) when the prophet observed a scribe marking the foreheads of the few faithful left in Jerusalem during the Babylonian Exile. The mark prevented the deaths of these faithful, but all others were destroyed. Something similar is noted in Haggai 2:23 when the Judean governor Zerubbabel was said to be God's signet ring, suggestive that the man and his talents belonged to God. The ordinance of baptism may somehow be involved in the sealing metaphor in certain instances. The seal of protection by God is a common enough theme in Scripture. We see the action as early as Genesis (the seal of Cain from vigilante justice of Genesis 4:15) to one of several noted as the last in Revelation, including the one that preserves the 144,000 evangelists. Others include Noah amidst the great flood, Rahab in besieged Jericho, Elijah the prophet, Jerusalem under Hezekiah and Isaiah, the deliverance of Elisha and Samaria from the Arameans, Moses in the Nile, the Passover and Red Sea Israelites in captive Egypt, the preservation of Daniel and his friends, Jonah in the sea creature, Job when convoluted with despair, Israel in the wilderness wanderings, Esther and her people in Persia, the holy family's escape to Egypt in defiance of Herod, the promise to Philadelphia among the seven churches, the protection of the two super witnesses of Revelation, Obadiah's 100 protected prophets (1 Ki. 18:4), God's promise to preserve the remnant of Israel, and many others. *See also* baptism; names (titles) for the Holy Spirit; 144,000, the; seal(s); seal of Zion; signet ring; six destroying warriors; Spirit of glory and of God.

seal of Zion: a mark of God's protection over Jerusalem, a phrase exclusive to the apocryphal writings. Such security was subject to withdrawal by God at any time. *See also* seal(s); seal of God.

seal up vision and prophecy: one of the six great proposals of God before He announces total victory over evil. In these times, we depend on preaching, study, and prophetic utterance (including dreams and visions), among other methods, to learn God's will for our lives. Someday, God will write His goodness "on our hearts" to the extent that we will need no external learning aids to know God and His righteousness. As some have phrased it: there will be no need for more expositions, for all will have been fulfilled. *See also* Big Six Clauses, the; anoint the most holy; atone for wickedness; end sin; eschatology, eschatological; finish transgression; inaugurate eternal righteousness; New Covenant, the; prophecy; sealed words of Daniel.

sea monster. See beast from the sea; Behemoth; Leviathan; Rahab.

séance: a necromancy or fortune-telling ritual designed to contact departed spirits, usually performed with a group. Fakery is common in the exercise, wherever it may be practiced. *See also* attending spirit(s); Fox sisters; Houdini, Harry; magic, magick; medium; meonenim; mystagogue; necromancy; paranormal; psychic(s); spirit guide(s); spiritism; Spiritualist churches; tutelary; witch of Endor.

Sea of Arabah. See Dead Sea.

Sea of Faith: a movement from 1984 described by Don Capitt. The idea is that faith is a human conviction only and not real. The name comes from a poem by Matthew Arnold entitled "Dover Beach"in which the author described faith as "slipping away"like the ebb tide. *See also* cult(s).

sea of glass: the appearance of a translucent threshold before the throne of God, or as a support for it, in Revelation 4:6. The presence of such a construct seems to represent God's unapproachable holiness. Exodus 24:9–11 also describes a sea of glass (*lapis lazuli*) at Mount Sinai as seen by Moses, the priests, and seventy elders of Israel that appears to represent the same idea of holy sanctity. Ezekiel 1:22 mentions a vast expanse above the chariot of God resembling ice. The *Qur'an* relates a charming incident when the queen of Sheba lifted her skirts to cross the glass threshold of Solomon's throne, thinking it was water. Revelation 15:3 speaks of the sea of glass as being mingled with fire, an undoubted reference to judgment. Some apocalypticists could not but notice the aftermath at ground zero from the first test-firing of an atomic bomb (called "Trinity") formed the silica of the desert sand into a sea of glass for eight hundred yards in all directions. *See also lapis lazuli;* sea(s); sea was no more; sapphire (emerald) throne; throne in heaven with someone sitting on it, a; water(s).

Sea of Reeds. See Red Sea.

sea peoples. See Philistia, Philistines.

seated at the feet: the early accepted body posture of a penitent in the presence of the confessor. The private audience of a confessional booth did not appear until the Council of Trent in the 16th century. To sit at the feet was also the proper and traditional position of a student before his teacher in biblical times. *See also* confession; Confiteor; confessor(s); gesture(s); *sigillum.*

sea was no more: a feature of the renewed earth wherein there are no oceans. Since seas usually depict confusion, separation, or masses of troubled humanity in apocalyptic language, it is logical to see their absence, in that sense, in the new age (Rev. 21:1). That symbolic application, however, does not exclude the possibility that the new world will hold literal expansive bodies of salt or fresh lakes, rivers, springs, and other sources of recreational and potable water. *See also* eschatology, eschatological; new heaven and new earth; sea(s).

Seba, Sabeans: the land of the Sudan or northern Ethiopia (Ps. 72:10; Isa. 43:3). The inhabitants were known as Sabeans, a wealthy, handsome race. The people were acknowledged as a cultured race situated in southwest Arabia. They occupy prophetic importance because they are someday to acknowledge Yahweh (Isa. 45:14). *See also* Arabia.

Sebastenians: the Roman garrison stationed in Caesarea at the time of Jesus and Pontius Pilate. It consisted of no more than 3,500 Greek mercenaries, the remainder of King Herod's force; they were not elite Roman troops. Consequently, Pilate had reason to be cautious when dealing with Jewish religious authorities since the residents of Jerusalem alone could have probably overwhelmed the soldiers in the city if angered enough; the real threat came from reinforcements in nearby Antioch where there was an Italian cohort consisting of about 400,000 veterans. *See also* centurion(s); Cornelius; Imperial Regiment, the; Italian Regiment, the; Julius; legion; Longinus; Pilate, Pontius; Praetorian Guard; Roman Empire; tribune.

Sebasterion: the so-called "temple of the holy ones" in ancient Aphrodisias near Ephesus. It may hold a reference to Satan's throne mentioned in Revelation. The site was a lavish and huge construct, some three stories in height. The city itself was based on the worship of Aphrodite, considered to be the divine protector of the metropolis. *See also* Aphrodite; Roman Empire; Satan's throne; temple(s); Venus; where Satan has his throne.

sebirin: a point of lower criticism in which a marginal note is supplied for an unusual or uncertain word or phrase in the biblical text. There are about 3,500 in different manuscripts in which they occur. *See also* accideme; alliteration; apostrophe; apothegm; assonance; autograph; Bible; Bible manuscripts; Bible translations; biblical criticism; chiasmus; conflict story; *constructio ad sensum;* context; contextualization; dittography; double sense fulfillment; doublets; doubling; edification; eisegesis; epanadiplosis; epigrammatic statements; etymology; exegesis; figure of speech; folio; form criticism; gattung; gloss; gnomic sayings; grammatical-historical interpretation; *hapax legomena;* haplography; hermeneutic(s); higher criticism; homographs; homonyms; homophones; *homoteleuton;* hyperbole; idiom; *inclusio;* interpolation; interpretation; inverted nun; irony; isagogics; *itture sopherim;* jot and tittle; kere; *kethib;* "L"; liberalists interpretation; literal interpretation; litotes; loan words; lower criticism; "M"; Masoretic Text; minuscule(s); mystery of God; omission; onomastica; onomatopoeia; palimpsest; papyrus; paradigm; parallelism; parchment; *paroimia; paronomasia;* pericope; personification; Peshitta; pointing; point of view; polyglot; principles of interpretation; proof texting; pun(s); "Q"; redaction; revelation, theological; rhetorical criticism; rhetorical devices; riddle; satire; *scripto continua;* scriptorium; simile; similitude; source criticism; sources, primary and secondary; special points; strophe; superscription; symbol(s); synecdoche; syntax; synthetic parallelism; text; textual criticism; *tiggune sopherim;* Time Texts; Torah; translation; transposition; trope; type(s); typology; uncial(s); vellum; verbicide.

Secchi, Pietro: *nee* Reggio nell'Emilia (1818–1910), an Italian astrophysicists and a Jesuit. He specialized in spectroscopic studies and was the first to suggest stars could be surveyed and classed by their spectra. *See also* clergy scientists; Society of Jesus; star(s).

Second Adam, the: a New Testament reference to Jesus Christ as our redeemer (Rom. 5:12–19; 1 Cor. 15:22, 45). In the paradigms, Paul compares the first Adam whose disobedience brought sin and death into the world with Christ who took it away. Jesus was also a man in his earthly sojourn, but unlike the first Adam, he did not yield to sin and thus qualified himself to be the world's redeemer—a second (and better) Adam. The phrase essentially declares Christ's role as federal head of the human race. His obedience to the Father renders his people righteous in the eyes of God. *See also* Adam; Eve; covenant of grace; covenant of works; names (titles) for Jesus; Second Eve, the.

Second Advent. See Second Coming.

second blessing, a. See glossolalia.

Second Coming: the anticipated return of Jesus Christ to earth in great glory. That grand event is mentioned by Jesus himself (forty-six times), by Paul (forty-nine times), by Peter (eight times), by John (six times), by James (three times), by Jude (one time), by Hebrews (two times) and by the angels at Jesus' ascension noting the promise of his return. In fact, for every verse about the First Advent, there are eight about the Second. The Old Testament records more than 1,500 references to the Messiah's return. Isaiah described the event, or his prayer that something like it would transpire, as "ripping the heavens" (Isa. 64:1-8). There are more than 300 references to the Second Coming in the New Testament—one out of every thirty verses. Jesus refers to his own return about twenty-four times. Of the Bible's 333 prophecies concerning the Messiah or Christ, only 109 were fulfilled with his first appearing; the rest await fulfillment in the second. For every prophecy in Scripture about Christ's first coming, there are eight featuring his return. With him will come the saints of heaven and the angelic hosts. He will set foot on the very mountain from which he departed, Mount Olivet. At that time, Satan, the Antichrist, the False Prophet, and all their wicked followers will have been defeated at Armageddon. Christ will then inaugurate his millennial kingdom, according to most conservative scholars. Perhaps Jesus himself best described his reappearance near the end of his earthly ministry: "In a little while you will see me no more, and then after a little while you will see me" (Jn. 16:16). The Second Coming is also termed the Second Advent, the Glorious Appearing, and the *Parousia*. *See also* advent(s) of Christ; appearing, the; appointed time, the; consummation, the final; day he visits us, the; day of God, the; Day of the Lamb's Wrath, the; day of the Lord; day of vengeance of our Lord; Day, that (the); *elthnen;* eschatology, eschatological; eschaton; Evangelical Alliance; Glorious Appearing; great and dreadful day, that; "here, there, or in the air"; "I am coming quickly"; *Parousia;* prophecy; rapture; rider on the white horse; Second Coming procession; termination dates; "until he comes"; worldwide preaching of the gospel.

Second Coming procession: an attempt to precisely trace the process of Christ's Second Coming. The theory encompasses a three-stage process: (1) Jesus or his eschatological sign will appear across the sky for all to see (Rev. 1:7), (2) he is next to pass through Edom, that is, modern Jordan (Isa. 63:1–6; Hab. 3:3–16), (3) the conclusion is a march to Jerusalem and the Mount of Olives (Ps. 24:7–10; Zech. 14:4; Rev. 19:17–21). Objections are easily surfaced since the time sequence of the Second Coming is difficult to discern from scattered scriptural references. Also, the passage from Zechariah implies a hard step on the Mount of Olives to split the mountain—not a casual stroll up the hill. *See also* eschatology, eschatological; Second Coming.

Second Coming Project, the: a hoax perpetrated by a group of eccentrics who claimed to have formed a not-for-profit organization designed to clone Jesus and bring him back to earth via DNA manipulation. The intent was to compel his appearance near the 2,000th anniversary of his nativity because we need him. The plan was to obtain an uncorrupted cell from the many blood relics of Jesus around the world, extracting its DNA, and inserting it into a human oocyte using nuclear transfer. The zygote would then be implanted into a virginal woman volunteer who was to give birth around December 25. The story made news for a time but who is to say it cannot or will not be done at some point? Hollywood movies and ego-mad scientists are already trailblazing the event.

second death, the. See death, the second.

Second Ecumenical Council: the Eastern Orthodox meeting in A.D. 381 with 150 bishops in attendance (also known as the Second Council of Constantinople). Among other discussions (mostly regarding Arianism and Macedonism), the delegates condemned chiliasm (millennialism) as a superstitious aberration. *See also* Councils of Constantinople; Eastern Orthodox Church; Macedonius; Millennium, millennial.

Second Eve, the: a concept of Roman Catholicism that sees Mary, the mother of Jesus, as the second Eve or lifegiver. The devotion functions as a quality of Mariolatry, with the hope that she will succeed where the first Eve in Eden failed because of humanity's personal and corporate sin. *See also* co-redemptrix; Eve; Marianist; Mariolatry; Mary; Mary Mother of God, Feast of; Our Lady of the Angels; queen of heaven; Roman Catholic Church; Second Adam, the.

second Exodus: or Exodus II, a more contemporary description of the Jewish remnant who are to enter the millennial age following the Second Coming of Christ. The depiction naturally evolves from the Israelite Exodus from Egypt under Moses; it can be interpreted as a crucial typical event (a type) for a similar one in the future. *See also* age of redemption; blindness of Israel;

curses of Isaiah; elect, the; eschatology, eschatological; Exodus II; Judaism; remnant; restoration of Israel (the Jews); seed of Israel; Shear-Jashub; spiritual Israel.

Second Great Awakening. See Great Awakenings, the.

second probation: the belief that non-believers will have a second chance for repentance after death. The concept is considered untenable and cultic by most orthodox Christian interpretations. *See also* great white throne judgment.

second resurrection, the. See resurrection, the second.

second sight: an uncanny psychic anticipation, usually concerning the imminent appearance of unscheduled visitors. Many cultures, in fact, retain folk names for such a precognitive trait. *See also* precognition; prediction; premonition; seventh sense; sixth sense; thoughtform.

second work of grace: a belief in some Christian circles that God may choose to execute a second great soul miracle or spiritual experience in one's life subsequent to salvation (counted as the first). John Wesley, among many others, taught the doctrine as does most of Pentecostalism today. What the second manifestation is, exactly, is broadly determined and individualized but usually involves a spiritual renewal or rejuvenation of some description. Some holiness preachers insist God can, and does, manifest an act of sanctification instantaneously as a life-changing experience in some individuals that could conceivably achieve sanctification (perceived as perfection). *See also* glorification; henosis; holiness; holiness movement; holy; holy and true; Holy Club, the; Palamism; perfectionism; sanctification; theosis.

Secreta. See *super oblata.*

Secret Chiefs. See Great White Brotherhood; Shambhala legends.

secret name, the: a key to the great oath of heaven that caused all of Paradise to tremble because of its sublime power. Such a talisman is mentioned only in the pseudepigraphal literature. *See also* Akae; Beqa; 'Emeth; Kesbul; "sign, the."

secret rapture: a landmark belief of dispensationalism. When Christ calls up his Church, the living and the dead, the occasion will be so swift and so unexpected that the event is sometimes called "secret." Some early followers of the doctrine believed that the rapture would be a secret event in that it would happen, but no one left would be aware. Most everyone has since abandoned that idea. *See also* blessed hope, the; eschatology, eschatological; rapture; translation.

secret societies: a collection of shadowy organizations, both past and present, and/or their esoteric doctrines. Often they are occultic and oligarchical in structure. There have been, and are, many such associations, but perhaps the most well-known are the Freemasons, the Rosicrucians, and the Knights Templar. More modern renditions include the Bilderberg Group, the Council on Foreign Relations, Bavarian Grove, The Group, the Trilateral Commission, Round Table, Skull and Crossbones Society, present-day Gnosticism, the Rite of Swedenborg, Royal Institute of International Affairs, and others. *See also* assassin(s); *Atlia Vendita;* Bilderberg Group; Bohemian Grove; Brethren of Light, The; Brotherhood of the Union; cantrip; conspiracy theorists; Crowley, Aleister; Damanhur; *Da Vinci Code, The;* Dionysian Artificers; "Dionysian Artificers, The"; fraternal organization(s); Gnosticism, Gnostic(s); Grand Design; Great White Brotherhood, the; grimoire; Freemasonry; Hashshashin; Hermeticism; Holy Grail; Illuminati; Illuminati Tyrant; John Birch Society; knighted orders; Mafia; magic arts; magic, magick; *mana;* mantic wisdom; mystery religion(s); Neo-Platonism; occult, occultic; *omerta;* Order of the Rosy Cross; *Ordo Templi Orientis;* Priory of Sion; Roman Phalanx; Rosicrucianism; secret wisdom; sect(s); Skull and Bones Society; spell names; *Spiritas Mundi;* synagogue of Satan; Thugs; Triads; underworld; Yakuza; Yeats, William Butler.

secret things of God. See mystery of God.

secret wisdom: wisdom from the Spirit of God as opposed to human intellect (1 Cor. 2:6–16). Paul termed the wisdom of God as "secret" or hidden since before time began. Now, however, it is being disclosed in Christ by the proclamation of the gospel and the power of prophecy—that very hope the prophets envisioned. By the influence of the Holy Spirit, God is able to impart spiritual truths, noted in the same context as "deep things from God," with spiritual terms to spiritual persons. Paganism also has a place for secret wisdom; in fact, it is central to the belief system that relies on the hierarchy knowing something the ordinary person does not know. Knowledge, reasonable or not, is power. *See also* Agrippa Books; alchemy; *arcanum arcandrum; Arcanum,* the; *Book of Abramelin, The;* cantrip; *Corpus Hermecticum; Da Vinci Code, The;* deep, the; deep things of God, the; Dionysian Artificers; deep things of God; *disciplina arcane;* dot within a circle; Emerald Tablet of Hermes, the; esoteric; esotericism; Gnosticism, Gnostic(s); *Golden Bough, The;* grimoire; Hermeticism; Hermetic wisdom; Hermetic writings; *Holy Blood, Holy Grail;* Holy Grail; magic arts; magic, magick; *mana;* mantic wisdom; mystery; mystical; mystery of God; mystery religion(s); occult, occultic; parapsychology; *Picatrix;* secret name, the; *Sophia;* spell; spell names; *Spiritas Mundi;* wisdom.

sect(s): an unconventional group of religious activists that usually holds doctrine outside of normal or orthodox Christian beliefs. Many feature apocalyptic themes. Some sociologists prefer to distinguish a sect from a cult if the former has a relatively long history or has managed consistent growth to some extent. A common distinction is that a sect has become an offshoot or radical branch of a more established or larger religious organ. That origin, however, is not always factual. At one point, the Christian faith was called a sect by its enemies (Acts 24:14). A sect may also be defined as a secular group in proper context. Or, if appropriate to its setting, a sect may be any religious organization. Frequently, the terms *cult* and *sect* are used interchangeably and are considered proper form. The period in and around the time of the civil war in England, (during the tumult of the Cromwellian revolt) seemed to produce a hotbed of small and radical sects including: 1. Adamites– an older cult with periodic revivals, which was antinomian and patterned on the innocence of Adam and Eve, even resorting to reveling and public nudity, 2. Antinomians– having no use and seeing no function for man-made laws in the land, 3. Behmenists– followers of the German mystic Jakob Bohme, most of whom seem to have been absorbed into the Quakers, Philadelphians, Gichtelians ("Brethren of the Angels"), New Harmony Community of Equality, Ephrata Cloister, Martinism, the Woman in the Wilderness society, and Christian Theosophy,

4. Diggers– Protestant agrarian socialist movement that tried to farm on common land, 5. Levellers– a political movement seeking religious grounds for universal suffrage, equality, and religious tolerance, 6. Ranters– a pantheistic, amoralist group of the antinomian persuasion, 7. Seekers– Legantine-Arians formed by three brothers Walter, Thomas, and Bartholomew Legate which was non-denominational, millennial, and anti-Trinitarian, 8. Soul Sleepers– believers that the soul is uncomprehending between death and judgment, 9. Muggletonians– a Protestant movement from two tailors named Muggleton, who claimed to be the two final witnesses in Revelation and were anti-evangelical, asserted the earth means nothing to God until He judges it, and prone to place curses on opponents, 10. various groups of Anabaptists, Seventh-Day Baptists, General Baptists, and many other brands. *See also* Adelphi Organization; Adamites; aikido; Aina religion; Akashic Records; Aladura; Albigenses; *Alpha Ovule;* Amyraldism; Anabaptists; ancestor reverence; Andreae, Johann Valentinus; Anglo-Israelism; animism; Anthropocentric Anti-Trinitarian churches; Anthroposophical Society; Ariosophy; Armstrong, Herbert W.; Asatru; Ascended Masters; Association for Research and Enlightenment; Astara; Badimo; Baha'i International; Basilideans; Besant, Annie; Bhakti; Blavatsky, Madame Helena Petrovna; Bod; Bon; Brahma Kumari; Brahmanism; Brethren of the Light; Brotherhood of Satan; Brotherhood of the Union; Brownsville Assembly; Buddhism; Burning Man Festival; Cainites; Camisards; Caodaism; Carpocratians; cargo cult(s); Catharists; Cathars; Catholic Apostolic Church; Cayce, Edgar; Cheonodoism; Chi; Chondogwan; Chopra Center; Chopra Center; Chrislam; Christadelphians; Christian Identity Movement (CIM); Christian Israelite Church; church bodies in America (typed); Church of Christ, Scientist; Church of Christ, Temple Lot; Church of Jesus Christ of Latter-Day Saints, the; Church of Satan; Church of the Firstborn; communal communities; Community of Christ (Mormon); Confucius, Confucianism; contemplative prayer movement; Convolution of Aries; Cosmerism; Council of Nine; Creativity Movement; Creole (Caribbean) religion; cult(s); Cult of the Supreme Being; Daejonggyo; Daesun Jinrihoe; Damanhur; Day of the Dead; deism; Dionysian Artificers; Divine Science, Church of; Donatism; Druidism; Druze; Dukhobors; Dunkards; Eddy, Mary

Baker; egocentric cults; Elian Gonzales Religious Movement; Emergent Church; Encratites; enneagram; Ephrata Cloister; Essenes; Euchite; *Falun Gong;* Fifth Monarchy Men; Finley, Robert; Five Percent Nation; firewalking; Flagellants; Flat Earth Society; Fourth Way, the; Fox, George; full gospel; Gichtelians; Gnosticism, Gnostic(s); Gurdjieff; Haile Selassie; Hellenistic Reconstructionism; Hellfire Club; Herodians; Hetrousians; Hinduism; Hoahaoism; Huguenots; Humanist Society; Human Potential Movement; Huna; Hussites; Illuminati; Indian Shaker Movement; Inner Light churches; Islam; Jainism; Janenism; Jehovah's Witnesses; Jesuism; Jeungsanism; John Frum religion; Jeungsanism; Johannite Church; Jehovah's Witnesses; Jonadabs; Juche; Karaites; Kalachakra Tantra; Katharoi; Kemeticism; Kimbang; Kirant; Kopimism; Kulam; labyrinth walk; Lee, Ann; Mandaeanism; Mani; Manicheanism; Manifest Sons of God; Marcosians; Mari; Marianists; Mar Thoma Church; Martinism; *Meher Baba;* Mennonites; Messianic Jews; Millennial churches; Millerites; Miller, William; mind science; Minim; Mithraism; Modekngei; monasticism; Moorish Science Temple of America; Moral Rearmament Movement; Moravian Church; Mugyo; Muhammad Ibn Abdul Wahhab; Mun; Muti; mystery religion(s); Nation of Islam; Native American Church; nature cult(s); *Neturei Karta;* New Age religion; new religious movement(s); New Thought Movement; Nichiren Buddhism; Nicolaitans; Novatian, Novatians; Odinism; Oecumenical Orthodoxy; Old Catholic Church; Oomoto; Ophites; Order of Perfectibilists; Order of the Rosy Cross; orders; Orphic religion; Pack, David C.; Panacea Society, the; parody religions; Parsees; Paulicianism; Pennsylvania Dutch; Peratae; Pharisees; Philadelphians; *Piagnoni;* Pietism, Pietists; Pilgrim(s); Pneumatomachi; prosperity religion(s); Qabbala; Quarmatians; Radhasoami Satsang; Rainbow Coalition; Ravidassia; Religious Science; Roganists; Rosicrucianism; Russell, Charles Taze; Rutherford, J. F.; Sadducees; Sanamahism; Sandemanianism; Sant Mat; Satanism; Schwarzenau Brethren; Schwenkfelders; scribe(s); secret societies; secular humanism; seior; Sethianism; Seventh-Day Adventism; Shakti; Shi'ite Islam; Shinto; Sibyl(s); Sikhism; Skull and Bones Society; Slocum, John; Smith, Joseph Jr. ; snake handling; Socinians, Socianism; Soka Gakkai International (SGI); Solara; Stiefel Freethought Foundation; Subud; Summum;

Sunni Islam; Swedenborg, Emanuel; Swedenborgianism; Syrian Orthodox Church; Tantric Buddhism; Taoism; Tatian; Tenrikyo; Theosophical Society; Theosophy; Therapeutae; Therapeutate; Theravada Buddhism; Thugs; Thule Society; Transcendental Meditation (TM); 24/7 Prayer Movement; Ultraquists; Unitarian Universalists; Unity Church; Universal Life Church; Urantia Foundation; Vendanta Society; Watch Tower Bible and Tract Society; Web-Bot; Wiener, Norbert; Westboro Baptist Church; Whirling Dervishes; White Buffalo Calf Woman; White, Ellen G. (Hamon); World Pantheist Movement; Worldwide Church of God; Wotanism; Wroe, John; Yakuza; Yama; *ya sang;* Yezidism; Yiguandao; Young, Brigham; Young-Earth Creationist Movement; Zionism; Zionites; Zoroaster, Zoroastrianism; *zos kia* cultus.

Secular Babylon: the derived name for the political portion of Babylon the Great, mostly described in Revelation 18–19. Commercial Babylon is an alternative title for the same entity. Wealth and corruption are its hallmarks. It should be remembered that when nations trade goods and services, they also export ideas, values, behaviors, and morals, which may or may not be compatible with righteous standards. The enterprise is destined for destruction at the end of days by God Himself. *See also* angel of Babylon's fall; Babylon the Great; city of power; desolate and naked; eschatology, eschatological; filth of her adulteries; "glorified herself"; great city, this; haunt (prison) for every unclean and detestable bird; merchant(s); Mystery Babylon the Great the Mother of Prostitutes and of the Abominations of the Earth; Religious Babylon; smoke of her burning; song of the harlot; wine of her adulteries.

secular humanism: probably the most popularly held belief of the present age, so much so that it was declared a religion by the United States Supreme Court. The properties of secularism are not to be confused with the humanist movement of the 15th century though both might be called philosophies of religion and sociology. Modern practice attempts to promote a better life through human self-effort, applied science, and improved political and social arrangements. The philosophy of such beliefs stems from a wide variety of mindsets from Marx to Freudian psychology to New Age thinking, but all aspects imply that human behavior can be defined in purely this-worldly terms with no reference to God. *See also* church decline; cultural relativism; culture war; human condition, the; humanism; Humanist Society; human nature; philosophy of religion; relativism; sect(s); social issues; sociology of religion.

secular institutes: a Roman Catholic initiative for the education of secular priests. The schools enroll consecrated individuals who are not ordained priests and not living in structured communities. These chosen concentrate on charity, chastity, and obedience since they were allowed by canon law in 1964. They have their own training centers (like Howden College) and incardinate their own membership (like the Schoenstatt fathers or the Institute of the Maids of the Poor in India). Protestants have a similar program in their Bible Colleges and courses open to ordained and non-ordained students. Alternate names for the training centers include Institutes of the Consecrated Life, Religious Institutes, Societies of the Apostolic Life, or Vocational Discernment in the Catholic Church. *See also* religious education; religious organizations; Roman Catholic Church.

secularization: sometimes modernism, or rarely sacralization, a relatively contemporary term to describe the usually adverse reaction to religion by the general public. Some have claimed secularization has already killed such cherished doctrines as hell, purgatory (for Roman Catholics), and even heaven. Today's retort by the unbelieving masses is often polite indifference. Many ecclesiologists blame the trend as the reason for low worship attendance almost everywhere. Certainly, that is a cause but hardly the only hindrance to religious attention. By way of illustration, organized religion's response is often overcorrection. Pope Paul VI defied the secularist influence during his tenure by reaffirming clergy celibacy, disapproval of contraceptive measures, feminism, homosexuality, the too-long delay in answering priest sexual abuse and its cover-up, and other issues. Today, the debate seems to be centered on newer issues like global climate change, marriage standards, and corporate greed. The process is such that there remains but little distinction between religious and secular institutions. All rituals, mores, and cultures seem to be fused until the unique religious contributions have virtually dissolved in many instances. *See also* Catholic Church abuse scandal; church decline; metaphysics; modernism; postmodernism; social issues; theism; Zionism.

secular Zionism. See Zionism.

Secundus: a traveling companion of Paul from Thessalonica (Acts 20:4). He and his fellow missionaries were sent ahead of Paul to Troas to prepare for a possible evangelistic campaign there. *See also* missions, missionaries.

Seder: the Jewish commemoration of Passover. At the Passover meal (*Seder* means "set order"), the accompanying traditions, the pronouncements of the season, and all other activities of the celebration constitute the *Seder.* There are fifteen divisions to the traditional service: (1) *Kadush–* the blessing or sanctification, (2) *Urechatz–* ritual washing without a blessing, (3) *Karpas–* vegetables (usually dipping parsley in salt water to resemble tears), (4) *Yachatz–* breaking of matzahs, (5) *Maggid–* the story of the Passover recited, (6) *Rachtzah–* a second washing, this time with a blessing, (7) *Motzi–* two prayers of blessing for the matzah, (8) *Matzah–* eating a bit of the matzah, (9) *Maror–* bitter herbs, a blessing of herbs (usually horseradish to symbolize the bitterness of slavery, (10) *Koresh–* "the sandwich," eating matzah and moror, (11) Shulchan Orekh– dining with family and friends, enjoying the fellowship and the traditional foods, (12) *Tzafun–* hiding of the afikomen, (13) *Berekh–* grace after the meal, 14) *Hallel–* praises, 15) *Nirtzah–* the closing with a prayer that the next Passover will be in Jerusalem or that the Messiah will come this year. The traditional foods are objectified on the *k'arah,* the ceremonial plate sectioned off to hold the representative elements of the ceremony: (1) *baytzah* (a roasted egg that is either a fertility symbol or expression of sorrow for the loss of two temples), (2) *charoset* ("clay," made of apples, cinnamon, nuts, honey, and wine representing brick mortar, (3) *charoset* (for the "Hillel sandwich" of matzah and *moror*)—an optional item, (4) *korpas* (green vegetables for sorrow), (5) *moror* (bitter herbs symbolizing the pain of slavery), (6) *zervoa* (the shank bone of a lamb for the Paschal sheep)—a reminder of the tenth plague on Egypt. Some homes add a small bowl of salt water to remind the diners of the tears shed by the slaves and of the Red Sea through which they passed. Other foods are permissible for the meal where the afikomen (dessert) and wine (at least four cups are drunk in ritual alone) are essential. *See also* Elijah's chair; feasts and special days of Judaism; "four cups, the"; "four nights, the"; "four questions, the"; Four Species, the; Judaism; liturgy, Jewish; "next year in Jerusalem"; Paschal; Paschal lamb; Passover; Unleavened Bread, Feast of; wine.

Seder Olam: also called "The Great Order of the World," the *Ancient Seder Olam,* and the *Seder Olam Rabbah.* The work is said to be around 2,000 years old in its original form from the second century and is written in Hebrew. The text details and dates biblical events from the creation to the time of Alexander the Great. Tradition says that the author was Yose ben Halafta. Subsequent additions carry the history to the bar Kokhba revolt under the emperor Hadrian. *See also* Judaism.

Sedevacantists: a Latin derivative meaning "the seat being vacant." The Sedevacantists are a dissident group of Roman Catholic priests who claim that those popes following the compromising spirit of Vatican II are antipopes or that the chair of Saint Peter is unoccupied. Some date the absence of a true pope since Pius XII (1958) or John XXIII (1963). *See also* Roman Catholic Church.

see: the geographic jurisdiction of a bishop of the Roman Catholic Church with a similar designation for Episcopalian, Anglican, and Greek Orthodox (such as a pentarchy) authority. The Holy See or Apostolic See is the central governing seat for the Vatican. *See also* church field; cure; diocese; eparchy; episcopate; fold; katholikon; ministry; missions, missionaries; parish; patriarchate(s); pentarchy; presbytery; Roman Catholic Church; titular sees; Vatican, the.

seed of Abraham. See Abraham's seed.

seed of Israel: descendants of Israel, the generations of Jews perhaps started around 2000 B.C. and destined to be ever persecuted but never annihilated. A seed is the pod or ovum containing the genesis of life and capable of growth after planting and cultivation. So, with God's people, a mighty offspring was promised through Abraham. David was also promised a perpetual lineage and that was not limited to his son Solomon, nor even to the followers of the Messiah Jesus who was in the line of David. *See also* Abraham's seed; Jew(s); Judaism; remnant; second Exodus; Seed, the.

seed of the serpent: Lucifer. Satan's evil influence throughout all of his history has been pronounced upon the world. *See also* dragon; Light-Bringer; Lucifer; Morning Star, the; red dragon; serpent; serpent seed doctrine, the.

Seed, the: a title for the promised Messiah whom the Law has foretold—a pledge so potent that it was affected by angels (Gal. 3:19; Heb. 2:2–4). Moreover, the guarantee of the coming Savior was often accompanied by signs and wonders in many descriptions. The apocalyptic flavor of the name is obvious since this "Seed" will flower to ultimate victory in the coming age of glory. *See also* Abraham's seed; names (titles) for Jesus; seed of Israel; Messiah.

Seeker: 1. one who professes Christianity but claims no official sect affiliation. 2. one who endeavors to find truth and satisfaction in religion, a suitable identifier, until she discovers it. 3. a believer who holds basic doctrine but endeavors to delve into deeper knowledge.

Seelie Court, Unseelie Court: pronounced SHEE, a classification of the fairies and creatures of Celtic folklore as either benevolent or unfriendly. The designation may derive from an early Celtic world for "silly" but the Seelie came to stand for "happy" and the Unseelie for "unhappy." The Seelie were considered the aristocrats of faerie, the judges and administrators. Their group was made up of political factions, like any other court, and full of intrigue. They were, however, fond of humans and were labeled the "blessed ones" of light. The Unseelie were the "unblessed ones," malevolent faerie and monsters of darkness bent on evil. They hated humans and were prone to kidnap them to be part of their hosts since they could not reproduce their kind. Within the set were sluagh—hosts of unforgiven dead akin to those told about in stories of the Wild Hunt. Shellycoat was a Trickster of the coastline. Redcap wore his cap drenched in human blood. *See also* attending spirit(s); banshee; bogle; brownies; bugbears; Celtic folklore and religion; clurichauns; daemons; deceiving spirits; demon(s), demonic; devils; disa; dryad(s); elemental(s); fairy, fairies; Furies; ghost(s); ghoul; gnome(s); Green Man, the; Gregori; hobgoblins; homunculus; household deities; huldafolk; Lares; leprechaun(s); Loa Loas; Manes; mythological beasties, elementals, monsters, and spirit animals; nereid; nisse; nymph(s); nyx; Oniropompi; Orisha; Oya; para; paredri; penates; Robin Goodfellow; satyr; selkie; Sidhe; siren(s); spiritual warfare; sprite(s); sylph(s); teraphim; territorial spirits; Trickster; Tuatha de Danann; tutelary; undine; wight(s).

Sefer Torah. See Torah Scroll.

Sefirot: a mystical design said to picture God's ten emanations according to Qabbalist lore. *See also* Aqiba, Rabbi Joseph ben; Bible Code; Cheiro; emanations, doctrine of; *gematria;* Haggada; Halakha; Husk(s); *isopseplia;* Kaduri, Rabbi Yitzchak; Lux; Masseket Hekalot; Noor, noor; *notarikon;* primal light; Qabbala; seventy-two; *temoorah;* Zevi, Shabbatai; *Zohar.*

Segub: youngest son of Hiel, the adventurer who attempted to rebuild Jericho, even in the face of Joshua's curse on the place. Hiel sacrificed Segub, his youngest son, to set up the gates of the city (1 Ki. 16:34). *See also* Abiram; Hiel; Jericho.

seior: or seid, a form of Norse sorcery. Worship was conducted by either sex and was likely shamanistic in structure. At one point, at least, it was directed to Odin. *See also* Aesir; Armanenschafft; Asa; Asatru; blyt; Norse and Old Germanic pantheon; sect(s); shaman, shamanism; skald(s); Valupsa; volva; Wotanism.

Seir: the hilly land in the mountains of Edom. The original inhabitants were Horites (Gen. 14:6), but Esau moved there and dispossessed them. Some Amalekites were there as well but were destroyed by the Simonite tribe (1 Chr. 4:42–43). *See also* Amalek, Amalekites; Edom; Horites; Idumea, Idumeans; Mount Seir.

Sele: also Sela or Selah, a term in ancient Hebrew for the city of Petra but most commonly spelled Sele. *See also* Azel; Bozrah; Edom, Edomites; Joktheel; Mount Paran; Nabateans; Pella; Petra.

Selah: likely a musical or metrical term of uncertain properties, perhaps used as directions to the musician or worship leader for chanting or singing the Psalms, where it is mentioned some seventy-one times; also indicated at several points in Habakkuk 3 amid that prophet's plaintive prayer. Speculation abides that the term is a note to the music director to sound the orchestra while the singers are silent. Some linguists claim that the word identifies a riddle, but that hypothesis seems weak. *See also alamoth;* Amen; music; Petra; riddle; *sheminith; shigionoth.*

Select Followers, the: a recent apocalyptic cult in Oklahoma who tried to sacrifice a virgin because their astrological analysis appealed for it. Police stopped them before the deed was done. *See also* cult(s).

Bernie L. Calaway

Seleucia: the government and trade center of Mesopotamia after the decline of Babylon. The seat of power had now shifted from Babylon on the Euphrates to Seleucia on the Tigris.

Seleucia, Seleucids: the conquerors and despoilers of the exiled Jews during the Syrian Greek occupation of the Holy Land. The despot and type for Antichrist, Antiochus Epiphanes, was of this line. The Seleucid kings were: Seleucus I Nicator (312–281 B.C.), Antiochus I Soter (281–261), Antiochus II Theos (261–246), Seleucus II Callinicus (246–226), Seleucus III Keroneos (226–223), Antiochus III the Great (223–187), Seleucus IV Philopater (187–175), Antiochus IV Epiphanes (175–163), Antiochus V Eupator (163–162), Demetrius I Soter (162–150), Alexander Balas (150–145), Demetrius II (145–139), and Antiochus VII (139–129). Seleucid influence failed in Judea when the Jews gained their independence under the Hasmoneans. The territory of the Seleucids was largely the modern state of Turkey. *See also* Antiochus Epiphanes; Antiochus II Theos; Antiochus III the Great; Antiochus IV Epiphanes; anti-Semitic; Demetrius the Syrian; Hasmonean dynasty; king(s); kings of the North; Ptolemy, Ptolemies; Seleucus I Nicator; Seleucus II Callinicus; Seleucus IV Philopater; Syria; Tobias.

Seleucus I Nicator: the first Seleucid ruler (312–281 B.C.), one of the Diadochi who took the provinces of Syria, Babylon, and Media. His story is likely covered in Daniel 11:4–5. *See also* Diadochi; king(s); Seleucia, Seleucids; Syria.

Seleucus II Callinicus: a son of Laodice who was married to (and then murdered) Antiochus II Theos, who ruled the Syrian North 261–246 B.C. Seleucus succeeded Antiochus (246–226 B.C.) but was defeated twice and then killed by Ptolemy III Euergetes, the brother of Berenice who had been in turn killed by Laodice. The story with its many feuds is likely taken up in Daniel 11:7–9. *See also* king(s); Seleucia, Seleucids; Syria.

Seleucus IV Philopater: ruler of Syria (222–205 B.C.) and son of Antiochus the Great. His history is likely the one covered in Daniel 11:20. *See also* king(s); Seleucia, Seleucids; Syria.

self-fulfilling prophecy: a prediction that causes itself to come true because we desire it or dread it as a psychological need, either consciously or unconsciously. Biblical prophecies are immune from such realizations because they do not originate with people and they are recorded in sacred scripture. *See also* prophecy types.

Selivanov, Kondrati: founder of the notorious castration cult known as the Skoptsy. *See also* cult(s); Skoptsy, the.

Seljuk Turks: a people of Tartan extract who carved out an Islamic Empire in Anatolia (now Turkey) and remained in existence amid the Byzantine territories from 1060–1307. The First Crusade of Christendom was launched against them. Even so, the Seljuks almost destroyed the Byzantine Empire. They were conquered and replaced by the Ottoman Turks early in the 14th century. *See also* atabeg; Ottoman Turks; pasha; Saracens; Toghuzghu.

selkie: in Celtic legend, a seal, a sea lion, or a legendary race of seal people who could shed their skins temporarily and venture on land as human. If their coats were lost or stolen, they could not return to the sea. *See also* attending spirit(s); banshee; bogle; brownies; bugbears; Celtic folklore and religion; clurichauns; daemons; disa; dryad(s); elemental(s); fairy, fairies; Fomorians; Furies; ghost(s); ghoul; gnome(s); Green Man, the; hobgoblins; homunculus; household deities; huldafolk; Lares; leprechaun(s); Loa Loas; Manannan mac Lir; Manes; mythological beasties, elementals, monsters, and spirit animals; nereid; nisse; nymph(s); nyx; Oniropompi; Orisha; Oya; para; paredri; penates; Robin Goodfellow; satyr; Seelie Court, Unseelie Court; Sidhe; sirens; spiritual warfare; sprite(s); sylph(s); teraphim; territorial spirits; Trickster; Tuatha de Danann; tutelary; undine; wight(s).

semeion: the Greek form for "sign" or a divine demonstration. *See also* semiotics; sign(s).

semi-classical post-Tribulationism: a theological position that agrees with traditional post-Tribulation doctrine but posits some events that are still future. The semi-classical position asserts that such occurrences as the rapture and the Second Coming cannot be imminent. *See also* post-Tribulation, post-Tribulational.

seminaries, theological: schools at the post-graduate level training ministers and priests. In early America, the founding universities were responsible for minister training including Harvard and Yale (Congregationalists) and the College of New Jersey (now Princeton) by the Presbyterians. The first true seminary in the states was started by the Dutch Reformed Church in New Brunswick, New Jersey, in 1784. The Baptists followed with a school in Newton, Massachusetts; the Lutherans at Gettysburg, Pennsylvania; and the Catholics in Baltimore called Saint Mary's. Jewish seminaries came online with Hebrew Union College in Cincinnati in 1875 (Reformed), Jewish Theological Seminary in New York City (Conservative), and Yeshiva University in New York (Orthodox). Bible colleges serve the same purpose but usually on a more basic level offering a Bachelor's degree. *See also* Reformed Churches; religious education; religious organizations.

semiotics: the systematic study of signs and symbols. *See also semeion;* sign(s); symbol(s); type(s).

Semi-Pelagianism: a doctrinal thesis that adopts a view somewhat between Pelagius and Augustine which asserts that man's will has been weakened or diseased by Adam's sin but not totally depraved as a result of the Fall. Such a compromise was considered by some to be weak-kneed and coined the name "Semi-Pelagianism" as a sort of left-handed insult. Nevertheless, the doctrine is a natural consequence as it was founded by Cassian of Gaul and is still viable today. *See also* Cassian, John of Gaul; Pelagius; Pelagianism.

Semiramis: the supposed queen or consort of the early version of the god Marduk in Nimrod's ziggurat. She was likely the forerunner of later goddesses, including Ishtar, Astarte, and Aphrodite (Venus). Babylonian legend says that when Nimrod died, he became a sun god or Orion, the hunter of the zodiac. His wife, Semiramis (called "the Supreme One"), then gave birth to a son named Tammuz, whom she claimed to be the child of the deified Nimrod; she also claimed she was the "seed of woman," as referred to in Genesis 3:15. She then demanded that both she and her son be worshiped. The Semiramis myth started when an egg of great size fell into the Euphrates and was pushed ashore by a large fish. From this egg, Semiramis was born and later helped to lead in the idolatrous worship in the ziggurat. *See also* Babel, tower of; Levant pantheon; Nimrod-bar-Cush; queen of heaven; Sumerian and Babylonian pantheon; queen(s); Tammuz.

Semitic(s): or Semites; in ethnology, those peoples of a language family by that name. Any Bible student should know that the term for it represents many races (some named in Scripture), including the Hebrews, Amorites, Edomites, Assyrians, Arameans, Amalekites, Moabites, Chaldeans, Arabs, Meunites, Mandaeans, Druze, Eblaites, Phoenicians, Shebans, Nabateans, Carthaginians, Samaritans, Mhallami, Arabs, and some few other cultures—all in the Fertile Crescent region. *See also* anti-Semitic; philo-Semitic.

sempect: a Benedictine monk of extreme age. *See also* Benedict, Order of; monk(s).

Semyaza: the leader of the evil Watcher angels (also called Azazel) who initiated sexual perversions with earth women (Gen. 6:1–4) according to *1 Enoch*. Other participants were called Ananel, Artqoph, Asael, Baraqel, Danieal, Gregori; Hermoni Kokabel, Matarel, Ramel, Ramtel, Sahriel, Samsiel, Stawel, Tummiel, Turiel, Yhaddiel, Yomiel, and Zeqiel. *See also* angel(s); Azazel; fallen angel(s); giant(s); Gregori; Watchers, the.

Seneca, Lucius Annaeus: Roman philosopher, naturalist, and writer of tragedies who was prime minister under Nero (4 B.C.–A.D. 65). He was a Stoic, not a Christian, yet was respected for centuries by most Christian philosophers and theologians because of his moral doctrines. He foretold that the world would go up in smoke, a prediction that prompted many to believe that the Mount Vesuvius eruption of A.D. 79 was a fulfillment. Roman thinking admonished those volcanic eruptions could release demons into the world. Seneca was said to have corresponded with the apostle Paul, but these letters, though widely quoted, were most likely forgeries. He eventually fell from Nero's favor and was forced to commit suicide. Nevertheless, his influence endured and his thoughts resided in many Renaissance leaders, not the least of whom were Shakespeare, Ben Jonson, Milton, and Bacon. *See also* philosophy of religion; philosophy of the Greeks; Roman Empire.

seneschal: a title for the grand commander of the Knights Templar, second in rank only to the grandmaster. *See also* knighted orders.

Senites: a cultural society possibly referenced in Isaiah 49:12 (there called "Sinim"), which is now commonly identified with China. If the research is solid, China's vast populations and 4,500 years of unbroken civilization could presage the "kings of the East" noted in Revelation 16:12. A footnote in the NIV Bible suggests that they may be the Syene (in the Aswan region). *See also* kings of the East; Middle Kingdom.

Senmut: a low-born Egyptian said to be the intimate counselor of Queen Hatshepsut of Egypt and tutor to her daughter. He was Hatshepsut's strongest advisor, friend, and confident and perhaps her stepson. It is speculated Senmut was Hebrew (the name means "mother's brother") and circumstantial evidence, as interpreted by some, suggests he may have been none other than Moses himself. *See also* Moses.

Sennacherib: king of Assyria (705–681 B.C.), a younger son of Sargon. His term was coincidental with the reign of Hezekiah, the king to whom Isaiah prophesied Jerusalem's deliverance from the Assyrians. After Hezekiah's prayer for rescue, 185,000 Assyrian soldiers mysteriously perished (2 Ki. 18:9–19:37). As promised, Sennacherib's army was defeated by an angel of God while besieging Jerusalem and lost vast numbers of troops, forcing the king to retire back to Nineveh after the puzzling (to him) defeat of his forces. Sennacherib was a boastful and cruel leader, like most of the Assyrian kings, but was not particularly effective. Sennacherib was subsequently assassinated in a palace *coup d'état* by his own sons. It is possible that the king was planning to eliminate his sons before his own demise so the attack could have been preventive self-defense. *See also* Assyria, Assyrians; Esarhaddon; king(s); Nisroch; Sennacherib's Prism; Shalmaneser.

Sennacherib's Prism: an important archeological discovery about 2,700 years old. The stele details how Sennacherib destroyed forty-two walled cities of the Jews. Concerning Jerusalem, however, the record says only "Hezekiah...himself I made a prisoner in Jerusalem, his capital city, like a bird in a cage. I surrounded him." The wording is surely a "saving face" boast from a mighty kind not willing to fully admit that Jerusalem was never overrun by him. *See also* Assyria, Assyrians; Sennacherib; stele.

sentences: in liturgical settings, short Scripture readings voiced at various points in the liturgy. *See also* liturgy, Christian.

Separatists: English Christians of the 16th and 17th centuries who desired separation from the established Church of England. In essence, they were the radical dissension wing of the Puritan cause. Resentment spurred them to abandon England for Holland in 1609 where they formed the nucleus of what was to become Plymouth Colony in America. Their preference was to establish independent local congregations but eventually they were classed together as Congregationalists. Separatists held the support of Oliver Cromwell, who was himself a Separatist, but many migrated to America as Puritans and other dissident groups. One might say, this body of believers began as Anglicans, then were called Separatists, who morphed into Puritans, who branched into Baptists and other conservative denominations. *See also* Congregationalists; Cromwell, Oliver; Half-Way Covenant; Massachusetts Body of Liberties; Hutchinson, Anne; Pilgrim(s); Puritanism, Puritans.

Sephardim: Spanish-Portuguese Jews, a designation taken from the Hebrew word for "Spain," *Sefarad*. The name is mentioned in Obadiah 20. *See also* Abraham's seed; Ashkenazi; Jew(s); Scythians; seed of Israel.

Sephiroth: the ten attributes or emanations of God as described in Qabbala. The term represents a corruption of the Tree of Life which is supposed to have twelve spheres but is now presented with distortions that have reduced them to ten. Sephiroth is also displayed in some tarot cards as the twenty-two paths between the branches of the Tree of Life. *See also* emanations, doctrine of; Qabbala; Sephirotic Tree; tarot; tree of life, the.

Sephirotic Tree: or "Tree of Science," a summary of the most famous and important teachings of the Jewish Qabbala. The practice can be traced back to about the tenth century, though some scholars date it to the third. Belief is derived from the allegory of God's perfect light which became blemished during its reflected journey to earth. From there, certain emanations emerged to make ten linked centers joined by pathways. This pattern makes a device, quite complex in its design, to which are added the twenty-two letters of the Hebrew alphabet. Each of the resultant thirty-two pathways was chosen by God to create the universe and as a means for Him to descend to the material world. The pathways are also a means for enlightened humans to ascend to God. Each emanation is called a Sephiroth, the elements of which actually spell the sacred name of God. The base of the tree design (Malkut) represents the world and the pinnacle (Keter) is God, or the supreme crown. The remainder of the tree make up *Chokma* (Wisdom), *Binah* (Understanding), *Chesed* (Mercy), *Gevurah* (Strength), *Tiferet* (Beauty), *Netzach*

(Victory), *Hod* (Splendor), and *Yesod* (Foundation). On the whole, the entire system is complex, mystical, and can be manipulated as a sort of "game board" to pursue the primary mysteries of life. *See also* Judaism; light; Qabbala; Sephiroth; Shemhamforesh; tree of life, the; *Zohar*.

Sepphoris: a walled city serving as the capital of lower Galilee, about six miles northeast of Nazareth. Herod Antipas rebuilt the metropolis to unrivaled beauty after its destruction by Varus, the governor of Syria around 4 B.C.

septa-millennial: an outdated end time dating method that counted 6,000 years from creation to the last days. *See also* calendar (Julian); Hippolytus; Irenaeus; Lactantius; Sabbatical millennialism; "six-day theory, the"; Ussher, James.

Septimus Severus: Roman emperor (A.D. 145–211). Severus was emperor from 193 until he died in Britain in 211 where he was strengthening the Hadrian wall against the Britons. By all accounts, he was an able, if brutal, ruler. During his reign the fifth great Christian persecution broke out. Severus forbade anyone to convert to Christianity or Judaism. *See also* Christianity in the Roman Empire; Perpetua and Felicity; Roman Empire.

Septuagesima: in Catholicism, the ninth Sunday before Easter and the third before Ash Wednesday. Sometimes the term is used to identify the start of Lent. *See also* feasts and special days of high liturgy faiths; liturgical year; liturgy, Christian; Roman Catholic Church.

Septuagint, the: the Greek translation of the Old Testament, completed around 300 B.C. under the sponsorship of Ptolemy II Philadelphus. Frequently, the term is abbreviated as LXX because legend reports that the work was accomplished by seventy scholars in seventy days. This story of the seventies may be recognition of that same number (or seventy-two) for a similar body of elders assisting Moses (Ex. 24:9–10). Some historians particularize the Septuagint version of the Pentateuch as having been translated by seventy scholars from Jerusalem while the rest of the Old Testament was prepared by seventy Jews of Egypt. The entire translation differs slightly from previous copies of the Hebrew Bible, and parts of the contents are arranged somewhat differently. The LXX moved the books of Ezra-Nehemiah and the Chronicles from the Writings to the historical section and placed Daniel from the Writings to the prophetic section. *See also* Aquila, translation of; Bible translations; Hexapla; LXX; Pentateuch; Ptolemy II Philadelphus; seventy-two; seventy elders; seventy, the.

sequence: the liturgy of a hymn sung in many High Church faith orders after the second lesson and before the Gospel acclamation at the Eucharist. *See also* hymn(s); liturgy, Christian; music.

Serafim of Sarov: one of the best beloved of the Orthodox saints (1759–1833). He was an ebonite in his early life but switched to an effective preacher to the masses in his later years. Once, when he was severely beaten and permanently crippled by robbers, he prayed alone for 1,000 days, kneeling or standing on a rock. He is quoted as saying, "Achieve stillness and thousands around you will find salvation." *See also* Eastern Orthodox Church.

Seraiah: 1. one sent by King Jehoiakim to arrest Baruch and Jeremiah (Jer. 36:26). 2. the chief priest of Judah when Nebuchadnezzar captured Jerusalem. He was commissioned by Jeremiah to carry a prophetic scroll to Babylon but could not personally complete the mission because he was executed at Riblah (2 Ki. 25:18–21; Jer. 52:24–27). This Seraiah was the father of Jehozadak (1 Chr. 6:14-15), who was carried into exile, and the grandfather of Jeshua, who was high priest after the return to Judah. He was also a progenitor of Ezra the scribe (1 Chr. 6:14–15; Ezr. 3:2; 7:1). 3. Other priests, both before and after the exile were named Seraiah as well as certain officials within Jewish history. *See also* priest(s); scroll of Babylon's doom.

Serapeum: a magnificent temple in Alexandria dedicated to the syncretic Greek-Egyptian god Serapis. It was constructed on the highest point of the Alexandrian Acropolis overlooking the city and its busy harbor and classed as the finest construct outside of the Capitol in Rome. The sanctuary of beautifully crafted marble and sculpture was not free-standing but part of the famous Library of Alexandria. A sarcophagus containing the body of Alexander the Great was said to reside in the temple library. A model of the bearded god rested solidly in its majestic chamber encased in gold. Regrettably, the marvelous structure was razed to the ground and its treasures trashed or looted by the zealous reformers of the idol-hating emperor Theodosius after 380 A.D. *See also* Library of Alexandria; Serapis; Theodosius I.

Seraph, Seraphim: angelic beings who take their name from the Hebrew derivative "fiery serpents." In Isaiah's vision of God's throne (Isa. 6), they are described as having six wings, a face, hands, and feet; they fly, speak, and worship their God reverently. From their rather spectacular descriptions and appearances, we cannot actually define their true form. One of them (Seraph is singular; Seraphim is plural) uses his facility with light or fire to touch the lips of the prophet to cleanse and empower his speech. In Numbers 21:6, an invasion of fiery serpents attacked the Israelite camp, but we are unsure if they are actual snakes or seraphic serpents acting in their stead. One reference (Psalm 104:4 and quoted in Hebrews 1:7) may be an allusion to the order's association with fire: "He makes his angels winds, his servants flames of fire." Some theologians of the Middle Ages held that the Seraphim were associated with love, whereas the Cherubim represented knowledge. As a group, the Seraphim may very well be the highest angelic authority. In the noncanonical slant, *2 Enoch* calls them "Chalkydri," who, along with the Phoenixes, tend the sun. The creatures are described as purple in color with a crocodile's head and the feet and tail of a lion with twelve wings. *Chalkydri* means "serpents" but *Seraphim* "to burn." *See also* angel(s); archangel(s); authorities; Bene Elohim; Chashmallim; Chayoth; Cherub, Cherubim; dominions; *elohim;* Erelim; fire; Galgallim; Hashmallim; Hayyot; Husk(s); Ishim; *mal'ak;* Ophanim; powers; principalities; serpent; thrones; twenty-four elders, the; Virtues; Watchers, the.

Serapis: a Greco-Egyptian god worshiped in Alexandria in the third century as ordered by Ptolemy I; it was an invented deity by which the king hoped to unite the crowded Egyptian pantheon. The magnificent Serapeum was constructed as his temple, but it was destroyed by Christian zealots in A.D. 389; it was one of the last sanctuaries to fall with the decline of paganism. To the ancient Egyptians, the prototype Serapis was Osiris, and when pictured as a bull, Apis. Isis was his powerful consort. The ancient church fathers relate that Serapis was one of the names the Egyptians gave to the Hebrew Joseph. Since Joseph knew that the people of Egypt would eventually try to deify him, as was a common custom in the land of the Nile, he constructed a library to house the true oracles of God and carved a prophecy into its walls.

According to Socrates's *Ecclesiastical History*, these inscriptions were found at the destruction of the Serapeum (Joseph's original library now corrupted), causing many to convert to Christianity. In brief, it is an amazing fact that humans could so easily be led into a "one-size-fits-all" religion in the name of expediency only. *See also* Egyptian pantheon; Olympian pantheon; Serapeum.

Serene: one who claimed messiahship (ca. A.D. 720) in Syria. He advocated the expulsion of all Muslims and the relaxation of some Jewish laws. Serene was arrested by the Muslim caliph, then turned over to the Jews for punishment, at which time he recanted. Serene was born a Christian and even had followers as far away as Spain. *See also* Jew(s); Syria.

Sergianism: an Orthodox position of somewhat recent appearance centered in the craven submission to the communists and atheism of the former Soviet Union. The hierarchy of the Russian Orthodox Church has been accused of the developing doctrine led by the late patriarchate of Moscow and all Russia. The "Sergi" comes from Patriarch Sergi of Moscow who endorsed the shift, supposedly on behalf of all the Russian people. *See also* Eastern Orthodox Church; Russian Orthodoxy.

Sergius and Bacchus: two Roman soldiers of the third century who became Christians, only to face martyrdom for their faith under Diocletian. Sergius, especially, is much venerated in almost all Western, Byzantine, and Arminian churches with a Catholic feast day of October 7. He remains the patron saint of the Arabs. The relationship of the two men was unique, and their names seldom appear singularly. Whether the relationship was a romantic one remains a question. Bacchus was tortured to death, followed by Sergius's beheading some time later. Legend reports Bacchus's spirit appeared to Sergius to encourage him during torture; then the same spirit is said to have appeared to a Mongol khan leader seven centuries later (around 1007) to solicit the pagan's conversion and to ignite the spread of the gospel among the Mongols. The apparition is said to have saved the Kerait chieftain from certain death in a blizzard. *See also* adelphopoiesis; apparition; ghost(s); martyr(s); Mongols; spirit; vision(s).

Sergius Paulus: the Roman proconsul at Paphos on the island of Cyprus (Acts 13:6–12). He is described as an intelligent man and was not deceived away from the gospel despite the persuasions of his attendant, the sorcerer Bar-Jesus (Elymas). *See also* Christianity in the Roman Empire; Roman Empire.

Seriah: a prophet mentioned in *2 Baruch*, along with another named Jabish; but the book also mentioned the more familiar Jeremiah and Iddo. His name does not appear in Scripture, nor does Jabish. *See also* Jabish; Jew(s); prophet(s).

sermon: a religious address, usually given by a minister or preaching layperson, in most forms of liturgical worship. Most seminaries and Bible colleges agree that the delivery may be instructional, consecrational, biographical, seasonal, exortational, doctrinal, evangelical, supportive, inspirational, or almost any form but is usually constructed around a given biblical text. The sermon is often equated to a homily, but technically the latter is shorter and more focused. *See also* exhortation; homily; *kerygma;* liturgical year; liturgy, Christian; message; preach(ing); "sugar stick"; "three points and a poem."

Sermon on the Mount, the: Jesus' homily, or more properly, a series of lectures in which he outlined the perfect society and the particulars of how a true believer should live (Mt. 5:1–7:29; Lk. 6:20–7:1). In his remarks, the Lord stressed perfection in the believer, an ideal impossible to be completely realized in our time. The concepts of the Sermon, however, make an excellent constitution for the period and rule of the Millennium, as well as a contemporary model of righteousness. Theological debate has raged over time as to how we are to consume Jesus' teaching in the Sermon since the admonitions are obviously impossible to perfectly obey in this world. Answers have been put forward: 1) the Sermon applies to the Millennium era only, 2) it relates to any time the Messianic kingdom is offered, 3) it relates both to the time of Jesus' earthly ministry and the Tribulation as well as the millennial kingdom. Our only practical response, perhaps, is to strive for the perfection demanded in the sermon but resigned to await its full potential. *See also* beatitude(s); Beatitudes, the; cheap grace; *opinio legis;* Mount of Beatitudes; Millennium, millennial; poverty; Sermon on the Plain, the; theocracy; theocratic kingdom; Tribulation.

Sermon on the Plain, the: the address by Jesus recorded in Luke 6:17–49. The phrase should be seen in the plural since the "sermon" is really a series of discourses on any number of subjects and days. *See also opinio legis;* Sermon on the Mount, the.

serpent: a snake, adder, asp, or viper. In Scripture, serpents as small as a ground-crawler (a "darter") to as large as a dragon usually represent evil. Satan is pictured as both creatures (in Genesis as small in size and in Revelation as large). Wherever we meet them, snakes are usually presented as deceiving, biting, raging, or acting in violence against God and humanity when speaking apocalyptically. Jeremiah recorded a threat that God will send venomous snakes (the basilisk or cockatrice) among the unfaithful, serpents that could not be charmed (Jer. 8:17). A correlate to this negative appellation may be found in Matthew 10:16 when Jesus admonished his followers to be "as shrewd as snakes and as innocent as doves." It is probably apocalyptically significant that the evil career of Satan begins as a fallen angel serpent in Eden and ends in the lake of fire with Revelation as a defeated dragon. Serpents had paganish associations as well in that they were linked with the gods Asclepius, Dionysus, and Zeus. A golden cobra (the *bureaus*) adorned the double crown of Egyptian pharaohs symbolizing power in the land. *See also* animals, birds, and insects, symbology of; *Bel and the Dragon;* bronze serpent; Draco; dragon; mythological beasties, elementals, monsters, and spirit animals; Nehushtan; Ophites; ouroboros; Python, python; red dragon; reptilian theory; seed of the serpent; serpent seed doctrine, the; Seraph, Seraphim; snake handling.

serpent meditation. See contemplative prayer movement; kundalini.

serpent seed doctrine, the: a common racist theme of many patriot movement groups that promotes the scheme that the Jews are a by-product of sexual coitus between Eve and Satan (Gen. 3). Satan, either in human or demonic form, impregnated Eve resulting in the birth of Cain, whereas the righteous Abel was born by the union between Adam and Eve. The Jews were then sired by Cain when he intermarried with non-whites known as "mud people" or "beasts of the field." The belief also asserts that Satan tainted the bloodline of the pre-Adamic races and eventually crucified Christ (who was a "white man" and not Semitic). Most advocates use 1 John 3:12, a verse speaking of Cain as an individual, as a base for their opinion. Their position is destroyed by Genesis 4:1, which clearly states Cain was born of Adam and Eve. *See also* anti-Semitic; Braham, William Marrion; Cainites; Gadreel; Missler, Chuck; Ophites; panspermia theory; Patriot Movement, the; reptilian theory; seed of the serpent; serpent; two natures, doctrine of the; Sethites; Watchers, the.

serpent's egg: an ancient Druid talisman (thus sometimes called a Druid's egg) which was said to bring victory in any court of law. According to the Roman historian Pliny the item was like a crystal about the size of a medium-sized apple. It was said to be produced of the foam from the mouths of snakes which formed into a viscous slime that became a ball tossed in the air and caught by a Druid. It could then be used to counteract incantations. Eggs in general were considered potent fertility symbols in much of the ancient world. *See also* charm(s); Druidism; talisman(s).

Serpent's Rock. See En-Rogel.

Serra, Junipero: Franciscan missionary (1713–1784) who founded the first nine Roman Catholic missions in California. He also established another at San Diego with the aid of Gaspar De Portola. Serra visited each setting annually. *See also* Franciscans; missions, missionaries; Roman Catholic Church.

Serto. See Estrangela.

servant: one who is subject to another and performs service for the master. In the Judeo-Christian view, it is acceptable to view the follower of God as His servant, and, in Christian thinking, as Christ being the servant to his Father's will (Phil. 2:7). According to the context, a servant may be a son, a slave, an apprentice, a helper, or even an angel. As an exception in Scripture, Jesus declared his followers to be *friends* instead of servants (Jn. 15:15) as they practice faith and obedience. *See also* angel(s); *poverello;* servant of God, the; servant of Yahweh; servant's heart; servants, my; servants of our God, the; servant, the suffering; slave, slavery.

servant of God, the: one who serves God in a general sense, but specifically the title identifies Moses *(i.e.,* Daniel 9:11). *See also* Moses; servant.

servant of Yahweh: an Old Testament title for a prophet. *See also Chozeh;* interpreter; *Kohen; Lewi;* man of God; man of the Spirit; messenger of Yahweh; *Nabhi';* prophet(s); *Ro'eh;* servant; servants, my; *Shamar;* watchman.

servant's heart: Christianese jargon for one possessed of the gifts and desire to serve humanity in kindness and with a mindset of humble servanthood. *See also* Christianese; *poverello;* servant; servant of God, the.

servants, my: specifically, the prophets of old claimed by God as His own (*i.e.,* Daniel 9:10). Also numbered among God's servants are those chosen by God to be a specific leader for a specific time and purpose. Furthermore, one of God's chosen could also be a non-believer or even a pagan, such as Cyrus or Nebuchadnezzar (Jer. 25:8). *See also Chozeh;* interpreter; *Kohen; Lewi;* man of God; man of the Spirit; messenger of Yahweh; *Nabhi'; poverello;* prophet(s); *Ro'eh;* servant; servant of Yahweh; *Shamar;* watchmen.

servants of our God, the: the Tribulation saints who carry the protective seal of God (Rev. 7:3). The indicated shielding does not equate to physical safety but does pledge eternal redemption to those faithful ones. As such, the sealing probably has some connotation to baptism or protective action of the Holy Spirit. *See also* brothers of mine; 144,000, the; servant.

Servant Songs. See servant, the suffering.

servant, the suffering: a prophetic description of the Messiah's sacrificial offering of himself as an abused and lowly savior. The portrayal is an encapsulation of Isaiah's five "Servant Songs" (Isa. 42:1–7; 49:1–7; 50:4–9; 52:13–53:12; 61:1–3). Taken together, the Songs picture the appearance, ministry, and destiny of the Messiah, particularly his humiliation at his first coming. Christians name that savior as Jesus Christ. *See also* Everlasting Father; Mighty God; names (titles) for Jesus; Prince of Peace; servant; Wonderful Counselor.

Servetus, Michael: (1511–1553) a European who ran afoul of the Calvinist-run politics and religion of Geneva. Servetus, in his zeal and radicalism, was determined to loose Calvin from his theological "delusions" and challenged his right to govern. He well knew the consequences of his mission as we know from his words, "If I win, Calvin will burn and I will rule Geneva. If I lose, the other will be true." Servetus was also an apocalypticist, predicting the end of the age in the year 1585. Calvin then warned Servetus that if he came to Geneva, he would never leave alive. Even the gentle-minded Philip Melanchthon called for his death. Servetus persisted until he was convicted and executed as a heretic because he refused to conform to Calvin's Geneva style of government. More than heretical, however, Servetus was a direct threat to Calvin's leadership and the promulgation of Calvinistic theology outside of Switzerland. *See also* Calvin, John; Geneva theocracy of John Calvin; Consistory, the.

Servite Order: one of the five original mendicant orders of the Roman Catholic Church. They served as preachers and devotees of Mary both in and out of recluse but the first members in 1233 were communally situated on Mount Senario in Italy. All seven of the original founders were canonized by Pope Leo XIII in 1888. *See also* Assumptionist Orders; Augustinian Order; Barnabites; Benedict, Order of; Black Canons; canon(s) of the church; canons regular; Capuchin Order; Carmelites; Carthusians; Celestines; Cistercians; clergy; discalced; Dominicans; Franciscans; friar(s); liturgical year; Minim; monasticism; monk(s); orders; Paulist Fathers; Premonstratensian Order; priest(s); religious organizations; Roman Catholic Church; Spirituals of the Franciscan Order; Trappist Order.

Sesotris: a pharaoh of ancient Egypt, or one of several with the name in more than one dynasty, whose title may appear as Senusret, Senwosret, Sistosis, Sesortosis, Sen-Was-Ret I, or Sesoosis. The name has been put forth as a candidate for the Pharaoh of the Exodus but which one is unclear, although Sesotris II has received some prominence among supporters of the Sesotris contenders. *See also* Amasis; Amenhotep II; Ay; Egypt, Egyptians; Hophra; king(s); Menes; Merneptah; Neco II; pharaoh; Pharaoh of the Exodus; Ramses II; Shabaka; Shishak; So; Tirhakah.

session: a function of Presbyterian polity by which elected elders act as a governing board for the local church. The word derives from the Latin *sessio*, meaning "sitting" and consists of the pastors and elders of a local congregation. As a body, it concerns itself with local administrative concerns, including the conduct of worship and oversight of deacons. It also acts as a referral agency to the regional presbytery and national general assembly. *See also* consistory; deacon(s), deaconess(es); elder(s); general assembly; Presbyterians; presbytery; synod.

session of Christ: a theological term for "sitting at the right hand" as mentioned in the Apostle's Creed. The doctrine claims that Christ is now seated at the right hand of the Father in a co-ruling position. *See also* right hand of the Most High; right hand, the.

Set: an Egyptian god described as a man with an animal head. He was worshiped as the god of darkness and symbolized by a black pig. Certain Illuminati groups and pagan religions claim the name is an alternative to Satan. *See also* Council of Nine; Egyptian pantheon; Satan.

Seth: 1. son born to Adam in his 130th year. Seth was then the father of Enosh (Gen. 5:3–4). 2. an Egyptian weather god (Typhon to the Greeks) and murderer of the chief god Osiris. At one point in Egyptian prehistory, he was the most worshiped idol by the indigenous populations of Upper Egypt. His parents were Geb and Nut, the earth god and sky goddess. He was brother to Osiris and Isis and wife to Nephthys but friendly to none of them. Nephthys gave birth to Anubis, but the dog-child was reared by Isis. Seth was the conveyor of disharmony and destruction—the opposite of Egypt's model of *maat*. The god's form is most bizarre—a general man shape but with the head like an aardvark, a curved snout, square-shaped ears, and a forked tail. He was finally exiled, more or less, and became the governor of seacoasts, desert places, and the region of Libya, plus being the guardian of the great sun chariot. Some place him among the Ennead. 3. a Gnostic name for the Son of Man (their equivalent of Jesus). Because Seth was a son of Adam, he could represent us as a savior-type figure (Adam means "man.") *See also* Adam; Allogenes; Anubis; Cave of Treasures; Demiurge; Egyptian pantheon; Ennead, the Great; Enosh; Geb and Nut; Gnosticism, Gnostics; Isis; Mandaeanism; Nephthys; Olympian pantheon; Osiris; Rock of Truth; Sethianism; Sethites; Typhon.

Sethianism: a major Gnostic sect prominent in the second and third centuries that seems to be patterned on Judaism and Platonism. The name is taken for Seth, the third son of Adam and Eve. Seth had attained Gnosis (secret knowledge) as recorded in the pseudo-gospel, *The Apocryphon of John*. Sethian theology, in brief, says that an "unknown god" called the Primal Father produced "Barbelo"—Thought—and began to emanate himself in the universe in the form of female Aeons. These "Barbeloites" produced angels, including Adamas, who was the perfect man. The youngest of the emanations, *Sophia*, decided to create her own version of the world without consulting the other Aeons. The disruption caused the appearance of the Demiurge (called *Yaldabaoth*) named "the serpent with a lion's head." The Demiurge then created Adam, followed by Eve from his rib. Meanwhile, the spirit of *Sophia* entered the tree of knowledge, which was, of course, forbidden to Adam and Eve. After the Fall, Yaldabaoth seduced Eve, who then birthed Cain and Abel. In typical Gnostic fashion, the Sethians were trying to explain how a good and righteous God could create a world of evil. *See also* Aeons; Allogenes; Demiurge; Gnosticism, Gnostic(s); reptilian theory; Seth; Sethites; sect(s); Seth.

Sethites: a group of men or angels called the "sons of God" who are to be judged in the final days. By some interpretations of Genesis 6, one view identifies the Sethites as a godly and faithful race before the great flood while their companion Cainites were worldly and rebellious. *See also* Cainites; daughters of men; serpent seed doctrine, the; Seth; Sethianism; sons of God; sons of God to be revealed.

Seton, Elizabeth Ann: (1774–1821) founder of the Sisters of Charity of Saint Joseph in America. Seton was born to a Protestant family in New York City and educated parochially. She helped organize many Catholic orphanages, hospitals, and maternity centers in the nation. The same church provided for her canonization in 1975, a rare honor for an American. *See also* nun(s); Roman Catholic Church.

settlement houses: a collection of comprehensive social service centers located in many major cities. The first was in New York City (1886) known as New York City's Neighborhood Guild (now University Settlement). The associations seek better working conditions, immigrant assimilation, public education, and good government. Most were, in the beginning, administered by churches. *See also* religious organizations; social issues; Woods, Robert Archey.

seven: the number most often used in apocalyptic language to symbolically represent "perfection" or "completion." To name but a few examples: Passover and Tabernacles are seven-day festivals, the Day of Atonement and Tabernacles both fall in the seventh month; the number is of frequent use in sacrifice and often noted by the prophets. To illustrate further: Proverbs 26:25 states that the heart of a gossiper is "full" of abominations even though they are counted as seven. Seven is also heavily prominent in Revelation. In the Apocalypse alone, there are seven descriptions of Christ, seven condemnations to the churches, seven affirmations, and seven commands. Further in the letter are seven each of angels, bowls, churches, eyes, heads, hills, horns, kingdoms, lamps and lampstands, seals, spirits, stars, trumpets, and world governments. When used with the multiples of seven, the existence and significance of the number are multiplied. Its frequent use almost demands it be called a sacred number in many instances, as well as an apocalyptic motif. Later, Judaism claimed God had created seven special things before the creation of the world, one of them being Israel herself. *See also* apocalyptic calculation; four; heptad(s); law of the sevens, the; names, symbology of; numbers, symbology of; seventy; seventy-two.

"seven and four" ritual: a Coptic hymn session in which seven theotekons and four hoos are sung. *See also* Coptic Church; Epsalmodia; hoos; liturgical year; liturgy, Christian; music; Tasbeha; theotekons.

seven churches of Asia Minor, the: seven church congregations of ancient Asia Minor addressed as the initial and direct recipients of Revelation's content. Chapters 2 and 3 name them as Ephesus, Smyrna, Pergamum, Thyatira, Sardis, Philadelphia, and Laodicea. Six of the seven mentioned were dominated by pagan temples. Each is commended or condemned according to its individual and collective merits and failures as a church body. Every fellowship is instructed with a series of commendations, condemnations, admonitions, commands, promises, and warnings posited as Christ's direct communication to each. Sometimes, these seven churches are said to represent seven distinct, if imprecise, periods of church history. The premise is commonly known as *dispensationalism* or the *church age theory*. It is a striking observation that of the seven churches, the two "good" ones (Philadelphia and Smyrna) exist today as Alasehir and Izmir, Turkey, but the two "bad" ones (Sardis and Laodicea) are ruins. *See also* angels of the churches; church; church age theory; dispensation(s); dispensational theology; Ephesus; Laodicea; Pergamum; Philadelphia; Sardis; Smyrna; Thyatira.

seven deadly sins: a collection of Catholicism that recognizes seven "major" sins named as Pride, Envy, Wrath, Sloth, Avarice, Gluttony, and Lust after the list was finalized in the sixth century. When the inventory was compiled in the fourth century, strangely enough, the index included Sadness but was dropped for obvious reasons. The reasoning for such a division may be that the process demonstrates how people may err in their free will in three ways: 1. by seeking bad goals (the pride of self-love that seeks to raise one's nature above others, by envy that resents the success of others, or by wrath that covets revenge at the cost of another's safety); 2. by sloth, the pivotal sin, identified as not mere laziness but indolence or disinterest in the things of God; 3. by too much love or attachment for the good things of this world (avarice, gluttony, and lust). *See also* mortal sin; pride; Roman Catholic Church; seven heavenly virtues; sin(s); venial sin.

7-11 songs: Christian contemporary music with a recurring beat and simple lyrics. To describe the practice is to merely state it is loud, prolonged, and repetitive. Singers can expect to voice the same seven words eleven times. 7-ll, get it? *See also* blended worship; Christianese; liturgical year; liturgy, Christian; music; slurs, religious.

seven great prophecies of world peace, the: a collection of what some believe to be the seven most important prophecies concerning world peace and its aftermath in all of the world's history. They may be listed as: 1. the Magi's prophecy of world peace and the single universal language (Num. 24:17; Dan. 8:15–26; 9:21–27), 2. the Sibylline prophecy of world peace and universal justice, 3. Enoch's prophecy of world peace and the giving of instructive books to the righteous, 4. Micah's prophecy of world peace and the freedom of religion (Mic. 4:1–5), 5. the *Elder Edda* with its prophecy of world peace and the return of ancient wisdom, 6. the Bible's prophecies of world peace and how it will be accomplished (summarized in Isaiah 52:6), and 7. Merlin's prophecies of world peace using symbolic words such as gold, silver, wine, and the planets—each of which carries varying interpretations. Universal peace is also discussed from Proclus, Plutarch, the Sibyllines, and Bible references from Deuteronomy, Isaiah, Ezekiel, Zechariah, and the Psalms. *See also Book(s) of Enoch;* Daniel as Old Testament prophecy; Deuteronomy as Old Testament book; eschatology, eschatological; *Edda,* the; Enoch; Ezekiel as Old Testament prophecy; Isaiah as Old Testament prophecy; Magi; Merlin; Micah as Old Testament prophecy; Numbers as Old Testament book; Psalms as Old Testament book; *Sibylline Oracles,* the; seventy weeks, prophecy of the; star of Bethlehem; Zechariah as Old Testament prophecy.

seven-headed beast: Antichrist as described in Revelation 13. Here, he appears as a beast from the sea with seven heads, ten horns, and ten crowns, showing his power and authority delegated to him by Satan, a part of the description of the beast from Revelation 13:1–10. The heads likely represent nations and the crowns are leaders of those nations (thus one set is a triumvirate). As a unit, they assist the beast (Antichrist) until they are defeated by the Lamb, Jesus Christ. Historical millennialists, among others, see only ancient Rome or imprecise language in these descriptions. *See also* Antichrist; beast(s); beast from the sea; beast, image of the; dragon; horn(s); seven; seven hills; seven kings; ten crowns.

seven-headed cobra: a creature of ancient Eastern lore similar to the dragon of Revelation 13. It anticipated the seven days of the week and was sought after by many Oriental rulers who thought it assured them of a stable reign. The image anticipates as well the day of Buddhism, which envisions the day when the world is divided into seven continents. Reputedly, Buddha himself embraced its worship. *See also* animals, birds, and insects, symbology of; mythological beasties, elementals, monsters, and spirit animals; dragon; reptilian theory.

seven heavenly virtues: a compilation of seven special qualities that make for a moral and selfless life. They are named by some denominations as Prudence, Temperance, Justice, Fortitude, Charity; Hope, and Faith. Another list of human merits, which were intended to be the opposite of the seven deadly sins, comes from the poet Prudentius (ca. A.D. 410). The virtues noted there are humility, meekness, charity, chastity, moderation, zeal, and generosity. *See also* seven deadly sins; temperance.

seven hills: part of a dual vision recorded in Revelation 17:9. The promontories described are pronounced to be the seven hills upon which the Great Prostitute sits (the false religion of Babylon the Great), which some interpret to represent the seven hills of Rome. The image also purports to be seven kings, five of whom are fallen, one is, and the other yet to come. In actual geography, the seven hills were Palatine, Aventine, Caelian, Equiline, Viminal, Quirimal, and Capitoline. Today, only Palatine is recognizable. (Technically, there are ten hills in Rome—not seven—but Vatican, Pincian, and the Janiculum hills are not counted in the traditional seven.) Wholesale belief that the seven hills of Rome (or any other city) are symbolized here, however, should be taken cautiously. Jerusalem, too, is surrounded by seven heights: Moriah, Bethsaida, Scopus, Olives, Opel, Zion, and Ghareb (Calvary), as are Moscow and Istanbul. *See also* Babylon the Great; king(s); seven; seven-headed beast; seven kings; ten crowns.

seven holy brothers: seven sons of Saint Felicity martyred by Emperor Marcus Aurelius after they refused to venerate idols. All died while hearing encouragement for their faith and courage from their mother, who also suffered death. Their names surprising remain: Januarius (scourged by leaded whips), Felix and Philip (beaten with clubs), Silvanus (dashed from a height), Alexander, Vitalus, and Martialis (beheaded). *See also* liturgical year; martyr(s); Perpetua and Felicity.

seven horns and seven eyes before the throne: part of the description of the Lamb given in Revelation 5:6. He is depicted as having seven eyes to imply the perfect prophetic vision enabled by the Holy Spirit and seven horns denoting complete power. Most likely the number 7 here, and elsewhere in Revelation is numerical symbology for perfection or completeness. *See also* horn(s); names (titles) for the Holy Spirit; numbers, symbology of; law of the sevens, the; seven.

seven kings: part of the detailed description of Mystery Babylon (Rev. 17). This "whore of Babylon" is pictured as riding the great scarlet beast with seven heads. She is also said to be sitting atop seven hills (the same sign as the seven kings). The hills and kings represent a series of Tribulation rulers, five of whom have fallen, one is, and the other as yet to come; but when he does come, he will remain a short while. This last will reappear, however, in a more virulent form as a kind of "eighth" king. The imagery of the seven kings (hills) seems to portray seven Tribulation rulers, one of whom is Antichrist who is in control of the others. Antichrist probably becomes the eighth king when he recovered from his grievous wound noted in Revelation 13:3 and is now in complete control of Tribulation earth. Some theologians try to identify the seven kings with historical ones, or nations represented by the rulers, but the process is speculative since there are far more than seven historical choices. A common approach is to cite the emperors Augustus (r. 27 B.C.–A.D. 4), Tiberius (14–37 A.D.), Caligula (37–41), Claudius (41–54), Nero (54–68), Vespasian (69–79), Titus (79–81), and Domitian, sometimes said to be the reincarnation of Nero (81–96) as the reborn eighth king. *See also* Antichrist; Babylon the Great; beast from the sea; eighth king, the; king(s); ninth power, the; seven; seven hills; ten crowns.

Seven Laws of Noah, the: according to Judaism, the seven operative laws given to non-Jews known as the Noahide Commandments or the Seven Laws of Noah. Although God has a unique mission for the Jewish people, He gives directives to all of humankind. By following these seven standards, all Gentiles can be judged righteous and can share in the world to come. The Torah contains 613 commandments for the Jews but only seven for others. The Judaic view, however, does not account for this numbering system as favoring the Jews but does see a special obligation to everyone else. The seven principles of righteousness are expressed as 1. believe in one God, 2. do not curse God, 3. do not murder, 4. do not steal, 5. do not commit adultery, 6. do not eat the limb of a living animal (do not act inhumanely), and 7. set up just governments and judicial systems. Sometimes two more or added—to honor parents and to give to charity. Similarity to the Ten Commandments cannot escape notice. *See also B'nai Noach*; Judaism; Ten Commandments, the.

seven levels of heaven: the names and contents of heaven according to the pseudepigraphal *Testament of Levi* and certain other pseudepigraphal writings. In the text of *Levi*, Level 1 is a place of dark and gloom, holding unrighteous deeds of people; Level 2 is fire, snow, and ice to be used as punishments plus the abode of wicked spirits that will perish; Level 3 holds warrior hosts ready to combat Beliar; Level 4 features thrones and powers (angels) engaged in worship; Level 5 contains more angels as does Level 6; Level 7 is the place and throne of God. *See also* "cloud nine"; heaven; heavenly realms; heavens, number of; third heaven; three levels of heaven, the.

seven mountains. See seven hills.

seven mountains dogma: a feature of the Reformed Restoration Movement that involves living the gospel in seven common

213

realms of life—business, education, government, media, family, religion, and entertainment. Those objectives are the "seven mountains" to be conquered when the righteous reclaim the earth for Christ. *See also* dominion theology; Reformed Reformation Movement; postmillennial, postmillennialism; Reconstructionism; replacement theology; theonomy.

seven psalms, the: a special selection of Psalms suitable for the liturgy of penance, especially adept for use in Lent. Roman Catholicism is the most frequent user. Those psalms composing the list are: Psalm 6, 32, 38, 51, 102, 130, and 143. *See also* commination; liturgical year; liturgy, Christian; Psalms as Old Testament book; Roman Catholic Church.

seven-sealed scroll, the: the pictorial image covering much of the content of Revelation in which a scroll with seven seals is given to the Lamb (Jesus Christ) for opening. The scroll holds part of God's plan to chastise and purify Tribulation earth and eventually help bring in the full kingdom of God. As each of the seals is broken, certain specified revelations or disasters are unleashed, which constitute God's action plan to accomplish those ends. *See also* scroll(s).

seven shepherds and eight princes: a mysterious vision that appears within the context of the prophecy announcing that the Messiah would be born in Bethlehem (Mic. 5:5–8) and seems to be an expansion on that prediction. The discussion declares that Assyria (which can properly be considered an example of many future conquerors and oppressors of Israel) will not prevail against united Judaism. Some theologians have speculated that the reference to mortal deliverers (princes or leaders) is a later interpolation since the Messiah is delayed in his coming. Until he does arrive, God will provide sufficient leadership to protect His people, then continue to expand Israel's influence in the world. Historically perhaps, the seven shepherds and eight rulers may represent the leaders of the Jews against Antiochus Epiphanes, specifically the valiant efforts of the Hasmoneans. The shepherds might even be designated religious leaders or chaplains and the princes the political rulers or military personnel. The most expansive and provocative explanation of the seven shepherds and eight leaders sees them in action between 1948 and the Second

Coming. The leaders then are called Prime Ministers and the "shepherds with the sword" are Defense Ministers. For named individuals to be counted in either category, they must have, in some political or military action, opposed modern Syria (ancient Assyria or Basham). So, the eight leaders most often mentioned are David ben Gurion (1948), Levi Eshkol (1967), Golda Meir (1973), and Menachem Begin (1981). The final four have not yet been revealed but the last will be the Messiah at Armageddon. The seven shepherds are David ben Gurion (Jewish War of Independence in 1948), Moshe Dayan (Six-Day War and Yom Kippur War), and Ariel Sharon (Golan annexation). The next three are not disclosed as yet but the last will again be the Messiah at Armageddon. There was an invasion of Lebanon in which Syria participated in 2006, but Begin and Sharon were still in office so that conflict is counted under the fourth leader and third shepherd. In any case, the messianic deliverer will raise up seven or eight helpers—or as many as necessary—to see that the nation gains its due glory. *See also* ben Gurion, David; Dayan, General Moshe; Hasmonean dynasty; Judaism; Meir, Golda; prince(s); prince of the covenant (testament), a; shepherds of Israel; shepherd/shepherdess.

seven signs, the: a short list of seven end-of-the-world type of events that are commonly referenced in many apocalyptic discussions ranging from the Bible to Nostradamus. The typical seven are: 1. the three major religions will decline. 2. there will be revolutions, terror, riots, and bloodshed worldwide. 3. there will be wars and rumors of wars. 4. famine, floods, drought, volcanic eruptions, and other natural disasters will be prolific. 5. air and water will become polluted. 6. earthquakes will be pronounced everywhere. (The "Big One" may be in the American Midwest or California.), and 7. plagues, diseases, and pandemics of all sorts will occur. *See also* birth pains, illustration of; eschatology, eschatological; myths universally duplicated in the Bible; "nation against nation"; Olivet Discourse, the; "sings of the times"; war on earth.

seven sleepers of Ephesus: the Christian version of a legend that seven martyrs were interred in a cave near Ephesus. They awoke during the persecution of Decius (ca. A.D. 250) and again in the fifth century. At the second stirring, they were taken to Emperor Theodosius II where they strengthened the ruler's faith. The martyrs then returned to their cave to await Judgment Day. The feast date for the event in high liturgy churches is July 27. *See also* martyr(s).

seven sons of Sceva. See Sceva.

seven spirits before his throne: the Holy Spirit as named in Revelation 1:4, *et al.,* who may be pictured as burning lamps in other instances. Some claim the seven located here do not represent the Holy Spirit but are instead representative angels such as mentioned in Acts 23: 8–9 and Isaiah 11. Nevertheless, the logical suggestion of the Trinity in this Revelation context is a powerful stand-alone argument against the angelic interpretation. *See also* Holy Spirit; lamp, lampstand(s); names (titles) for the Holy Spirit; spirits of God, the seven.

seventh day: the Jewish Sabbath celebrated as the ending of God's creative actions of beginnings. This special day may not be peculiar to the Jews alone, however, but for all the earth's history. Some ancients called it "the birthday of the world" and similar encomiums. *See also* Judaism; Sabbath; Seventh-Day Adventism.

Seventh-Day Adventism: an apocalyptic sect systematically evolved from the Millerite movement of the mid-1800s but formally established in 1863. The group is known for its belief in the infallibility of Scripture, the strict interpretation of the Fourth Commandment to honor the Sabbath (which they observe as Saturday), and a distinct penchant for setting a date of the Second Coming of Christ. Despite assertions that Adventism has never predicted the date of Christ's Second Advent, their denomination is predicated on that emphasis and the group has been repeatedly forced to justify that stance. They fear enforced legislation making Sunday the only official day of worship, a sure sign of the end of days. The denomination asserts that the pope of Rome is the Antichrist (certainly not the first to do so) and sees the three and a half years of Daniel 7 as historical time beginning in 538 B.C. and terminating in A.D. 1798. The first date marks the time the pope was taken captive by the French army, thus lessening the power of the Roman Church; the second marks the birth of the United States of America. The "image of the beast" represents that form of Protestantism that will develop when those persuasions shall seek the aid of civil power for ecclesiastical gains, especially as the population is forced to accept the Sunday Sabbath. Baptism is by immersion and non-salvable; the Lord's Supper is normally observed four times a year and usually proceeded by a foot-washing ceremony. Adventists are Trinitarian and premillennialists with two resurrections expected (one each for the good and evil of the world). To loyal followers, hell eventually dissolves into annihilation, and the faithful dead will lie in "soul sleep" until their resurrection to heaven. Adventists abstain from alcohol, tobacco, recreational drugs, and even coffee and tea as a practice but not a requirement; preferred dress is plain and modest. There is an emphasis on holistic health. Most are prone to be conscientious objectors in military service but many are willing to serve in some humanitarian capacity or chaplaincy. The official prophetic journal of the sect is called *History's Crowded Climax*. The most influential leader of the Adventists was Ellen G. White, whom they hold in special honor and authority as a prophet. Oddly enough, however, Seventh-Day Adventist publications normally disguise or omit the White contributions as if acknowledgment might somehow lessen the acceptability of the message as revealed publically. Should Seventh-Day Adventism be classed as a denomination, cult, or sect? The issue is much debated and advocates of the false rankings are numerous while others see them as within the Christian community if somewhat unorthodox. Critics are prone to point out legalism in faith practice, the paradoxical investigative judgment doctrine, the devotion to Ellen White, the conditional immortality doctrine, the literal interpretation of Genesis, the suggestion of the group that Satan is actually the incarnation of the archangel Michael who will eventually bear out sins, that Satan and his emissaries will rule the earth before the Millennium, the penchant for date-setting, naming the pope as Antichrist, and their comfort that they are the true Church remnant in the world have fueled mistrust from traditionalists. *See also* apocalyptic calculation; church bodies in America (typed); cult(s); date-setting; holistic; holistic health; investigative judgment; Millennial churches; millennial madness; Miller, William; Pankhurst, Christabel; sect(s); seventh day; soul sleep; White, Ellen G. (Harmon); Wyatt, Ronald Eldon.

Seven, the: the designation for the original seven deacons, an ordination that began after Jesus' resurrection (Acts 6:5). As selected by the insight of the Holy Spirit, the church chose Nicanor, Nicholas, Parmenas, Philip, Procorus, Stephen of Jerusalem, and Timon to assist in the daily obligations of the assembly. Their efforts made way for the apostles to concentrate on more pastoral and evangelistic duties. *See also* deacon(s), deaconess(es); evangelist(s), evangelism; Nicanor; Nicholas; Parmenas; Philip; Procorus; Stephen of Jerusalem; Timon.

seventh sense: an idea embraced by some whereby the born-again Christian can possess an unnatural sense of the spirit because the wall between the spirit realm and the flesh has been weakened. The renewal of the mind (Rom. 12:2) is operative here and allows the believer to use his or her gifts freely under the New Covenant. *See also* second sight; sixth sense.

seven thunders. See thunder revelations.

seven times: the length of time decreed by God for Nebuchadnezzar's imposed madness due to the king's arrogance and pride (Dan. 4:16 and other notations). Most interpreters assume that the duration is seven years; however, the symbolic number 7, meaning completion, could indicate the time was "just enough" for God's will to be accomplished in the king's attitude adjustment. A shorter period of derangement may be a preferable interpretation because seven years is a lengthy time for his kingdom to be held for him before reassuming the throne.

seventy: a number often carrying symbolic meaning (sometimes noted as seventy-two). Seventy was the number of disciples sent out by Jesus (Lk. 10:1), and the number of the Exodus elders (Ex. 24:1). Also, seventy is frequently noted as a multiple of the numeral seven. The count may also be the ideal membership of the Sanhedrin. *See also* Sanhedrin; Septuagint; seven; seventy elders; seventy, the; seventy-two.

seventy elders: assistants to Moses in the government of Israel (Num. 11:16, 24) during the wilderness wanderings. *See also* Eldad and Medad; Jew(s); seventy, the.

seventy-five days of transition: the time between the Second Coming of Christ and the actual start of the Millennium (according to dispensationalists and other conservative interpreters). Such a period of "time out" can help us account for a seed of confusion that started germinating in the last chapter of Daniel (Dan. 12:11–12). There, a mathematical anomaly or "error" seems to be present. At one point, the new age is said to begin after 1,290 days (the length of the Tribulation), but a bit later the number has changed to 1,335 days. The difference is said to allow time for necessary "housekeeping" millennial preparations—thirty days added to 1,290 for removing the abomination of desolation from the Temple, plus another forty-five added to 1,290 for the judgments of the nations and the Jews. In all, the interim of 1,335 leaves time for such events as the Temple cleansing and judgments noted above, not to mention the vast clean-up effort necessary to cleanse the land from slaughter. Then, there must be actions to cast the Antichrist and False Prophet into hell (Rev. 12:20), bind Satan for thousand years (Rev. 20:1–3), raise the Old Testament saints to new life (Isa. 26:19; Dan. 12:2), raise the Tribulation saints who were martyred (Rev. 20:4), set up a governmental structure for the Millennium (assumed) and assign governing responsibilities, and celebrate the Marriage Supper of the Lamb (Rev. 19:9)—to which is added an assumed timing. Likely, the new Millennial Temple must be built, or at least started. So, we now have 1,290 days for the Tribulation plus thirty for removal of the abomination of desolation to get to 1,290 (Dan. 12:1). Then comes another forty-five added to the original 1,290 to reach 1,335 (Dan. 12:12). *See also* evenings and mornings; "extra days" of Daniel prophecy, the; 1,290 and 1,335 days of prophecy; seventy weeks, prophecy of the.

seventy nations: the concept that God intended the world to be populated by seventy (or seventy-two) nations and no more, at least for the world of the day. The idea is explored in *1 Enoch*. Those countries outside the seventy true ones are implied to be manmade and thus false. There is some indication the seventy nations are associated with references that there are also seventy sons of God mentioned in Genesis 32:8 as well as Ugaritic texts that state the god El and his consort Asherah had seventy sons. *See also* nations, the; seventy shepherds; Table of Nations.

seventy sevens, prophecy of the. See seventy weeks, prophecy of the.

seventy-seven times: the curious response to Peter's inquiry of Jesus as to the number of times he was obligated to forgive another's wrongs (Mt. 18:21–22). The apostle even hinted toward a desired answer: "Up to seven times?" The surprising answer from the Lord instructs us we are to forgive, not seven times, but seventy-seven (some translations say seventy times seven). Jesus' answer did not imply a specific number of seventy-seven, or even 490 (seventy times seven). Who's counting? Rather, the hyperbole sets the standard of an unlimited pardoning disposition.

seventy shepherds: a rendition most clearly related in the Ethiopian Book of Enoch (chapters 83–90) known as "dream visions." Various interpretations have been offered as to the identity of these characters depicted there but no common consensus has surfaced. The most logical, perhaps, is that they are the *sarim*, those nations or their angelic leaders of the world—the so-called national guardian angels. In general, those entities are hostile Gentile nationalities opposed to Jews throughout history who are bent on destroying the Hebrew state and its population with excessive cruelty. *See also* angels of the nations; anti-Semitic; book(s) of Enoch; guardian angels; nations, the; prince of Greece; prince of Persia; seventy nations; Table of Nations.

seventy, the: seventy persons, or perhaps seventy-two, who were selected, trained, and sent out as evangelists by Jesus (Lk. 10:1–20). They were to work humbly, simply, and with no view toward personal gain. Their actions serve today as a lesson in how missions should be conducted according to Christ's design. We do know that the traditional number of the Sanhedrin was seventy-two and the legend of the LXX translation consisted of the same number who supposedly finished their work in seventy days. *See also* Bible translations; evangelist(s), evangelism; missions, missionaries; Septuagint, the; seventy-two; seventy elders.

seventy times seven. See seventy-seven times.

seventy-two: a number sometimes substituted for the round number of seventy. When groups are named, it is perhaps impossible to guess which was the more accurate as the calculating methods of the times seem to make no particular distinction. Numbers of all descriptions in the Bible are often irreconcilable in their accounts or imprecise in some way. Qabbalist rabbis say that the number was given to Enoch when he became Metatron (*3 Enoch* 9:2) and enumerate the number of kosmokrators over the people of Earth. Conspiracists consider it important that the pyramid on the Great Seal of America has seventy-two stones. *See also* kosmokrators; Metatron; Qabbala; seventy.

seventy weeks of Daniel. See Daniel's vision of the seventy "sevens"; seventy weeks, prophecy of the.

seventy weeks of years. See seventy weeks, prophecy of the.

seventy weeks, prophecy of the: Daniel's prophecy for Israel (Dan. 9:20–27) stated in weeks of years (*shabuwa'* in Hebrew). The exposition is critical to eschatological study, for it notes positions of history that can act as a sort of "checkpoint" system to trace God's plan through the ages. The calculations are not literal years but a bundle of heptads totaling seventy. The time span may be displayed as prophetic weeks, the first being seven weeks (49 years), a second of sixty-two sevens (434 years), and a third of one more week (7 years) for a sum of 490 years. The first two sections have passed into history, but most scholars (other than preterists) name the last seven years as coexistent with the Tribulation. Such a configuration requires a hiatus of indeterminate length between the close of the second group of 434 years (or sixty-nine prophetic years) and the restart of the last seven—sometimes called "the great parenthesis" of our own age. The seventieth week then is the Tribulation or "the time of Jacob's trouble." The most accepted calculation is that the seventy weeks began with a pronouncement from Persian authorities that the Jews were free to return to the Holy Land and rebuild Jerusalem. Historically, there are three proclamations of emancipation—in 539 B.C. from Cyrus, in 458 B.C. under Artaxerxes, and in 444 B.C., again, from Artaxerxes. The first cannot be the start for it makes no mention of rebuilding the city, nor does the second decree, although the scribe Ezra may have interpreted it that way. The third specifically states that Nehemiah can begin rebuilding the walls. Either the second or the third proclamation can serve as a start date but will end with slightly different events along the way to the sixty-ninth week. The year 444 is a common assumption as the ancient historian Prideaux said that Nehemiah completed his work under the Persian ruler Darius Nothus (423–404 B.C.).

The termination date then would be somewhere in the ministry of Jesus. A less accepted theory of the seventy weeks states that they began their course at the death of Jesus and continued to the Jewish War starting in A.D. 66. The book of *1 Enoch* records that we are presently in the seventieth week. That analysis is matched by the dispensational idea that our generation is the last, represented by the church of Laodicea in Revelation 3:14–22. For students of the seventy weeks prophecy, the work of Sir Robert Anderson is definitive. *See also* Anderson, Sir Robert; Anointed One, the; apocalyptic calculation; Babylonian Captivity; Babylonian restoration decrees; covenant of death; Daniel as Old Testament prophecy; date-setting; eschatology, eschatological; "great parenthesis, the"; heptad(s); Nehemiah as Old Testament book; Newton's Riddle; Palm Sunday; seven years covenant with Israel; seventy-five days of transition; seventy years of captivity; Tribulation; War of Jewish Independence.

seventy years of captivity: the time predicted by the prophet Jeremiah for Judah's exile in Babylon (Jer. 25:8–14). The prediction was a welcome aid to Daniel as that prophet considered the nation's approaching restoration. *See also* Babylonian Captivity; seventy weeks, prophecy of the.

seven wonders of the ancient world: the agreed-upon seven most magnificent structures in the ancient world, some of which bore significant religious expression. The constructs are listed as the pyramid of Giza in Egypt, the Hanging Gardens of Babylon, the Temple of Artemis in Ephesus, the statue of Zeus in Olympia, the mausoleum of Halicarnassus in Turkey, the Colossus of Rhodes, and the lighthouse of Alexandria. *See also* Alexandria as city; Artemisium; Artemis; Colossus of Rhodes; Ephesus; Hanging Gardens of Babylon; Helios; pyramid(s); Zeus.

seven words from the cross, the: the utterances of Christ from his cross of crucifixion, his final speaking offered before death. What he said then is intrinsically linked to prophecy and the future life. Likely, the pronouncements were voiced in the following order: 1. "Father, forgive them, for they do not know what they are doing" (to the Father) (Lk. 23:34), 2. "I tell you the truth, today you will be with me in paradise" (to the penitent thief) (Lk. 23:43), 3. "Dear woman, here is your son" (to Mary) and "Here is your mother" (to John) (Jn. 19:26–27), 4. *"Eloi, Eloi, lama sabachthani?"* (to the Father) (Mt. 27:46). 5. "I am thirsty" (to the soldiers) (Jn. 19:28), 6. "It is finished" (to the crowd) (Jn. 19:30), and 7. "Father, into your hands I commit my spirit" (to God) (Lk. 23:46). The words are the most poignant prophecy in all of Scripture. Of the seven last pronouncements, it has been said that they can be heard as: propitiatory—to seek forgiveness, promissory—granting paradise, provisionary—providing for his mother, protestatory—asking why God denies, peremptory—asking for drink, proclamatory—describing the end, and pacificatroy—reconciliation to God's will. *See also* crucifixion; *"Eloi, Eloi, lama sabachthani?"*; "It is done"; sacred wounds, five.

seven years covenant with Israel: the treaty to be negotiated between the Jewish leadership and the Antichrist that guarantees the Tribulation Jews a place to live and worship in peace under national protection in the land they claim as their own. It is by permission of the Antichrist that the Jews will be allowed to construct their millennial Temple. The agreement, however, is a deceptive one, and Antichrist will break it around the middle of the Tribulation period, and then desecrate the new Temple according to dispensational theology and other belief systems. Historical precedent is not lacking since God always displays His intentions in past events before He moves to implement a prophecy, namely, Rome concluded a great number of treaties of non-aggression and friendship with the Jews, only to abrogate them when convenient. Most of these pseudo accords were provided by Caesar to the Jews under Hyrcanus II. Many dispensational premillennialists agree that the signing of the false treaty will mark the start of the Tribulation and provide the signal for the rapture of the Church. The prophesied treaty then is an eschatological one drawn from Daniel 9:27 anticipating a future alliance between the Jews and the coming Antichrist. According to futurist theology, it can thus labeled "the covenant of the Antichrist." The contract reads: "He will confirm a covenant with many for one 'seven,' but in the middle of that 'seven,' he will put an end to sacrifice and offering. And one who causes desolation will place abominations on a wing of the temple until the end that is decreed is poured out on him." Just before the Tribulation the Antichrist will pledge freedom to exist and to worship for the beleaguered Jews, only to betray them at mid-point. In a radical departure from the common understanding, some apocalypticists view the "he" in the Daniel passage—not as naming the Antichrist—but as Christ himself. To them, the agreement being discussed is the New Covenant. Such an interpretation is usually considered flawed by most theologians. *See also* Antichrist; covenant(s), biblical; covenant of death; covenant theology; elect, the; eschatology, eschatological; Middle East peace initiatives; New Covenant, the; Palestinians; rapture; rebuilding the Temple; seventy weeks, prophecy of the; testament(s).

seven years, the: an alternative or "shorthand" name for the seven years of Tribulation. *See also* Days of Awe; eschatology, eschatological; Great Tribulation; "hard times"; hour of testing; hour of trial; seventy sevens, prophecy of the; time of Jacob's trouble; Tribulation.

Seven Years' War: a conflict that might technically be called the world's first global war (fought 1756–1763). The struggle was, at its base, a contention between Great Britain and France (with Spain), which eventually cost over a million lives in Central and North America, the subcontinent of India, the Philippines, Germany, Scandinavia, and even Africa. In North America, the clash was known as the French and Indian War, in Sweden the Pomeranian War, and the Third Silesian War in Austria and Prussia. It was fought to a standstill and ended with the Treaty of Paris in 1763 that made Britain a world empire. Religious difference certainly paid a part in the conflict, though it was not the major cause.

Severus Sebokht: a Christian scholar from Nisibis and bishop of a monastery on the Euphrates of the Syrian Orthodox Church. In the mid-seventh century, he formulated a system of mathematical signs from India that were then absorbed into Islamic scholarship and became known to us as Arabic numerals. *See also* Syrian Orthodox Church.

Sexagesima: in liturgical terms, the second Sunday before Ash Wednesday on the Roman Catholic and some Protestant church calendars. The designation is most prominent in the Anglican and Lutheran persuasions. *See also* liturgical year; liturgy, Christian; Quadragesima; Quinquagesima.

sext: prayers at noon in the canonical hours. *See also:* Agpeya; complain; canonical hours; lauds; liturgical year; liturgy; liturgy, Christian; matins; nones; novena; prayer(s); prime; terce; vespers.

sexton: a church caretaker with janitorial, repair, upkeep, and similar duties. *See also* beadle; verger.

Shabaka: pharaoh who assumed the throne of Egypt when conquered by the Ethiopians. He attempted to enlist Judah in an uprising against Assyria but was rebuffed by God's word through Isaiah (Isa. 19:1–15) under King Hezekiah. *See also* Amasis; Amenhotep II; Ay; Egypt, Egyptians; Hophra; king(s); Menes; Merneptah; Necho II; pharaoh; Pharaoh of the Exodus; Ramses II; Sesotris; Shishak; So; Tirhakah.

Shabbat angels: spirit beings (angels) whom many Jews believe attend Sabbath worship and are to be welcomed by the singing of s*halom aleichem,* the song of welcome. The Talmud suggests that, upon returning from synagogue, each person is accompanied by a good angel to encourage him and a bad one to discourage him. If the person keeps the Sabbath attitude through the week, the good angel has prevailed and is permitted to enter the home. *See also* angel(s); Judaism; liturgy, Jewish; Sabbath.

Shabu'ot: Hebrew name for the Feast of Weeks (Pentecost). *See also* flora, fruit, and grain; symbology of; feasts and special days of Judaism; Judaism; Pentecost.

shackles: a device for incapacitating a prisoner, usually by use of cuffs and manacles to the legs or arms. The term is a symbol of confinement, oppression, or restriction in prophetic language (*e.g.,* Nahum 1:13). In Scripture, sin can be portrayed as the burden of hindering shackles that represses joy and acceptance. *See also* sin(s); slave, slavery; yoke.

Shad: one of the major gods of ancient Babylon and likely the one for whom the Hebrew champion Shadrach was named. *See also* Shadrach; Sumerian and Babylonian pantheon.

shade(s): 1. a word with many meanings but, in religion or superstition, a disembodied spirit is implied. Usually spoken of in the plural, a shade may be a lost soul, the essence of a dead person that has failed to gain a fortunate afterlife—a ghost. 2. in the vernacular, to "throw a shade" at someone is to offend with some degree of disrespect, judgment, or animosity. *See also* apparition; evil eye; ghost(s); soul(s); spirit.

shadow(s): the darkened image exposed when any object blocks the sun's rays. In prophetic terms, a shadow can foretell an event—a foreshadowing—with a welcome or fearsome outcome. Peter's shadow is said (Acts 5:15) to have healing powers. It appears death has its own special shadow in some sense. Some apocalypticists use the term much like "signs," but holding the idea that the paradigm conceals the future and states those events may repeat themselves, thus making the shadow a true prophecy. *See also* cycles of history; prodigy; prophecy; shadow of death; sign(s); symbol(s).

shadow of death: or "deep shadows." The phrase intends a state of despair or fear in which the sufferer can only resort to God for rescue. Job 38:17 places the situation squarely with the Lord when he could find no earthly remedy. *See also* shadow(s).

Shadrach: the Babylonian name for one of the three wise companions of Daniel who were rescued from the fiery furnace. Shadrach's Hebrew name was Hananiah ("God is gracious"), but it was altered to honor one of the gods of the Babylonian pantheon, most likely Shad. *See also* Abednego; Azariah as exile; Belteshazzar; Daniel; Hananiah the exile; Meshach; Mishael; Shad; Sumerian and Babylonian pantheon.

Shakers. See United Society of Believers.

shake; shaken: the act of violently moving a body, usually in anger or agitation. The term is apocalyptic when used in this fashion (Ezk. 12:17–20; Mt. 24:29). The psalmist declared, to the contrary, that his presence in the Lord assured he will not be shaken (Ps. 16:8).

Shakti: 1. the divine mother goddess of the Hindu tradition. The name means "power" or "empowering" because not only was she the creator goddess but was also the cosmic energy that moved the universe and initiated change. She is the one who gives birth to all things sometimes referred to as Devi. The goddess is further personified as Maha Diva, the divine mother or "great goddess," the nurturing force of the universe. She may appear as the gentle, loving Parvati but also as Kali and Durga—the terrible and threatening. 2. an Eastern practice of discipline related to yoga. It is the starting point that inspires the serpent-type energy to coil up the spine through the body, often accompanied by the recitation of a mantra. The goal is to unite with the male power of Shiva. The belief, a. k. a. Chiti, Chit Shakti, or Kundalini, is essentially the creative principle of Hinduism. *See also* chakra; Chi; contemplative prayer movement; Hinduism; kundalini; mantra; sect(s); yoga.

Shalem: the Canaanite god of dusk or sunset. He was said to have appeared over Jerusalem at the hill of Ophel affirming it was a sacred place. *See also* Levant pantheon.

Shallum: 1. fifteenth king of Israel who gained the position by slaying King Zechariah and ruled over the ten tribes for only one month before being killed by Menahem (2 Ki. 15:8–15). 2. a second name for Jehoahaz, king of Judah. 3. the husband of Huldah the prophetess; Josephus praised him for possessing great dignity. Shallum was a common name in the Old Testament, but only the three cited above appear to hold significant prophetic impact. *See also* Huldah; Jehoahaz of Judah; king(s); kings of Israel and Judah; kings of Israel and Judah in foreign relations.

Shalman: most likely an abbreviation for Shalmaneser of Assyria, although this identification is not wholly proven. He (or perhaps one Salamanu of Moab) was, according to the prophet Hosea (Hos. 10:14), the conqueror of Beth Arbel in Galilee. That exploit acts as a warning from the prophet to all of Israel that it could happen again elsewhere and at any time. *See also* Assyria, Assyrians; Beth Arbel; king(s); Shalmaneser.

Shalmaneser: the name of several Assyrian kings, probably four in all. Two are of interest to prophecy. Shalmaneser III (859–824 B.C.) was the first Assyrian king to come into contact with Israel. He was an energetic warrior and fought his neighbors (including Ahab of Israel) on several occasions. Shalmaneser V (ruled 726–722 B.C.) was the successor to Tiglath-pileser III (727–722 B.C.) and was equally ambitious in warfare; he battered the Northern Kingdom under Hoshea and chained her king, then left the final disposal of Samaria to his younger brother, Sargon II who ruled 721–705 B.C. (2 Ki. 17:1–6). Later, Sennacherib also tried to subdue both Samaria and Judah but fell short. *See also* Assyria, Assyrians; Beth Arbel; Hoshea; king(s); Sargon II; Sennacherib; Sennacherib's Prism; Shalman; Tiglath-pileser III.

shalom: The Jewish term for "peace," usually pronounced as a blessing. The word carries more meaning than a mere greeting or gesture of friendship, however. *Shalom* is a pointed desire for another's happiness, well-being, life balance, prosperity, and contentment in one's faith. *See also* grace and peace; *maat;* peace.

shaman, shamanism: the title of a tribal leader, priest, or medicine man who claims and exercises occultic powers and the ability to contact the spirit world through trance, dance, drugs, etc. The practice is an ancient one, and some primitive tribes still retain that culture today. The more common term is "witch doctor." *See also* animism; attending spirit(s); Cheonodoism; conjure; conjure man; dance; divination; Ghost Wolf, Robert; hierophant; Inuit; kahuna; Kirant; lower world; magic arts; mambo; medium; meonenim; Mugyo; Mum; mystagogue; occult, occultic; pagan practices; priest(s;) Sangoma(s); seior; soothsayer(s); sorcery, sorceries; spirit guide(s); Tenskwautawa; tutelary; witchcraft; witch of Endor.

Shamar: a Hebrew word for the prophet as a watchman or guardian. *See also Chozeh;* interpreter; *Kohen; Lewi;* man of God; messenger of Yahweh; *Nabhi';* prophet(s); *Ro'eh;* servant of Yahweh; servants, my; watchman.

Shamash: the ancient Babylon god of prophecy and justice and the sky god of the Middle East. This welkin deity was also the chief god of Sumer, the sun god responsible for justice in the land. *See also* Sumerian and Babylonian pantheon; Sumer, Sumerian(s); Utu; welkin.

Shambhala legends: also known as the Secret Chiefs, Hidden Masters, or the Great White Brotherhood. Myths emerged from Tibet and surrounding territories that reported a hidden locale where perfection reigned—an unspoiled paradise. Perhaps "Xanadu" is an acceptable alternate description. Usually, the Tibetan lamas are said to have governed the area, and explorers from all over the globe have attempted to find such a place. The lamas alone claim to know its location, or someday will learn it. *See also* Abraham's bosom; afterlife; Annwn; Aralu; Arcadia; Asgard; Avalon; Dalai

Lama; Dis; Duat; Elysium; eternal life; future life, doctrine of the; Gehenna; Great White Brotherhood; Hades; happy hunting ground; heaven; hell; Hy-Breasail; Hyperborea; Jade Empire, the; Jahannam; Janna; lake of fire; life after death; limbo; *Limbus Puerorum;* Mictlan; Nirvana; Otherworld; Paradise; paradise of God; Pardes; Perdition; Promised Land, the; Pure Land, the; Roerich, Nicholas K.; *Sheol;* soul sleep; space doctrine; Summerland; Thule, land of; Tir na nOg; underworld; Utopia; Valhalla; world to come, the; Xibala.

Shamgar: a judge of Israel (Jud. 3:31) who is reported to have slain 600 Philistines with an ox goad. Deborah's victory song (Jud. 5:6) mentions some of his exploits. He is named as the third judge in the land and ruled for an unknown number of years. *See also* judge(s); Judges as Old Testament book.

Shammai, Rabbi: founder of a rabbinic system that interpreted the Torah in a strict and controlled manner. Shammai was born around 50 B.C. and died in A.D. 30 and was destined to be highly influential in Jewish scholarship. He was afraid the Roman influence would become too strong if the Jewish manner of torah and behavior was too lax. The Law of Moses was decidedly rigid, with no flexibility in interpretation or action. Shammai's approach was markedly different from that of his rival, Rabbi Hillel, though reportedly the competition was friendly. Shammai was reputedly dour, quick-tempered, impatient, and not surprisingly, the less favored of the two. Both men lived during the time of Herod the Great. *See also* Hillel, Rabbi; Jew(s).

Shango: a.k.a. Chango, Jakuta, Xango, or *Siete Rayos,* a Yoruba king in Nigeria who is venerated as a god there and in parts of the Caribbean. Shango was a warlike ruler (his name means "to strike") but his worship today seeks to empower the life of the devotee. The cult is often mixed with other Caribbean sects. Ritual involves a unique combination of red cloth, a peculiar diet, beads (numbering four to seven called "sacred numbers"), and dancing with drum music. *See also* animism; Brujeria; Candomble; Creole (Caribbean) religions; cult(s); king(s); Kumina; Macumba; magic, magick; Obeah; occult, occultic; Orisha; Quimbanda; Rastafarianism; Santeria; shaman, shamanism; spiritism; Spiritual Baptists; Umbanda; Voodoo, Voudou; Yoruba.

Shapash: the Canaanite goddess whose worship entailed ritual prostitution. *See also* demimondaines; Levant pantheon; sacred prostitution.

Shari'a: the sacred law of Islam containing the will of Allah as to religion, ritual, legal, ethical, and social aspects of living. The term means "way" or "path," and its statutes apply to all Muslims to some degree. More precisely, the word springs from the notion of "the road to the watering hole," a clue important in desert regions where Islam began. Shari'a law is a curious mixture of political function and the Islamic religion in that the boundaries of the two are blurred. There is no line of separation between mosque and state, whereas a democracy tries to discriminate between church and state. The severity and jurisdiction of the courts, legislatures, and educational institutions vary from region to region but are present in some form in all Islamic nations. In more modern Islamic societies (*e.g.*, Turkey and Egypt), the Shari'a has given way to more secular codes of law, but fundamentalists everywhere are continually trying to return the nations to "the true Islam." Shari'a is rooted in the *Qur'an* and its *Hadith* and is considered inviolate, but its interpolations are wholly in the control of the imams and mosques. Even so, from the 13th century four schools of interpretation had already arisen as to how the law should be applied. Each was named for its originator: the Shafi'i, the Hanbali, the Hanafi, and the Maliki. Even today, there are variations of administration from region to region of Islam with perhaps the Shafi'i being dominant and the imam's opinion weighing heavily. *See also* Abu 'Abdallah Muhammad ibn Idris al-Shafi'i; Daesh; decapitation; *fatwa; Hadith;* House of War; imam; Islam; jihad; Qur'an; Salafi.

Sharon: the coastal plain of Israel running about fifty miles from south of the Carmel Mountain range to the city of Jaffa, and extending about six miles inland. The area might be called the "breadbasket" of the land because of its rich and vital agriculture (*i.e.,* Isaiah 35:1–2). An earlier description (1 Chr. 5:16) places the location near the territory of the tribe of Gad known for its good pasturage. *See also* Valley of Achor.

Sharpton, Charles "Al" Jr.: an American Baptist minister and political activist, (b. October 3, 1954). Sharpton's actions, however, are far more political than pastoral. He is a media personality with frequent TV and radio appearances in which he promotes civil rights and other social issues with a radical slant. Sharpton was a Democratic presidential candidate in 2004 but fared poorly. He is frequently investigated for tax evasion, conspiracy, and incite to riot. His critics (of which there are many) see him as a radically political agitator and a threat to peaceful law and order. *See also* Afro-American theology; Baptists.

shaved head and beard of Ezekiel. See Ezekiel's demonstration of his shaved head and beard.

Shaw, Anna Howard: a Methodist minister (1847–1919), physician, and president of the National Woman Suffrage Association from 1904 to 1915. Shaw worked with the likes of Susan B. Anthony and held several pastorates in Massachusetts. She was awarded the Distinguished Service Medal for her work as a member of the Council on National Defense in World War I. *See also* Methodists.

Shaw, George Bernard: Irish playwright, drama critic, and polemicist (1856–1950), undoubtedly controversial in both his work and persona. He was a supporter of eugenics and alphabet reform but avidly antagonistic toward religion. Shaw's comment on the book of Revelation, for example, is symptomatic: "[the book is]...a curious record of the visions of a drug addict."

Shay, John Dawson Gilmary: Catholic historian and co-founder of the United States Catholic Historical Society (1884) where he served as editor and president. Shay was also a member of the New York and other historical societies, a rare honor for Catholics in his era. His most famous writing is the five-volume *History of the Catholic Church in the United States* (1886–1892). *See also* Roman Catholic Church.

Shayler, David: a British-born (December 24, 1965) journalist and former operative for MI5. Shayler claims to be the reincarnation of several deities, including the Son of God. His most famous pronouncement, other than the above, seems to be his allegation that the September 11, 2001, attacks in New York City did not involve airplanes but disguised missiles. He is anti-Zionist and claims to be able to predict the weather and football scores, as well as coming terrorist attacks. He remains in British legal trouble for violation of the nation's security laws and secrecy acts.

Shaytan: the Islamic Satan—the devil or *a* devil. *See also* accuser of our brothers; angel of light; Anointed Cherub; Apophis; Baal-zebub; Baphomet; Beelzeboul; Beelzebub; Behemoth; Belial; binding of Satan; *Book of the Dead;* Cupay; Day Star; dragon; Evil One, the; father of lies; genie(s); goat; Ghede; goat; god of this age, the; guardian Cherub; Hahgwehdaetgah; Iblis; *Kategor;* kingdom of the air; kingdom of this world; king of Babylon; king of Tyre; Leviathan; Light-Bringer; lion; Lucifer; Mastema; Morning Star, the; names, symbology of; pentagram; prince of demons; prince of the power of the air; prince of this world; Rahab; red dragon; ruler of the kingdom of the air; Sammael; Sanat Kumar; Satanic Bible; satanic salute; Satanism; Satan's so-called deep secrets; seed of the serpent; serpent; Shaytan; son of the morning, son of the dawn; Venus.

Shealtiel: likely the second son of Jeconiah and father of Zerubbabel (Hag. 2:23), or possibly Jeconiah was his uncle or grandfather, who is listed in the genealogy of Jesus (Mt. 1:12). In the Luke genealogy, Shealtiel is named as the son of an unknown man named Neri and thereby traced through David's son Nathan. Whether or not he is considered within the royal bloodline by family or position, he was considered the legitimate successor to Jehoiachin and Zerubbabel and thereby the link to the royal line. His name is listed as a separate entry in Matthew's genealogy of Jesus. Shealtiel could also be an alternate or last name for Zerubbabel, as some surmise. *See also* Babylonian Captivity, return from; Ezra as scribe; Nehemiah as governor; Sheshbazzar; Zerubbabel.

Shear-Jashub: the young son of Isaiah who accompanied his father to visit King Ahaz (Isa. 7:3). On that occasion, Isaiah pronounced his vital messianic prophecy that "a remnant shall return," which promises prosperity for Israel and is the literal meaning of the child's name (Isa. 8:18). The reference to Shear-Jashub may be connected to Isaiah's further prophecy that the Messiah, called Immanuel (Emmanuel), would come as the Messiah or Christ—the Anointed One (Isa. 7:14). *See also* Emmanuel; remnant; second Exodus.

Sheba: 1. a Benjamite who tried to take advantage of the turmoil following Absalom's rebellion and win the kingdom for the northern tribes against the recently victorious David (2 Sam. 20:1–22). David commissioned Abishai to chase after and subdue the rebel. Abishai, accompanied by Joab, was successful when a wise woman of the town at Abel of Beth-Maacah, where Sheba had taken refuge, counseled that the rebel's head be thrown over the wall to placate the pursuing army. 2. a country contemporary with that of Solomon located most likely in southern Arabia or coastal Africa at Yemen or Ethiopia. The Queen of Sheba, a possible ruler there, visited Solomon when she learned of his wealth and wisdom (1 Ki. 10:1–10). The country trafficked in precious gems, spices, and other exotic products. *See also* Arabia; Belkis; Candace; Cush, Cushites; Makeda; queen(s); Queen of Sheba; Queen of the South.

Shebna: steward of the king's palace under Hezekiah (Isa. 22:15–25). Isaiah prophesied against him as a disgrace in his trusted position and foresaw his replacement by the more noble and efficient Eliakim. *See also* Eliakim.

Shechem: 1. an old city of Canaan and an important one to the history of the Israelites, situated within the boundaries of the tribe of Manasseh in the hill country. Shechem was the site of the spark of rebellion by Jeroboam over Rehoboam, making the former the king of the ten northern tribes (1 Ki. 12:1–19). The place was also the site of the covenant renewal by Joshua (Jos. 24). 2. the name of the Canaanite rapist who ravaged Dinah, the daughter of Jacob. Two of her brothers, Levi and Simeon, retaliated against the perpetrator with severity (Gen. 34). *See also* Dinah; Levi; Simeon.

shechitah: the slaughtering of animals in accord with Hebrew kosher laws. *See also* Judaism; *kosher*.

Sheen, Fulton J.: a popular Catholic (archbishop and theologian) broadcaster (1895–1979) whose pragmatic and positive expositions resonated well with all types of listeners from the 1930s into the 1960s. His radio program was called the "Catholic Hour" and the TV episodes were familiar as "Life is Worth Living." He was a two-time Emmy Award winner and one of the early televangelists but short of the typical evangelistic appeal. *See also* Roman Catholic Church; televangelism, televangelists.

sheep: ruminant livestock valued for their meat, skin, and wool. Sheep are a frequent metaphor in Scripture, usually representing the "meek" (modest but strong in the Lord) followers of Christ, of whom he is chief shepherd. To be sheepheaded, however, is to appear simple or fatuous. The animals were the principal blood sacrifice of Old Testament Judaism. In Revelation, Jesus is pictured both as a lion (powerful) and a Lamb (humble but in this instance strong as well). In Jesus' parable of the sheep and goats, the former are considered worthy because of their goodness in action. Sometimes the animal represents Israel herself (Ps. 80:1). *See also* animals, birds, and insects, symbology of; flocks and herds; lamb; parable(s); parables of the New Testament; ram; sheep and goats, judgment of the; "sheeple."

sheep and goats, judgment of the: a judgment of Gentile survivors just prior to the establishment of the millennial kingdom. The process will determine who is eligible to enter the Millennium according to their benevolent actions during the Tribulation, especially enacted by their aid to the persecuted Jews at that time. The sheep will enter for blessing, but the goats will be denied and condemned. Jesus used the parable of the sheep and goats (Mt. 25:31–46) to illustrate that event when speaking in his Olivet Discourse. It is permissible to interpret this parable in a more contemporary sense as well, even if that is not its primary intent (*viz.*, that believers should practice benevolence to those less fortunate and in need of basic subsistence in our own day). *See also* eschatology, eschatological; eschatological parable(s); parable(s); parables of the New Testament.

"sheeple": an insulting name placed on those of us whom the political elitists consider inferior and incapable of knowing what is best for ourselves. These "enlightened ones" regard themselves to be experts in politics and economics and must direct the normal population as to how to live our ordinary lives. We are simply too dumb to make our own decisions. *See also* Brights, the; Christianist(s); sheep; slurs, religious.

"sheep stealing": the deliberate act of attempting to lure a member of one denomination or faith tradition to one's own. Some consider the action unethical while others view it as acceptable recruitment. *See also* Christianese; comity; proselyte(s); proselytism; slurs, religious; "souper."

sheik: an honorary title of respect used by Muslims in the way Christians employ "reverend." *See also* Islam.

shekel: ancient coinage consisting of about 2/5 of an ounce of silver. Other forms of currency included the talent (75 pounds), the mina (1 ¼ pound), the pim (1/3 ounce), the beka (1/5 ounce), and the guah (1/50 ounce). *See also* denarius; gold, golden; kondrantes; lepta; mammon; *Mene, Mene; Tekel, Parsin (or Uparsin)*; silver; talent.

Shekinah glory: a brilliant light or cloud so intense that it is reserved for a singular description of God's glory in His divine presence. Such glory light suggests it will be even more brilliant because of the anticipated total darkness surrounding the Second Coming event prior to Christ's appearance. It was in place at the consecration of the tabernacle, at the dedication of Solomon's Temple (2 Chr. 5:13–14; 7:1-3), at Isaiah's call to ministry (Isa. 6:1–7), and some other high biblical reference points. Ezekiel saw it depart from the Temple in his vision as God abandoned that edifice, no longer a worthy dwelling for Himself (Ezk. 10). It is eschatologically noteworthy that the Shekinah did not return to the Second Temple. Other biblical instances of the Shekinah appearance include: as the guide for the Israelites from the Exodus, as protection from Pharaoh at the Red Sea, at the wilderness of Zin, with Moses on Mount Sinai, above the mercy seat in the Holy of Holies, when God appointed the seventy elders, when Miriam spoke against Moses' Cushite wife, when Moses pleaded for Israel (Num. 14:13-14), at Korah's rebellion, with the shepherds at the birth of Jesus, and at Jesus' baptism, transfiguration, and ascension. Other bright lights may qualify including Jesus described as the light of the world (John 8:12), the angels at the empty tomb (Mt. 28:2), the heavenly light that blinded Paul (Acts 9:3), the light of Peter's angelic deliverer (Acts 12:7), and the appearance of New Jerusalem that needs neither sun nor moon (Rev. 21:28). The Shekinah is predicted to reappear at the ascension of the two great witnesses (Rev. 11:12). Revelation 15:5-8 describes the heavenly Temple filled with the "smoke" of God's glory so that the place could not be entered. Paul seemed to describe the same phenomenon as "unapproachable light" (1 Tim. 6:16). The Shekinah brilliance could very well be the final and most intense "sign" of Christ seen in the heavens at his coming (Mt. 24:30); the *Apocalypse of Peter* hints it will be the sign of the cross moving before him at his appearance. In some instances, the Shekinah may be associated with the clouds, as may be seen at the rapture of the Church (1 Th. 4:17). Qabbalistic adherents claim that the Shekinah is the feminine aspect of the deity, or "the bride of God." Some Jewish synagogues of that order welcome the Shekinah at sunset on Friday (the start of the Sabbath). They assert that only through the female Shekinah can creation be manifested. For most Jews, the Shekinah signifies the presence of God with them. The most unusual feature of the Shekinah is that it both attracts and repels (Ps. 39:13; 143:7) and conceals and reveals (Isa. 1:1–8). *See also* astronomy, astronomers; Branch of the Lord; celestial disturbances; eschatology, eschatological; Ezekiel's call and vision of the Cherubim; Ezekiel's vision of the Cherubim and the departed glory; cloud(s); emanations, doctrine of; empyreanism; eschatology, eschatological; Ezekiel's vision of the fiery man and the wicked Temple; glory; glory, the surpassing; great sign, the; great signs, the; heavenly Temple; Holy of Holies; house of My glory; light; illumination; *kavod;* Lux; manifestation of the Spirit; "next year in Jerusalem"; Noor, noor; primal light; Qabbala; Second Coming; sign of the Son of Man, the; smoke; Solomon's prayer of dedication; Son of God; Tabor light; tent of meeting; Transfiguration, the.

Sheldon, Charles Monroe: a Congregational minister (1857–1946), novelist (he wrote some thirty books), editor, and social reformer. Sheldon was editor of the *Christian Herald* magazine, but it was one of his books, *In His Steps* (1896), for which he is best-known. He emphasized the Social Gospel movement that is featured in the book which sold more at the time than any, except the Bible and the works of Shakespeare. *See also* Congregationalists; Social Gospel; social issues.

Shem: a son of Noah (Gen. 10:21), probably the firstborn, although, in the Genesis genealogy, it can be interpreted that he was either an older brother or a younger one. He acted respectfully upon discovering his father nude and in a drunken stupor. Consequently, he was blessed with his brother Japheth, but the other sibling, Ham, was not so favored. Shem is usually pronounced to be the ancestor of the chosen people, the Jews. *See also* Ham; Japheth.

Shema: the high declaration of faith and the most famous of all Jewish creeds. The fullest explanations of the meaning are in Deuteronomy 6:4-9 and 11:13–21. The recitation (to be spoken twice daily by Orthodox Jews) is central to the faith and is the first prayer taught to young children. The declaration is called the *Shema*, from the first word meaning "hear." The pronouncement (in short form) is: *Shema Yisrael Adonai Elohaynu Adoai Echad*— "Hear, O Israel, the Lord is our God, the Lord is One." Any misuse, disbelief, or neglect of the *Shema* was, and is, considered a breach of torah. *See also Amidah*; Judaism.

Shemaiah the false prophets: 1. an unworthy prophet bribed by Tobiah and Sanballat in an effort to frighten Nehemiah and thereby hinder the rebuilding of Jerusalem's walls (Neh. 6:10–11). 2. a false prophet among the exiles who wrote the priests at Jerusalem, insisting that the Babylonian Captivity would be brief, a direct repudiation of Jeremiah's official prediction. Shemaiah urged that Jeremiah should be disciplined for treason (Jer. 29:24–32), an attitude that resulted in Shemaiah's demise by divine intervention. *See also* False Prophet, the.

Shemaiah the true prophets: 1. a seer who informed Rehoboam of Judah that he should not take any soldiers of Israel to war against Jeroboam (1 Ki. 12:22–25; 2 Chr. 11:1–4) in an attempt to dethrone the new king of the Northern Kingdom. Five years later, he counseled Rehoboam on the occasion of Pharaoh Shishak's siege of Jerusalem by telling him that the battle was caused by Judah's rebellion against God. After repentance, the siege was lifted even though Shishak carried off the treasure of Jerusalem, including all the riches of the Temple. Shemaiah eventually wrote a history of Rehoboam's reign. 2. the father of Uriah (Urijah) put to death by King Jehoiakim because of his true but censorious prophecies against Judah (Jer. 26:20-23). His preaching paralleled that of Jeremiah, but his life was forfeit despite his attempted escape to Egypt. Several other characters in the Bible are also named Shemaiah, but they are of marginal interest to eschatology. *See also* martyr(s); prophet(s); prophets as martyrs; Uriah.

Shemhamforesh: the first four letters of God's name (the Ineffable Name or the Tetragrammaton) that can be combined in seventy-two ways to represent the powers, laws, and energy of nature (according to Qabbalism). Such a magical manipulation of the title could be invoked to bind or loose supernatural agents. *See also 'Emeth; hadavar; Ha Shem;* Ketef Hinnom amulets; names, symbology of; names (titles) for God; Qabbala; Sephiroth tree; Yahweh.

Shemini Atzeret: a Jewish festival also known as the "eighth-day assembly" because it follows the seven-day celebration of *Sukkot.* Though related to the Feast of Tabernacles, it stands as its own holiday in the September/October time slot. The day is recognized by joyful prayer and celebrations as a sort of postlude to the previous week of worship for the harvests. *See also* feasts and special days of Judaism; Judaism; *Simchat Torah;* Tabernacles, Feast of.

sheminith: a musical term noted in 1 Chronicles 15:21 and elsewhere. Perhaps, in contrast to the *alamoth,* the tune was in a lower octave or the bass voice. *See also alamoth;* music; *Selah; shigionoth.*

Shemitah. See Jubilee Year.

Shenazar. See Sheshbazzar; Zerubbabel.

Sheol: the Hebrew term for "grave" or "Hades," which designates the abode of the dead until the resurrection. The term occurs some sixty-five times in the Old Testament. In ancient times the dead were buried in communal caves, their bones growing to piles as additions were made. The terms *Gan Eden, Gilgul,* and *Olam Haba* also apply. As Jewish thought developed, it was concluded that somewhere underneath all the clutter was a literal place where, in some sense, the spirits of the deceased dwelled. *Sheol* is to be distinguished from the place of torment officially termed "the lake of fire." The place was considered to be an eerie, dreary situation with little or no consciousness. Job described the region as "the place of no return...the land of gloom and deep shadow... and disorder, where even the light is like darkness" (Job 10:20– 22). *See also* Abaddon; Abraham's bosom; Abyss, the; afterlife; Amente; Annwn; Aralu; Arcadia; Asgard; Avalon; Bolos; death; Death and Destruction; Dis; Duat; Elysium; eschatology, eschatological; eternal life; future life, doctrine of the; Gehenna; grave; Hades; Harrowing of Hell, the; heaven; hell; Hy-Breasail;

Hyperborea; intermediate state; Jade Empire, the; Jahannam; Janna; Kidron Valley; lake of fire; life after death; limbo; *Limbus Puerorum;* Mictlan; *nephesh;* new heaven and new earth; Nirvana; Otherworld; Pardes; Paradise; paradise of God; paraeschatology; Perdition; Promised Land, the; Pure Land, the; purgatory; *rephaim;* soul sleep; space doctrine; Summerland; Thule, land of; Tir na nOg; Tophet; Tyropoeon Valley; underworld; Upper Gehenna; Utopia; Valhalla; Valley of Decision; Valley of Hinnom; Valley of Jehoshaphat; Valley of Slaughter; world to come, the; Xibala.

Shephelah: (foothills) of the Judean mountains, about midway between Jerusalem and Tel Aviv. It overlooked the coastal plain and served as the north/south trade junction linking Egypt to Asia Minor and the east/west road from the sea to Jerusalem. The principal town was Gezer, now an important archeological research site.

shepherding (cultic): granting personal freedoms to a charismatic or demanding leader, the "shepherd" who controls every aspect of life in the faith community. The practice is commonplace in most cults, so much so that it has become a guiding principle for evaluating a group as to its purpose and administration. The techniques display characteristics of mind control except the base is likely to be a demeaning religiosity for the benefit of the dictatorial leader or small group supervisors alone. *See also* acephali; autocephalous; Catholic Church abuse scandal; church abuse; church, administration of the early; church discipline; churching; church models; conciliarism; congregational polity; connectional polity; cult(s); ecclesiology; episcopate; faith and order; Free Church(es); hierarchical polity; magisterium; papal revenue; plebania; polity; prelacy; presbytery; representative polity; sect(s); shepherding (discipleship); shepherding (pastoral); shepherdless flock, the; shepherd/shepherdess; sobornost; Zechariah's oracle of the stricken shepherds and the scattered sheep.

shepherding (discipleship): a description using rather euphemistic language for the church polity of pastoral education or guidance. Such a political and religious mold positions the pastor or priest and/or elders (deacons) as the supreme authority in the church organization with almost absolute control over all matters practical and theological. The congregation, willing or not, has but token representation, or as much as they are willing to concede. As of today, the reconstituted Southern Baptist Convention may be the premier model of shepherding/discipleship as it has reverted to strict fundamentalist doctrine and practice. Either word in the depiction, shepherding or discipleship, can be a positive trait when used wisely and compassionately. However, the terms today tend to denote something more sinister in many contexts. *See also* acephali; autocephalous; church, administration of the early; church models; church abuse; conciliarism; congregational polity; connectional polity; deacon(s), deaconess(es); ecclesiology; episcopate; faith and order; Free Church(es); hierarchical polity; magisterium; pastor(s); plebania; polity; prefect(s); prelacy; prelate(s); *presbuteros;* presbytery; priest(s); priesthood of the believer; primate; religious education; representative polity; shepherding (cultic); shepherding (pastoral); shepherds of Israel; shepherd/shepherdess.

shepherding (pastoral): the practices and attitudes of some church leaders who strive for caring and constructive management of their charges that will advance the congregation as a whole and sustain the individual church-goer. The pastor, priest, or another manager of title bases his or her plans on compassion, the care of souls, and shared administration of church affairs. No techniques of control are in evidence and self-aggrandizement of the pastor is not utilized. Christ-like principles are attempted at all times and the Holy Spirit is allowed freedom to guide the congregation as the members comprehend him. *See also* acephali; autocephalous; church, administration of the early; church abuse; church models; conciliarism; congregational polity; connectional polity; ecclesiology; episcopate; faith and order; Free Church(es); hierarchical polity; magisterium; minister(s); ministry; "pass under my staff"; pastor(s); pastoral care; plebania; polity; prelacy; presbytery; priest(s); priesthood of the believer; representative polity; shepherding (cultic); shepherding (discipleship); shepherds of Israel; shepherd/shepherdess.

shepherdless flock, the: a parable or vision of the prophet Micaiah to illustrate the defeat of Ahab and Jehoshaphat before Ramoth Gilead (1 Ki. 22:13–28). The phrase has become a metaphor for hopeless, dissolute, or discouraged peoples without a strong leader. *See also* Ezekiel's curse of the neglectful shepherds; parable(s); parables of the Old Testament; shepherding (cultic); shepherds of Israel; Zechariah's oracle of the stricken shepherds and the scattered sheep.

shepherd, my. See Cyrus the Great (Cyrus II).

Shepherd of Hermes, The: a Christian extrabiblical literary work composed sometime in the second century. Some early church leaders, including Irenaeus, considered it to have great authority, and it was subsequently included in the canon of some early biblical collections. The book is composed of some five visions, twelve commandments, and ten parables. The "good shepherd," which can be taken as the central theme, may be a symbol of Christ. The author is known only as a former slave who claims to have received visions concerning the sad state of affairs in the Christian Church at that time and consistently appeals for repentance and reform. Nevertheless, the work seems to carry an optimistic tone throughout. *See also* canon; Hermas; parable(s).

shepherd of the sheep, that great: a description of Christ as head of his Church as named by the writer of Hebrews (Heb. 13:20). *See also* names (titles) for Jesus; shepherd/shepherdess.

shepherds of Israel: Israel's leaders (often called princes or "captains" as well) or military protectors at the time of the Babylonian Exile and in other periods of history (*i.e.,* Ezekiel 34). A nation's leaders may be worthy or they may be failures in line for God's judgment—they are either good shepherds or poor ones. *See also* Ezekiel's curse of the neglectful shepherds; Hasmonean dynasty; prince(s); prince of the covenant (testament), a; seven shepherds and eight princes; shepherdless flock, the; shepherd/shepherdess; Zechariah's oracle of the stricken shepherds and the scattered sheep; Zechariah's oracle of two shepherds and two shepherd's staffs; Zion.

shepherd/shepherdess: a caretaker or producer of domestic sheep. Shepherd is a frequent scriptural metaphor for one who protects and cherishes, especially on behalf of God's people. Jesus Christ is often named the good shepherd or the Chief Shepherd (Jn. 10:14; 1 Pe. 5:4) who is coming again to earth. Sometimes, a mortal ruler of an empire or nation is called a shepherd (*e.g.,*

Nahum 3:18). On occasion, a pastor or elder is also described as a shepherd or undershepherd. A shepherd's life is lonely and not easy and the occupation has not always enjoyed honor, especially in ancient Egypt or from cattlemen of the old West. Even so, some have aspired to greatness including Saint Benezet, Cyrus the Great, Mithridae Eupator, Romulus of Rome, King Artaxerxes III and, of course, King David of Israel. *See also* angel(s); elder(s); Hasmonean dynasty; pastor(s); priest(s); prince(s); prince of the covenant (testament), a; seven shepherds and eight princes; shepherding (cultic); shepherding (discipleship); shepherding (pastoral); shepherdless flock, the; shepherds of Israel; shepherd of the sheep, that great; Zechariah's oracle of the stricken shepherds and the scattered sheep; Zion.

Sheshack: a cryptogram for Babylon or Babel (Jer. 25:26; 51:41) using an adaptation of the Atbash code. Almost certainly, the name mocks an idolatrous god somewhere in the pagan pantheon of the time. *See also Atbash*; Babylon, Babylonians; Babylonia; Leb Kamiah.

Sheshbazzar: the Persian court official who was granted permission to return to Jerusalem with the sacred treasures and begin restoration of the Temple there. Oddly, the same task is assigned to Zerubbabel. A satisfactory solution to this anomaly has not been provided. However, the answer likely lies in one of two or three suggestions. First, Sheshbazzar could be another name for Zerubbabel, not an uncommon practice since the Jews often had a foreign name and a Hebrew one; however, both of these names are Chaldean. Or, Sheshbazzar could be a relative of Zerubbabel, probably his uncle, and superior to him in rank. Because of age or some other reason, the actual construction work was left to Zerubbabel. To further complicate the matter, Sheshbazzar may also have been Shenazar, who was possibly designated as the first governor of Judea, a son or other relative of Jehoiachin, and whose nephew was Zerubbabel (1 Chr. 3:18). Perhaps the only definitive fact we know of Sheshbazzar is that he laid the foundation of the restored Temple (Ezr. 5:14). The author of *1 Esdras* called him Sanabasser and does not distinguish his work from Zerubbabel's; he was there again named as governor of Judah. *See also* Babylonian Captivity, return from; Ezra as scribe; Nehemiah as governor; Shealtiel; Zerubbabel.

she who is in Babylon: an unnamed woman who seems to have been dear to Peter (1 Pe. 5:13) and helpful to him at some point. Or perhaps the phrase identifies the local congregation in Rome (Babylon) because the noun is feminine. Other theologians are more literal and cite the letter's origin in the city of Babylon itself. The latter supposition is unlikely since the ancient city was in ruins by the time of Peter's epistle.

Shia Islam. See Shi'ite Islam.

shibboleth-sibboleth test, the: a peculiar examination at the fords of the Jordan immediately after Jephthah's defeat of the Ammonites (Jud. 12:4–6). The tribe of Ephraim had upbraided Jephthah for not allowing them to share in the glory of battle and spoils of war even though they had earlier spurned their champion's call to arms. Subsequently, Jephthah's men went to war against the Ephraimites as well and put them to flight. Some escapees were intercepted at the Jordan, where they endeavored to cross to safety. Since both armies were Israelites, it was difficult to distinguish between the warring parties. Those who held the fords, the men of Jephthah, required all refugees to speak the word "shibboleth" (which can mean an ear of grain or a stream). Since the men of Ephraim had no "h" sound in their vocabulary, the sound emerged as an "s." If the word was pronounced as "sibboleth" Jephthah's men killed them without ceremony. The word *shibboleth* has entered our language as a kind of litmus test for orthodoxy considered characteristic of a given party, sect, or even a religious persuasion. *See also* Jephthah.

shield: an instrument of war designed to protect the soldier from missiles or other harm. Paul used the term to signify the faith of the believer (Eph. 6:16). Solomon made 200 large gold shields and 300 small ones as ornamentation for the Temple (1 Ki. 10:16-17). In many Bible translations, the word is often translated alternately as "chariots" for some reason. *See also* armor; buckler.

Shift, the: a New Age notation for a time of great cataclysm, perhaps to be initiated after the Mayan doomsday prophecy of December 21, 2012. Some astronomers and scientists study the potential for such an event as well but with a scientific view rather than religious speculation. *See also* galactic superwave, the; polar shift.

shigionoth: likely a musical or literary term of uncertain properties as used in Habakkuk's poem/prayer (Hab. 3:1). Technically, a *shiggaion* is a wild, raving type prayer or lamentation, so perhaps the music was rather lively as well. *See also alamoth;* music; *Selah; sheminith.*

Shi'ite Islam: usually printed as "Shiite" or simply "Shia." Shi'ites are centered mostly in Iran, (with a minority in Iraq), Yemen, and parts of Lebanon and consider themselves descendants of the mighty Persians. The Shiite branch of Islam is similar in outlook to other Muslim theology and practice but with two distinct and important differences. First, Shia Islam believes that the family of Mohammed, the *Ahl al-Bayt* ("the people of the House"), along with certain others of his descendants called imams, have special spiritual and political authority over the believers. Second, the Shia hold strongly that Ali, Mohammed's cousin and son-in-law, was the first of the imams and was the rightful successor to the prophet. The name means "the party of Ali." Ali was said to be sin-free. There have been a dozen legitimate imams but the last disappeared into history in A.D. 931. He will reappear at the end of days, however, to establish Muslim rule over the earth as the true *Mahdi.* Those Shi'ites who claim this doctrine name this savior as the "Hidden Imam" or "Twelfth Imam" are commonly called "twelvers." A splinter group arose called the Ismailis, most of whom reside in Pakistan, India, and Afghanistan, but there are groups scattered in the Middle East and Africa. The Ismailis number the so-called "seveners" (the Sabiyya) among them, a group believing the seventh imam was the concealed Mahdi who will return and restore Islamic purity. Another splinter group, the Nizaris, insist their imams will never perish from the earth. This rival segment has proven to be the more militant of the groups and was the name given to the Hashshashin assassins by Muslims. Twelvers are the larger assembly, composing 90 percent of the Iranian population and 60 percent of Iraqis. The two distinctive agendas divide Shia Islam and the Sunnis, the largest of the community, and are a source of severe friction between the two sects. Future reconciliation seems highly unlikely. *See also* Abode of Learning; Alawis; Ali ibn Abi Talib; anti-Semitic; Husain; Druze; Fatimid Caliphate; Horite(s); Islam; Quarmatians; religious organizations; Safavid; sect(s); Sunni Islam; terrorism; terrorist(s); Twelfth Imam, the.

Shiloh: an enigmatic term meaning "to be secure" or "at rest." In Genesis 49:10, the word or the commentary on that word, seems to identify the coming Messiah. In its eschatological sense then, the term introduces a time when the ruling scepter will be reconfirmed in the tribe of Judah and the Messiah will become the great "rest-giver" to Israel. The New Testament does not mention this name in such a context that has led some to deny any association with the Messiah. In other scriptural references, the word designates a physical place, usually where the tabernacle resided in premonarchical days. Josephus said it was first set up there, which would give it some precedence. Shiloh is mentioned in one situation or another in Genesis, Judges, 1 Samuel, Jeremiah, and Ezekiel. Hebrews 4 appears to be an essay on the same topic of *rest* but without the name "Shiloh." Genesis 2:2 declares the day God "rested" from His creation efforts (in the sense of completion, not because He was weary). The word has eschatological implications wherever it is found. *See also* eschatology, eschatological; Judah; rightful sovereign, the; Sabbath rest, the.

Shimei: a name occurring some twenty times in the Old Testament to identify various personalities. The individual with prophetic importance, however, is one Shimei of the house of Saul (2 Sam. 16:5–14; 19:16–23; 1 Ki. 2:8–9, 36–46). When David was routed from Jerusalem during the rebellion of Absalom, Shimei cursed his fallen king, and did so with insulting language. David forgave him since he was inclined to believe that pointed upbraid was from God at that time. Later, however, he hinted that Solomon should secure vengeance for such an impious outburst. As king, Solomon ordered Shimei to remain in Jerusalem under penalty of death should he leave the city. The directive was obeyed for three years but violated afterward; Shimei was then put to death by Solomon's general Benaiah.

Shinar: the ancient name for Mesopotamia, the "land between the rivers" (the Tigris and Euphrates) where Nimrod was active. The place is also called "Land of the Watchers" or "Land of the Shining Ones" since it is sometimes identified with the theory that evil angels descended there in order to have intimate relations with female humans and propagate the infamous Nephilim as related in Genesis 6. *See also* Babylon; giant(s); Mesopotamia; Neo-Babylon; Nephilim; Nimrod-bar-Cush; Sumer, Sumerian(s); Watchers, the.

Shinto: one of the principal religions of Japan akin to the *Tao* system meaning "spirit" or "way." Its singular place in the nation was virtually unchallenged until elements of Buddhism and Confucianism seeped in causing the imperial court to consolidate and systematize the religion; texts like the *Kojiki* ("Record of the Ancient Masters") and *Nihon Shoki* ("Continuing Chronicles of Japan") were subsequently recorded. Originally, Shintoism was a form of nature worship, with the sun as the supreme god. The soul of the sun god, when on earth, was said to have founded the reigning house. Hence, the emperor was worshiped as a divine being until the end of World War II when the imperial cult was abolished. Natural phenomena such as earthquakes, storms, and the environment (especially any event related to Mount Fuji) are held to be particularly sacred. The essence of worship today is ancestral veneration and sacrifice or votives to departed heroes. The common people of Japan typically invoke the deities with various occult practices, such as divination, fortune-telling, and magic facilitated by using small household shrines (*kamidona*); other public temples may be as huge as a village or as small as a roadside display. Every Shinto temple features a simple structure with a gateless entry called the *torii* consisting of a pair of uprights with a crossbar. Susanoo, the storm god, Tsukuyomi, the moon god, and Amaterasu, the sun goddess are important deities. The *kami*, spirits of natural forces and personalities, form the basis of worship (not all *kami* are benevolent, however). Concepts like purity and impurity are vital, with death considered the ultimate fouling. Thus, no Shinto master will conduct funerals. These impurities, or *tsumi*, must be eradicated or purified via precise ritual (*harai*). Numbers of splinter groups have developed from Shintoism including Tenrikyo, Konkokyo, Omotokyo, Shinrikyo, Sekai Shindokyo, Zenriko, the Mahikari movement, the Church of Perfect Liberty, Gion, Seicho-no-le, and the Church of World Messianity. *See also* Mount Fuji; Oomoto; sect(s); Tenrikyo.

Shirazi, Siyyid Ali Muhammad. See Bab.

Shishak: the pharaoh of Egypt who invaded Judah under King Rehoboam and carried off the Temple treasures (1 Ki. 14:25–28; 2 Chr. 12:1–11) in 910 b.c. In Egypt he was known as Shoshenq. *See also* Amasis; Amenhotep II; Ay; Egypt, Egyptians; king(s);

Hophra; Menes; Merneptah; Necho II; pharaoh; Pharaoh of the Exodus; Ramses II; Sesotris; Shabaka; So; Tirhakah.

Shittim: 1. the last encampment of the Exodus Hebrews before crossing the Jordan into Canaan, also called Abel-shittim (Josh. 3:1; Num. 33:49). It was from here that Joshua dispatched two spies to Jericho and the place where Balaam managed to seduce some of the Israelites into idolatry (Num. 25:1–3; Mic. 6:5). 2. a barren vale near the Dead Sea, possibly the terminus of the Kidron Valley. Nothing will grow in the area except the hardy acacia tree, otherwise called the shittah or shittim (Joel 3:1). The prophet Joel (Joel 3:9–21) identified it as a lush valley that will spring up following God's final judgment. Perhaps it is the valley of decision or the Valley of Jehoshaphat, where that very apocalyptic judgment of God will take place. *See also* shittim; valley of decision; Valley of Shittim.

shittim: a hearty type hardwood tree, also called the acacia or *shittah*, which grew primarily in the Jordan Valley and the wilderness of Sinai. Its timber was extensively used in the construction of the tabernacle, the ark of the covenant, and many accessories of that project. The Egyptians used it for shipbuilding. The name "acacia" means "beneath the goddess Saosis" so it had mystical meaning to the ancients. The wood was worshiped as the birth site of gods and goddesses and called "the tree of divine children." It symbolized Egyptian afterlife and was venerated as a magical healing tree. The acacia is associated with themes of rebirth and new growth since it is an evergreen. In Freemasonry, a sprig of it was planted on the grave of Hiram Abiff and some traditions say the crown of thorns on Jesus' brow was made from its wood. *See also* flora, fruit, and grain, symbology of; Shittim; tree(s).

Shiva: a.k.a. Mahadwa ("Great God"), a popular deity among the several traditions of Hinduism. He is both benevolent and fearsome, a recluse who lives apart with his wife and demon children. Shiva is also considered the patron of yoga and the arts. *See also* Brahma; Hinduism; Rudra; Sri Ramakrishna; Trimurta; Vishnu; yoga.

Shoa: a people mentioned in Ezekiel 23:23 who, along with the Babylonians, Chaldeans, Assyrians, Pekod, and Koa, will rise against Judah on some future day. The Shoa may be Arameans. *See also* Aram, Arameans; Koa; Pekod.

shoah: a Hebrew word for "disaster" or "catastrophe." The slaughter of vast populations of Jews, including mass crucifixions by the Romans after the siege of Jerusalem, the Holocaust of Nazi Germany, and other wonton persecutions of the Jewish people are certainly examples of its manifestations in human history. *See also* anti-Semitic; Holocaust, holocaust; Inquisition, the; Judaism; Jewish persecution; persecution(s); pogrom; Porajmos; terrorism; *Tisha b'Av.*

shoe(s): footwear. Most ancients wore sandals, an element of dress essential for protection, health, and travel. Besides the practical aspects of shoes, they could also figure prominently in the culture of the time. The articles were involved in legal transactions as a ritual of agreement (1 Samuel 12:3; Ruth 4:7). To remove one's shoes and shake the dust from them was a sign of contempt and a sign that the owner was forever done with his enemy. *See also* discalced; sandal(s).

shofar: the Hebrew name for a trumpet-like instrument made from the horn of a male goat. The instrument was essential as an instrument for a call to worship, communication in warfare, and heralding important announcements or ceremonies. War signals could be heard by the army as the *shofar* signaled for assembly, advance, attack, ambush, pursue a retreating enemy, retreat, or to regroup. The chief of chaplains of the Israeli army sounded the *shofar* when Jerusalem and the Temple mound were secured after the Six-Day War. *See also* Goren, Shlomo; horn(s); Judaism; musical instrument(s); ram; *Rosh Hashanah;* trumpet(s); Trumpets, Feast of.

shoot from the stump of Jesse. See Branch from (of) Jesse, the.

"shortening the time": a promise from Jesus in his Olivet Discourse that he would abridge the time of persecution in the last days lest the world's population be utterly decimated. Perhaps his meaning was not that the days will be less for we know the Tribulation is seven years, but that the days themselves will be shorter. Or, more likely, he may have intended that he could have *extended* the Tribulation to more than seven years but opted not to do so for the sake of the world's preservation. *See also* eschatology, eschatological; "short time, a."

Shorter Catechism, the Westminster. See Westminster Confession.

"short time, a": a phrase from Revelation 12:12 that describes Satan's dilemma as he contemplates his final effort for world domination in the face of Armageddon. Most theologians assume the dragon is concerned or anxious because he knows he has a short time in which to wreak havoc before his defeat. It is equally possible, however, that he fears he has but a short time to *win*. The latter concept might be more in the character of his arrogance. *See also* eschatology, eschatological; "shortening the time."

shoulder(s): the part of the body between arm and torso so necessary for heavy work and burden carrying. The apocalyptic symbolism emphasizes strength, responsibility, obligation, and support (Zeph. 3:9; Isa. 9:6; Mt. 23:4). That body part can also be a refuge for the distraught where one's troubled head can be laid on another's empathetic shoulder.

shout: a loud exclamation of exultation, praise, command, surprise, or warning (Ps. 47:1; 1 Th. 4:16; Jer. 31:7). Some prophecies involve a cry from heaven to announce certain end time events. *See also* eschatology, eschatological; last trumpet, the; loud command, a; praise paradigms of Revelation; rapture; Shout of the Overcomers; sounds of the rapture; trumpet call of the elect; voice of God; voice of the archangel, the; voice out of heaven.

Shout of the Overcomers: a contrived but descriptive title of a loud voice in heaven calling for rejoicing because the saints have "overcome" (triumphed) due to the Lamb's victory, but expressing sorrow for the trials brought on by Satan's sojourn on Tribulation earth in Revelation 12:10–12. Loud voices are a common feature of the book of Revelation in keeping with its apocalyptic style. *See also* music; praise paradigms of Revelation, the; shout.

showbread. See Bread of the Presence.

shrine(s): a designated holy site said to be worthy of special veneration and pilgrimage. A shrine may have been the location of the death of a saint, a locale for a relic, or the place where a miracle or some other extraordinary event of religious significance was said to have occurred. Shrines are fairly well limited to Catholicism, Eastern religions, and paganism with few Protestant associations. *See also* al-*Aqsa* Mosque; Bamah; Buddhism; dog(s); icon, iconography; Eastern Orthodox Church; fane; Iconoclasts, War of the; Jeroboam I; *Ka'aba;* Mandylion, the Holy; Oracle of Delphi; pagan, paganism;

pilgrimage; Pillars of Mina, the Sacred; Roman Catholic Church; sacellum; Shroud of Turin; Spear of Destiny; temple(s); veil of Veronica; Well of Souls; Well of Zam-Zam; Xylolaters.

Shrine of the Book: a building of great architectural beauty in Jerusalem. The structure serves as the depository for most of the Dead Sea Scrolls where they are preserved and studied in a lab-like atmosphere. Dead Sea archivist authorities have come under considerable criticism in the past from anxious scholars who see a reluctance to display the artifacts or to publish enough of them. *See also* Bible manuscripts; Copper Scroll; Dead Sea Scrolls; Essenes; Isaiah Scroll; Jerusalem, landmarks of; Manual of Discipline; Qumran; religious organizations; *War of the Sons of Light Against the Sons of Darkness*; War Scroll.

shrive: to cleanse or scrub clean, as to shrive one's soul of unworthy habits and sins through confession, recompense, or other means. *See also* absolution; atonement; redemption.

Shroud of Turin: a controversial measure of cloth now residing in Turin, Italy, purportedly holding the image of the crucified Christ in his burial sheet. An early tradition claimed the disciple Thaddeus carried it to Edessa, where he served as an early Christian missionary. Some scientific investigations have been conducted, including sindonology testing, on the material since 1969, but their research results have never been universally accepted, whether positive for identification or not. The image itself appears to be scorch from a burst of radiation emitted from the corpse, as during resurrection. Otherwise, it is a brilliant hoax and other factors seem not to square with the miraculous origin of the icon. There is some scant evidence it once belonged to the Knights Templar who believed it to be authentic. A growing number of scholars have come to believe the image is not Jesus Christ but that of the Templar leader during the purge of the early 1300s, Jacques de Molay. Others are convinced the relic is an utter fraud. *See also* cross; de Molay, Jacques; Holy Rood; knighted orders; Mandylion, the Holy; Prepuce, the holy; relic(s); Roman Catholic Church; shrine(s); Spear of Destiny; Sudarium of Oviedo; veil of Veronica; vernicle.

Shrove Tuesday: a time for "shriving," or stripping the soul of unwanted sin and mental hindrances so that one may properly prepare the self for approaching the season of Lent. Such a discipline is the religious expression of the Lenten observances that directly contradicts the excessive decadence of the secular application of the time commonly called "Fat Tuesday." *See also* Ash Wednesday; Easter; Fat Tuesday; feasts and special days of high liturgy faiths; feasts and special days of Protestantism; Good Friday; Holy Saturday; Holy Week; Lent; liturgical year; liturgy, Christian; *Mardi Gras;* Maundy Thursday; Palm Sunday.

shucklen: the body stance for Orthodox Jewish males in prayer. The position and its movements consist of the methodical bobbing or swaying of the head and upper torso in short bows. The motion is constant while engaged in prayer, a scene often evident before the Kotel in Jerusalem. Supposedly, the stance provides aid to concentration and memory. *See also* gestures; Judaism; liturgy, Jewish; orans.

shul: a synagogue. *See also* Judaism; synagogue; temple(s).

Shunammite: a feminine name from the book of Songs with the most likely meaning of "bride." The word's origin is unknown, nor do we know for certain which nationality the Shunammite represented, although some students surmise she was black. *See also* Song of Songs as Old Testament book; woman (women).

shunning: a form of disfellowshiping whereby a condemned member is denied basic social graces, not even speaking. The Amish and Jehovah's Witnesses are prone to use the technique, which can be quite disturbing to the victim. *See also* church abuse; church discipline; disfellowshiping; excommunication; rumspringa; slurs, religious.

Sibbecai: twice as Sibbechai in the King James Version, one of David's mighty men (2 Sam. 21:18; 1 Chr. 20:4) also known as Mebunnai the Hushathite (2 Sam. 23:27). He was recognized for slaying the Philistine Saph, the son of a giant. *See also* giant(s).

Sibyl(s): or Sybil(s). Women, usually imagined to be elderly (one was said to be over 600 years old) but probably represented in all ages, who pronounced ecstatic oracles professionally in various locations. Sources for the name are unknown, but the *Sibylline Oracles* were probably titled for one or more of them. Sibyls were located in Cumae in Italy, Erythrea, and Marpessus in

Asia Minor as well as Persia, Greece, Libya, Egypt, Babylonia, and Palestine. One or more main Sybil sects were centered in Italy, although they grew from the cultic actions at Delphi and caused the Romans to adopt an ever-increasing number of the Greek pantheon into Western Asian and Etruscan religion—a cult concept foreign to basic Roman religion that was centered in the farm, field, and hearth. The most prominent, however, would likely be the Erythraean (Eastern), the Delphic (Greek), and the Cumaean and Tiburtine (Italian) Sibyls who wielded considerable influence in the various times of their notoriety. Coins were even struck in their image. The prophetess of the famous Oracle of Delphi was called a Sibyl as well as the Pythia. The most famous, however, resided near Naples as a guild of Sibyls who maintained a strong degree of political and religious influence in the city of Rome. The Sibyl cult was somehow inextricably linked to the preservation of the empire in the minds of most citizens and politicians. They are prominently depicted by Michelangelo on the Sistine Chapel dome where the lead Sibyl is shown with a sixth finger on the left hand (called "the sign of the sixth knuckle"), considered by some to be an occultic sign relating to the Watchers. The Sibyls predicted what may be modern-day transhumanism when they presented the inevitability of the emergence of "men and heroes" (demi-gods) co-mingling with humans. The pagan god Jupiter was considered the ultimate source of the Sibyls' prophecies but all of them considered themselves to be most closely associated with Apollo, who was also deemed the special protector of Roman colonists and thereby a world-recognized deity. The priestesses considered themselves permanently wedded to Apollo, much as Roman Catholic nuns do today in Christ. The women of the guilds had been in practice at least 400 years before the first Christian century, and certainly had some connection to the early pagan *Magna Mater* cults. Some legends say the first Sibyl was named Herophile of Erythrea and the first at Delphi was Phemonoe who spoke her prophecies in Greek hexameters until that process was taken over by the male priests in later years. The first Cumaean Sibyl was said to be enamored of Apollo and was given the prophetic gift as a bribe for hoped-for sexual favors along with great longevity of life. She spurned him after his presentation but was destined to live a long and unhappy life for her betrayal. One legend says Phemonoe was the daughter of a simple fisherman named Glaucus who was magically metamorphosed into a merman with prophetic powers so great he was the teacher of Apollo. As to the Tiburtine Sibyls, proximity eased travel to Rome so consultations were not uncommon, and almost always they were treated with deference. *See also* Apollo; Delphi, Oracle of; *Dies Irae;* dove; Gaia (Gaea); Isadore of Seville; *Magna Mater;* Mother Shipton; prophetess(es); *Pytho;* Python, python; Roman Empire; sect(s); *Sibylline Oracles,* the; Sibyl of Tivoli, the; transhumanism; Watchers, the; woman (women).

Sibylline Oracles, the: a collection of non-Christian prophecies that nevertheless received some respect from early Jewish and Christian scholars. The writings are twelve in number, first published in the 16th century and predominately apocalyptic and eschatological in theme. Some of these later pseudo-sibylline oracles are of Jewish origin, some are Christian, and still others are Jewish with Christian editing. These, along with certain certified Sibylline papers of an earlier age, are often classed together but the originals were supposedly produced by the Sibyl(s) of Cumae, near the Bay of Naples originally colonized by the Greeks or from more remote Sibyl conclaves. New augurs had sprung up among Christian writers that appear to have adapted their works to the legitimate Sibylline books and attributed to the ancient Sibyls, who were said to have been inspired to teach the faith to the heathen. The earlier authentic Sibylline books were prophetic pronouncements considered so valuable and necessary they were kept under constant protection on the Capitoline Hill in Rome. Copies of the Erythraean prophecies were taken to Rome at great expense where they were added to the collection in the temple of Jupiter Optimus Maximus. There they were locked away and made accessible to only a group of fifteen nobles appointed by the Senate called the *quindecimviri sacris faciundis.* The writings were consulted by them alone and only in the most dire emergency and inspected with great care. There they stayed for 400 years until the temple burned down some eighty years before the birth of Christ. Their loss caused great consternation in the empire. Attempts to replace the precious documents were only partially successful. Christianity did not deny that the oracles held spiritual power despite their pagan background even though they may have harbored manifestations of evil spirits. The Sibyls, supposed by some early church fathers and writers, were said to have borne witness to Christ by some of their mysterious and uncanny predictions. When Emperor Augustus inquired of the Sibyl of Delphi, for example, concerning the longevity of his new empire, he was pleased with the result. The oracle told him the rule would last until a young maiden would deliver a child but remain a virgin. Since everyone considered that an impossibility, the emperor assumed the empire would last forever. As time went on, the oracles such as these gained a measure of recognition from the church, especially in the second and third centuries. The emperor Constantine appealed to the oracles, and Augustine had a place for them in his *City of God.* Not all Romans, however, were so trusting. Julius Caesar was so fearful of their influence, he once ordered the confiscation and incineration of some 2000 copies. The Erythraean Sibyl's revelations were originally written on dry leaves, a practice so commonplace then that even today a sheet of paper is called a *leaf.* The compositions were then allowed to be blown freely about the cave by the prevailing winds. She may have also been the inventor of the acrostic form by uttering the short phrase *Iesous Chreistos Theou Uios Soter*—Jesus Christ Son of God and Savior. Even Bishop Eusebius ends his commentary by stating, "it is evident that the virgin uttered these verses under the influence of Divine inspiration." The traditional Christmas Eve mass offering called the Song of the Sibyl has been performed since the eighth century, the words of which are based directly on Augustine's Latin translation of the Erythraean Sibyl's apocalyptic verses. *See also* Apocryphal Apocalypses; Delphi, Oracle of; *icthus;* seven great prophecies of world peace, the; Sibyl(s); Sibyl of Tivoli, the.

Sibyl of Tivoli, the: a supposedly accomplished seeress summoned to the court of the emperor Trajan in the early second century to interpret a dream that had miraculously disturbed the sleep of 100 Roman senators in the same night. She construed the visions to be an elaborate prophecy of the end times wherein the Eastern and Western factions of the church would be reunited by the efforts of a certain handsome young man. She also concluded that Gog and Magog would be defeated and that the Adonis-type hero she envisioned would rule over an abundant kingdom for 112 years. Anxiety over the simultaneous dreams of the judges seems to have been heightened in Rome at the time because the Eastern Empire had just experienced (in 378 A.D.) the massacre of Emperor Valens and his army by barbarians at Adrianople, a Thracian city on the Bulgarian frontier. The 100 dreamers were certainly present and attentive when the Sibyl gave her interpretation. The most famous Italian seeress, however, was probably Albunea operating out of the idyllic resort city of Tivoli near Rome. Legend marks her beginnings as a river nymph of the Anio with its inspiring waterfalls, a tributary of the Tiber, but graduated to an influential correspondent to the emperor's court. She was even called to Rome by Emperor Augustus and the Senate to arbitrate between them over the question of human deity. The Senate was determined to make Augustus a god but the leader steadfastly refused to accept such a title, unlike many of his unscrupulous successors. While in the meeting on Capitoline Hill, Albunea repeated her forecast that the Messiah would come when a fountain began to spurt oil instead of water. Reportedly, that curious episode had already happened a few days earlier, so the Sibyl then escorted the emperor outside to witness a vision in the sky of the sun encircled by a halo with a young woman seated in the center holding an infant. That event came down in history as the so-called *tableau vivant*. Augustus marveled, then offered incense to the newborn on that first Christmas Day. The spot of the encounter became a Christian monastery, then a church called Santa Maria Ara Coeli (*Ara Coeli* means "altar of heaven"), soon after. Every year since the church of Santa Maria Ara Coeli was established, a Christmas Eve Mass is celebrated with great pomp and ceremony in honor of the blessed event. *See also* nymph(s); rescuers of the church; Roman Empire; Sibyl(s); *Sibylline Oracles,* the.

Sicarii: a body of assassins who represented the extremist of the Zealot sect. The name is taken from the term for the concealed dagger they preferred to use in their bloody work. Their preferred *modus operandi* was to mingle in a crowd, strike swiftly, then join in the resulting outcry and lamentation as if they were innocent bystanders. They even managed to murder one of the high priests, Jonathan. *See also* assassin(s); Hashshashin; Jew(s); religious organizations; sect(s); terrorist(s); Thugs; Zealots.

sickle: a hook-shaped edged farm implement smaller than a scythe used to harvest grain cereals or to mow weeds and grass. It is the instrument of choice in Revelation 14:14-20 for harvesting the grain and grapes of that paradigm. As a tool, the sickle is a suitable enough implement for harvesting grain but not grapes. The apocalyptic image then emphasizes the safety of the "grain" saints but the damage and destruction of the "grape" rebels. The name is used in Joel 3:13 with basically the same meaning. *See also* grain; grapes; harvest; harvest of the earth; pruning hooks; threshing; threshing floor; threshing sledge; winepress; winnowing fork.

Sicilian vespers: a phrase marking the revolt of Sicilian commoners against the tyrannical Count of Anjou in 1282. The signal to begin the rebellion was the first toll of the vesper bell on March 30. Almost all the occupying French men, women, and children were massacred. Earlier, in 1263, Pope Urban IV had wrested the rule of Sicily from the Holy Roman Emperor Henry VI and granted it to the Count. *See also* canon(s) of the church.

sic transit gloria mundi: the Latin phrase, "thus passes the away the glory of the world," a favorite quote for many Christian authors. The saying is much older than Christianity but expresses the clear teaching of the Bible as found most eloquently in 1 John 2:17: "The world is passing away, and the lust of it; but he who does the will of God abides forever." *See also* eschatology, eschatological.

Siddhartha Gautama. See Gautama Buddha.

"sides of the north": the description of Satan's declaration or boast that he will rule the world from "the sides of the north," which many consider to be an apostate Jerusalem. "On the utmost heights of the sacred mountain" (Isa. 14:13) is another, and perhaps better, translation. *See also* north.

Sidhe: (pronounced Shee) a supernatural race of beings similar to fairies or elves common in the folklore and mythology of Ireland and Scotland, or the mounds in which they were said to dwell. The Sidhe lived underground (the name means "hills,") in what were termed the "fairy mounds" and were later identified as the Tuatha de Danann. *See also* attending spirit(s); banshee; bogle; brownies; bugbears; Celtic folklore and religion; clurichauns; daemons; disa; dryad(s); elemental(s); fairy, fairies; Fir Bolg; Fomorians;

Furies; ghost(s); ghoul; gnome(s); Green Man, the; hobgoblins; homunculus; household deities; huldafolk; Lares; leprechaun(s); Loa Loas; Manes; mythological beasties, elementals, monsters, and spirit animals; nereid; nisse; nymph(s); nyx; Oniropompi; Orisha; Oya; para; paredri; penates; Robin Goodfellow; satyr; Seelie Court, Unseelie Court; selkie; sirens; spiritual warfare; sprite(s); sylph(s); teraphim; territorial spirits; Trickster; Tuatha de Danann; tutelary; undine; wight(s).

Sidon, Sidonians: a town mentioned by Jesus in Matthew 11:21-24 as a pagan populace who would fare better on the day of judgment than the Jewish cities of Bethsaida and Korazin because of their willingness to repent more readily than their Jewish counterparts. The actual site was an ancient Phoenician city-state on the coastal plain of the Mediterranean. Sometimes the city's name is meant to encompass all the Phoenicians depending on the narrative's context.

sigil: a magical symbol, often referring to the signature of a demon in chaos magic. *See also* chaos magic; demon(s), demonic; demonology; egregores; magic, magick; occult, occultic; sign(s).

sigillum: the seal of the confessional. Clergy are legally protected, in almost all instances, from divulging the specifics of confession rendered in the sanctity of the confessor/supplicant relationship. Few denominations, however, enforce the rule more stringently than Catholic priests for whom it is ecclesiastical as well as civil law. The problem becomes sticky when faced with a court order, for instance, soliciting testimony. *See also* confession; confessor(s); Roman Catholic Church; seated at the feet.

sign(s): (*semeion*) 1. a momentous event, real or imagined, which Articulates divine authority and intent. From time to time, God may explain or demonstrate His supremacy via a dramatic or miraculous exhibition of power. He may also use figurative language that conveys prophetic understanding indicative of special instructions or warnings to mankind. Matthew 12:39–40, for example, is a narrative illustration that anticipates Christ's death, burial, and resurrection on the third day. Jesus called that prediction "the sign of Jonah" since it paralleled that prophet's three days' stay in the belly of the great fish. At one point, even the prophet Ezekiel was declared to be a sign to exiled Judah

(Ezk. 24:24). Matthew 24:3 relates that the disciples asked Jesus for such a *sign*, which he proceeded to give them in some detail. On the contrary, when the Pharisees asked for a sign to prove Christ's divinity (Mt. 12:38–40; Mk. 8:11–12; Lk. 11:16), they were chastised for their impertinence. Furthermore, Acts 1 may even be interpreted as a *sign* of the coming new age as related in parts of Peter's sermon on that occasion. 2. an idea, event, or object that looks beyond the immediate significance to some more profound or vital event in the future. For example, certain portions of the Lord's Supper ritual are said to be precursors to Christ's Second Coming (*i.e.,* Mark 14:24–25). In other words, a sign is really a divine mystery that hints of events waiting to be revealed. The emphasis is always on the message of the indicator—not the sign itself, even as highway signs interest us because of the information they convey and not their material of construction. Certain signs may be classed as "close" in that they represent the soon coming advent of Christ in glory. These include, at least, the darkening sun, the moon turned to blood and accompanying celestial disturbances, the great "falling away" into apostasy, the revelation of the Antichrist, and the return of Elijah. Some theologians have collected five signs that they consider significant and essential before the Tribulation strife unfolds: 1) Israel must be regathered in their homeland called Palestine (the process began as early as 1871, received a big boost with statehood in 1948, and continues to this day), 2) apostasy will surge, both doctrinally and morally (today's behavior and beliefs in most of the population can only substantiate this prediction), 3) the Middle East "road to peace" will be found (but will only manage to set the stage for the onslaught of the Antichrist), 4) the old Roman Empire must reinvent itself (not as ancient Rome but a New World Government—the NWO— of evil), 5) globalism must be mature (today's sophisticated technology, travel, and communication are necessary to enable the NWO to erupt). Revelation speaks of three important signs, even naming them as such: the first two are in Revelation 12 unfolding as the woman of the sun and the great red dragon; the third is in Revelation 15:1 but is unclear if it represents the start of the seven seals or the Tribulation martyrs pictured there. Finding and interpreting true eschatological signs is essential to apocalyptic study. *See also* foreshadow; Godwink; great sign, the; *Jerusalem Journey;* miracle(s); paranormal; prodigy; rainbow; *semeion;* semiotics; shadow(s); sigil; sign of Jonah; sign of the Jew; sign of the Son of Man, the; signposts of the end time; signs and wonders; signs in heaven; "signs of the times"; super-sign, the; tabernacle, the; type(s); symbol(s); telegnosis; "wonders in the heavens and in the earth."

signet ring: a special finger ring, or by extension, a gem usually engraved with the owner's private seal or official logo. When such a ring was pressed into sealing wax on an official document, it carried the authority of the writer. Or when it was worn by family members, the ornament signified ownership or clan unity (*e.g.,* Daniel 6:17, Exodus 39:6). One of the gracious acts of the father of the returning prodigal son was to present the young man with the family ring (Lk. 15:22). Zerubbabel was called "the Lord's signet ring." *See also bulla;* seal(s); seal of God; white stone secretly written on; Zerubbabel.

sign of Jonah: a reference from Jesus in response to those of his listeners who were demanding a sign to affirm who he was (Mt. 12:38–45; Lk. 11:29–32). The Lord was teaching that only an evil generation seeks such a portent; the people of Nineveh and the South (Sheba) will rise up to judge those kinds of nonbelievers. The Queen of the South cherished Solomon's wisdom and profited by it; the Ninevites repented at Jonah's preaching and were saved. Yet even one greater than Jonah and Solomon was standing before them in the form of the Christ, but they would not acknowledge him as the Son of God. The only sign they were to receive was that of the burial and resurrection of Jesus—as Jonah was three days in the belly of the great fish, so Jesus would be in the earth three days before resurrection. *See also* Jonah; resurrection(s); resurrection of Jesus; resurrection, the first; resurrection, the general; resurrection, the second; sign(s); sign of the Son of Man, the.

sign of the covenant: a visible demonstration that the believer is in compliance with God's will as a member of God's family of believers. He or she, in a real sense, is offering a manifestation of faith as a testimony to belief. For the Old Testament saints, the sign of the covenant was circumcision; for Christians, it is baptism. The latter is also noted sometimes as "token of salvation." *See also* baptism; circumcision; covenant(s), biblical.

Bernie L. Calaway

sign of the cross: a ritual tracing in the air the outline of the cross intended as a blessing. The sign may be administered by clergy on another or done for oneself. The practice is almost universally employed by the Catholic and Orthodox bodies. The proper form is to begin at the forehead, move to the heart, cross to the left shoulder, then to the right. The ritual is formally performed appropriately at the invocation, the Absolution, the Creed Recital, at Communion, and at the benediction. Even this simple maneuver has not escaped controversy in church history. In 1667, the Russian Orthodox patriarch Nikon ordered all Orthodox, clergy and laity alike, to make the sign of the cross with three fingers, representing the Trinity, instead of the usual two, symbolizing the twin natures of Christ. *See also* Eastern Orthodox Church; genuflection; gestures; liturgical year; liturgy, Christian; Roman Catholic Church.

sign of the Jew: a rarely used phrase denoting the relevance of the Jewish nation to eschatological thought. The idea intended is to incorporate the perseverance of the Jewish people throughout history and their seeming advance or retreat toward welcoming their Messiah. As such, the political restoration of Israel (1948), their many Holocaust survivals, and their inevitable inheritance of the messianic kingdom are important eschatological considerations. *See also* apocalyptic, apocalypticism; apocalyptics; apocalyptic time; eschatology, eschatological; eschaton; Judaism; sign(s); sign of the Son of Man, the; signposts of the end time; signs and wonders; "signs of the times"; super-sign, the.

sign of the Son of Man, the: the mysterious and perhaps the greatest of the portents of Jesus' Second Coming. A majestic "sign" of some description is to appear in the heavens at his Second Advent (Mt. 24:30) as the final prelude to Christ's descent to Earth. An exact definition of what that omen may be is elusive. Some declare it to be an image of the cross emblazoned in the heavens, a great cloud, or some other anomaly. The best guess as to what the sign may be could include the idea that the Shekinah glory of God is present with the Lord at that time. It is interesting to note that signs (an angel chorus, brilliance in the heavens, a moving star, etc.) were present to announce his *First Advent* as well. *See also* apocalyptic, apocalypticism; apocalyptics; apocalyptic time; eschatology, eschatological; eschaton; great sign, the; great signs, the; Judaism; Shekinah glory; sign(s); sign of Jonah; signposts of the end time; signs and wonders; signs in heaven; "signs of the times"; Son of Man; super-sign, the; "wonders in the heavens and in the earth."

signposts of the end time: a contrived identification coined by some conservative and dispensationalist scholars to name those events that must transpire before the Second Coming of Christ. These three are usually listed: 1. Israel must be in existence as a nation (fulfilled in 1948), 2. the emergence of the so-called Revived Roman Empire (also referred to as the ten-nation confederacy of Antichrist), and 3. the rebuilding of Babylon in Iraq or designation of another place that will take on the same evil connotations as Babylon's secular dominance. *See also* apocalyptic, apocalypticism; eschatology, eschatological; great sign, the; great signs, the; miracles of Jesus with eschatological emphasis; sign(s); sign of the Jew; sign of the Son of Man, the; signs and wonders; signs in heaven; "signs of the time"; super-sign, the; "wonders in the heavens and in the earth."

signs and wonders: a biblical expression intended to relate the marvelous works of God. The word "wonder" never appears alone, but "signs" do. Both words are a medium of revelation— one a portent and the other a miracle used to validate divine disclosure. Signs and wonders are sure to be a hallmark of the end of days. *See also* eschatology, eschatological; Godwink; great sign, the; great signs, the; miracles; prodigy; sign(s); sign of the Son of Man, the; signposts of the end time; signs in heaven; "signs of the times"; "wonders in the heavens and in the earth."

signs in heaven: celestial phenomena to be evidenced in the latter days before Christ's Second Coming. Several cosmic events are foretold, including a darkening moon, falling stars, and various other heavenly disturbances (Mt. 24:29). Revelation enacts many such fantastic perturbations in partial fulfillment of those portents. *See also* apocalyptic, apocalypticism; blood moon(s); celestial disturbances; eschatology, eschatological; great sign, the ; great signs, the; sign(s); prodigy; Shekinah glory; sign of the Son of Man, the; signposts of the end time; signs and wonders; "signs of the times"; star(s); supermoon; "wonders in the heavens and in the earth."

"signs of the times": any number of prophesied occurrences that help predict the approach of Christ's Second Coming. Many are listed in Scripture (no few from the Olivet Discourse of Matthew 24) that are both prolific in number and intense in the description. Jesus once lamented that the Pharisees and Sadducees could interpret the appearance of the sky and weather but could not interpret the more important signs of the kingdom of heaven at that time (Mt. 16:1–3). **That makes Jesus himself the originator of the familiar phrase.** Some writers have identified seven signs that must-see action before the end of days: 1. a time of false peace precedes all others, 2. cosmic disturbances, 3. earthly disturbances, 4. famine, 5. pestilence, 6. war, and 7. persecution of the saints and Jews. *See also* apocalyptic, apocalypticism; birth pains, illustration of; eschatology, eschatological; eschaton; great sign, the; great signs, the; names, symbology of; "nation against nation"; Olivet Discourse, the; seven signs, the; sign of the Jew; sign of the Son of Man, the; signposts of the end time; signs and wonders; signs in heaven; "wonders in the heavens and in the earth."

"sign, the": a special knowledge or password needed by Paul (from the Gnostic *Apocalypse of Paul*) in order to defeat the guardian Archons during his allegorical ascent to heaven. *See also* Akae; Beqa; Kesbul; secret name, the; symbalon.

Sihon: an Amorite king ruling east of the Jordan who attacked the Israelites on their way to the Promised Land. He was defeated at Jahaz (Num. 21:21–30). This victory of the Hebrews seemed to be of significant importance because the battle is commemorated often in the Old Testament. Sihon's prominence as a king may arise in part because he was possibly one of the wicked Nephilim and therefore a giant like his confederate, Og. *See also* giant(s); king(s); Og.

Sikhism: an Indian (actually the Punjab which is now Pakistan) sect most recognizable by their elaborate orange turbans, long beards, and a reputation of being fierce fighters among the male membership at one time in their five centuries of history. They call themselves saint-soldiers (with "saint" holding the priority of position). The religion was founded by Guru Nanak (1469–1539) who claimed God gave him a cup of nectar and told him his vocation was to spread the message of his Name. Thus began the formulation of the fundamentals of the faith. Among its most famous rules are the "five Ks" that constituted the outward expression of the group. The letter "k" is noted in the original language for each rule but translated as: 1. wear the hair and beard unshorn (*kesh*), 2. always carry a comb (*kangha*), 3. wear a pair of shorts (*kachera*), 4. wear a steel bangle on the arm (*kara*), and 5. always carry a saber (*kirpan*). The original plan of the Sikhs was to mingle Hinduism and Buddhism so as to obtain the good of both. However, their last guru, Gobind Singh Ji, decided to form them into a fighting force to combat the Mughal and Afghan empires and to defend the weak. It was he who formed the order of the Khalsa ("the pure" or "the free") into which all are now baptized since 1699. He and the previous guru leaders contributed to the holy writings called the *Adi Granth* which became so persuasive Gobind renamed it *Adi Granth Sahib* and made it his successor—the eleventh guru. The Sikhs (meaning "learner" or "disciple") do not aim for paradise because there is no heaven or hell; there is only the desire to obtain freedom from rebirth through virtues like honesty, simplicity, monogamy, and avoidance of alcohol or drugs. They do not proselytize. All wrong springs from the five vices (also called "the five thieves of Sikhism"): lust (*kaam*), anger (*krodh*), greed (*lobh*), emotional attachment (*moh*), and egotism (*ahkankar*). Whether they still wear their shorts is unknown, but their sect still thrives today though they are no longer primarily a warrior clan. Houses of worship are called gurdwaras, men and women are considered equals, and Sikhism is the fifth-largest faith in the United States. Their motto might be recognized: "fear not, frighten not." *See also* gurdwara; Khalsa; langar; Nanak Ji, guru; sect(s).

Silas: a co-missionary and friend of Paul. Peter also called him a friend (1 Pe. 5:12). Silas was also a part of a delegation from Jerusalem to the church at Antioch (Acts 15:22–35) and called a prophet. He, along with his companion, Judas (Barsabbas), encouraged the believers in Antioch. His Greek name was Silvanus. *See also* missions, missionaries; prophet(s).

silence in heaven: a mysterious hiatus of time mentioned in Revelation 8:1 lasting half an hour. The purpose of the quiet moment is not precisely explained but most likely represents a respite between the sixth seal and the seventh, a pause for dramatic effect, a brief opportunity for reflection, or to ease the transition from the first account of Armageddon (the sixth seal) to other Revelation events. It could also be the indicator that the seventh seal represents Armageddon and is necessarily delayed from its climax. We can also picture the event as God's careful listening to the prayers of His people before the tumultuous soundings of the trumpets and unleashing the chastening bowls of wrath. The Talmud ritual reserves a time of quiet for the priests to retire to the Chamber of Hewn Stone in the Temple to prepare for the offering of incense. The length of time noted is probably not a literal thirty minutes. Some scholars declare the half-hour might typify a week in real-time. Depending on interpretation, the programmed silence could also be a form of judgment in and of itself. *See also* contrapuntal approach to Revelation; eschatology, eschatological; half an hour; heaven; hour; interlude.

Silva Mind Control: or the Silva method, an intense meditation self-help program developed by Jose Silva. The practice may be quasi-religious and is designed to improve brain function. Some, including the inventor, believe that the routine can achieve ESP. *See also* cult(s); extrasensory perception (ESP); New Thought Movement.

Silvanus. See Silas.

silver: a precious metal used for currency or beauty. Sometimes it is taken to represent wisdom, prosperity, opportunity, redemption, and perhaps the soul (Ecc. 12:6) but can also signal greed. *See also* bronze; gold, golden; mammon; shekel; talent; thirty pieces of silver.

Simchat Torah: the Jewish festival day that commemorates the complete yearly reading of the Torah. The recognition is closely aligned with the time of *Shemini Atzeret* and is celebrated by dancing in the synagogue with the Torah Scroll held aloft. *See also* feasts and special days of Judaism; Judaism; *Shemini Atzeret*; Torah Scroll.

Simeon as prophets: 1. an elderly and devout Jew living in Jerusalem at the time of Christ's birth who was longing for the "consolation" (salvation) of Israel (Lk. 2:25–38). He had received assurance by the Holy Spirit that he would not die until he could see the Messiah and is considered a prophet. Again, prompted by the

Spirit, Simeon made his way to the Temple and met the infant Jesus and his parents there for the child's dedication. He blessed the baby and offered praise to God for him and for Mary. His hymn of thanksgiving is known by its opening words in its Latin title, *Nunc Dimittis,* ("now dismiss"...your servant). 2. a Christian prophet or teacher in the church at Antioch when Paul and Barnabas were ordained to missionary service (Acts 13:1). His Latin name was "Niger," meaning "black," so he may have been of African descent. 3. an ancestor of Jesus who lived after David but before Zerubbabel (Lk. 3:30). 4. the replacement for James the Just, who was killed by the priestly leadership in A.D. 62, when he was president of the Jerusalem Church. *See also* Barnabas; liturgical year; Lucius; Manean; *Nunc Dimittis;* Paul; prophet(s); Sameas; Saul; Simeon as tribe; Simeon Stylites; Simon.

Simeon as tribe: one of the twelve tribes of Israel descended from the patriarch Jacob and his wife Leah. Jacob's deathbed blessing for the tribes describes Simeon and Levi (Gen. 49:5–7) together as brothers who are to be chastised for their violent attack against the Shechemites who had ravished their sister, Dinah. Like the tribe of Levi, there is no record of the Simeonites receiving a territorial grant in the Promised Land but for entirely different reasons. Jacob's prediction sees them scattered throughout the land. Upon entry to Canaan, they were the smallest of the tribes, numbering only 22,000. The tribe is, however, listed with the 144,000 servants of Revelation 7:7. *See also* Dinah; Levi; lost tribes, the ten; Seir; Shechem; Simeon as prophets; Simon; tribes of Israel, the; twelve tribes.

Simeon Stylites: one of the more notorious "pillar monks" of fifth century Christianity in the Roman Empire. He lived atop a high pillar east of Antioch for thirty-six years. It was said that he could touch his forehead to his feet 1,244 times in one exercise session. Reportedly, his body fairly dripped with vermin. He died in 459. Simeon's excesses were not singular. Some self-effacing monks ate grass they harvested themselves, others crammed themselves into cells that allowed them to neither fully stand nor lie down. Some starved themselves, endured sleep deprivation, and the like. Not surprisingly, such monastics were called "athletes of God." Each seemed to be swayed by the erroneous assumption that God requires needless suffering to acquire piety. *See also* Flagellates; hairshirt; monasticism; monk(s); mortification of the flesh; near-death experiences (NDEs); pillar(s); Roman Catholic Church; Simon.

simile: a figure of speech that compares two dissimilar ideas or objects with the use of adverbs such as "like" or "as." Scripture, including its eschatological concepts, sometimes employs similes as does all good writing. *See also* accideme; alliteration; apostrophe; apothegm; assonance; autograph; Bible; Bible manuscripts; Bible translations; biblical criticism; chiasmus; conflict story; *constructio ad sensum;* context; contextualization; dittography; double sense fulfillment; doublets; doubling; edification; eisegesis; epanadiplosis; epigrammatic statements; etymology; exegesis; figure of speech; folio; form criticism; gattung; gloss; gnomic sayings; grammatical-historical interpretation; *hapax legomena;* haplography; hermeneutic(s); higher criticism; homographs; homonyms; homophones; *homoteleuton;* hyperbole; idiom; *inclusio;* interpolation; interpretation; inverted nun; irony; isagogics; *itture sopherim;* jot and tittle; kere; *kethib;* "L"; liberalists interpretation; literal interpretation; litotes; loan words; lower criticism; "M"; Masoretic Text; minuscule(s); mystery of God; omission; onomastica; onomatopoeia; palimpsest; papyrus; paradigm; parallelism; parchment; *paroimia; paronomasia;* pericope; personification; Peshitta; pointing; point of view; polyglot; principles of interpretation; proof texting; pun(s); "Q"; redaction; revelation, theological; rhetorical criticism; rhetorical devices; riddle; satire; *scripto continua;* scriptorium; *sebirin;* similitude; source criticism; sources, primary and secondary; special points; strophe; superscription; symbol(s); synecdoche; syntax; synthetic parallelism; text; textual criticism; *tiggune sopherim;* Time Texts; Torah; translation; transposition; trope; type(s); typology; uncial(s); vellum; verbicide.

similitude: a comparative story or illustration. *See also* accideme; alliteration; apostrophe; apothegm; assonance; autograph; Bible; Bible manuscripts; Bible translations; biblical criticism; chiasmus; conflict story; *constructio ad sensum;* context; contextualization; dittography; double sense fulfillment; doublets; doubling; edification; eisegesis; epanadiplosis; epigrammatic statements; etymology; exegesis; figure of speech; folio; form criticism; gattung;

gloss; gnomic sayings; grammatical-historical interpretation; *hapax legomena;* haplography; hermeneutic(s); higher criticism; homographs; homonyms; homophones; *homoteleuton;* hyperbole; idiom; *inclusio;* interpolation; interpretation; inverted nun; irony; isagogics; *itture sopherim;* jot and tittle; kere; *kethib;* "L"; liberalists interpretation; literal interpretation; litotes; loan words; lower criticism; "M"; Masoretic Text; minuscule(s); mystery of God; omission; onomastica; onomatopoeia; palimpsest; papyrus; parable(s); paradigm; parallelism; parchment; *paroimia; paronomasia;* pericope; personification; Peshitta; pointing; point of view; polyglot; principles of interpretation; proof texting; pun(s); "Q"; redaction; revelation, theological; rhetorical criticism; rhetorical devices; riddle; satire; *scripto continua;* scriptorium; *sebirin;* simile; source criticism; sources, primary and secondary; special points; strophe; superscription; symbol(s); synecdoche; syntax; synthetic parallelism; text; textual criticism; *tiggune sopherim;* Time Texts; Torah; translation; transposition; trope; type(s); typology; uncial(s); vellum; verbicide.

Simius Dei: Augustine's description of Satan as "the ape of God." By that droll title, he meant to name Satan as a mimic of the true God with his own church (the synagogue of Satan– Rev. 2:9), his own ministers (false prophets– 2 Cor. 11:4–5), his own theology (demonic teaching– 1 Tim. 4:1; Rev. 2:24), his own gospel (a "different" proclamation of bad news– Gal. 1:6–8), his own throne (evil power and authority– Rev. 13:20), his own followers (unbelievers and demons– Rev. 13:4), his own teachers (destructive heresies– 2 Pe. 2:1), his own false teachers (deceivers– Mt. 24:11), and his own wonder-working talents (supernatural and/or Grade B tricks– 2 Th. 2:9). *See also* image of God.

Sim Kiel: the angel who supervises the Jewish Purgatory from an odd reference in *3 Enoch. See also* angel(s).

Simon: a name found only in the New Testament and certain pseudepigraphal writings, probably a contraction of "Simeon." Those of apocalyptic interest can be named as: 1. the surname for the apostle Peter, 2. Simon Zelotes (the Zealot), one of the twelve original disciples, 3. the father of Judas Iscariot, 4. a brother of Jesus, 5. a Pharisee who hosted Jesus at dinner, 6. a leper who entertained Jesus at his home, 7. Simon of Cyrene, who carried the cross of Jesus part-way to Golgotha, 8. a tanner in Joppa who showed hospitality to Peter even though he was a Gentile, 9. a sorcerer popularly known as Simon Magus, 10. one of the Maccabee brothers, 11. the possible successor to James the Just (usually spelled Symeon) in the Jerusalem church, 12. various prophets, 13. several Jewish rebel leaders in the historical revolts against Rome, 14. Simon the Essene and, 15. certain church notables and martyrs throughout church history. *See also* Alexander the son of Simon; apostle(s); *desponsyni;* disciple(s); Hasmonean dynasty; martyr(s); Pella; Peter as apostle; prophets as martyrs; Simeon as prophets; Simeon Stylites; Simon bar Giora; Simon bar Kokhba; Simon Magus; Simon, Menno; Simon of Gerasa; Simon of Peraea; Simon the Essene; Simon the priest; zeal; Zealots; *Zelotes.*

Simon bar Giora: an Essene notable who insisted that the end of the age would be A.D. 70, the date of the Roman-Jewish war. Coins were even minted to celebrate the redemption of Zion. *See also* Essenes; Jew(s); Simon.

Simon bar Kokhba: or bar-Cochba, leader of a failed but bloody Jewish revolt against Rome in A.D. 122–135. This heresiarch and others like him were a frequent bane to Israel's history. Over a million were killed. Stirring the large crowds on the high holy days seems to have been a common tactic for recruitment. Most of the radical revolutionaries, Bar-Kokhba included, managed to secure public support because they were called true prophets or savior figures. Even the great Rabbi Akiba hailed him as the Messiah. Kokhba's revolt was initially successful, but he was eventually killed by the Romans. He treated his fellow Jews harshly if they chose not to join his rebellion—a very un-likable quality for a savior. He did manage to establish a short-lived Jewish state before his death. Because he based his claim on being the Messiah, he was known as "son of the star" (Venus), since *star* was an eschatological label for savior. His true name was bar Koseva but the change suited because of the sign of a "star" shining out of Judah—a messianic reference in Numbers 24:17. When his true character was revealed, he was renamed once again to bar Kozeba, "son of a lie." *See also* Jew(s); Jewish War; Simon; star(s).

Simonini Letter: an anti-Semitic document penned by a French army officer named J. B. Simonini in 1806. Obviously a fabrication, the letter was intended to disfavor Napoleon toward the Jews. All conceivable lies were presented regarding atrocities committed by Jews and making connections to Freemasonry and the Illuminati, both of which were said to be started by Jews. The letter was used extensively by the French political police and caused incalculable harm worldwide. *See also Adversus Judaeus;* anti-Semitic; *Entdectes Judenthum;* Freemasonry; Illuminati; "Protocols of the Elders of Zion."

Simon Magus: a sorcerer or magician of Samaria, also called Simon the Sorcerer (Acts 8:9, 13), who tried to buy the power of the Holy Spirit (Acts 8:18–25) after he witnessed the preaching power of Philip the evangelist. His foolish action gave rise to our word "simony," the attempt to procure a position through influence ("connections") or bribery for which one is neither qualified nor deserving. Some early Christians named him the first Gnostic. Simon called himself "the great one" and sustained a sizable following. He then, according to some legends, built up a stronger sect in Rome. He is reputed to be able to levitate, work magic tricks, and even consort with demons, some of which he demonstrated before Nero. Legend says he once levitated above the Forum to challenge the apostle Peter. The disciple prayed for his defeat, causing Simon to crash to Earth where he was stoned to death as a fraud. In a writing called *Recognitions of Clement,* Simon is recorded as having bragged: "I have flown through the air; I have been mixed with fire, and have been made one body with it; I have made statues move; I have animated lifeless things." His proud assertions nearly hint at the powers of the False Prophet of the end time who makes the statue of Antichrist move and speak. *See also* Dositheos the Samaritan; False Prophet, the; Gnosticism, Gnostics; Great Power, the; magic, magick; Magus; Menander the heretic; Oniropompi; Philip; Saturnius; Simon; simony; soothsayer(s); tonsure.

Simon, Menno: an Anabaptist leader (1496–1561) and founder of the movement later known as Mennonites. Simon was born of a poor family but rose in the Roman Catholic system until he was ordained a Dutch-speaking priest. As he matured, Simon began to renounce certain Roman Catholic doctrines, especially transubstantiation and infant baptism (thus, *ana* baptism—to baptize again). He renounced his Catholic ordination and worked with the Reform movements of the time. Despite the perceived Mennonite exclusivity, Simon rejected asceticism. Like most of the Reformers, Simon was not particularly apocalyptically minded, a movement that began in earnest after him. *See also* Anabaptists; Inner Light churches; Mennonites.

Simon of Gerasa: one of those several robber barons and Zealot leaders who ravished their fellow Jews during the war with the Romans. This Simon may have been the worst of the lot as he was even successful in subduing his notorious Zealot rival, John of Gischala, in Jerusalem. He and his cohorts executed the occupants of Jerusalem, stole food from them, and raped and pillaged indiscriminately. Certainly, he had no regard whatsoever for the sanctity of the Temple. Simon was captured by the Romans and executed in Rome as a trophy of victory. *See also* Jew(s); Jewish War; John of Gischala; Simon.

Simon of Peraea: a slave of Herod the Great (ca. 4 B.C.) who led a revolt as a false Messiah but was killed by the Romans. *See also* Jew(s); Simon.

Simon the Essene: an Essene prophet who predicted that Herod Archelaus would reign but nine or ten years. *See also* Essenes; Herod Archelaus; Jew(s); prophet(s); Simon.

Simon the priest: the climax of a list of Israel's heroes recorded in *Ecclesiasticus*. In this writing, he represents the son of Onias II, high priest at the beginning of the second century B.C. He was active in the building up the Temple and the defenses of Jerusalem. As such he had some political power under the Syrians. *See also* Jew(s); priest(s); Simon.

simony: the unworthy act of buying a church office via bribe or political favoritism. Pope Gregory VI (d. 1048), for example, probably purchased his papal seat from the previous pope, Benedict IX, for 2,000 silver pounds but the practice was not uncommon. The term is coined from Simon Magus, who tried to buy the power of the Holy Spirit after seeing the actions of Philip the evangelist. *See also* bribery; papal revenue; Simon Magus.

Simpson, Albert Benjamin: the recognized founder of the Christian Missionary Alliance denomination (1843–1919). *See also* Christian and Missionary Alliance; missions, missionaries. *See also* Christian and Missionary Alliance; missions, missionaries.

simulacra: when speaking theologically or psychologically, the ability of the mind to draw recognizable images where none exist.

simulacrum: a copy or image of someone or something, often considered inferior to the original. Some religions might consider an avatar or a doppelganger, for example, to be a simulacrum of the original. Even a "straw man" set up to represent the ideal could be so classed. *See also* avatar; Dead Sunday.

simultaneum: a church facility shared by more than one congregation.

Sin: 1. a fortress city in Egypt that the Greeks called Pelusium. Ezekiel proclaimed it was slated for God's judgment (Ezk. 30:15–16). The city was, as predicted, overrun at least three times—by Nebuchadnezzar, Cambyses, and Antiochus IV. 2. a wilderness region in the Sinai through which the Israelites journeyed in their exodus from Egypt. 3. the moon god of Babylon, also called Nanna. Nabonidus was a devotee and spent much of his reign after Nebuchadnezzar out of state repairing its temples and offering worship. The name may be a derivative of the larger land of Sinai. *See also* Sumerian and Babylonian pantheon; Sinai.

sin(s): disobedience to or transgressions against the law of God or defiance of His existence and holiness, an attitude leading to spiritual and physical death. Men and women are sinful by nature and by practice—a religious doctrine recognized almost universally. Personal sin, no matter what action is displayed from it, usually sprouts and bloats from an obsession for one of the four selfish p's—power, prestige, pleasure, or possessions. It seems aberrant behavior is somehow programmed into the human psyche and only God within us can control it. What, one may ask, was the first sin? A case can be made that the initial offense of Adam and Eve was a rebellion against the goodness of God. When that trust is lost, all is lost. What, along those lines, was the first doctrinal error emanating from the denial of God's goodness? Surely it was a dismissal of God's judgment because Satan's basic lie was that to disobey God would not engender death since sin didn't matter that much to God (Gen. 3:4). Ancient Judaism even held the idea that sin was something tangible and was contagious if not physically removed from the community and individual. Most apocalyptic writings poetically and dramatically delineate the results of sin as punishment, death, or retribution. There are over fifty words for "sin" in the Old Testament alone. Each has to do with human failure, moral deficiency, or violation of a ritual, ethical, or behavioral principle or law. The most common Hebrew term, usually transliterated simply as "sin" is [c]*hata,* which covers any violation of God's precepts but with regret and yearned-for restoration. There are other variations of meaning in Hebrew theology, however. *Avon* is iniquity in the form of weakness or a tendency to fall into temptation. *Shagah* is to "miss the mark," or "losing one's way,"—a deliberate transgression or rebellion. Further distinctions might be presented in the use of "iniquity,"—a deep-seated (more so than common sin) which is a premeditated choice to do wrong. Or, a "transgression" might be called a presumptuous failure—an intentional and willful disobedience. Even unintended offense is included in the definition. The remedy of sin is the covering atonement of Christ, which is clearly emphasized in apocalyptic literature as it discusses the coming Messiah. Perhaps because of the complexity of the subject, Jesus spoke of sin metaphorically to illustrate the havoc it can bring on an individual or nation. He described it as "blindness" (Mt. 23:16–26), "sickness" (Mt. 9:12), "being enslaved" (Jn. 8:34), and "living in darkness" (Jn. 8:12; 12:35–36, 44–46). Jesus also taught that sin springs from within the human heart producing evil thoughts, sexual immorality, theft, murder, adultery, greed, malice, deceit, envy, slander, arrogance, and folly (Mk. 7:21–23). He insisted that the Father knows every person's sin, both external and internal (Mt. 22:18; Lk. 6:8; Jn. 4:17–19). Perhaps we might view the singular *sin* as the attitude of rebellion and disobedience and the plural *sins* as those specific acts generated from such a mindset. Roman Catholicism distinguishes between two types of sin: mortal and venial. Mortal sin accrues to spiritual death whereas venial sin is a voluntary transgression of God's law that retards man's attainment of final union with the Father but does not destroy the clarity or union with Him. Catholicism also recognizes seven "deadly sins" named as Pride, Envy, Wrath, Sloth, Avarice, Gluttony, and Lust after the list was finalized in the sixth century. Protestantism seldom distinguishes between sins on a technical basis as all are acts or attitudes against the sanctity and prohibitions of God. The sole exception may be the so-called "unpardonable sin" but technically known as "the sin unto death." Since the doctrine and experience of personal and corporate offense are so deeply personal and complex, an examination of the basic paradigms of the sin tenet can be helpful. First, as most Western cultures and Augustinian and Reformed theology are familiar with, the idea can be illustrated in a courtroom environment of guilt and innocence. The feeling is that innocence has been lost and regret of conscience has come. How can my sins be forgiven and how can I be assured of heaven? Next, we may struggle with the honor or shame of holy defiance. My position with my family and society has been compromised for which I sense shame and betrayal. How can I still be a part of and respected by my community? Asians are most familiar with this process which they may term "saving face." Thirdly, there exists a dynamic of power vs. fear. God is an all-powerful entity with Whom I have no influence except tremulous worship or gestures of sacrifice and personal punishment to placate Him. How can I access the power to control my life and be free of dread? The final two paradigms are common to underdeveloped/animalistic cultures and some charismatics. Resultant thinking compels us to affirm we are personally helpless to avoid sin, control it, or bring about forgiveness for it. So then, God's loving initiative to care for us and save us is of primary and essential belief. Only there, in the substitutionary atonement of His Christ, is the assurance of salvation and the energy to combat our sinful tendencies. Wisdom writing (as in *The Wisdom of Solomon*) graphically describes the nemesis of sin as ritual murder of children, secret ceremonies and frenzied orgies of unnatural cults, abandonment of purity in marriage, bloody murder of one's neighbor and corruption of his wife to break his heart, theft and fraud, adultery, idol worship, indulgence to madness, sexual perversion, debauchery, dishonesty, oath-breaking, and perjury. Who could sum it up better? When all is said and done, we are left with the single and only effective remedy for sin that is the basis of faith—acceptance of Christ's pardon through his sacrifice on the cross. *See also* after one's own lusts; antinomianism; atonement;

body; carnal; casuistry; concupiscence; death; debauchery; demimondaines; depravity; dissipation; five sins of Revelation; flesh; free will; harmartiology; hedonism; human condition, the; human nature, the; immorality; iniquity; leaven; *metanoia;* moral relativism; moral uncleanliness; mortal sin; noetic effects; orgies; penance; Phibionites; pride; prostitute, prostitution; redemption; repent; repentance; ritual defilement; sacrilege; salvation; seven deadly sins; seven heavenly virtues; shackles; sinful nature, the; sin unto death; slave, slavery; social issues; tabernacle, the; total depravity; trespass; unclean; venial sin; wicked, wickedness; "world, the"; worldly; yeast.

Sinai: the peninsula between the Red Sea and the Gulf of Suez, now called Saudi Arabia. The land holds the traditional site of Mount Sinai and was the main geography traversed by the Exodus Israelites. The land was also called Sin, though that site was more accurately precise in its location within the larger land area. *See also* Arabia; Mount Sinai; Saint Catherine's Monastery; Sin.

sine qua non: that which is essential or indispensable to the whole, including church doctrine, faith, and other theological subjects. For example, an automobile must have certain parts, like a motor and wheels, before it will function; even as faith is necessary to salvation. *See also* faith.

sinful nature, the: that aspect of human existence that seems bent on sin, rebellion, and disobedience to God (Eph 2:1–3). The concept likely springs from the Fall of Adam and Eve in Eden that infested the human race with a proclivity to transgression, or even a spiritual disease that infects every generation. The sinful nature can be somewhat controlled by the actions of the Holy Spirit in the world and in individual believers who strive for moral excellence (actions we are enjoined to do as commands of Christ). The sinful nature cannot, however, be eradicated until the world and the resurrected faithful are renewed by the power of the returning Christ. *See also* after one's own lusts; antinomianism; Big Six Clauses, the; body; carnal; concupiscence; debauchery; demimondaines; depravity; dissipation; flesh; human condition, the; human nature, the; immorality; moral uncleanliness; noetic effects; *opinio legis;* philosophy of religion; sin(s); social issues; unclean; wicked, wickedness; worldly; "world, the."

singing. See music.

single eye: the *ophthalmos haplous* (from the KJV translation of Mt. 6:22 and Lk. 11:34). The single (focused) eye is one that perceives an object clearly and then understands what is being seen—a sound observation that cannot be confused in reference to the physical eye or the one which is the metaphorical light of the body. *See also* eye(s).

single-horned goat. See flying goat, the.

single sense fulfillment: the assignment to a specific biblical prediction of but one legitimate accomplishment. Multiple sense prophecy is the opposite approach by which more than one outcome can be discerned. *See also* allegorism; double sense fulfillment; prophecy types.

singularity: the scientific term for that theoretical point of infinity when all mind-sponsored equations break down and cease to provide logical answers. There is today, however, a concept of singularity as a religious event as well, a time when human consciousness will expand beyond itself throughout the universe–a time when humans will transcend their biology and be transformed into essentially superhuman or spiritual beings of some description. The process has acquired the name "transhumanism." Singularity, in the realm of speculative science, denotes the point at which human ability is overtaken by artificial intelligence and begins to design new technology on its own. In this arena, a singularity is more closely defined as a created being that is part human and part machine, a cyborg. Religious cabals and churches have already been established centered on such a principle. Among those researchers who name themselves transhumanists, it has been estimated that about one-fourth are favorable to or active in such a religious system. *See also* "going here and there"; GRIN; Human Animal Hybrid Prohibition Act; Human Enhancement Revolution (HER); lulu; Overman; panspermia theory; point of infinity; transhumanism.

Sinhue: an important official under Pharaoh Amenhotep (1991–1962 B.C.) who was exiled to Canaan, then pardoned to return to Egypt. His story parallels much in the Bible book of Genesis. *See also* Egypt, Egyptians.

"Sinners in the Hands of an Angry God": Jonathan Edward's most famous sermon (delivered on July 8, 1741, in Enfield, Connecticut), one that has been reprinted to the near exclusion of all others he preached. Tradition says he spoke "Angry God" in fiery words but in his usual unemotional monotone style of reading. Nevertheless, most listeners moaned or cried out for salvation throughout the delivery and did so in genuine fear. Due to the theme of hell's condemnation and human sin of which he spoke, Edwards has been subjected to the stereotype of a fully negative preacher. All contained in the sermon is true, of course, but Edward's mind had a more engaging side as well. "A Divine and Supernatural Light," as an example from 1734, proclaims the glory of God contained in the human heart as well as all of creation. *See also* Calvinism; Edwards, Jonathan; Puritanism, Puritans.

sinner's prayer: a phrase, used mostly in evangelical circles, for the plea of a non-Christian for God to accept him or her as a new believer. There is no set formula for the appeal but most contain some element of repentance, confession of sin, an entreaty for acceptance, and perhaps a pledge to be of service to the Lord with one's life. *See also* Christianese; conversion; liturgy, Christian; prayer(s); recant.

sin of the innocents: the controversial theological debate concerning the fate of infants and children not yet attained to an age of accountability for their transgressions. Are they born into sin needing immediate remedy, or does God accommodate them in their blamelessness? *See also* baptism; credo-baptism; Original Sin; pedobaptism; vicarious faith.

sin (rebellion) of the angels: a probable reference to the rebellion of Satan and his angelic followers far back in the unknown past. Biblical references to the event are rare and obscure, either as history or allegory, but some scant discussion is contained in 2 Peter 2:4–9. *See also* angel(s); fallen angel(s); Gregori; Watchers, the.

sins of Revelation. See five sins of Revelation.

sins of Sodom, the: a designation paraphrased in Luke 17:26–30 as an age of appetite, sexual abuse (probably including sodomy), and greedy industrialization and commerce. Ezekiel adds three more: pride, an "age of bread" (overindulgence or gluttony), and idleness (Ezk. 16:49–52). Such sins constitute a just cause for apocalyptic punishment from the God of righteous judgment that can be readily visited on those who indulge in them. *See also* Sodom; Sodom and Gomorrah.

sin unto death: the great grievance against the Holy Spirit, the so-called "unpardonable sin," which cannot be forgiven (1 Jn. 5:16–17). The phrase does not imply that there are one or more sins which Christ will not, or cannot, pardon but that absolution is impossible if the Holy Spirit is not allowed to convict the conscience (*i.e.,* if the wrong is not acknowledged). The gravity of the act centers on the idea that sin cannot be covered if the unrepentant offender will not appeal to the Holy Spirit or recognize and confess his actions in the salvation experience. One cannot find the goal of salvation without acknowledging its source in the redeeming savior Jesus. This serious and deadly transgression is mentioned in all the Gospels except John wherein Jesus says, "I say to you, all sins will be forgiven the sons of men, and whatever blasphemies they may utter; but he who blasphemes against the Holy Spirit never has forgiveness, but is subject to eternal condemnation" (Mk. 3: 28–29). Many do not recognize that the fatal sin is implicit in the most quoted and famous lines of the Bible, John 3: 16–18, noted particularly in verse 18: "Whoever believes in him is not condemned, but whoever does not believe stands condemned already because they have not believed in the name of God's one and only Son." In a somewhat different slant on the meaning, some theologians interpret the unpardonable sin as ascribing the works of Jesus to the power of Satan. At times (Mt. 12:22–32 *et al.*), the Pharisees accused Jesus of operating under the authority of the devil and not the Father. Jesus' harshest condemnations follow an accusation by his enemies that the Lord's power to cast out demons came from Satan. In other words, they attributed God's power to the realms of darkness—calling Jesus a servant of Satan. They were professing good to be *evil* and evil to be *good* (Isa. 5:20). Hebrews 10:26-31 is an excellent commentary on the subject of contemptuous and unrepentant shame heaped upon the Spirit of life. In such an understanding, the view of some that the unpardonable sin is blasphemy may be an acceptable, though perhaps not a totally acceptable, definition. The theological debate continues and asks: 1) Can a Christian persist in sin to the point where God must impose physical death upon her? 2) Can one who is unremitting in the sin of denial of God's son ever find salvation? 3) Do adamant and implacable sinners who deny Christ expect only salvation exemption like atheists, antichrists, and unrepentant blasphemers? *See also* blasphemy; death; hardening of the heart; obduration; salvation; Sin; sin(s); strong delusion.

Sira: the third holy book of Islam. It consists of a series of biographies of Mohammed. *See also Hadith;* Mohammed ibn 'Abdallah; Islam; *Qur'an.*

sirens: marine temptresses of Greek mythology. Sailors were lured to their deaths if they succumbed to the sirens' haunting melodies at sea. In apocalyptic theology, sirens are sometimes named as the human women who mated with fallen angels to produce the savage Nephilim. *See also* attending spirit(s); banshee; bogle; brownies; bugbears; clurichauns; daemons; deceiving spirits; demon(s), demonic; devils; disa; dryad(s); elemental(s); fairy, fairies; Furies; ghost(s); ghoul; gnome(s); Green Man, the; Gregori; hobgoblins; homunculus; household deities; huldafolk; Lares; leprechaun(s); Loa Loas; Manes; mythological beasties, elementals, monsters, and spirit animals; nereid; nisse; Nephilim; nereid; nymph(s); nyx; Olympian pantheon; Oniropompi; Orisha; Oya; para; paredri; penates; Robin Goodfellow; satyr; Seelie Court, Unseelie Court; selkie; Sidhe; spiritual warfare; sprite(s); sylph(s); teraphim; territorial spirits; Trickster; Tuatha de Danann; tutelary; undine; wight(s).

Sirion. See Mount Hermon.

Sisera: commander of the Canaanite army opposed by Deborah. He was defeated by the Israelites under Barak and was killed by a woman named Jael (Jud. 4:2; 5:26). *See also* Deborah; Jael.

sister(s): a common expression of affection or recognition directed to women, the companion term of "brothers." Most early writers rarely communicated directly with women on an individual basis as was normal for the age. The early Christian congregations, however, clearly intended the message of the gospel and church affairs to include women of the faith as well, *e.g.* Mark 3:35. For Protestants, a "sister in Christ" usually addresses the female believer in general or in particular. For Roman Catholics and other liturgical groups, the name is synonymous with "nun," although there is a difference between nuns and teaching or religious sisters within those bodies. Today, politically correct (and properly so) attempts to more closely individualize women normally avoid the all-encompassing "men" except as a generic name for mankind. *See also* brother(s); fellow servant; novitiate; nun(s); postulate; woman (women).

Sisyphus: king of Corinth who was judged by the gods to be avaricious and murderous. As punishment, Zeus declared he was to push a giant boulder uphill, only to have it roll back, for all of eternity. *See also* king(s); Olympian pantheon.

Sitchin, Zecharia: arguably the most polished and prolific academic writer (1920–2010) in favor of the Ancient Astronaut Theory and the presence of gods and demi-gods in ancient Sumer. *See also* Anunnaki; Ancient Astronaut Theory; *Chariots of the Gods?*; demi-god(s); Human Enhancement Revolution (HER); Igigi; lulu; panspermia theory; von Daniken, Eric; UFO.

situational ethics. See moral relativism.

Sitz im Leben: the "setting of life," a situation correctly presented as it is or was. The idea is critical to such disciplines as archeology and history. Prophetically, if the setting in life or the historical record is misplaced, the insight may be skewed. *See also* archeology, archeologists.

"six-day theory, the": a method of biblical calculation too often employed in an attempt to predict the end of the age. Certain rabbis and Christian leaders from the first to the sixth century A.D. promoted the idea that God would allow mankind 6,000 years of existence, and then establish his earthly kingdom. Later, the Irish Archbishop James Ussher (1581–1656) claimed he could count the years of genealogies listed in Genesis and ascertained that Adam and Eve were created in 4004 B.C. (calculated by use of the old Julian calendar). Each "day" of creation supposedly equals thousand years. Genesis 3, Psalm 90:4, and 2 Peter 3:9 were used as proof texts for the theory. The process is thoroughly unscholarly and totally unreliable. Still, some modern-day preacher celebrities endorse the shopworn system. The theory itself is of dubious origin; it first showed up in the spurious *Secret Book of Enoch* then later in *The Epistle of Barnabas.* The theory is also called the "day-age principle." *See also* analogical day theory; big bang theory; big crunch theory; chaos theory; cosmogony; cosmology; creation; Creator; *creatio ex nihilo;* day-age theory; dispensation(s); economy; evolution; framework hypothesis; gap theory of creation; Hippolytus; intelligent design; involution; Irenaeus; Lactantius; naturalism; *oikonomo;* Omphalos Hypothesis; progressive realism; Sabbatical millennialism; Scopes Trial; septa-millennial; six (or seven) ages of the world; Ussher, James; uniformitarianism; Young-Earth Creationist Movement.

Six-Day War: Modern Israel's remarkable defeat of an Arab coalition of invaders launched in June of 1967. *See also* Judaism.

six destroying warriors: six devastating angels called warriors or "guards" featured in Ezekiel's vision of the desolate Temple in Jerusalem (Ezk. 9). They were directed by God to execute without compassion any person found within Jerusalem who did not bear the mark (seal) of the scribe clothed in linen who preceded them throughout the city and thereby identified those who were to be spared. *See also* angel(s); seal of God.

six directions, the: compass points that are significant to certain religious beliefs. Those named usually include north, south, east, west, up, and down. There is even space for degrees of the compass between cardinal points like southeast, northwest, etc. The theory is especially important to certain primitive tribes, Aboriginals, and some Native American bands.

616: the "mark of the beast" according to some translations of Revelation. Most Bibles use 666. Those references to 616 instead of 666 may have arisen from the church fathers Irenaeus and Polycarp. According to the story, the two of them were discussing the mark of the beast but neither knew the interpretation. Since Polycarp knew the apostle John, it was agreed he should be consulted for the answer. John's explanation was to forbid the calculation of 666 until the ten-nation-confederacy of Antichrist has been formed. After, a copyist erred in recording John's exegesis by writing "one" in place of the middle "six." Another possible origin is said to have arisen because of an early attempt to make Gaius Caesar (Caligula) into an alphanumeric name for the Antichrist.

The number 616 evolved when the Latin name for Nero Caesar (if strict interpretation rules are soft enough) was converted to Hebrew. *See also* alphanumeric code; Antichrist; apocalyptic calculation; 888; eschatology, eschatological; *gematria;* numbers, symbology of; 666; theomatic number(s).

666: the "mark of the beast" cited in Revelation 13:18. A stamp, implant, tattoo, or some other mark that is to be placed on the right hand or forehead of the followers of the Antichrist, an inscription that is necessary in Tribulation times for anyone seeking food, medical care, or other succor. The Greek word in use is *charagma* or "mark," as impressing an image on the old Roman coins. Once taken, the mark is both irreversible and unpardonable. It will embody the flesh, soul, and spirit of any person who takes it and will be completely visible. The program is to be initiated and administered by the False Prophet. Those not wearing the mark are subject to extermination, but the true saints will refuse it despite the risks; thus the Tribulation world will be decidedly polarized. Many and varied are the interpretations of this strange code. A literal approach sees the mark as it is described in Revelation—an allegiance to the Antichrist. A common less plain construal assumes that since seven declares perfection, six must represent a failure to attain it; thus Revelation is saying Rome (or even mankind itself) is "imperfect, imperfect, imperfect." Qabbalists venture the numbers represent 600 (false religion), 60 (greed), and 6 (this world). Most of the remaining attempts at decoding usually involve complicated and unreliable alphanumeric systems to form a man's name, either identifying someone of the past (usually Nero) or an evil person of the future. Irenaeus, for example, thought that the cipher was Greek *gematria* for *Latcinos* (Rome) and represented the last kingdom in Daniel's prophecy (the bear). The most obscure of definitions involves the 666 calculation by involving the Divine Proportion, an aberration of the perfect number of creation. Some assert that the name Nero Caesar can be programmed to spell 666 when translated from Greek to Hebrew. All we know is that the mark is promoted as 666, the "number of the beast" (Antichrist) and the number for man, but calculating its exact meaning is difficult and probably futile to our generation. *See also* alphanumeric code; Antichrist; apocalyptic calculation; beast from the sea;

Bitcoin; devil's mark; Divine Peroration, the; 888; eschatology, eschatological; *gematria;* great fire of London; names, symbology of; numbers, symbology of; Nero; 616; theomatic number(s).

six (or seven) ages of the world: a Christian compilation from several sources that name the six distinct ages of the world from a biblical and historical base. A seventh is sometimes added to account for the future Millennium and further eternity. The first composition may be from Augustine around A.D. 400 but each account lasts about a thousand years. They are named as: 1) Eden – Noah, 2) Noah – Abraham, 3) Abraham – David, 4) David – the Babylonian Exile, 5) Babylonian Captivity – nativity of Christ, 6) Jesus– Armageddon or the end of the age. Such an enumeration is critical to dispensational theology. *See also* church age theory; dispensation(s); dispensational theology; economy; *oikonomo;* progressive dispensation; "six-day theory, the."

Sixteen Fundamentals of Truth: the sixteen doctrines favored by the theologians and leaders of the Assemblies of God denomination. They are expected to be promulgated and expounded among the membership. *See also* Assemblies of God.

sixth sense: the mysterious faculty that allows a person to perceive, to some degree, more of her surroundings than can be gained through the five physical senses. The term "intuition" is often applied as a simple definition. Whether the prophets or others in the religious realms experienced such gifts is not clear but possible. *See also* names, symbology of; second sight; seventh sense.

skalds(s): a Norse poet or bard of the Viking age who wrote and narrated much of the poetry and history of the North. Their writing style has been dubbed the Skaldic—as opposed to the Eddic. *See also* Asa; Asatru; blyt; disa; *Edda,* the; Norse and Old Germanic pantheon; rune(s); storyteller, a good; Valupsa.

Skandas: Buddhism's five principal components of personality—form, sensation, perception, impulse, and consciousness. *See also* Buddhism.

Skeptic's Credo: the unofficial but popular mantra of dubious scientists who have eliminated any need for any sort of faith-based belief system in their professional persuasions. Except, of course, for their own exponential leaps of faith in science and the scientific method. The saying was originated by Carl Sagan and is commonly expressed as "extraordinary claims require extraordinary evidence." *See also Doctor Mirabilis.*

Skinner, Burrhus Fredric (B. F.): American atheistic psychiatrist, inventor, author, and philosopher (1904–1990). He believed human free will to be an illusion and instead was the consequence of some action. If the consequence was bad, it was not likely to be repeated. But if the result was good, the odds of repetition were higher. From this idea, he developed his theories of radical behaviorism so invested in religion and social action today. *See also* Behaviorism; human condition, the; humanism; Humanist Society; human nature, the; philosophy of religion.

Skoptsy, the: a Russian cult founded late in the 18th century by Kondrati Selivanov and others. The order was devoted to eliminating sexual lust from the populace. The errors of obedience sprang from Selivanov's thinking (he was a self-taught peasant) because he thought the word in his Russian Bible for "Redeemer" was "castrator" and the command to "be fruitful" meant "castrate yourselves." The name of the group means "castrated ones," something the males did invariably; the women often performed mastectomy—all to achieve purity. The cult persisted into the 20th century, then suddenly died out, an extinguishment not particularly surprising considering its bizarre practices. In its history, the movement was highly apocalyptic in keeping with the tenor of times throughout most of Russia. *See also* cult(s); Selivanov, Kondrati.

Skull and Bones Society: sometimes called the "Brotherhood of Death" or "Chapter 322," the oldest fraternity at Yale University (since 1832) and the most secretive, giving rise to rampant conspiracy theories. Whatever secrets it holds, the Bonesmen are beyond a typical Yale fraternity of spoiled college boys. The organization was originally set up as a rival to Phi Beta Kappa but has remained exclusively at Yale. Only selected seniors are "tapped" (literally on the shoulder) and given an opportunity to join; only fifteen a year are selected. Members meet in their reserved building, called the Tomb, which is dedicated to the goddess of eloquence and elegance, Eulogia. Therein is rumored to be a large cache of historical artifacts, all of them purloined—a practice called "giving gifts to the goddess."

Prescott Bush, the grandfather of George Bush, is reported to be the procurer of "the flying skull of Geronimo," which he dug from the grounds of Ft. Sill, Oklahoma. Rumors are that new members are required to confiscate a worthy skull for the collection so, considering their 160 years of existence, there might be a hefty number of bizarre tokens somewhere in the Tomb. Other treasures include the skulls of Poncho Villa and Martin Van Buren, along with some of Hitler's silverware. The number 322 honors the date of the death of the Greek orator Demosthenes in 322 B.C., the mystical year in which Skull and Bones was founded. Walls of the Tomb are reportedly covered with license plates containing the numbers because members are obligated to steal any of that description that they encounter. Members dress as both historical and fictional characters and rituals are alleged (after all, the sect is a *secret* society) to be shrouded in sexuality and physical abuse. During initiations, the actors for the pope, Don Quixote, and the devil are most active. Candidates are led into a darkened room one at a time. At appointed moments they are nude and forced to lie in coffins while the Bonesmen shriek at them, although the order may have progressed past that particular rite. Finally, the initiates kneel before Don Quixote as the shouting quiets, at which time he taps the new member on the left shoulder and recites, "By order of our order, I dub thee knight of Euloga." New members are rewarded with a grant of $15,000.00 cash and "a good-quality grandfather clock." Meanwhile, the pope sits nearby with his slippered foot atop a stone skull. Both Bush presidents, John Kerry, and other contemporary celebrities have been members. Other famous on the roster include Lewis Lapham, Tex Avery, Averell Harriman, Henry Luce, McGeorge Bundy, William Howard Taft, Alonzo Stagg, Archibald MacLeish, Robert Lovett, Potter Stewart, William F. Buckley, Jr., Stephan A. Schwarzman, Austin Goolsbee, and Henry Sloan Coffin. *See also* conspiracy theorists; Eulogia; secret societies; sect(s).

skull of an ass: the skull bone of a donkey necessary for the practice of placing the artifact on a stake to protect one's crops. The superstition dates back as far as the ancient Etruscans. *See also* hex; magic, magick; pow-wow; ward.

Skull, the place of The. See place of The Skull.

Sky-Bellower: the ox belonging to the Norse hero Hymir. The great god Thor used the head of the beast as a river lure to hook the sea serpent Midgard. *See also* animals, birds, and insects, symbology of; mythological beasties, elementals, monsters, and spirit animals; Norse and Old Germanic pantheon.

sky pole: a.k.a. the "world pole," the link (according to ancient belief) that connected the earth and the heavens. Considerable attention was afforded the belief because the pole because kept the world stable and prevented the sky from falling on us. To the Norse, the pole was called Yggdrasil. *See also* lion; pillar(s); pillars of the universe; Pole Star(s); totemism; Twi; Yggdrasil.

"slain in the Spirit": an expression, almost linguistic slang in our day that describes an experience of Spirit-filled anointing, often accompanied by various mental and physical manifestations that may seem bizarre to the outside observer. The recipient may, for instance, fall to the ground after being touched by a charismatic healer or evangelist. Some moderate observers consider the phenomenon sectarian or even demonic but others see it as a powerful Holy Spirit manifestation. *See also* Azusa Street revival; baptism of the Holy Spirit; Brownsville Assembly; Christianese; ecstasy; glossolalia; holy laughter; "in the Spirit"; Pentecostalism; theolepsy; tongues; "Toronto Blessing, the"; tremendum; xenoglossy.

slander: false and damaging reports promoted mostly by gossip and innuendo. Most religions condemn both slander and gossip as evil acts that too frequently damage reputations and well-being (Ps. 15:3). *See also* flesh; social issues.

slaughter of the innocents: the attempt by Herod the Great to slay all the male children two years of age or under near the time of Jesus' birth (Mt. 2:13–18). Such draconian action was the king's attempt to thwart the prophecy of the Magi anticipating that the baby would grow to leadership over all kingdoms, certainly including his own. Herod's actions are said to be prophesied by Jeremiah (Jer. 31:15) under the theme of "Rachel weeping for her children." The same dreadful actions were taken by the pharaoh holding slavery over the Israelites (Ex. 1:22) when he ordered the deaths of all male babies born to that race lest they become unmanageable. Josephus said that Pharaoh decreed the heinous order because an Egyptian priest soothsayer predicted the birth of Moses, a powerful man who would be a threat to the kingdom of Egypt. Josephus further claimed that this pharaoh was none other than Ramses the Great. Neither inference is mentioned in Scripture. *See also* Christmas; Columbine; columbine; escape into Egypt; Herod the Great; Holy Innocents, Feast of the; liturgical year; Rachel weeping for her children.

slave girl of Philippi: a young demon-troubled soothsayer who earned a hefty profit for her masters by fortune-telling at Philippi (Acts 16:16–21). She followed Paul and his companions, daily shouting, "These men are servants of the Most High God, who are telling you the way to be saved." The annoyance finally became too intense, and Paul exorcised the evil spirit within her, causing her owners to attempt to prosecute or sue the apostles for loss of revenue. *See also* Abaddon; Abezi-Thibod; Apollyon; Azazel; Dibbuk; demon(s), demonic; Gadreel; Jannes and Jambres; Legion; Lilith; Sammael; Sceva; slave, slavery; soothsayer(s); Syrophoenician woman; woman of Canaan.

slave, slavery: persons under bondage to another, either as individuals, ethnic group, or a nation. An equivalent reference today is termed "human trafficking," including outright enslavement, predatory sexual exploitation of adults and children, forced prostitution, or any other of its nefarious forms. Slavery was common in biblical days and was a subject of commentary by preachers and prophets. Sometimes they described it as a yoke about one's neck or bondage in chains. No Hebrew could permanently become the slave of another except by the subject's consent; all Hebrew slaves who desired emancipation must be freed in the year of Jubilee. Gentile slaves were mostly war captives or purchased from a slave trader for about thirty shekels (the exact amount Judas was paid for his betrayal of Jesus). Roman slaves often held privileged positions in the owner's household. In the heyday of the Roman Empire, the slave population outnumbered official citizens. Christianity was instrumental in promoting the alleviation of slave misery but remained more or less loyal to the customs and laws of the time (1 Cor. 7:21; Eph. 6:5–8; Phm.). In a New Testament context, slavery could even take on a positive aspect metaphorically. Jesus was named a bondservant of God the Father. Paul considered himself, or desired himself to be, a slave to the gospel as he posited all believers should be. He even considered himself an "under-rower," in reference to those unfortunates shackled to the oars of Roman war galleons in the lowest deck—no doubt the most gruesome circumstance of servitude. Christianity did, however, recognize that there is no difference in Christ as to whether one was a slave or freeman (1 Cor. 7:21–22; Gal. 3:28; Col. 3:11). Scripture also warns that one can be a slave to depravity (2 Pe. 2:19), and it is perhaps the most common metaphor for sin (*cf.* Gal. 4–5:1). Paul expressed a desire to subdue his own body and make it a slave to righteousness, not indulgence (1 Cor. 9:24–27). Opposition to slavery in the United States has been a moral and political divide almost unequaled in the country's history. For at least one generation of Americans, the abolition of slavery and the emancipation of women was one way to hasten the advent of the millennial kingdom. After the Civil War, the movement in religious circles at least, attached itself to the Social Gospel movement. Those favoring emancipation were called abolitionists who fostered such opposition that the Civil War erupted in the mid-nineteenth century. Those supporting slavery were mostly southern plantation owners and those loyal to the culture of the antebellum South. Freedom, when granted, is termed "emancipation." *See also* Afro-American theology; Allen, Richard; Anthony, Susan Brownell; Babylonian Captivity; Beecher, Edward; Beecher, Henry Ward; Beecher, Lyman; bitter herbs; Boko Haram; bondservant; Brown, John; captivity; Cartwright, Peter; chain(s); *chrestus/Crestos;* Christian Identity Movement (CIM); Clapham sect; classes of humanity in the Apocalypse; Congregationalists; corvee; *dulia;* Emerson, Ralph Waldo; Exodus; Finney, Charles Grandison; Hagar and Sarah; Hale, Edward Everett; Higginson, Thomas Wentworth; "invisible institution, the"; Jubilee Year; Knights of the Golden Circle; Knights of the White Camellia; Ku Klux Klan; Ladd, William; Leland, John; liberation theology; Lovejoy, Elijah Parish; Lovejoy, Owen; Mameluke(s); Mott, Lucretia Coffin; Newton, John; offscourings; Onesimus; Palfrey, John Gorham; Parker, Theodore; Pastorius, Francis Daniel; Philemon as slave owner; servant(s); seventy years of captivity; shackles; sin(s); slave girl of Philippi; snowflake(s); Social Gospel; social issues; Society of Friends; Stanton, Elizabeth Cady; Stowe, Harriet Beecher; thirty pieces of silver; Turner, Nat; Vesey, Denmark; watchnight; Weld,

Theodore Dwight; Wheatley, Phillis; Wilberforce, William; Woolman, John; yoke.

sleep: the unconscious state of repose. Biblical usage is usually a euphemistic term for death (Acts 13:36; 1 Cor. 15:18) or a metaphor for not being alert. The Old Testament is fond of using the phrase "slept with the fathers" as a reference to dying. Of prophetic importance, sleep is the normal vehicle for dreams. *See also* death; dream(s).

Sleipnir: the eight-legged horse of power in Norse mythology belonging to the god Loki. *See also* animals, birds, and insects, symbology of; Buraq; horse; Loki; mythological beasties, elementals, monsters, and spirit animals; Norse and Old Germanic pantheon; Pegasus.

Slocum, John: a Native American of the Pacific Northwest who founded (in 1881) a "Shaker"—style religion similar to that of Ann Lee's earlier sect. Slocum's beliefs sprang from trances he experienced from illnesses suffered but from which he miraculously recovered, and from at least one perceived heavenly visitation. *See also* Indian Shaker Movement; sect(s).

slurs, religious: any pejorative term for people of differing religious background or ethnicity from a prejudicial user. Common examples may be cited as: Bible thumper (Protestant evangelical), Fundie (Protestant fundamentalist), Orangie (pro-British Ulster Protestant of the Orange Order in Ireland), Spike (high church Anglican or Anglo-Catholic), left-footer or left-legger (Roman Catholic of Ireland or Scotland); mackerel-snapper (Roman Catholic in the United States drawn from the abstinence from meat on Fridays), Mick (an Irish-Catholic—a hypocorism of Michael), Hodgie (Muslim), Majoos (Zoroastrian or Magi), clam or clamhead (Scientologist), Moonie (Unification Church); Jack Mormon or Peter Priesthood (a non-faithful Latter-day Saints male), Polly Mormon (non-faithful Latter-day Saints female), happy-clappy (charismatic Pentecostal), Qadiani (South Asian reference to Pakistani Muslims), Campbellites (followers of the Restoration Movement in America, especially associated with Thomas and Alexander Campbell), Fenians (Irish Roman Catholics), towel heads (Muslims), bead-mumblers (Roman Catholics from saying the rosary), Shakers (United Society of Believers), Prots or Proddy dogs (schoolboys of Protestant schools from those of parochial schools), Irvingites (members of Edward Irving's Catholic Apostolic Church). It is reasonable to state that certain words or phrases some would term an epithet are not intended as a derogatory aspersion. Rather, some (not all) expressions are more colorful than cruel. On the opposite extreme, however, religious slurs can be fantastically obnoxious and vicious, especially those from those antagonistic to Christians based in deeply seated resentment. Inter-denominational or in-house Christianity is certainly not exempt when used disparagingly. *See also* Alka-Seltzer Christians; anti-Semitic; back-biting; backslide; benefit of clergy; "Bible thumper"; Brights, the; buzzard Christians; cafeteria Christians; Campbellites; carnal Christians; charismania; "christened on a Sunday"; Christianese; Christianist(s); C and E Christians; church abuse; "church-hopper"; churchianity; churching; "churn" (religious); "clobber passages"; Conversos; Creeping Jesus; denominational mutt; dial-a-prayer; "dones"; doors of evangelism; doubting Thomas; drive-by evangelism; fanatic; fire insurance; frozen chosen, the; fundamentalism, fundamentalist(s); *giaour;* God talk; *goy;* "Great Satan"; heretic; "holy roller"; hyper-grace; "I just want to love Jesus"; infidel; in-fighting; Jesus freak; Jesus junk; "Little Satan"; Marrano; McChurch; "nickels and noses"; nominal Christians; "nones"; "no-shows"; papist; Pharisaism; parody religions; "popery"; praying around the world; preacher's kid(s); pulpit theft; purpling; raghead; Rice Christians; 7-11 songs; "sheeple"; "sheep stealing"; shunning; snowflake(s); social issues; "souper"; "sugar stick"; Sunday Christians; Sunday school answers; "sweet Jesus"; televangelism, televangelists; "three points and a poem"; United Society of Believers; Wandering Jew; WASP; wildfire; Xylolaters.

Smalcald Articles: a summary of Lutheran doctrine assembled by Martin Luther (1537) in anticipation of an important meeting of the Schmalkaldic League. *See also* confession(s) of faith; Credo; creed(s); Luther, Martin; Schmalkaldic War.

small city, a: an illustration or short story (Ecc. 9:13–18) that tells of a little town saved by the wisdom of a poor man resident there. The point of the story is that "wisdom is superior to strength." *See also* parable(s); parables of the Old Testament.

Small(er) Catechism, Luther's: Martin Luther's formulation (1529) of basic Lutheran doctrine into a catechism intended for teaching children. Subjects included the Ten Commandments, the Apostle's Creed, the Lord's Prayer, baptism, the Eucharist, and other subjects. Its content is displayed in the Book of Concord. *See also* Book of Concord; confession(s) of faith; Credo; creed(s); Large(r) Catechism, Luther's.

smashing of the wineskins. See wineskin(s).

smashing rock of Daniel, the. See crushing stone that became a mountain.

smelting: the process of heating base metals in a crucible until all dross (the alloy) is removed. The technique was used as a metaphor by some of the prophets (*e.g.*, Ezekiel 22:17–22) as God's punishment for the impure silver that made up the pre-exilic population of Judah.

Smerdis: also Pseudo-Smerdis, Gomates, or Gaumata. Smerdis was a pretender to the Persian throne and was active for a short time after the reign of Cambyses (522 B.C.). Cambyses had earlier killed his brother Bardiya to prevent his ascension to the throne and subsequently left on a campaign to conquer Egypt and Ethiopia. On his way home, he learned that someone named Gaumata (or Smerdis) was pretending to be Bardiya and had taken control. Since Cambyses had murdered his brother in secret, he had no way of proving otherwise and committed suicide. Gautama's success was short-lived, however, as he was removed from power by Darius Hystaspes, who restored the Persian throne to its legitimate dynasty. Smerdis is probably included in the final Persian list of kings in Daniel 11:1–3. *See also* Cambyses II; Darius I Hystaspes; king(s).

Smith, Chuck: *nee* Charles Ward Smith (b. 1927), fundamentalist pastor and founder of the Calvary Chapel Movement. He has set the date for Christ's return in 1981 (in his 1978 book *End time*), then again for 1992 and 1995. His ministry was plagued with allegations of various scandals and missteps, such as comparing the 9/11 attacks as punishment for homosexuals, abortionists, and others of their ilk.

Smith, Gerald Lyman Kenneth: (1898–1976), a member of the Disciples of Christ and a dedicated anti-Semitic. Smith aligned himself with such compatriots as William Dudley Pelley (organizer of the "Silver Shirts," a Nazi-style group intent to "disenfranchise the Jew"), Governor Huey Long, Dr. Francis Townsend, and the radio priest Charles. E. Coughlin. Smith also aimed his ire at the United Nations and Dwight E. Eisenhower. Smith helped organize the Union Party, a political racist organization, and ran for president in 1936. *See also* anti-Semitic; Christian Identity Movement (CIM); Coughlin, Charles E.; Disciples of Christ; militant domestic organizations; Patriot Movement, the.

Smith, Joseph Jr.: the founder of Mormonism (December 23, 1805–June 27, 1844). Smith was a treasure hunter of rather ne'er-do-well character (known in the local parlance as a "juggler") from the upstate of New York. Smith claimed to have had his first "vision" in 1820, followed in 1823 by a series of appointments from the angel Moroni. Those visitations, and others, prompted him to uncover some golden plates near Palmyra, New York, left there by the angel Moroni. He and a pair of compatriots managed to translate the plates from the original "reformed Egyptian hieroglyphics" by the use of magic spectacles he called the Urim and Thummin. He and his family were Freemasons, as was his successor, Brigham Young. He and his followers moved the sect steadily from place to place because of localized persecution. The church's doctrine of permissive polygamy caused considerable controversy both within and without the sect; Smith himself had at least twenty-seven wives, numerous dalliances with married women, and was once tarred and feathered in Hiram, Ohio, for having sex with a teenager. He and some associates (including his brother Hyrum) were eventually killed by a mob near Nauvoo, Illinois. Smith tried to shoot his way out of jail, wounding and/or killing up to four men before he was gunned down. While at Nauvoo, Smith ruled as a virtual monarch with his own bank (uncharted and failed), government positions, and his own trained and uniformed militia. The city was the largest in Illinois at the time. The Mormon leader had ambitions further than Illinois and even ran for president in 1844 on the "theodemocracy" ticket—a democracy under religious rule—and tried to establish such a theocracy wherever he settled. Brigham Young sought the same in the western United States. Smith is known to Mormonism as a prophet, but by Christian and Hebrew standards, he would be classed as a false prophet. He predicted the end of the age in

1891; such predictions were routinely made by sticking his head into a bag of magic rocks. He claimed the people on the moon were gentle conservative people dressed like Quakers. Smith's legacy was described by one dissenter who deemed him "the most pernicious and diabolical character that ever stained the pages of the historian." His central philosophy, "God himself was once as we are now, and is an exalted man," became the hidden core of Mormonism. *See also* Church of Jesus Christ of Latter-Day Saints, the; Doniphan, Alexander William; golden plates; Moroni; sect(s); Space Doctrine; white horse prophecy; Young, Brigham.

Smith, Rodney "Gypsy": British evangelist (1860–1947) who led gospel campaigns in the United Kingdom and America for seventy years. Smith was born to generally disfavored Romani people but was enlisted in the Salvation Army by General William Booth himself who saw great potential in the young man. One of Gypsy's most famous quotes reads: "There are five gospels: Matthew, Mark, Luke, John, and the Christian. But most people never read the first four." *See also* evangelist(s); evangelism; revivalism; Roma; Salvation Army.

smoke: the lighter-than-air refuse of burning material. The term is an apocalyptic reference to obscurity or mystery (as the Shekinah glory of God), ascending prayers (symbolized by burning incense), or the flux of evil (the locusts of Revelation 9:3 emerging from the smoke of the Abyss when opened at the fifth trumpet). Smoke can also be a metaphor for an irritant (Isa. 65:5) or represent the reality and beauty of sacrifice. Old Testament sacrifice was sometimes phrased as "a pleasant odor to God." Revelation 18:9 describes Babylon's demise as "the smoke of her burning." *See also* incense; Shekinah glory; smoke of her burning.

smoke of her burning: the description of the doom of Babylon the Great (Rev. 18:9; 19:3). The demise of Commercial Babylon is said to be thorough, violent, and brief—"in one hour." *See also* angel of Babylon's fall; Babylon the Great; city of power; desolate and naked; great city, this; filth of her adulteries; "glorified herself"; Great Prostitute, the; haunt (prison) for every unclean and detestable bird; merchant(s); Mystery Babylon the Great the Mother of Prostitutes and of the Abominations of the Earth; Religious Babylon; Secular Babylon; smoke; wine of her adulteries.

Smyrna: the second of the seven churches addressed in Revelation (Rev. 2:8–11). That congregation was commended for her endurance under persecution but received no condemnations. The worshippers (one of whom is said to be a young Polycarp) were alerted that they would endure persecution for "ten days." That phraseology seems to spring from Daniel 1 where the young prophet and his friends set that period as a time of testing for themselves—seeing if they could serve Nebuchadnezzar yet remain uncompromised in their faith. The ten days indicate that their inconvenience would be real but of relatively limited duration. Smyrna was situated near Ephesus. It was an ancient city, not counting some 200 years it lay desolate after being destroyed by the Lydian king Alyattes in 500 B.C. Alexander the Great rebuilt it, intending it to be a model of beauty in his day. Her harbor was fine and safe and well situated on the India-to-Persia trade route. The population claimed that their city outline resembled a crown, an image they duly stamped on their coins and monuments. The town featured fabulous libraries, music, art, and other cultural amenities, including the Homerium, a public building dedicated to the writer Homer, who was said to have been born there. Paganism was rampant; even the main thoroughfare was called "the goddess street" because the city held temples to Zeus, Roma, Cybele, Apollos, Asclepius, and Aphrodite. Dispensationalists count the Smyrna church as representing the age of Christian persecution from A.D. 100 to 313. *See also* church; crown of life; dispensational theology; new name, a; Persecuted Era; seven churches of Asia Minor, the; ten days.

Smyth, Charles Piazzi: a 19th century Scottish astronomer and pyramidologist. He measured the great pyramid at Giza and converted inches to years, concluding that the Second Coming would be between 1892 and 1911. *See also* astronomy, astronomers; pyramidology.

Smyth, John: (ca. 1570–1612), a Separatist co-founder of the General Baptist denomination along with Thomas Helwys. Smyth put himself at risk from the Church of England authorities (as did all dissidents) and worked fervently for free-formed liturgy in worship, church administration led by pastor and deacon, and in opposition to infant baptism. Since he determined there was no one else to properly do it, Smyth baptized himself (called se-baptism from the Latin for "self") by affusion, then proceeded to enact it for his followers. He later regretted the action and apologized. Smyth felt compelled to leave England and his Anglican associations and established his church in Holland in 1608–09 where he was influential to the Pilgrim fathers who fled to America in 1620. Both he and Helwys held sympathies with the Mennonite group at some point and some of Smyth's congregation joined them after his death. Smyth's views caused Helwys to expel him from the Baptist fellowship. *See also* Baptists; Helwys, Thomas.

snake. See serpent; reptilian theory; serpent seed doctrine, the.

snake handling: a fundamentalist sect centered mostly in the Blue Ridge and Appalachian Mountains. The religion began in 1909 under the sponsorship of George Hensley of Grasshopper, Tennessee. The basis of the movement focuses on Mark 16:17–18, which speaks of a faith that will sustain a snake bite or swallowed poison. Hensley called his group the Church of God until snake handling fell out of favor with many in the denomination and the general public. He then changed the name to the Church of God with Signs Following in 1922. Some groups also drink poison as a demonstration of their faith, but all are defended by the American Civil Liberties Union in their right to practice such a faith. A recent lawsuit against a snake handling pastor was overturned when the preacher testified that he owned no reptiles—the church did. *See also* firewalking; ordeal(s); reptilian theory; sect(s); serpent.

snipe: a short-legged, brown, black, and white, angular-winged shorebird with a long flexible bill. Its legendary appearance, however, is entirely different. According to practical jokers fond of "snipe hunting," the critter is small, black, and furry with one red eye and one green—a sort of cross between a jackrabbit and a squirrel. To catch the elusive creature, one must sit in the dark of night with a pillowcase until the prey is captured and shown back at the campsite. No one has ever snared one, of course, because they don't exist. The joke is similar to the "crossing the line" maritime games at the Equator. The Shellback requires the Pollywogs to see the "sea bat" under an overturned bucket. When bent over, the reward is a swat on the behind with a large paddle. In ancient Bohemia, the approved cure for fever was to snare a nestling snipe (the real kind), keep it on one's person for three nights, then release it back into the woods. Immediately the fever would vanish. *See also* animals, birds, and insects, symbology of; mythological beasties, elementals, monsters, and spirit animals.

snow: cold flakes of moisture formed in winter. In Scripture, snow may transcend the basic definition to represent God's creative greatness (Job 37:6), the necessity of irrigation from the snow-capped mountain peaks to valleys below, or, most significantly, the soul that is forgiven and cleansed (Isa. 1:18-20; Ps. 51:7). *See also* hail; rain; snowflake(s).

snowflake(s): beyond the obvious meaning of snow crystals from the sky, a term that has taken on several derogatory meanings. 1) in the 1860s a snowflake named a pro-slavery advocate in the Missouri territories based on the conviction that whites are superior to blacks. 2) in the 1970s, whites (especially attractive petite girls and women), were snowflakes and considered vulnerable for exploit; or, they were blacks who tried to masquerade as whites. 3) in the 2016 presidential election campaign, a snowflake was a disparaging term for political or religious liberals implying they were fragile or delicate. 4) the term has now morphed into the name for many in the younger generation, a millennial perhaps, who appear to be coddled, egotistical, credulous, and oversensitive to criticism. Such personalities seemingly cannot grasp any reason why they can't be the CFO of a large organization the day after college graduation or why they should be opposed on any issue. *See also* slurs, religious; slave, slavery; snow; woman (women).

So: perhaps also called Sais or Osorkon, the Egyptian mentioned in 2 Kings 17:4 during the reigns of Ahaz and Hoshea. Hoshea allied with him, thus bringing down the wrath of Assyria upon Israel that caused the annihilation of the Northern Kingdom and its capital, Samaria. *See also* Amasis; Amenhotep II; Ay; Egypt, Egyptians; Hophra; Hoshea; king(s); Menes; Merneptah; Necho II; pharaoh; Pharaoh of the Exodus; Ramses II; Sesotris; Shabaka; Shishak; Tirhakah.

sobornost: a Russian theological term favoring a conciliar or ecumenical ideal functioning for a church or faith group. The intent is to decree that the interior communion of the body takes precedence over any individual belief one may hold. Such a communistic-style doctrine may be the one most basic affront to Protestantism which lifts up the priesthood of every believer— not the dictates of a ruling class or governmental authority, regardless of whether the dictator is secular or ecclesiastical. *See also* acephali; autocephalous; church, administration of the early; church models; conciliarism; congregational polity; connectional polity; ecclesiology; episcopate; faith and order; Free Church(es); hierarchal polity; magisterium; plebania; polity; prelacy; presbytery; priesthood of the believer; representative polity; rite; ritual; shepherding (cultic); shepherding (discipleship); shepherding (pastoral).

Social Darwinism: an economic survival-of-the-fittest concept often used to justify rampant (and often unscrupulous) capitalism. The idea was a near-natural and inevitable product of Darwinism and evolutionary theory. As such, it is often a target of Christian ethics. The main tenet of Social Darwinism is that wealthy people are more favorably endowed with biological superiority and are thereby privileged to be the superior class of any society. Any attempt to alter the *status quo* was dangerous tinkering with nature and would produce genetic corruption in the human race. Society advances because of class warfare, whereby the fittest emerge as advanced and the poor are best left to remain so. Two important supporters of Social Darwinism were William Graham Sumner of Yale and Daniel Coit Gilman of Johns Hopkins. Prominent promoters should also include John Fiske of Harvard (1743–1798), perhaps the most vocal lecturer and popularizer of the cause, along with other notables like Henry Ward Beecher and Lyman Abbott. *See also* Abbott, Lyman; evolution; Beecher, Henry Ward; Groton School; Fiske, John; Social Gospel; social issues; Society of Christian Socialists; Sumner, William Graham.

Social Gospel: a late 19th century humanitarian/religious movement, the name by which it was known in the United States, that tried to convince believers that they should address the physical, social, political, and economic well-being of people along with, or even before, the spiritual condition of humanity. The emphasis, more particularly played out in Europe, was to accentuate justice and equality in the world. One stated objective emerged stating that the effort was a call "to build on American soil a society worthy of the exalted vision of the New Jerusalem found in the book of Revelation." Springing from the abolitionist movement a few years earlier, the emphasis became focused on the empowerment of women, prison reform, homeless shelters, care for the indigent, and asylums for the mentally afflicted. Eschatology played but a minor role in the movement. The early prophets were surely interested in society's ills but their theological priority was on the power and obedience of God. Some historians have labeled the Social Gospel groundswell (probably erroneously) as America's Third Great Awakening. *See also* Abbott, Lyman; Beecher, Henry Ward; Bushnell, Horace; Conway, Russell H.; Gladden, Washington; Groton School; Interchurch World Movement; McPherson, Aimee Semple; meliorism; Muhlenberg, William Augustus; Niebuhr, Reinhold; prosperity religion(s); Rauschenbusch, Walter; Sheldon, Charles Monroe; slave, slavery; Social Darwinism; social issues; Society of Christian Socialists; sociology of religion; Strong, Josiah; Willard, Francis.

social issues: also called social problems or social ills, those real or potential disruptions to normal community and civil interaction so necessary to a peaceful and productive civilization. Social issues are normally not personally based nor economic, though those influences are certainly present in many of society's troubles. The prophets, most legitimate religions, most good governments, and caring citizens are deeply concerned about social issues that affect lives worldwide. Among religion's many contributions to the issues, the prophets must rank high with their ideas of social justice. Church responses such as charitable ministries, the ethics imperative, the Social Gospel movement, and other initiatives have made real contributions. Numerous agencies—private, ecclesiastical, and political—have come and gone over the centuries in an attempt to alleviate the problems of society. Work of the settlement houses, American Red Cross, YMCA, Family Services organizations, Salvation Army, Hebrew and Christian charities, and countless others have contributed but not eliminated the predicament. Social maladjustment in this century is certainly complex and multifaceted, but major problems can be listed as: class and economic distinctions regarding wealth, poverty, and status; discrimination of sex, religion, ethnicity, physical condition, or age; alcohol, drug, tobacco, and firearms regulation; crime and punishment; violence and terrorism; political corruption and favoritism; environmental and animal rights concerns; judicial abuse and reform; scientific research and reproduction protocols; sexuality; disease; immigration; child and gender exploitation; domestic abuse and use of force for selfish ends; pollution; cultism and religious freedom; journalistic or media bias; personal privacy and national security; urban sprawl and rural depletion; rampant crime; and a host of other issues. Most religious or apocalyptic views are convinced that such conditions will get worse, not better, as time goes forward to an end of civilization as we know it. *See also* Abbott, Lyman; Abernathy, Ralph David; abortion; *ad hominem* argument; after one's own lust; American Society for the Promotion of Temperance; antidisestablishmentarianism; antinomianism; Anti-Saloon League; anti-Semitic; blasphemy; artificial conception; *B'nai B'rith;* bribery; capital punishment; cardinal virtues; church decline; civil religion; civil unions; Columbine; concupiscence; conscience; contraception; corporate guilt; covet; cultural relativism; culture war; demimondaines; deontology; disestablishmentarianism; divorce; ethics; exemplar motif; Faustian; Government Regulations Index (GRI); "hard times"; "hate crimes"; holistic redemption; human condition, the; humanism; human nature, the; iniquity; Interchurch World Movement; Judeo-Christian ethic; kinism; LGBTQ; malice; Manifest Destiny; matrimony; metathesis; militant domestic organizations; misanthropy; modernism; moral relativism; moral uncleanliness; murder; norm; oppression; occult, occultism; *odium theologicun;* orgies; orthopraxy; partiality; persecution(s); PC; postmodernism; "post-secularists"; poverty; prodigal; prostitute, protection of marriage; Protestant ethic; prostitution; public square; racism; Rainbow Coalition; Religious Left, the; Religious Right, the; religism; relativism; reprobate; reprobation; Salvation Army; scruples; "secular but not religious"; secular humanism; secularization; settlement houses; Sharpton, Charles "Al"; sin(s); sinful nature, the; slander; slave, slavery; slurs, religious; Social Darwinism; Social Gospel; Socialists; Society of Christian Socialists; sociology of religion; spirit of the age; state church; "stews"; temperance; temptation; terrorism; terrorist(s);

theft; Thomas, Norman Mattoon; total depravity; vengeance; violate; wicked, wickedness; Wines, Enoch Cobb; Woman's Christian Temperance Union; woke; Woods, Robert Archey; "world, the"; worldly; World War III; xenophobia; youth religious organizations.

social protest movements. See militant domestic organizations.

Society for the Propagation of the Gospel in Foreign Parts: also called the Venerable Society, the timely response to an appeal from the Anglican clergyman Thomas Bray, who had arrived in Maryland from England in 1700. There, he discovered only seventeen Anglican ministers trying to serve thirty-one churches. Bray immediately asked the Church of England to send forty men "of a true missionary spirit" to meet the spiritual and material needs of Anglican colonists. The Society sent the needed aid in the form of more clergy, schoolmasters, books, and nursing care. By 1776 the Society had made possible the establishment of 300 churches and placed 250 Anglican priests. After the Revolutionary War, the Society moved its operation to Canada, the Orient, and Africa. *See also* Bible societies; missions, missionaries; religious organizations.

Society for the Propagation of the Gospel in New England: an organized attempt by the Puritan settlers of New England to convert the Native Americans to Christianity. The effort was both missionary-modeled and politically practical because conversion of the Indians heightened security. The colonists believed that their native neighbors were descendants of the ten lost tribes of Israel which made the program even more appealing. The Society was formed in 1649 and set about to support their primary preacher, John Eliot. Funds were collected from English churches and goods shipped to America. Quarters for "praying Indians" were established at Natick, Massachusetts, in 1651 with fourteen more planted later. Most of the Indian settlements vanished after King Philip's War, and the success of the Society was severely curtailed. *See also* Bible societies; Bray, Thomas; Chief Philip; Eliot, John; missions, missionaries; "praying Indians"; religious organizations.

Society of Believers. See United Society of Believers.

Society of Christian Socialists: organization started with the efforts of
economist Richard T. Ely in 1889 to promote culture and politics
more in line with the principles of Christ. It was essentially a
group who had given up on salvaging what they imagined to
be the unfair economic climate in America at that time. Many
in the Social Gospel movement were drawn to the body, and it
held definite left-leaning philosophies. *See also* Groton School;
Herron, George Davis; Social Darwinism; Social Gospel; social
issues; Thomas, Norman Mattoon; religious organizations.

Society of Friends: the Quakers. The Society is a pacifist movement
begun in England by a dissenter from the Church of England,
George Fox. The first members are today remembered as "the
valiant sixty." Members do not call themselves "Quakers" (they
prefer "Friends"), but the name adhered because Fox often
admonished his listeners to "tremble before the Lord." The
core doctrine is adherence to the doctrine of the priesthood of
all believers—each person is responsible to God for himself or
herself. Worship may be programmed (with structure and ritual)
or unprogrammed (silent worship in the Inner Light style).
Speech and behavior are central to Quaker living: pacifism, plain
dress, refusal to swear oaths, opposition to slavery, teetotalism,
and, in the earliest records, dissent from such "idle recreation" as
stage plays, gambling, revels, masques, cock-fighting, and bear-
baiting. Even so, Quakers may be variously classed as evangelical,
holiness, liberal, or conservative, as many denominations are
today, and welcomed women preachers early on. Furthermore,
Quakers are active in many civic, educational, and charitable
causes. Use of "thou" is a preferred pronoun when speaking.
Quakerism was brought to America by William Penn, a friend
of George Fox, who established a strong colony reserved for
religious dissenters in Pennsylvania. The first major split among
the Friends occurred under the headship of Elias Hicks (1748-
1830), an itinerant preacher within the group, resulting in
the "Hicksites" branch, a more liberal group theologically but
stressing the "Inner Light" aspects of the faith over biblical
interpretation. *See also* Anthony, Susan Brownell; anti-Semitic;
Behmenism; church bodies in America (typed); Coddington,
William; denomination(s), denominationalism; Fox, George;
Fry, Elizabeth "Betsy"; Hicks, Elias; Inner Light churches;

Mott, Lucretia Coffin; Penn, William; Pastorius, Francis Daniel; Pennsylvania Dutch; quietism; Wilkinson, Jemima; Woolman, John.

Society of Jesus: the Jesuits, a religious order established by Ignatius Loyola in 1540. The organization was militaristic in structure and has had a tremendous impact on Roman Catholicism then and now. Loyola had designed a series of spiritual exercises for Christian soldiers, which served as a manual for the group, supplemented by a two-year novitiate followed by further testing and training. Their watchword was "obedience" (to the pope), and some credit them with literally saving the Roman Catholic Church during and after the Protestant Reformation. The society is unique in that it is led by its own superior-general and not technically the pope. Lay-persons may belong. Nevertheless, by the time the year 1759 rolled around, the pope was forced to suppress, or at least restrict, the entire society through political pressure. They were not fully reinstated until 1814. As a result, Roman Catholic missions suffered, then almost died after the French Revolution. That task then fell more and more to the Protestants. The strict lifestyle of the Jesuits and their passion for obedience tended to represent their doctrine as *probabilism* (any course is justified if an authority can be found in its favor), *intentionalism* (if the intention is good, other considerations may be overlooked), and *mental reservation* (the whole truth does not necessarily have to be told, even under oath). Many Jesuit leaders deny these applications, but the history of the order seems to support its validity. Assassination of tyrants and "the end justifies the means" philosophy were early accepted modalities. The Jesuits were enthusiastic missionaries, among the most celebrated being Francis Xavier. The political power and influence of Roman Catholic politics and spirituality today is unquestionably intense, especially since the present pope, Francis, is of the order. At one point, because of their great influence, the order was disbanded for a time. *See also* Allouez, Claude Jean; Berrigan, Daniel and Philip; Counter-Reformation; de Chardin, Teilhard Pierre; De Smet, Pierre Jean; Francis, Pope; Lacunza, Emmanuel; Lalemant, Gabriel; Loyola, Ignatius; mental reservation; missions, missionaries; Mount of the Jesuits; relativism; religious organizations; Ricci, Matteo; Roman Catholic Church; Xavier, Francis.

Society of Saint Vincent de Paul (SVP): a women's charity organization associated with the Roman Catholic Church. *See also* religious organizations; Roman Catholic Church.

Socinianism, Socinians: or Socinusism, the anti-Trinitarian doctrine of Polish-born Fausto Paolo Sozzini (1539–1604) and his uncle Laelius Sozzini (1525–1562). The sect proved to be a radical form of the Reformation. Both men denied any divine satisfaction was necessary as a condition for the remission of sin. The deity of Christ was denied and salvation by grace rejected as truth. Their work became more or less fixed in communes. Socinianist thinking eventually fed into Unitarianism. As a group of Reformation times, they disavowed the deity of Christ and his atoning work, with or without the supernatural elements in Jesus. The Christ was in some manner divinely endowed with righteousness and truth, and he *almost* became divine at his resurrection. An uproar ensued soon after growth began, and the death penalty was even pronounced for Socinian ministers in 1658. Socinianism was, at the center, a biblical rationalism repudiating not only the Trinity but the atonement and divinity of Christ. *See also* Adoptionism; Anomoeans; appropriation; Arianism; Arius; communal communities; complementarian view of the Trinity; Donatism; dualism; Dynamic Monarchianism; dynamism; dyophysitism; eternal subordination of the Son; "four fences of Chalcedon"; *homoiousios; homoousios;* hypostatic union; incarnation; *kenosis;* kenotic view of Christ; monoenergism; miaphysitism; modalism; monarchianism; monophysitism; monoenergism; Nestorianism; Nestorius; *ousia;* patripassianism; Pelagianism; *perichoresis;* psilanthropism; Sabellianism; sect(s); subordinationism; theanthroposophy; *Theophorus*; Trinity; two natures, doctrine of the; unipersonality; Unitarian Universalists.

sociobiology: a scientific philosophical endeavor having arisen in the past twenty or thirty years claiming that individuals are born with a kind of evolutionary "selfish gene" that moves us toward certain behaviors. Sociobiology has become a systematic attempt to explain notions of right and wrong, not on some moral level, but purely at the naturalistic genetic basis. *See also* evolution; God gene, the; human condition, the; sociology of religion.

sociology of religion: study of religion in its many doctrines, forms, organization, and typology using standard sociological methodologies and research. Prominent religious sociologists through the ages might include Aristotle, Plato, Emile Durkheim, Max Weber, Karl Marx, Peter Berger, Robert Bellah, Thomas Luckmann, Rodney Stark, William Bainbridge, Robert Wuthnow, Christian Smith, Bryan Wilson, Michael Foucault, Ernest Gellner, and many others. *See also* civil religion; cultural mandate; cultural relativism; culture war; dialectic materialism; Groton School; higher criticism; human condition, the; Interchurch World Movement; Lenin, Vladimir; Malthus, Thomas Robert; Marx, Karl; moralistic therapeutic deism; Nietzsche, Friedrich; "opiate of the people"; philosophy of religion; religion; religiosity; relative deprivation; religious capital; relativism; secular humanism; sinful nature, the; Social Gospel; social issues; sociobiology; Stark effect; transhumanism.

Socrates: Greek philosopher (469–399 B.C.), perhaps the most famous of all in the company of thinkers. He challenged stories about the gods of Olympus and preached a great concern for the soul, as well as the body. Because of these and other radical ideas, the council of Athens forced him to drink poison. His ideas lived on under his pupil Plato. *See also* philosophy of religion; philosophy of the Greeks.

sodality: a Roman Catholic and Anglican lay organization (also called a syndiakonia) of some description established to promote the Christian life or a religious project. *See also* laity; missions, missionaries; religious organizations; Roman Catholic Church.

Sodom: the town (already famous for its immorality) mentioned in Matthew 11:23 that is said to fare better on the day of judgment than the Jewish city of Capernaum because of the latter's refusal to repent of its sins or acknowledge the miracles performed in the city. The prophet Ezekiel recorded essentially the same message in Ezekiel 16:48–50. Even long after the destruction of Sodom, the name remained a common byword for evil peoples and practices. There are many such references in Scripture. *See also* Admah; Gomorrah; Pentapolis; Samaria and Sodom; sins of Sodom, the; Sodom and Egypt; Sodom and Gomorrah; Zeboiim; Zoar.

Sodom and Egypt: a derogatory tag name for Jerusalem from Revelation 11:8. The condemnation is placed on the city because of its rejoicing for the death of the two super witnesses of God and for the refusal of the citizens to bury their bodies for three and a half days. *See also* Jerusalem as city; Sodom; Sodom and Gomorrah.

Sodom and Gomorrah: the two cities of the plain destroyed by God because of their wickedness (Gen. 19). Only Lot and his daughters escaped with their lives. Often the two towns are used as illustrations for the sin of the people in the extreme. The grievous sins of Sodom and her sister cities were many and varied, including sensual appetite, sexual deviation or homosexuality (from which we get our word sodomy), and lack of moral restraint. Some believe the citizens' lack of hospitality was the most serious error. Ezekiel compared Jerusalem unfavorably to Sodom, saying the sins of that city exceeded even those of that wicked city (Ezk. 16:48–50). *See also* Admah; angelic miracles; cities of the plain; hospitality; Pentapolis; sins of Sodom, the; Sodom; Sodom and Egypt; Zeboiim; Zoar.

Soka Gakkai International (SGI): the largest splinter group from Buddhism in Japan. The sect was formerly called Nichiren Shoshu in America. Practitioners promote enlightenment through the *gongyo*—kneeling before a *gohonzon* (a black wooden box containing passages from the *Lotus Sutra*), quoting the words, and chanting the *dainoku*, ("nm-myoho-renge-kyo") over and over. Unlike other characteristics of Buddhism, this cult is aggressive in its recruitment and mission and is said to harbor a desire for world power. *See also* Buddhism; sect(s).

Sol: Roman sun god celebrated as *Sol Invictus*. Norse mythology also references Sol but as a goddess of the sun. *See also* Norse and Old Germanic pantheon; Olympian pantheon; Saturnalia; sun worshipers.

sola Christo, sola fide, sola gratia, sola Scriptura, soli Dei gloria: the Latin formula that most theologians and church historians attribute as Martin Luther's bases for faith and the core of the Reformation. The terms translate to Christ alone, faith alone, grace alone, Scripture alone, and "for the glory of God alone." Each component underpins Protestant belief and is commonly labeled "the five solas" or "the Five *Solae.*" Other theological maxims were superfluous elements, especially man-made or ecclesiastical ones, and were to be eliminated or brought into conformity with the gospel. *See also* Bible; faith; grace; instrumental clause; Luther, Martin; *norma normans non normata;* Protestant Reformation, the; rule of faith; *Soli Deo Gloria;* solifidianism.

Solara: a New Age celebration event in which thousands gather, dressed in white, to dance at 11:11 a.m., 11:11 p.m., and 11:11 GMT. The demonstration is said to open the "doorway" to a higher consciousness, but we were given only until December 31, 2001, to attain it. *See also* dance; New Age religion; sect(s).

Solar Temple, the: an apocalyptic cult in Canada and France late in the 20th century. Some fifty of them, along with their leader, Luc Jouret, committed mass suicide in October of 1994. The organization held many vaunted objectives to achieve power in the world. They wanted to re-establish the correct notions of authority and power, affirm the primacy of the spiritual over the temporal, return the conscience of dignity to humanity, help society transition, promote the human framework of body, soul, and spirit, and unify religions, especially Islam and Christianity. Suicides in at least three events claiming the lives of fifty-three in the headquarters at Chiery, Switzerland, sixteen at a chalet in the Alps, and five at St. Casimir, Quebec. *See also* cult(s); Jouret, Luc.

solecism: a mistake or blunder in speech or grammar.

solemnity: in liturgical circles, the highest-ranking type of feast day observance in recognition of holy persons and events. Solemnities are closely related to holy days of obligation and appear frequently on the liturgical calendar of most high church offices. *See also* feasts and special days of high liturgy faiths; liturgical year; liturgy; liturgy, Christian; liturgy, Jewish; memorial(s); octave(s).

Solemnity of the Sacred Heart: Roman Catholic devotion to the sacred heart of Jesus; such reverence can be discerned in the church as far back as the 11th century. *See also* feasts and special days of high liturgy faiths; liturgical year; Roman Catholic Church; Sacred Heart, Feast of the.

Soli Deo Gloria: the Latin phrase "for the glory of God alone." The great musical composition masters like Bach, Handel, and Christoph Graupne were prone to add the words as a superscription to their scores to affirm they had labored for the glory of God as their only motivation. *See also sola Christo, sola fide, sola gratia, sola Scriptura, soli Dei gloria.*

solifidianism: the conviction or doctrine that faith alone will accomplish salvation. *See also* Amyraldism; antinomianism; Arminianism; autosoterism; condign merit; congruent merit; covenant of grace; covenant of works; grace; monergism; salvation; stone of stumbling; synergism; works, salvation by.

Sol Invicti **cult.** See Saturnalia.

sologism: a proposition or literary piece consisting of reasoning understood by only one person, usually the author.

Solomon: son of David and Bathsheba, born in Jerusalem about 900 B.C. (whom Nathan the prophet called Jedidiah). He succeeded to the throne of Israel (reigning about 970–931 B.C.) and became renowned for his wisdom and wealth. His name means "peaceful," which fits because he was selected by God as one suited to build the Temple since he was of that nature and disposition, whereas his father was a soldier and even a murderer. In the Song of Songs the name appears as *Salma* (S. of S. 1:5); the Muslims call him a major prophet and name him Sulayman. Solomon's rule of forty years saw only one minor military action even though he maintained a huge army, a fledgling merchant navy, and an elite chariot corps. He was granted these monarchial rights, and others, because of the effect of the Davidic Covenant granting perpetual kingship to David's line. His rule ended badly, having slipped away into many questionable relations with foreign women—it is claimed he had 700 wives and 300 concubines. One dalliance involved the Queen of Sheba. He even consecrated altars to pagan idols, much to God's displeasure. Legend reports he had power over demons and used their strength for construction and other purposes. Most legendary tales of his life spring from the apocryphal *Testament of Solomon.* Josephus hinted that he and King Hiram of Phoenicia frequently challenged each other to solve complex problems or puzzles. Neither he nor his nation was severely punished, however, because of his father's faithful legacy, and he lived and served as king to the age of sixty. Solomon was more than a builder and statesman, however. He is said to have written two of the Psalms, 3,000 proverbs, 1,005 songs, the book of Ecclesiastes, and the

Song of Songs. Solomon's kingdom was extensive, wealthy, and expensive to maintain. His scientific, biological, and diplomatic skills were unsurpassed. The united kingdom fell apart, however, early in the succession of his arrogant son Rehoboam when the Israel tribes of the north broke away. Not all share in his high ratings, however, even seeing him as an early Antichrist type or anti-Messiah. There is perhaps some validity in the matter because Solomon seemingly did everything opposite of what God expected of him, particularly during his later reign. He multiplied wives and consorts, amassed armies and horses, hoarded gold and silver, built pagan altars, was an arms merchant to the kingdoms about, used slave labor, reveled in luxury, and even gave away portions of his realm. Legend says he regularly consorted with demons. *See also* Antichrist; atrahasis; concubine; David; demon(s), demonic; Davidic Covenant; goetia; Haile Selassie; Hiram I, King; Jedidiah; king(s); kings of Israel and Judah; kings of Israel and Judah in foreign relations; key of Solomon; Lemuel; Mount of Offence; Menelik, Prince; Nathan; Proverbs as Old Testament book; *Qoheleth;* Queen of Sheba; Solomonic Covenant; Solomon's prayer for wisdom; Solomon's prayer of dedication; Solomonic Covenant; Solomon's Stables; Solomon's Temple.

Solomon ben Isaac. See Rashi.

Solomonic Covenant: a feature of the Davidic Covenant allowing Solomon to rule after his father, David, and to construct the first Temple. Although Solomon's reign did not end faithfully, he was not dismissed because of the Lord's pledge to David. *See also* covenant(s), biblical; covenant(s); covenant theology; Davidic Covenant; Solomon.

Solomon's prayer for wisdom: the king's unselfish appeal to God that he might be a wise ruler to the people of Israel, his subjects (2 Chr. 1:1–12). The prayer was pleasing to God at that time and precipitated many material and spiritual blessings on Judah. *See also* Solomon; Solomon's prayer of dedication.

Solomon's prayer of dedication: the king's prayer of dedication for the Temple of God in Jerusalem that he had sponsored (1 Ki. 8:22–61). Much of the content of the appeal is prophetic in that it rehearses the holy purposes of the structure just completed and the blessings it would facilitate for the nation. *See also* Shekinah glory; Solomon; Solomon's prayer for wisdom.

Solomon's Shield. See Star of David.

Solomon's Stables: part of the vast subterranean complex beneath the Temple Mount. Perhaps Crusaders stabled their horses there, but originally the spaces were storerooms for Solomon's treasures and supplies. The Muslim Waqf has vindictively destroyed or sealed off most or all of these archeologically significant areas. Still, the Muslims insist there is no Jewish history on the Temple Mount. *See also* Jerusalem, landmarks of; Solomon.

Solomon's Temple: the first Temple of the Jews in Jerusalem. It was constructed under the auspices of King Solomon from plans drawn up by his father, David, to completion in about 1000 B.C. The structure was magnificent by any architectural standard. To begin, Solomon had access to over 10 billion dollars in gold, just for the lining of the walls and the utensils; silver was priced at over 100 million dollars. Conservative estimates today claim such a construction could not be duplicated for less than 100 billion dollars. Thousands were conscripted as corvee laborers necessary for construction, along with numerous skilled workers and craftsmen. The resulting edifice stood as a wonder in the age until destroyed by the Babylonians in 536 B.C. *See also* religious organizations; Solomon; Temple(s).

someone "like a son of man": Jesus in theophany form seated on the throne of heaven (Rev. 1:13, *et al.*). *See also* names (titles) for Jesus; throne in heaven with someone sitting on it, a.

song. See music.

Song of Moses: the victory hymn of thanksgiving raised to God by the voices of Moses and the people who escaped from Pharaoh through the Red Sea (Ex. 15:1–18). The section is also called the Song of the Sea. Many modern Jews consider the anthem to be properly read in the future tense, indicating that Moses' words of praise cannot be fully rendered until the Lawgiver Himself is present and mankind has experienced its final redemption. The urban anecdote persists today that the rock song "American Pie" (which some negativists claim predicts the downfall of America) was based on the Song of Moses. Liturgical churches call the passage *Cantemus Domino. See also* "American Pie"; music; Song of Moses and the Lamb.

Song of Moses and the Lamb: a contrived but descriptive title for the praise to the victorious God in Revelation 15:3–4. The song emanates from the seven bowl angels on behalf of the saints who were victorious over the beast. The words are a compilation of the song of Moses (which was actually composed to accompany dancing and performed by his sister Miriam in Exodus 15:1–21) and a variety of other liturgical sources, including Psalms, Amos, Malachi, and Deuteronomy. *See also* deliverance motif; music; praise paradigms of Revelation, the; Song of Moses.

Song of Salvation: a contrived but descriptive title for the praise section of Revelation 7:10, which offers thankfulness from the great multitude in white for their victory in Christ despite their martyrdom. *See also* martyrdom; music; praise paradigms of Revelation, the.

Song of Solomon. See Song of Songs.

Song of Songs as Old Testament book: an Old Testament book of poetic expression extolling love, also known as the Song of Solomon. Later, the Song came to be called *Canticles* as well. The text is the last of the five poetic writings and certainly the most sexually sensuous. The composition is a love song expressing the king's adoration for his favorite bride. At the time, Solomon had only 60 wives and 80 concubines; that situation later grew to 700 wives and 300 concubines (1 Ki. 11:3). Some claim that the writing is a metaphor for God's love, but that idea requires a stretch of implied theology. Jewish commentators referred to the poem as allegorical and a reference to God's dealings with Israel, His chosen people. The Song holds no discernible apocalyptic matter. *See also* blazon; Canticles; Hagiography; love; poetry (biblical); Shunammite.

song of the harlot: an odd phrase found in Isaiah 23:13–18 as derision of the ancient seaport city of Tyre. The ridicule seems to involve the greed and heavy trading so characteristic of that land. A similar meaning can be applied to the great harlot of Revelation 18. *See also* Babylon the Great; Great Prostitute, the; merchant(s); Mystery Babylon the Great the Mother of Prostitutes and of the Abominations of the Earth; Phoenicia, Phoenicians; Religious Babylon; Secular Babylon; Tyre, Tyrenians; whore of Babylon.

"song of the sword": a vision from Ezekiel 21 in which Babylon is named as the Lord's weapon against unrepentant Israel. Verses

309

9–17 are spoken poetically, producing a vivid and bloody image of slaughter and mayhem. *See also* Babylonia; sword.

Song of the Vineyard: a lament for Judah and Israel as recorded in Isaiah 5:1–7 in which Jerusalem and Judah are compared to a vineyard. When the people are faithful, the land prospers, but when they are neglectful, the beauty and fertility are marred and unproductive. The song can be compared to Jesus' parable of the wicked tenants (Mt. 21:33–46) with some interest. *See also* curses of Isaiah; parable(s); parables of the Old Testament.

songs of ascent: some fifteen psalms composed to be sung by pilgrim worshipers as they made their way from their homes and "ascended" the hill of Zion to worship in the Temple of Jerusalem. *See also* music; psalm; Psalms as Old Testament book.

Son of a Woman: the Messiah, according to some pseudepigraphal writings. *See also* male child, a; names (titles) for Jesus; Pseudepigrapha.

Son of David: a reference to Christ as descended in the line of Judah, or David's lineage. *See also* Davidic Covenant; names (titles) for Jesus.

son of destruction. See son of perdition.

Son of God: Jesus as he described himself for the church at Thyatira (Rev. 2:18). The title is frequently used throughout Scripture, sometimes promoting eschatological implications and sometimes not. Even the Centurion guarding the cross of Christ pronounced Jesus the Son of God (or *a* son of god) as death approached (Jn. 27:54). The entire address to Thyatira is "the Son of God, whose eyes are like blazing fire and whose feet are like burnished bronze." *See also* Lord and his Christ, our; names (titles) for Jesus; Son of Man; son(s) of man (men).

Son of Man: a title for Christ that carries a strong prophetic emphasis, along with its reference to his humanity. It is a frequent and important name for the Messiah noted in both Daniel and Revelation, most particularly. Ezekiel is named often as "son of man" or "son of Adam," perhaps to magnify his status as a priest in the Zadok line. Daniel also used the phrase, on a less frequent basis, but those accounts refer to his humanity only. Perhaps no other apocalyptic title bears as much weight for eschatology as does *Son of Man*. How does such a designation carry so much credence for prophetic supremacy? The Jews should not have been marveled at the novelty of such a title. They would have recognized its meaning from Daniel (Dan. 7) because God had bestowed the name on His champion—a pronouncement of the Ancient of Days to one who holds the power of the universe in both the physical and spiritual worlds. The Son of Man will make and break kingdoms, establish eternal dominions, and receive the fealty of untallied millions upon trillions. The central question in the name, after all, is one of authority. To Jesus alone has it been bequeathed by the Father and he alone shall wield it in righteous power. *See also* apocalyptic, apocalypticism; crushing rock that became a mountain; Daniel's vision of end time; Daniel's visions of the mighty kingdom; eternal kingdom, the; Ezekiel's pledge to the Jewish remnant; Ezekiel's vision of the restored theocracy; great sing, the; Lord and his Christ, our; names (titles) for Jesus; New Covenant, the; prophet(s); sign of the Son of Man, the; Son of God; sons of God to be revealed; son(s) of man (men); super-sign, the.

son(s) of man (men): a typical biblical phrase for human beings (*e.g.,* Psalm 14:2). Both Daniel and Ezekiel were addressed as "son of man," which carries a distinct impression of humanity. *See also* Adam; Ezekiel as prophet; man (men); Son of God; Son of Man; woman (women).

son of perdition: 1. a name for Judas the betrayer (Jn. 17:12). 2. a synonym for destruction (Rev. 17:8, 11, *et al.*). 3. another name for Paul's identification of the Antichrist (2 Th. 2:3). All three definitions use the term "destruction" in the New International Version. The terms "son of perdition" and "man of lawlessness" seem almost interchangeable. *See also* Antichrist; man of lawlessness; man of sin; perdition.

son of the dawn. See son of the morning, son of the dawn.

son of the gods, a: the title used by King Nebuchadnezzar to identify the mysterious theophanic figure aiding Shadrach, Meshach, and Abednego within the fiery furnace (Dan. 3:25). *See also* angelic miracles; Daniel's account of the image of gold and the fiery furnace; theophany.

son of the morning, son of the dawn: Isaiah's name for proud Babylon (Isa. 14:12). Standard thinking holds that this section of Isaiah also cryptically describes Satan, or Lucifer, as an exalted angel before his rebellion. *See also* accuser of our brothers; angel of light; Anointed Cherub; Babylon, Babylonians; Beelzebub; Belial; Day Star; dragon; Evil One, the; father of lies; god of this age, the; guardian Cherub; kingdom of the air; kingdom of this world; king of Babylon; king of Tyre; Light-Bringer; Lucifer; Mastema; Morning Star, the; prince of demons; prince of the power of the air; prince of this world; red dragon; ruler of the kingdom of the air; Sammael; Satan; Venus.

"sons and daughters" prophecy. See generational prophecy.

Sons of Darkness: those who will oppose the Sons of Light in the eschaton when they clash at the end of days, according to the Essenes. The conflict is thoroughly explained by many of the Qumran commentaries. *See also* Angel of Darkness; Angel of Light; Dead Sea Scrolls; Manual of Discipline; Renewal, the; Sons of Light; Teacher of Righteousness; *War of the Sons of Light Against the Sons of Darkness;* War Scroll; Wicked Priest.

sons of God: a frequent Old Testament identification for angels, also known as "messengers" or "ministering spirits." Paul (Gal. 3:26) also called Christians who have been baptized with Christ as "sons of God." He used the phrase again in Romans 8:19 where, once more, the reference is pointed to the redemption of God's mortal creation (the believers in Christ) and not to the angels. On the other hand, Jude 6 seems to state that evil angels (sons of God) that inhabited earth in Noah's day are those now imprisoned in the depths where they are prevented from further devastation until released for eternal judgment. The context determines whether angel or mortal is the proper subject. A group called the Sethites or Cainites are also called sons of God when distinguishing those to be judged at the end of time. *See also* angel(s); Cainites; daughters of men; prophet(s); Sethites; sons of God to be revealed.

sons of God to be revealed: Paul's description of those children of God [sons and daughters] who are destined to be fully redeemed, along with all of creation, when the Son of Man appears (Rom. 8:18–19). *See also* Cainites; daughters of men; eschatology, eschatological; Sethites; Son of Man; sons of God.

sons of Korah: Korahites (a tribal entity in Israel that numbered Haman, Jeduthun, and Asaph as members) whom David organized as singers in the Temple (1 Chr. 15:17; 16:41-42; 25:4–5). A number of the Psalms bear a subscription to indicate that the verse was written for or by one or more of them. Some of them may have been prophets as well. Other Korahites were gatekeepers and bakers for the sanctuary (1 Chr. 9:19, 31–32). *See also* Asaph; Haman; Jeduthun; prophet(s).

Sons of Light: those who will oppose the Sons of Darkness in the eschaton when the final battle is fought at the end of the age according to the Essenes. The conflict is thoroughly explained by many of the Qumran manuscripts. *See also* Angel of Darkness; Angel of Light; Dead Sea Scrolls; Manual of Discipline; Renewal, the; Sons of Darkness; Teacher of Righteousness; *War of the Sons of Light Against the Sons of Darkness;* War Scroll; Wicked Priest.

Sons of Solomon. See Dionysian Artificers.

sons of the light and sons of the day: Paul's description of the righteous who will not be surprised or alarmed at the Second Appearing of Christ (1 Th. 5:5). Such believers are never named as among those bound in the darkness of evil.

sons of thunder: in Aramaic "Boanerges," meaning "outbursts" or "wrath." The term spots the nicknames given to James and John by Jesus (Mk. 3:17) because of their occasional rash flare-ups of temper. Once, the two brothers even offered to rain down judgment on a Samaritan village they perceived as rude or inhospitable to their mission (Lk. 9:54). *See also* James; John as apostle.

sons (school) of the prophets: bands of roving young men, around the time of Samuel and after, who traveled from place to place praising God in a sort of ecstatic, slavering, frenetic, shouting, and dancing sort of exhibition. Such groups were first noted in the writings of Samuel (1 Sam. 10:5) and were mentioned elsewhere in the histories (1 Ki. 20:35; 2 Ki. 2:3, 5, 7, 15; 4:1, 38; 6:1). Saul was seen among their number at least once. Supposedly, their style of praise and display was mentally or psychologically contagious to some extent and seemed more oriented to ecstasy than discernible preaching. The scriptural record notes that the sons of the prophets had sanctuaries or training communes at

Bethel, Gibeah, Rama, Jericho, and Carmel. *See also* Assemblies of the Wise; communal communities; ecstasy; prophet(s); prophetic associations; religious organizations.

sons (seven) of Sceva. See Sceva.

soon: a measurement of estimated time with the assumption that the wait will be short. It is an important apocalyptic word because the Second Coming is frequently mentioned in the New Testament as appearing "soon." The exact meaning may be impossible to determine as we have no point of reference from the Scriptures. There is little question that the early Christians expected Christ's return in their own lifetimes. However, that hope was not to be realized, even 2,000 years later. It must be then that "soon" is presented within the context of God's time, not our own. In Hebrew, the term is often an expression of eagerness or expectation, not time. *Soon,* in its Greek form as *en takhei or tachys* (a synonym), might also mean that an event may not happen in the near term but that, when it does, the action will be swift and sudden. Even "at hand" can also refer to prophetic measures related to nearness—not only that something is about to transpire immediately but can hint of a differing kind of prophetic alertness. *See also en takhei;* eschatology, eschatological; "soon, but not yet"; time; time is near, the.

"soon, but not yet": a catchphrase prone to be spoken by eschatologically aware Jews who are actively looking for the coming Messiah, and for some, the rebuilding of the Temple. *See also* eschatology, eschatological; soon; time is near, the.

soothsayer(s): more of a sorcerer than a prophet. Such performers claimed supernatural or occultic powers and were prone to use spells, incantations, and other thaumaturgic wonders. The office and its practices were forbidden to God's people. Some prominent soothsayers in Scripture include the Philippian girl whom Paul led to Christ (Acts 16:16–18) and the seven sons of a man named Sceva who tried to practice magic in the name of Jesus (Acts 19:13–16). Others include Jannes and Jambres, who opposed Moses before Pharaoh (2 Tim. 3:8); the witch of Endor (1 Sam. 28); Simon the Samaritan sorcerer (Acts 8:9–24); the wife of Pontius Pilate (Mt. 27:19); and Elymas (Acts 13:6–11). *See also* conjure man; Elymas; filidh; hierophant; hungan; Jannes and Jambres; magic, magick; medium; meonenim; mystagogue; mystery religion(s); occult, occultic; Pilate's wife; priest(s); psychic(s); Sangoma(s); Sceva; shaman, shamanism; Simon Magus; slave girl of Philippi; sorcery, sorceries; spirit guide(s); storyteller, a good; tutelary; witchcraft; witch of Endor.

Sopater: (possibly Sosipater) a traveling companion of Paul from Berea (Acts 20:4). His assistance was mainly rendered during the return trip of Paul's third missionary journey. *See also* missions, missionaries; Sosipater.

sopherim. See scribe(s).

Sophia: the personification of wisdom (also named Sophia) as expounded by the ancient philosophers, considered by some of them to be the first creation of Yahweh. The idea became a prominent feature of Gnosticism when a lesser Sophia (a female emanation) descended from the realms of light and spirit into the mundane world of matter. Thus, most Gnostic teachers claimed the Sophia was two-fold—the upper called *ano* Sophia and the lower called *kato* Sophia (or Achamoth). The wisdom of the book of Proverbs is hardly mythological or other-worldly writing, yet it nevertheless holds a certain content of aspiration and reverence for God and Goodness. Solomon's wisdom was of the more practical type (*i.e.,* knowledge, but it, too, hinted of a certain kind of esoteric understanding). The Gnostics conceived of Sophia as the consort of the unknown god dwelling in the Ogdoad, their highest heaven. Achamoth herself was born with another female consort, not a male, and is entirely a Gnostic concoction. *See also* Aeons; Archons; "Book of Thunder"; bridal chamber ceremony; Demiurge; Gnosticism, Gnostic(s); Lady Wisdom; *nous;* Ogdoad; Olympian pantheon; philosophy of religion; Pleroma; *protennoia;* Proverbs as Old Testament book; unknown god, the; wisdom; woman (women).

Sophronius: the patriarch of Jerusalem who surrendered the city to the Muslims under Caliph Omar in A.D. 636. *See also* Eastern Orthodox Church.

Sophronius, Eusebius Hieronymus. See Jerome.

sorcery, sorceries: pagan practices, (*pharmakeia*) sometimes perhaps involving hallucinogens. As it pertains, some apocalypticists insist one form of sorcery involves the modern experience with illicit drugs—which may or may not be the case when referenced in the biblical context. The intended meaning in Scripture points to deception and occultic-like expression. The prophets were vitally interested in sorcery since the pagan societies around them were steeped in its practice, as were many Hebrews from time to time. Several types can be distinguished. A diviner (*kesem*) gazes into an object until he is transfixed and an altered state of mind is achieved; an observer of the times (*me'onen*) is a Chaldean astrologer and, later, a cloud reader and observer of the flights of birds; an enchanter (*nachash*) controlled animals, especially snakes and scorpions or burned incense; a sorcerer (*kashap*) is a general term for any occult manipulator using drugs, meditation, or shamanism; a charmer (*cheber*) used charms (jewelry or talismans) for achieving his wants or for protection (Acts 19:19); one with a familiar spirit (*ob*) conjured ghosts or spirits by using teraphim or soothsaying (as was the witch of Endor); a wizard (*yidde'oni*) used a bone of an animal or person by placing it in his mouth to speak to the dead by incantation; a necromancer (sometimes dreamer) spent nights in cemeteries to invoke the spirits of the dead; a magician or soothsayer (*chartumim*) uses ceremonial or non-ceremonial magic to call upon the spirits for aid. *See also* anthropomancy; anthroposophy; apotropaic magic; aretology; Ariosophy; astral plane; astral projection; astrolabe; astrology, astrologers; athame; audition; augury; automatic writing; bagua; belomancy; *besom*; bibliomancy; black arts; black mirror; blood moon(s); cartomancy; chaos magic; chiromancy; clairaudience; clairsentience; clairvoyance; cone of power; conjure; cryptesthesia; crystallomancy; crystal skulls; curious acts; curse(s); divination; dream(s); dreams and visions; dweomer; ecstasy; enchantment; enneagram; ensorcell; esoteric sects; evil eye; extrasensory perception (ESP); foreknowledge; foretelling; geomancy, grimoire; gris-gris; hepatoscopy; Hermetic wisdom; Hermetic writings; hex; hierscopy; horoscope(s); hydromancy; Ifa; incantation; juju; labyrinth walk; lecanomancy; literomancy; locution; magic arts; magic, magick; magic square; magnetism; *mana*; mantic wisdom; mantra; Mass of Saint Secaire; miracle(s); monition; mystery religion(s); necromancy; New Age religion; numbers, symbology of; occult, occultic; omen; oneiromancy; oracle(s); otherworldly journeys; ouija board; out-of-body experiences (OBEs); paranormal; parapsychology; past life regression; peace pole(s); pentagram; philosopher's stone; poppets; precognition; prediction; prefiguration; premonition; prodigy; prognostication; prophecy, general; psi; psychic healing; psychic(s); psychic reading; psychomancy; psychometry; psychonautics; pyramidology; rebirthing; reincarnation; remote viewing; revelation; rhabdomancy; scrying; séance; secret societies; secret wisdom; soothsayer(s); spell; spell names; spiritism; stigmata; supernatural; superstition; tarot; telegnosis; telepathy; telesthesia; talisman(s); teraphim; theugry; third eye, the; thoughtform; totemism; vision(s); vision quest; visualization; Voodoo; Voudou; wanga; warlock(s); Web-Bot; witchcraft; wizard(s); *ya sang*; yoga; Zen; zodiac; *zos kia* cultus.

sore(s): afflictions to the skin, often painful. They are marks of punishment by God when speaking eschatologically. The pouring of the first bowl (Rev. 16:1–2) produced boils or sores on the people carrying the mark of the beast. The Philistines suffered something like "tumors" (some translations say "hemorrhoids," or "rats" possibly carrying bubonic plague) when they refused to release the captured ark of the covenant (1 Sam. 5). Many other Scripture references relate to the presence of leprosy (usually a generic name for various diseases of the skin) or some eruptions of the body as punishment from God. *See also* boil(s); leprosy; ritual defilement.

Soreg. See middle (dividing) wall of partition.

Sosipater: (perhaps Sopater), a believer who joined Paul in sending greetings to the Roman church (Rom. 16:21). He is identified as a relative of Paul. *See also* Jason; Lucius; Sopater.

Sosthenes: the synagogue ruler at Corinth (Acts 18:17) during the ministry of Paul. He was punished in court by the Judaizers of Corinth in frustration because the Roman proconsul, Gallio, refused to hear their complaint against Paul. Thus, we may see him as a scapegoat or one who suffers for no legitimate reason. One of that name is also mentioned as a Christian from whom Paul's first letter to the Corinthians was sent as if he might have been a co-author or consultant (1 Cor. 1:1). It is uncertain if the two names are the same, but the tendency is to think of them as separate individuals.

soteriology: theology's technical word for that which deals with salvation in Christ. The word is derived from the Greek *soteria* (salvation, deliverance) and *logos* (word). The act of salvation began early but will be completed in the eschaton, for we are now "working out our own salvation with fear and trembling" (Phil. 2:12–13). *See also* anthropology; apology, apologetics; eschatology, eschatological; history of the church; salvation; theology.

Sought After: a name for redeemed Israel likely reserved for the millennial era in which the people of God will live in harmony and good reputation (Isa. 62:12). Their guidance and advice will be esteemed, particularly in ritualistic and religious matters. *See also* Beulah; City No Longer Deserted; Deserted/Desolate; Hebrews as a people; Hephzibah; Holy People, the; eschatology, eschatological; Jerusalem as city; Jew(s); Judaism; name, a new; Redeemed of the Lord, the.

soul(s): the spiritual or fundamentally created nature of a person—the life principle or undying essence of God inherent in the individual. The term (*nephesh* in Hebrew and *psyche* in Greek) embraces the meaning of "a living being," both human and animal. It, along with the heart and mind, is capable of loving God and others (Deut. 6:5), a fact which Jesus reaffirmed (Mk. 12:30). The soul can be "lost" to moral depravity or spiritual neglect, which in essence, is the ultimate and irretrievable catastrophe. The central theme of eschatology may very well be the mysterious and continuous battle between God and the devil (good and evil) for the accumulation of souls for eternity. Assuming the existence of the soul, what is its locus? Does it have substance? Can it be subjected to the scientific method of investigation? Herophilus of Alexandra, in the third century B.C., may have been the first to dissect a human corpse spurred by pure curiosity. His conclusion was that the soul is to be found in the fourth ventricle of the brain. The ancient Egyptians differed in that they claimed it was the heart, an organ they preserved in the dead to be weighed by the god Anubis; the brain they cast away as irrelevant. The Roman physician Galen theorized that the soul animated consciousness by breathing the soul force of the world (*Spiritus Mundi*) which heated and cooled the body and helped its function. Rene Descartes concluded the soul was in the pineal gland, which we know governs the levels of melatonin in the body. Franz Gall (19th century Vienna) theorized the soul was diffusely located throughout the body, a theory that gave rise to phrenology—the study of bumps on the head. An American doctor named Duncan MacDougal (19th century) tried to weigh the soul. His conclusions said the mass (which was not exactly mass or substance) was three-quarters of an ounce. Devotees of Haitian Voodoo believe every man has two souls—the *gro bonanj* animates the body while the *ti bonanj* protects it. The West African Fon people say everyone has three souls and an adult male has four. *See also* aspect; breath; Christoplatonism; evangelist(s), evangelism; heart, heart and spirit; heart, soul, mind; *Ka;* life; love; mind; *nephesh; psuche;* psyche; *qi;* shade(s); sleep; soulmate; "soul bone"; "soul hole"; soul sleep; souls under the altar; soul-winning; spirit; *Spiritus Mundi;* strength; *zoe.*

"soul bone": a part of the body that some Jewish spiritualists believed existed as the residence of the life force, an element they called *luz.* It was believed to be located somewhere along the spine and claimed to be indestructible. Other theories set the location in the sacrum, the coccyx, and even the sesamoid bones of the big toe. In the first century, Emperor Hadrian ordered Rabbi Joshua ben Hananiah to produce one for his examination. Experiments concluded, Hadrian reported, that the *luz* could not be consumed by fire, crushed in the mill, or cracked by hammer and anvil (though both anvil and hammer were split). *See also* bone(s); soul(s).

"soul boxes": in ancient belief, a temporary container or amulet, natural or man-made, intended to hold a person's soul for a time until some danger or misfortune was overcome. In parts of Kei Island, for example, the soul of an infant could be protected in an empty coconut shell until it could be safely released to the body.

"soul-carriers". See *psychopomps.*

soul catcher: a computer chip, predicted to be available in 2025, which can be implanted behind the eye to record a person's every lifetime thought and sensation. It is reported the device is being perfected by British scientists. *See also* eschatology, eschatological; "wearable tech."

Soulcraft: a term used by William Dudley Pelley, a publisher of metaphysical and philosophical books exclusive to himself as author. His firm was called Fellowship Press, a publishing arm devoted solely to esoteric teachings similar to Gnosticism. Pelley was also the organizer of an American pro-Hitler group in 1933 called the Silver Shirts. *See also* Gnosticism, Gnostic(s); Hitler, Adolf.

soul freedom: freedom of conscience in religious matters. The conviction is also known as "free agency" and by other names. Individuals are free to choose their own faith outlook as personal decision-making. The right extends to those who choose no religious affiliation or action whatsoever but it also applies to those attracted to faith to examine their convictions with no outside influence forced upon the mind. Even God does not force His will on any person. *See also* free will; priesthood of the believer; will.

"soul hole": a purposefully-drilled hole in a wall or tomb through which an offering to the gods could be passed. It also allowed the arriving soul of a newborn to enter the world or the spirit of the deceased to depart. Often the opening was positioned to view a significant part of the heavens to ease the passage and to observe the heavenly movements. Archeologists are prone to call the porthole *seelenlochker*, the German designation. *See also* archeology, archeologists; hole on the Isle of Derg; soul(s).

soulmate: (or soul mate) in contemporary language, one of a couple settled in love and companionship that may be described as God-ordained. In the original sense, however, a soulmate was the spouse or marriage partner in a previous life. Edgar Casey and the followers of Theosophy further modified the meaning to refer to God's creation of humans whom they saw as androgynous souls. *See also* matrimony; reincarnation.

soul sleep: the condition that some believe occurs between death and resurrection in which there is no consciousness until the eternal awakening. More technical names for the idea are presented as hypnopsychism, thnetopsychism, psychopannychia, Christian mortalism, conditional immortality, or the "intermediate state." The idea is not compatible with most orthodox doctrine, although Scripture is not particularly verbose as to the particulars of the intermediate state. We do know, however, that the soul is aware and in contact with Jesus but not yet ignited to a perfect body. *See also* Abraham's bosom; afterlife; annihilationism; Aralu; Arcadia; Asgard; Avalon; Dis; Duat; Elysium; eschatology, eschatological; eternal life; future life, doctrine of the; Gehenna; Hades; happy hunting ground; Harrowing of Hell, the; heaven; hell; intermediate state; Jade Empire, the; Jahannam; Janna; lake of fire; life after death; limbo; *Limbus Puerorum*; Mictlan; new heaven and new earth; Nirvana; Otherworld; Paradise; paradise of God; paraeschatology; Pardes; Perdition; Promised Land the; Pure Land, the; purgatory; sect(s); Seventh-Day Adventism; Shambhala legends; *Sheol*; space doctrine; Summerland; Thule, land of; Tir na nOg; underworld; Upper Gehenna; Utopia; Valhalla; world to come, the; Xibala.

souls under the altar: those martyrs of Revelation 6:9–11 revealed in the fifth seal. They are safe in the Lord but cry out for justice from the Lord to satisfy the vindication they deserved and demanded from the righteousness of God. *See also* eschatology, eschatological; martyr(s); martyrdom; witnesses, great crowd of.

soul-winning: the more casual manner of recruiting people to salvation in Christ by means of personal or mass evangelism. *See also* altar call; "asking Jesus into my heart"; blood of the Lamb; Christianese; evangelist(s), evangelism; fishers of men; gospel; lost; missions, missionaries; "nail-scarred hands, the"; "turn your life [heart] over to Jesus"; "washed in the blood"; witness(es); worldwide preaching of the gospel.

sound of marching in the trees: God's signal or sign to David to attack the Philistines at the Valley of Rephaim (2 Sam. 5:23–25). At the sound of marching in the tops of the balsam trees, where David's army was positioned, he was to launch an assault behind God's advance toward the enemy.

sound of marching troops: a ploy from God which frustrated Ben-Hadad's attempt to subdue Samaria. The troops of Aram heard the sound of chariots and horses and a great army, causing them to panic and flee (2 Ki. 7:5–7). *See also* Ben-Hadad; Hadadezer.

sounds of the rapture: the audio (as described in 1 Thessalonians 4:16–17 and elsewhere) said to emanate from heaven when Christ arrives to seize his Church. The expressions are noted to be a shout, a cry of the archangel, and the blare of a trumpet. Though not specified in the Thessalonian paradigm, nor its rehearsal in 1 Corinthians

15:51–52, it is tempting to speculate that the voice of the archangel is primarily a general announcement of what is to ensue, the trumpet to call forth the dead in Christ, and the "voice" as that of Jesus himself calling the living believers to him. *See also* "Come up here"; eschatology, eschatological; last trumpet, the; lightning; loud command, a; rapture; shout; Shout of the Overcomers; thunder; trumpet(s); trumpet call of the elect; voice of God; voice of the archangel, the; voice from the throne; voice out of heaven.

"souper": a malicious name coined by the Irish peasantry in the 19th century. The tag identified any Catholic dealing with Protestant gentry suspected of currying favor with the poorer classes, especially if the actor was proselytizing—seeking to lure converts from Catholicism. The byword developed because some Catholics enduring the potato famine would abandon their faith for a bowl of soup from Protestants—a "soup-taker." *See also* Christianese; comity; Dow, Lorenzo; proselyte(s); proselytism; Rice Christian; slurs, religious; "sheep stealing."

source criticism: the process of discovering the social, linguistic, and geographical origins of a given biblical pericope. It was a prime tool for developers of the documentary hypothesis theory. *See also* accideme; Agrapha; allegorical interpretation; alliteration; analogical interpretation; apostrophe; apothegm; assonance; autograph; Bible; Bible manuscripts; Bible translations; biblical criticism; chiasmus; conflict story; *constructio ad sensum;* context; contextualization; dittography; documentary hypothesis; double sense fulfillment; doublets; doubling; edification; eisegesis; epanadiplosis; epigrammatic statements; etymology; exegesis; figure of speech; folio; form criticism; Fourfold Interpretation; gattung; genre; gloss; gnomic sayings; Gospel(s); grammatical-historical interpretation; *hapax legomena;* haplography; hermeneutic(s); higher criticism; homographs; homonyms; homophones; *homoteleuton;* hyperbole; idiom; illumination; *inclusio;* inspiration; interpolation; interpretation; inverted nun; irony; isagogics; *itture sopherim;* jot and tittle; kere; *kethib;* "L"; liberalists interpretation; literal interpretation; litotes; loan words; lower criticism; *logia;* lower criticism; "M"; Masoretic Text; minuscule(s); mystery of God; omission; onomastica; onomatopoeia; palimpsest; papyrus; paradigm; parallelism; parchment; Pardes; *paroimia; paronomasia;* pericope; personification; Peshitta; plenary inspiration; pointing;

point of view; polyglot; principles of interpretation; proof texting; pun(s); "Q"; redaction; revelation, theological; rhetorical criticism; rhetorical devices; riddle; satire; *scripto continua;* scriptorium; *sebirin;* simile; similitude; sources, primary and secondary; special points; strophe; superscription; symbol(s); synecdoche; syntax; synthetic parallelism; text; textual criticism; threefold sense of interpretation; *tiggune sopherim;* Time Texts; Torah; translation; transmission history; transposition; trope; type(s); typology; uncial(s); unwritten prophecy; vellum; verbicide.

sources, primary and secondary: tools for the students of lower criticism. Primary sources for biblical criticism and research are usually those of earlier date and not copied. Secondary sources are considered less reliable as they may be copies or copies of copies. Both, however, are valuable to accurate investigation. *See also* accideme; allegorical interpretation; alliteration; analogical interpretation; apostrophe; apothegm; assonance; autograph; Bible; Bible manuscripts; Bible translations; biblical criticism; chiasmus; conflict story; *constructio ad sensum;* context; contextualization; dittography; double sense fulfillment; doublets; doubling; edification; eisegesis; epanadiplosis; epigrammatic statements; etymology; exegesis; figure of speech; folio; form criticism; Fourfold Interpretation; gattung; gloss; gnomic sayings; grammatical-historical interpretation; *hapax legomena;* haplography; hermeneutic(s); higher criticism; homographs; homonyms; homophones; *homoteleuton;* hyperbole; idiom; illumination; *inclusio;* inspiration; interpolation; interpretation; inverted nun; irony; isagogics; *itture sopherim;* jot and tittle; kere; *kethib;* "L"; liberalists interpretation; literal interpretation; litotes; loan words; lower criticism; "M"; Masoretic Text; minuscule(s); mystery of God; omission; onomastica; onomatopoeia; palimpsest; papyrus; paradigm; parallelism; parchment; *paroimia; paronomasia;* pericope; personification; Peshitta; plenary inspiration; pointing; point of view; polyglot; principles of interpretation; proof texting; pun(s); "Q"; redaction; revelation, theological; rhetorical criticism; rhetorical devices; riddle; satire; *scripto continua;* scriptorium; *sebirin;* simile; similitude; source criticism; special points; strophe; superscription; symbol(s); synecdoche; syntax; synthetic parallelism; text; textual criticism; threefold sense of interpretation; *tiggune sopherim;* Time Texts; Torah; translation; transmission history; transposition; trope; type(s); typology; uncial(s); vellum; verbicide.

sour grapes, proverb of the: the keywords within the proverb found in Ezekiel 18:1–4 (among other places) that states: "The fathers have eaten sour grapes, and the children's teeth are set on edge." The saying is intended to broadcast the truism that the ills of a given generation are, at least in part, brought on by the more wicked acts of the previous ones. God is said to punish past a single generation in certain instances. Ezekiel's prophetic message now states that this proverb may no longer be used as an excuse for bad behavior since each person is responsible for his or her own faults. Ezekiel's presentation, however, does not adequately deal with God's indisputable ability to punish generations past the originator of a sin failure. *See also* corporate guilt.

Southcott, Joanna: self-proclaimed prophetess of the 1800s who reported a vision in which she was told that Jesus would return on October 19, 1864. She had gained notoriety by accurately predicting a poor harvest and the death of the local bishop in 1792. Joanna called herself "the greatest prophet that ever came into the world" and named herself the woman clothed with the sun in Revelation 12. At age sixty-four, the virginal Southcott claimed she would give birth to Jesus on Christmas Day of 1814. An autopsy revealed she was not pregnant. Her actions initiated a cult following later led by John Turner and John Wroe, both of whom offered end time predictions. Charles Hindley published Southcott's writings in 1862. At that time, Hindley discovered that the famous apocalyptic couplet supposedly composed by her was a forgery. The doggerel reads: "The world to an end shall come in eighteen hundred and eighty one." *See also* cult(s); Panacea Society, the; prophetess(es); woman clothed in (with) the sun, the; Wroe, John.

Sovereign and Lord, our only: the title for Jesus rendered by Jude (Jude 4). *See also* names (titles) for Jesus.

Sovereign Lord: the name for God used by the martyred souls under the altar in Revelation 6:10. It is also a common address for God throughout Scripture when God's dominion or majesty is to be emphasized, especially in the prophecies of Ezekiel. The title was in use as far back in history as the time of Abraham (Gen. 15:2). The judge Gideon also used the label (Jud. 6:22). *See also* Almighty; Author of Mighty Deeds; God, the great and awesome; names (titles) for God.

Sovereign of Creation: God as addressed by the archangel Michael in *The Testament of Abraham. See also* Creator; Maker of All Things; Maker, the; names (titles) for God; Pseudepigrapha.

sovereign will of God. See will of God.

space doctrine: a.k.a. Mormon cosmology, a rather bizarre Latter-Day Saints doctrine featuring eternal marriage for observant male members who will continually reproduce spirit children to become gods in the afterlife, thus perpetuating the human-to-god cycle theology so prominent in Mormonism. The most faithful will rule as deities from his individual planet. Others are to have lesser prestige and more humble bases of power. *See also* Abraham's bosom; afterlife; Aralu; Arcadia; Asgard; Avalon; Church of Jesus Christ of Latter-Day Saints, the; cosmology; Dis; Duat; Elysium; eschatology, eschatological; eternal life; future life, doctrine of the; Gehenna; Hades; happy hunting ground; heaven; hell; Hy-Breasail; Hyperborea; intermediate state; Jade Empire, the; Jahannam; Janna; lake of fire; life after death; limbo; *Limbus Puerorum;* Mictlan; new heaven and new earth; Nirvana; Otherworld; Paradise; paradise of God; paraeschatology; Pardes; Perdition; Promised Land, the Pure Land, the; purgatory; Shambhala legends; *Sheol;* soul sleep; Smith, Joseph Jr.; Summerland; Thule, land of; Tir na nOg; underworld; Upper Gehenna; Utopia; Valhalla; world to come, the; Xibala.

span: a rather imprecise unit of measure in the ancient world. The calculation is based on the width of a man's four fingers and thumb taken three times, or with the fingers splayed. A "handbreadth" then would be one width of the hand measured in such a manner. *See also* cubit.

Spangler, Lee J.: a grocery clerk in York, Pennsylvania, who predicted the end of the world in October 1908. He received some temporary notoriety at the time.

Spare, Austin Osman: English artist and draughtsman (1886–1956), an accomplished occult expert and developer of automatic writing and drawing. The form called the *zos kia* cultus emerged from his techniques. Spare's work was continued by his friend and successor, Kenneth Grant, into the 20th century. *See also* automatic writing; *zos kia* cultus.

Bernie L. Calaway

Sparks, Jared: editor, teacher, historian, and Unitarian clergyman (1789–1866). Sparks wrote American history by using original documents and became known as the "patriarch of American history" even though he was known to embellish his accounts of national heroes like George Washington, Benjamin Franklin, and others. He edited the *North American Review,* then *The American Almanac and Repository of Useful Knowledge.* His ministerial duties were limited. *See also* Unitarian Universalists.

Spark Sunday: a custom of ancient Switzerland consisting of lighting bonfires on high places on the evening of the first Sunday in Lent. The belief was that it helped secure light and safety for the coming year. Further, when the fire died down, it was good luck to jump over it. *See also* Easter; Easter fires; Lent; liturgy, Christian;

spared from the hour of trial: a promise to the Philadelphian church of Revelation 3:10 that would exempt that assembly from further ordeal because of their fidelity and endurance. Many accept this indicator as a voucher that the Church as a whole will not be forced to go through the seven years of Tribulation on earth but will be raptured to safety. *See also* rapture.

sparrow: a common and unremarkable bird mentioned in Scripture as a metaphor for the inconsequential and less recognized among us. Jesus reminded his hearers that sparrows were then sold for two birds per penny. Yet not one went unnoticed by the Father Who knows when each falls to the ground (Mt. 10:29). We are neither forgotten nor overlooked by Him. *See also* animals, birds, and insects, symbology of; bird.

spasmos. See holy kiss.

speaking in tongues. See glossolalia.

spear(s): or lance or javelin, an ancient weapon consisting of a shaft with a point at one end. Its advantage was that it could reach an opponent via close-in combat or thrown at the enemy in a distance. A Roman soldier thrust one into the side of Jesus on the cross to ascertain if he was truly deceased (Jn. 19:34). The Bible also speaks of turning these instruments of war into pruning hooks of peace. *See also* pruning hooks; Spear of Destiny.

Spear of Destiny: also called the holy lance or the spear of Longinus. The artifact has been identified by some as the lance used to thrust into the side of Jesus (the story found in John's Gospel only) to assure the Romans that he was truly dead and in no need of the standard act of breaking his legs to hasten death. The wielder of the lance (according to the *Acts of Pilate* and the *Gospel of Nicodemus*) is said to be the centurion Longinus, whom Pilate had placed on limited duty because of severe cataracts of the eyes. He was cured of his sight difficulties when the gash produced blood and water. Longinus then became an immediate believer. The most famous relic of the type is in Vienna, although it was coveted and stolen by Adolf Hitler and kept throughout most of World War II. There are other replicas in Poland, Russia, Antioch, and Armenia, but, so far as can be determined, none are authentic. Legend claims that whoever possesses the spear is invincible. It is put forward that the spear of Vienna was carried by the Holy Roman emperors as part of their battle standard. *See also* cross; Longinus; Mandylion, the Holy; relic(s); Roman Catholic Church; shrine(s); spear(s); veil of Veronica.

special points: *(puncta extraordinaria)* unique "pointing" of the Hebrew text placed over certain words or letters (occurs fifteen times) indicating that the scribe had reservations about the correct translation but dared not alter it. *See also* accideme; alliteration; apostrophe; apothegm; assonance; autograph; Bible; Bible manuscripts; Bible translations; biblical criticism; chiasmus; conflict story; *constructio ad sensum;* context; contextualization; dittography; double sense fulfillment; doublets; doubling; edification; eisegesis; epanadiplosis; epigrammatic statements; etymology; exegesis; figure of speech; folio; form criticism; gattung; gloss; gnomic sayings; grammatical-historical interpretation; *hapax legomena;* haplography; hermeneutic(s); higher criticism; homographs; homonyms; homophones; *homoteleuton;* hyperbole; idiom; *inclusio;* interpolation; interpretation; inverted nun; irony; isagogics; *itture sopherim;* jot and tittle; kere; *kethib;* "L"; liberalists interpretation; literal interpretation; litotes; loan words; lower criticism; "M"; Masoretic Text; minuscule(s); mystery of God; omission; onomastica; onomatopoeia; palimpsest; papyrus; paradigm; parallelism; parchment; *paroimia; paronomasia;* pericope; personification; Peshitta; pointing; point of view;

polyglot; principles of interpretation; proof texting; pun(s); "Q";
redaction; revelation, theological; rhetorical criticism; rhetorical
devices; riddle; satire; *scripto continua;* scriptorium; *sebirin;* simile;
similitude; source criticism; sources, primary and secondary;
strophe; superscription; symbol(s); synecdoche; syntax; synthetic
parallelism; text; textual criticism; *tiggune sopherim;* Time Texts;
Torah; translation; transposition; trope; type(s); typology;
uncial(s); vellum; verbicide.

species: theologically speaking, the word takes on the meaning of
"form" or "appearance." When the wine of the Eucharist is
elevated, according to High Church dogma, it turns to literal
blood of Christ and the bread becomes actual flesh. However, as
to appearance, texture, and taste, each remains in its recognizable
"species" as bread and wine. *See also* bread; consubstantiation;
element(s); Eucharist; Lord's Supper; transubstantiation; wafer;
wine.

spell: words in a formula usually intended to cast a curse or hex. *See
also* apotropaic magic; cantrip; charm(s); conjure; curse(s);
dweomer; enchantment; ensorcell; evil eye; execration; *geis*;
hex; imprecation; incantation; magic, magick; Magickal Circle,
The; magnetism; Mass of Saint Secaire; New Age religion;
occult, occultic; *pharmakeia;* pow-wow; psychonautics; sorcery,
sorceries; spell names; taboo; thoughtform; Voodoo; Voudou;
ward; warlock(s); Wicca; witch(es); witchcraft; wizard(s).

Spellman, Cardinal Francis Joseph: Roman Catholic archbishop
of New York (1889–1967). Cardinal Spellman was interested
in education and charity and advocated state aid for parochial
schools. He served as vicar to the United States Armed Forces.
Spellman defended Joseph R. McCarthy's radical congressional
investigations of Communism in the country and later supported
the Vietnam War. Spellman is remembered, not necessarily
fondly, as one who campaigned shamelessly for a papacy election
inspired by the "Prophecy of the Popes" document. *See also*
Hughes, John Joseph; parochial school(s); "Prophecy of the
Popes"; Roman Catholic Church.

spell names: magical utterances of a demon's name or string of names
said to bring them forth for use and control of the conjurer.
Whether the attempt was by force or pleading, the use of names

in ancient times was a powerful tool. Knowing the name of something or someone, especially the secret or "second" name, granted control over that entity. Magicians used the spells to aid in matters of romance, business, politics, health, etc. King Solomon was, according to some mythical writings, able to hold power over demons, which he used to construct the Temple in Jerusalem. *See also* Agrippa Books; apotropaic magic; *arcanum arcandrum; Arcanum,* the; *Book of Abramelin, The;* cantrip; charm(s); conjure; *Corpus Hermecticum;* curse(s); dweomer; Emerald Tablet of Hermes, the; enchantment; ensorcell; evil eye; execration; *geis; Golden Bough, The;* grimoire; Hermeticism; Hermetic wisdom; Hermetic writings; hex; imprecation; incantation; Key of Solomon; magic arts; magic, magick; *mana;* New Age religion; occult, occultic; parapsychology; *pharmakeia;* psychonautics; *Picatrix;* pow-wow; secret wisdom; spell; sorcery, sorceries; *Spiritas Mundi;* taboo; thoughtform; Voodoo; Voudou; ward; warlock(s); Wicca; witch(es); witchcraft; wizard(s).

Spener, Philipp Jakob: considered the father of German Pietism (1635–1705) though he was not strictly a Pietist of the "quiet and contemplative" stereotype. He was, contrarily, a renowned writer, Lutheran pastor, teacher, and a pioneer of the nascent foreign missions movement. He did, however, launch "piety groups" for self-improvement of the personal spiritual life and renewal. August Francke, also an influential Pietist of the age, was a spiritual protégé. *See also* Holy Club, the; missions, missionaries; Pietism, Pietists.

Sphinx, sphinx(es): 1. the great Egyptian monument at Giza, near Cairo. The mysterious statue has the head of a man (probably a pharaoh) and the body of a crouching lion. The giant figure was originally named for the god Hor, an eagle-like deity, but was given the name "Sphinx" by the Greeks from one of their myths. Other Egyptian sphinxes had rams' heads or that of hawks. 2. a Greek goddess featuring a woman's head and a lion-like body. Whereas the Sphinx of Cairo is male and wingless, the Greek version had wings and breasts. The so-called "riddle of the sphinx" concerned the goddess who was prone to destroy any Theban citizen unable to answer her enigmatic riddle. When Oedipus Rex finally did so, she threw herself off a rock and Thebes was saved. Alternate versions of sphinxes are found throughout the world. *See also* Egyptian pantheon; Gilgal Refa'im; *Gobekli Tepe;* *masseboths;* megaliths; mythological beasties, elementals, Moai; monsters, and spirit animals; Oedipus; Olympian pantheon; riddle; sacred stones; stone(s).

spices. See perfumes, ointments, and spices.

spirit: 1. the essential or animating force that sustains life. In the Old Testament, the Hebrew word *ruach* (found an astonishing 377 times) translates to "breath," "wind," or "spirit." Each has a slightly different connotation. According to the context, *ruach* may mean something akin to the soul, the breath we take in and out of the lungs, or it may refer to a person's temperament or vigor. Another word, *pneuma,* has a similar intent but centers more heavily on the literal blowing wind of nature (if the context implies) and the life-being of the inner man (if a more theological intent is expressed). The spirit is that which constitutes the immaterial but basic essence of the human being; it is what is "saved" when one becomes a repentant believer, it is what lives in Paradise, with or without a body of some description, and it is what makes us sensitive to God's own Holy Spirit. The spirit's relation to the soul is similar but distinct. 2. In another context, a spirit is a ghost or deceptive demon or sometimes even a heavenly angel. *See also* apparition; angel(s); astral body; breath; bugbears; Christoplatonism; deceiving spirits; familiar spirit; ghost(s); heart; heart and spirit; heart, soul, mind; Holy Spirit; *Ka;* life; *mana;* mind; names (titles) for the Holy Spirit; nostrils; numen; *pneuma; psuche; qi; ruach;* shade(s); soul(s); Spirit, the water, and the blood, the; wind(s); *zoe.*

Spiritas Mundi: an ancient description of magic and its processes by which wonders were possible. The term means "cosmic breath of the universe" or the like. *See also* Agrippa Books; alchemy; *arcanum arcandrum; Arcanum,* the; *Book of Abramelin, The;* cantrip; *Corpus Hermecticum;* Emerald Tablet of Hermes, the; *Golden Bough, The;* grimoire; Hermeticism; Hermetic wisdom; Hermetic writings; magic arts; magic, magick; *mana;* mantic wisdom; occult, occultic; parapsychology; *Picatrix;* secret wisdom; soul(s); spell names; spirit.

spirit guide(s): a primarily New Age, Spiritualist, and early Native American belief that a familiar spirit manifests itself in the life of the seeker to help him or her reconnect to the light (sometimes seen as Lucifer) through meditation or other means. Shamanist religions feature them prominently as do cosmic consciousness connections. The concept is that every person of faith has one or more guiding spirits to help tutor and protect the individual. Usually, they are described as a woman or man, who may formally have been a human soul, who is assigned to collaborate with us in creative endeavors, especially growth in faith and in the practice of our humanity. Many assert the guides can be named and can interact with us on some level. *See also* Akashic Records; ancestor reverence; attending spirit(s); automatic writing; bugbears; cosmic consciousness; daemons; ectoplasm; guardian angel(s); hierophant; medium; meonenim; mystagogue; mythological beasties, elementals, monsters, and spirit animals; New Age religion; paredri; psychic healing; Reiki; séance; shaman, shamanism; soothsayer(s); spiritism; Spiritualist churches; testament(s); Third Man, the; tutelary.

spiritism: the supposed practice of calling forth the spirits of the dead, usually by use of a séance. Sometimes the practice is called spiritualism. Spiritism as a movement was started by a French educator of the 19th century named Hippolyte Leon Denizard Rivail, operating under the pen name Allan Kardec. He believed humans are immortal spirits that temporarily inhabit mortal bodies, one of several incarnations necessary to achieve moral and spiritual improvement. Mediumship may assist the living to contact the departed spirits, who may choose to exhibit beneficent or maleficent influence on the world. Kardec's book was called *The Spirits' World*, which does not equate spiritism to spiritualism. *See also* Caodaism; Candomble; Creole (Caribbean) religions; ectoplasm; Fox sisters; Kumina; Lily Dale Assembly; Macumba; medium; meonenim; mystagogue; mystery religion(s); mythological beasties, elementals, monsters, and spirit animals; necromancy; Obeah; occult, occultic; parapsychology; Quimbanda; Rastafarianism; séance; Santeria; shaman, shamanism; Shango; sorcery, sorceries; spirit guide(s); Spiritual Baptists; spiritualism; Spiritualist churches; Voodoo; Voudou; Yoruba.

spirit of error: a translation of the "spirit of antichrist" used in some Bible translations (1 Jn. 4:3). *See also* antichrist, spirit of.

Spirit of glory and of God: an approbation of the Holy Spirit as an essence of the Father Who rests on the persecuted Christians so that they might survive their tribulations in unremitting faith (1 Pe. 4:14). *See also* names (titles) for the Holy Spirit; seal(s); seal of God.

spirit of prophecy: the angel's testimony to the faithfulness of Christ and the truth of the prophetic product (Rev. 19:10). The affidavit applies to the book of Revelation itself and to godly prophetic output wherever it occurs. It is Christ's personal testimony that substantiates all of it in truth. *See also* God of the spirits of the prophets; Holy Spirit; names (titles) for the Holy Spirit; restrainer, the; spirit of truth; spirits of the prophets, the; testimony; testimony of Jesus.

spirit of the age: those values, ideas, and attitudes that influence the human culture of every age (*Zeitgeist*). For believers, the phenomenon invariably produces a kind of growing consensus that tends to lull our morals to sleep, gradually and subtlety urging us to accept society's latest mores and fads. The apostle Paul spoke of such danger (Eph. 2:1–10), calling it the "course of this world" and announcing that such peer pressure is satanic because it cultivates a lifestyle independent of God. Today, we might summarize the description as humanism (love of self), materialism (love of money), and hedonism (love of pleasure)—all to the exclusion of God and His righteousness. The spirit of the age is real and holds more significance as the world limps speedily to a culmination when we are to see its intensification and degradation in the extreme. Therefore, the concept is a vital eschatological consideration. *See also* kingdom of this world; social issues; "world, the"; worldly.

spirit of the Lord. See hand of the Lord.

Spirit of truth: a name for the Holy Spirit as expressed by John (Jn. 14:17; 15:26; 16:13; 1 Jn. 4:6). Jesus predicted the Spirit's arrival as our counselor who will lead us to all truth, including the exposition of prophecy. If "Spirit" is not capitalized, it may be permissible to describe the spirit of truth as an affinity for truth-telling in one's daily conduct. *See also* Holy Spirit; names (titles) for the Holy Spirit; restrainer, the; spirit of prophecy.

spirits. See deceiving spirits.

spirits in prison: noncorporal entities now restrained in another dimension by the power of God. The identity of the "spirits in prison" introduced in 1 Peter 3:19–22 is a source of some debate. One idea is that they are unregenerate souls awaiting their final destination in Hades. Perhaps a better explanation is that they are the populations of Noah's day who dismissed the antediluvian preaching and were destroyed by the flood. Yet the best explanation may be that they are the spirits of fallen angels or demons who corrupted the human race before Noah's flood. The passage in 1 Peter reveals that Christ descended into the lower depths to preach to the resident souls there during the time between his death and resurrection. On that occasion, did he announce his victory over sin and death to those with no hope of claiming the benefits of it? Or did he alert those on the redeemed or "good" side of Hades that he had won his Father's great triumph and secured their eventual release? Though the 1 Peter passage is not definitive, the latter proposition seems more reasonable, particularly when studied alongside other scriptural passages of similar subject matter, especially Hebrews 2:14–18, Psalm 16:10, Acts 2:30–32, and Ephesians 4:8–10. *See also* angel(s); bound angels; fallen angel(s); Harrowing of Hell, the; Tartarus; wandering stars.

spirits of righteous men [and women] made perfect: a category of faithful believers mentioned in Hebrews 12:23 otherwise not fully identified. The group is one of three collections of saints (the others being innumerable angels and the assembly of the firstborn enrolled in heaven) who are more easily recognized. Some theologians assert they are people who came to God without knowing Christ in the ante-Messianic age, which is a reasonable deduction. The group may, then, refer to Old Testament believers who will have their proper place in heaven along with all the firstborn ones.

spirits of the prophets, the: a descriptive phrase from Revelation 22:6 that testifies to the veracity of the prophetic utterance, especially (in this instance) of the truths of heaven. As an oath, the passage assures us that everything described about heaven is accurate and trustworthy since God Himself confirms the facts. *See also* God of the spirits of the prophets; spirit of prophecy.

Bernie L. Calaway

Spirit, the. See Holy Spirit.

Spirit, the water, and the blood, the: the apostle John's apology [defense] of the divinity, humanity, and ministry of Jesus (1 Jn. 5:6–8). In order to refute the Gnostics and other opponents, and to fortify the faith of believers, John "called up" three witnesses to affirm the messiahship of Jesus and his authentication as the Son of God. To comprehend the doctrine, we must first amplify the text. The King James Version reads: "For there are three that bear record in heaven, the Father, the Word, and the Holy Ghost: and these three are one." Verse 8 begins: "And there are three that bear witness on earth." That wording could be an interpolation, for it has not been seen in any Greek manuscript before the 16th century and is correctly omitted in later translations. Rather, John named the three witnesses only as the Spirit, the water, and the blood—each one affirming the truth of the others. How this trio divulges its witness is a bit of an enigma. However, the generally accepted interpretation is that the Holy Spirit may call upon "the water" as representing Jesus' earthly baptism by John the Baptist, or secondarily, from his body on the cross that issued blood and water when speared by the Roman guard. The Spirit may also count on "the blood" as representative of Christ's death on the cross to affirm the New Covenant. An alternative interpretation is that the water represents Christ's natural birth from Mary's womb and the blood his divine sacrifice. In any case, the true verification of the divine and human nature of Jesus is affirmed by the inner conviction of the believer as prompted by the Spirit of God. In Mosaic Law, three witnesses were required to verify a truth or legal transaction, a likely source of the trinity of witnesses in John. *See also* baptism of John; blood; Holy Spirit; names (titles) for the Holy Spirit; New Covenant, the; spirit; water(s).

spiritual: a condition assumed by some who claim they are receptive to religious matters, including ethics, but not affiliated with any form of organized religion. *See also* "spiritual but not religious."

Spiritual Baptists: one of the so-called Creole religions mostly composed of black and some Asian believers in Trinidad and Tobago, Granada, Guyana, Venezuela, Toronto, Los Angeles, and New York City. The group is most noted for its complex

334

rituals, especially the *mourning rite* involving lying on a dirt floor, fasting, and other ordeals. *See also* animism; Brujeria; Candomble; cult(s); gris-gris; hungan; juju; Kumina; Loa Loas; Macumba; magic, magick; mambo; Obeah; ordeal(s); Orisha; Quimbanda; Rastafarianism; Santeria; shaman, shamanism; Shango; Umbanda; veve; Voudou; Voodoo; wanga; Yoruba.

spiritual body, terrestrial body: two phrases that accentuate the body of the spirit (spiritual body) and the body of flesh (the natural body) (1 Cor. 15:42–58). *See also* resurrection(s).

"spiritual but not religious": a familiar refrain of the modern era intended to present the speaker as a "spiritual" or devout or believing person but not inclined to be affiliated with any orthodox worshiping community or set of doctrines. The phrase is so common that the acronym SBNR is often used for convenience. At first blush, this trend seems to be a forward step away from the perceived corruption and self-serving spirit of today's congregations. Then, however, this new spirituality took on the aspects of modern society to the point that it marked a highly individualistic kind of attitude. Modern peoples came to diagnose churches as they might an experiment in sociology. Factors such as the sociological condition of the community, the maturity of the church's development, the prestige (or lack of it) in the land, the worship style of its leadership and laity, its internal dynamics of administration, its reputation in the surrounding locale, and the like were measures of success. Often enough, the traditional church comes up short in such examination and is replaced by the individual's own adaptation of what "spirituality" really is. "Spiritual but not religious" is characterized by an anti-institutional mindset and hostility to organized religion. Even among those who are not enthusiastic church-goers, people today tend to be shoppers and seekers with an appeal for temporary worship experiences rather than long-term commitment. It has become one of the most pervasive marks of contemporary culture, particularly in Europe and America. *See also* Christianese; church; megachurch; "nones"; "dones"; "no-shows"; NOTA; postmodernism; spiritual.

spiritual forces of evil. See authorities.

spiritual interpretation. See allegorism.

spiritualism: 1. devotion to the mystic or contemplative arts and religion. The practitioners intend to achieve a higher intimacy with the divine and fill out the soul. 2. an alternate term for spiritism. *See also* Doyle, Arthur Conan; Lily Dale Assembly; medium; mythological beasties, elementals, monsters, and spirit animals; spiritism; Spiritualist churches.

spiritual Israel: a term sometimes used to name the physical descendants of Abraham who, through faith, are God's chosen and true to Him. It may also refer to the faithful remnant of Judaism to be redeemed at the end of the age. *See also* Jew(s); remnant; second Exodus.

Spiritualist churches: organized spiritist congregations most of which are independent, although there are Spiritists organizations modeled on the esoteric teachings of the sect. Congregants and liturgy are led by a medium and usually have an attached space called the lyceum for study and practice. *See also* cult(s); séance; medium; meonenim; mystagogue; spirit guide(s); spiritism; spiritualism.

spiritualization. See allegorism.

spiritual milk. See elementary teaching of Christ.

spirituals: religious songs composed and sung by Southern slaves based on the hymns they overheard in the camp meetings and the white churches. The musical style is a blend of African rhythms and European harmonies, which suited black yearnings for freedom of body and soul. Modern popularization of the tunes was spurred by Colonel Thomas Wentworth Higgenson when he reported on the stirring singing from his black regiments of the Civil War. After 1870, the music was raised to further general awareness by the tour performances of the Fisk University Jubilee Singers. *See also* Afro-American theology; Jubilee Singers; liturgy, Christian; music; sacred music.

Spirituals of the Franciscan Order: sometimes called Zealots or Conventuals, certain Roman Catholic men and women of the 14th century who refused to favor or condone the obvious corruption in the Roman Church of the time. Most were in the Franciscan Order but the same designator could extend to others in alternate places of service. A few so classed included

Hildegard of Bingen, Joachim of Fiore, the Beguines, Peter John Olivi (c. 1248–1298), John of Rupescissa ("Brother John") (c. 1310–1366), Ubertino da Casale (c. 1259–1330), Marguerite Porete (d. 1310), na Prous Boneta (1290–1325), and some others. In 1317, Pope John XXII convened a papal court to try at least one of the Spiritual disturbances of the Franciscan Order. The defendant was actually a book, a commentary on the book of Revelation. Since the author, Peter John Olivi, was already dead the trial served as a substitute for the accused. Olivi had accused the papacy of being "infected from head to toe and turned, as it were, into a New Babylon." A verdict of guilty ensued and copies were burned as "offensive to the faith." The Spirituals were, oddly enough, quite instrumental in deciding the question as to whether a pope could or could not abdicate his office. The issue was decided in the affirmative and has since been used by Popes Celestine V and Benedict XVI. The Spiritual Franciscans calculated that the new age would begin in 1260 A.D. which they supported with Revelation 13:5, where John refers to forty-two months which they named the end of the conclusion of the present age at forty-two generations. They were to be the model community for a new world in a millennial "Age of the Spirit." *See also* Assumptionist Orders; Augustine Order; Barnabites; Beguines; Benedict, Order of; Black Canons; canon(s) of the church; canons regular; Capuchin Order; Carmelites; Carthusians; Cistercians; clergy; da Casale, Ubertino; discalced; Dominicans; Franciscans; friar(s); Hildegard of Bingen; Joachim of Fiore; John of Rupescissa; Minim; monasticism; monk(s); na Prous Boneta; Olivi, Peter John; orders; Paulist Fathers; poverello; Premonstratensian Order; priest(s); Roman Catholic Church; Saint Francis of Assisi; Servite Order; Trappist Order.

spiritual warfare: the unseen but intense, all-pervasive, and unrelenting conflict between good and evil. Such warfare has been, and is even now, enacted on an eternal and celestial scale between the Trinity and Satan and his minions. It is also described as warfare being waged within the human spirit, and, in some more supramundane capacity, encompassing our inward struggle with personal sin. Such supernatural warfare may be conducted by angels or humans and may involve fervent prayer as basic, and, on occasion, exorcism in the extreme. The apostle Paul explains it best: "For our struggle is not against flesh and blood, but against the rulers, against the authorities, against the powers of this dark world and against the spiritual forces of evil in the heavenly realms" (Eph. 6:12). *See also* armies of heaven; attending spirit(s); authorities; banshee; bogle; brownies; bugbears; clurichauns; daemons; deceiving spirits; demon(s), demonic; demonology; devils; disa; dryad(s); elemental(s); evil (unclean) spirit(s); fairy, fairies; familiar spirits; frog(s); Furies; ghost(s); ghoul; gnome(s); Green Man, the; Gregori; hobgoblins; homunculus; household deities; huldafolk; Lares; leprechaun(s); Loa Loas; Manes; nereid; nisse; nymph(s); nyx; Oniropompi; Orisha; Oya; para; paredri; penates; Robin Goodfellow; satyr; Seelie Court, Unseelie Court; selkie; Sidhe; sirens; spirit guide(s); sprite(s); sylph(s); teraphim; territorial spirits; things taught by demons; Trickster; Tuatha de Danann; tutelary; undine; wight(s).

spit: to expectorate or the resulting product of spitting. Jesus warned the church at Laodicea that he would "spit out" their presence from him if they did not overcome their lackadaisical spirit (Rev. 3:16). Jesus used his saliva at one point to make a mud patch which he applied to a blind man to allow him to regain his sight (Mk. 8:23). To spit in the face was, and is, considered a great insult, as was done to Jesus before his crucifixion (Job 17:6; Deut. 25:7–10; Mt. 27:30). *See also* "have a good spit"; vomit.

split of the great city: part of the results of the seventh seal (Rev. 16:19) in which the great city is split into three parts. Whether the city referenced is Jerusalem or the Babylon headquarters of the Antichrist is not clear. The context seems to suggest the latter. On a more positive note, Scripture (Zech. 14:4) predicts that the Mount of Olives will split in two from east to west when the Lord sets foot there at his Second Coming. *See also* eschatology, eschatological; Mount Olivet.

spoons, apostle: a series of thirteen silver spoons—one for Jesus and each of the apostles. Each has a unique design and is used primarily as gifts for the baptisms to godchildren. *See also* apostle(s); Coptic Church paraphernalia; Roman Catholic Church.

spreading the gospel: ecclesiastical jargon for all forms of evangelism, missions, witnessing, and otherwise broadcasting the message of salvation everywhere. *See also* Christianese; evangelist(s), evangelism; fishers of men; missional; missions, missionaries; preach(ing); soul-winning; witness(es); worldwide preaching of the gospel.

spring of living water: a metaphor for God used by the prophet Jeremiah (Jer. 2:13; 17:13). The title names Yahweh as the source of blessing and refreshment while concurrently lamenting that the people have fallen away from that grace. *See also* fountain; water(s); waters, living; water of life.

sprite(s): supernatural fairy-like and ethereal creatures of folklore. The entities encompass a wide variety of spirits ranging from the diminutive elves and fairies to water species (sirens and naiads) to flyers like Shakespeare's Ariel. Some nature-based religions like neo-Druidism and Asatru still reverence them. Sprites may be more particularly referenced as dagons, dokkaebi, elves, fairies, gnomes, goblins, jengu, jinn, kelpie, kobolds, mami wata, melusine, mermaids and mermen, merrow, morgens, naiads, Nakki, nix, nymphs, pixies, rusalka, salamanders, selkies, sirens, nymphs, tritons, undine, vodyanoy, or yakashini. *See also* Ariel; attending spirit(s); banshee; bogle; brownies; bugbears; clurichauns; daemons; deceiving spirits; demon(s), demonic, Dogon Nommos; dryad(s); disa; elemental(s); fairy, fairies; Furies; ghost(s); ghoul; gnome(s); Green Man, the; Gregori; hobgoblins; homunculus; household deities; huldafolk; jinn; Lares; leprechaun(s); Loa Loas; Manes; mythological beasties, elementals, monsters, and spirit animals; nereid; nisse; nymph(s); nyx; Oniropompi; Orisha; Oya; para; paredri; penates; Robin Goodfellow; satyr; Seelie Court and Unseelie Court; selkie; Sidhe; sirens; spiritual warfare; sylph(s); teraphim; territorial spirits; Trickster; Tuatha de Danann; tutelary; undine; wight(s).

Sproul, Robert Charles: (1939–2017) arguably, in his lifetime, the most influential contemporary exponent of present-day preterism. *See also* Presbyterians; preterism.

Sri Ramakrishna: b. Gadadhar Chatterjee to a poor Brahmin family in Bengal in 1836, a claimant to be a reincarnation of the Hindu god Shiva. He put forward the idea that all religions lead to the same god. Rather than attempting to convert people from one religion to another, we should encourage everyone to follow his or her own inclinations and allow the natural spiritual convergence to take place. To prove the point, he even became a Muslim for a short time and seemed comfortable in the position. Muslims doubted his sincerity, however. Not surprisingly, his ideas spread and were made more systematic by his able disciple Swami Vivekenanda (1836–1902) who wanted to prove that the Hindu religion was not a matter of trying to believe certain doctrines or philosophies, but one of entering into an experience. *See also* Hinduism; Shiva.

Stachys: a disciple in Rome praised by Paul (Rom. 16:9).

stadia: a Roman unit of linear measurement. Revelation 21:16 says New Jerusalem is 12,000 stadia on all sides (about 1,400 miles or 2,200 kilometers). The "blood" from the winepress of God's wrath in Revelation 14:20 is said to crest at 1,600 stadia (about 180 miles or 300 kilometers).

staff: a long stick used as an aid to walking or as a symbol of authority in Israel. Moses' staff was an example of the latter definition and was used as a tool to enact many miracles from the Lord. Almost all shepherds carried a staff, usually crooked on one end (along with a rod for offensive action), to aid in the tending of sheep. Today, such a device is featured in the symbol of the office of Roman Catholic bishops and the pope. Crossed shepherd's staffs were at one point considered a suitable uniform device for United States Navy chaplains and may prove to be so again because of the multiplicity of religions within the Corps today, each with its own insignia device. *See also* rod; rod of iron.

staff of bread: a phrase in some Bible translations (not the NIV) of Ezekiel 4:16; 5:16; and 14:13 pertaining to famine prophesied by God on Jerusalem. The same occurs in Leviticus 26:26 and Psalm 105:16 with the same meaning.

stake: 1. a pointed stick or shaft used to pin a tent to the ground. 2. a regional association of churches of the Church of Christ of Latter-Day Saints (Mormons). *See also* Church of Jesus Christ of Latter-Day Saints, the; peg; ward.

Stalin, Joseph: *nee* Joseph (Josef) Jughashvili (1878–1953), leader of the Soviet Union from the 1920s until his death. He may well fit into history and the greatest of all brutal dictators, being responsible for the condemnation of countless victims to the

Gulag labor camps and the death of millions. He was a virulent enemy of freedom and religion, doing all he could to destroy faith and churches in the countries under his tight control. *See also* terrorism; terrorist(s).

Stanton, Elizabeth Cady: one of the first and most effective organizers of the effort to promote women's suffrage in America, as well as the abolitionist cause during the Civil war. Stanton (1815–1902) was skeptical and even critical of organized religion and rebelled early against her Presbyterian background in favor of hard science. She was a close associate to Susan B. Anthony and Lucretia C. Mott, each of whom was a superb manager. *See also* Anthony, Susan Brownell; Mott, Lucretia Coffin; slave, slavery; suffragan.

star(s): heavenly bodies in space often including planets when discovered in the Bible. Some astronomers estimate there are at least 100 billion trillion of them in the universe. In apocalyptic language, however, stars are seen falling from heaven to warn us of trouble to come or already upon us. Also, stars can be figurative nouns for angels or an eschatological sign for the Messiah. In other instances, they can represent a large number; God promised Abraham that his offspring would be as numerous as the stars of heaven. The stars, or their pagan representatives, were often worshiped in the ancient world. They were considered to be the controllers of the destinies of nations (Dan. 1:20; 2:2, 10, 27; 4:7; 5:7, 11, 15), and the Babylonian priests attempted to predict their movements to use the knowledge to the benefit of the empire. Sidereal practices are still important in many areas of the world, particularly those who manipulate horoscopes. According to Isaiah (Isa. 40:26), God brings out the starry hosts one by one and calls each by name. The metaphor is profound as scientists tell us there are about ten stars for every grain of sand on earth. Paul admonished believers to shine as lights in this dark and broken world (Phil. 2:14–16). Wandering stars are unstable guides (Jude 13). Other biblical references appear to attach apocalyptic significance to the starry hosts (Gen. 1:14; Lk. 21:25; Joel 2:30–31; Rev. 6:12). *See also* angel(s); angels of the heavens; Aries; astrology, astrologists; astronomy, astronomers; celestial disturbances; constellations; de Stella, Eudo; dust; Fabricius, David; fallen star; heavenly bodies; horoscope(s); host(s) of heaven; Magi; moon; Pisces; planets as gods, the; Pole Star(s); Rahati'el; sand; Secchi, Pietro; signs in heaven; Simon bar Kokhba; star and crescent; star of Bethlehem; Star of David; woman clothed in (with) the sun, the; zodiac.

star and crescent: 1. a pair of enduring symbols for fertility religions, primarily those overseen by a goddess. The images are closely associated with the waning and waxing moon. 2. a recognized sign for Islam. *See also* Islam; pagan, paganism.

Star Constellation Prophecy, the. See Rattlesnake Prophecy, the.

starets: venerable and respected Russian Orthodox monastic advisor. Usually an elder in age, the task of the starets is to spiritually guide the troubled and the inexperienced younger monks to excellence in their calling. *See also* archimandrite; clergy; divine; ecclesiastic(s); episcopate; man of God; metran; "old man"; monasticism; monk(s); patriarch(s); prelate(s); prefect(s); priest(s); primate; Russian Orthodoxy.

stargazers. See astrology, astrologers.

star god(s). See Rephan, star of; Saccuth.

Stark effect: conclusions from a study of juvenile delinquency by Rodney Stark and associates in 1982. Among the findings, it was determined that "religious" youths reared in "religious" homes and neighborhoods are less attracted to crime and mischief than those more secularized, but with the exception that a secularized environment lowers resistance in both classes. *See also* moralistic therapeutic deism; religiosity; sociology of religion.

star of Bethlehem: the wondrous celestial display that guided the Magi, the "wise men," to Bethlehem to honor the infant Jesus. What the phenomenon was, exactly, has never been determined. Some believe it might have been a conspicuous conjunction of Jupiter with Saturn, Mars, or the moon. Some speculate it may have been a comet, a supernova (once observed by Kepler in 1604), or some other bright light in the sky capable of being calculated and observed by those who possessed the skills of astrology, astronomy, and prophecy. Most modern astronomers agree that the planet Jupiter was somehow involved with the appearance of the "star" because its movements were conspicuous at that time. Furthermore, Jupiter represented a new king to come while Saturn named the old king. The constellations were also important to the Magi studies and most certainly were part of their observations near the era of Christ's birth. Quite possibly, the heavenly movements were subtle, so that only the trained eye could discern the celestial message. Many scholars see the prophecy of Balaam in Numbers 24:17–19 as a direct reference to the star of Bethlehem. *See also* Aries; astrology, astrologers; astronomy, astronomers; Balaam; Bethlehem; Jupiter; Magi; Pisces; Saturn; star(s); zodiac.

Star of David: the ancient and modern signature of Judaism, known by many names including "Shield of David" (*Mogen [Magan] David)* and "Solomon's Shield." The basic design consists of two equilateral triangles (some say pyramids) that are superimposed—one of them being inverted and producing a hexagram. Otherwise, the origins and functions of the star are a mixed bag of legend and lore. Tradition roots as far back as King David, or perhaps more closely with Solomon. We see glimpses of the logo in use by the Qabbalists as early as the third century and more recent renditions in the fourteenth. Some historians date the symbol even more remotely, to the time of the Judges; the sigil or family crest of Jesse, the father of David, was said to be a six-pointed star. What is the symbolism? Take your pick: 1. the twelve resulting angles representing the twelve tribes, 2. the Hebrew letters *dalet* and *yod* to represent the tribe of Judah, 3. the ruling tribes of Judah and Benjamin, 4. an early *mezuzah*, 5. a form of ancient Jewish amulets worn for protection (*segulot),* 6. representative of the twelve or thirteen-month cycle of the Jewish solar/lunar calendar, 7. a representation of the six directions (north, east, south, west, up, and down), or 8. something else lost to us in its original meaning. Grail buffs see the two crossed symbols as the blade of the male (the traditionally based pyramid) and the chalice of the female (the inverted pyramid). Certainly, the symbol is readily recognized today as the flag of Israel. Some Jewish groups reject the star outright because of its magical associations (it does resemble the pentagram) or because it was a Nazi "badge of shame" which was required identification for all Jews and their habitations before and during World War II. *See also* Judaism; pentagram.

state church: a religion partially or fully supported by the state and is identified as the only officially recognized religious institution by that country. The Church of England in the United Kingdom and Lutheranism in Denmark are examples of state-supported churches. *See also* Abington School District vs. Schempp; Allegheny County vs. ACLU; antidisestablishmentarianism; Caesar cult; caesaropapacy; civil religion; collegialism; disestablishmentarianism; Emerson vs. Board of Education; emperor worship; Establishment Clause and Free Exercise Clause; Geghan Bill; Government Regulation Index (GRI); *instrumentum regni;* Johnson Amendment; Lemon vs. Kurtzman; *Pontifex Maximus; princeps; principis;* public square; Roman Catholic Church; Shubert vs. Verner; ultramontanism; Virginia's Religious Disestablishment law.

stationary men. See representatives of the people.

stations of the cross: a religious devotional act in which the faithful process from place to place to contemplate the passion events marked off by signs and objects. At each station, representing a significant occurrence along Jesus' route to Golgotha, the penitent may pray, meditate, or review the significance of the incident. Many Roman Catholics and any number of liturgical-type Protestants participate yearly in Holy Week. *See also* liturgy, Christian; *Via Dolorosa;* Way of the Cross.

statue erected by Nebuchadnezzar: a grandiose depiction of the human form erected by Nebuchadnezzar on the plains of Dura in Babylon. In his pride, the king commanded all his citizens and conquered peoples to worship the image. He was defied by the three friends of Daniel—Hananiah, Mishael, and Azariah. The three Hebrew servants were thrown into a fiery furnace for their disobedience but were miraculously rescued by God. The statue may be considered a sign of the abomination of desolation because of their similar designs and intent. *See also* Abednego; abomination of desolation, the; Daniel's account of the image of gold and the fiery furnace; Dura; furnace; Meshach; Nebuchadnezzar II; Shadrach; stratified man, dream of the.

statue of the beast. See beast, image of the.

statute(s): codified law. *See also* apodictic law; Capitulary; canons of the church; Mosaic Law; rede.

statuary: a generic name for statues but, in religious circles, the veneration of the cross, sometimes including icons and secular sculptures as well. *See also* Eastern Orthodox Church, Roman Catholic Church; veneration of the cross.

stauropegion: a Greek monastery or church not under the jurisdiction of a local bishop but depending on the local head primate or synod for legitimacy. *See also* Eastern Orthodox Church, monastery; monasticism.

stele: an upright column common in the ancient world in almost all cultures. They marked boundaries, celebrated the deeds of kings, served as funerary markers, or honored the gods. The Hebrews invariably used stone for their altars and markers and served to identify land ownership or commemorate great acts of Yahweh. *See also* Ariel; astrological megaliths; Black Obelisk; Boaz and Jachin; boundary stones; Chintamani Stone; Coronation Stone; crushing stone that became a mountain; Delphi, Oracle of; Ebenezer; En-Rogel; Georgia Guidestones; harg; *Ka'bah;* Kamehameha, King and Emma; *masseboths;* megaliths; Merneptah Stele; Moabite Stone; Mount Behistun; pillar(s); Pillars of Mina, the sacred; Rosetta Stone; Sennacherib's Prism; stone(s); Stonehenge; Sun Stone; Zechariah's vision of the seven-eyed stone.

Steno, Nicholas: *nee* Niels Stensen (1638–1687), a Danish churchman and geologist specializing in fossils and their formation. His thesis disputed the common belief that the fossil record is the unfinished model of God's handiwork or the deposits of the Genesis flood. Steno became a Roman Catholic bishop though born a Lutheran. His famous work, *Solids Contained in Solids,* was published in 1669. *See also* clergy scientists; evolution; Roman Catholic Church.

Stephanas: a family head, one of the few persons Paul personally baptized (1 Cor. 1:16). The record implies that Paul suddenly remembered he had performed this immersion while explaining how few baptisms he had actually conducted. Stephanas was the first convert to the Christian faith in Achaia, along with his family. The kin of Stephanas developed as valued servants to the saints. Stephanas was welcomed by Paul on a visit to the apostle and received as a refreshing messenger (1 Cor. 16:15–17).

Stephen of Jerusalem: one of the early Christian deacons (Acts 6:8–7:60), a disciple of great power and grace. He was a Greek-speaking convert from Judaism, a powerful witness to the risen Christ, and the first known martyr of the new faith. As he was being stoned, Stephen proclaimed he could see heaven opened and the Son of Man standing at the right hand of God. This vision alone would qualify him as a prophet. *See also* deacon(s), deaconess(es); liturgical year; martyr(s); prophet(s); Raphan, star of; Synagogue of the Freedmen.

Stephen of Perm: *nee* Stefan (Stephen) Khrap, an effective missionary of the Russian Orthodox church (1340–1396). He desired to take the gospel north into uncharted lands as far as the foothills of the Ural Mountains. His mission at that time was fired by the millennial fever then sweeping the Muscovite church. Stephen created an alphabet for his new converts and even translated the Bible and appropriate church liturgies for them. His writing was short-lived because the imperial officials in Moscow soon substituted the language for Slovak, but his preaching effectiveness remained. *See also* missions, missionaries; Russian Orthodoxy.

stern-faced king, the: Antiochus IV Epiphanes as described in the book of Daniel (Dan. 8:23). There he is depicted as not only grim-faced and resolute but also completely wicked, arrogant, cruel, and a master of intrigue. *Fourth Maccabees* calls him an "arrogant and terrible man," and *1 Maccabees* labels him a "sinful root." As such, he is the perfect prefigurement of the Antichrist. *See also* anti-Semitic; Antichrist; Antiochus IV Epiphanes; *Armilus;* Black One, the; contemptible person, a; king(s); king who exalts himself, the; little horn, the; vile person, a; willful king, the.

Stevens, John Robert: (1919–1983) founder of the Living Word Fellowship, or "The Walk," a cult-like unorthodox collection of churches set in the United States, Mexico, Brazil, and Canada. They fit as an extension of the Manifest Sons of God. Some ex-members claimed Stevens used mind control or hypnotism on his congregants and was known to pray for the death of certain political figures. *See also* cult(s); Living Word Fellowship, the; Manifest Sons of God.

stewardship: the fair and careful administration of assets available to the believer seen as blessings from God. Even talent or abilities are to be so utilized. Generous and just stewardship is considered a valuable Christian virtue. In earlier times, a steward was the caretaker of a superior's goods and finances. *See also* economy; *oikonomo.*

Stewart, Rollen: known as "Rock'n' Rollin'" and "the Rainbow Man" (b. 1944) famous for showing up at major sporting events (and even the Miss America pageant) in the United States displaying a John 3:16 sign before national TV. He is known to have traveled some 60,000 miles to sporting events everywhere, the bane of sports broadcasters, and notorious in the 70s and 80s. He was ubiquitous and easily recognized by his rainbow-colored wig (he is bald) and fur loincloth. Stewart led a bizarre life with multiple marriages, a stint as a marijuana farmer, multiple psychiatric problems, and is now serving three lifetimes of imprisonment for kidnapping. He is a radical apocalypticist and disciple of televangelist Charles Taylor.

"stews": a peculiar expression surprisingly found in the Westminster Confession, specifically Question 139 of the Larger Catechism. The term is slang recognizable in the 1640s as springing from its original reference to "stewing" in the public hot baths of the time. After, however, it came to refer to houses of prostitution. The answer to the catechism question denounces prostitution as part of the condemnation cited in the seventh Commandment. *See also* Christianese; prostitute, prostitution; social issues; Ten Commandments, the; Westminster Confession.

sticheron: a short hymn suitable for divine worship. *See also* Cathisma; canticles; hymn(s); invitatory; liturgical year; liturgy, Christian; music; praise; theody.

stichometry: originally a line of poetry formed from the Greek *stichos*, also called a colon. Later, the term came to designate a unit of measure or word count for poetry or prose. *See also* acrostic poem; antithetic parallelism; climatic parallelism; colon; doubling; poetry (biblical); psalm; synthetic parallelism.

sticks, prophecy of the two. See Ezekiel's demonstration of the folded boards.

Stiefel Freethought Foundation: a newly minted 21st century sect seeking to confederate those who are atheist, agnostic, humanist, non-religious Jews, and other "openly secular" persons. The founder and main pusher of the movement is Todd Stiefel, who envisions a coalition of non-religious individuals who wish to promote resources for those with a secularist worldview. The group is also sympathetic to openly gay, lesbian, bisexual, and transgender people who are welcome to publicize their stories. *See also* sect(s).

stiff-necked: a metaphor for stubbornness or implacability. God often labeled the Israelites as "a stiff-necked people" when they were behaving rebelliously. *See also* frozen chosen, the; hardening of the heart; obduration; sin unto death; strong delusion.

stigmata: the phenomenon of persons (or even objects) that seem to spontaneously experience bleeding from the hands, head, or feet as if in imitation of Jesus' blood loss on the cross. The fantastic stigmata of Saint Francis even has its own feast day. *See also* audition; dream(s); dreams and visions; ecstasy; Francis of Assisi; liturgical year; locution.

Stiles, Ezra: (1727–1795) a New England theologian, scientist, and political advisor. Stiles was an associate of Benjamin Franklin when they collaborated on various scientific projects. He was ordained as a Congregationalist minister in 1755 to pastor in Newport, Rhode Island. While there, he studied ecclesiastical history, foreign languages, and science. After fleeing Newport in fear of a British invasion, Stiles moved to New Haven, Connecticut, continued his support of the colonists in rebellion, and eventually became president of Yale. *See also* clergy scientists; Congregationalists.

stipend: a gratuity or donation (a prebend) to one (usually a professional) who grants special services. Many names exist for clergy payments (some not so complimentary) including stole fee, gratuity, altarage, and others. Most clergies expect a small stipend for performing weddings or similar duties which is certainly within the bounds of acceptability. Stipends and the like are not considered part of ecclesiastical salary or benefits. Some clerics prefer the term "stole fee" or something else. *See also* altarage; benefice; benefit of clergy; carrodian; *cathedraticum;* love offering; mensa; oblation; offering; papal revenue; pounding; prebend; sustentation; tithe.

Stir-up Sunday: a Christ the King liturgy adapted by the Church of England (but not celebrated in the Episcopal Church) for the Sunday before Advent. The name evolves from the first words of the Collect for the day: "Stir up your power, O Lord, and with great might come among us" from the *Book of Common Prayer. See also* Christ the King, Feast Day of; Church of England; feasts and special days of high liturgy churches; liturgical year.

Stoddard, Solomon: the most influential clergyman evangelist (1643–1729) on the New England frontier working from his pastorate at the Congregational Church in North Hampton, Massachusetts. He was the grandfather of Jonathan Edwards. Stoddard preached and published his belief that all persons should be permitted to church membership upon profession of faith. His most telling writing was the *Doctrine of the Instituted Churches* (1700). In all other respects, however, Stoddard was a strict Puritan, even objecting to long hair, extravagant dress, clergy dominance of the churches, and insistence on proclaiming the hellfire judgment of God. *See also* Congregationalists; evangelist(s), evangelism; Great Awakenings; Puritanism, Puritans; revivalism.

Stoeffler, Johannes: an astronomer, astrologer, and prominent religious figure at the University of Tubingen who observed a celestial conjunction in the order Pisces, the water sign, on February 20, 1524. He took this to be a trigger to the end of the Millennium and the finish of the world by flood. His calculations differed from certain astrologers in London who saw the flood occurring earlier, on February 1. In that panic, 20,000 people abandoned their homes. All this, despite the clear promise God made in the Noahic Covenant not to destroy the world a second time by water. Stoeffler tried again and set the doomsday date to 1528. *See also* astrology, astrologers; astronomy; astronomers; clergy scientists.

Stoicism, Stoics: a philosophical school founded by Zeno (335–263 B.C.) in Athens. The Stoics believed that everything in the universe, including God, is material. They also believed in the doctrine of what we would call predestination. They practiced a fairly virtuous life and carried a rather strong influence into early Christianity. Perhaps the most singular aspect of the philosophy is the concept that emotion, physical sensation, worry, and the like are to be endured with no discernible feeling or display, a concept they called *ataraxia*. Stoicism became the most popular philosophy in first and second century Rome. To be of stoic nature today is to be seemingly impervious to hardship or disappointment in both attitude and demeanor. *See also* philosophy of the Greeks; Word of God.

stole fee. See stipend.

stone(s): geological formations of density used frequently for many practical and symbolic advantages. One or more stones could be used as: 1. a pillow (Gen. 28:18), 2. a seat (Ex. 17:12), 3. shade or shelter (Isa. 32:2), 4. a covering for a well (Gen. 29:2), 5. closing the entrance to a cave or tomb (Josh. 10:18; Jn. 11:38), 6. as weaponry (1 Sam. 17:40; 2 Chr. 26:15), 7. to execute a criminal and use as burial material (Josh. 7:25–26), 8. utensils, 9. grinding (Deut. 24:6), 10. cutting (including circumcision) (Ex. 4:25; Josh. 5:2), 11. harvesting with a stone-edged sickle, 12. cairns or memorials (Gen. 31:46–52; Josh. 4:9), 13. guideposts or boundary markers (Jer. 31:21; Deut. 19:14), 14. stele or dolmens (1 Sam. 7:12), 15. idol worship or altars (Isa. 37:19; Ex. 20:25–26.), 16. weights (Lev. 19:36), 17. durable writing material (the Ten Commandments, for example, were written on stone tablets) and stone, clay, or leather was used for some of the Old Testament (approximately 1500–400 B.C.), 18. paving (Esth. 1:6) and construction of public and private roads, walls, or buildings, 19. precious or semi-precious stones were used medicinally or in lapidary, especially quartz, obsidian, river rocks, and black tourmaline. In metaphorical usage, stones were symbols of hardness, obstinacy, or endurance. The Lord can also picture Himself as the apocalyptic stone, the one who crushes evil (*e.g.,* Daniel 2:44–45), and Christians are named as "living stones" (1 Pe. 2:4–6) of the faith. Jerusalem was designated a heavy stone, a burden to the world, so that hostile nations who try to move it will be injured (Zech. 12:2–3). *See also* altar; Ariel; astrological megaliths; Boaz and Jachin; Black Obelisk; boundary stones; Caelum Moor; Chintamani Stone; clay; Coronation Stone; crushing stone that became a mountain; Delphi, Oracle of; Ebenezer; En Rogel; Georgia Guidestones; Gilgal Refa'im; *Gobekli Tepe;* harg; Jerusalem as city; Judaculla Rock; *Ka'bah;* Kamehameha, King and Emma; *masseboths;* megaliths; Merneptah Stele; Moabite Stone; Moai; Mount Behistun; obsidian; papyrus; parchment; pillar(s); Pillars of Mina, the sacred; rock(s); Rosetta Stone; sacred stones; Sennacherib's Prism; Sphinx, sphinx(es); stele; stone circles; Stonehenge; stone of stumbling; stones, living; Stone, the living; stoning; Sun Stone; vellum; Zechariah's vision of the seven-eyed stone.

Stone, Barton W.: American preacher (1772–1844) during the Second Great Awakening. At one point (at Cane Ridge, Kentucky) he preached before nearly 20,000 seekers over several days. Following disagreements with the Presbyterian Church to which he belonged, he and some colleges formed the Christian Church as a new denomination without any creedal statements, except the Bible. Eventually, Stone allied with Thomas and Alexander Campbell (also dissident Presbyterians) and became active in the Restoration Movement of the day. *See also* Campbell, Alexander; Cane Ridge camp meeting; Christian Church (denomination); Churches of Christ; evangelist(s), evangelism; Great Awakenings, the; Restoration Movement in America; revivalism; "sawdust trail, the."

stone circles: (sometimes identified as "Druid circles") a spherical arrangement of undressed stones, more or less pillar-shaped, set on end around the circumference. Most were likely pagan worship centers, observatories, or burial mounds. Stonehenge in England is probably the most recognized. The circles differed as to size, location, the interval of the placed stones, and numbers of stones. Sometimes they are found with outside trenches, cairns, or mounds inside with dolmens or menhirs at or near the center. An avenue, or more than one, might lead to an entrance. Some even contain concentric circles. The structures are common enough in Europe, particularly Scandinavia, but also exist in Asia, Arabia, and North Africa, but the best examples are in Britain, Ireland, and Scotland. *See also* Druidism; *masseboths;* megaliths; sacred stones; stele; stone(s); Stonehenge.

Stonehenge: the world-famous prehistoric monument at Wiltshire in southern England. The evolution of the site on the Salisbury Plain is believed to have occurred over time around 3000 to 2000 B.C. The magnificent (and mysterious) structure is a subject of debate as to its purpose, method of construction, and significance to the primitive culture of the times. The design is a rough circle of standing stones amid earthworks. Some of the trilithons (huge dolmens) and accompanying smaller pillars, the heel stone, and an entrance avenue are speculated to be a burial site or astronomical observation station, or both. The position and design of the arrangement indicate the entryway aligns to the sunset of the winter solstice while the back opens to the summer solstice. The intent of the placement, an architectural wonder of the Neolithic period, still suggests it is most likely an observatory or a religious site, but all its secrets are yet to be revealed, if they are ever to be discovered. Who the builders were has never been proven, though plenty of theories have come forward. In 1624, Edmund Bolton credited Queen Boudicca with the building as her monument. Others claim the Romans erected it although the circle is far older than any Latin appearance in Britain. Dr. Walter Charleton (1663) claimed it was erected by Danish Vikings. Some say the Saxons are responsible and, of course, Merlin remains a contender for many. Even today, modern "Druids" descend on Stonehenge for ceremonies. *See also* Caelum Moor; Druidism; Gilgal Refa'im; *Gobekli Tepe;* megaliths; Merlin; Midsummer Day; Moai; New Age religion; sacred stones; stele; Sphinx, sphinx(es); stone(s); stone circles.

stone of stumbling: a reference to the hindrance of the Pharisees and other Jews like them who were so bound to their rigid interpretation of the Law of Moses that they could see no value in the Messiah (Rom. 9:31–33) or his preaching. They pursued the religious life in terms of works and not faith. So, the stumbling stone is Jesus Christ himself. *See also* autosoterism; covenant of grace; covenant of works; monergism; names (titles) for Jesus; solifidianism; stone(s); works, salvation by.

stone of Tarshish. See Tarshish stone.

Stone of Zoheleth. See En-Rogel.

Stone Pavement, the. See Gabbatha.

stones, fiery: a perplexing description of the king of Tyre (Ezk. 28:14, 16) and the splendor in which he lived. This passage, and another in Isaiah 14 describing the king of Babylon, is commonly viewed as markers for the power and prestige of pre-fallen Lucifer. The devil was prominent in the heavenly realms, and even called a guardian Cherub, before his rebellion demanded a change of name and destiny for him. *See also* gem(s); guardian Cherub; Lucifer.

stones, living: a metaphorical description of believers (*cf.* 1 Peter 2:5). Followers of Christ may then be affectionately called "little rocks" as intended by Jesus (Mt. 16:17-19) and reasserted by the writings of Peter. "Live" stones are the people of God who are being built into a spiritual house and holy priesthood—those who follow the living Stone, Jesus Christ (1 Pe. 2:4–5). *See also* binding and loosing; cornerstone (capstone); rock(s); stone(s); Stone, the living.

Stone, the living: a metaphor for Christ, the perfect material for building one's life of holiness (1 Pe. 2:4–8), or if disobedient, a cause for spiritual stumbling. *See also* Cornerstone, Capstone; names (titles) for Jesus; stones, living.

stone with seven eyes. See Zechariah's vision of the seven-eyed stone.

stoning: death by the action of throwing stones at the victim, or by crushing him or her under their weight. Execution by stoning was a common enough method of capital punishment in the Old and New Testaments. Stephen the evangelist was executed in such fashion (Acts 7:54–60), and the apostle Paul suffered that abuse, from which he was fortunate to recover. Islam condones stoning in some locations even today. Stoning could also be practiced as a scapegoat measure. *See also* stone(s).

"stoning of Satan." See Pillars of Mina, the Sacred.

storehouse(s): a place for storing crops or goods, a warehouse. The Hebrew ancients were known to assume that the blessings of heaven were stored by God in His heavenly warehouses, particularly in the apocalyptic writings. Wind, sun, moon, precipitation, etc., were reserved there and dispensed or withheld at the will of God or by an angel overseer. There was even a storehouse for human souls awaiting resurrection and judgment. *See also* Guph; under the altar.

stork: large, long-necked, long-legged, strong-billed wading birds of the family *ciconiidae*. The species is mentioned in Psalm 104:17 as having nests in the pine tree. In nature, the stork's nest can indeed be huge—up to ten feet in height. Of course, the prevailing myth that they deliver babies to new parents is universally known and perpetuated. As a related concept, many ancient peoples saw storks as "soul carriers" of the deceased to the gods. *See also* animals, birds, and insects, symbology of; *psychopomps.*

story: a tale or chronicle of adventure or narrative. In Christian use, however, it implies one's status with the Christian life, its essence, and its involvement on a daily basis. The expression usually comes forth as "my story' (what's happening in my walk with Christ) or "your story" (as in "What's your story?"). One's testimony or relation of involvement with the Holy Spirit can be deeply personal, all-inclusive, and passionate and must be developed with sensitivity. *See also* authenticity; Christianese; "in this place"; on mission; storyteller, a good; testimony; walk with God; will of God.

Story of Ahikar, The: or *The Wisdom of Ahikar,* a popular romance legend discovered on the island of Elephantine, where there was a Jewish colony in exile during the fifth century b.c. The tale is even older, however, and is said to have inspired Aesop's fables and other proverbs and stories of the time. The main character, Ahikar, is reported to be an Assyrian official in the court of Sennacherib, so the origin of the fable is supposed to be Assyrian. The writing likely had some influence into the Hebrew forms of proverbial wisdom writing. *See also* Ahikar.

storyteller, a good: someone adept or talented as a relater of tales, stories, parables, and the like—a raconteur. The prophet Ezekiel expressed a complaint or fear that his facility with words and his dramatic antics as a spokesman for God would be classed as merely good storytelling; thus his prophecy would be received in the wrong manner (Ezk. 20:49). Like all worthy prophets, he did not want his skill with words to be interpreted as merely a good yarn or charming tale. *See also* conjure man; filidh; hungan; hierophant; meonenim; mystagogue; parable(s); preacher(s); priest(s); Sangoma(s); shaman, shamanism; skald(s); story; Valuspa; volva.

Stoughton, William: (ca. 1631–1701), a Massachusetts clergyman, magistrate, public official, and acting colonial governor of the state from 1694–1701. Stoughton was the chief justice of the Salem witch trials (1692) when he exhibited a lack of compassion for the defendants and took on deserved blame for admitting "spectral evidence" into court. He was largely responsible for much of the hysteria and corrupted justice in Puritanism at that time. *See also* Puritanism, Puritans; Salem witch trials.

Strabo: learned Greek historian and geographer (64 B.C.– c. 24 A.D.). He was an extensive traveler and familiar with the geographical of many areas, especially Asia Minor. Strabo is often called the father of geography and his best-known work is titled *Geographia*.

straight gate, the: known in the King James Version as the strait gate, a metaphor used by Jesus to define the difficult path of righteousness and obedience as opposed to the broader undemanding way leading to death (Mt. 7:13-14; Lk. 13:23). Few enter the narrow entrance, Jesus says, but many choose the easier but destructive way of life. *See also* broad and narrow way; parable(s); parables of the New Testament.

Straight Street: the address Paul used from rented property in Tarsus after his dramatic Damascus Road experience with Jesus. It is still an important and much-traversed thoroughfare in the modern city. The layout is also remarkably straight, contrary to most meandering and confusing roadways of the ancient cities. *See also* Tarsus.

strange fire: ridicule or abhorrence for the unauthorized offering of incense to Yahweh. Only Aaron and his sons could officiate in this role as priests. Today, the expression may take on a rebellion or "takeover" attitude in any religious organization that seeks to usurp existing authority and function in a ministry area where they are unwelcome, unqualified, or disruptive. Nadab and Abihu were exterminated for disregarding the holy ritual as prescribed for the true priests of God (Lev. 10:1–3). *See also* Abihu; Nadab.

"strange work": or "alien work." The odd phrase notes God's anticipated eschatological work when He will "rise up" as once happened at Mount Perazim and pronounce judgment on the land (Isa. 28:21; 2 Sam. 5:20). *See also* eschatology, eschatological; Mount Perazim.

stratified man, dream of the: Nebuchadnezzar's dream as recorded in Daniel 2–3. The statue represents the parade of kingdoms from Nebuchadnezzar's Babylon (the head of gold) to the futuristic Revived Roman Empire (the feet and toes of iron and clay). *See also* Babylonia; belly and thighs of bronze; chest and arms of silver; crushing rock that became a mountain; Daniel's account of the image of gold and the fiery furnace; dream(s); feet and toes of iron and clay; Greece; head of gold, the; Hesiod; legs of iron; Medo-Persia; Nebuchadnezzar; Roman Empire; statue erected by Nebuchadnezzar.

Strauss, David Friedrich: German philosopher (1808–1874), a liberal Protestant who, while not denying the historicity of Jesus, criticized the sources of the New Testament. He claimed that the reports about Jesus found there were unreliable and "mythical" based on tales from the Old Testament. His influential book, *Life of Jesus* (1835), made him famous but also destroyed his peace of mind and physical health because of the hostility it generated. *See also* philosophy of religion.

streets of gold: a description of the city and the streets in New Jerusalem (Rev. 21:18, 21) that are described as pure gold so refined as to be almost luminous. *See also* amber; names, symbology of; New Jerusalem.

streets of the city: an apocalyptic expression sometimes denoting a city's physical or spiritual condition. For example, in times of disaster or divine punishment, the streets of the city are said to be flowing with blood. In modern parlance, we would say "the streets are not safe."

stregheria: a form of witchcraft practiced in southern Europe and some Italian-American communities. *See also* magic, magick; occult, occultic; Wicca; witchcraft.

strength: a common secular and biblical term usually denoting physical (Jud. 14:6) or spiritual (Mk. 12:30) prowess. *See also* heart; heart and spirit; heart, soul, mind; love; mind; *psuche;* soul(s); spirit; *zoe.*

strictness theory: the theory that religious groups or denominations tend to retain membership and promote growth if their doctrine and practice are strict and mostly unyielding. Conversely, more lenient persuasions tend to lose membership and lessen involvement.

striking hands and striking the thigh: a typical Hebrew gesture to register the conclusion of some significant event, either political or personal, much as we might "fist bump," shake hands, or applaud. *See also* Aha!; clapping hands and stomping feet; gestures.

strong delusion: an initiate of God's will to irrefutability dismiss the gospel or reject it with contempt, mockery, or disbelief (2 Th. 2:8–12). The risk for the non-believer is to know the truth but refuse it so vigorously and consistently that God will abandon His appeal to salvation. The doctrine has been compared to the so-called "unforgivable sin." *See also* hardening of the heart; obduration; sin unto death.

stronghold of the Daughter of Zion: a millennial name for Jerusalem (*e.g.,* Micah 4:8).

Strong, Josiah: internationally known author, lecturer, and Congregationalist minister (1847–1916). Strong's work was well received after the publishing of *Our Country* (1885) and its sequel, *The New Era* (1893). The works are prophetic in theme, with favoritism shown to the Social Gospel. He is just as often mentioned as the originator of the phrase "safety first." *See also* Congregationalists; Social Gospel; social issues.

strophe: an irregular division of an ode or poem, taken from the actions of the ancient Greek chorus as the singers or narrators turned themselves to the left or the right of stage. Much of the book of Isaiah is divided into strophes, each with its own subject theme. *See also* accideme; alliteration; apostrophe; apothegm; assonance; autograph; Bible; Bible manuscripts; Bible translations; biblical criticism; chiasmus; conflict story; *constructio ad sensum;* context; contextualization; dittography; double sense fulfillment; doublets; doubling; edification; eisegesis; epanadiplosis; epigrammatic statements; etymology; exegesis; figure of speech; folio; form criticism; gattung; gloss; gnomic sayings; grammatical-historical interpretation; *hapax legomena;* haplography; hermeneutic(s); higher criticism; homographs; homonyms; homophones; *homoteleuton;* hyperbole; idiom; *inclusio;* interpolation; interpretation; inverted nun; irony; isagogics; *itture sopherim;* jot and tittle; kere; *kethib;* "L"; liberalists interpretation; literal interpretation; litotes; loan words; lower criticism; "M"; Masoretic Text; minuscule(s); mystery of God; omission; onomastica; onomatopoeia; palimpsest; papyrus; paradigm; parallelism; parchment; *paroimia; paronomasia;* pericope; personification; Peshitta; pointing; point of view; polyglot; principles of interpretation; proof texting; pun(s); "Q"; redaction; revelation, theological; rhetorical criticism; rhetorical devices; riddle; satire; *scripto continua;* scriptorium; *sebirin;* simile; similitude; source criticism; sources, primary and secondary;

special points; superscription; symbol(s); synecdoche; syntax; synthetic parallelism; text; textual criticism; *tiggune sopherim;* Time Texts; Torah; translation; transposition; trope; type(s); typology; uncial(s); vellum; verbicide.

Student Volunteer Movement: a youth-led foreign mission emphasis begun about 1886 and unofficially led by Arthur Tappan Pierson. The first organized mission effort may have begun with five students at Princeton College in 1888 who declared their intent to promote the gospel worldwide. Growth quickly followed until the movement became a strong impetus to missions in and from America. *See also* missions, missionaries; religious organizations; youth religious organizations.

stupa: an Eastern-style reliquary or monument.

Styx: a river, or more accurately, the marshy center of the underworld according to Greek mythology. The goddess Styx was ruler there and was believed to have possessed the power to grant invulnerability (Achilles was a recipient) and was authoritative in some measure over all the other gods. The term means "hate" or "detest," an apt title considering the river's function. The myth shows the ferryman Charon transporting the dead from earth to Hades for a fee. In certain locales of both ancient Italy and Greece, actual tours of the underworld could be arranged for a paid ticket (complete with a boat ride to hell) in order to consult the Sibyl oracle stationed there. No doubt, a visit to Styx, or any other river in hell like the Acheron, was a dreadful and fearful prospect for both living and dead. *See also* Acheron; Charon; hell; Olympian pantheon; Oracle of Delphi; Sibyl(s); Underworld.

sub-atomic consciousness. See Quantum Entanglement.

sublapsarianism: See infralapsarianism.

subliminal messaging: supposed communication at a level below the conscious mind's ability to perceive it directly. The message instead goes directly to the subconscious, thus bypassing the rational screening center of the brain. Commercial advertisers and church or cultic promotions are sometimes accused of the practice, which is considered unethical at best. *See also* backmasking.

subordinationism: the theological idea, probably originated by Arius (256–336), stating that Jesus was subordinate rather than equal with the Father. Christ is not co-eternal with the Father but was simply given the rank of divinity by divine decree. The idea was favored by Origen and other influential statesmen early on. *See also* Adoptionism; Anomoeans; appropriation; Arianism; Arius; complementarian view of the Trinity; Donatism; dualism; Dynamic Monarchianism; dynamism; dyophysitism; eternal subordination of the Son; "four fences of Chalcedon"; *homoiousios; homoousios;* hypostatic union; incarnation; *kenosis;* kenotic view of Christ; monoenergism; miaphysitism; modalism; Monarchianism; monophysitism; monoenergism; Nestorianism; Nestorius; *ousia;* patripassianism; Pelagianism; *perichoresis;* psilanthropism; Sabellianism; Socianism, Socinian; theanthroposophy; *Theophorus;* Trinity; two natures, doctrine of the; unipersonality.

Subramanya: the Hindu deity worshiped mainly in Southern India, Sri Lanka, and Malaysia, a.k.a. Murugan. The name also incorporates the Vedic priests' connection with certain local religious and civil observances in which they act as chaplains. Sixteen Subramanian priests and their assistants are required to preside over the specified rituals and ceremonies. *See also* Hinduism.

substance dualism: the theory that the mind and brain are separate as to construct and purpose. The brain is a corporeal organ; the mind is not physical.

Subud: an international spiritual awareness movement begun in Indonesia by Muhammad Subuh Sumohadiwidjojo in 1920. The religion is based upon testing and fasting to achieve experience with what the adherents call the "life force" of God. Today the sect has about 10,000 members in seventy countries. *See also latihan;* sect(s).

Succoth-Benoth: or Sakkuth, Sikkuth—a false god worshiped by the Babylonians and by those refugees returned to Samaria as part of the Assyrian resettlement campaign (2 Ki. 17:29–30). Worship of the idol was somehow combined with the worship of Yahweh by these repatriated Israelites. He may be the same as Marduk and probably associated with Saturn (Amos 5:26). *See also* Levant pantheon; Marduk; Sumerian and Babylonian pantheon.

succubus: a female demon who torments men in their dreams or in real time. *See also* demon(s), demonic; devils; incubus; Lilith; mythological beasties, elementals, monsters, and spirit animals.

Sudarium of Oviedo: a bloodstained cloth kept in Oviedo, Spain, and venerated as a church relic. It is said to be the wrapping of Jesus' head during his burial. A face is not discernible but some claim the faint markings match the face on (or in) the Shroud of Turin. *See also* relic(s); Shroud of Turin.

suffering servant. See servant, the suffering.

suffragan: an assistant or subordinate to a bishop overseeing a diocese. A suffragan bishop does not automatically succeed to the office of the one he assists. *See also* bishop(s); ecclesiastic(s).

suffrage: 1. the right to vote. A suffrage promoter, then, is a campaigner for voting rights. Some subtle distinctions, however, should be noted when discussing the advocates. In England, for example, *suffragists* were formed in 1879 and led by Millicent Fawcett (whose sister Elizabeth Garrett Anderson, was the first woman doctor in Britain). Their tactics were pacific using demonstrations, petitions, and the like. The follow-on *suffragettes,* however, were more militant employing radical acts including arson, vandalism, hunger strikes, etc. Still, it was five years before Parliament responded to their demands. Conditions in America were similar and lawmakers were slow to accede; nor is universal suffrage yet a reality worldwide. 2. in liturgical terminology, suffrages are prayers prescribed for a specific purpose, especially obsequies. Such prayers are short intercessory appeals and are usually recited in a series. *See also* Anthony, Susan Brownell; liturgy, Christian; Mott, Lucretia C.; obsequy; prayer(s); Stanton, Elizabeth Cady; Willard, Francis.

Sufi: Muslim mystics. The sect is generally more liberal than traditional Islam and holds interests in spirituality rather than politics or Islamic doctrine. They are also coeducational, whereas most other Muslim sects are strictly male in membership. The name "sufi" comes from the Arabic term for *wool* in reference to the rough woolen clothing they preferred in protest to the rich silks of other Muslims whom they considered worldly. For Sufis, an individual's focus should remain on the denial of the self to pursue a deep experience with God. As the movement developed, some became ascetic—breaking ties to the material world in poverty, fasting, or celibacy; others became more public in faith demonstrations (such as the Whirling Dervishes). *See also dhikr;* Green Man, the; Islam; langar; Whirling Dervishes.

Sufyani: according to Muslim eschatology, the one-eyed *Sufyani* (*Dajjal*) will arrive in the end time to oppose the *Mahdi* (the savior) and will make an issue of killing innocent children and pregnant women. *See also Dajjal;* Islam.

"sugar stick": a favorite sermon held by any given number of preachers and pastors who are prone to revive it for proclamation over and over if time and effort for new material is, for some reason, not exercised. *See also* Christianese; homily; sermon; preaching; slurs, religious; "three points and a poem."

Sukkot. See Tabernacles, Feast of.

Suleiman the Magnificent: Turkish sultan of the 16th century who restored the walls of ancient Jerusalem and repaired the *al-Aqsa* Mosque. It was also he who sealed the east gate of Jerusalem facing the Mount of Olives. Muslims then, and many today, fear that the Messiah will enter the city through this gate. Many Christians and Jews certainly believe the same. Thus, the gate is sealed by Muslim authority and a cemetery is planted nearby as a further preventive. *See also al-Aqsa* Mosque; gates of Jerusalem and the Temple; Islam.

sulfur: a chemical element with the scientific designation S and the atomic number 16. The product is sometimes noted as an ingredient of the lake of fire, along with brimstone. The chemical had other practical uses in the ancient world as it does today. *See also* brimstone.

Sumerian(s). See Sumer, Sumerian(s).

Sumerian and Babylonian pantheon: a designed list (severely abbreviated) of the gods, goddesses, and demi-gods of the ancient Sumerian civilization and the follow-on Babylonian culture. The major goddess entries are: 1. Antu (wife of Anu the god of heaven), 2. Damkina (wife of Enlil the god of earth), 3. Eriskegal or Allatu (goddess of the dead and the underworld), 4. Ishtar (the ubiquitous fertility goddess, love, and war), 5. Kingu (or Kingsu goddess of death and ally of Tiamat sacrificed by Marduk), 6.

Nanshe (dreams and prophecies), 7. Ningal (Babylonian mother goddess), 8. Nin-kharsag (goddess of life and reproduction), 9. Semiramis, queen of heaven (mother of Tammuz), 10. Succoth-Benoth (Marduk or his spouse, fertility goddess, prostitution), 11. Tiamat (goddess of the deep who formed earth and sky). The main gods are listed as: 1. Adad (storms, rain, tempest), 2. Anu (highest heaven or sky god, part of a triad with Enlil and Enki), 3. Apru or Apsu (underwater oceans), 4. Dagon (originally associated with fish but later more with fertility and agriculture, also worshiped among the Philistines), 5. Ea or Enki (chief god of Babylon, estranged half brother to Enlil), 6. Ebeh (a mountain god), 7. Enlil (Sumerian god of the earth later succeeded by Marduk, estranged half brother to Enki), 8. Erra (war, death, and disaster), 9. Girra or Gibil (light and fire), 10. Irra (plague), 11. Marduk or Bel (patron god of Babylon and creator of heaven and earth), 12. Mot (Canaanite and Babylonian god of death), 13. Nabu (Babylonian god of learning, oration, and literature), 14. Namtar (herald of death), 15. Nebo (son of Marduk), 16. Nergal (fire, heat, pain, disaster, underworld darkness), 17. Nisroch or perhaps Nushu (fire god or agriculture), 18. Oannes (founder god and patron of learning), 19. Saccuth (a star god), 20. Shad (one of six warrior gods and goddesses with Irene, Esmund, Enki, Menphia, and Kul'Zak), 21. Shamash or Utu (Babylonian god of prophecy, law, truth, and justice and Sumerian sun god), 22. Sin (or Nanna the moon god), 23. Tammuz (husband to Ishtar), 24. Tartak (prince of darkness), 25. Utnapishtim (survivor of the great flood and made immortal), 26. Zahar (dreams, divine messages. There were hundreds more as well. Recent interest in alien space invader ancestor theories has suggested: 1. Anunnaki (space visitors to Earth), 2. Enki and Enlil (sons of the chief god Anu set to govern Earth for visiting space aliens), 3. Igigi ("watchers" of Earth employed by space gods), 4. lulu (humanoid created by space gods). *See also* Abednego; Abzu; Akitu; Akkad; Aloros I; Anammelech; Anak; Ancient Astronaut Theory; Anu; Anunnaki; Apse; Aralu; Aruru; Ashtoreth, Ashtoreth(s); Assyria, Assyrians; atrahasis; Baal-zebul; Babylon, Babylonians; Babylonia; Bel; Belteshazzar; Berossus; Bull of Heaven; *Chariots of the Gods?;* chimera; cities of the gods; Dagon; Day Star; demon(s), demonic; *dingir;* Ea; Ebeh; Egyptian pantheon; Enki and Enlil; Enmeduranki; *Enuma Elish; Epic of Gilgamesh, The;*

Eriskegal; Hadad; Igigi; "Keeper of the Bridge"; Kingu; Kish; Levant pantheon; Lilith; Lucifer; lulu; Marduk; Meshach; Mesopotamia; Mot; mushrishu; mystery religion(s); Nabu; Nanna; Nanshe; Nebo; Nergal; Nibiru; Ningal; Nin-kharsag; Nisroch; Oannes and the Seven Sages; Olympian pantheon; panspermia theory; Pazuzu; Qadesh; queen of heaven; Saccuth; Saturn; satyr; Semiramis; Shad; Shadrach; Shamash; Sin; Succoth-Benoth; Sumer, Sumerian(s); Sumerian Tablets; Table of Destinies; Tablet of Destinies; Tablet of Nineveh; "Tablets of Faith"; Tammuz; Tartak; Tiamat; transhumanism; underworld; Utnapishtim; Utu; Watchers, the; Zuism.

Sumerian Tablets: a.k.a. the Eridu Genesis, or in some articles "an alternative Genesis." Sumerian clay tablets and engraved markings on other surfaces have long been in evidence and were originally deposited in the museum at Nippur in Southern Babylonia. Recently, in 2006, a new record was serendipitously found in Iraq and collected on the promise that the contents would be disclosed to the general public. The authorities typically reneged, but the finds have been subsequently leaked in both video and text format. The new tablets were contained in a copper box and engraved on *lapis lazuli*. The epics described were written long before the Bible and include a creation story and great flood account told from a common, or "farmer-type," perspective. The tale has bestirred anew the idea that Earth's civilizations were seeded by aliens. *See also* Anunnaki; cities of the gods; cuneiform; demi-god(s); *Enuma Elish; Epic of Gilgamesh, The;* Igigi; lulu; Mesopotamia; Nibiru; Nin-kharsag; panspermia theory; Sumer, Sumerian(s); Sumerian and Babylonian pantheon; Table of Destinies; Tablet of Nineveh; Utnapishtim.

Sumer, Sumerian(s): an ancient civilization (possibly the oldest ever according to the majority of archeologists and historians though that assumption has recently come under question) situated in lower Mesopotamia near the Persian Gulf. Indeed, the designation "first" fits because these remarkable people produced the first of many disciplines ranging from an alphabet to the wheel. The settlement existed from at least the fifth millennium B.C. and was the source of numerous cultural contributions, including law and leadership techniques, cuneiform writing, and star mapping. The early society launched all of the follow-on kingdoms of

Mesopotamia, including Assyrian and Babylon. Perhaps their greatest kings were the three Sargons: Sargon of Akkad, who ruled an astonishing sixty-one years (dates uncertain), Sargon I, and II of Assyria. The population was polytheistic and counted some important deities—Anu, the sky god, and his consort, Ki, the earth goddess, Enki, the god of beneficence and the arts; Enlil, the god of spells and incantations; Inanna—a deification of Venus; Atu, the sun god; Nanna the moon god; and hundreds of minor deities. The patriarch Abraham was from Sumer and undoubtedly carried the memory of some of their beliefs and practices to Canaan. It was Abraham, as related in historical legend, who despoiled his father's idols before heeding God's call to form new peoples. *See also* Abraham; Abzu; Aruru; alphabet; Anunnaki; Aramaean(s); Berossus; cities of the gods; cuneiform; demi-god(s); Enki and Enlil; Enmeduranki; *Enuma Elish; Epic of Gilgamesh, The;* Hammurabi; Igigi; lulu; Mesopotamia; Nibiru; Nin-kharsag; panspermia theory; Sargon II; Shinar; Sumerian and Babylonian pantheon; Sumerian Tablets; Table of Destinies; Tablet of Nineveh; Tiamat; Utnapishtim; "Tablets of Faith"; Zuism.

Summa Theologica: the definitive work of Thomas Aquinas that details his commentary of the Christian faith and doctrine. The influence of the writing, particularly for Roman Catholic theology, has been tremendous. *See also* Aquinas, Thomas; Five Ways, the; *Quinque Viae;* Roman Catholic Church.

summer fruit: the last of the harvest, or the poor fruit that was somehow missed in the main gathering. The prophet Micah (Mic. 7:1) used the phrase to note the bare remainders of the crop after the gleaners have gone through behind the harvesters. What is left is a bare minimum and hardly worth the effort to save, which conveys his metaphorical meaning well enough. *See also* fig(s); Firstfruits; flora, fruit, and grain, symbology of; fruit, basket of ripe (summer); grapes; olive(s); peach; two baskets of figs.

Summerland: name for a type of heaven described by any number of New Age enthusiasts. *See also* Abraham's bosom; afterlife; Annwn; Aralu; Arcadia; Asgard; astral plane; Avalon; Dis; Duat; Elysium; eschatology, eschatological; eternal life; future life, doctrine of the; Gehenna; Hades; happy hunting ground; heaven;

hell; Hy-Breasail; Hyperborea; intermediate state; Jade Empire, the; Jahannam; Janna; lake of fire; life after death; limbo; *Limbus Puerorum;* Mictlan; New Age religion; new heaven and new earth; Nirvana; Otherworld; Paradise; paradise of God; Pardes; Perdition; Promised Land, the; Pure Land, the; purgatory; Shambhala legends; *Sheol;* soul sleep; space doctrine; Thule, land of; Tir na nOg; underworld; Upper Gehenna; Utopia; Valhalla; world to come, the; Xibala.

Summum: a cult sprung from 1975 but based on the ancient religions of Egypt, particularly the god Amon Ra. American Claude Nowell claimed to have met beings he called "summa individuals" directed by Ra who explained to him the great law of life: "The grand principle of creation is that Nothing and Possibility come in and out of bond infinite times in a finite moment." Nowell then changed his name to Summum Bonum Amon Ra, but his nickname, "Corky," stuck. Summum produces what the followers call the seven principles of their religion—psychokinesis, correspondence, vibration, opposition, rhythm, cause and effect, and gender. The group practices a ritual involving some type of alcoholic drink and meditation and is serious about mummification within their pyramidal structures in preparation for future life. *See also* Egyptian pantheon; sect(s).

summum bonum: the "highest good." Such a philosophy for life is important to many cultures but was particularly revered in ancient Greek philosophy. *See also* philosophy of the Greeks.

Sumner, William Graham: American sociologist and economist, an advocate of *laissez-faire* economics and a strong supporter of Social Darwinism (1840–1910). Sumner insisted that all "weak" elements of society must be minimized, a thrust that gave political and industrial monopoly interests a friend in America. He was an ordained Episcopal deacon and priest but best remembered as a teacher of political and social science at Yale. Sumner was a specialist in the study of what he termed "folkways" and published his brilliant *Folkways: A Study of the Sociological Importance of Usages, Manners, Customs, Mores, and Morals* in 1910. He was also a champion of the small tax-payer whom he called "the forgotten man." *See also* clergy scientists; Protestant Episcopal Church; Social Darwinism.

sun: Earth's star and our source of natural heat and light. In apocalyptic language, the sun is often portrayed as being darkened in times of distress or divine destruction. Revelation 12:1 shows the woman Israel clothed with the sun the moon as her footstool. The reference to the sun here is a symbol of Israel as drawn from Isaiah 42:6 and elsewhere. There was a solar eclipse at the crucifixion of Christ. The fourth trumpet of Revelation (Rev. 8:12) resulted in the sun's light being diminished by one-third. The fourth bowl (Rev. 16:8-9) produced a blazing heat wave. The midday sun was regarded as punishing (Ps. 121:6; Isa. 49:10; Jon. 4:8) because of its scorching heat. In a quotation from the lost book of Jasper (Josh. 10:1–15), the sun was made to stand still until the Israelites could defeat the Amorite king Adonizedek and his allies. A reflection of that miracle event, in a more poetic style, is found in Habakkuk 3:11. The sun, or its pagan personifications, was often worshiped in the ancient world. *See also* eclipse(s); heavenly bodies; hosts of heaven; life; moon; planets as gods, the; Saturnalia; star(s); sun stood still; swastika; twelve-starred crown; woman clothed in (with) the sun, the.

Sunday: also, the Lord's Day or "the first day of the week." The reference to Sunday, or more preferably, "the first day of the week" is found only in Revelation (Rev. 1:10) as the day John received the Apocalypse vision. The mention of *Sunday* at the start of Revelation may not refer to the first day of the week at all. There is strong suspicion here that John is somehow projecting himself to the future "day of the Lord" at the end of the age. Such thinking fits well with the eschatological nature of the Apocalypse and avoids naming the day before Monday, a rather unnecessary tidbit of dating. Furthermore, it is difficult to imagine John received all the revelations in a single day— an exhausting experience for an elderly man already suffering in slavery and banishment. The words "write this down" occur twelve times in the text, suggesting there is a command to do so after each distinct revelation. Nevertheless, the day has long been associated with the Lord's Supper (1 Cor. 11:20) and the weekday is generally recognized to consecrate the occasion for the Lord's worship since Jesus rose from the dead on a Sunday. He also appeared to the disciples on a Sunday, and it was the day that unleashed the miracles of Pentecost. The emperor

Constantine decreed it a day of rest, much to the relief of soldiers and slaves. His bold action of 321 A.D. was a radical decision (as are all attempted calendar manipulations) so why did he do it? Historians disagree on the reason. Some say the edict was meant to mirror the Genesis account of creation—six days ending in a day of rest. Another group claims the days of the week were named for the seven planets known in the emperor's day—Mars, Mercury, Jupiter, Venus, Saturn, and the moon and sun. A third group says the days of the week grew from the phases of the moon, each having a duration of about seven days. In any case, the proclamation was a momentous event. Gradually, the church came to revere the date as the desired day of formal worship for Christendom. Sunday differs from the Jewish Sabbath in both occasion and observance, although both are sacred days. *See also* calendar; day of (our Lord Jesus) Christ; feasts and special days of high liturgy faiths; feasts and special days of Protestantism; liturgical year; liturgy, Christian; Lord's Day, the; Sabbath; Saturnalia.

Sunday, Billy: accurately William Ashley "Billy" Sunday, an ex-professional baseball player turned evangelist (1862–1935) from the Presbyterian denomination. Sunday became extremely popular (and wealthy) during the first two decades of the 20th century because of his charisma, anti-drink stance, and frenetic style of preaching. Sunday's life was shaken when he and a few friends walked out of a bar on a night of drinking to listen to the rescue mission musicians outside. Under conviction of his sin, he began to weep copiously, much to the amusement of his buddies. Sunday was known for his pulpit antics, such as throwing chairs, pounding the pulpit or floor, and other flamboyant displays. Sunday's support of prohibition and the Eighteenth Amendment were mainstays of his message but it should be noted that estimates of converts range from over 300,000 to 1,000,000 persons who walked the "sawdust trail" to publically profess personal convictions of some description during his evangelistic tours across America. *See also* evangelist(s), evangelism; Presbyterians; revivalism; "sawdust trail, the."

Sunday Christians: those who are more or less faithful in attendance at regular worship services but are known to not observe the moral or ethical principles of the faith. Most also refuse to officially join a church roll lest they be tasked with some duty other than their presence. *See also* C and E Christians; Christianese; Creeping Jesus; slurs, religious.

Sunday of the Five Loaves. See Laetare Sunday.

Sunday school(s): an organized and usually effective method of teaching the Bible to all ages. Much of the credit for Sunday school formation goes to the Wesley brothers and Methodism in search of a methodical and organized teaching program without boring catechism instruction. The first organized classes, however, were instituted in 1780 by the Englishman Robert Raikes, who taught Bible studies to slum children. The first Sunday school in America was in Acomac County, Virginia, where William Elliott held classes on his plantation for slaves and servants. Benjamin Rush, the physician and signer of the Declaration of Independence, helped organize the movement in Pennsylvania. Most prominent Protestant churches have excelled in the practice by graded classrooms, dedicated volunteer teachers, and active church support. Good Sunday schools have proven to be an effective evangelistic tool, an asset to the church body, and satisfactory training in fundamental biblical knowledge and moral precepts. *See also* Chautauqua Movement; Methodists; quarterly; Raikes, Robert; religious education; religious organizations; youth religious organizations.

Sunday school answer: response to a theological or religious question so undemanding even a Sunday school child could answer. The phrase may also refer to a trite, simplistic, or "churchy" answer without much informational substance. *See also* Christianese; slurs, religious.

sundial, miracle of the: a phenomenon experienced by King Hezekiah of Judah. During a severe illness, the king prayed for healing, which prompted Isaiah to promise the king fifteen more years of life (Isa. 38:1–8). The king's prayer was an unselfish one since it was prompted by his need to produce sons to succeed him. Therefore, recovery was allowed as announced by Isaiah. Furthermore, as a pledge or sign of God's favor, the sun's shadow backed up ten degrees in some discernible fashion, either on a sundial as described (a shadow clock) or by some other means. Such an unusual astronomical episode, many scholars claimed, is said to have marked the shadow's descent ten steps on the stairway of Ahaz instead of proceeding naturally in the expected direction. This movement of light and shadow continues to be a subject of controversy. Was it a genuine miracle whereby the Earth revolved east to west for a time before restoring itself to the usual west to east rotation? Could clouds somehow manipulate events? The historian Josephus insisted that the shadow moved *up* the steps of the palace before it went *down* again at the same speed, thus ensuring that the day would be no longer than normal. This astronomical event seems to have been noticed elsewhere, so Josephus may be quite correct. Indeed, it is possible that the ambassadors to Hezekiah from Babylon under Merodach-Baladan had this astronomical anomaly on their diplomatic agenda for discussion at the time of their visit (Isa. 39). *See also* Hezekiah; miracle(s); Merodach-Baladan; sun stood still.

Sunnah: Mohammad's way of life, taken as a model for Muslims and recorded in the *hadiths*. *See also* Abu 'Abdallah Muhammad ibn Idris al-Shafi'i; *fatwa; Hadith*; Islam; Shari'a.

Sunni Islam: the branch of Islam that makes up 90 percent of the Muslim population and is generally considered the orthodox group. The word "Sunni" derives from an Arabic term referring to the sayings of Mohammed as recorded in the *Hadith*—the collection of texts regarding the prophet. The translation is "one on the path." Sunnis believe the first four caliphs—Mohammed's successors—are the right rulers of Islam, and their heirs have continued consistently until the breakup of the Ottoman Empire after World War I. This doctrine places them in direct opposition to the second largest community of Islam, the Shi'ites, who deny the authority of the first caliph, Abu-Bakr. Sunni theology revolves around four distinct schools of interpretation, each with its peculiar explanation of the faith protocols. Sunni eschatology consists of a series of beliefs, including the defeat of Satan by the *Mahdi*, rewards in Paradise for the faithful according to their deeds or works, and condemnation to hell of those with insufficient merit. *See also* Abu-Bakr; anti-Semitic; Fatah; grand mufti; Hamas; Islam; sect(s); religious organizations; Safavid; Shi'ite Islam; terrorism; terrorist(s).

sun of righteousness: a title for the rescuer of Israel following the terrible day of the Lord. This savior type is described as rising with healing in his wings to trample down the oppressors and give liberty to the subjugated (Mal. 4:2–3). "[T]he rising sun will come to us from heaven" is part of Zechariah's praise song for the birth of John the Baptist (Lk. 1:78–79). *See also* John the Baptist; names (titles) for Jesus.

Sun Stone: one of a few names for the ancient Aztec calendar. The object is about twelve feet in height, four in thickness, and weighs about twenty-four tons. *See also* Aztecs; calendar; Chilam-Balam; Eagle Bowl; five stages of the earth, the; Inca; Itza-Maya; Maya; Mesoamerica; Moai; Montezuma II; prophecy, advocates of; 2012, prophecy of; Quetzalcoatl; Xolotl; zodiac.

sun stood still: a miracle of some description at Gibeon, about ten miles northwest of Jerusalem. The Gibeonites, who were frightened at the fall of Jericho and Ai, were eager to ally themselves with the Israelites. This action angered the kings of Jerusalem, Hebron, Jarmuth, Lachish, and Eglon. Joshua rushed to the rescue, but in the ensuing battle, he found the need for extended daylight to secure a total victory. God provided for a day's extra sunlight by miraculous means, perhaps as a perihelion, a supernatural miracle, or some other means we do not know. The story seems to have sprung from the lost book of Jasper as recorded in Joshua 10:1–15. This amazing story seems to be referenced also in Isaiah 28:21 (where the prophet refers to it as God's "strange work" at Gibeon), Habakkuk 3:11 (which says the moon joined the suspension), and is examined in the Apocryphal book of Ecclesiasticus (Ecclu. 46:4). Josephus said these events were recorded in the "Books of the Temple," but we know nothing of those. A similar miracle occurred during the reign of Ahaz when time seemed to reverse itself to some degree. *See also Book of Jashar*; miracle(s); sun; sundial, miracle of the.

sun worshipers: a vision of Ezekiel (Ezk. 8:16–18) at the Inner Court of the Temple. The sight revealed twenty-five men with their backs to the Temple and facing east. They were bowing down to the sun and "putting the branch to their nose." The ritual of smelling the branch is of uncertain definition but likely refers to a part of the idolatrous ceremony they were enacting. *See also* cult(s); planets as gods, the; Re (Ra); Saturnalia; Sol.

supererogation: the doctrine, almost exclusively Roman and Eastern Catholic, that states certain saints in heaven have acquired an abundance of virtue (more than they need) that can be shared with those in the purgatory. The merits of Jesus himself are sometimes counted as a source of supererogation. *See also* hyten; Roman Catholic Church; treasury of merits; veneration of the saints.

supermoon: the astrological point at which the moon in its elliptical orbit about the earth is closest to our planet, a.k.a. a "full moon." For some religions, Judaism, Christianity, Islam, Wicca, and paganism included, the supermoon holds real ritual meaning. *See also* astrology, astrologers; astronomy, astronomers; blood moon(s); celestial disturbances; *compuctus;* eclipse(s); heavenly bodies; hosts of heaven; New Moon(s); planets as gods, the; signs in heaven.

supernatural: any event, such as a miracle, that does not necessarily conform to the laws of science or nature. In Scripture, the supernatural event is always at the discretion of God Who is capable of suspending natural causes. Revelation and other apocalyptic writings report a vast number of such occurrences, many of them initiated by the prophets. Theologically speaking, the current idea of the supernatural as being ghostly or other-worldly does not apply in this context. All of God's miracles are supernatural to our experience and beyond the realm of the ordinary. *See also* anthropomancy; anthroposophy; apotropaic magic; aretology; Ariosophy; astrology, astrologers; audition; augury; automatic writing; bagua; belomancy; bibliomancy; black arts; cartomancy; chiromancy; clairaudience; clairsentience; clairvoyance; cleromancy; cone of power; conjure; cryptesthesia; crystallomancy; curious acts; divination; dream(s); dreams and visions; ecstasy; enchantment; enneagram; evil eye; extrasensory perception (ESP); foreknowledge; foretelling; geomancy; Godwink; grimoire; hepatoscopy; Hermetic wisdom; Hermetic writings; hex; hierscopy; horoscope(s); hydromancy; Ifa; incantation; lecanomancy; literomancy; locution; magic arts; magic, magick; magic square; magnetism; *mana*; mantic wisdom; mantra; miracle(s); monition; necromancy; New Age religion; Nicene Creed; numbers, symbology of; occult, occultic; omen; oneiromancy; oracle(s); otherworldly journeys; ouija board; out-of-body experiences (OBEs); paranormal; parapsychology; peace pole(s); pentagram; portent; precognition; prediction;

prefiguration; premonition; prodigy; prognostication; prophecy, general; psi; psychic healing; psychic reading; psychic healing; psychomancy; psychonautics; pyramidology; remote viewing; retrocognition; revelation; rhabdomancy; scrying; séance; secret wisdom; sorcery, sorceries; spell; spell names; spiritism; stigmata; tarot; telegnosis; telepathy; telesthesia; theugry; third eye, the; totemism; vision quest; visions; visualization; Voodoo; Voudou; witchcraft; *ya sang*; yoga; Zen; *zos kia* cultus.

super oblata: "prayer over the offerings," earlier called the *Secreta* (secret) because it was recited in a soft voice. The prayer pleads for the gifts just offered to be acceptable to God and used wisely. *See also* liturgical year; liturgy, Christian.

superscription: 1. the heading above most literary works—a title. 2. the reverse of a coin. 3. the titulus, the placard tacked to a cross naming the crime for which the victim is to be crucified. *See also* accideme; alliteration; apostrophe; apothegm; assonance; autograph; Bible; Bible manuscripts; Bible translations; biblical criticism; chiasmus; conflict story; *constructio ad sensum;* context; contextualization; dittography; double sense fulfillment; doublets; doubling; edification; eisegesis; epanadiplosis; epigrammatic statements; etymology; exegesis; figure of speech; folio; form criticism; gattung; gloss; gnomic sayings; grammatical-historical interpretation; *hapax legomena;* haplography; hermeneutic(s); higher criticism; homographs; homonyms; homophones; *homoteleuton;* hyperbole; idiom; *inclusio;* INRI; interpolation; interpretation; inverted nun; irony; isagogics; *itture sopherim;* jot and tittle; kere; *kethib;* "L"; liberalists interpretation; literal interpretation; litotes; loan words; lower criticism; "M"; Masoretic Text; minuscule(s); mystery of God; omission; onomastica; onomatopoeia; palimpsest; papyrus; paradigm; parallelism; parchment; *paroimia; paronomasia;* pericope; personification; Peshitta; pointing; point of view; polyglot; principles of interpretation; proof texting; pun(s); "Q"; redaction; revelation, theological; rhetorical criticism; rhetorical devices; riddle; satire; *scripto continua;* scriptorium; *sebirin;* simile; similitude; source criticism; sources, primary and secondary; special points; strophe; symbol(s); synecdoche; syntax; synthetic parallelism; text; textual criticism; *tiggune sopherim;* Time Texts; titulus; Torah; translation; transposition; trope; type(s); typology; uncial(s); vellum; verbicide.

supersessionism. See replacement theology.

Super-Shemitah: a take on the Jubilee Year observance (now mostly disregarded by Jews) that has been set to the date of September 2015 through September 2016. It was so designated by some apocalypticists who suspect the time will see a major stock market crash. Their reasoning grows from past events which have seen Wall Street failures before—six days after the 911 terrorist attacks and a second on September 29, 2008, amid a global economic meltdown. Each took place on the same biblical day exactly seven years apart. Most scholars see the Super-Shemitah speculation as another Y2K debacle. *See also* Jubilee Year; Judaism; Y2K.

super-sign, the: a non-technical reference used by some authorities to designate the return of the Jews to their homeland in Palestine in 1948. They consider it to be a pivotal point in prophecy. Another super-sign has to be the destruction of Jerusalem in 70 A.D. and others not yet come to pass. *See also* eschatology, eschatological; Ezekiel's vision of the new Temple and new land; Ezekiel's vision of the restored theocracy; Ezekiel's vision of the valley of dry bones; miracles of Jesus; miracles of Jesus with eschatological emphasis; "next year in Jerusalem"; prodigy; restoration of Israel (the Jews); sign(s); sign of the Jew; sign of the Son of Man, the; signposts of the end time.

superstition: any belief or attitude that is inconsistent with natural law and rationality, such as confidence in charms, omens, sympathetic magic, and the like. Often such convictions become ritualized into religious form and take on symptoms of idolatry. Both science and the Christian religion condemn such beliefs but many primitive or occultic practices harbor them as basic to their worship style and spirit. *See also* magic, magick.

supper of God, the great: a scene of Revelation 19:17 that appears in direct contrast to the supper of the Lamb. In the great supper of God description, evil and what remains of it is devoured by scavengers and decay. In the supper of the Lamb, believers who have overcome in the faith enjoy sweet communion and delight with Christ in God's heaven. *See also* Babylon the Great; marriage supper of the Lamb.

supplication psalm: an Old Testament psalm directed to God as an appeal for aid and comfort to the writer or on behalf of another. *See also* creation psalm; cry to the Lord; enthronement psalm; historical psalm; imprecatory psalm; messianic psalm; penitential psalm; psalm; psalm of judgment; psalm of lament; Psalms as Old Testament book; royal psalm; thanksgiving psalm; wisdom psalm; worship psalm.

supply clergy: or supply preaching, temporary clergy assistance on a *per diem* basis. Churches or other religious organizations may employ substitutional assistance when needed usually with specified and limited duties. *See also* auxiliary ministries; clergy; ecclesiastic(s); laity; lay minister(s).

supralapsarianism: Calvinist theology relating how God determined to provide salvation "before the fall" or "after the fall." Did he save people, then allow sin? Or did He allow sin, and then save? If the former, the correct term is supralapsarianism; if the latter, the act is infralapsarianism. Supralapsarianism insists that God granted election to some and reprobation to others before the world was introduced to sin, a failure of human nature which God allowed since His plan for deliverance was already in place. *See also* Calvinism; Lambeth Articles; infralapsarianism.

Supreme Muslim Religious Council. See Waqf.

sura(s): a chapter of the *Qur'an*. There are 114 to be found there. *See also* Islam; *Qur'an*.

Sursum Corda: a popular Christian ritual expression meaning "lift up your hearts." It appears in many early church liturgies. *See also* liturgical year; liturgy, Christian; music.

Surt: the greatest fire giant in Norse mythology. He wields a great flaming sword and will have much to do in the final battle of Ragnarok. *See also* frost giants; giant(s); mythological beasties, elementals, monsters, and spirit animals; Norse and Old Germanic pantheon; Ragnarok.

survivalist(s): a "preppie," one who makes ready for calamity or end-of-the-world pronouncements by stockpiling foodstuffs, water, and other necessities. A bomb shelter may be in the plans as well. Examples of the survivalist mode may be seen in the recent Y2K fear and are present in many paramilitary groups today. Most faithful believers prefer to trust God with their destinies rather than prepare elaborate escape schemes that may prove futile or, at best, temporary. A careful study of end time prophecy seems to imply such desperate action will be futile anyway. *See also* Y2K.

Susa: (Shushan) the winter residence of the Persian kings during the time of Daniel. It was the capital of Elam and the site of the nearby Ulai Canal, where Daniel received some of his revelations and a base of operations for Queen Esther.

Susanna: 1. a valued helper of Jesus and the traveling disciples (Lk. 8:3). Little is known of her history. 2. another Susanna who appears in one of the apocryphal stories as an addition to the book of Daniel. In that title, Susanna is a chaste woman falsely accused of misconduct but vindicated by Daniel's ingenious strategy. *See also* Apocrypha, the; Jew(s); liturgical year.

sustentation: a monetary collection or funding to more fully sustain a Presbyterian minister. *See also* altarage; benefice; benefit of clergy; carrodian; *cathedraticum;* mensa; pounding; prebend; love offering; Presbyterians; stipend.

Suttanipata: a Buddhist scripture portion, part of the Pali Canon, of Theravada Buddhism divided into five mostly poetic sections. It is a companion piece to the Dhammapada. *See also* Buddhism; Dhammapada; Gautama Buddha; Pali Canon, the; *Sutta Pitaka;* Theravada Buddhism.

sutra: a written text concerning ancient and medieval Vedic writings or aphorisms. They are common in Indian compositions of Hinduism, Buddhism, and Jainism. Many are considered canonical. *See also* apothegm; Buddhism; Hinduism; Jainism.

Sutta Pitaka: a portion of Buddha's recorded sayings. Within the writings, Buddha says the world will endure a time of moral deterioration during which his teachings and the ten moral behaviors of the faith will gradually disappear over some 500 years to be replaced by ten amoral behaviors. The results will be poverty and lawlessness. The *Sutta Pitaka* is one section of the Pali Canon called the "basket of discourses," the other two being the *Abhidhamma Pitaka* and the *Vinaya Pitaka. See also* Buddhism; Dhammapada; Gautama Buddha; Mahayana Buddhism; Pali Canon, the; Suttanipata; Theravada Buddhism.

suzerainty treaty: a type of covenant in which a sovereign (a ruler) pledges to benefit some or all of those under his authority (his vassals). In return, certain obligations are usually required from the subjects, such as obedience to the king or fealty to his reign. All of God's covenants may be properly labeled as those of the suzerainty type, but most are unconditional (*i.e.,* their fulfillment does not depend on the faithfulness of the people). *See also* Code of Hammurabi; conditional covenant(s), biblical; covenant(s), biblical; covenant theology; king(s); unconditional covenant(s); vassal treaty.

Swaggart, Jimmy Lee: Pentecostal televangelist (b. 1935) and gospel musician (he was cousin to Jerry Lee Lewis and Mickey Gilley) who rose from poverty to a successful media personality. His career, however, was stunted in the late 1980s and early 1990s due to exposure of failures of moral turpitude involving prostitutes. The incidents caused his defrocking from the Assemblies of God denomination. His TV show, nevertheless, continued. *See also* Pentecostalism; revivalism; televangelism, televangelists.

swami: "one who possesses"—a lord. The term is a title of respect for some religious or political leader, most often associated with an Eastern ascetic or yogi. The designate is commonly abbreviated as "sw."

Swami Vivekenanda. See Sri Ramakrishna.

swastika: a srivatsa, an ancient symbol of the life cycle or the sun before it became a Nazi symbol. Some Native American tribes used it as well. The corruption of the swastika meaning gave rise to its recognition by some with a religious bent as a "twisted cross." *See also* black sun; cross; cross of Nero; Fascist millennialism; Fascist salute; Hitler, Adolf; life; Mussolini, Benito; Neo-Nazi(s); sun; symbol(s).

sweat lodge: a crude structure, similar to a sauna, intended by some religious practices to eliminate impurities from the mind and body. Most use steam in combination with other ingredients along with prescribed rituals and ceremonies. The practice is common in some Native American tribes.

Swedenborg, Emanuel: German philosopher, scientist, and mystic (1688–1772). Swedenborg's early life exhibited strong gifts for mathematics, mechanics, physiology, and astronomy. He became almost exclusively interested in religion, however, and reported numerous visions, some of them dealing with the last judgment. His most famous work was entitled simply *Heaven and Hell.* Swedenborg's doctrine espoused that everything tangible and visible represents something spiritual, invisible, and astral, a concept he called "correspondence." He recognized Jesus as savior but dismissed the Trinity and excluded the writings of Paul from the New Testament. According to Swedenborg, man in his highest form may actually see God. Swedenborg was a strict vegetarian and urged his many followers to copy that lifestyle. He saw himself as called of God to end current Christianity and begin the New Jerusalem dispensation. He insisted angels informed him that the end of the age would occur in 1757, but few heeded his statement. *See also* Anthropocentric and Anti-Trinitarian churches; clergy scientists; philosophy of religion; sect(s); Swedenborgianism.

Swedenborgianism: an eschatological sect of some influence established in the British Isles by Emanuel Swedenborg (1688–1772). Swedenborg claimed to have had a special revelation that promoted the idea that we are now "marking time" in the "old church" (Christianity) until this age will pass away in favor of the arriving New Jerusalem. He wrote prolifically, most of the literature being ultra-allegorical and fantastic in style. The sect called themselves the Church of the New Jerusalem (fully organized around 1821). The philosopher/theologian Henry James Sr. used some of Swedenborg's mysticism to formulate a number of his theoretical ideas. *See also* Chapman, John; Anthropocentric and Anti-Trinitarian churches; sect(s); New Thought; sect(s); Swedenborg, Emanuel.

"sweet Jesus": the fashioned reasoning of those who prefer the easy or less troublesome ideas of Jesus and the gospel. One's theology is padded, in the sense that only the more positive aspects of the faith need to be entertained at the expense of more difficult concepts like justice, condemnation, obedience, sacrifice, morality, and the like. Even choice of art and literature may bolster the idea when Jesus is pictured as the effeminate kindly shepherd but not the stern condemner of sinfulness or when shallow devotional preferences exclude deep theological inquiry. *See also* Christianese; hyper-grace; "I just want to love Jesus"; slurs, religious.

sword: a bladed weapon of varying lengths and designs. In symbolic terminology, the sword represents power and precision in cutting, often when referring to speech or to recorded Scripture (Heb. 4:12). The psalmist David spoke of (Ps. 59:6) "spewing out swords from the lips." The term is also frequently used in apocalyptic imagery to denote warfare, death, and destruction. Revelation describes Jesus as having a sharp double-edged sword emerging from his mouth (Rev. 1:16; 19:15). The apocalyptic rider of the second seal (Rev. 6:3–4) wields a large sword. God often used destruction, war, famine, drought, or plague as punishment for the unrighteous nations. One of the more interesting prophetic references to the sword can be found in Ezekiel 21. *See also* double-edged sword; Excalibur; Mjollnir; "song of the sword"; "Sword of God"; sword of the Lord; sword, famine, and plague; Zolfaghar.

sword drill: a contest in which the participants, normally young people, scramble to find Bible passages presented to them as quickly as possible. Certain rules are applicable and sometimes extra points are added for identifying specific words hinted at in the text instructions. With practice, users can learn the Bible books thoroughly and locate the specific passages in remarkably short periods of time, even seconds. The name for the game surely comes from the description of the Bible as "the sword of the Lord" (Eph. 6:17; Heb. 4:12) but the title "Bible drills" has virtually replaced the older name. Regional and state competitions are still popular in some areas of the country. *See also* Bible; Bible baseball; Christianese; religious education; sword of the Lord.

sword, famine, and plague: a tripartite formula for God's severe punishments when expressed as a lament (Jer. 14:12). The phrase sounds eerily descriptive of the four horsemen of the Apocalypse. *See also* four horsemen of the Apocalypse; sword of the Lord.

"Sword of God": Halley's Comet of 66 A.D. as named by Josephus when it appeared over Jerusalem before the city's destruction in A.D. 70. The body returned to view in 451 at the time of Attila's invasion of Western Europe and again in 1066 when William the Conqueror invaded England. Comets had, until Edmond Halley diagnosed them scientifically in 1682, been counted as harbingers of doom and catastrophe. Josephus also named other unusual phenomena around the time of the Roman invasion including a bright light at night over the altar and Holy Place lasting half an hour, a heifer being led to sacrifice which calved a lamb, chariots, soldiers in full battle dress racing to and fro in the sky, an earthquake, and voices shouting "Let us remove hence." *See also* astronomy, astronomers; Halley's Comet; Jerusalem, invasions of; Josephus, Flavius; sword; sword of the Lord.

Sword of God Brotherhood: a group of twenty-five or so in southern France who claimed that the end of the world would be on January 1, 2017. *See also* cult(s).

sword of the Lord: 1. a frequent prophetic description of God's periodic acts of punishment for unfaithfulness, idolatry, or other serious indiscretion by His people or the rebellious populations. Incidents of God's wrath, known generally as "the sword of the Lord," may be found in Deuteronomy 32:41–42; Isaiah 27:1, 34:5–6, 66:16; Jeremiah 12:12, 47:6; Ezekiel 14:17–18, 21:3–5, 32:10, 24; Zephaniah 2:12; and Revelation 1:16,19:15, 21. 2. a metaphor for the Word of God (Heb. 4:12). Scripture is described as living and active, sharper than a two-edged sword that penetrates even to diving the soul and spirit to judge the thoughts and attitudes of the heart. God's speech then, created in Genesis, redeems in the present and will conquer in the end. *See also* Bible; Howe, Julia Ward; sword, famine, and plague; sword drill; "sword of God."

Sworn Book of Honorius: or *Liber Juratus,* a Latin grimoire (magical textbook) supposedly composed by Honorius of Thebes. The author, even though named, is of uncertain identity since he could be Pope Honorius I, Pope Honorius III, another individual, or even a totally mythical character. In any case, the book's appearance in several manuscripts starting around the 13th century has proven to be one of the oldest and most influential magical texts of the medieval period. The term *juratus* pertains to oath-taking or "sworn." *See also* grimoire; occult, occultic.

Sybil(s). See Sibyl(s).

sycamore tree(s). See fig tree(s).

Syene. See Elephantine.

Syllabus of Errors: the Vatican's published intent to stamp out secret societies that the church considered dangerous, such as

Freemasonry. Pope Pius IX issued the first bull on the subject in 1864 followed by Pope Leo XIII in 1884 and Pius X in 1907, with Freemasonry as their primary targets. The syllabus declared that all doctrine exclusive from the Roman Church was condemned, including the policy of separation of church and state, freedom of religion, all forms of Protestantism, and personal preferences of the religious conscience of the individual. *See also* Freemasonry; Roman Catholic Church.

sylph(s): a slender and elfish-type young girl often depicted as a tease. Alexander Pope drolly called them the humors of a peevish woman. The mythological sylph, however, began with Paracelsus and was seen as an invisible fairy-like creature or elemental prominent in hermetic literature but with little impact on Christianity or prophecy. Sylphs are usually considered to be soulless creatures. *See also* attending spirit(s); banshee; bogle; brownies; bugbears; clurichauns; daemons; deceiving spirits; disa; dryad(s); elemental(s); fairy, fairies; Furies; ghost(s); ghoul; gnome(s); Green Man, the; hobgoblins; homunculus; household deities; huldafolk; Lares; leprechaun(s); Loa Loas; Manes; May Day; mythological beasties, elementals, monsters, and spirit animals; nereid; nisse; nymph(s); nyx; Olympian pantheon; Oniropompi; Orisha; Oya; para; paredri; penates; Robin Goodfellow; satyr; Seelie Court, Unseelie Court; selkie; Sidhe; sirens; spiritual warfare; sprite(s); teraphim; territorial spirits; Trickster; Tuatha de Danann; tutelary; undine; wight(s); woman (women).

symbalon: a "password" necessary to participate in most of the pagan religious mysteries. Only initiates could share the experience since secrecy was paramount. *See also* Akae; Beqa; Mason's Word, the; secret name, the; "sign, the."

symbol(s): an object, word, or idea that has meaning in itself but at the same moment represents another more profound concept. Symbols are convenient and powerful in that they can simplify complex ideas with their suggestive attributes without resorting to lengthy interpretations of those thoughts. For example, the flag of the United States normally conjures images of patriotism, sacrifice, loyalty, national unity, sovereignty, etc., more poignantly and clearly than mere words. Biblical examples may be noted as Moses' staff (representing his leadership authority). Many common expressions represent the Holy Spirit: a descending dove, the purging fire, the invisible wind, and cleansing water. There are twenty-one symbols used in Revelation alone—the first being the seven lampstands in chapter one. Symbols may appear as numbers, names, colors, jewels, metals, directions, creatures, actions, objects, or ordinances. Biblical symbology is consistent throughout Scripture but can be abused by the ill-informed. *See also* accideme; Advent wreath; alliteration; apostrophe; apothegm; assonance; autograph; Bible; Bible manuscripts; Bible translations; biblical criticism; chiasmus; chrismon(s); Christmas tree; Christingle; conflict story; *constructio ad sensum;* context; contextualization; cross of Nero; dittography; double sense fulfillment; doublets; doubling; edification; eisegesis; epanadiplosis; epigrammatic statements; etymology; exegesis; figure of speech; folio; form criticism; gattung; gloss; gnomic sayings; grammatical-historical interpretation; *hapax legomena;* haplography; hermeneutic(s); higher criticism; homographs; homonyms; homophones; *homoteleuton;* hyperbole; idiom; *inclusio;* interpolation; interpretation; inverted nun; irony; isagogics; *itture sopherim;* jot and tittle; kere; *kethib;* "L"; liberalists interpretation; literal interpretation; litotes; loan words; lower criticism; "M"; Masoretic Text; minuscule(s); mystery of God; omission; onomastica; onomatopoeia; palimpsest; papyrus; paradigm; parallelism; parchment; *paroimia; paronomasia;* peace symbol; pericope; personification; Peshitta; pointing; point of view; polyglot; principles of interpretation; prodigy; proof texting; pun(s); "Q"; redaction; revelation, theological; rhetorical criticism; rhetorical devices; riddle; satire; *scripto continua;* scriptorium; *sebirin;* semiotic(s); shadow(s); sign(s); simile; similitude; source criticism; sources, primary and secondary; special points; strophe; superscription; synecdoche; syntax; synthetic parallelism; text; textual criticism; *tiggune sopherim;* Time Texts; Torah; translation; transposition; trope; type(s); typology; uncial(s); vellum; verbicide.

Symmachus: a translator writing in Greek of the Old Testament from the third century who tried to combine literalness with some literary style. Both Lucian and Jerome favored the work. Some histories claim he was a Samaritan converted to Judaism. *See also* Jew(s); Lucian; Theodotion.

Symphony of the Marriage Feast: a contrived but descriptive title for praise offered in Revelation 19:6–8 as the marriage feast of the Lamb is celebrated. *See also* music; praise paradigms of Revelation, the.

synagogue: a Jewish assembly (the *Beit Knesset*) or its building (sometimes called a shul or temple) established after the Babylonian Captivity. When Ezekiel, Daniel, and Jeremiah assured the exiles that God was with them in their captivity, the people more or less accepted this as permission to carry on a form of worship that would necessitate the lack of a Temple (Jer. 29:1–9). The synagogue structure was used for community meetings, school, and worship; in fact, the word means "assembly." Jesus and the early apostles preached in the village synagogues often, and even as a priority, before they approached the Gentiles with the gospel. We know that all synagogue goers were not Jews. Luke (writing in Acts) called these non-Jews by various names, one of which is "God-fearers." The Christian equivalent would likely be a church building, classroom, or lecture hall. *See also* furniture and furnishings of the tabernacle, temples, and modern synagogue; Judaism; liturgy, Jewish; religious education; religious organizations; shul; Synagogue of the Freedmen; temple(s); Touro Synagogue.

synagogue of Satan: a nefarious group mentioned in the address to the church at Philadelphia (Rev. 3:9). The reference appears to be a description of false Jews who were disturbing the church there. Jesus declared those persons to be liars and promised that they would be forced to humble themselves before the Philadelphians and acknowledge that Christ does, indeed, love his faithful. Some apocalypticists see the synagogue of Satan as a code for secret societies in general. *See also* Judaizers; secret societies.

Synagogue of the Freedmen: a disputed investigation exists as to who the so-called "Freedmen" or "Libertines" composed these synagogues. Some say they were of two collections of emigrant Jews—one from the Greek-speaking regions of Cilicia and Asia and another from Aramaic-speaking North Africa (Alexandria and Cyrene). Other studies suggest they were freed prisoners of war under Pompey (63 b.c.) who had settled in Jerusalem. They were not recognized as pure-blooded Jews but were now free of their former slavery under the Romans and had chosen orthodox Judaism as their religion. Perhaps they could be classed among the "God-fearers." In any case, they were the prime instigators of Stephen's martyrdom (Acts 6:8–7:60). Stephen probably preached to the men of these synagogues as he was a Greek-speaking convert to Christianity and could communicate with some of them. The Freedmen, probably lacking the respect of the Hebrew-speaking Jews, deferred to the authority of the Sanhedrin but presented false accusations against Stephen because they could not defeat his testimony. Stephen was quickly condemned and stoned to death. *See also* "God-fearers"; Judaism; Pompey; religious organizations; Stephen of Jerusalem; synagogue.

synaxarium: "to bring together." The synaxarium is an Eastern Orthodox compilation of hagiographies listing the saints or their biographies. It corresponds in some ways to the Roman Catholic martyrologies. *See also* Eastern Orthodox Church; *Golden Legend;* martyrologies.

synaxis: Greek for "meeting" or "assembly." The ancients used the term to name any type of public worship, but a more modern application is reserved for readings and prayers before the Eucharist celebration in most liturgical churches. More precisely, the term names the liturgy said in common by Eastern Orthodox priests on Saturday or Sunday. It also defines the rule of prayer followed by a solitary monk. *See also* Eastern Orthodox Church; monk(s).

synchronic: "together time," the study of events in one specific moment. The synchronic view is an immediate examination of an event without reference to what happened before or after—a sort of snapshot in time. *See also* historicism; diachronic.

synchronicity: theologically speaking, any event that happens without a cause, or a process that ties together events into meaningful coincidences.

syncretism: a mix of the ritual and beliefs of numerous religious persuasions. Syncretism weakens the core of faith by making "all things to all men" and was strongly condemned by the prophets because the Jews were prone to combine polytheistic paganism and the monotheism of Yahweh. There were those in ancient Israel, for example, who practiced a syncretistic form of Yahwism, equating Yahweh with Baal (Hos. 2:18) and worshiping the stars of heaven. Later, orthodox Jews campaigned against the syncretism of Judaism with Hellenistic and Oriental ideas. Today, the tendency is to combine elements of many religions to a modernistic, palatable but insipid spiritual consistency. *See also* indigenization; postmodernism.

synecdoche: a literary technique whereby a part is put forth as a whole or the whole put forth as a part. "Everyone who heard him [the boy Jesus] was amazed at his understanding and his answers" (Lk. 2:47) may be a synecdoche because surely *everyone* did not share that opinion. *See also* accideme; alliteration; apostrophe; apothegm; assonance; autograph; Bible; Bible manuscripts; Bible translations; biblical criticism; chiasmus; conflict story; *constructio ad sensum;* context; contextualization; dittography; double sense fulfillment; doublets; doubling; edification; eisegesis; epanadiplosis; epigrammatic statements; etymology; exegesis; figure of speech; folio; form criticism; gattung; gloss; gnomic sayings; grammatical-historical interpretation; *hapax legomena;* haplography; hermeneutic(s); higher criticism; homographs; homonyms; homophones; *homoteleuton;* hyperbole; idiom; *inclusio;* interpolation; interpretation; inverted nun; irony; isagogics; *itture sopherim;* jot and tittle; kere; *kethib;* "L"; liberalists interpretation; literal interpretation; litotes; loan words; lower criticism; "M"; Masoretic Text; minuscule(s); mystery of God; omission; onomastica; onomatopoeia; palimpsest; papyrus; paradigm; parallelism; parchment; *paroimia; paronomasia;* pericope; personification; Peshitta; pointing; point of view; polyglot; principles of interpretation; proof texting; pun(s); "Q"; redaction; revelation, theological; rhetorical criticism; rhetorical devices; riddle; satire; *scripto continua;* scriptorium; *sebirin;* simile; similitude; source criticism; sources, primary and secondary; special points; strophe; superscription; symbol(s); syntax; synthetic parallelism; text; textual criticism; *tiggune sopherim;* Time Texts; Torah; translation; transposition; trope; type(s); typology; uncial(s); vellum; verbicide.

synergism: the doctrinal error that we cooperate with God in securing salvation for our souls as opposed to the fact that it is entirely God's initiative (except concerning our decision to allow His intervention). Almost all cults are synergistic in that they continually add works, rituals, obedience, bodily denial, or harsh regimen to the saving process of simple grace. Such was the great failing of the Pharisees. *See also* Adamic Covenant; autosoterism; covenant of grace; covenant of works; monergism; salvation; solifidianism; stone of stumbling; works; works, salvation by.

synod: 1. in some ecclesiastical circles (especially Roman Catholicism), an official church gathering. 2. in Presbyterianism, a religious court ranked between a presbytery and the general assembly provided the participating presbyteries are large enough to support one. The organization is essentially an expansion of member presbytery duties and a liaison between them and the general assembly. *See also* Cadaver Synod, the; elder(s); general assembly; Presbyterians; presbytery; session; Roman Catholic Church; Synod of Dort; Synod of Whitby.

Synod of Dort: a Protestant conference held in Holland in 1618. The delegates debated its hottest topic—the controversy between Arminianism and traditional Calvinism. The latter seemed to be more favored by the attendees. *See also* Arminianism; Calvinism; Canons of Dort; conditional election; election; eternal security; fall from grace; free will; "once saved, always saved"; perseverance of the saints; predestination; Protestantism, Protestants; Remonstrants; *Remonstrants,* the; synod; total depravity; TULIP.

Synod of Whitby: a synod held in 664 A.D. at the double monastery of Hilda of Whitby in Northumbria of England, later named Whitby Abbey. At the time, the celebration of Easter and the various monastery rules followed both Rome and the Celtic isle of Iona practices. King Oswiu of Northumbria finally ruled that Roman Catholic procedures would take precedent giving some rise in prestige to Catholic rites and influence in early England. *See also* Celtic folklore and religion; synod; Roman Catholic Church.

synoptic: having a similar viewpoint. The first three Gospels of the New Testament are called synoptic because they are capable of being "viewed together." *See also* Gospel(s); harmony of the Gospels.

synoptic Gospels. See Gospel(s).

legomena; haplography; hermeneutic(s); higher criticism; homographs; homonyms; homophones; *homoteleuton;* hyperbole; idiom; *inclusio;* interpolation; interpretation; inverted nun; irony; isagogics; *itture sopherim;* jot and tittle; kere; *kethib;* "L"; liberalists interpretation; literal interpretation; litotes; loan words; lower criticism; "M"; Masoretic Text; minuscule(s); mystery of God; omission; onomastica; onomatopoeia; palimpsest; papyrus; paradigm; parallelism; parchment; *paroimia; paronomasia;* pericope; personification; Peshitta; poetry (biblical); pointing; point of view; polyglot; principles of interpretation; proof texting; pun(s); "Q"; redaction; revelation, theological; rhetorical criticism; rhetorical devices; riddle; satire; *scripto continua;* scriptorium; *sebirin;* simile; similitude; source criticism; sources, primary and secondary; special points; strophe; superscription; symbol(s); synecdoche; syntax; text; textual criticism; *tiggune sopherim;* Time Texts; Torah; translation; transposition; trope; type(s); typology; uncial(s); vellum; verbicide.

Syntyche: one of two women (the other being Euodia) who were involved in some sort of disagreement in the church at Philippi (Phil. 4:2). Paul wrote to urge their reconciliation with the help of Syzygus. *See also* Euodia; Syzygus.

Syria: 1. the land area of the Middle East that today makes up the region of the same name. Now, as in ancient history, the capital of the country is Damascus. Ancient Syria was an implacable enemy of Israel during and after the monarchy under the Seleucids of the Maccabean era. 2. the region south of Cappadocia on the extreme eastern edge of the Roman Empire around A.D. 300. It, along with Armenia and Cappadocia, made up the main regions of the early Christian church in the East. Antioch of Syria was a major center of evangelism and learning. Syrian Christianity was notable for several innovations in worship and theology. The believers there were pioneers in creating hymns and chants; a second century compilation known as the "Odes of Solomon" was popular. They were also first to feature Mary, the mother of Jesus, as a virgin. Furthermore, they seemed to view the Holy Spirit as female. *See also* al-Assad, Bashar; Alawis; Antioch of Syria; Amram, Arameans; Aretas IV, King; Armenia; Bardesanes; Bedouins; Canneh; Cappadocia; Coptic Church; Damascenes, city of the; Damascus; Demetrius the Syrian; Druze; Eber; Ebla;

Ephraem the Syrian; Hadad; Hadadezer; Hadrach; Hamath; Hazael; Helbon; Horites; Jacobites; Marka; Maronite Church; Naaman; Nimrud; Nusra Front; Patronius; Qetesh; Quirinius; Rezin; Rezon; School of Antioch; Seleucia, Seleucids; Seleucus I Nicator; Seleucus II Callinicus; Seleucus IV Philopater; Serene; Syria and Samaria; Syriac; Syrian Orthodox Church; Syria-Palestine; Syro-Ephramitic War; Tatian; Theodoret; Varus.

Syria and Samaria: the two kingdoms referred to by Isaiah (Isa. 7:14, 16) that were troublesome to Judah. Before the Messiah (Jesus) reached his *Bar Mitzvah,* the prophecy said that these two nations would be abolished. Syria was conquered and divided by the Romans and Parthians in 60–20 B.C., and Samaria was absorbed into the Roman Empire in 6 A.D., four years before Jesus' presentation in the Temple. *See also* Samaria; Syria.

Syriac: the language of ancient Syria, akin to Aramaic. There originally existed a simple alphabetic script for its literature called Estrangela. *See also* Aramaic; Estrangela; Peshitta; Syria, Syrian Orthodox Church.

Syrian Orthodox Church: the Jacobites, with a tradition of being founded in India by the apostle Thomas. The Jacobite name is taken from a Syrian Orthodox organizer of the sixth century, Jacob Baradaeus. The faithful are also called the "Syrian Orthodox Church of Antioch and the All the East" with most congregations located in India, Syria, and Iraq. The church was disbarred by the stronger Roman Catholic contingency in the fifth century because they were monophites. Accepted scriptures include the standard canon of Roman Catholicism plus the *Letter of Baruch. See also* abba; Council of Chalcedon; Eastern Orthodox Church; Ephraem the Syrian; Jacobites; *Mar;* Melkite; Monophysitism; patriarch(s); Severus Sebokht; Syria; Syriac.

Syria-Palestine: a derogatory name for Judea applied by the Romans during their long occupation of the land of Palestine. *See also* Aelia Capitolina; Judea; Palestine; Philistia, Philistines; Roman Empire; Syria.

Syro-Ephramitic War: the conflict between Pekah of Israel and Rezin of Syria that quickly involved Judah as well. One of Hosea's oracles may have predicted that rebellion, which lasted from approximately 743 to 734 B.C. *See also* Holy War; Syria; Israel.

Syrophoenician woman: a Canaanite woman who approached Jesus during his visit to the region of Tyre and Sidon (Mt. 15:21–28). She begged for the Lord's help because her daughter was demon-possessed. The disciples urged Jesus to send her away because she was a foreigner, a request the Lord seemed to have temporarily acceded. The woman's intellect and faith were evident, however, so Jesus commended her faith and healed her child. Her intellect and humility were evident to that end in that she reminded those present that even the "dogs" (foreigners) were allowed to eat scraps from the master's table. *See also* dog(s); woman (women); woman of Canaan.

systematic theology: the study of theology in an orderly or "systematic" manner. The process is valuable for understanding prophecy or any other hermeneutic concept. The method can be accommodated by comparing Scripture with Scripture. The system is particularly helpful in the study of prophecy because one biblical paradigm often illuminates another if the subject matter is related. Some more liberal commentators decry the practice and call it "proof texting" or some other epithet. Comparative religion, a related discipline, critiques the form and process of faiths other than the student's choice of denomination. Both studies are considered to be important issues and are taught in most seminaries and Bible colleges. Several subjects are traditionally treated as worthy of systematic study: 1. Bibliology– study of the Bible, 2. Theology– study of the nature of God and His actions, 3. Christology– study of the Christ, 4. Pneumatology– study of the Holy Spirit, 5. Angelology– study of angels, both glorious and fallen, 6. Anthropology– study of mankind and our environment, 7. Soteriology– study of salvation, 8. Ecclesiology– study of the Church, 9. Eschatology– study of the end time. If theological study can be properly systematized, its content can be comprehended far more readily. *See also* didactic theology; proof texting; religious education.

Syzygus: an elder or other leader in Philippi whom Paul called his "loyal yokefellow." The apostle desired him to intervene in the dispute then being experienced between Euodia and Syntyche in an attempt at reconciliation of those two women (Phil. 4:3). *See also* Euodia; Mani; Syntyche; yoke.

T

"tabernacle (dwelling) of God is among men, the": the phrase in Revelation 21:3 promising that the fellowship of Christ will be personal and eternal in heaven.

Tabernacle of Testimony: an alternate name for the ark of the covenant, sometimes not capitalized on the word "testimony." In Revelation 15:5, however, it appears in its heavenly prototype with little distinction made between the Temple there and the ark of the covenant within. *See also* ark of the covenant; heavenly temple, the; tabernacle, the.

Tabernacles, Feast of: in Hebrew, *Sukkot* (the Hebrew word for "booths"), the third of the Jewish pilgrimage feasts, also called the "Feast of Ingathering." The festival commemorated the autumn harvests, and, as part of the significant ritual for the celebrants, the people lived in temporary brush arbor structures outdoors for seven (eight in the land of Israel itself), followed by an eighth day of holy thanksgiving. The day's observance has eschatological significance in that it is to be celebrated in the Millennium, along with the basic Sabbath observance (Isa. 66:22–13; Zech. 14:16–19). Part of the present-day celebration involves the "Four Species," or the *Lulov.* On the day, each man in Israel was to present a tall palm branch surrounded by willow on one side and myrtle on the other (Lev. 23:40). These were bound together and held in the right hand with an etrog (yellow citron) in the left. The former represented the Messiah and the latter, held upside down (blossom end on top), was the Israelite lost in the world. When the fruit was held upright, the symbology saw a reunification or a marriage to make the world complete in the four species of creation. The Three Stars rule obligated the family's temporary tabernacle to have a hole in the roof large enough to see three stars (Gen. 1:14). At least one meal was to be taken in the shelter *(Ushpizin),* with an extra place setting for any grand Hebrew ancestor who might visit. The House of the Water Pouring *(Biet HaShoevah)* was performed each day of *Sukkot.* At that time, the priests left the Temple to cut willow branches about twenty-five feet long, and process back with them whistling in the air to sound like wind. They would then meet with fellow priests who had been to the Pool of Siloam carrying a golden vessel with living water. They could then begin the traditional tabernacle rituals at the altar. So many people attended the festival that all the priests were on duty the entire week. The officiants were divided into three groups: the first was responsible for slaying the sacrifices; the second, headed by the high priest, brought water in a golden vessel from the Pool of Siloam; the third group exited the Beautiful Gate to the Motzah Valley to cut willow strips twenty-five to thirty feet in length. The water was poured on the altar and the willow branches were waved in a parade of celebration. The last day was called "the Great Day" *(Hoshana Rabbah)* teaching of the great Messianic kingdom to come. It was likely the time when Jesus stood to cry out to those who thirst to come and drink of him (Jn. 7:37–39). It is generally assumed, with good evidence, that the Feast of Tabernacles will be the premier worship occasion of the millennial kingdom. Zechariah says God will send a plague on any who dare not gather and celebrate the annual observance at that time (Zech. 14:17-18). *See also* feasts and special days of Judaism; Firstfruits; Four Species, the; fruit; Ingathering, Feast of; Judaism; millennial sacramentalism; Millennium, millennial; myrtle; New Moon(s); palm; Pentecost; *Shabu'ot; Shemini Atzeret;* tree(s); willow.

tabernacle, the: the tent structure designed by God and erected under the leadership of Moses to house the ark of the covenant and other holy furniture. Its full dimensions were 75 feet x 150 feet with the entrance to the east. The encampment surrounded the structure in a prescribed order. Worship and sacrifice were performed inside and in its courtyard by the high priest Aaron and his designated sons, assisted by the Levites. The structure saw service on the high places at Gibeon, Shiloh, the plain of Gilgal, and Jerusalem. Later, the movable structure was superseded by the more permanent Temple. Common wisdom has long understood that both the tabernacle and Temple hold significant messianic and eschatological symbolism for both Jews and Christians. Possibly, the so-called tent of meeting became an alternative name for the tabernacle after the latter was constructed and consecrated. It is also probable that the tent of meeting served before construction of the tabernacle according to the specifics of God. What was the purpose and prominence of the tabernacle/Temple construct to both the Hebrews and Christians? Practically, of course, both provided a place for worship ritual and the focus of God's method of meeting with His people and residing with them. The Creator, naturally, does not need an enclosure of any sort to dwell in but we humans find a synagogue or church building to be convenient if not necessary for public devotion, fellowship, and learning. More importantly, however, the tabernacle and Temple serve as tangible signs of how God relates to us, His people. Even the paraphernalia and equipment in use serve such a holy purpose. What, then, were the contents of the first tent and the first stone structures and what function did they serve? Let us walk into the tabernacle from its eastern entrance and explore the items there. First, in the courtyard, stood the bronze altar of sacrifice. No one could approach the divine presence until sin was dealt with in some prescribed manner, and that process was through the sacrifice of innocent animals (Lev. 17:11). Sacrifices and their scripted enactment varied according to the purpose envisioned but were necessary for the human-divine connection to even commence. The altar was 7 1/2 feet long and just as wide but only 4 1/2 feet in height and made of bronze so the meat could be roasted or consumed. To Christians, Jesus is our perfect offering (Jn. 1:29) and our own bodies can house our lives as living sacrifices (Rom. 12:1). The next step brings us to the bronze laver (called the Great Sea in the Temple), set aside for the priests for washing their hands and feet before ministering before the Lord. Cleansing was necessary so they could enter the Holy Place without suffering immediate death. Believers need cleansing also because sin, though forgiven in Christ, ever smears us daily with its vileness (1 Jn. 1:8–9). Next, we encounter the golden lampstand just inside the Holy Place, one of three holy objects there. The lamp was on the south side to give light to the interior and was fueled by oil, not wax. The stand was of a single piece of beaten gold with seven branches—three on each side of the stem and one atop (now called a Menorah). Jesus called himself the light of the world (Jn. 12:46) and we, ourselves, are urged to be lights of faith in the world (Acts 13:47). To the north sat the table of showbread, an ornate table 3 feet in length x 1 ½ in width x 2 ¼ in height. On it rested twelve loaves of unleavened bread (the bread of the presence), one for each of the tribes. The display represented the provisions of God for the people and a reminder of the unbreakable covenant with them. Jesus called himself the bread of life (Jn. 6:35, 51) and promotes the blessing that we today enjoy a better (new) covenant through him (Heb. 8:6–7; 10:16); and bread is one element of the Communion ritual. Fifth, just before the veil hiding the Holy of Holies, was the altar of incense. The structure was 1 ½ foot long, 1 ½ wide, and 3 feet high. Sweet incense, a special recipe, burned continually assuring all that the prayers of God's people are heard. Incense always represents the faithful prayers rising as illustrated in Revelation 5:8 and 8:3–4. Now we face the barrier of the holy veil measuring at least fifteen feet in width. It shields the Holy of Holies where the high priest could enter but once per year on the Day of Atonement. The covering was heavy cloth, exquisitely woven, but with no central entrance cut; entry was through the side. It was the item split from top to bottom at the moment of Jesus' death of the cross to show the separation was forever gone. For centuries, the Israelites depended on their high priest to intercede for them but now our perfect high priest is in Christ himself (1 Tim. 2:5; Heb. 8:1; 9:11; 10:11-12). Inside the Holy of Holies, representing God's presence, rested the ark of the covenant and the mercy seat (3 ¾ feet long, 2 ¼ feet wide, and 2 ½ feet tall). Atop of the mercy seat (the covering or lid) were two Cherubim with wingtips touching, waiting to receive the drops of blood offered by the high priest to atone for all the sins of the people. Inside were three items: the stone tablets of the Ten Commandments given to Moses, Aaron's rod that budded, and a sample of manna. Not only was the ark Israel's greatest talisman, but it was also a powerful symbol of the nation and even a deadly weapon of war. (Christianity, in contrast, is not a religion in which we approach God but how He finds us in love (Jn. 6:44; Eph. 2:8–9).) All the religious paraphernalia were portable, including the tabernacle itself, which was erected and maintained by the Levites wherever they encamped. *See also* Aaron's rod that budded; altar; altar of sacrifice; altar of incense; "approach the holy altar"; ark of the covenant; Atonement, Day of; Bread of the Presence; Communion; covenant(s), biblical; Eucharist; furniture and furnishings of the tabernacle, temples, and modern synagogue; Great Sea, the; Holy of Holies; incense;

lamp, lampstand(s); Levite(s); manna; Menorah; mercy seat; Most Holy Place (One); New Covenant, the; prayer(s); priest(s); sacrifice; sign(s); Tabernacle of Testimony, Temple(s); Temple utensils; Ten Commandments, the; tent(s); tent of meeting; veil(s).

Tabitha: a woman of noble character raised from the dead by Peter (Acts 9:36–43), thus relating another resurrection miracle. She was also called Dorcas. Tabitha is a Hebrew and Aramaic name meaning "doe," as is true for the Greek rendition of Dorcas. *See also* Joppa.

Table of the Nations: the recorded dispositions and migrations of the peoples of the world after the great flood. The table is reproduced in Genesis 9 and 10, then selects certain heads or chieftains for follow-up discussion in later chapters. Modern ethnologists have some difficulty in applying the various persons and places to modern geography. The table is important to eschatological study because of its record of origins and identification of the nations. *See also* nations, the; seventy nations; seventy shepherds.

Table of Destinies: an unknown device, or more than one, that alien settlement advocates name as the power source of the visiting Anunnaki spacemen. The power station was said to be housed in the great Mission Control Center at Nippur, humming with instrumentation and exuding a blue light. The table was said to be essential to their survival and productivity on earth. *See also* Anunnaki; *Chariots of the Gods?;* cities of the gods; demi-god(s); Enki and Enlil; *Enuma Elish; Epic of Gilgamesh, The";* Igigi; lulu; Mesopotamia; Nibiru; panspermia theory; Sumerian and Babylonian pantheon; Sumerian Tablets; Sumer, Sumerian(s); "Tablets of Faith"; Tiamat.

Tablet of Destinies: mythological symbols used by the Babylonians in enacting their important Babylonian New Year ritual. As such, they decided the fate of individuals and possibly nations. Supposedly, whoever controlled the Tablet controlled the world. In *Jubilees* and *The Testaments of the Twelve Patriarchs,* the Tablets seem to have morphed into the Jewish version of the heavenly tablets of God. *See also Jubilees, Book of;* Sumerian and Babylonian pantheon; *Testament of the Twelve Patriarchs.*

Tablet of Nineveh: ancient Sumerian text (dated prior to 1100 B.C.) dealing with the interaction between the Sumerian gods and the peoples of Nippur, Sippar, and Babylon. *See also* Assyria, Assyrians; Enmeduranki; Nineveh, Ninevites; Sumerian and Babylonian pantheon; Sumer, Sumerian(s).

"Tablets of Faith": a Babylonian myth linked to the epic of that culture and the drama enacted before their gods annually at the important New Year's pageant. *See also* Sumerian and Babylonian pantheon; Table of Destinies.

taboo: or tabu, that which is forbidden, especially in religious practice but also in recognized cultural mores. The word taboo is of Tongan origin; it is one of the few English terms incorporated from Polynesian languages. *See also* apotropaic magic; ban(s); cantrip; charm(s); curse(s); enchantment; evil eye; execration; *geis;* hex; imprecation; magic, magick; *mana;* mores; New Age religion; occult, occultic; *pharmakeia;* pow-wow; psychonautics; sorcery, sorceries; spell; spell names; Voodoo; Voudou; ward; warlock(s); Wicca; witch(es); witchcraft; wizard(s).

Taborites: an apocalyptic sect of the 1400s–1500s organized in reaction to Roman Catholic Church persecutions of those the ecclesiastical hierarchy determined to be heretics. The Taborites developed themselves as a protest movement in dissent for the execution of Jan Hus, a popular reformer who favored the translation of the Bible into English accomplished earlier by John Wycliffe. The Taborites established communal communities, even populating a mountaintop near Prague that they named Mount Tabor. This Bohemian sect was convinced that Christ would return, cleanse the world of sinners, and set up the millennial kingdom. The dissenters fought pitched battles against the Roman Church, led by their blind general named Ziska, often against great odds. They were annihilated in 1434. *See also* Hus, Jon; Hussites; Mount Tabor; White Mountain, battle of; communal communities; Ultraquists; Ziska.

Tabor light: the Eastern Orthodox view (as presented by Gregory Palamas) that describes the divine light experienced by Jesus at his transfiguration and the brilliance of that surrounding Paul at his conversion on the road to Damascus. Obviously, Palamas has taken the name from the mountain of transfiguration. *See also* Eastern Orthodox Church; illumination; light; liturgical year; Lux; Mount Tabor; Noor, noor; Palamism; Paul's conversion; primal light; Shekinah glory; Transfiguration, the.

tabot: "Holy Ark"—a name for altars or Communion tables in Ethiopian Christian churches that are said to contain the ark of the covenant, or a replica of it. The original ark is said to reside in Aksum at the Church of Saint Mary of Zion. *See also* ark of the covenant; Axum; Ethiopian Church; *Kebra Nagast;* Menelik, Prince; Queen of Sheba.

tabu. See taboo.

Tacitus: a notable Roman historian who produced a more or less accurate historical account of the Roman Empire in the first century. He was not favorably disposed to Christians, however, calling them "enemies of the human race" and labeling their God an ass' head. He was brought to task by Tertullian. Tacitus was a contemporary of Josephus who also wrote a history of the Jews. Most scholars consider that work inferior to the account of Josephus because Tacitus's rendering of the origin of the Jews is decidedly biased even though his writing on the Jewish War seems to follow Josephus's version carefully. *See also* Roman Empire.

Tafurs: the innumerable masses of camp followers and poor of the land who trailed the Crusader armies to the Holy Land. They were described as dirty, ill-clothed in sackcloth, covered in open sores and filth, and living on roots and grass—sometimes even roasting the corpses of their enemies for food. They left a trail of destruction wherever they ventured. Since none could afford swords, they used sharpened sticks, clubs, shovels, hatchets, and whatever weapons they could fashion themselves. The Crusaders made no effort to control them (to do so would have been both dangerous and futile), and the Muslims were terrified of them. *See also* Crusades.

***Taheb*:** the Samaritan name for their Messiah. *See also* Messiah; names (titles) for Jesus; Samaritan(s).

Tahpanhes: also Tehaphanehes, a city in Egypt to which the Jewish refugees—carrying a reluctant Jeremiah—of the Babylonian invasion fled (Jer. 43:8–13). The prophet took stones with him from Jerusalem and buried them in the pavement before

Pharaoh's palace in Tahpanhes. He intended to confirm the prediction that Nebuchadnezzar would invade Egypt as he had Judah and set up his throne on that very spot. *See also* Egypt, Egyptians; Jeremiah.

tail of the dragon: the phrase in Revelation 12:4 that describes an enormous red dragon with seven heads and ten horns and with seven crowns on its heads. The giant tail of the beast sweeps a third of the stars out of the sky and flings them to earth. The narrative drama represents Satan recruiting his army of fallen angels and their forced descent to earth where they are now in a position to wreak havoc on the vulnerable people of Tribulation earth, especially the Jews. *See also* dragon; eschatology, eschatological; red dragon; Satan; serpent.

Taiowa: the Hopi name for God. *See also* Hopi; names (titles) for God.

Taj Mahal: a magnificent ivory-white mausoleum on the banks of the Yamuna River near the city of Agra, India. The construction, being a sacred tomb, makes it a religious structure since it was planned and dedicated by the Mughal Emperor Shah Johan (1628–1658) as a memorial to his favorite wife Mumtaz Mahal. She died giving birth to their fourteenth child and the tomb expresses the husband's love and grief. The site is considered holy to some, including some New Age enthusiasts. Contrary to what many understand, the Taj Mahal is not a Hindu site but an Islamic one expressing Muslim architecture and reverence for the dead. *See also* burial; Islam; New Age religion; temple(s).

talent: a frequent designation in Scripture to a unit of money or precious metals. In New Testament times (as in the parable of the talents found in Matthew 25:14–29), a talent was worth about a thousand dollars. Today, we use the word to illustrate an aptness for a given artistic or craft skill. *See also* denarius; gold, golden; kondrantes; lepta; mammon; parable(s); parables of the New Testament; shekel; silver.

Tales of the Patriarchs: a pseudepigraphal writing also known as the *Genesis Apocryphon. See also Genesis Apocryphon.*

Taliban: militant and fundamentalist Muslims formed in the 1960s in Afghanistan. The term means "students of religion" because the Muslim Youth Movement at that time rallied against Zionism,

American politics, and class differences. Over time they became increasingly linked to Osama bin Laden and his al-Qaeda network. Inside Afghanistan, the group sought to establish literal Islam based on the *Qur'an* and Shari'a law and to rid the country of all Shi'ite Muslims. They managed to virtually destroy the country and rendered life there, particularly for women, to a primitive level. The various groups in-country are highly tribal in loyalty but do manage to function together as terrorists or Jihadists. The United States and allied military intervention may have reversed this trend somewhat for the present. *See also Alluha Akbar;* al-Qaeda; al-Shabab; anti-Semitic; Boko Haram; Daesh; Hamas; Hezbollah; Islam; Islamic State in Iraq and Syria (ISIS or ISIL); *jihad;* Mujahedeen; Muslim Brotherhood; Nusra Front; Palestinian Islamic Jihad (PIJ); Palestinian Liberation Organization (PLO); radicalized; Salafi; terrorism; terrorist(s); Turkistan Islamic Party; Velayat Sinai.

talisman(s): small objects said to have magical powers or supernatural qualities to protect or prosper the owner. Such items were disfavored in Hebrew law. *See also* ankh; amulet(s); apotropaic magic; Celtic wheel; charm(s); crucifix; gris-gris; juju; magic, magick; Medusa; serpent's egg; teraphim; "thunderstones"; wanga.

"*Talitha koum!*": an exclamation from Jesus, speaking Aramaic, as he revived the dead child of Jairus. The interpretation results as: "Little girl, get up!" or words to that effect (Mk. 5:41). *See also* Aramaic.

tallit: or *tallis,* a garment of green and white stripes edged with fringes used as a prayer shawl to remind the wearer of the Commandments and of God's presence. Orthodox men are the primary users but some women of the Conservative and Reformed groups wear them as well. There are two styles—a long one for ceremonial use and a shorter one for everyday wear. *Tzitzit* cords may be attached. *See also* Judaism; *tefillin; tzitzit; yarmulke.*

Talmud: the body of Jewish civil and sacral law consisting partly of the Mishna and the Gemara, which are Aramaic commentaries associated with it. The Palestinian Talmud was finished about the fourth century A.D. and the Babylonian version around the fifth or sixth. The latter is considered more authoritative. With its more than 6,000 pages, it is generally more widely used by students of Judaism. Among the many prophetic pronouncements in the Talmud is a list of 613 commandments, many of which concern the building of the future Temple in Jerusalem. Many see an end of the world prediction in the Talmud in the year 2239. *See also* Gemara; Halakha; Judaism; Masseket Hekalot; Midrash; Mishna; Targum(s).

Talmudic Sages: a Jewish apocalyptic document that presents a bleak picture of the end time dispersion of the Jews undergoing intense anti-Semitism. Accordingly, one of the sages wrote: "Let him [the Messiah] come, but let me not see him." *See also* Jew(s); Judaism.

Tamar: 1. the wife of Judah's sons Er and Onan (Gen. 38:1–10). She tricked her father-in-law into a sexual liaison when he refused his third son to her in marriage (Gen. 38:11–30) in defiance of the law of the kinsman-redeemer. 2. a daughter of David who was raped by her brother Amnon (2 Sam. 13). Amnon was later killed in revenge by Absalom. *See also* Judah; kinsman-redeemer; Onan.

tamarisk tree: an evergreen native to Eurasia and Africa; also called the salt cedar because it can survive in saline soil. The growth is found in over fifty species with slender branches, dull green leaves, and smooth bark in its youth. Some of the more literal-minded Bible scholars suspect that the tree's sap was a source for the Israelite's supply of manna in the wilderness. *See also* flora, fruit, and grain, symbology of; manna; tree(s).

tambourine: a simple hand-held percussion instrument sometimes sporting bells or small cymbals around the outside of its round drumhead. Women often used it to supplement their dancing, and it was a necessary musical implement for worship for Jewish worship (Ps. 150:4). *See also* musical instrument(s).

Tammuz: a god of the Babylonians, Syrians (as *Dumuzi*), and other cultures said to be the husband or consort of Ishtar (Ashtoreth). In other regions he was Adonis. One of Ezekiel's visions (Ezk. 8:14–15) shows some women of Jerusalem weeping for Tammuz, one of the causes for God's abandonment of the Temple. Some historians claim that Tammuz is the divinity corresponding to the later Adonis of Rome, where the name was a title more than a personal identifier. The cult origin of Tammuz probably dates to the time of Nimrod in Shinar, where he is presented as the offspring of Nimrod and Semiramis. When he died, his lover Inanna determined to descend into the Great Below for a rescue. Under the pretext of arranging funeral rites for her brother-in-law (the Great Bull of Heaven recently slain by Gilgamesh and Enkidu), she made the attempt, leaving instructions behind for her retrieval in case of problems. At each of the seven levels of the depths, she was required to remove one layer of her clothing until she arrived in shame before the queen of the underworld, Eriskegal. The queen killed her and hung her corpse from a hook in the wall. Her servant Ninshubar, as instructed, pleaded with the gods to save her. Only Enki agreed to try. He fashioned two sexless beings from dirt under the fingernails of the gods and gave them the food and drink necessary to sprinkle on Inanna's body. She was released then, but Eriskegal demanded a substitute. When Ianna returned, she discovered Tammuz reveling in her place without remorse. He became the substitute, of course, but his sister Geshtinanna was so devoted she insisted on taking half the time in the underworld for him—a plan actually instigated by Inanna. *See also* Adonis; Ashtoreth, Ashtoreth(s); Babel, tower of; Bull of Heaven; Enki and Enlil; Ereshkigal; Ezekiel's four visions of Israel's demise; Levant pantheon; Nimrod-bar-Cush; queen of heaven; "resurrection gods"; Semiramis; Sumerian and Babylonian pantheon; underworld.

Tanakh: the Jewish Bible. The name is derived from an acronym from the first letters of the names of its three major components— *Torah* (Law), *Nevi'im* (Prophets), and *Ketuvim* (Writings). The Tanakh is also the Christian Old Testament but arranged somewhat differently. *See also* Aggadah; Bible manuscripts; Book of the Covenant; Book of the Law; Gemara; Hagiographa; Halakha; Hebrew Bible; Judaism; Masseket Hekalot; Midrash; Old Testament; Talmud; Targum(s); Pentateuch; prophet(s); Prophets, the; Torah; Torah Scroll.

tantra: the Hindu position stating that the holy practices of the religion will lead to enlightenment. *See also* Hinduism.

Tantric Buddhism: or Vajrayana Buddhism, a combination of the Theravandan and Mahayanan traditions of that faith, all of which is permeated by a single power (*Shakti*) emanating from God. As it developed from the fifth century, the tantric arm consists of positive masculinity, positive femininity, and the union of both. It features a number of esoteric rituals, including the sexual act. *See also* Buddhism; Great Rite, the; *Kama Sutra*; Padmasambhava.

Tantalus: a character of Greek mythology (from which we devise our word *tantalize)* who committed an atrocity against the gods. His punishment in the underworld was to see food and drink just within reach, but snatched away when he grasped for them. Such ideas of eternal deprivation found their way into Christian theology regarding hell. *See also* Olympian pantheon.

Taoism: also Daoism, an Eastern religion or philosophy stressing the duality of the universe, a central theme of Taoism. Within its structure are two sets of opposing forces, called *yin* and *yang*— both of which are needed for harmony in the universe. The two principles seem contrary to each other yet are interdependent but complementary. *Yin* is the creative principle (femininity) with aspects of negativity, slowness, softness, diffusion, coldness, wetness, and passivity. It is associated with water, earth, the moon, and nighttime. *Yang* is the aggressive principle (masculinity), with aspects of quickness, solidity, focus, heat, and dryness. It is associated with fire, the sky, the sun, and the daytime. The concept of *yin* and *yang* is also a key element of Chinese philosophy in general. The *yin* and *yang* in the *I Ching* are represented by solid lines for *yin* and broken lines for *yang*. By way of interest, the largest collection of Taoist statues (numbering 4,643 in 2013) belongs to the Beigang Tien Temple in Taiwan. *See also* bagua; Daesun Jinrihoe; dialectic monism; *Feng Shui; I Ching*; Jade Empire, the; Pure Land, the; sect(s); *Tao Te Ching*.

Tao Te Ching: or *Dao De Jing*, the classic Chinese text of Taoism by the sixth century scholar Laozi (although both the date of composition and content are disputed). The writing has also influenced Buddhism and Confucianism and is one of the most heavily translated works of Eastern thought. *See also* Buddhism; Confucius, Confucianism; Taoism.

Tara Centers. See Crème, Benjamin.

Targum(s): oral and eventually written paraphrases or translations of the Old Testament. The plural is sometimes written as *Targumin*. Something like them was required when the Jews returned from the Babylonian Exile, with many of them no longer able to read Hebrew. Ezra and his scribes made the Scriptures known by reading and writing about them in the common language of Aramaic (Neh. 8:8). Two of the most authoritative appeared based on the official text and interpretation. The first was called the Oneqelos; the second was the Targum of Jonathan ben Uzziel. Others were extant both before and after the pair of official ones and remain as valuable translation aids for scholars of all stripes. *See also* Aquila; Bible translations; Gemara; Halakha; Judaism; Masseket Hekalot; Midrash; Mishna; Talmud; Targum Pseudo-Jonathan; torah; Written Torah and Oral Torah.

Targum Pseudo-Jonathan: a western version of the Torah, also known as Targum Jerusalem I. The text is not to be confused with Targum Jonathan; the Pseudo tag is appended because it was erroneously attributed to Jonathan ben Uzziel and resembles the Onkelos rendition. Pseudo-Jonathan is a mix of rabbinic and didactic material. One of its most unique features is the thought that God heals or saves with His right hand but kills with His left. *See also* Aquila; Judaism; Targum(s).

tarot: a method of fortune-telling using specially marked cards and by reading the patterned display and images. The earliest pack surfaced around A.D. 1445. *See also* augury; cartomancy; *Corpus Hermecticum;* divination; magic, magick; New Age religion; psychic(s); Sephiroth.

tarry: 1. a traditional Protestant term describing an attitude of prayerful anticipation or quiet acceptance until a given spiritual struggle is resolved in the heart of the believer. 2. another traditional expression defining the hesitancy of a penitent believer before fully converting to an acceptance of personal salvation. Complete acceptance or gradual rejection of the Holy Spirit's manipulations is possible until the issue resolves into the will of the candidate.

Tarshish: a city known for gold mining and export mentioned fairly frequently in the Bible. Suggestions have been advanced that Tarshish was located at Sardinia, Africa, or even Spain. Other scholars insist that the place is ancient Britain, but the lack of gold deposits there tends to cool the theory. Modern scholarship seems to favor the city of Tartessos in southwestern Spain as the ancient location. Identifying the city as being the site of ancient Atlantis seems to be taking on archeological favor, being located on the southern coast of Spain. Tarshish was the destination of the prophet Jonah in his desperate seaborne attempt to escape God's call to Nineveh. *See also* Atlantis; Gog and (of) Magog; gold of Uphaz; Jonah as prophet; lions, the young; Pul the nation; Tarshish stone.

Tarshish stone: an adornment of the angel in some translations of Daniel 10:5–6. What the item might be exactly is unknown but is possibly related in some fashion to the gold resource available for trade and commerce. One creditable suggestion is that the stone of Tarshish refers to a precious gem, likely a beryl, frequently occurring in a yellow or green hue. *See also* gold of Tarshish; gold of Uphaz; Pul the nation; Tarshish.

Tarsus: one of the oldest cities in the ancient world lying astride the Cydnus River in Cilicia about ten miles from the Mediterranean Sea and about 170 miles north of Jerusalem. It hosted a great university of learning that rivaled the one in Alexandria and was a successful trading port and capital city for the province of Cilicia. Paul was born in Tarsus and received his early education and Roman citizenship there (Acts 21:39) and it was the hometown of the learned Gamaliel, his teacher. The place has been named the oldest most continuously inhabited city in the world. It was situated on the edge of the Syrian desert and at various times controlled by the Greeks, Assyrians, Babylonians, Persians, Nabateans, and Armenians, and was particularly favored by the Romans of Paul's day. *See also* Straight Street.

Tartak: a false god worshiped by the Avvites and by those refugees returned to Samaria as part of the Assyrian resettlement campaign (2 Ki. 17:29–31). Worship of the idol, under the form of an ass, was somehow combined with the devotion to Yahweh by these repatriated Israelites. *See also* Levant pantheon; Sumerian and Babylonian pantheon.

Tartars: (Tatars) a diverse ethnic group known widely by the early church as inhabitants of Central Asia and Russia, but they were also found in Turkey, Poland, the Baltics, and elsewhere. As conquerors of the Byzantine East (1060–1307), the Tartars were generally tolerant of Christians but extracted tribute until they were overrun by the Ottoman Turks. As a people and an empire, the Tartars worshiped *Mongke Koko Tengre,* "The Eternal Blue Sky," who controlled good and evil. Powerful spirits were said to live in fire, wind, and running water. As a consequence, Tartar law (also applied to those conquered) forbade bathing in moving water. The word "Tartar" has always been synonymous with violence and uncivilized behavior. *See also* emir, emirate; khan.

Tartarus: the term used in 2 Peter 2:4 (an alternate reading in the New International Version) sometimes translated as "hell" but more technically referring to the "Abyss" since the author is speaking of the abode of fallen angels and the prediluvian giants. There the wicked angels are bound with chains awaiting eternal judgment. In Greek mythology, Tartarus was the chasm below Hades where Zeus and the Olympians hurled the Titans. The place is said to be surrounded by bronze walls and iron gates. The Greeks perceived Tartarus as the place where spirits, defeated gods, and monsters are tormented and situated it as far below earth as earth is below heaven. Some Christian concepts see Tartarus as the deepest and most vicious chamber of hell but there is no hint from Peter that Tartarus is a place of eternal punishment, at least for humankind. The Abyss of Revelation 9 may be, or even likely be, the same as Tartarus. *See also* Abyss, the; Bolos; fallen angel(s); giant(s); Hades; hell; lake of fire; Perdition; spirits in prison; Titians; underworld; wandering stars; Xibala.

Tasbeha: a Coptic collection of doxologies and praises. *See also* Coptic Church; Epsalmodia; hoos; liturgical year; music; "seven and four" ritual; theotekons.

Tatian: a second century disciple of Justin Martyr and a Christian apologist born c. 172. His most famous work is the *Diatessaron,* a harmony of the Gospels. The product was originally written in Greek, but Tatian translated it into Syriac. He also wrote an apology steeped in his disgust with paganism and its practices. The same Tatian deviated to heresy after the death of Justin Martyr and became a leader of the Encratite sect, an ascetic group in Syria. *See also Diatessaron;* Encratites; harmony of the Gospels; parallelism; Roman Catholic Church; sect(s).

Tattenai: the governor of Trans-Euphrates at the time of the return of the Jews to Judea (Ezr. 5:3) from the Babylonian Exile. He was a fierce opponent to the rebuilding effort but his obstructionist efforts were eventually thwarted.

taurobolium: the ritualistic process whereby initiates, particularly those of Attis worship and Mithraism, participated in the blood bath (tauroctony) from a slaughtered bull positioned overhead. *See also* Attis; Mithraism; tauroctony.

tauroctony: to be bathed in the blood and entrails of a bull, such as was practiced by worshipers of Attis and Mithra. The ritual of initiation was technically known as the *taurobolium*. *See also* Attis; Mithraism; *taurobolium*.

tautology: in the practice of rhetoric, using different words to say the same thing. Also, the term is a series of self-reinforcing statements that cannot be disproven because the declarations are assumed to be disambiguous from the first. In logic, tautology is a technical term for universal truth—facts that are always valid. The prophets, preachers, and teachers of the Bible often used both approaches to affirm their messages, assuming their hearers were believers, or potential believers, in God.

taxiarch: an Eastern Orthodox reference from the Greek word for "brigadier" or "brigade." The name refers to the archangels Gabriel and Michael. *See also* archangel(s); Eastern Orthodox Church; Gabriel; Michael.

Taxil, Leo: a pseudonym (one of many *noms de plume*) for a Frenchman named Marie Joseph Gabriel Antoine Jorgand-Poges (1854–1907). He was a hustler, pornographer, journalist, and hoaxer of international repute. Among his many schemes and cons, none is more infamous than his treatment of Freemasons, whom he accused of being devil worshipers and sexual deviates. He was himself a Mason but was expelled from the order for moral reasons before achieving meaningful rank. In retaliation, Taxil invented his own lodge ritual, which he called Palladism. The focus of his attacks was aimed at the Arkansas grandmaster and Masonic scholar Albert Pike. The religious and secular world was thoroughly duped by Taxil until his public exposure in 1897; he had successfully managed his campaign of deception for an amazing twelve years. In the end, he confessed the dupe himself to the embarrassment of the Masons and even the Catholic Church because he was patently aided in the scheme by the Jesuits. Even so, the action only fueled an already intense anti-Masonic epidemic that has hardly diminished among conspiracists. Taxil was sharply anti-Catholic and anti-cleric. *See also* conspiracy theorists; Freemasonry; Palladium; Society of Jesus.

tax collectors. See publicans.

Taylor, Charles: editor of the popular *Bible Prophecy News* who predicted the rapture in September of 1984. *See also* Baptists, Stewart, Rollen; televangelism, televangelists.

Taylor, Edward: Puritan minister (ca. 1645–1729) affectionately known as "Father Taylor." He is now recognized as America's finest poet from colonial times, though he saw none of his work in the public domain during his lifetime. Remarkably, he tried to ensure his heirs would never publish his poems. Taylor pastored in Westfield, Massachusetts, but his work was passed to descendants. His poems (in some 400 manuscripts) are sensual, mystical—a style he likely suspected would not have pleased his Puritan constituency. *God's Determinations Touching His Elect* is long and semi-dramatic. The collection was published in 1939 and the originals now rest with Yale University. *See also* Puritanism, Puritan(s).

Taylor, Edward Thompson: a Methodist missionary (1793–1871) and dynamic preacher to New England coastal towns and seamen. Taylor was unschooled but gifted with a galvanizing oratory. An orphan at infancy, he survived to sign on in the fleet as a cabin boy at age seven. Taylor was later captured by the British in the War of 1812, and most agree he was the model for Father Mapple's sermon in the novel *Moby Dick* by Herman Melville. He was praised by Ralph Waldo Emerson, Charles Dickens, and Walt Whitman. *See also* Methodists; missions, missionaries; revivalism.

Taylor, Graham: a Reformed Church in America minister (1851–1938). He was active in race relations and concerned with graduate education and social reform. *See also* Reformed Churches.

Taylor, Hudson: intrepid missionary to China (1832–1905). Taylor became disenchanted with his country's fractured Methodism back in England and set about to form what is likely the first truly indigenous church on foreign soil. He and his helpers set up the China Inland Mission to be entirely self-supporting and adaptive to native Chinese customs. *See also* Methodists; missions, missionaries.

Teacher of Righteousness: (Righteous Teacher), a term for an apocalyptic type—a virtuous and powerful leader central to the eschatological expectations of the Essene sects. Possibly the figure was the coming Messiah or one of their own number. Other terms for the same hero include Unique Teacher, Expounder of the Law, the Priest, or the Chosen One. *See also* Angel of Darkness; Angel of Light; Dead Sea Scrolls; Manual of Discipline; Qumran; Renewal, the; Sons of Darkness; Sons of Light; *War Against the Sons of Light and the Sons of Darkness;* War Scroll; Wicked Priest.

tear: to rend or rip, usually a garment. The ancient Hebrews were prone to shred their clothes in times of great distress or lamentation. *See also* gestures; rending of garments.

tear(s): natural saline drops from the eyes precipitated by intense emotion. The term is a frequent metaphor for the sorrow of loss, death, trouble, or repentance. One of the grand heavenly promises is that there will be no more tears in the eternal home of the believer (Rev. 21:4). If it seems anachronistic that tears should appear in heaven, we may assume God wipes away the tears brought on by the cursed earth and the past Millennium, and so preparing the believer for the eternal and griefless life of heaven. *See also* bread of affliction; bread of despair; thorn in the flesh; trial(s); vale of tears; water of affliction.

tears of Michael: tears wept by the archangel Michael (*Mikail* in Arabic), according to the *Qur'an*. In the story, each drop of sorrow for the sins of the faithful formed the Cherubim. Christians, of course, would reject the tale as pure fantasy. *See also* Cherub, Cherubim; Islam; Michael.

technical language: terminology that is peculiar and helpful to a given discipline of study, or "shop talk." Theology, like all fields of scholarly or scientific expertise, has its own technical language and works best when the definitions and procedures of biblical study remain standard and are utilized appropriately. *See also* theology.

Te Deum Laudamus: also known as the "Song of the Church" or the Ambrosian hymn. The phrase is taken from the principal words in Latin for a praise recitation spoken as: "Thee, O God, we praise." The devotion has long been a staple of worship for Roman Catholics, Anglicans, and some Lutheran congregations. *See also* liturgical year; liturgy, Christian; music.

teeth. See tooth (teeth).

"teetotaler": one who abstains from strong drink. Frequently, the same dissenter urges the same stance for everyone. *See also* abstinence; American Society for the Promotion of Temperance; Anthony, Susan Brownell; Anti-Saloon League; Beecher, Lyman; blue laws; Booth, Evangeline Cory; cardinal virtues; Christianese; Church of the Brethren; Dunkards; Hare Krishna; Higginson, Thomas Wentworth; intoxication; Seventh-Day Adventism; seven heavenly virtues; social issues; Stanton, Elizabeth Cady; suffragan; Sunday, Billy; Theobald, Matthew; virtue(s); Weld, Theodore; Willard, Francis; Woman's Christian Temperance Union.

tefillin: phylacteries worn by orthodox Jews, consisting of straps holding a small box with Torah portions inside. They are worn on the forehead and arm as a safeguard to faith in literal obedience to the injunction of Deuteronomy 6:8. *See also* Judaism; *tallit; tzitzit; yarmulke.*

Tehaphanehes. See Tahpanhes.

Tekoa: also Tekoah, the hometown of the prophet Amos. Amos was from the Southern Kingdom but did much of his preaching in the northern land of Israel. The place was also home to the so-called "wise woman of Tekoa" who acted as a ploy to King David after the loss of his son Absalom. *See also* Amos; wise woman, a.

telegnosis: supernatural or occult knowledge. *See also* anthropomancy; anthroposophy; apotropaic magic; aretology; Ariosophy; astrology, astral projection; astrologers; audition; augury; automatic writing; bagua; belomancy; bibliomancy; black arts; cartomancy; chaos magic; chiromancy; clairaudience; clairsentience; clairvoyance; cone of power; conjure; cryptesthesia; crystallomancy; curious acts; divination; dream(s); dreams and visions; enneagram; ecstasy; enchantment; esoteric sects; evil eye; extrasensory perception (ESP); foreknowledge; foretelling; geomancy, Gnosticism, Gnostic(s); Godwink; grimoire; hepatoscopy; Hermetic wisdom; Hermetic writings; hex; hierscopy; horoscope(s); hydromancy; Ifa; incantation; labyrinth walk; lecanomancy; literomancy; locution; magic arts; magic, magick; magic square; magnetism; *mana*; mantic wisdom; mantra; monition; miracle(s); necromancy; New Age religion; numbers, symbology of; occult, occultic; omen; oneiromancy; otherworldly journeys; ouija board; outof-body experiences (OBEs); paranormal; parapsychology; past life regression; peace pole(s); pentagram; philosopher's stone; planets as gods; portent; precognition; prediction; prefiguration; premonition; prodigy; prognostication; prophecy, general; psi; psychic healing; psychic reading; psychomancy; psychometry; psychonautics; pyramidology; rebirthing; reincarnation; remote viewing; revelation; rhabdomancy; scrying; séance; secret societies; secret wisdom; sorcery, sorceries; spell; spell names; spiritism; stigmata; supernatural; superstition; tarot; telepathy; telesthesia; theugry; third eye, the; thoughtform; totemism; vision(s); vision quest; visualizations; Voodoo; Voudou; witchcraft; *ya sang*; yoga; Zen; zodiac; *zos kia* cultus.

Telemachus: 1. a desert monk of the late fourth century credited with abolishing the gladiatorial circuses (as chronicled by Bishop Theodoret of Syria). On a visit to Rome, Telemachus became appalled at the bloodbath of animals and humans in the arena. He leapt into the combat zone in a bold attempt to stop two gladiators from killing each other. He cried out to end the violence but was either stoned to death by the crowd, stabbed by a contestant, or both. When Emperor Honorius learned of Telemachus' courageous act, he ordered an end to the brutal games. History says the final gladiatorial "entertainment" was January 1, 404 A.D. 2. a figure of Greek mythology, the son of Odysseus and Penelope, and a major character in Homer's *Odyssey*. The first four books of the epic center on Telemachus' search for his father who had not returned from the Trojan War. Eventually reunited,

Bernie L. Calaway

father and son returned to their land and rid the infestation of suitors in the palace trying to seduce Penelope and gain the throne. *See also* desert mystics; martyr(s); monasticism; monk(s); Olympian pantheon; Roman Catholic Church.

teleology: a term dealing with the philosophical study of design and purpose, especially of the world. The word is useful in discussing eschatology because it introduces the problem of final causes or of having an ultimate purpose. In Christianity, teleology centers on nature as being motivated by an omnipotent Cause, as well as a mechanical or natural process. *See also* Anaxagoras; dystelelogical theory; eschatology, eschatological; Five Ways, the; adjacent possible; Jumping Jesus Phenomenon, the; Law of Accelerating Returns, the; point of infinity; *Quinque Viae;* zero state.

telepathy: the ability to transmit information over distance from one person to another using only the power of the mind. The term has been in use since 1882 but more modern names have entered the research including "thought transference," or even "mind reading." The effort is surely pseudoscience and has never produced positive evidence of its existence except in certain New Age experiments. *See also* anthropomancy; anthroposophy; apotropaic magic; Ariosophy; astrology, astral projection; astrologers; audition; augury; automatic writing; bagua; belomancy; bibliomancy; black arts; cartomancy; chiromancy; clairaudience; clairsentience; clairvoyance; cone of power; conjure; cryptesthesia; crystallomancy; curious acts; divination; dream(s); dreams and visions; enchantment; enneagram; evil eye; extrasensory perception (ESP); geomancy, grimoire; hepatoscopy; Hermetic wisdom; hex; hierscopy; horoscope(s); hydromancy; incantation; labyrinth walk; lecanomancy; literomancy; locution; magic arts; magic, magick; magic square; magnetism; *mana*; mantic wisdom; mantra; monition; necromancy; New Age religion; numbers, symbology of; occult, occultic; oneiromancy; otherworldly journeys; ouija board; out-of-body experiences (OBEs); paranormal; parapsychology; peace pole(s); pentagram; portent; precognition; prediction; prefiguration; premonition; prodigy; prognostication; prophecy, general; psi; psychic healing; psychic reading; psychomancy; psychometry; psychonautics; pyramidology; remote viewing; revelation; rhabdomancy; séance; secret wisdom; scrying; sorcery, sorceries; spell; spell names;

spiritism; stigmata; superstition; tarot; telegnosis; telesthesia; theurgy; third eye, the; totemism; vision quest; visions; visualizations; Voodoo; Voudou; witchcraft; *ya sang*; yoga; Zen; *zos kia* cultus.

telescoping prophecy. See foreshortening prophecy.

telesthesia: sensation of perception received from a distance without the use of the recognized sense organs. *See also* anthropomancy; anthroposophy; apotropaic magic; Ariosophy; astral projection; astrology, astrologers; audition; augury; automatic writing; bagua; belomancy; bibliomancy; black arts; cartomancy; chiromancy; clairaudience; clairsentience; clairvoyance; cone of power; conjure; cryptesthesia; crystallomancy; curious acts; divination; dream(s); dreams and visions; enchantment; enneagram; evil eye; extrasensory perception (ESP); geomancy, grimoire; hepatoscopy; Hermetic wisdom; hex; hierscopy; horoscope(s); hydromancy; incantation; labyrinth walk; lecanomancy; literomancy; locution; magic arts; magic, magick; magic square; magnetism; *mana*; mantic wisdom; mantra; monition; necromancy; New Age religion; numbers, symbology of; occult, occultic; oneiromancy; otherworldly journeys; ouija board; out-of-body experiences (OBEs); paranormal; parapsychology; peace pole(s); pentagram; precognition; prediction; prefiguration; premonition; prodigy; prognostication; prophecy, general; psi; psychic healing; psychic reading; psychomancy; psychometry; psychonautics; pyramidology; remote viewing; revelation; rhabdomancy; scrying; séance; secret wisdom; sorcery, sorceries; spell; spell names; spiritism; stigmata; superstition; tarot; telegnosis; telepathy; theurgy; third eye, the; totemism; vision quest; visions; visualizations; Voodoo; Voudou; witchcraft; *ya sang*; yoga; Zen; *zos kia* cultus.

televangelism, televangelists: media savvy preachers who use the airways to ostensibly promote the gospel. Some are dedicated missionaries, certainly, but more are guilty of serious moral, ethical, and legal violations in the "Elmer Gantry" persona. Concerning the latter type of televangelists, almost all are criticized because 1. they are not structured denominationally so they are accountable to no authority, 2. they are fast and loose with sound accounting procedures, 3. many preach the "prosperity gospel" (but with most of the prosperity going to themselves), 4. they practice greed and flaunt ostentatious living, 5. they are aggressive and calculating fundraisers, 6. their miraculous and astonishing claims of success are not verified, 6. many are morally lax, including sexual liaisons, 7. many are involved with political intrigue to further either their standing or their peculiar broadcast stance. End time theology and the warnings of Jesus alert us to the certain explosion of such manipulation in the future closing phase of the earth. *See also* Bakker, Jim and Tammy; Camping, Harold; Christianese; dial-a-prayer; *Elmer Gantry;* eschatology, eschatological; evangelist(s); evangelism; "falling into sin"; Falwell, Jerry; Fuller, Charles E.; Graham, William Franklin (Billy); Hinn, Benny; Kuhlman, Kathryn; McPherson, Aimee Semple; prosperity religion(s); Roberts, Granville Oral; Robertson, Marion Gordon "Pat"; Sheen, Fulton J.; slurs, religious; Swaggart, Jimmy Lee; Taylor, Charles; Van Impe, Jack.

tell: or tel, a mound or heap of earth that may contain objects of archeological interest. Ancient cities were commonly built atop those destroyed or abandoned earlier, which are significant for identification and exploration by archeological digs. This process caused layers of civilization left in Earth's strata.

telos: a Greek philosophical word pertaining to an "end," "purpose," or "goal." In eschatological usage, we may apply *telos* to the inevitable working out of God's plan in an unswerving and unhindered manner. In 1 Thessalonians 2: 13–16, Paul spoke of the gospel as being advanced despite opposition, along with the sure recompense for those who oppose the goals of God. *See also* due time, in; eschatology, eschatological; *en takhei;* eschaton; *kainos; kairos; kronos;* things that must soon take place, the; "which must soon (shortly) take place."

teloumemoi: those undergoing mystery religious initiations passing through the degrees of the ritual, instructions, training, and the like. Aristotle spoke of them by advising that those involved should not be "learning" from the event so much as "suffering" or "experiencing" it.

Te Lucis: a hymn attributed to Ambrose of Milan in which God's help is invoked against nocturnal spirits. The full title reads *te Lucis ante termenum*—"to Thee before the close of day" and is traditionally sung at compline. One line reads: "May dreams and phantoms of the night go far away." Some of the music when sung resembles a lullaby. *See also* Ambrose; hymn(s); liturgical year; liturgy, Christian; music.

Teman: a site currently unknown in the territory of Edom; also known as Gebal. The inhabitants were renowned for their wisdom (Jer. 49:7). The prophet Habakkuk named it as the place (metaphorically) from which the Holy One has come (Hab. 3:3) in his wrath. *See also* Edom, Edomites; Gebal; Mount Paran.

temenos: a sacred grove commonly used as a pagan worship site. *See also* pagan, paganism.

temoorah: a method of Qabbalistic study whereby new meanings are produced by interchanging given letters or words of the text. A common method of such transposition was to substitute each letter of a chosen word that stands in equivalent order to another part of the Hebrew script. Yet another practice involved changing the words of a specific text into other words that resemble them in form or sound. *See also* Aqiba, Rabbi Joseph ben; Bible Code; Cheiro; *gematria;* Haggada; Halakha; *isopseplia;* Judaism; Masseket Hekalot; *notarikon;* Qabbala; *Sefirot;* Zevi, Shabbatai; *Zohar.*

temperance: abstinence from any form of alcohol, a state known informally as teetotalism. The virtue has sparked a strong political and social temperance movement in American history culminating in the passage of the Eighteenth Amendment banning the sale and transportation of liquor; the act was repealed later due to its unpopularity and enforcement difficulties. There were vast numbers of advocates of the temperance movement and multiple organizations to promote the issue nationwide but notable leaders included: Benjamin Rush, P. T. Barnum, Billy Sunday, Carry Nation, Amelia Bloomer, Susan B. Anthony, Elizabeth C. Stanton, Frances Willard, Daisy Douglas Barr, Wayne Wheeler, William H. Anderson, Ernest Cherrington, Andrew Volstead (for whom the prohibition legislation was named), William and Evangeline Booth, Lucy Webb Hayes, and many many others. The movement, as it developed, tended to be Protestant conservative church-led in many instances with a strong dose of anti-foreign, anti-Catholic, and anti-Semitic elements. Even the Klu Klux Klan joined the protest against the sale and consumption of alcohol. The Prohibition Party was the primary political faction driving the movement and it was often closely aligned with anti-slavery efforts before the Civil War and the women's struggle for the vote. Temperance is also be classed as a virtue absent of any alcoholic connotation if taken as an emotion of tolerance, mildness, and self-control. *See also* abstinence; American Society for the Promotion of Temperance; Anthony, Susan Brownell; Anti-Saloon League; Beecher, Lyman; blue laws; Booth, Evangeline Cory; cardinal virtues; Church of the Brethren; Dunkards; Hare Krishna; Higginson, Thomas Wentworth; intoxication; Seventh-Day Adventism; seven heavenly virtues; social issues; Stanton, Elizabeth Cady; suffragan; Sunday, Billy; "teetotaler"; Theobald, Matthew; virtue(s); Weld, Theodore; Willard, Francis; Woman's Christian Temperance Union.

Templar Knights of Saint Andrew. See knighted orders.

Temple(s): one of the three great historical centers of worship in Jerusalem replacing the tabernacle, or any prospective one, but with the same purposes of worship and sacrifice. Eschatological significance is always uppermost when considering the Temple, whether it is a relic of the past or a structure promised in the future. Revelation 15:5–8 describes a heavenly Temple from which the seven bowl angels emerge to begin their apocalyptic tasks on Tribulation earth. The passage, however, is not clear as to whether a heavenly Temple alone is indicated or if the ark inside is included in the depiction. There, the name applied is "the ark of Testimony." The heavenly Temple is important to Jewish eschatology because, with the creation of the Throne of Glory, it shows that God did not make the world once in time only to abandon it. No Temple of any description is found in the New Jerusalem, for God and the Lamb are its resident Temple (Rev. 21:22). The word may or may not be capitalized, depending on editorial preference. Those Jewish Temples named in history include those of Solomon, Zerubbabel, and Herod. (Most rabbis name Herod's Temple as the second, a reconstruction of Zerubbabel's, but renovations were so extensive it could rightly be called a new structure.) The first was built by Solomon from plans and materials collected by his father, David, and completed in about seven years, in about 960 B.C. It was, no doubt, the most magnificent structure of the ancient world; this grand edifice was destroyed by the Babylonians in 586 B.C. The replacement, called the Second or Zerubbabel's Temple, saw the foundations laid in 535 B.C. after the return of the Jews from the Babylon Exile; it was not completed until around 515 B.C. at the urging of Haggai and Zechariah because of hindering opposition by the resident Samaritans. Herod's Temple, which the Jews call their second since they consider it a remodeling of the postexilic building, was initiated in 18 or 19 B.C. and was still under minor construction at the time of Jesus; this one was destroyed by the Romans in A.D. 70. Much of our information about the Temple sources comes from Alexander Polyhistor, the Greek historian, in his writing *On the Jews,* and from Josephus. Each Temple erection and each destruction were carefully compassed with prophetic insight. Both the first (Solomon's) and the second (Zerubbabel's) were destroyed on the same day—the seventh of Ab. The last, to be constructed by permission of the Antichrist and that of the Millennium, is yet to come. *See also* Abijah as priestly division; ark of the covenant; ark of the Testimony; Court of the Gentiles; Court of the Israelites; Court of the Priests; Court of the Women; crushing rock that became a mountain; *Devir;* election; elect, the; Freemasonry; furniture and furnishings of the tabernacle, temples, and modern synagogue; gates of Jerusalem and the Temple; Hall of Hewn Stones; Heikhal; Herod's Temple; Holy of Holies; house of My glory; house of prayer; House of Yahweh; Jerusalem, siege of (literal); Jerusalem, siege of (pantomime); kingdom that cannot be shaken, a; kingdom, the; messianic age, the; middle (dividing) wall of partition; millennial geography; millennial Sabbath; millennial Temple; millennial worship; *Miqdash;* Most Holy Place (One); *naos;* New Covenant, the; New Eden; New Jerusalem; pillars of the Temple; rebuilding the Temple; religious organizations; remnant; rod of iron; Sabbath rest; shul; Solomon's prayer of dedication; Solomon's Temple; tabernacle, the; temple(s); Temple guards; Temple utensils; third Temple; times of refreshing; Tribulation Temple; *Ulam;* Zerubbabel's Temple.

temple(s): a place of worship, whether monotheistic, polytheistic, or pagan. The Revelation "temple" denotes a sanctuary or safe house for believers where they are eternally secure and welcome. When speaking metaphorically, a temple can be the housing for the spirit (*i.e.,* the believer's body). In John 2:19, 21, Jesus spoke of his temple/body which will rise again with him. Paul speaks of the human frame as the temple of the Holy Spirit (1 Cor. 3:16) and made the same analogy for the Church, the body of Christ (1 Cor. 12:27; 2 Cor. 6:16; Eph. 2:21–22). As such, the body as its temple constitutes the flesh, blood, and soul of the believer and can even refer to Christ's body or the Church universal. For Jews, a physical temple for worship is an important institution because (according to Exodus 25:8) God established a special place to call home on earth: "And have them make me a sanctuary, so that I may dwell among them." Notice that God did not say He was to dwell *in it* but *among them. See also* adytum; bethel; body; body of Christ, the; cathedral(s); cella; chantry; chapel; Church; church; cornerstone (capstone); fane; fold; furniture and furnishings of the tabernacle, temples, and modern synagogue; *Gobekli Tepe;* house of prayer; kirk; katholikon; mission; *naos;* religious organizations; sacellum; shrine(s); shul; Taj Mahal; Temple(s).

Temple guards: a corps of Levites or their assistants specifically trained to secure the Temple precincts. Their watch commander was called "captain of the Temple" (Acts 4:1) and was to supervise the 240 Levites (plus another twenty-four in the evenings) who patrolled the grounds, storehouses, and treasuries. They were also charged to keep the keys of the gates and various auxiliary buildings. The reference in Revelation 16:15 (an urgent appeal to be alert) can be more readily understood since an officer was prone to set afire the robes of those who malingered or slept on duty. A contingent of these sentries was no doubt present in the Garden of Gethsemane to arrest Jesus (Mk. 14:43–51), and one of their officers assisted in the detention of Peter and John for preaching the gospel (Acts 4:1). *See also* Temple(s).

Temple Institute: an unofficial but active association of orthodox rabbis and others whose aim is to plan the location and building of the new Temple in Jerusalem. *See also* cornerstone (capstone); Judaism; Menorah; religious organizations; Temple Mount and Land of Israel Faithful Movement.

Temple Mount: Mount Zion, a thirty-five or more acre complex in Jerusalem, the traditional site of the Jewish Temple in any of its manifestations. The place is now dominated by the Dome of the Rock and other Islamic shrines, but many Orthodox Jews look for the day when they can rebuild a third Temple on the prescribed spot. The area is today the most sacred, contentious, and prophetic real estate on planet earth and is likely to remain so until the Second Coming of Christ. *See also Haram esh-Sheif;* Jerusalem, landmarks of; Judaism; Mount Zion; Temple Mount and Land of Israel Faithful Movement.

Temple Mount and Land of Israel Faithful Movement: active associations of volunteer historians and artisans in Israel dedicated to securing rights and privileges to the Temple Mount for Jews and for recovering or duplicating worship items for the projected third Temple. The founder and director of the Land of Israel Faithful is Rabbi Gershom Solomon; he and his organization are pledged to the rebuilding efforts of the third Temple. Rabbi Israel Ariel directs the Temple Institute. The work there is dedicated to fabricating and storing Temple paraphernalia that will be needed in future construction as well as making preparations for the necessary priesthood. Their work includes finding a pure-bred red heifer, securing sacred vessels, weaving priestly garments, etc. Hope soared in 1996 when a bright red Holstein calf was born on a dairy farm in northern Israel; her name was Melody. Perhaps a suitable and unblemished red heifer could at last produce the ashes needed for a rededication sacrifice. Unfortunately, white spots developed later. Half-shekel coins of pure silver are also minted, suitable for the treasury of the new Temple. The sympathetic Jerusalem Temple Foundation, headquartered in Los Angeles, managed to raise some ten million dollars to fund the construction in Jerusalem. Supporters have indeed laid the cornerstone for the new Temple, either ceremonially or literally, and periodically parade it through the streets for public viewing. The work is carefully done to follow the pattern used as far back as the tabernacle days. Most in the group are convinced the Menorah and other Temple treasures are hidden in the Vatican; a belief that has prompted their leader to demand that the pope act for their immediate release. *See also* ashes of the red heifer; cornerstone (capstone); foundation of New Jerusalem; furniture and furnishings of the tabernacle, temples, and modern synagogue; Judaism; Menorah; Temple Institute; New Jerusalem; religious organizations; Temple Mount; Temple utensils.

Temple of Set. See Council of Nine.

Temple of the Psychedelic Light and the Church of the Realized Fantasy: an ominous cult led by Daniel Rahowitz said to practice Satanism, human sacrifice, and cannibalism. *See also* cult(s).

Temple Sermon: an exposition preached by Jeremiah (Jer. 7:1–15) based on events related in chapter 26 of the Jeremiah prophecy. His speech was rendered from the gateway to the Temple's Inner and Outer Courts, thus deriving its name. The tone of the discourse was a denunciation of Jehoiakim and the populace, coupled with an appeal to repentance. The admonition was rejected and the prophet was nearly executed for his preaching.

temples in Egypt. See City of Destruction; Elephantine; Heliopolis.

Temple utensils: small vessels or tools needed for ritual practice in the tabernacle and Temples of Judaism. There were many such articles, both practical and beautiful, all of which must be painstakingly reproduced if a third Temple is to be built in Jerusalem. The altar of incense alone, for example, needed a copper tray (*kaf*) to hold a silver chalice (*bazikh*) and a silver ring covered in cloth (*mitultelet*). A large quantity of tools and ritual objects were, and are, necessary—snuffers, tongs, cutlery, bindings, wick trimmers, cups, ewers, and dozens of related paraphernalia to name a few. *See also* furniture and furnishings of the tabernacle, temples, and modern synagogue; tabernacle, the; Temple Mount and Land of Israel Faithful Movement; Temple(s).

temptation: an unworthy allurement, usually toward some object, person, or action that is damaging to the self or others. Scripture reports the prime source for temptation is Satan (Mk. 1:13), and the Lord's Prayer (Mt. 6:13) specifically pleads for us to be free of it. *See also* Lord's Prayer; Satan; social issues.

temporal punishment: a Roman Catholic doctrine that specifies punishment for sin in this life or in purgatory. *See also* purgatory; Roman Catholic Church.

ten: the basic number, when used symbolically, that normally identifies human government. The figure may also, of course, name a precise count or even represent a large (but imprecise) counting. *See also* numbers, symbology of; ten days; ten horns; ten kings (kingdoms) of Revelation; ten-nation confederacy.

ten Boom, Corrie: a saintly Dutch woman (whose complete given name was Cornelia Arnold Johanna) watchmaker who authored the world-famous books *The Hiding Place, Tramp for the Lord,* and other classics (1892–1983). She and her family were Christians but dedicated their lives in World War II to rescuing persecuted Jews. Eventually, Corrie and her siblings were captured and sent away to Nazi concentration camps; only Corrie survived. *See also* missions, missionaries.

Ten Commandments, the: the Decalogue—the ten basic rules for moral living delivered to Moses from Mount Sinai on the front and back of stone tablets. Though they are a specific ten in number, we should regard them more as foundational principles rather than merely a short list of dos and don'ts. The Jews called them "the ten words." The Ten Commandments are the foundational laws for the prophets' moral teaching and indeed for all persons who desire to live an honorable and ethical life. The laws do not have the power to transform us nor can they liberate us from our addiction to sin. What they do is lay out the standards of good morality with an obligation to obedience and thereby illuminate our faults and failures. That, in itself, makes them invaluable. The Decalogue was the fundamental teaching for facilitating the prophets' mandate to "tell forth" (expound or broadcast) God's message and advertise His righteousness to the world. As listed in Exodus 20:1–17 and in a later form in Deuteronomy 5:6–21, the ten great rules for a moral and just society are: 1. Hold no other gods other than Yahweh. 2. Make no idols. 3. Respect God's name. 4. Honor the Sabbath. 5. Honor parents. 6. Do not murder. 7. Do not commit adultery. 8. Do not steal. 9. Do not lie. 10. Do not covet. In the Millennium, the basic laws of God will be enforced and not optional for all the inhabitants. The first five are said to deal with our relationship with God (a vertical approach); the second set deals with our relationships to each other (a lateral stream). There are also two systems of numbering, both totaling ten but divided differently. One method, favored by Roman Catholics and Lutherans and based on Augustine, names three commands of God on one tablet, then seven more for man. The prohibition against coveting is divided into people and property. The second, preferred by the Reformed churches and springing from Josephus, Jews, Origen, and Philo is older and divides the ten in an alternate way. The prohibition against having other gods and making idols are counted as two. This difference in numbering was especially important during the iconoclast disputes, for the reading could support either side depending on how they are collected. *See also* adultery, adulteries; antinomianism; blasphemy; Book of the Covenant; covet; deceit; ethics; forthtelling; Iconoclasts, War of the; lie(s); iniquity; injustice; Law, the; monotheism; moral relativism; Mosaic Law; murder; *opinio legis;* rod of iron; Sabbath; salvation; Seven Laws of Noah, the; sin(s); slander; social issues; "stews"; synteresis; tabernacle, the; theft; theonomy.

ten crowns: part of the description of the beast from the sea in Revelation 13:1–10. The monster has ten horns on seven heads, with ten coronets around the horns. The crowns represent ruling leaders and the heads are nations. Thus, three of the rulers must be a triumvirate ruling one of the kingdoms. All assist the beast (Antichrist) until they are defeated by the power of the Lamb (Jesus). The number 10 may be symbolic numerology for governmental perfection. *See also* Antichrist; beast from the sea; diadem; eschatology, eschatological; horn(s); numbers, symbology of; seven; seven-headed beast; ten; ten hills; ten kings (kingdoms) of Revelation.

ten days: the period designated for the church at Smyrna to endure persecution (Rev. 2:10). The length of moment intended is not ten literal days of twenty-four hours each; rather, the days are symbolic usage of numbers—a short but indefinite period of duration that will end when the desired effect has been achieved. *See also* numbers, symbology of; Smyrna; ten; ten days of awe.

ten days of awe: also, "the awesome days" or "ten days of repentance." In Judaism, the ten days of awe are those between Rosh Hashanah and Yom Kippur (*Yamim Noraim*), a time of introspection and repentance. In a more eschatological sense, some apocalypticists claim to see a ten-day hiatus in the book of Revelation following the sounding of the trumpets and continuing for some duration. This period will allow people to repent and accept the Messiah before their fate is forever sealed. However this interlude may be calculated, the results tend to be tenuous at best. Still another Jewish designation (not particularly popular) names the time from September 13, 1993 (when the "Jericho-Gaza First" concords were signed between Arabs and Israel) to the end of days. Most such computations, according to this countdown method, have not proven to be reliable. *See also* Days of Awe; feasts and special days of Judaism; ten days.

Tenebrae: a worship theme for Maundy Thursday, Good Friday, or Holy Saturday in Holy Week. During the ceremony, candles are extinguished as readings, prayers, psalms, etc., are recited. The name is explained, then, as "darkness" or "shadows." *See also* feasts and special days of high liturgy faiths; feasts and special days of Protestantism; Good Friday; Holy Saturday; Holy Week; liturgical year; liturgy, Christian; Maundy Thursday.

tenet: an opinion, principle, dogma, doctrine, or belief that is accepted as true. *See also* doctrine(s); dogma, dogmatism.

10/40 window, the: a phrase coined by a Christian missionary named Luis Bush in 1990. The idea refers to those regions of the eastern hemisphere between ten and forty degrees north of the Equator. There, it is purported, are held those populations of highest resistance to the gospel and the most difficult cultural challenge to the evangelistic world at large. The area includes Northern Africa and most of Asia, where about two-thirds of the world's people reside. The religions of the region are mostly Muslim, animists, Jewish, atheists, Hindu, and Buddhist. Most representative governments are legally or culturally opposed to Christianity and most Western influences or expressions. *See also* indigenous religion; missionary eschatology; missions, missionaries.

ten heads. See seven-headed beast.

ten horns: part of the description of the scarlet beast of Revelation 17. The monster described has seven heads with ten horns, thus necessitating the perception that three of the horns are on a single head. Horns represent kings or kingdoms, so in this instance, the ten horns are Tribulation rulers. They are evil governors because they make up parts of the evil dragon. The chapter further describes the ten as kings who have not yet received their authority, but they will eventually gain it for a short time at the discretion of the great beast (Satan). As a confederation, the ten will make war on the Lamb but will be defeated. The imagery seems to say that the Antichrist's Tribulation rule consists of ten confederates under his direction, all of whom are destined to be crushed. Some theologians see references to ancient Rome only, or purely symbolic language, in these descriptions. The ten horn illustration in Daniel 7 is probably best viewed as the ten Seleucid rulers, or aspiring rulers, before Antiochus IV Epiphanes, including three contenders who were bested by Antiochus. *See also* horn(s); king(s); numbers, symbology of; Roman Empire; ten; ten kings (kingdoms) of Revelation; ten-nation confederacy.

ten kings (kingdoms) of Revelation: a title in Revelation 17:12 representing ten future kings (or nations) that will assist the Antichrist in his Tribulation rule. They are said to be identical in apocalyptic definition to the ten horns noted in the same passage. Both the kings and the horns symbolize a powerful but brief governmental authority on Tribulation earth. Alternate views see only references to historical Rome, or else pure symbolism only, in these references. *See also* horn(s); king(s); numbers, symbology of; Roman Empire; ten horns; ten-nation confederacy.

ten lepers: the recitation of Jesus' encounter with ten lepers (Lk. 17:11–17). All were healed of their disease at their request. All were likewise ordered to report to the priests for certification of cleansing. The poignant moment of the incident is that only one of the ten returned to thank Jesus for his healing. This rudeness prompted Jesus to comment on the failure of favored people to render praise to God. In the eschatological future, praise to God will be spontaneous and cosmically inclusive. *See also* leprosy.

ten martyrs, legend of the: a story in the Jewish Mishna telling of the martyrdom of ten sages or rabbis during the reign of Hadrian. The emperor decided to randomly destroy ten Jews to correspond to the ten sons of Jacob who sold their youngest sibling Joseph into slavery in Egypt. The tale is much loved in Judaism and stresses the idea that each of the sacrificed men accepted his fate and was confident of his place in heaven. The story teaches that a good life is necessary to attain the positive afterlife but those yearning for it must also firmly *believe* in heaven. Perhaps a better explanation is that the only people in heaven will be those who hoped to see it. *See also* Judaism; martyr(s).

ten-nation confederacy: a collection of Tribulation rulers, actually under the authority of the Antichrist, who will assist him in his battle with the saints and the Lamb. Some theologians view the confederacy as representative of ancient Rome only or view them as merely symbolic. Others, however, have taken the description literally, even to the point of attempting to name the final confederacy. Both the United Nations and the Club of Rome have already divided the globe into ten sections, the latter saying it is the best way to approach a cashless society. One list names the ten as North America, Western Europe, Japan, Australia (including South Africa and the remainder of the market economy of the developed world), Eastern Europe (including Russia), Latin America, North Africa and the Middle East, Tropical Africa, South and Southeast Asia, and China. Another list cites Greece, Turkey, Syria, Egypt, and perhaps Saudi Arabia and Iraq. How these few are designated is never indicated. No prophetic theory has clearly demonstrated if the confederacy will be made exclusively of Muslims or if there will be a mix of Islam and Middle East countries. Theoretically, when the Antichrist assumes complete dominance, he will usurp three of the kingdoms similar to what happened in Daniel's vision (Dan. 7: 8). Some even name the three fallen kingdoms as North America, Eastern Europe, and the Middle East. *See also* Club of Rome; European Union, the; king(s); numbers, symbology of; Roman Empire; ten horns; ten kings (kingdoms) of Revelation.

Tennent, Gilbert: a Presbyterian Scotsman, apocalypticist, and participant of the New England Great Awakenings (1703–1764). His father, William, and three brothers, also ministers, were all active in the same pursuits. Tennent was known as a firebrand revivalist and compared other ministers not keen on Great Awakening evangelism to the Pharisees in the Gospels. He was associated with Theodorus Frelinghuysen, George Whitefield, and other apocalyptic leaders of the age. He was pastor of the First Presbyterian Church of New Brunswick from 1726 to 1743. Tennent's ardor for revivalism was somewhat "cooled" when he met Count Nikolaus Ludwig von Zinzendorf on one of his American mission trips with the Moravians. Zinzendorf somehow convinced him that his theology and revivalist methods were somewhat suspect. *See also* evangelists, evangelism; Great Awakenings, the; New Side, Old Side; Presbyterians; Restoration Movement in America; revivalism; Tennent, William; Zinzendorf, Count Nikolaus Ludwig von.

Tennent, William: Scottish clergyman and educator (1673–1764) born into the Church of Ireland but became Presbyterian in America. Tennent emigrated to the thirteen colonies in 1718 and started pastoring in Pennsylvania. There he established a rural school for poor aspiring clergy known simply as the "log college" which many consider the forerunner of Princeton University. He became active in the First Great Awakening and fostered a dynasty of Tennent Presbyterian evangelists, all of whom were vital to the American cause and national evangelistic reform. *See also* evangelist(s), evangelism; Great Awakenings, the; Presbyterians; Restoration Movement in America; revivalism; Tennent, Gilbert.

Tenrikyo: the teaching of Divine Wisdom (Tentiism), a form of Japanese Shinto. The movement was spawned by a peasant woman named Nakayama Miki—called Oyashma—(1798–1887) who began to receive visions from 1838 onward from the god Tenri O No Mikoto by whom she was possessed. Some Buddhism philosophy is mixed in. The sect claims about two million followers, making it one of the most successful Shinto-based sects in Japan. Doctrine centers on the promotion of the joyous life through ecstatic dance, charitable acts, and study of the oracles delivered by their revered founder and current leaders. Other Shinto-derived sects include Konkokyo, Omotokyo, Shinrikyo, Sekaishindokyo, Zenriko, the Mahikari movement, the Church of Perfect Liberty, Seicho-no-le, the Church of World Messianity, and many more. *See also* dance; sect(s); Shinto.

Tenskwautawa: a Shawnee shaman known to his contemporaries as "the Prophet" or "the Shawnee Prophet" (ca. 1770–1813). He was the brother of the famous Chief Tecumseh and claimed to have supernatural power over the whites after the Revolutionary War. This attribute was dispelled when the Shawnee were defeated by William Henry Harrison at the battle of Tippecanoe. Tecumseh was soon after killed in the War of 1812, and Tenskwautawa's influence faded to obscurity. *See also* shaman, shamanism; "zero years" prophecy, the.

tent(s): a portable and usually temporary shelter. Goat skins were a popular construction material used by most of the nomads of the day. Metaphorically, a tent denotes protection, shade in the heat, or a nomadic lifestyle in both practical living and worship (*e.g.,* Revelation 7:15). Destruction or damage to a tent was considered a misfortune, but to see one repaired or restored was a symbol of forgiveness and prosperity (*i.e.,* Amos 9:11). The tabernacle in the wilderness of the Exodus was an ornate and holy tent sanctuary. A "tent" can also represent the perishable and temporary human body (2 Cor. 5:4; 2 Pe. 1:13–14). The apostle Paul made his living as a tentmaker, as did Priscilla and Aquila. *See also* earthly tent, the; Ezekiel's Oholah and Oholibah allegory; peg; tabernacle, the; tent of meeting.

tent, earthly. See earthly tent.

Tenth Crusade, the: a modern-day rhetoric adopted by some to define the war on terrorism as a continuation of the Crusades. The phrase was first mentioned by political journalist Alexander Cockburn in 2002 as he tried to build an analogy to the U. S. led coalition against terrorism in the world. *See also* Crusades; terrorism; terrorist(s).

10,000 × 10,000: (thousands upon thousands), a reference in Revelation 5:11–12 indicating a number too large to calculate.

tent of meeting: also called the "tent of testimony," "tent of witness," and "dwelling of the testimony," a temporary meeting place erected by Moses during the Exodus from Egyptian slavery. The structure was 150' x 75' whereas the tabernacle was about 45' x 15' with two rooms. It is possible the latter could be fitted into the dimensions of the former. Its purpose seemed to have been to serve as a place for conference between God and Moses in order that revelations and instructions might be received and for Moses to inquire about matters for the people's welfare and mission. Also, it was the locale where judicial proceedings could be conducted. When God was present, the area was covered with the Shekinah glory. Joshua was in charge of its security and maintenance. Evidently, a corps of women attendants also served at the tent in some capacity. Later, the tent of meeting seems to have evolved into an alternate name for the tabernacle. *See also* Shekinah glory; tabernacle, the; tent(s).

TEOTWAWKI: the modern-day acronym for "the end of the world as we know it." *See also* apocalyptic, apocalypticism; end time world conditions; eschatology, eschatological.

Terah: the father of Abraham whose genealogy is recorded in Genesis 11. According to both Scripture and extra-biblical material, he was a worshiper (or even a manufacturer) of idols. Terah moved his family toward Canaan but stopped to settle in Haran shortly after Abraham (then called Abram) destroyed his father's icon statues and received God's call to a new location. *See also* Abraham; Haran.

teraphim: small portable household gods also known as "household deities." Such items were considered idolatrous as they were likely used for divination or talismans for luck and, in certain instances, could be recognized as living creatures to be feared. Rachel stole her father Laban's teraphim (Gen. 31:30–35), possibly to guarantee Jacob's estate after his death, but more likely because she had not totally abandoned her polytheistic beliefs. Josephus asserted she took the articles so that, in case her father should overtake and capture the escapees, she could mitigate his anger. This possibility is not reasonable since she hid the idols in her saddlebags and sat upon them on her camel, claiming she was menstruating and could not rise to be searched. The *Book of Jasher* records that there were *two* types of teraphim. The first involved decapitating the firstborn son, putting a magic copper or gold piece under the tongue with a secret word inscribed, and mummifying the head. When worshiped, the head was said to speak as a conduit between the living family and the departed ancestors. An Egyptian and Canaanite version involved interring an infant into the walls of family dwellings. The second type consisted of figurines of various materials with signs of the zodiac engraved. It was this design used by Laban. *Jasher* also says that when the death angel passed over Egypt in the last plague before the Exodus, he ripped out the bodies of the entombed children, as well as slaying the eldest living. The Babylonian version of creating teraphim burned the firstborn to Molech by placing the child in the idol's metal hands. Loud drumming masked the screams from parents and children. In a certain sense then, the great animated and speaking statue of the Antichrist to be erected in the Tribulation Temple could be described as a teraphim. *See* *also* amulet(s); ankh; attending spirit(s); banshee; beast, image of the; bogle; brownies; charm(s); clurichauns; daemons; demon(s), demonic; devils; disa; dryad(s); evil (unclean) spirits; fairy, fairies; familiar spirits; Furies; ghost(s); ghoul; gnome(s); Green Man, the; Gregori; gris-gris; hobgoblins; homunculus; household deities; huldafolk; gris-gris; juju; Lares; leprechaun(s); Loa Loas; magic, magick; Manes; Molech; nereid; nisse; nymph(s); nyx; Oniropompi; Orisha; Oya; para; paredri; Passover; "pass through the fire:; penates; Robin Goodfellow; satyr; Seelie Court, Unseelie Court; selkie; Sidhe; sirens; spirit guide(s); sprite(s); spiritual warfare; sylph(s); talisman(s); territorial spirits; Trickster; Tuatha de Danann; tutelary; undine; wanga; wight(s).

terce: prayers at nine in the evening according to the canonical hours. *See also* Agpeya; canonical hours; compline; lauds; liturgical year; liturgy; liturgy, Christian; matins; nones; novena; prayer(s); prime; sext; vespers.

Teresa of Avila: female mystic of the Carmelite order for women (1515–1582). Teresa reported she saw visions that either made her ecstatic with joy or enveloped her with periods of silence, making her wonder if God would ever speak again. In one visualization, which she called the "transverberation," she claimed a beautiful and fiery angel appeared to her in bodily form and plunged a golden spear into her heart several times. She described the pain as, oddly, "sweet." The artist Bernini's depiction of the incident, a sculpture called *The Ecstasy of St. Teresa,* may be the most famous statue of an angel ever produced. She managed to reform her order and write her biography entitled *Interior Castle.* Sister Teresa's career was remarkable in that she managed prominence despite the usual male objections to female leadership. The secret of her success, it has been said, is that she possessed "a gift for making men give her the orders she wanted to obey." She and John of the Cross were contemporaries and both were Carmelites. Teresa was eventually made co-saint of Spain with Santiago (the apostle James). *See also* Carmelites; desert mystics; James; John of the Cross; liturgical year; near-death experiences (NDEs); nun(s); pilgrimage; Roman Catholic Church.

Teresa of Calcutta: more affectionately known as "Mother Teresa" (August 26, 1910–September 5, 1997). Mother Teresa worked in India during her long life of service to the "poorest of the poor," including care for victims of HIV/AIDS, the dying, leprosy, tuberculosis, and others many would not touch. Teresa was a woman of intellect and possessed of a buoyant disposition who claimed to have periodic visions from heaven concerning her and her mission. She founded the Missionaries of Charity, now functioning in over 100 nations with the same purposes but including orphanages and schools. Teresa was born in Albania and became a Roman Catholic nun when of age. She has since become the modern-day model of selfless service and giving, even receiving the Nobel Peace Prize in 1979. *See also* nun(s); Roman Catholic Church.

termination dates: a derivation of scholarly thinking trumpeted by some theologians that claims to designate, as closely as possible, those historical dates critical to worldwide apocalypticism. That pattern might be reproduced as: 1. September 8, 70 A.D. (the fall of Jerusalem to the Romans), 2. May 14, 1948 (establishment of the nation as Israel—the "regathering"), 3. June 7, 1967 (the capture of Jerusalem and the Temple Mount by the Jews), 4. the rapture (future date unknown), 5. Second Coming (future date unknown). *See also* eschatology, eschatological.

territorial spirits: the belief by some that evil entities plague cities, towns, locales, or regions and they must be opposed and checked before evangelism can have full effect. Aboriginals and certain charismatic denominations are prone to claim the idea most closely. Something akin to the doctrine is discussed in Daniel 10:12–14. *See also* attending spirit(s); authorities; banshee; bogle; brownies; bugbears; clurichauns; daemons; deceiving spirit(s); demon(s), demonic; devils; disa; dryad(s); elemental(s); evil (unclean) spirits; fairy, fairies; familiar spirits; Furies; ghost(s); ghoul; gnome(s); Green Man, the; Gregori; hobgoblins; homunculus; household spirits; huldafolk; Lares; leprechaun(s); Loa Loas; Manes; mythological beasties, elementals, monsters, and spirit animals; nereid; nisse; numen; nymph(s); nyx; Oniropompi; Orisha; Oya; para; paredri; penates; Robin Goodfellow; satyr; Seelie Court, Unseelie Court; selkie; Sidhe; sirens; spirit guide(s); spiritual warfare; sprite(s); sylph(s); teraphim; territorial sprits; things taught by demons; Trickster; Tuatha de Danann; tutelary; undine; wight(s).

terrorism: or the war on terror. Terrorism, whether local (often labeled "domestic" terrorism) or sponsored internationally by organized groups worldwide (particularly Islamic militants), is a constant threat to individuals and nations that must suffer unprovoked attacks on the innocent and infrastructure as a tortuous expression of some religious or moral extremism. As seen in Islamic terrorism, it is the legal and the theological aspects of the faith that are at the heart of extremism since religion and politics are so closely combined in Islam. There are even observers who say Islam is really a violent political entity disguised as a religion. Some of the more publicized terror groups active today include: the Muslim Brotherhood, Islamic State in Iraq and Syria (ISIS or ISIL), Fatah (the former PLO), Islamic Jihad, Hezbollah, Hamas, Al Qaeda, Salafist Group, al-Aqsa, and the Martyrs Brigade. There are at least twenty radical Islamic groups in operation at the moment worldwide. Each may exhibit different ideologies and methods, but they all have one goal: to place the world under Islamic rule. Hezbollah and Islamic Jihad are Shi'ite sponsored and many terrorist groups are funded and promoted by Iran. Beyond the borders of Israel are some twenty-three Muslim nations with one hundred million in population also yearning for the destruction of the Jewish state and other democratic countries. The richest terrorist organization is the relatively new Islamic State in Iraq and Syria (ISIS or ISIL), with assets of some two billion dollars annually as reckoned around the year 2017. ISIS is followed in financial support by the Irish Republican Army (IRA), the Taliban, the Revolutionary Armed Forces of Colombia, *Lashkar e Taiba* or *Lashkar-e-Tayyiba* ("Army of the Righteous") in Pakistan, and Boko Haram in West Africa. Their unbelievable wealth is gained (especially foreign terrorism) by sympathetic donations, extortion, kidnapping, assassination, human trafficking, counterfeiting, and the illicit drug trade. Some view such acts of terror as symptomatic "birth pains" explained by Jesus and predicted for a time near the end of the age. Some theologians assert that the "wild animals" encountered in the book of Revelation are not animals at all but terrorists. Terrorism, in general, may be centered in the political (Shining Path guerrillas of Peru, Peoples Mujahedin of Iran), religious (numerous Islamic, Christian, Buddhist, Jewish, or Saffron [Asian] separatists), or independent (lone wolf) extremists (domestic and criminal violators). "Soft targets" such as schools and churches are often a favored point of attack. There are around 300 groups on most international terrorists watch lists at any given time. *See also* Abu Bakr; Ahmad, bin Abd Allah Muhammed; Ahmad, Mirza Ghulam; Ahmadinejad, Mahmoud; al-Baghadi, Abu Bakr; Aleph; *Alluha Akbar;* al-Qaeda; Ali ibn Abi Talib; al-Shabab; al-Zarqawi, Abu Musab; American Party; anti-Semitic; Arafat, Yasser; Aryan Nation; assassin(s); Atta, Mohammed ibn 'Abdallah; beast(s); Bhagwan Shree Rajneesh; bin Laden, Osama; birth pains, illustration of; Boko Haram; Branch Davidians; Brothers and Sisters of the Red Death; Brown, John; Christian Identity Movement (CIM); Columbine; Covenant, The Sword, and the Arm of the Lord, The (CSA); cult(s); Daesh; decapitation; Elijah Mohammed; eugenics; Family International; Fascist millennialism; Fatah; *Fedayeen;* Fenians; Final Solution; genocide; ghost dance cult; Hamas; *harem;* Hashshashin; "hate crimes"; Heaven's Gate; Hezbollah; Hitler, Adolf; Holocaust, holocaust; House of Yahweh; House of War; Husain; Hussein, Saddam; Inquisition, the; Intifada; Iranian military; Irish Republican Army (IRA); Islam; Islamic State in Iraq and Syria (ISIS or ISIL); Jewish persecution; *jihad;* Jones, Jim; Juhayman al-Otaibi; Khlysty, the; *Khojas;* Khomeini, Grand Ayatollah Ruhollah Musavi; Knights of the Golden Circle; Knights of the White Camellia; Ku Klux Klan; madrassa(s); militant domestic organizations; Manson, Charles; Molly Maguires; Mohammed ibn 'Abdallah; Movement for the Restoration of the Ten Commandments of God; Muhammed Ibn Abdul Wahhab; Mujahidin; murder; Muslim Brotherhood; Neo-Nazi(s); Nusra Front; Palestinian Islamic Jihad (PIJ); Palestinian Liberation Organization (PLO); Patriot Movement, the; Peoples Temple; persecution(s); pogrom; Porajmos; *Quds* Day; radicalized; Rahman, Sheikh Oman; Red Shirts; Salafi; Scientology, Church of; Shi'ite Islam; *shoah;* Sicarii; social issues; Solar Temple; Stalin, Joseph; Taliban; Tenth Crusade, the; terrorist(s); Turkistan Islamic Party; Turner, Nat; Vesey, Denmark; Villa Baviera; Velayat Sinai; Wahhabism; Waqf; wild beasts (animals) of the earth; Zealots.

terrorist(s): those individuals and radicals within their organizations who do not hesitate to use indiscriminate bombings, small-arms fire, improvised explosive devices (IEDs), staged destruction, or deadly attacks of any description as weapons of terror. Their agendas may be personal, political, religious, or combinations of misguided motives but the innocent are always the victims of their destructive rampages. One recognized ranking list of the ten most dangerous foreign terrorist organizations is presented as (in ascending order): the Lord's Resistance Army (Uganda, Sudan, Congo, Central African Republic), Forcas Armadas Revolutionaries de Colombia (Columbia), Tehrik-i-Taliban Pakistan (Pakistan), Lashkar-e-Tayyiba (India, Pakistan), Al-Shabab (Somalia, Kenya, Uganda), Hezbollah (Lebanon), Boko Haran (West Africa, Syria), Taliban (Afghanistan), Al-Qaeda (worldwide), and the Islamic State of Iraq and the Levant/Syria (Iraq, Syria). *See also* al-Baghadi, Abu Bakr; Ahmad, bin Abd Allah Muhammed; Ahmad, Mirza Ghulam; Ahmadinejad, Mahmoud; al-Baghadi, Abu Bakr; Aleph; *Alluha Akbar;* al-Qaeda; Ali ibn Abi Talib; al-Shabab; al-Zarqawi, Abu Musab; Ahmad, bin Abd Allah Muhammad; Ahmadinejad, Mahmoud; al-Assad, Bashar; American Party; anti-Semitic; Arafat, Yasser; Aryan Nation; Atta, Mohammed ibn 'Abdallah; beast(s); Bhagwan Shree Rajneesh; bin Laden, Osama; birth pains, illustration of; Boko Haram; Branch Davidians; Brothers and Sisters of the Red Death; Brown, John; Christian Identity Movement (CIM); Covenant, The Sword, and the Arm of the Lord, The (CSA); cult(s); Daesh; Elijah Mohammed; Family International; Fatah; Fenians; ghost dance cult; Hamas; *harem;* Hashshashin; "hate crimes"; Heaven's Gate; Hezbollah; Hitler, Adolf; House of Yahweh; House of War; Husain; Hussein, Saddam; Inquisition, the; Intifada; Iranian military; Irish Republican Army (IRA); Islam; Islamic State in Iraq and Syria (ISIS or ISIL); *jihad;* Jones, Jim; Juhayman al-Otaibi; Khlysty, the; Khomeini, Grand Ayatollah Ruhollah Musavi; Knights of the Golden Circle; Knights of the White Camellia; Ku Klux Klan; militant domestic organizations; Manson, Charles; Molly Maguires; Mohammed ibn 'Abdallah; Movement for the Restoration of the Ten Commandments of God; Muhammed Ibn Abdul Wahhab; Mujahidin; murder; Muslim Brotherhood; Mussolini, Benito; Neo-Nazi(s); Nusra Front; Palestinian Islamic Jihad (PIJ); Palestinian Liberation Organization (PLO); Patriot Movement, the; Peoples Temple; *Quds* Day; radicalized;

Rafsanjani, Akbar Hashemi; Rahman, Sheikh Oman; Red Shirts; Salafi; Scientology, Church of; social issues; Solar Temple; Stalin, Joseph; Taliban; Tenth Crusade, the; terrorism; Turkistan Islamic Party; Turner, Nat; Vesey, Denmark; Villa Baviera; Velayat Sinai; Wahhabism; wild beasts (animals) of the earth.

tertiary: a member of a confraternity of lay persons pledged to follow the same regulations as the friars. Such tertiaries are called the "third order" behind the Franciscan orders (the first in the 13th century) and the Poor Clares (the second order). *See also* confraternities; friar(s); monk(s); nun(s); orders; religious organizations.

Tertius: Paul's amanuensis who prepared the letter to the Romans for him. He appended a personal greeting for himself near the end of the epistle (Rom. 16:22).

Tertullian: famous North African apologist, moralist, philosopher, and theologian (ca. A.D. 160–220) who has been described by at least one reporter as a "bad-tempered but classy journalist." Tertullian was the son of a Roman army officer who converted to Christianity at age forty. He was zealous against Jews, pagans, heretics, and abusive administrators. He was an early advocate of the Trinitarian doctrine and the first genuine theologian to write in Latin. His doctrine supported the millennial approach to eschatology and asserted Ezekiel's and John's description of the thousand years' rule of Christ as literal. The tenet of traducianism can be traced to his thinking. He also supported the idea that God does indeed speak to His people in dreams and visions from time to time. Around the year 207, he surprisingly became an ardent adherent of Montanism. Tertullian's most famous works are probably his five books against the heretic Marcion, including a volume *Against Marcion* in which he discussed the Antichrist and other eschatological matters. Interestingly enough, he seemed inordinately afraid of the evils and terrorism of the spirit world. Tertullian is the reported source of the oft-quoted ecclesiastical saying: "The blood of the martyrs is the seed of the Church." In his later years, he became increasingly more ascetic and finally died, distanced from the very faith he had so strenuously advocated. Even then, he continued to battle heresy, especially Gnosticism. *See also* anti-anti-Semitic; "blood of the martyrs"; martyr(s); philosophy of religion; traducianism; Roman Catholic Church.

Tertullus: a Roman lawyer and orator employed by the Jews to head the prosecution trial of Paul before Governor Felix (Acts 24:1–2). *See also* Roman Empire.

testament(s): a covenant or treaty. Our Bible is composed of the Old and New Testaments, which are expanded covenants—one for Judaism and the other for the Church in their first intended readership. The explanation of Old and New Testament theology and history would be difficult or pointless without reference to the many covenants God has initiated with Judaism and the Church. Some people reject the terms "Old" and "New" when referencing the Scriptures as being too politically incorrect; they substitute "the Hebrew Scriptures," "the Christian Bible," or some other less pejorative identification. In more mundane terms, a testament is a farewell speech or legal document of an aged or dying person giving possessions, blessing, instruction, advice, and even future predictions. In apocalyptic testaments, the fictional author (as in *The Testament of Moses*) is giving a revelation, whereas, in an apocalypse, the fictional author is the receiver of a revelation. These revelations are often mediated by an angel guide. See *also* Bible manuscripts; covenant(s), biblical; covenant theology; New Testament; Old Testament; seven years covenant with Israel; spirit guide(s).

Testament of the Twelve Patriarchs: an apocryphal Christian rendition of the final words of Jacob to his sons (following the explanation in Genesis 49) but with more detail. *See also* Apocryphal Apocalypses; *Jubilees, Book of;* Tablet of Destinies.

Testimonium Flavianum: the scholarly title for at least one reference to Jesus within the works of Flavius Josephus. The historian's allusions to Jesus appear twice, in Books 18 and 20 of his *Antiquities of the Jews.* Whether the appearance of these notes is genuine or blatant interpolations is an issue of continuing debate. Academic discussions render no final judgment on their authenticity, or partial acceptance, but the larger consensus seems to discredit them. Speculation in some circles suggests that the great churchman, Eusebius himself, forged at least one of the commentaries. The fact that Josephus was a Jew with no love for Christianity seems to mitigate much of the fervor that the quotes are authentic. *See also* Caius; Eusebius; Josephus, Flavius.

testimony: 1. an oral or written presentation offered by one who wishes to offer evidence that her pronouncements are true and trustworthy. 2. an expression of one's faith publically, as in worship, often spoken extemporaneously. The rendition usually mentions the individual's conversion experience, a profession of faith, and any number of other personal observations that seem appropriate to the purpose. One's testimony can also be written but such a rendering somehow makes the revelations a bit more aloof. The exception may be encountered in 1 John 5:10-11 which gives a biblical testimony of faith that is both instructive and hopeful. Oral testimony was once a popular evangelistic tool and remains so in some religious venues. The manner of presentation, however, matters. The verbal witness can be dry and uninspired, delivered with bravado or subtlety, and directed toward self-aggrandizement. *See also* confession; confession(s) of faith; conviction; core beliefs; Credo; creed(s); evangelist(s), evangelism; fishers of men; liturgy, Christian; Christianese; lost; missional; soul-winning; spreading the gospel; spirit of prophecy; story; testimony of Jesus, the; "turn your life [heart] over to Jesus"; "washed in the blood"; witness(es).

testimony of Jesus, the: Christ's assurance that he and his ministry were God-ordained (Jn. 5:31-40). The Lord cites three impeccable sources for his assertion—the testimony of John the Baptist (which Jesus then labels as trustworthy but of human origin and thereby not unassailable), his own work (the ministry, miracles, etc.), God the Father, and the Scriptures. The list then comes to four sources of testimony so the first (re John the Baptist) is relegated to an ancillary position. *See also* Old Testament; spirit of prophecy; testimony.

test(ing): a check, assessment, or ordeal designed to verify some knowledge or skill. God sometimes chooses to test his servants as to faith and fortitude (Lk. 8:13; 1 Th. 2:4; Jas. 1:2–3). *See also* ordeal(s); rite of passage; tests of the prophet.

tests of the prophet. See prophet, tests of the.

Tethys: the Titaness daughter of Gaia and Uranus and wife of Oceanus. She was considered to be a marine deity but not venerated with a cult following. *See also* giant(s); Olympian pantheon.

Tetragrammaton. See Shemhamforesh.

tetramorph: an artistic rendition of the four evangelists as one figure. *See also* icon, iconography.

Tetrapolitan Confession: a Protestant confession of faith produced in the 16th century by Wolfgang Capito, Martin Bucer, and Caspar Hedio for the edification of four major cities in Germany. The articles were intended to aid the Diet in its deliberations about theology, but the offering was eventually rejected in favor of the Augsburg Confession. Nonetheless, the Tetrapolitan was useful, especially in its definition of the Lord's Supper and the discussions of the images controversy. *See also* Augsburg Confession; confession(s) of faith; Credo; creed(s); icon, iconography.

tetrarch: a Roman appointee who ruled over but a fourth portion of a kingdom or province, the divisions of which were called a tetrarchy. Eventually, the word was used loosely for any petty prince, or as a courtesy, one who was allowed to be titled a "king." The New Testament names three of these dignitaries: Herod Antipas (Galilee), Philip (Ituraea and Trachonitis), and Lysanias (Abilene). In one instance, Augustus gave half the kingdom of Herod the Great to Archelaus, whom he named an "ethnarch." The latter title may indicate that a bit more territory was governed than that of a tetrarch or that a tad more honor was due, although its true definition is somewhat imprecise. Josephus also used the term "ethnarch" for Simon Maccabee, the high priest and governor of Judea, so the term may not have been exclusive to the Romans. *See also* Herodian dynasty; king(s); Roman Empire.

Tetzel, Johann: a Dominican priest known as a successful seller of indulgences (1465–1519). These scripts, he preached, were effective donations to free loved ones from purgatory. He clashed often, and heatedly, with Martin Luther on many occasions. His sales pitch could be heard throughout the land: "When a coin in the coffer rings, a soul from purgatory springs." *See also* Dominicans; papal revenue; Roman Catholic Church.

Teutonic Knights. See knighted orders.

text: a selected Bible reading used to base a sermon or homily. In a broader sense, a text is a Scripture portion selected from among many to be read or studied. *See also* accideme; allegorical interpretation; alliteration; analogical interpretation; apostrophe;

apothegm; assonance; autograph; Bible; Bible manuscripts; Bible translations; biblical criticism; chiasmus; conflict story; *constructio ad sensum;* context; contextualization; dittography; double sense fulfillment; doublets; doubling; edification; eisegesis; epanadiplosis; epigrammatic statements; etymology; exegesis; figure of speech; folio; form criticism; Fourfold Interpretation; gattung; gloss; gnomic sayings; grammatical-historical interpretation; *hapax legomena;* haplography; hermeneutic(s); higher criticism; homily; homographs; homonyms; homophones; *homoteleuton;* hyperbole; idiom; illumination; *inclusio;* inspiration; interpolation; interpretation; inverted nun; irony; isagogics; *itture sopherim;* jot and tittle; kere; *kethib;* "L"; liberalists interpretation; literal interpretation; litotes; loan words; lower criticism; "M"; Masoretic Text; message; minuscule(s); mystery of God; omission; onomastica; onomatopoeia; palimpsest; papyrus; paradigm; parallelism; parallel passage; parchment; *paroimia; paronomasia;* pericope; personification; Peshitta; plenary inspiration; pointing; point of view; polyglot; principles of interpretation; proof texting; pun(s); "Q"; redaction; revelation, theological; rhetorical criticism; rhetorical devices; riddle; satire; *scripto continua;* scriptorium; *sebirin;* sermon; simile; similitude; source criticism; sources, primary and secondary; special points; strophe; superscription; symbol(s); synecdoche; syntax; synthetic parallelism; textual criticism; threefold sense of interpretation; *tiggune sopherim;* Torah; translation; transmission history; transposition; trope; type(s); typology; uncial(s); vellum; verbicide.

textual criticism: the science of determining as closely as possible what the original author wrote. The examiners are looking for solid history in the writing and reliable proof of authenticity. *See also* accideme; allegorical interpretation; alliteration; analogical interpretation; apostrophe; apothegm; assonance; autograph; Bible; Bible manuscripts; Bible translations; biblical criticism; chiasmus; conflict story; *constructio ad sensum;* context; contextualization; dittography; double sense fulfillment; doublets; doubling; dynamic equivalence; edification; eisegesis; epanadiplosis; epigrammatic statements; etymology; exegesis; figure of speech; folio; form criticism; Fourfold Interpretation; gattung; genre; gloss; gnomic sayings; grammatical-historical interpretation; *hapax legomena;* haplography; hermeneutic(s); higher criticism;

homographs; homonyms; homophones; *homoteleuton;* hyperbole; idealism; idiom; illumination; *inclusio;* inspiration; interpolation; interpretation; inverted nun; irony; isagogics; *itture sopherim;* jot and tittle; kere; Ketef Hinnom amulets; *kethib;* "L"; liberalists interpretation; literal interpretation; litotes; loan words; lower criticism; "M"; Masoretic Text; minimalism; minuscule(s); mystery of God; omission; onomastica; onomatopoeia; palimpsest; papyrus; paradigm; parallelism; parchment; Pardes; *paroimia; paronomasia;* pericope; personification; Peshitta; plenary inspiration; pointing; point of view; polyglot; principles of interpretation; proof texting; pun(s); "Q"; redaction; revelation, theological; rhetorical criticism; rhetorical devices; riddle; satire; *scripto continua;* scriptorium; *sebirin;* simile; similitude; source criticism; sources, primary and secondary; special points; strophe; superscription; symbol(s); synecdoche; syntax; synthetic parallelism; text; threefold sense of interpretation; *tiggune sopherim;* Time Texts; Torah; translation; transmission history; transposition; trope; type(s); typology; uncial(s); vellum; verbicide.

Textus Receptus. See Masoretic text.

TGAOTU. See Great Architect of the Universe, the.

Thaddaeus. See Judas.

thalassocracy: from a Greek combination of thalassic words for "sea" and "rule," referring to rule of the oceans or sea lanes. The term has theological significance only in that many of the ancient religions were centered on the seacoasts or maritime provinces controlled either by naval supremacy or marine commerce. There were many such empires, including ancient Phoenicia, Tyre, Sidon, Carthage, the Minoans, and the Delian League of Greece. Later times saw the rise of Venice, Alexandria, Genoa, Pisa, and the Srivijaya and Majapahit of Southeast Asia; then came the Portuguese, Dutch, Spanish, and English Empires. Many sultanates were also heavily engaged in the sea trade. Hardly any other human enterprise facilitated interaction and communication among the races, including the spread of the gospel and other faith notions.

Thales: reputedly the first extensive traveling Greek historian to return from Egypt endowed with substantial practical and esoteric lore of that ancient land, especially the art of geometry. Many Greek philosophers and their teachings developed from his experience and coaching in many educational disciplines. *See also* philosophy of religion; philosophy of the Greeks.

Thanatos: Greek god of the peaceful dead (those who died non-violently). To the Romans he was Mors, the personification of Death. *See also* attending spirit(s); banshee; bogle; brownies; bugbears; clurichauns; daemons; Death; deceiving spirits; demon(s), demonic; disa; dryad(s); elemental(s); fairy, fairies; Furies; ghost(s); ghoul; gnome(s); Green Man, the; Gregori; hobgoblins; homunculus; household deities; huldafolk; Keres; Lares; leprechaun(s); Loa Loas; Manes; mythological beasties, elementals, monsters, and spirit animals; nereid; nisse; Norse and Old Germanic pantheon; nymph(s); Olympian pantheon; Oniropompi; Orisha; Oya; para; paredri; penates; Robin Goodfellow; satyr; Seelie Court and Unseelie Court; selkie; Sidhe; sirens; spiritual warfare; sprite(s); sylph(s); teraphim; territorial spirits; Trickster; Tuatha de Danann; tutelary; undine; wight(s).

thanksgiving: an attitude of gratitude. Jews (strongly encouraged by the prophets) and Christians are constantly enjoined to be grateful to God for His beneficence (Ps. 100:4; Col. 3:15). Gratitude to others for received kindnesses is also appropriate and desirable. Insincere thanksgiving can be perverse (Amos 4:5), an attitude that is insulting to God. *See also* grace; liturgy, Christian; liturgy, Jewish.

thanksgiving psalm: an Old Testament psalm expressing thanks to God for received blessings or answered prayer. *See also* creation psalm; enthronement psalm; historical psalm; imprecatory psalm; messianic psalm; penitential psalm; psalm; psalm of judgment; psalm of lament; Psalms as Old Testament book; royal psalm; supplication psalm; wisdom psalm; worship psalm.

Tharbis: the first wife of Moses. According to Josephus, she was the daughter of the king of Ethiopia whom Moses defeated as Pharaoh's military leader against this Cushite's invasion of Egypt. Some believe Moses brought her with him when he led the Israelites to freedom in the Exodus. Most agree she was the object of Miriam's racist remarks against the "Cushite wife"(Num. 12) resulting in her punishment from God. Some authorities claim Tharbis and Zipporah (another wife, the daughter of Jethro) were the same person, but the idea seems incompatible with history and chronology. *See also* Cush, Cushites; Miriam; Moses; Zipporah.

that day: the time referenced by Jesus when he told his disciples of his return to heaven—a time when their prayers and his teachings would be directly and plainly spoken (Jn. 16:25–28). The words may also carry a more mundane or ordinary sense of time of something that will happen in the future. *See also* eschatology, eschatological; the day; judgment on the great Day, the.

"that number". See Meni.

Thaumaturgus, Gregory: a.k.a. Gregory of Neocaesarea, a Christian bishop of Asia Minor (c. 213–270 A.D.). The name means "wonder-worker." Gregory's fame, despite the unique title, does not derive from miracle making but as a church leader, pastor, and theologian. He was later canonized by both the Eastern Orthodox and Roman Catholic churches. He studied under the great Origen and participated in several church councils of the day. Part of his career included fleeing from persecution, epidemic among the population, and the demise of his congregation, which at his death had declined to less than twenty souls. Much of his written contributions are in disarray but his most famous work is probably *The Exposition of Faith.*

thaumaturgy: stage magic entertainment. The name applies even when the audience seems enraptured or under a sort of artistic spell due to the skills of the magician. *See also* abracadabra; Crowley, Aleister; hocus-pocus; Houdini, Harry; magic, magick; mumbo jumbo; Randi, James.

Thayendanegea. See Brant, Joseph.

theanthroposophy: the belief that Christ was truly a man. *See also* Adoptionism; Anomoeans; appropriation; Arianism; Arius; complementarian view of the Trinity; Donatism; dualism; Dynamic Monarchianism; dynamism; dyophysitism; eternal subordination of the Son; "four fences of Chalcedon"; *homoiousios; homoousios;* hypostatic union; incarnation; *kenosis;* kenotic view of Christ; monoenergism; miaphysitism; modalism; monarchianism; monophysitism; monoenergism;

Nestorianism; Nestorius; *ousia;* patripassianism; Pelagianism; *perichoresis;* psilanthropism; Sabellianism; Socianism, Socinian; subordinationism; *Theophorus*; Trinity; two natures, doctrine of the; unipersonality.

Thebes: undoubtedly the most important city of ancient Egypt, known in the Bible as No Amon. It contains the magnificent artifacts of the pharaohs at Luxor and Karnak. *See also* Egypt, Egyptians; No Amon.

Thecla: a female Christian convert from Iconium, according to the apocryphal *Acts of Paul and Thecla*, from about A.D. 180. Her presence and actions with the apostle may be legendary but she is described as an ardent missionary living a life of virginity and danger, having escaped martyrdom several times. She had heard Paul preach in her city and became a tireless supporter. The same text is the one that describes Paul's unimposing physical appearance—the only hint we have of how he may have looked. *See also* Paul as apostle.

the day: a (usually) prophetic stipulation that something important will happen on a given day. For example, the prophet Ezekiel referred to "the day" as the coming downfall of Jerusalem and the mass exoduses of the population from Judah to Babylon. The words may also have a more pointed apocalyptic thrust. *See also* eschatology, eschatological; that day; judgment of the great Day, the.

theft: the act of taking another's property by force or stealth, a violation of the Eighth Commandment. The Law of Moses (radically enforced by the prophets) and Christian ethics condemn the action thoroughly, especially when perpetrated against the poor and weak. *See also* social issues; Ten Commandments, the; thief, thieves; thief (thieves) on the cross, the.

theism: the belief in one God as Creator and Ruler of the universe, including a capacity for revelation to the human mind and spirit. Such a definition identifies something different from either atheism or deism. *See also* atheism, atheist(s); atheism, the new; deism; metaphysics; modernism; possibilianism; secularization.

Thelema: a philosophical law turned religion with the motto: "Do what thou wilt shall be the whole of the law. Law is the law, love under will." The sect developed around 1900 from the notorious English writer and magician Aleister Crowley, who called himself the prophet for the "Aeon of Horus." Crowley claimed that a sort of non-corporeal being called Aiwass dictated the text of *The Book of the Law* to him and his wife Rose Edith during a trip to Egypt in 1904. The Thelemites, as believers are called, honor many Egyptian gods, including those they name as Nuit, Hadit, and Ra-Hoon-Khuit. Crowley, of course, added his own stinging brand of occultism, mysticism, and the Qabbala. Sometimes the Thelemists are called "# 93" because that number is sacred to them. *See also Astrum Argentum;* Crowley, Aleister; cult(s); Damanhur; Egyptian pantheon.

The Lord is There: the final phrase of Ezekiel's prophetic description of the coming New Jerusalem. *See also* Ezekiel's vision of the new Temple and new land; Holy to the Lord; Jerusalem as city; millennial geography; Millennium, millennial; names (titles) for God; New Jerusalem.

theocracy: literally, the rule of God. The best example of a theocracy is the millennial kingdom. At that time, the Lord will rule supreme and governance will be exacted via enforced righteousness, thus making that era a government or society under the rule or law of God. In any definition of the term, however, every citizen has a personal and corporate responsibility for maintaining the prescribed religious and social order in a theocracy as the will and purpose of God are made known to the population. Many have attempted to create a humanity-based theocracy on earth with varying, but usually terminal, success. Nevertheless, teaching those obligations is the mandate of prophecy and divine law. The injunctions constitute an absolute standard of belief and conduct binding on the nation and the individual to live in a holy society. This is especially true of the Millennium. *See also* Beza, Theodore; communal communities; Geneva theocracy of John Calvin; Millennium, millennial; New Jerusalem; Protocratics; rod of iron; Sermon on the Mount, the; theocratic kingdom.

theocratic kingdom: the kingdom of God in its fullness. The Millennium will be ruled by Christ with an iron rod, thus making it the ultimate and only real theocratic kingdom with the possible exception of pre-Fallen Eden. *See also* communal communities; Geneva theocracy of John Calvin; Millennium, millennial; New Jerusalem; Protocratics; rod of iron; Sermon on the Mount, the; theocracy.

theodidact: a student of God; a person taught by God in special circumstances.

theodicy: a vindication of the divine attributes, especially those of holiness and justice, in contrast to the existence of evil in the world. Essentially, the word defines God's justice in His creation. Theodicies, in all their various expressions, are set to declare that God is not responsible for evil. If God is not omnipotent (Manichaeism or Zoroastrianism) or if He is not fully good but causes all forms of behavior (determinism and causality), or if He rejects the reality of evil (pantheism and Christian Science) He, as God, is not responsible for evil in the world. But neither is He necessarily the Cause of goodness.

Theodora: co-ruler of the Eastern Roman Empire as the wife of Justinian I (ca. 500–548). She was at the start a mere courtesan but later achieved great feats of humanity, especially on behalf of women. Undoubtedly, she was a woman of fortitude, beauty, and ambition. Her marriage to Justinian was solid despite their outward differences, and both shared a deep interest in religion. The two disagreed strongly, but agreeably, in their theology. Her husband was a staunch supporter of Chalcedonian Orthodoxy while she favored the Monophysites. Theodora managed to reinstate the use of icons in the East even though her husband had deeply opposed them. *See also* Eastern Orthodox Church; Iconoclasts, War of the; Justinian I; Monophysitism; queen(s).

Theodore of Mopsuestia: or Macedonius, influential figure in the Antiochian School (ca. A.D. 350–428). Though the training at Antioch supported the literal method of interpretation, he does not mention millennialism. Theodore's most helpful teaching was that Christ in his human nature was the second Adam, a theology akin to Paul's understanding of the same theme. As such, a belief arose that people could imitate the holiness of Christ. *See also* Eastern Orthodox Church.

Theodoret: scholar of the Antiochian School (A.D. 386–458) and bishop of Cyrus in Syria. He was a proponent of literal interpretation but does not discuss millennialism. *See also* Eastern Orthodox Church.

Theodoric the Great: king of the Ostrogoths (454-526). Theodoric was an Arian Christian who established a Gothic presence in the West by invading Italy. Ravenna was captured in 493, and subsequent Lombardic rulers began a long run of kingship in southern Italy for 774 years. *See also* Eastern Orthodox Church; king(s); Lombards.

Theodosius I: known as "the Great" (ca. A.D. 346–395). He was emperor of the Eastern Roman Empire who was called the "destroyer of paganism" because of his zeal to punish unbelievers for noncompliance to the Christian faith. He was a strict anti-Arian in theology and aggressively helped accelerate the denouncement of those who would not accept the Nicene Creed. Theodosius was converted later in mid-life but once committed he became the implacable enemy of anything smacking of paganism. He ordered the destruction of pagan property, propaganda, and any semblance of ancient god worship wherever it was within his reach or that of his zealous followers. His rule, as is true of most of the emperors of East and West in the empires, was at the same time strongly involved with Christian church affairs during that era. Nevertheless, Bishop Ambrose of Milan once refused his presence in worship until he apologized and recanted his wanton massacre of certain Thessalonicans in 390. The king complied, thus exhibiting the competing power of the church at that time. It was Theodosius who convened the Council of Constantinople in 381 that finally sounded the death knell of Arianism. *See also* Ambrose; Arian; Arianism; Eastern Orthodox Church; Gregory of Nazianzus; Iconoclasts, War of the; king(s); Serapeum.

Theodotion: author of a revised Septuagint in the second century that depended heavily on the Hebrew text. He was a Jewish proselyte from Ephesus. *See also* Bible translations; Greek Orthodox Church; Lucian; Symmachus.

theody: a hymn of praise to God. *See also* canticles; cathisma; hymn(s); hymnal; invitatory; liturgical year; liturgy; liturgy, Christian; liturgy, Jewish; music; praise; sacred music; sticheron.

theogamy: divine marriage. The image is of gods and goddesses becoming wedded in elaborate ceremonies. *See also* pagan, paganism.

theogony: a study of the origins or descent of the gods. *See also* apotheosis; avatar.

Bernie L. Calaway

theolepsy: the exuberant expression of one seized or overcome by the Spirit of God, or by a god. *See also* baptism of the Holy Spirit; charismatic movement; demon(s), demonic; demon possession; ecstasy; glossolalia; holy laughter; inspiration; "in the Spirit"; intoxication; numinous; Pentecostalism; psychopathology; *Pytho*; revivalism; "river, the"; "slain in the Spirit"; tongues, gift of; tongues, interpretation of; tremendum.

theologaster: a petty or shallow theologian not worthy of recognition as a teacher or spiritual leader.

Theologia Germanica: an anonymous mystical work held dear by nearly all individual mystics and organized mystical societies during the Protestant Reformation. Even Martin Luther praised it early on in his career. *See also* mysticism, mystics.

theologoumenon: debate with a faith commitment in place—not to dispute basic doctrine but to discuss the particulars of belief, perhaps drawing leads that may progress to further dialogue and learning. An example: we do not know the date of Christ's return—we only know the doctrine that pledges it—so any speculation or investigation of the matter is theologoumenon. Some name the discipline "presuppositional apologetics." A theologoumenon, then, is a theological opinion. Given a disagreement regarding mostly orthodox subjects, the debaters could concede that not all knowledge is possible but the matters can be explored reasonably. *See also a priori.*

theology: literally, the study of God. The word is formed from two Greek terms meaning "God" (*theos*) and "word" (*logos*). Various academic and spiritual disciplines are employed in order to examine and comprehend the nature of God and His works. The theological ideas explored in the book of Revelation, for example, include anthropology, harmartiology, angelology, ecclesiology, eschatology, and soteriology. The subjects attempt to harvest the knowledge of God from the most basic tenets to the most complex. How is God known? He is recognized in many ways, but it should be remembered that without intimacy between the inquirer and his or her faith, there can be no interaction or purpose. We find God in creation/nature (a real but limited revelation), through human experience (provided it is generally fortified by faith and interaction), and from wisdom (both intelligence and the arts) as typically expressed in the wisdom literature of Scripture. It must be acknowledged that true discernment of the Word of God is impossible without the illuminating power of the Holy Spirit. Diligent study, prayer, and a correct hermeneutical procedure are also important. Even so, the complete and thorough knowledge of God will never be known. God is one (monotheistic) and holy (radiating glory and love) but just as assuredly the epitome of holy mystery (inscrutability). *See also* accideme; Afro-American theology; allegorical interpretation; analytical interpretation; anthropology; apology, apologetics; Bible manuscripts; Bible translations; biblical criticism; Christianese; covenant theology; Death of God theology; dialectic theology; dialogical critical method; dispensational theology; doctrine; dogma, dogmatism; dominion theology; edification; eschatology, eschatological; exegesis; feminist theology; form criticism; God talk; grammatical-historical interpretation; hermeneutic(s); higher criticism; history of the church; idealism; illumination; inspiration; knowledge of God; *mujerista* theology; mystery; liberation theology; lower criticism; mystery of God; negative theology; neo-orthodoxy; open theism; orthodoxy; plenary inspiration; process theology; progressive revelation; proof texting; prophecy; physico-theology; plenary inspiration; replacement theology; revelation, theological; salvation; soteriology; source criticism; systematic theology; technical language; tenet; wisdom.

theomachist: one who strenuously resists God and His will.

theomatic number(s): certain numbers which are said to be discernible in Scripture as "theomatics," having special significance because they are capable of being divided into the sum values of words, phrases, or verses of the Bible with no remainder (within plus or minus two). The basis of the theory is the fact that Greek or Hebrew letters carry a numeric value. In both alphabets, the letter could even be used as a substitute for a number. As one example, the Greek name for "Jesus" has a numeric value of 888. When those values are collected from a given portion of Scripture and added together, they can then be divided by one of the theomatic numbers. The figure thirty-seven seems to be particularly momentous to the system's users. Judgment is needed to ascertain if theomatic numbers have real relevance to theology, but if they do, the theory could have a heavy impact on prophetic interpretation. *See also* alphanumeric code; apocalyptic calculation; Divine Proportion, the; 888; fingerprint of God, the; numbers, symbology of; thirty-seven; 616; 666; *Vesica Piscis.*

theonomy: a combination of Greek words meaning "God" and "law." Theonomists believe that the Mosaic Law should be operative in the world today and enforced with appropriate standards and penalties. In such a situation, the world will prepare itself properly for the arrival of Christ. In its extreme form, the death penalty is to be allowed, even mandatory, for such crimes as murder, kidnapping, homosexuality, rebellious children, false prophets, and other offenders as named in the Mosaic Code. *See also* dominion theology; Law, the; Mosaic Law; postmillennial, postmillennialism; Reconstructionism; replacement theology; seven mountains dogma; Ten Commandments, the; Whitby, Daniel.

theopaschitism: a doctrine from the sixth century that essentially states "one of the Trinity was crucified." The idea fell out of favor, not necessarily because it is false, but because it can be misleading.

theophagy: literally, eating the body of a god. Protestant churches usually practice such a Eucharist symbolically, but Roman Catholicism insists that the bread and wine of the ceremony are the "real presence" of Christ in which his flesh and blood are experienced in some mystical yet substantive way. Theophagy was likely the spark of revulsion from pagan Rome because they thought the early Christians were cannibals. *See also* capernaitic eating; concomitance; consubstantiation; Eucharist; Lord's Supper; means of grace; real presence; sacrament(s); transubstantiation.

theophany: 1. a method allowing God to show Himself to His people in a safe and more understandable manner. The term is formed from the Greek words *theos* (God) and *phainein* (to manifest) so the idea is a manifestation of God, sometimes called an "apparition." The Lord may choose to present Himself in human or symbolic form in such a way that the mortal is aware of the presence being demonstrated but can remain secure from the Shekinah righteousness of God that would otherwise slay him. God's appearance to Moses in the form of a burning bush is one example of theophany. Perhaps the most awesome theophany was experienced by the prophet Isaiah (Isa. 6) and others by Micaiah (1 Ki. 22:19–22), two by Ezekiel (Ezk. 1; 10), Stephen (Acts

7:54–60), and John of the Revelation, to mention some. Some scholars equate the appearance of angels (an angelophany) with a theophany but the two' phenomena are not exactly alike. The appearance of the Holy Spirit is called a *pheumatophany*. 2. the Eastern Orthodox term for the celebration of the baptism of Jesus. *See also* angelophany; anthropomorphism; apotheosis; apparition; avatar; Baptism of the (Our) Lord, Feast of; beatific vision; Christophany; *epiphaneia;* Eastern Orthodox Church; feasts and special days of high liturgy faiths; hieraphony; manifestation of the Spirit; pneumatology; revelation, theological; vision(s).

Theophilus: 1. a friend to Luke, otherwise unknown, to whom his Gospel and the book of Acts are addressed (Lk. 1:3; Acts 1:1). Possibly Theophilus was a patron of the disciple or an influential potential convert to Christianity. 2. a second century bishop of Antioch and a Christian apologist. He was the first person to use the technical word "triad" to define the mystery of the Father, Son, and Holy Spirit.

Theophorus. See Ignatius of Antioch.

theory of everything, the: the theoretical concept (TOE) that postulates that it may someday be possible to isolate a single hypothesis of quantum physics that will explain the complexities of particles of nature, general relativity, electromagnetism, and nuclear interactions. The conception also goes by the simplified term "the Final Theory" popularized by Mark Alpert's sci-fi novel by the same name. Religiously oriented persons, and perhaps many individual physicists as well, can readily intuit the theological implications of the TOE model although it is theoretically impossible to know everything, even in heaven. *See also* all-encompassing theory; creationism; evolution; God gene, the; God particle, the; transhumanism.

theosis: or divinization, the Christian principle stating that one can participate in the life of God without sharing His essence. In the minds of some theologians, the belief runs even deeper with the implication that humans can achieve deification. The definition, however, varies somewhat among the several denominations. In Eastern Orthodoxy, for example, theosis is the call for one to become holy. The most objectionable theory regarding theosis, perhaps, is the idea that a person can evolve into material union with the divine, or some description of sainthood, by human efforts of piety and good works. The whole concept is practically anathema to most Protestants. *See also* apotheosis; exaltation; glorification; henosis; Palamism; perfectionism; saint(s); sanctification; second work of grace.

Theosophical Society: an esoteric group founded in 1875 by a Russian medium, Madame Helena Blavatsky. Her intent was to synthesize Eastern religious forms and occultism, including Hinduism and Tantric yoga, in conjunction with Western Rosicrucianism, Hermeticism, Freemasonry, and the Qabbala. Much of the sect's teaching springs from mystics like Meister Eckhardt, Jakob Boehme, and Emmanuel Swedenborg. Her teachings had considerable influence for some time, a phenomenon continued by her successor, Annie Besant. The first Theosophical Society, or "lodges" as the groups were called, was formed by Blavatsky and sixteen disciples in 1875 in New York City. *See also* Akashic Records; Besant, Annie; Blavatsky, Madame Helena Petrovna; egocentric cults; sect(s); Theosophy.

Theosophy: esoteric teachings that attempt to order and maintain mystical contact with God, or the god entity. Its concepts greatly influenced Nazism in the 20th century, particularly Hitler and Himmler. It is also considered the precursor to the modern New Age movement. The mission of the sect followers is motivated by the integration of certain Eastern beliefs with Western mysticism. It interprets science through occultic means and describes itself as the "science of religion." Humanity, then, must evolve itself until it assimilates into the great "World Soul." *See also* Akashic Records; anthroposophy; Besant, Annie; Behmenism; Blavatsky, Madame Helena Petrovna; Damanhur; Divine Science, Church of; Hitler, Adolf; Huna; mind science; New Thought Movement; Religious Science; sect(s); Suttanipata; Theosophical Society; Yeats, William Butler.

theotekons: hymns of praise to Mary, the mother of Jesus, in the Coptic ritual. Two melody types are in vogue when reciting the theotekons. One, called the *Watus,* is a chanting term referring to the bush Moses saw burning of Mount Sinai and sung on Thursdays. The second is the *Tasbeha,* concerning Adam and vocalized on Mondays. *See also* Coptic Church; Epsalmodia; hoos; liturgical year; Mariolatry; Mary; music; "seven and four" ritual; Tasbeha; *Theotokos.*

theotherapy: treatment of disease or illness by prayer and religious exercises of various descriptions. The methods were developed by Peter Lumesurier (a prolific arcane author known as a Nostradamus expert). The process seems to be that the afflicted person is to select a Greek god or goddess of choice, then try to actively adopt the deity's positive characteristics. *See also* homeopathy.

Theotokos: a term from Eastern Orthodoxy meaning "birth giver of God," the Madonna. The word suits the tenets of Nestorianism, which asserted that even though Jesus was both human and divine, he did not hold these natures as a solid unit of being. In essence, the belief holds that Christ is the "God-Bearer," a doctrine critical to Greek Orthodox thinking. According to the policy, Jesus is not authentically God but merely the body the Father used for earthbound teaching. Mary then birthed the savior and is to be reverenced for it. *See also* Adoptionism; Anomoeans; appropriation; Arianism; Arius; *Christotokos;* complementarian view of the Trinity; Donatism; Dormition of the Theotokos; dualism; Dynamic Monarchianism; dynamism; dyophysitism; Eastern Orthodox Church; Entry into the Temple of the Theotokos; eternal subordination of the Son; "four fences of Chalcedon"; *homoiousios; homoousios;* hypostatic union; incarnation; *kenosis;* kenotic view of Christ; Mariolatry; Mary; miaphysitism; modalism; monarchianism; monophysitism; monoenergism; names (titles) for Jesus; Nestorianism; Nestorius; *ousia;* patripassianism; Pelagianism; *perichoresis;* psilanthropism; Sabellianism; Socianism, Socinian; subordinationism; theanthroposophy; *Theophorus;* Trinity; two natures, doctrine of the; unipersonality.

Therapeutae: an alternate name for many early Christian monks set in Alexandria. They mixed prayers with a corrupt form of Egyptian Essene meditation, a fact confirmed by Eusebius. Most historians count them as the first recorded "Christian" monastic sects. Celibacy was normal for the group, perhaps having been suggested by the Roman Vestal Virgins; they also voiced prayers to the sun. Their communities were widespread and more secluded than the Essenes. *See also* desert mystics; Essenes; monastery; monasticism; monk(s); orders; sect(s).

Therapeutate: a derivation of the so-called "White Brotherhood"— Pharaoh Thutmose III's master craftsmen at Karnak operating as healers in honor to the goddess Hathor. The Therapeutate were said to be a pattern for the later establishment of Essene communities of the Dead Sea at Qumran. The brotherhood claimed to have earned its ancient prestige due to its mastery of a mysterious white powder (an ingredient for the philosopher's stone), thus suggesting the name of their brotherhood. *See also* Essenes; philosopher's stone; powder of projection; sect(s).

therapeutic touch. See Reiki.

Theravada Buddhism: one of the oldest Buddhist sects framed by the worship of Sanputra, an early disciple of Buddha who stressed conservatism and monasticism. Theravada, with its conservative and austere approach, is closer to Buddha's original teachings but became quite localized in southern India and Sri Lanka, more so than any rivals. It experienced a revitalization in the 12th century when travelers took it into Burma, Thailand, Cambodia, and Laos. *See also* Buddhism; Dhammapada; Gautama Buddha; Mahayana Buddhism; Pali Canon, the; sect(s); Suttanipata; *Sutta Pitaka*.

therianthropy: the supposed magical ability, also called lycanthropy, to shapeshift—to morph from human form to that of an animal. *See also* alukah; *nagual;* occult, occultic; wolf.

The Skull. See place of The Skull.

Thessalonian Church: citizens of the city of Thessalonica (named for the sister of Alexander the Great) on the Gulf of Salonika. They were perhaps the earliest date setters for the end of the age on record. The Thessalonian Christians thought Jesus was returning soon, so some quit their work and settled in to wait. Paul rebuked them and urged them to restart their lives (2 Th. 2:1–2; 3:10–12). Their eschatological thinking also convinced some that loved ones preceding them in death would miss the resurrection or rapture, necessitating a corrective from Paul. Then would they themselves miss out on the Parousia? *See also* church.

Theudas: 1. a false Messiah mentioned in Acts 5:36. His rebellion with 400 men failed and the hapless leader was killed. 2. a false prophet whom Josephus called a "magician." During the procuratorship of Cuspius Fadus, this Theudas claimed to be a prophet and managed to lead a large contingent of Jews to the Jordan that he promised to part for them. Governor Fadus intercepted the group and killed or captured almost all of them. Theudas himself lost his head, which was carried to Jerusalem as a warning to other insipient rebels. *See also* Jew(s).

theugry: the working of a divine or supernatural agency in human affairs. The term also describes the practice of rituals, usually magical in nature, often intended to invoke a god. *See also* anthropomancy; anthroposophy; apotropaic magic; *arcanum arcandrum; Arcanum*, the; Ariosophy; astral projection; astrology, astrologers; audition; augury; automatic writing; bagua; belomancy; bibliomancy; black arts; cartomancy; chiromancy; clairaudience; clairsentience; clairvoyance; cone of power; conjure; cryptesthesia; crystallomancy; curious acts; divination; dream(s); dreams and visions; enchantment; enneagram; evil eye; extrasensory perception (ESP); geomancy, grimoire; hepatoscopy; Hermetic wisdom; hex; hierscopy; horoscope(s); hydromancy; incantation; labyrinth walk; lecanomancy; literomancy; locution; magic arts; magic, magick; magic square; magnetism; *mana*; mantic wisdom; mantra; monition; necromancy; New Age religion; numbers, symbology of; occult, occultic; oneiromancy; otherworldly journeys; ouija board; out-of-body experiences (OBEs); paranormal; parapsychology; peace pole(s); pentagram; precognition; prefiguration; premonition; prodigy; prognostication; prophecy, general; psi; psychic healing; psychic reading; psychomancy; psychometry; psychonautics; pyramidology; remote viewing; retrocognition; revelation; rhabdomancy; séance; scrying; secret wisdom; sorcery, sorceries; spell; spell names; spiritism; stigmata; superstition; tarot; telegnosis; telepathy; telesthesia; third eye, the; totemism; vision quest; visions; visualization; Voodoo; Voudou; witchcraft; *ya sang*; yoga; Zen; *zos kia* cultus.

The Way International: one of the more damaging cults on the world scene crammed with proven allegations of rampant homosexuality, mind control, fraud, and other abuses. The organization began as a radio broadcast in 1942 by its founder Victor Paul Weirville from his headquarters in New Knoxville, Ohio. By 1947, it had become known as the Vesper Chimes or the Chimes Hour

Youth Caravan, the Way Over the World (WOW), The Way Bible Research Institute, and the Way Corps, but officially The Way as of 1955. The latest president, L. Craig Martindale, has been arrested for sexual abuse and other crimes. The Way classes are strict, aimed at demonizing all other beliefs, and exploitation of the membership with advanced mind control and enforced labor. Absolute loyalty is required, even dismissing family and all former associations. *See also* cult(s).

thief, thieves: one who steals. Jesus used the thief in his illustration of hoarding as a caution not to store up treasures that can be stolen (Mt. 6:19). The recitation is also a warning to watch for his appearing in which he will come unexpectedly like a thief in the night (Mt. 24:42–43). Two thieves, or malefactors guilty of other crimes, were present at the crucifixion of Jesus, one of whom became a believer before his demise. *See also* Ten Commandments, the; theft; thief (thieves) on the cross, the.

thief (thieves) on the cross, the: one or both of two criminals executed on the cross contemporary with Jesus who are of interest to eschatology. One of the malefactors, because of his repentance and appeal to Christ, was granted salvation and a place in Paradise at that very time (Lk. 23:32–43). Christian tradition says his name was Dismas. The other offender also may hold apocalyptic interest but for the opposite reason. Unreliable Christian tradition says their names were Demas (meaning "dying") and Gestas. Others name them Titus (the good one) and Dumachus (the bad). One legendary story relates that the two robbers earlier accosted the Holy Family during their flight to Egypt. When Titus bribed Dumachus to spare the travelers, Jesus predicted the manner of their deaths to him. *See also* theft; thief, thieves.

things taught by demons: an eschatological prediction from Paul (1 Tim. 4:1) asserting that an evil age is imminent in which hypocritical liars will issue evil messages from Satan and his minions rather than the true Word of God. *See also* attending spirit(s); authorities; daemons; deceiving spirits; demon(s), demonic; demonology; disa; evil (unclean) spirit(s); frog(s); Oniropompi; Orisha; para; paredri; spirit guide(s); spiritual warfare; territorial spirits; thrones; tutelary; wight(s).

things that must soon take place, the: a reference from Revelation 22:6 affirming that those subjects announced by the angel of revelation to all of God's servants are trustworthy and true. Those disclosures, the passage emphasizes, will transpire soon. *See also* eschatology, eschatological; "which must soon (shortly) take place."

Thiota: a so-called prophetess and false Christ of the mid-800s who gained a sizable following by predicting the end of the age in A.D. 848 or sooner. She was eventually condemned by the Roman Church and forced to confess her "presumptions" were invented for money and due to the influence of a young priest of her acquaintance. She was publically flogged and offered no more predictions. *See also* prophetess(es).

3 and 4 Maccabees: two writings pertaining to the era of the struggle for Jewish independence. *Third Maccabees* has nothing to do with the Maccabee dynasty but deals with Jewish affairs under the Ptolemies of Egypt in the third century B.C. *Fourth Maccabees* is a moralistic essay on the Maccabean martyrs, written late, perhaps at the beginning of the Christian era. *See also 1* and *2 Maccabees.*

Third Church Restoration. See Reformed Reformation Movement.

Third Church, the: a modern-day reference to the growing number of Christians and the rise of Christianity outside the Western world while the old order is stagnant or declining. The First Church is said to have blossomed in the East A.D. 0–1000, the Second in the West A.D. 1000–2000, and the Third is designated A.D. 2000 to the present. *See also* Church.

third eye, the: an additional eye, or a substitute for one or both of the natural ones, that is said to grant the bearer supernatural perception and superhuman powers. It is reputed to be particularly effective when used in conjunction with certain "dark sentences" of the ancient occult mystery religions and consortiums. The most common assertion is that such power is organically inherent in the human brain within the pinecone-shaped pineal gland. The concept of a third eye is an old one, having seen the expression in the Greek Cyclops, the Norse Odin, the Irish Fomorians, and Horus of the ancient Egyptians. The presence of such an organ is common to perceptions of the Antichrist as he is described in Zechariah as the false shepherd, in the wounded head of the beast of Revelation, and in the Islamic tradition of the one-eyed *Dajjal. See also* Antichrist; Astaru; chakra; *Dajjal;* Fomorians; Horus; Norse and Old Germanic pantheon; occult, occultic; Odin; worthless (wicked) shepherd, the.

third heaven: a reference to the highest heaven where God dwells. Paul hinted that he had glimpsed such a place or state of being when he was "taken up," either bodily or in the Spirit, to Paradise (2 Cor. 12:3–4). Paul's description of the event is couched in vague language since he was attempting not to boast to the Corinthians of his superior apostleship at the time and even told his audience that the heavenly visitor was "a man." There is little doubt the "man" was Paul himself who heard inexpressible things he could not repeat. *See also* heaven; heavenly realms; heavens, number of; paradise of God; seven levels of heaven; three levels of heaven, the.

Third Man, the: an entity whom some believe may appear to someone under duress or danger in order to render comfort and, in some cases, actual rescue. These companions may be visible or invisible and may or may not speak. Each instance, however, is one of consolation and confidence. Many adrift sailors, endangered soldiers, stranded mountaineers, and explorers (including polar adventurer Sir Ernest Shackleton and his followers), have reported the existence of the Third Man when most needed. Similar stories have emerged from survivors of the 9/11 attack on the World Trade Center and many other instances of calamity. *See also* guardian angel(s); spirit guide(s); tutelary.

third order. See tertiary.

Third Quest: a new way of investigating the historical Jesus that sprang up in the 1970s. The process was an attempt to formulate a different process for looking at the portrait of Jesus from the Gospels and diverged somewhat from the first quest which began in the 19th century. The second quest started in the 1950s. *See also* biblical criticism; higher criticism; historical Jesus, the; Jesus Seminar, the.

third Temple: the planned and hoped-for replacement of the Temple of Herod destroyed by the Romans in A.D. 70. It is legitimate to name Herod's edifice as a third Temple since his renovations were so extensive as to render it a new construction. Nevertheless, the Jews call it their second, with the third to be built during the Messianic era. Problems of international politics and local culture plague any plans for the new Temple at this time. For one, the Temple Mount is occupied by several Islamic holy sites that would surely spark a world war if disturbed. There are three possible locations on Mount Zion where the new building could take place: 1. on the rock where the Holy of Holies is said by some to have existed—inside the Dome of the Rock, 2. north of the Dome of the Rock opposite the Eastern Gate, 3. South of the Dome of the Rock near the *al-Aqsa* Mosque. The second location would require minimal hubris to Muslim shrines. Some people claim that the Jews themselves will rebuild the third Temple, but others suggest they must await the Messiah who will do it himself. There are some stipulations for rebuilding the Jerusalem Temple, namely, 1. the Jews are to rebuild, with or without the aid of the Messiah, 2. the altar is to be of unhewn stones, 3. ascension to the altar will be via ramp, not stairs, 4. all are to reverence the new Temple as the seat of God, 5. the Temple must be guarded at all times, and 6. the Jews must never cease watching over and using the Temple as long as it is in existence. Should there be a Tribulation Temple, it should technically be the third, but according to Judaism, the third is to be the millennial Temple. There is no precise indication as to when the third Temple will be constructed except to place it near events of the Tribulation at a time near the beginning or end of the seven year treaty between Israel and the Antichrist. Five prophets have predicted the third erection—Daniel, Ezekiel, Zechariah, Malachi, and Jesus; one more, Isaiah, hints strongly of it. We conceive that worship there will be, not only incorrect according to God's instructions, but abominable because the Jews will not pay attention nor understand its true intent and spiritual impact. Isaiah 66:1-4 explains God's displeasure at all aspects of the construction and ritual, even calling it "evil." Interestingly, verse 6 of chapter 66 (which particularly discusses God's problem with the third Temple) ciphers to 666. Certainly, when the Bible was composed there were no chapter and verse divisions but it could be no accident that the numbers evolved to the alphanumeric designation of the Antichrist who will personally spoil its worship. Heaven will contain no Temple for Christ will serve that purpose for that era. *See also* crushing rock that became a mountain; election; elect, the; kingdom that cannot be shaken, a; kingdom, the; messianic age, the; millennial geography; millennial Sabbath; millennial sacramentalism; millennial Temple; millennial worship; Millennium, millennial; New Covenant, the; New Eden; restoration of all things; restoration of Israel (the Jews); restoration Temple (and land); rod of iron; Sabbath rest; Temple(s); times of refreshing; Tribulation Temple.

Third Wave: Alvin Toffler's futuristic prediction from his book of the same title (1980). The Third Wave is to be a new existence, a sort of Utopia that he calls "practopia"—a practical and pleasant world. The assumed First Wave is passed as representing the post-agrarian era; the Second Wave is the industrial revolution that has wrought much havoc on humanity. *See also* Toffler, Alvin.

Thirteen Principles of Faith, the: as recited in the Jewish liturgy, the thirteen principles of faith that constitute the summary of the essence of torah. They have been extant for 800 years and hold a central place in the understanding and practice of the Jewish faith. 1. God is Creator, 2. God is one, 3. God is incorporeal, 4. God is eternal, 5. all prayer is to be offered to God alone, 6. the directives of the prophets are true, 7. Moses is the greatest prophet, 8. the written torah and the oral torah were both given to Moses, 9. the Torah will never be superseded, 10. God knows the thoughts and actions of human beings, 11. God rewards the righteous and punishes evildoers, 12. God will send a messiah, 13. God will resurrect the dead. *See also* confession(s) of faith; Judaism; Maimonides, Moses.

Thirty-Nine Articles, the: the historic and official definitions of the doctrine and practice in the Church of England communion. The project was started in 1536 as a response to the Anglican position somewhere between Roman Catholicism and Protestant convictions (especially Calvinism). The Articles were revised and expanded a number of times until the final edition in 1571. Much of the content of the *Book of Common Prayer* is derived from the Articles. *See also Book of Common Prayer;* confession(s) of faith; Church of England; sacraments.

thirty pieces of silver: the traditional price of a slave in ancient times. It was the sum paid to Judas Iscariot for the betrayal of Jesus and the purchase price of Jeremiah's land purchase (*cf.* Zech. 11:12–13; Jer. 32: 6–15). *See also* Judas; potter's field; silver; slave, slavery; Zechariah's oracle of two shepherds and two shepherd's staffs.

thirty-seven: the number which some historians and theologians have nicknamed "the fingerprint of God." This integer is called a "theomatic," along with a few others, as having special significance because all are capable of being divided into the sum values of words, phrases, or verses of the Bible with no remainder (within plus or minus two). The number thirty-seven is said to be discernible thousands of times in Scripture via the theomatic process and seems to appear most prominently when God desires to speak of a particularly significant event of history, thus casting it as the keystone of the theomatic system. Thirty-seven is also considered by many such scholars to be the most likely age of Jesus when he died; others imply his age was thirty-three. *See also* apocalyptic calculation; "fingerprint of God, the"; numbers, symbology of; theomatic number(s).

Thirty Years' War: a series of bloody and devastating conflicts in Europe between 1618 and 1648, primarily between Catholics and Protestants of the Holy Roman Empire. The Peace of Augsburg was somewhat failing early in the 17th century, and new crises quickly developed. The victorious Lutherans (now called Protestants) became disunited over doctrine. Simultaneously, Roman Catholicism resurged and solidified. Violations of the Treaty of Augsburg became commonplace, and political rivalry, as usual, stirred the coals of religious intolerance. The struggles began in Bohemia under Emperor Matthias (1612–1619) when he refused to allow Protestants to erect certain churches in the country. The war quickly spread to Germany, France, Denmark, Holland, Switzerland, and elsewhere. Catholics were initially successful but Gustavus Adolphus of Sweden eventually defeated them. Nevertheless, battles raged interminably for the next sixteen years until the exhausted armies simply agreed to stop fighting and signed the Peace of Westphalia. *See also* Holy Roman Empire; Holy War; Peace of Westphalia; Protestant Reformation; Roman Catholic Church.

"this calls for wisdom": the phrase of Revelation 13:18 that tells the reader that the identification of the 666 mark of the beast will be difficult, even impossible, for our generations. The phrase occurs again in Revelation 17:9 when trying to decipher the sign of the Great Prostitute and the scarlet dragon. The same utterance could well serve as an interpretive caution for all of Revelation and for apocalyptic reading in general. *See also* "let the reader understand."

this generation. See generation.

thistle(s). See briars and thorns; thistle and the cedar, fable of the; thorn(s), thornbush(es).

thistle and the cedar, fable of the: a fable related by King Jehoash of Israel to King Amaziah of Judah (2 Ki. 14:9–10). Jehoash warned Amaziah not to threaten or trouble him and illustrated the danger by analogy to a trampled thistle. It was true that Amaziah had triumphed over Edom, but the same result was not guaranteed if he attacked Israel. The fable proved accurate since Amaziah was defeated in the ensuing combat. *See also* fable(s); Jehoash; riddle.

Thomas as apostle: one of the original twelve disciples, also called Didymus because he had an unnamed twin. Though serving faithfully for years, he doubted the resurrection of Jesus until it was proven to him. At that point, he returned to his former spiritual fervor (Jn. 20:24–29). Some Mesoamerican legends claim he was a missionary to that area, an unlikely occurrence. A legend that is more probable, however, is that he traveled to India along the busy trade routes of the time to proclaim the gospel there. *See also* apostle(s); disciple(s); doubting Thomas; liturgical year; Mar Thoma Church; martyr(s); Mesoamerica; missions, missionaries; prophets as martyr(s).

Thomas a' Kempis: mystic and canon of the Germanic priesthood (ca. 1820–1471), a Bible copyist and author of renown. His name springs from his hometown but was called "the little hammer." Thomas passed much of his life as a monk at the monastery of Saint Agnes. His best-known work has to be the classic *Imitation of Christ*. *See also* desert mystics; monastery, monasticism; monk(s); Roman Catholic Church.

Thomas, Norman Mattoon: a six-time Socialist Party candidate for the United States presidency (1884–1968). Thomas was a

Presbyterian minister serving poverty-stricken churches in New York City, where his attachment to Socialism was cemented. He resigned his pastoral duties in 1926 to head the Socialist Party, relieving Eugene V. Debs. Thomas helped found the National Civil Liberties Bureau (now the American Civil Liberties Union) and became a prolific author, pacifist, and journalist. *See also* Groton School; Presbyterians; social issues; Society of Christian Socialists; Social Gospel; social issues.

Thomas the Contender, Book of: one of the more interesting finds of the Nag Hammadi library. The book is Gnostic, claiming to be authored by the apostle Thomas. It consists of eight pages of Coptic text, a dialogue between the risen Christ and his twin (Didymus Thomas). One "Mathias" (presumed to be Matthew) is the recorder. The work is in two parts—a kind of philosophical treatise on "knowing one's self" and a vivid description of hell, a place of punishment for those who do not trust Christ and his teachings. *See also* Apocryphal Gospels; hell; Nag Hammadi library.

Thor: the Norse god of lightning, storm, thunder, and oak trees. He is known by at least fourteen other names but is identified specifically as the son of Odin and the personified earth and husband of the blonde goddess Sif. Thor's war equipment is almost as famous as his name. Among his gear is the deadly hammer Mjollnir, his power-pack belt Megingjaro, the gloves Jarngripr, and his staff Grioarvolr. *See also* Loki; Mjollnir; Norse and Old Germanic pantheon; oak; Odin; Ragnarok.

thorn in the flesh: a malady suffered by Paul (2 Cor. 12:7) that he called a "messenger of Satan." The exact nature of his complaint is not known, but guesses range to demonic affliction, a human contender who harassed him, anxiety, depression, ophthalmia (possibly an aversion to bright light as a lingering aftereffect of his traumatic conversion experience), or even malaria. The phrase has become a sort of metaphor for any grievance borne by the believer from time to time that must be endured without relief. In Paul's case, the purpose seemed to have been to guard against spiritual pride so evident in his missionary and theological talents. *See also* bread of affliction; bread of despair; messenger of Satan; tear(s); trial(s); vale of tears; water of affliction.

thorn(s), thornbush(es): prickly growth, often seen paired with "briars," "nettles," "brambles," or "thistles." Thorns are a frequent biblical metaphor for hindrance, harm, or persecution (Mt. 13:7; Heb. 6:8). Jesus was made to wear a crown of thorns in ridicule (Mk. 15:17) at his crucifixion. Joshua warned the people that God was liable to use "whips on your backs and thorns in your eyes" if they were unfaithful to His commandments (Jos. 23:12–13). Gideon the judge punished the elders of Succoth by whipping them with thorns and briars (Jud. 8:7; 15–16). Jesus used the thornbush as an example of the inconsistency between the products of good and evil: "People do not pick grapes from thornbushes" (Lk. 6:44). Something similar occurs as a proverb: "Like a thornbush in a drunkard's hand is a proverb in the mouth of a fool" (Pro. 26:9). In Hosea 2:6 the thornbush is presented as a barrier or a hedge, and again in 9:6 and 10:8 as ruination. The ancient peoples commonly burned thornbushes as a nuisance, causing a fast-burning and consuming fire. *See also* briars and thorns; flora, fruit, and grain, symbology of; Sabra; sabra.

Thoth: Egyptian god of wisdom, knowledge, healing, the moon, and resurrection. His guidance was essential to the healing of Horus from a scorpion sting. He can be noted as the historian of the gods and was considered to be a sage in ancient Egypt when he was called "very great, great." *See also* Egyptian pantheon; Hermes Trismegistus; Hermetic writings; Horus; Isis; Osiris.

thoughtform: a process, said to be a living entity, created by a large number of people worshiping a particular god over a long period. We then create our gods by our worship. Thoughtform is common belief in Tibetan Buddhism and some New Age and Wiccan thinking. Some descriptions relate that a thoughtform master can create a three-dimensional image or form that has been fashioned from an astral substance, usually by the efforts of a trained mind. Several such strong minds can build the same thoughtform and maintain its existence for a time. Manifestations of gods or saints are usually thoughtforms discerned by the highly intuitive, such as children or those possessed of second sight. Untrained minds may occasionally see imaginary or ill-defined images like UFOs. *See also* Akashic Records; Buddhism; dweomer; egregores; enchantment; ensorcell; magic, magick; magnetism; New Age religion; second sight; sorcery, sorceries; spell; spell names; Wicca; witchcraft.

three: the number obtained from adding one and two. Its symbolic meaning most often refers to the Trinity, or the completeness of the Godhead. Some theologians claim more significance in that God does everything in bundles of three. To illustrate, they see three apartments in the tabernacle (courtyard, Holy Place, and Holy of Holies), the frequent division into thirds (Zech. 13:9), and sometimes even history is sectioned into thirds. *See also* numbers, symbology of; Trinity.

three and one half days: the length of time (Rev. 11:9) in which the two great witnesses will lie unburied and dishonored before their resurrection back to heaven. Whether the time is literal or symbolic of some length of days is uncertain. In other instances, the three and a half days are apocalyptic language for three and a half years.

three announcing (flying) angels. See flying angels, the three.

three antichrists theory: a rather unorthodox belief held by some end-of-the-world theorists stating that our history will see three distinct antichrists before the end of the age instead of the commonly assumed one. The first is usually named Napoleon Bonaparte, the second Adolph Hitler, and the third as the yet unnamed Antichrist of the Tribulation. An alternative concept shows the first antichrist to be the "terrifying beast" of Daniel 7:7 who will manifest at the end of "the times of the Gentiles." His task is to act as a sort of John the Baptist preparing the way for the second antichrist. That second is the "666" beast of Revelation 13:1–10. Because of the timing, this man of perdition could easily be mistaken as the Messiah and subject to worship. The third figure is the leader of the Gog and Magog incursion following the Millennium (Rev. 20:7–10). *See also* Antichrist; Bonaparte, Napoleon; Hitler, Adolph.

three cornerstones of Anglicanism, the: the summary doctrine of the Church of England stating that reason, Scripture, and tradition are the keys to correct belief. No one holds all truth all the time, but together they form a spiritual and ecclesiastical guide. *See also* Anglicanism; confession(s) of faith.

three days of darkness: the belief among some Catholics that God has decreed three days of darkness at the end of the age for sin punishment. The idea is modeled on the Egyptian plagues in pre-Exodus Israel. Noted personalities like Hildegard of

Bingham and Padre Pio affirmed the tenet, but the official Roman see does not condone its veracity. The Apocalypse, however (Rev. 8:12), does mention something similar. *See also* darkness; darkness in earth and sky; eschatology, eschatological; Roman Catholic Church.

threefold sense of interpretation: a method of allegorizing Scripture accepted by some scholars in the Middle Ages and popularized by Origen. The idea is that there are three possible interpretations of Scripture: the literal, the moral, and the spiritual. Sometimes a fourth called the anagogical was added. According to Origen and those like him, the spiritual interpolation is clearly superior. *See also* analogical interpretation; biblical criticism; Fourfold Interpretation; grammatical-historical interpretation; hermeneutic(s); higher criticism; interpretation; literal interpretation; Origen; plenary inspiration; principles of interpretation; revelation, theological; rhetorical criticism; source criticism; text; textual criticism; translation; transmission history.

Three Jewels of Buddhism, the: key doctrines of the Buddhist concept of faith that can be summarized as Buddha, *Dharma,* and *Sangha.* The first is the historical Buddha himself (sixth–fifth centuries B.C.) who recognized his preeminence. The second is truth as taught by the Buddha combined with ontological insight. The third is the Buddhist community, both monks and nuns and laypersons. *See also* Buddhism; confession(s) of faith; Dharma; Eight Adversities of Buddhism, the; Five Hindrances of Buddhism, the; Five Poisons of Buddhism, the; Five Precepts of Buddhism, the; Four Constituents of Buddhism, the; Four Noble Truths of Buddhism, the; monasticism; Sangha; Three Marks of Existence of Buddhism, the.

390 days and 40 days: the length of time Ezekiel was ordered to lie on his side to demonstrate the sin of the Southern and Northern kingdoms—390 on his left side for Judah and forty on his right for Israel. The time is intended to represent one day for each year of the nation's rebellion leading to the Babylonian Exile. *See also* Ezekiel as Old Testament prophecy; Jerusalem, siege of (pantomime).

three kneelings: a ritual of Coptic worship performed at Pentecost in honor of the descent of the Holy Spirit. *See also* Coptic Church; gestures; liturgical year.

three levels of heaven, the: the atmosphere, the realm of the heavenly bodies, and the headquarters of God. The ancients viewed the cosmos as being of at least three levels, and often many more. The pseudepigraphal writings in particular note that there are many planes from us to God, and frequently they are barriers between Yahweh and us who dwell on earth. However, the Christian perspective is that God is close to us in Christ—only a prayer or thought away. *See also* heaven; heavenly realms; heavens, number of; seven levels of heaven; third heaven.

Three Marks of the Existence of Buddhism, the: a short list of Buddhist belief that almost sums up the cardinal doctrines: impermanence, suffering, and "no soul"—a concept of human reality. The first indicator is *anicca*, everything is impermanent and subject to change; second, people have a dissatisfaction with life, *dukkha*, because of the quest for stability, and finally *anata*, in that since everything is constantly changing, nothing has a fixed self or essence. For the good life, *dukkha* must be minimized even if cannot be eliminated. See *also* Buddhism; confession(s) of faith; Eight Adversities of Buddhism, the; Five Hindrances of Buddhism, the; Five Poisons of Buddhism, the; Five Precepts of Buddhism, the; Four Constituents of Buddhism, the; Four Noble Truths of Buddhism, the; Three Jewels of Buddhism, the.

"three points and a poem": a somewhat disparaging or droll description of how to prepare a rather dull or routine sermon. The expression is often quoted to seminary students as symptomatic of a shortcut or inoffensive preaching style that incorporates a triad of simplistic points with a poem or other insertion serving as an illustration. *See also* Christianese; homily; preaching; sermon; slurs, religious; "sugar stick."

three poisons of Yoga Sutra: greed, anger, and delusion. Yoga practices are said to cure such distractions and to avoid other mental afflictions as ignorance, ego-centered living, and extremes of emotion. The theory is shared by Buddhism. *See also* yoga.

three-self principle, the: a mission strategy that saw adoption around the 19th century as perhaps the most desirable standard for fostering native or indigenous churches—that they should be self-supporting, self-governing, and self-propagating. *See also* indigenous religion; missions, missionaries.

three sisters, the: a trio of cherished deities among the Iroquois, and perhaps some other of the more Native American agricultural tribes, representing the staples corn, beans, and squash. *See also* flora, fruit, and grain, symbology of.

three stages of judgments: the judgment process, according to the pseudepigraphal *Testament of Abraham*. In the source, three acts of judgment are ordained for every person upon death: by Abel, by the twelve tribes of Israel, and by God Himself. Those souls found guilty (those whose bad deeds overbalance the good ones) are carried off to "a most disagreeable place of punishment." The righteous inherit Paradise. Then those who endure perpetual death may atone for their sins and avoid the eschatological condemnations. If the good and bad deeds are equal, that soul is placed "in the middle" with neither rewards nor punishments. The entire process, according to the text, seems to base itself on the Mosaic Law, which says that any evidence must be presented by three witnesses to be valid. *See also* day of the Lord.

three that testify. See Spirit, the water, and the blood, the.

three traitors, the: a triumvirate of evil, named by a number of organizations. In Christianity, the betrayers are Judas, Pilate, and Caiaphas. In Freemasonry, the reference is to the murderers of Hiram Abiff. In Egyptian myth, they are the three demons who killed Osiris. *See also* Caiaphas; Egyptian pantheon; Freemasonry; Judas; Osiris; Pilate, Pontius.

three uses of the Law: God's purposes, according to some theologians, for His rule of life as seen in scriptural interpretation. The first use is political—to be practiced as a restraint to the wicked; the second is theological—as a prompt to bring us to Christ; the third is didactic—to act as a guide for the unregenerate or the attempt to live ethically. *See also* Law, the.

threnody: a dirge; plaintive poem, speech, or lament, especially for the dead—a funeral requiem. *See also* chant; death; dirge; exequy; funeral; jeremiad; *kinah;* kontakion; lament; liturgy, Christian; liturgy, Jewish; music; obit; obsequy; Pannychis; Requiem; requiescat; vigil.

threshing: the agricultural practice of beating the harvested wheat or other grain crops to separate the good kernels from the head and chaff. In apocalyptic language, threshing often represents God's chastisement of His creation or His people. *See also* eschatology, eschatological; harvest; harvest of the earth; sickle; threshing floor; threshing sledge; winepress; winnowing fork.

threshing floor: a hard-packed round surface or pavement used for threshing grain to separate the germ from the chaff. The identification holds prophetic significance since many holy places, not the least of which was the Temple in Jerusalem, were established on threshing floors. *See also* harvest; harvest of the earth; sickle; threshing; threshing sledge; winepress; winnowing fork.

threshing sledge: a farming implement for threshing grain that is pulled by draught animals. It consists of two heavy planks secured by cross-pieces and set with sharp stones. A threshing *cart* by contrast had rollers. Another method was to toss the grain into the air, hoping the wind would separate the chaff. Apocalyptically speaking, the sledge is a metaphor for annihilation or severe punishment (Isa. 41:15; Amos 1:3; Job 41:30). *See also* harvest; harvest of the earth; sickle; threshing; threshing floor; winepress; winnowing fork.

threshold, not stepping on the: a superstitious act common in some cultures (including our own) in which one avoids stepping on the threshold of a doorway. Biblical references include Zephaniah 1:9, which likely has its antecedent in 1 Samuel 5:1-5. In the latter passage, the priests of the Philistine god Dagon found the idol edifice toppled at the entrance of his temple due to the proximity of the captured Hebrew ark of the covenant. The head and hands were broken off the statue. From that time, the worshipers refused to step on the threshold of the shrine. Zephaniah reported this action as one more sign of pagan idolatry worthy of ridicule and condemnation. *See also* Dagon.

throat: inside of the human neck through which food and drink enter the body and sounds exit. The psalmist declared that the throat can be an open grave (Ps. 5:9), and one of the Proverbs (Pro. 23:2) reminds us it is better to put a knife to one's throat rather than to overindulge in gluttony.

throne in heaven with someone sitting on it, a: God in theophany as noted in Revelation 4:3 and elsewhere. In other Scriptures, as in portions of Ezekiel, God's throne is described as a magnificent chariot with fiery intersecting wheels controlled by the Cherubim. *See also* court of heaven; eschatology, eschatological; heaven; someone "like a son of man"; sapphire (emerald) throne; throne(s); Throne of the Lord, the.

throne of David: or David's throne—the designation from God that King David or his descendants will always occupy the ruling position of Israel. The promise is centered on Gabriel's words to Mary as he announced the savior's birth (Lk. 1:30–33). There, the angel spoke of David's *house* (a dynasty), a *kingdom* (Israel, with occasional reference to Gentiles sharing the rulership), and *throne* (ruling authority). All believers are in a sense deputy rulers, whether we are of David's relatives, Jews, or Gentile saints (Mt. 25:21; 2 Tim. 2:12), but the pledge to David from God was a personal one and applies particularly to the governorship in the Millennium. *See also* David; House of David; Judaism; king(s); throne(s).

throne of grace: a metaphorical description of God's willingness to grant access in prayer, His favor, and His forgiveness to any who sincerely seek Him in conversation. *See also* Christianese; "prayed up"; prayer(s).

throne of the beast: the headquarters of the Antichrist (Rev. 16:10) that suffers the effects of the fifth bowl. Whether this location is an actual capital city or a generalization for the rule of Antichrist is unclear. *See also* throne(s).

Throne of the Lord, the: a holy name for restored Israel or Jerusalem, most likely referring to the millennial age of peace and universal worship of God (Jer. 3:17). *See also* throne(s); throne in heaven with someone sitting on it, a.

thrones: 1. a classification of angels according to rank and authority. Thrones fit into the so-called "highest" rating in the number three position—those secular and evil entities named as enemies of the righteous God and His people. The ranking of "thrones" as evil beings or holy powers is somewhat uncertain but the early church considered them both extant and viable (Col. 1:16) so the term may also be a rank of evil entities in the demonic order. Sometimes evil entities can occupy thrones of rulership as well. 2. the seat of kings. Apocalyptic language often denotes God and the Lamb

(Christ) as occupying thrones in heaven. The twenty-four elders also occupy heavenly thrones (Rev. 4:4), and perhaps we also will utilize them as believers helping to govern in the Millennium (Mk. 10:39–45; Rev. 20:4–6) and following. Sometimes, as in *3 Enoch,* the throne may equate to a "chariot." To place the name "throne" in biblical perspective, we may note that the Bible mentions them four times in respect to their rightful owners—one for God the Father (Dan. 7:9; Heb. 12:2; Rev. 22:1), one for Christ the Son (Mt. 20:23; Lk. 1:32; Heb. 1:8), one each for God's children [the redeemed of heaven], including David and the disciples destined to rule over the tribes of Israel (Ps. 89:3; Mt. 19:28; Dan. 7:26–27; Rev. 4:4, 11:16), and one for Satan (Rev. 2:13). God's claim to sovereignty is absolute and irrevocable; ours is tentative and temporary, that is, we await our kingdom responsibilities provided we are proven children of God and we may periodically abandon them in deference to Christ's authority (as do the twenty-four elders); Satan's seat and his tenuous rule are doomed. In Scripture, there appears to be a close but indistinct connection between the chariot of God and the throne of God. *See also* angel(s); archangel(s); attending spirit(s); authorities; Bene Elohim; chariot(s); chariot of God; Chashmallim; Chayoth; Cherub, Cherubim; court of heaven; daemons; deceiving spirits; demon(s); demonic; devils; disa; dominions; *elohim;* Erelim; evil (unclean) spirits; fallen angels; frog(s); Gilgulim; Hayyot; Husk(s); Ishim; king(s); *mal'ak;* Merkabah; Merkabah mysticism; oniropompi; Ophanim; Orisha; para; paredri; powers; principalities; queen(s); sapphire (emerald) throne; scepter; Seraph; Seraphim; someone "like a son of man"; spirit guide(s); spiritual warfare; territorial spirits; things taught by demons; throne in heaven with someone sitting on it, a; throne of David; throne of grace; throne of the beast; Throne of the Lord, the; Virtues.

Thugs: "to conceal," an assassination cult, the Thuggee, bent on robbery and strangulation for the glory of their goddess Kali by providing human sacrifices. The murderers were located in northern and central India from ancient times until finally subdued in the 19th century. Since then, the term has become a tag name for gangsters, robbers, and the like. *See also* assassin(s); Hashshashin; Kali; Mafia; religious organizations; secret societies; sect(s); Sicarii; Triads; underworld; Yakuza

Thule, land of: an unknown land envisioned by the ancient geographers and cartographers, first imagined by the Greeks. It was a place of mystery, possibly an island, thought to be in the unexplored northern regions and may have had connections to the so-called Native American land bridge in the Bering Strait. The place has been variously identified as Norway, Iceland, the Orkney or Shetland Islands, Greenland, or parts of Canada. The term has remained in our culture and now bears place names in several locations. *See also* Abraham's bosom; afterlife; Annwn; Aralu; Arcadia; Asgard; Avalon; Dis; Duat; Elysium; eschatology, eschatological; eternal life; future life, doctrine of the; Gehenna; Hades; happy hunting ground; heaven; hell; Hy-Breasail; Hyperborea; Jade Empire, the; Jahannam; Janna; lake of fire; life after death; limbo; *Limbus Puerorum;* Otherworld; Paradise; Pardes; Perdition; Promised Land, the; Pure Land, the; purgatory; Shambhala legends; *Sheol;* soul sleep; space doctrine; Summerland; Thule Society; Tir na nOg; underworld; Upper Gehenna; Utopia; Valhalla; world to come, the; Xibala.

Thule Society: German occult and philosophical group formed in Munich after World War I. The organization was headed by Walter Nauhaus who set about, among other objectives, to promote the superiority of the Arian race. Adolf Hitler was initiated into the organization in 1919 by Dietrich Eckart. Other high-ranking Nazis were prominent members. *See also* anti-Semitic; Eckart, Dietrich; Fascist millennialism; Hitler, Adolf; occult, occultic; sect(s); Thule, land of.

thunder: atmospheric noise during or near a storm. Apocalyptic language often uses thunder to signify the voice of God in His power or the sound accompanying destruction (Job 26:14; 1 Sam. 7:10–11; Ezk. 7:7–9). *See also* thunder revelations; lightning; voice of God; voice out of heaven.

thunder revelations: a series of seven revelations (Rev. 10:4) that are announced but not explained in the Apocalypse. They were mentioned in addition to the seals, trumpets, and bowls. What they contain is unknown to us, for the revealing angel forbade their disclosure. The fact that they are concealed, however, simply means to some that they must crack the code. The revelations have been viewed by different interpreters as the seven Crusades, the seven wars between the time of the Reformation and the French Revolution, the seven kingdoms that promoted the Reformation, the seven decrees issued by the pope condemning the Reformation leaders, and other guesses. But that is all they are—pointless guesses. They will surely be of inestimable value to the Tribulation saints who will need to heed them, however. *See also* bowl(s); eschatology, eschatological; seal(s); thunder; Tribulation; trumpet(s).

"thunderstones": *peirdres tonnerres,* polished stone axes used in the Kele religious rites in Saint Lucia. The Amerindian stones are arranged in a sacred pattern, along with a variety of agricultural implements, as part of the ceremony to seek favors of the ancestors called the Shango. Devotees believe the thunderstones fell from the sky as their gifts from the gods. *See also* Creole (Caribbean) religion; talisman(s).

"Thus sayeth the Lord (Yahweh)": the common catchphrase for prophets who were to proclaim the word of the Lord. It was a sort of signature announcement and in use by all the prophets except Daniel. Modern translations update the title to more contemporary speech but the meaning remains the same. *See also* oath formula; prophet(s).

Thyatira: the fourth of the seven churches addressed in Revelation (Rev. 2:18–29). The congregation was praised for its good deeds, love, and faith but was criticized for immorality and weak doctrine. The congregation seemed unable to deal with the disconnect between being indulgent of the numerous trade guilds in the city yet simultaneously trying to remain loyal to their moral convictions. The guilds were prone to sponsor idolatrous and debauched parties for their members and were almost indispensable for maintaining jobs or perpetuating a market for trading and sales. A woman named Jezebel is cited within the Thyatirian membership as representative of the immorality in their city; her like will reappear in later Revelation as modeled by Madame Babylon the harlot. The church was rampant with Gnosticism. The city of Thyatira was colonized by Seleucus Nicator around 301–281 B.C. on the busy road between Pergamum and Sardis. The citizens worked in wood, clothing, tanning and dyeing, pottery, baking, bronze smelting, and slave trading. It was a city of trade guilds, which essentially monopolized the city. Lydia, the seller of purple dye at Philippi (Acts 16:14) came from Thyatira. The place was a center for emperor worship and heavy into occultism. Dispensational theologians name the church to represent the so-called Impious Age (630–1328) when the church was internally corrupt and divisive. *See also* church; dispensation(s); Impious Age; seven churches of Asia Minor, the; trade guilds.

Tiamat: or Tiamat, the Babylonian and Sumerian goddess of the deep from whence the cleaved bodies of the upper (atmospheric) and lower (earthly) realms were formed. The god Marduk was said to have attacked Tiamat twice until he finally managed to decapitate her. The head became earth and her seed was incorporated into the godly pantheon so Earth could be populated with lulu and demi-gods. The Genesis account of creation (Gen. 1:6–8) claims that action was by the creative power of God alone. *See also* Abzu; Akitu; Anunnaki; *Chariots of the Gods?;* demi-god(s); Enki and Enlil; *Enuma Elish; Epic of Gilgamesh, The,* Igigi; Kingu; Lotan; lulu; Mesopotamia; mythological beasties, elementals, monsters, and spirit animals; Nibiru; panspermia theory; Sumerian and Babylonian pantheon; Sumerian Tablets; Sumer, Sumerian(s); Table of Destinies.

Tiberius Caesar: son of Tiberius Claudius Nero, an evil and punishing Roman ruler. It was in his fifteenth year that John the Baptist began his preaching (Lk. 3:1). *See also* Christianity under the Roman Empire; king(s); Roman Empire.

Tiberius, Sea of. See Galilee, Sea of.

Tibetan Book of the Dead: Buddhist texts detailing the state between death and rebirth—a forty-nine-day journey wherein the traveler meets both good and evil entities along the path. *See also* Buddhism; Eight Adversities of Buddhism, the.

Tibetan Buddhism: a colorful and dramatic faction of Buddhism centered in Tibet. Padmasambhava was its founder in the eighth century that held some features of Buddhism and Hinduism. A central element is called Tantra which involves, not just thinking about spiritual matters, but demonstrating them. Worship then is dramatic, colorful, and engaging with bright costumes, headdresses, music (or at least noise), chanting, mudras, and dance. Private devotion is also practiced, led by a teacher (a lama). *See also* Buddhism; Dalai Lama; Hinduism; Padmasambhava.

Tibni: a rival of Omri for the kingship of Israel (1 Ki. 16:21–22). He did not succeed in gaining the throne.

tiger: a large and beautifully striped predator cat. For some ancients and the New Agers, the animal represents a sign of feminine occultic power over males, an Asiatic symbol of the supremacy over death and life, the gambler's emblem, the military valor of warriors, or a sign of senseless anger. *See also* animals, birds, and insects, symbology of; mythological beasties, bugbears; elementals, monsters, and spirit animals; New Age religion; occult, occultic.

tiggune sopherim: scribal corrections used in the pointing method of Jewish texts intended to remove objectionable expressions referring to God. *See also* accideme; alliteration; apostrophe; apothegm; assonance; autograph; Bible; Bible manuscripts; Bible translations; biblical criticism; chiasmus; conflict story; *constructio ad sensum;* context; contextualization; dittography; double sense fulfillment; doublets; doubling; edification; eisegesis; epanadiplosis; epigrammatic statements; etymology; exegesis; figure of speech; folio; form criticism; gattung; gloss; gnomic sayings; grammatical-historical interpretation; *hapax legomena;* haplography; hermeneutic(s); higher criticism; homographs; homonyms; homophones; *homoteleuton;* hyperbole; idiom; *inclusio;* interpolation; interpretation; inverted nun; irony; isagogics; *itture sopherim;* jot and tittle; kere; *kethib;* "L"; liberalists interpretation; literal interpretation; litotes; loan words; lower criticism; "M"; Masoretic Text; minuscule(s); mystery of God; omission; onomastica; onomatopoeia; palimpsest; papyrus; paradigm; parallelism; parchment; *paroimia; paronomasia;* pericope; personification; Peshitta; pointing; point of view; polyglot; principles of interpretation; proof texting; pun(s); "Q"; redaction; revelation, theological; rhetorical criticism; rhetorical devices; riddle; satire; *scripto continua;* scriptorium; *sebirin;* simile; similitude; source criticism; sources, primary and secondary; special points; strophe; superscription; symbol(s); synecdoche; syntax; synthetic parallelism; text; textual criticism; Time Texts; Torah; translation; transposition; transition; trope; type(s); typology; uncial(s); vellum; verbicide.

Tiglath-pileser I: an early monarch of Assyria near the time of Samuel and conqueror of Babylonia (1114–1076 B.C.). *See also* Assyria Assyrians; king(s).

Tiglath-pileser II: king of Assyria 966–935 B.C. He was not considered a capable ruler and of little interest to biblical study. *See also* Assyria, Assyrians; king(s).

Tiglath-pileser III: perhaps the most able of the Assyrian rulers (745–727 B.C.). He was also called Pul, the only monarch of the three bearing the name mentioned in the Bible. He was not only a conqueror but also an able administrator and governmental organizer. It was he who sacked the Northern Kingdom of Israel in 732 B.C. to be followed ten years later by another invasion that abolished the nation. *See also* Assyria, Assyrians; king(s); Sargon II; Shalmaneser.

Tigris River: one of the two great rivers of Mesopotamia. It, along with the Euphrates, was at the heart of the Assyrian and Babylonian empires as well as others in the same region throughout history. The Tigris is generally faster flowing than the Euphrates. *See also* Euphrates River; Mesopotamia.

Tiki: 1. a Polynesian god or the embodiment of his power called *mana*. According to Maori mythology, he was the first man created by Tumatauenga or Tane. In Hawaiian tradition the first human was Kumuhonua; in Tahiti he was Ti'i; in the Marquesas Islands, there exists a variety of legends concerning human creation. In the Cook Islands, Tiki guards the entry to the underworld called *Auaiki*. 2. carvings in wood or stone of ancestral or nature spirits of the Philippine Islands and other Polynesian, Micronesian, and Melanesian cultures. 3. a 20th century decorative style familiar to many Polynesian-themed restaurants or the gaudily colored strung lights or torches of an outdoor patio (not capitalized). *See also* cargo cult(s); Huna; John Frum religion; kahuna; Kokopelli; Loki; Lono; *mana*; Moai; Pele.

Tillich, Paul Johannes: a German-American Lutheran minister and existential philosopher (1886–1965) whom many consider to be the most influential theologian of the 20th century. Tillich's theology (or perhaps philosophy is a more accurate description) is based on what he called the "method of correlation" by which he attempted to explain ontology (the concept of "being") as a relationship between divine revelation and existential philosophy. The result was a ponderous three-volume work entitled *Systematic Theology* and some other publications. *See also* existentialism; Lutheran Church; philosophy of religion.

time: the measured progression of history and the seasons. Quantifying time is essential for human development and understanding but it should be remembered that God is immune to it except as a tool of divine power. It was the first creation and allows us a means of charting our lives (*e.g.* Ecclesiastes 3). All of human history transpires in time. Whatever method of calendar or time-keeping device we devise will always be an artificial invention, however, because God is above time and capable of intervening or manipulating it at any point. Peter reports that, to God, existence in the mind of God is alien to human thinking. He says, "With the Lord a day is like a thousand years, and a thousand years are like a day" (2 Pe. 3:8). Time truly is history and mystery. The essential Greek word for time, *kronos,* may also indicate a span of time ended or about to end. *See also* apocalyptic calculation; apocalyptic time; due time, in; *en takhei;* eschaton; "I am coming quickly"; *kairos; kronos;* present age, the (this); soon; "soon, but not yet"; time, the present; time is near, the; timeline, eschatological; things that must soon take place, the; times and the seasons, the; times of the Gentiles; time, the present; time, understanding (knowing) the; Today; "waiting for the Lord"; "which must soon (shortly) take place."

time, apocalyptic. See apocalyptic time.

time is near, the: an eschatological reference to the nearness of Christ's Second Coming. The season of the *Parousia* is readying itself for completion, a promise the Bible and Jesus called "soon." What "soon" implies for us is surely not in God's program since the divine mind moves in differing patterns. Peter says: "The Lord is not slow in keeping his promise, as some understand slowness. He is patient with you, not wanting anyone to perish, but everyone come to repentance" (2 Pe. 3:9). *See also* apocalyptic time; due time, in; *en takhei;* eschatology, eschatological; eschaton; "I am coming quickly"; *kairos;* soon; "soon, but not yet"; things that must soon take place, the; time; time is near, the; timeline, eschatological; times and the seasons, the; times of the Gentiles;

time, the present; time, understanding (knowing) the; "waiting for the Lord"; "which must soon (shortly) take place."

timeline, eschatological: a graphic designed to illustrate the various interpretations of end time events. The depiction is simple, the base of which is a horizontal line drawn on the page left to right. The *terminus ad quo* on the left is to represent eternity past (or some other arbitrary starting point) and the *terminus ad quem* is to point eternity future (or some other subjective point of ending desired). Intersecting vertical lines are commonly inserted on the base timeline periodically to represent those eschatological events deemed important to pinpoint chronologically so the end time scenario can be visualized and more easily interpreted. The spaces above and below the timeline may be filled with any notes, illustrations, or explanations the artist may deem helpful. The values of a pictorial representation of eschatological events are obvious. The production can be constructed by student or academic alike as a welcome study aid or teaching model. Moreover, all theories (*e.g.*, pre-Tribulational, mid-Tribulational, post-Tribulational, premillennial, postmillennial, amillennial, etc.,) can be readily displayed. Timelines are standard teaching tools for historical purposes, but an eschatological one emphasizes futuristic theology. *See also* apocalyptic time; *en takhei*; eschatology, eschatological; eschaton; *kairos;* present age, the (this); soon; "soon but not yet"; things that must soon take place, the; time; time is near, the; times and the seasons, the; time, the present; time, understanding (knowing) the; Today; "waiting for the Lord"; "which must soon (shortly) take place."

time of Jacob's trouble: the Old Testament designation for the end of days when the Jewish people will be harshly oppressed as never before. It will be the time of God's great disciplinary dealings with His chosen people. According to Zechariah 13:7–9, some two-thirds of the Jewish population then will lose their lives and only a third will survive. The same time in New Testament terminology is "the Tribulation." *See also* anti-Semitic; Days of Awe; eschatology, eschatological; Great Tribulation; hour of testing; hour of trial; Judaism; remnant; Tribulation.

time of restoration: the Bible's declaration (Acts 3:21) that Jesus is to remain in heaven until the proper moment to restore all in compliance with Christ's kingdom. *See also* eschatology, eschatological; time of fulfillment; times of refreshing.

times and the seasons, the: a generic phrase for countenancing the march of time until the end of days. In Daniel 2:21, God is described as the One who controls the times and the seasons, and Antiochus (Antichrist) is one who tries to alter them (Daniel 7:25). *See also* apocalyptic time; *en takhei;* eschatology, eschatological; eschaton; *kairos;* present age, the (this); soon; "soon but not yet"; things that must soon take place, the; time; time is near, the; timeline, eschatological; times of fulfillment; time of Jacob's trouble; time of restoration; times of refreshing; times of the Gentiles; time, the present; time, understanding (knowing) the; Today; "waiting for the Lord" "which must soon (shortly) take place."

times of fulfillment: Paul's explanation of the believers' perfection to be completed on the day when Christ brings all of heaven and earth under his governorship (Eph. 1:10). The consummation is presented as a coming together under Christ and the filling up of the mystery of God. *See also* apocalyptic time; eschatology, eschatological; time; time of restoration; times of refreshing; "waiting for the Lord."

times of refreshing: a description of the Millennium (Ps. 91; Acts 3:19–26) stressing rest and satisfaction. The theme is found as part of Peter's sermon at Pentecost when he reminded his listeners that the Messiah could (and would) bring refreshment to their souls after sin's forgiveness—both now in Christ's presence and in the future era of peace. The phrase then could easily hold a contented emotion for the believer of the present because sin has been forgiven and the birth, death, and resurrection of Jesus have accomplished it in the here and now, as well as the eternal future. *See also* crushing rock that became a mountain; election; elect, the; eschatology, eschatological; kingdom that cannot be shaken, a; kingdom, the; messianic age, the; millennial geography; millennial Sabbath; millennial sacramentalism; millennial Temple; millennial worship; Millennium, millennial; New Covenant, the; New Eden; rebuilding the Temple; restoration of all things; restoration of Israel (the Jews); restoration Temple (and land); rod of iron; Sabbath rest; Temple(s); third Temple; time of restoration; times of fulfillment.

times of the Gentiles: a period of unknown duration that most ascribe to be our present age. Jesus used the term in his Olivet Discourse to define an era in which the world's rough ethic and apostasy will hold sway until his return at the Second Coming event (Lk. 21:24). Most historians agree that the time referenced began in 606 B.C. and will continue until the Second Coming of Christ. *See also* age of grace; age of the Gentiles; apocalyptic time; fullness of the Gentiles; Gentile(s); "great parenthesis, the"; prophetic postponement; time is near, the; times and the seasons, the; time, understanding (knowing) the; "waiting for the Lord".

time texts: those biblical references that point to some hint of the time of Jesus' Second Coming. None gives a precise date, which is a futile and forbidden tactic, but all of them may reveal signs of the times that alert us to the approaching *Parousia*. *See also* apocalyptic, apocalypticism; eschatology, eschatological; *Parousia;* Second Coming.

time, the present: designation of the present moment of our lives. In apocalyptic thinking, however, the present time takes on another significance related to the time to come, the eschaton. Perhaps the most compelling discussion of present time in an eschatological context is from Paul as recorded in Romans 13:11–14. Therein, the apostle insisted that we "understand" it. Then, in Colossians 4:5, he urged us to redeem the time or "make the most of it." How are we to understand time in the present stretching into forever? Comprehension of the day and hour of our existence, with an outlook to the future, is realized by a conviction that: (1) it's time to "wake up" to end-of-the-age matters, (2) salvation (defined here as eternity) is near, (3) the night (our untenable presence in human form) is nearly over, (4) the day (of blessed redemption) is almost here, (5) putting aside dark deeds (sin), and (6) clothing ourselves with Christ (the only trustworthy guarantee of eternal life). *See also* apocalyptic time; eschaton; present age, the (this); time; time is near, the; timeline, eschatological; times and the seasons, the; Today.

time, times, and half a time: the length of time the woman Israel is to be cared for in safety (Rev. 12:14) and the period required to satisfy the prophecy of the angel in Daniel 12:1–7. It is also the predicted days of suffering for God's people noted in Daniel 7:25

under the sway of the terrible monster. Additionally, the time enumerates those days the two faithful witnesses of Revelation 11 are effective in their unique ministries. Undoubtedly, all references pertain to the troubles of the Great Tribulation as well as those experienced closer to Daniel's time. The actual length delineated is 1,260 days, or two years and a half. *See also* forty-two months; Great Tribulation; numbers, symbology of; Tribulation.

time, understanding (knowing) the: Paul's admonition (Rom. 13:11) for the people of Christ to "wake up," see what time it is (nearing the Second Coming), and put aside dark, evil deeds. Such attitudes are to be replaced in favor of redeeming the hours in Christian love and action. *See also* apocalyptic calculation; apocalyptic time; due time, in; *en takhei;* eschatology, eschatological; eschaton; *kairos;* present age, the; soon; "soon but not yet"; things that must soon take place, the; time; time is near, the; timeline, eschatological; time of Jacob's trouble; times and the seasons, the; times of fulfillment; times of the Gentiles; times of refreshing; times of restoration; time, the present; Today; "waiting for the Lord"; "which must soon (shortly) take place."

timewave, the: the idea that new forms and developments come into existence in our society at increasingly rapid rates. The progress of knowledge is said to evolve in an up-and-down sinusoid, not a smooth graph-like curve. Such a time wave peaked in the 1960s, according to the theorists, at a rate sixty-four times faster than a previous one in 500 B.C. (when Plato, Buddha, and other intellectuals were active). Such a spike is called an "ingression of novelty" as explained by Alfred North Whitehead. According to some thinkers, the timewave was predicted to surge to a point on or before December 21, 2012, to a state called "timewave zero." The 2012ologists Dennis (b. 1950) and Terence McKenna (d. 2000) predicted that moment as the time the human race would be overwhelmed or stymied in its reasoning abilities. *See also* adjacent possible; Jumping Jesus Phenomenon, the; Law of Accelerating Returns, the; point of infinity; zero state.

timewave zero. See timewave, the.

Timon: one of the seven deacons chosen by the early church to assist the apostles (Acts 6:5). *See also* deacon(s), deaconess(es).

Timothy: arguably Paul's favorite disciple whom he called "my son." Timothy's biological father was a Greek, but his mother, Eunice, and grandmother, Lois, were Jews who reared him devoutly. The young preacher enjoyed a good spiritual education and was well respected among the elders (Acts 16:1–2). Timothy was a frequent companion with Paul and served as pastor at Ephesus where he was martyred. His mentor wrote at least two letters to him, known in the New Testament and 1 and 2 Timothy. It is speculated that the young servant was of shy but dedicated personality and perhaps prone to some unknown physical weakness or illness. Timothy was evidently the subject of a number of prophecies about him (1 Tim. 1:18–19) to the effect that he would be an able minister during his lifetime. *See also* Eunice; 1 and 2 Timothy as New Testament epistles; liturgical year; Lois; Titus as New Testament epistle.

tippet: a long black cloth worn by Anglican clergy and some other ecclesiastical vocationists in various designs and styles. *See also* furniture and furnishings of the modern church; Anglicanism.

Tirhakah: Egyptian or Ethiopian pharaoh who tried to assist Judah in rebellion against the Assyrians (ca. 688 B.C.). The Assyrians, led by Sennacherib, crushed the uprising. Hezekiah was king of Judah at that time (2 Ki. 19:9). *See also* Amasis; Amenhotep II; Ay; Egypt, Egyptians; Hophra; king(s); Menes; Merneptah; Necho II; pharaoh; Pharaoh of the Exodus; Ramses II; Sesotris; Shabaka; Shishak; So.

Tir na nOg: a sort of Celtic heaven, a place for youth in another world beyond the western sea. *See also* Abraham's bosom; afterlife; Annwn; Aralu; Arcadia; Asgard; Avalon; Celtic folklore and religion; Dis; Duat; Elysium; eschatology, eschatological; eternal life; future life, doctrine of the; Gehenna; Hades; happy hunting ground; heaven; hell; Hy-Breasail; Hyperborea; intermediate state; Jade Empire, the; Jahannam; Janna; lake of fire; life after death; limbo; *Limbus Puerorum;* Mictlan; Nirvana; Otherworld; Paradise; paradise of God; Pardes; Perdition; Promised Land, the; Pure Land, the; purgatory; Shambhala legends; *Sheol;* Sidhe; soul sleep; space doctrine; Summerland; Thule, land of; underworld; Upper Gehenna; Utopia; Valhalla; world to come, the; Xibala.

Tirshatha: the Persian title for the governor of Judah. Nehemiah could have been said to bear the designation since he was appointed by the Persian ruler after the Babylonian Exile. *See also* Nehemiah as governor.

Tirza: the capital city of the Northern Kingdom of Israel until it was moved to Samaria by Omri. *See also* Samaria.

Tisha b'Av: a Jewish commemoration (on the ninth day of the Hebrew month of Av) in remembrance of the two most tragic events in Jewish history—the destruction of the temples of Solomon (586 B.C.) and Herod (A.D. 70). Today, even marriage ceremonies include the smashing of a drinking glass under the foot of the groom to recognize the despair of the Temple's destruction still fresh in Jewish memory. The observance is a day of mourning and fasting, consumed in contemplation without shoes on the feet, bathing, shaving, perfume, washing of clothes, or personal greetings. Other misfortunes for the Jews are also recognized on the day, including the expulsion of Jews from England in 1290 and the date in 1492 when Ferdinand and Isabella of Spain launched the Inquisition, all of which occurred in the month of Av. Further, the day commemorates Jacob's confrontation with Esau, the return of the unfaithful spies to start the forty years of desert wandering in the Exodus, the desecration of Solomon's Temple with Asherah poles, plowing of the Temple site with salt by the Romans under Turnus Rufus and the beginning of the city of Aelia Capitolina, the era of the Bar Kokhba rebellion that killed a 1,000,000 Jews, the martyrs of York where 500 died when mobs stormed a castle in York, England, the declaration of the first Crusade by Pope Urban II that saw 10,000 Jews slaughtered in the first month, the defilement of the Temple by Antiochus, the beginning of World War I, the day Jeremiah cursed the day of his birth because he despised being a prophet of doom for the land and people of Judah, France's persecution of the Jews in A.D. 1306, the massacre of Jews in Catalonia, Spain, the murder of 3,000 Jews in Poland in 1648, the expulsion from Austria, and the beginning of mass deportations of Jews to the Nazi Death Camps in 1942. As if that were not enough, the Temple was destroyed on the ninth of Av in 586 B.C. by the Babylonians and again by the Romans in 70 A.D. It was also the day of Hitler's proclamation to exterminate all the Jews and was the date all

Jews were expelled from the Gaza Strip in 2005. The anniversary is also called the "Between the Straits," a phrase taken from Lamentations 1:3: "All her [Judah's] persecutors overtook her *in dire straits.*" The books of Lamentations and Job are traditionally read on this day. Jewish tradition still includes prayer for the building of the third Temple in the days of the Messiah. A Christian conviction has surfaced, drawn from a similar Jewish tradition, which says that the Antichrist will be born on *Tisha-b'Av* and will commence building the third Temple. *See also* Alhambra Decree; anti-Semitic; Babylonian Captivity; feasts and special days of Judaism; Holocaust, holocaust; Inquisition, the; Jewish persecution; Judaism; Lamentations, book of; persecution(s); *shoah.*

Tishbe: the hometown of Elijah in Gilead.

Titanomachy: the legendary story of the epic battle between the giant Titans against the Olympians. The battle lasted ten years with victory finally coming to the Olympian court led by Zeus. There may be hints in the account of the legendary Atlantis. *See also* Atlantis; Olympian pantheon; Titans.

Titans: a legendary race of giants said to have emerged from the work and union of Gaia (Earth) and Uranus (Sky) to become the first of the Greek pantheon. The chief members were Oceanus, Hyperion, Coeus, Cronus, Crius, and Lapetus (males) and Mnemosyne, Tethys, Theia, Phoebe, Rhea, and Themis (females). Later generations produced other notable deities until the great war with the Olympians led by Zeus overcame them. The Greek writers, Homer and Hesiod, named the Titan and his children as counterparts of the scriptural accounts of Satan and his evil angels. The Titans, after defeat, were defeated and ceased to be seriously recognized except some place them as the present occupants of Tartarus. *See also* Anunnaki; Cronus; Cyclopes; Dionysus the god; Fir Bolg; Fomorians; frost giants; giant(s); Laestrygonians; mythological beasties, elementals, monsters, and spirit animals; Nephilim; Olympian pantheon; Tartarus; *Titanomachy;* Watchers, the; Zeus.

tithe: a tenth of some amount. The tithe, in both Old and New Testaments, was considered the minimum offering owed by the believer to the Lord. The prophets often condemned the withholding of the tithe and called it robbing God (Mal. 3:6–12). The scribes and Pharisees also tithed, but their attitude was a sham of the true intent and meaning of the practice. They habitually portioned off a trifle of the minuscule dill and cumin seeds but neglected the weightier matters of the law—justice, mercy, and faithfulness (Mt. 23:23). Some of them even declared their income "corban" (reserved for the Lord), so they were relieved of caring for their elderly parents. *See also* altarage; benefice; benefit of clergy; carrodian; *cathedraticum;* church abuse; delict; Leo X, Pope; liturgy, Christian; love offering; mensa; oblation; offering; papacy; "popery"; pornocracy; pounding; prebend; "Prophecy of the Popes"; ritual abuse; Roman Catholic Church; salvation; shepherding (cultic); simony; stipend; Tetzel, Johann.

Titian: heretical Gnostic who taught that Adam was condemned, drinking wine is a sin, the soul is not eternal, and medicine is demonic; he also disbelieved that Christ's divinity and pre-existence were accurate. *See also* Gnosticism, Gnostic(s).

tittle. See jot and tittle.

titular sees: Roman Catholic dioceses where the church once flourished but has since died or ceased to function. Bishops without a territorial diocese of their own (such as auxiliary bishops) are given titular sees. *See also* Roman Catholic Church; see.

titulus: a name plate placed above the head of a crucified victim by the Romans. Pontius Pilate affixed one over the head of Jesus at his crucifixion that named him as "Jesus of Nazareth, the king of the Jews." The inscription was written in Aramaic, Greek, and Latin so any visitor could read it (Jn. 19:19–20) and was usually carried ahead of the crucifixion procession so all could know the criminal and his deeds. If speaking of a relic, name could be capitalized. *See also* INRI; Pilate, Pontius; *Quad scripsi, scripsi;* relic(s); superscription.

Titus: 1. a young contemporary of Paul, a respected pastor and evangelist. He seemed to have been more aggressive in his personality than his fellow pastor in youth, Timothy. 2. the Roman general, the son of Vespasian (both of whom were later emperors), who led the final assault on Jerusalem in A.D. 70. *See also* Arch of Titus; Christianity in the Roman Empire; Jewish War; king(s); liturgical year; Roman Empire; Timothy; Titus as New Testament epistle; Vespasian.

Titus as New Testament epistle: Paul's letter to his younger fellow minster, Titus. False teaching and legalism are condemned. Additionally, the rapture and related events are discussed in the epistle. *See also* Paul as apostle; Titus.

Titus Justus: a worshiper of God in Corinth who lived next door to the synagogue there (Acts 18:7). Paul stayed in his home for a time and probably lectured from there.

Tobiah: an Ammonite living in devastated Jerusalem who mocked and hindered Nehemiah's efforts to refurbish the city (Neh.2:10; 4:3, 7). He was likely a governor of Ammon since he is called "the Ammonite official." *See also* Gesham; Sanballat.

Tobias: 1. a Jewish rebel leader during the occupation of Antiochus III who was allied on the Syrian side. He instigated an insurgence against Egypt, thinking treatment under the Seleucids would be preferable over the Ptolemies. Such proved not to be the case. Tobias's uprising is probably represented in the history of Daniel 11:13–16. 2. a character in the noncanonical short story *Tobit.* *See also* Jew(s); Ptolemaic, Ptolemies; Seleucia, Seleucids; *Tobit.*

Tobit: an adventure story with a moral taken from a combination of two folk tales called "The Grateful Dead" and "The Unlucky Bride." There are also some clear associations with *The Wisdom of Ahikar. Tobit* is replete with Old Testament theology from both the wisdom literature and the prophets, particularly Daniel. The account was popular with the Qumran ascetics, Jews, and Christians. It is especially admired as a Roman Catholic liturgy, which is used in certain worship contexts and in weddings. The main themes of the tale are family life and almsgiving. *See also* Apocrypha, the; Asmodaeus; Tobias; Raphael.

Today: this very date in our lives (Heb. 3:13). The term stresses the idea that people should make the most of the time given to them while the opportunities of life are still open. Some believers enjoy the accumulated time of religious history (Heb. 4:7) as if it were just another moment of living in the routine. From the time of the desert wanderings to the writing of Psalm 95:7–8 (which is quoted in the Hebrews passage), unbelief had stolen away the faith of many. Now, in the time since then, other generations also tend to waste the prospects of salvation and service to God—an attitude that could exclude them from the eternal glorification of heaven. *See also* present age, the (this); time; time, the present; time, understanding (knowing) the.

toe(s). See foot, feet.

Togarmah. See Beth Togarmah.

Toghuzghu: the Uighur people of Central Asia—the only Turkish group to profess the Manichaean religion. *See also* Manicheanism; Ottoman Turks; Seljuk Turks.

token: 1. a small object tendered in pledge or as a representation of some larger deed or material. 2. a sign from God in the form of a lesser miracle in pledge to a larger one to come. 3. a charm. *See also* charm(s); white stone secretly written on.

token of salvation. See sign of the covenant.

Tola: a judge of Israel from the tribe of Issachar (Jud. 10:1–2). He served for twenty-three years following the era of Gideon and Abimelech, but his administration seems to have been devoid of warfare. He is listed as sixth of the judges. *See also* judge(s); Judges as Old Testament book.

Toleration Act of 1649: a.k.a. the Act Concerning Religion, a production of a law passed by the Catholic majority Colonial Maryland legislature, the first of the settlements to grant religious freedom on American soil. Puritans later overturned the effort and oppressed the Catholics and other dissidents, only to see the law restored yet again by Lord Baltimore. The statute was passed when Protestants began to outnumber Roman Catholics in Maryland (a colony established as a Catholic refuge). Protestants were among the 200 passengers on the *Ark* and the *Dove* carrying colonists to the newly chartered lands. The act was limited to Christians, but Jews were not persecuted. The essence of the law was succinctly stated as "noe person...professing to believe in Jesus Christ shall from henceforth be any waies... discountenanced for or in respect of his or her religion nor in the free exercise thereof." Among the early New World settlements, only Maryland and Rhode Island held any semblance of religious toleration. Later, Puritans overtook the Maryland colony and began the harassment of Catholics, Anglicans, Quakers, and

Jews. *See also* antidisestablishmentarianism; anti-Semitic; *Booke of General Lawes and Liberties;* caesaropapacy; Calvert, Cecilius and George; civil religion; collegialism; disestablishmentarianism; Establishment Clause and Free Exercise Clause; Geghan Bill; Johnson Amendment; Massachusetts Body of Liberties; *Pontifex Maximus; princeps, principis;* state church; ultramontanism; Virginia's Religious Disestablishment law.

Tolkien, J. R. R.: accomplished professor of languages and enduring author of the prototype style of writing known as fantasy (January 3, 1902–September 2, 1973). His novels, *The Hobbit* and *The Lord of the Rings* trilogy, are widely read from first publication and have prompted a near cult following (in the secular sense). Though he denied any mindful intent to draw his scenes, characters, and action from any particular literary source, the kinship to biblical scenarios and prophetic themes is unmistakable, whether they were produced consciously or not. Tolkien told intimates that his visions of "Middle Earth" were inspired by recurring dreams experienced by him and one of his sons. The author confessed that these mental disturbances (in which he saw tsunamis) plagued him until he began to write his sagas. Tolkien's theory was that the images sprang for some "racial memory" or a past life (reincarnation) even though he was a staunch Catholic. It was he who voiced the rather brief but insightful definition of magic in its most debilitating sense: Magic is "the thirst for power." *See also* Lewis, Clive Staples; Roman Catholic Church.

"toll collectors." See archon(s).

Tolstoy, Leo: *nee* Count Syev Nikolayevich, Russian writer (1828–1910). He predicted that a Mongolian Slav will someday arrive to supplant monotheism and restore a benevolent pantheism. He was an avowed Christian but strictly non-violent, pacifist, and anarchist. *See also* Mongols.

Toltecs: an early and advanced Mesoamerican (A.D. 800–1200) tribe of Mexico that proved to be the seed civilization of many later advanced peoples of the area. Their ancient prophecies were remarkable and the basis for many Mesoamerican predictions of the future age. *See also* Aztecs; Chilam-Balam; *Dresden Codex;* eagle and the condor, the; Inca; Itza-Maya; Katun Prophecies; Maya; Mesoamerica; *Popul Unh;* Quetzalcoatl.

tones of hymns: various melodies that can be ascribed to hymns and praises commonly used in the Eastern Orthodox Church. There are eight modes in the music for the production of hymns and chants, most of which are proscribed in some manner for proper use in the church calendar. *See also* Eastern Orthodox Church; liturgical year; music.

Tongs. See Triads.

tongue(s): 1. the organ of the mouth aiding speech and taste. The tongue can also be a metaphor for verbal ridicule, abuse, lying, or gossip, or contrariwise, for blessing, praise, song, and worthy instruction. "With the tongue we praise our Lord and Father, and with it we curse men" (Jas. 3:9). The abuser via speech is said to have a "sharp" tongue whereas the gentle or gifted speaker has a "honeyed" tongue. 2. the less-technical name for glossolalia, ecstatic utterance that can be produced under the inspiration of the Holy Spirit. *See also* charisms; gifts of the Holy Spirit; glossolalia; liturgy, Christian; Pentecostalism; tongues, gift of; tongues, interpretation of.

tongues, gift of: the ability to facilitate glossolalia that Paul declared to be a gift of the Holy Spirit, though a lesser one (1 Cor. 12). *See also* charisms; gifts of the Holy Spirit; glossolalia; liturgical year; liturgy, Christian; Pentecostalism; tongue(s); tongues, interpretation of.

tongues, interpretation of: the ability, classed as a gift of the Holy Spirit, to translate the strange language of glossolalia into meaningful speech or religious instruction. According to the authority of Paul (1 Cor. 12:10), the interpretation of tongues is vital because it is necessary to prevent chaos in the church worship scene. *See also* charisms; glossolalia; liturgical year; liturgy, Christian; Pentecostalism; tongue(s); tongues, gift of.

tongues, speaking in. See glossolalia; tongue(s), tongues, gift of; tongues, interpretation of.

tonsure: a monastic hairstyle that exposes the bald head on top with a ring of hair around the head beneath. The look proclaimed the clerical status of the wearer. The hairstyle may have begun with the Celtic Druids, something the Roman Church denied stating it was the tonsure of Saint John; opponents of Christianity at the time claimed it was the tonsure of Simon Magus. In many other parts of the world, the cut was a distinctive mark of the warrior classes and priestly castes. *See also* bald, baldness; Druidism; Eastern Orthodox Church; monasticism; monasticism, degrees of Eastern Orthodox; Roman Catholic Church; Simon Magus.

tooth (teeth): the enameled outgrowth of the inner mouth used in speaking and eating. The term is a frequent figure of speech for sharpness or rending in anger. In metaphoric usage, the breaking of teeth demonstrated a hurtful or damaging blow (Ps. 3:7; Lam. 3:16). Sharp words were like tearing bites (Pro. 30:14). An unjust rebuke was to cast words "into the teeth" of another as Jesus suffered (in some early Bible versions of Matthew 27:44).

Tophet: "the place of burning" mentioned in Jeremiah 7:31–33 as the location of a conjunction of three valleys south of Jerusalem— the Tyropoeon, Hinnom, and Kidron. The site was the city garbage dump where fires were continually alight in an effort to consume some of the refuse. Isaiah seemed to allude to the custom of burning carcasses when speaking of the defeat of Sennacherib (Isa. 30:33), and that reference likely has apocalyptic implications as well. Jeremiah 30:33 identified the site as a hellish burning prepared by God Himself. Worship of the god Molech was practiced in the Tophet vale, including enacted child sacrifice. The kings Ahaz and Manasseh were especially noted for indulging in idolatrous worship at the site. The reforming King Josiah desecrated the place, so none could use it to sacrifice his son or daughter (2 Ki. 23:10). Jews and Arabs speak of it as the mouth of hell. The place was also known as the Valley of Slaughter. The name Tophet may mean "place of fire" or "a place to be spit upon," or it may derive from *toph,* the word for "drum" because such instruments were used to drown out the screams of the dying children. *See also* death; grave; hell; Hades; lake of fire; *Sheol;* Tyropoeon Valley; Valley of Decision; Valley of Hinnom; Valley of Jehoshaphat; Valley of Slaughter.

Torah: the first five books of the Old Testament (the Pentateuch) when capitalized. In a more expanded version of the term, the Torah was the Law of Moses, Israel's unique and treasured possession. At first, it consisted mainly of cultic expression and secularizations in the name of Moses, who received them from

God, and then rendered them to the people as detailed elements of the covenant between Israel and her God. Under the prophets after the eighth century B.C., the Torah was further infused with morals and instructions following the ethical standards of an all-righteous God. So then, the Torah may be named the Pentateuch or the expanded Law of God's chosen people. *See also* Aggadah; Bible; Book of the Covenant; Book of the Law; Gemara; Hagiographa; Halakha; Hebrew Bible; Judaism; Law, the; lower criticism; Masseket Hekalot; Midrash; Mishna; Mosaic Covenant; Mosaic Law; Old Testament; Pentateuch; Prophets, the; Talmud; Targum(s); Tanakh; torah; Torah Scroll; Written Torah and Oral Torah.

torah: the practices, traditions, and ethics (when not capitalized) of Orthodox Judaism as they are faithfully observed by all pious Jews. To dishonor the prophets, for example, would be a breach of torah. The word originally meant "omen." *See also* liturgy, Jewish; Judaism; Torah; Written Torah and Oral Torah.

Torah Code. See Bible Code.

Torah Scroll: treasured Hebrew Scriptures that are normally fixed on parchment or other special paper and wound around two wooden shafts. The bottom pair of rods have handles for unrolling the scroll (the *Sefer Torah*) and capped with a *Kisser* ("crown") on each spindle, typically silver. Other accouterments include the *Atzei Chayim* (the wooden shafts themselves), and the *Gartel* (Yiddish for "belt"), which secures the scroll writing within its ornamented covering when not in use. In addition, the *Mantel* (Yiddish for "cloak") makes up the cover which is usually beautifully embroidered with golden thread, silk, and beads on velvet. Finally, the *Yad* ("hand") accompanies the scroll—a small silver rod with one end resembling a human hand with the index finger extended and used as a pointer when reading the *Sefer*. All are housed at the head of the synagogue in its "Ark" near an eternal flame or light. Orthodox Jews consider the Torah Scroll a living document that requires special skill to repair and may even be ceremonially buried when too worn to be functional. *See also* Book of the Covenant; Book of the Law; Hebrew Bible; Judaism; *Shimchat Torah;* Torah; Written Torah and Oral Torah.

Toronto Airport Christian Fellowship (TACF). See "Toronto Blessing, the".

"Toronto Blessing, the": a.k.a. "that Toronto Thing," Toronto Airport Christian Fellowship (TACF), "Holy Laughter" movement. The movement, and others like it, was also called "the river" because the spirit of the event seemed to flow supernaturally; now it is officially called Catch the Fire Toronto. "The Toronto Blessing" was a near spontaneous revivalist type phenomenon springing up near the Toronto airport. Services featured ecstatic movement, barking, groveling, mock birthing, laughter, falling, and numerous other outrageous behaviors. The movement experienced a limited spread akin to the Brownsville Assembly in Florida and the Azusa Street revival in Los Angeles. *See also* Azusa Street revival; baptism of the Holy Spirit; Brownsville Assembly; glossolalia; holy laughter; Pentecostalism; revivalism; "river, the"; "slain in the Spirit"; theolepsy; tongues, gift of; tongues, interpretation of; tremendum.

Torquemada, Tomas de: arguably the most infamous of the inquisitors, the leader of the famous Spanish Inquisition. His actions were supported and approved by Pope Leo XIII who called the flames of the manifold burnings "blessed." *See also* Innocent VIII, Pope; Inquisition, the; *Malleus Malefiracum;* Roman Catholic Church.

Torrey, Reuben A.: arguably the most influential superintendent of the Moody Bible Institute (1856–1928). He was also a far-ranging evangelist in the premillennialist revivalist stripe. *See also* evangelist(s), evangelism; Moody Bible Institute; Moody, Dwight L.; religious education.

Tortosa: (Tartus), the Crusader name for the fortress site between the Mediterranean Sea and inland Syria, now the city of Homs. It was the last Crusader stronghold to fall, but its nearby island Arwad held out for eleven more years. Nearby was the castle of Krak des Chenciers, a Hospitaller strong point that was never really taken. *See also* Acre; Castle Blanc; Crusades; Horns of Hattin; knighted orders; Outremer.

Tory: a supporter of the mother country, England, during America's Revolutionary War. Many of the loyalists were members of the elitist Episcopalian Church of the time. Their persuasions disenfranchised the church to some extent among the colonies. *See also* Methodists; Protestant Episcopal Church.

Toseftas: a secondary compilation of Jewish laws. It dates to the time before A.D. 450. *See also* Judaism.

total depravity: the theological doctrine that supports the idea that humanity is forever tainted by sin and capable of redemption only by the act of the savior Jesus. The Fall event from Eden has broken us to moral damage, the severity of which we seldom contemplate. This dissoluteness need not be total, however, since being created in the image of God, we hold godlike attributes such as patience, love, compassion, self-awareness, etc. Total depravity does not mean that humans are as wicked as they can be but relates to the extent of our immorality—the depth of it in our consciousness and the expandability of its borders. The measurement of that spread is not to be plotted by human standards but by the fixed and unqualified imperatives set by God Himself. Nor can we quantify the severity of our moral decline (except to watch it do so) but can only await God's judgment of it. For now, we may seek only the remedy of forgiveness in Christ and redouble our feeble efforts to behave honorably. Many scriptural references support the doctrine of total depravity, including Romans 3:10–12. Calvinist doctrine posits that depravity is indeed *total* and salvation will not accrue to those not preordained to salvation by God's sovereign will, a doctrine known as "double predestination." *See also* BACON; Calvinism; conditional election; double predestination; election; elect, the; eternal security; fall from grace; Fall, the; Five-Point Calvinism; free will; grace; hyper-Calvinism; limited atonement; image of God; noetic effect; "once saved, always saved; Original Sin; perseverance of the saints; predestination; social issues; TULIP; Westminster Confession.

totemism: a conviction of one or more individuals who believe that a mystical connection exists between the owner and a totem that is constructed of selected natural materials and spiritual intent for him. A totem can be of any substance desired (so long as it derives from nature) or desired size if the maker ascribes a sacral or spiritual manifestation to the object. Some primitive cultures worship using totems. Most commonly known are Native Americans of the Pacific Northwest, Eskimos (the Aleut), Moluccans of the interior Amboina Islands of Indonesia, and certain Pacific islanders. The Maori of New Zealand are still excellent pole and decorative wood carvers. Traditions of the Tsimshian Indians of

British Columbia obligated a family totem outside each home. A totem *pole* was often used to distinguish the various tribal units. The word "totem" likely springs from the Algonquin dialect. The practice is akin to animism, but the two beliefs are not the same by definition. *See also* animism; Asherah pole(s); May Day; medicine wheel; Mongols; mythological beasties, elementals, monsters, and spirit animals; nature cult(s); peace pole; pillars of the universe; revitalization movement; sky pole.

Totensonntag: a. k. a. Sunday of the Dead, Eternity Sunday, Silent Day, or Totenfest, a German Protestant religious holiday commemorating the dead. *See also* Day of the Dead; Dead Sunday; Death; death; feasts and special days of Protestantism; liturgical year; liturgy, Christian.

Touro Synagogue: the first dedicated synagogue in America. It was established in Newport, Rhode Island, in 1763 and is still in operation. *See also* Judaism; synagogue.

tower: a high structure used as a lookout for danger, a refuge, or a defensive position. Metaphorically, the tower illustrates those functions, and if one is captured or destroyed, the outcome is considered a civic or military disaster (*i.e.,* Isaiah 30:25, Luke 13:4). *See also* Akra; Antonia Fortress; Babel, tower of; Galilean blameless victims; minaret; Tower of David; watchtower of the flock; ziggurat.

tower of Babel. See Babel, tower of; ziggurat.

Tower of David: a structure in the Old City of Jerusalem once thought to be part of David's palace; Byzantine Christians mistook it as such dating back to the eighth century B.C. The location was subsequently considered as the start of the *Via Dolorosa* until the 13th century A.D. That site eventually proved to be a reconstruction by Herod the Great of a Hasmonean edifice that he used to fortify his own palace. There remains but one of three historical towers in the city today—the Tower of David or the Jerusalem Citadel. *See also* Antonia Fortress; *ecce homo;* Jerusalem, landmarks of; Lithostrotos; Praetorium; tower; *Via Dolorosa.*

towers of silence: above ground structures upon which are placed the dead in Zoroastrian funeral ritual. The body remains there lest the sacred earth be defiled by corruption. *See also* burial; excarnation; Zoroaster, Zoroastrianism.

Toxcatl: perhaps the greatest Mexican festival of the year. The recognition comes from the barbaric Aztec practice of sacrificing a comely youth to Tezatlipoca, the "god of gods," after worshiping the victim for a full year. Oddly enough, the festival occurs close to the dates for Easter. *See also* Aztecs; Mesoamerica.

tract(s): 1. an older term for Lent when the Alleluias were omitted in the worship. 2. a religious pamphlet describing some doctrinal position (usually concerning repentance and salvation) intended to be distributed liberally. Many are cheaply produced, liberally illustrated, and quite parochial in content, sometimes to the point of being offensive and unwelcome. *See also* evangelist(s), evangelism; incunabula; plan of salvation; religious education; "Roman Road, the"; Tractarianism; witness(es).

Tractarianism: the policies and doctrines of the Anglican Church, particularly as it applied to the Oxford Movement. *See also* Anglicanism; Church of England; "high and dry"; High Church, Low Church; Oxford Movement; tract(s).

trade guilds: *collegia,* associations of related industries or crafts joined for mutual advantage in trade and commerce. Demetrius and his group of silversmiths (Acts 19:25–41) is one biblical example. Nevertheless, the real purpose of the guilds was primarily social and, most often, occasions for debauchery and revelry before the gods. We might call them rudimentary unions without the partying. Such cooperatives were common in the city of Thyatira and influenced the church there in a negative fashion (Rev. 2:18–29). *See also* orgies; religious organizations; Thyatira.

traditional church. See church models.

traditionalism: adherence to what has been believed in the past in preference to newer ideas or concepts. Churches and denominations can hold traditions of their faiths as naturally as any other organization. Some traditions, including religious ones, are worthy but others are proven to be hindrances or sources of pride (Mk. 7:8) *See also* church models; Eastern Orthodox Church; Roman Catholic Church; tradition (Eastern Orthodox and Roman Catholic).

traditional Zionism. See Zionism.

tradition (Eastern Orthodox and Roman Catholic): a critical precept of the Roman Catholic system of doctrinal formation derived from papal pronouncements, evolved ecclesiastical law, and general usage. Biblical authority is a separate source, but often enough, tradition holds greater authority. *See also* Eastern Orthodox Church; Roman Catholic Church; traditionalism.

traditions of the elders: the many laws and ritual expectations derived from early Jewish generations and diligently passed to the younger. They were supposedly drawn from the Law of Moses but Jesus condemned them as far too rigid with too many inventions and ridiculous codices promoted by the Pharisees and scribes. *See also* Judaism; Karaites; Law, the; Pharisees; Sadducees; "your own traditions."

traducianism: or transducianism and transducianist theology, the idea that the human soul is transmitted from parents to their children. The doctrine sprang from Tertullian and, later with his hearty emphasis on Original Sin, Augustine of Hippo as interpreted from Genesis 35:18 and Matthew 10:28. A parallel but opposite idea is that ensoulment is a gift of the Holy Spirit. *See also* Adam; Adamic Covenant; Augustine, Aurelius; ensoulment; Eve; Fall, the; federal theory of guilt; imputation; noetic effect; Original Sin; Tertullian; total depravity.

"trafficking in Masses": a Roman Catholic practice whereby its priests could claim a stipend for celebrating a Mass to heal a living person, speed a soul through purgatory, or for other religious reasons. The process was stopped by the dictates of Vatican II. It should be no surprise that a profitable scheme arose as independent priests developed a lively mail order system for personal benefit. In no way could a single celebrant keep up with the pay-to-order demand. Nevertheless, the money kept coming but was never returned because of pure penury. *See also* Mass; Mass of Saint Secaire; papal revenue; Roman Catholic Church.

Traill, Stewart: (b. 1936) founder of the modern cult called the Church of Bible Understanding, or the "Forever Family." Traill was Canadian but operated his cult in Allentown, Pennsylvania. He was a former vacuum cleaner repairman and son of a Presbyterian minister who gained a reputation as one of this century's most notorious cult leaders. *See also* cult(s).

Trajan: Roman emperor (ca. A.D. 53–117). Under his administration, the Roman Empire realized its greatest expanse. Trajan's legacy is a positive one, even in accounts of the early church. A medieval tale called "The Golden Legend" relates that Pope Gregory I resurrected him from the dead and baptized him into the Catholic faith—a farfetched idea indeed. He appears in Dante's *Divine Comedy* as a heavenly resident. *See also* Christianity in the Roman Empire; king(s); Roman Empire.

transcendence: a theological term declaring that God is "over" or superior to His creation. The philosophical message pertains to that which is outside or beyond the range of human experience or understanding. *See also* immanence; Merkabah mysticism; ultramundane.

transcendentalism: a quasi-religious and philosophical movement from the early 19th century in the Eastern United States. The group arose in protest against the intellectualism prevalent at the time, especially at Harvard Divinity School and in the Unitarian Church. A magazine called the *Dial* was the guiding organ of the movement edited by Ralph Waldo Emerson, George Ripley, and Margaret Fuller. Transcendentalist ideas were a curious blend of humanism, mysticism, and reason. Emerson's take on the movement has been called "intuitive perceptions of truth" held comfortably without the constrictions of Calvinism or individual convictions operating within well-defined limits and rules. Members honored the inherent goodness in both people and nature but were anti-Trinitarian and anti-predestination in doctrine. For them, the favored term "over-soul" represented a medium of communion and "God" was a causal agent, as well as a medium, to encounter the soul. Their motto might be found in their rallying cry: "plain living and high thinking." Prominent members included Ralph Waldo Emerson, Frederic Hedge, Orestes Brownson, George Putman, Henry David Thoreau, Emily Dickinson, Louisa May Alcott, Henry Wadsworth Longfellow, Walt Whitman, and the indomitable Elizabeth Palmer Peabody—close associate and facilitator to Hawthorne, Channing, Emerson, and others. Some transcendentalists even established several communal retreats, the best-known of which was Brook Farm at West Roxbury, Massachusetts, in 1841 under the leadership of Albert Brisbane (1809–1890). A number of prominent transcendentalists relocated to Concord, Massachusetts, where they were known as the Concord Group. All such experiments were failures, and the transcendentalists soon faded from influence. *See also* Clarke, James Freeman; Emerson, Ralph Waldo; Fruitlands Community; Heckler, Isaac Thomas; Parker, philosophy of religion; Theodore; Ripley, George.

Transcendental Meditation (TM): an altered state of consciousness favored by many of the New Age persuasion. The technique was popularized by Maharishi Mahesh Yogi who combined yoga, intense meditation, and similar techniques to train the mind to a higher plane. TM is said to expand creativity, nurture self-awareness, and promote world peace. Some actors have even tried (unsuccessfully) to levitate their bodies. An alternate name to the practice is sometimes seen as the World Executive Council. *See also* Beatles, the; holistic; New Age religion; Reiki; sect(s); yoga; Yogi, Maharishi Mahesh.

transducianist theology. See traducianism.

Transfiguration, Feast of the: the celebration of Christ's transfiguration practiced in both Roman Catholicism and Eastern Orthodoxy, although at different times of the year. *See also* Eastern Orthodox Church; feasts and special days of high liturgy faiths; liturgical year; Roman Catholic Church; Transfiguration, the.

Transfiguration, the: the experience by which Jesus and his clothing became luminously changed and charged in bright light in the presence of a select number of his disciples (Mk. 9:2–13). While in this exalted appearance, he conferred with Moses and Elijah, much to the amazement of those watching. The incident may have eschatological significance in that the Shekinah glory of God was manifest at that time as it will be again in the future. It may also be that Moses and Elijah are now prepared by the experience to assume the roles of the two faithful witnesses in Revelation 11:1–14, partly because of their experiences on the Mount of Transfiguration. *See also* liturgical year; Mount of Transfiguration; Mount Tabor; Shekinah glory; Tabor light; Transfiguration, Feast of the.

Transformational Church Assessment Tool (TCAT): a research and measurement process (with any number of related scientific evaluation tools) for assessing the goals and dynamics of a congregation or denomination. A congregation can use such instruments to evaluate and plan various strategies for growth, paradigm change, or modification in the manner of congregational operations and purpose. *See also* church models.

transgression(s). See sin(s).

transhumance: the movement of flocks or herds by nomadic peoples to varying locations to obtain forage and water while maintaining a central base for the family or clan (*e.g.,* Genesis 37). The method was a common ranching procedure for the ancients. *See also* "going here and there"; great migration(s).

transhumanism: a modern social and scientific concept sometimes called posthumanism. Its shorthand rendition is often written as a simple "H+." The idea deals with the notion that man can become more than human—a superman. (Interestingly, the original Superman of comic book fame was an evil character and based on Friedrich Nietzsche's view of humanity.) Accomplishment is almost universally considered possible by transhumanists through DNA manipulation of either the genes of humans or animals to make us better, or even to make us a new order of beings. (Also, interestingly, the Bible promises the same in Christ whereby we are made new creatures by regeneration and resurrection.) The scientific fields, including genetics, robotics, artificial intelligence, nanotechnology, neuropharmacology, cybernetics, and synthetic biology are well underway to "improve," or at least redesign, the human mind, memory, physiology, reproduction apparatus, philosophy, and perhaps even our very souls. In essence, the transhumant scientist views the human body as mere hardware that can, and should, be re-engineered and improved. Technically speaking, if one has a pacemaker, a hip replacement, or similar devices in the body, the user can be considered a model for incipient transhumanism. Few recognize or worry that a mutation or genetic error could be disastrous for the human race, preferring rather to praise the benefits of fighting disease and other medical advantages. Transhumanists have, therefore, discounted the biblical worldview and most class Christianity (and religion in general) as an outdated myth. Traditional religious views, which are shamefully seldom expressed, are of no consequence. Even so, despite protestations of some in the research fields, the transhumanist worldview itself fits the standard criteria of a religion. Our cultural institutions—the media, government bureaucracy, academia, medicine, and ever increasingly, the churches, have adopted the idea as a good one. The prediction is that within thirty years, no one will die; or, at least, we will all live to be one thousand years of age or more. There is little scientific doubt that given sufficient duration, funding, and legal disinterest, such a procedure will be possible on a practical level in a very short span of time. In truth, they have already succeeded since we can now create male eggs and female sperm, make hybrid human/animal specimens, and have set ourselves on a path to *Homo Evolutis* (a term from Juan Enriquez, CEO of Biotechonomy). Taiwanese scientists have mingled the genetic material of pigs with glowing jellyfish and produced real green eggs and ham! The moral and ethical repercussions, however, will be enormous. Primarily, the process violates God's law of reproduction according to kind—in His image and likeness. Transformation, at its center, seeks to disconnect us from God forever and meets the primary objective of the practice to "advance evolution" by jump-starting it. Not a few conservative apocalypticists have predicted the fulfillment of at least three end time prophecies as a direct consequence of transhumanism: 1. the replication of the "days of Noah" (Mt. 24:37) in which evil angels bred a race of hybrid human and animals upon the earth according to Genesis 6, 2. the imprecation of the "mark of the beast" (Rev. 13:16–17), and 3. the arrival of the end time "doctrine of demons" as indicated in 1 Timothy 4:1 and 2 Timothy 4:2. The mixing of human seed with animals is but a phase for a more sinister goal—the sabotage of human DNA, something Satan has already attempted in the past and probably will again at the end of the age. Speculation exists already that it may be the means by which the Antichrist escapes death and manages a functional recovery from his so-called mortal wound suffered in Revelation 13:3. *See also* alien Jesus; Anak; Ancient Astronaut Theory; Anunnaki; beast, image of the; *Chariots of the Gods?;* chimera; Eckart, Dietrich; egregores; *elohim;* eugenics; evolution; God gene, the; giant(s); Gregori; GRIN; Hitler, Adolf; Human Animal Hybrid Prohibition Act; Human Enhancement Revolution (HER); Igigi; Kurzweil, Ray; lulu; Mount Hermon; Nietzsche, Friedrich; Nephilim; Oannes and the Seven Sages;

Overman; panspermia theory; "post-secularists"; Sibyl(s); singularity; sociology of religion; Theosophy; Thule Society; transmutation; von Daniken, Erich; Watchers, the.

"transition of consciousness": the idea forwarded by the Mayan seer Pacal Votan stating that a great cosmic change would transpire on or before December 21, 2012, that would close the world-age cycles. The transition phase, which we are now experiencing, represents the death of the old world order and the birth of the new. That time will be brought about, according to Votan, when mankind completely abandons nature's ways in preference for all-consuming materialism. *See also* Chilam-Balam; eagle and the condor, the; Eagle Bowl; five stages of earth, the; Inca; Katun Prophecies; Maya; Sun Stone; 2012 prophecy, advocates of; 2012, prophecy of; Votan, Pacal.

Transjordan: land along the east side of the Jordan River in what is now the Hashemite kingdom of Jordan. *See also* division of Israel; forest of the south; Galilee; Gilead; Idumea, Idumean(s); Israel; Judah; Judea; Kinneret; Palestine; provinces of Palestine; Samaria; West Bank.

translation: 1. the process of rendering the Bible, or any other text, from one language to another. There are around sixty modern Bible translations in use today alone. 2. a term for the sudden seizure of believers from earth to heaven (1 Th. 4:16–17). 3. the transfer of a bishop or other official from one center of service to another. *See also* accideme; allegorical interpretation; alliteration; analogical interpretation; apostrophe; apothegm; assonance; autograph; Bible; Bible manuscripts; Bible translations; biblical criticism; chiasmus; conflict story; *constructio ad sensum;* context; contextualization; dittography; double sense fulfillment; doublets; doubling; dynamic equivalence; edification; eisegesis; epanadiplosis; epigrammatic statements; eschatology, eschatological; etymology; exegesis; figure of speech; folio; form criticism; Fourfold Interpretation; gattung; gloss; gnomic sayings; grammatical-historical interpretation; *hapax legomena;* haplography; hermeneutic(s); higher criticism; homographs; homonyms; homophones; *homoteleuton;* hyperbole; idiom; illumination; *inclusio;* inspiration; interpolation; interpretation; inverted nun; irony; isagogics; *itture sopherim;* jot and tittle; kere; *kethib;* "L"; lemma; liberalists interpretation; literal interpretation; litotes; loan words; lower criticism; "M"; Masoretic Text; minuscule(s); mystery of God; omission; onomastica; onomatopoeia; palimpsest; papyrus; paradigm; parallelism; parchment; *paroimia; paronomasia;* pericope; personification; Peshitta; plenary inspiration; pointing; point of view; polyglot; principles of interpretation; proof texting; pun(s); "Q"; rapture; redaction; revelation, theological; rhetorical criticism; rhetorical devices; riddle; Roman Catholic Church; satire; *scripto continua;* scriptorium; *sebirin;* secret rapture; simile; similitude; sources, primary and secondary; secret rapture; source criticism; sources, primary and secondary; special points; strophe; superscription; symbol(s); synecdoche; syntax; synthetic parallelism; text; textual criticism; threefold sense of interpretation; *tiggune sopherim;* Time Texts; Torah; transmission history; transposition; trope; type(s); typology; uncial(s); vellum; verbicide.

transmigration of the soul. See reincarnation.

transmission history: sometimes encountered as "tradition history," a method of hermeneutic analysis that seeks to unveil the hidden meaning of a text by examining the material behind the written document. Hermann Gunkel (1862–1932) was particularly interested in comparing oral traditions, the cults and mythos of ancient Egypt, and Mesopotamian legend to show relationships between them as they impacted Hebrew writing. The literary form has taken hold in some of the stories, laws, and poems of the Old Testament. Theologians Gerhard von Rad and James Robinson also used the methodology. *See also* allegorical interpretation; analogical interpretation; biblical criticism; Fourfold Interpretation; grammatical-historical interpretation; hermeneutic(s); higher criticism; interpretation; liberalists interpretation; literal interpretation; plenary inspiration; principles of interpretation; revelation, theological; rhetorical criticism; source criticism; text; textual criticism; threefold sense of interpretation; translation.

transmutation: the changing of the material of one object into the composition of another. In theological terms, transmutation applies to the believer whose basic make-up as a person is changed so that he or she can experience a spiritual existence, as well as a physical one. *See also* alchemy; *khemeia;* od; *ormus;* philosopher's stone; powder of projection; transhumanism; transubstantiation.

transporting angel of Ezekiel, the: one of Ezekiel's visions in which he saw an angelic figure (perhaps a Seraphim) who appeared as flame from the waist down and as burnished metal from his mid-section up (Ezk. 8:1–3). This holy being seized the prophet by the hair and transported him from his place of exile in Babylon to Jerusalem, so he could view the troubled conditions there. We assume that this trip not a literal conveyance although it could have been precisely that. *See also* angel(s); angels of touring; angels of transport; Ezekiel as Old Testament prophecy; Ezekiel as prophet.

transposition: a copyist error in which two or more letters are transposed. *See also* accideme; alliteration; apostrophe; apothegm; assonance; autograph; Bible; Bible manuscripts; Bible translations; biblical criticism; chiasmus; conflict story; *constructio ad sensum;* context; contextualization; dittography; double sense fulfillment; doublets; doubling; edification; eisegesis; epanadiplosis; epigrammatic statements; etymology; exegesis; figure of speech; folio; form criticism; gattung; gloss; gnomic sayings; grammatical-historical interpretation; *hapax legomena;* haplography; hermeneutic(s); higher criticism; homographs; homonyms; homophones; *homoteleuton;* hyperbole; idiom; *inclusio;* interpolation; interpretation; inverted nun; irony; isagogics; *itture sopherim;* jot and tittle; kere; *kethib;* "L"; liberalists interpretation; literal interpretation; litotes; loan words; lower criticism; "M"; Masoretic Text; minuscule(s); mystery of God; omission; onomastica; onomatopoeia; palimpsest; papyrus; paradigm; parallelism; parchment; *paroimia; paronomasia;* pericope; personification; Peshitta; pointing; point of view; polyglot; principles of interpretation; proof texting; pun(s); "Q"; redaction; revelation, theological; rhetorical criticism; rhetorical devices; riddle; satire; *scripto continua;* scriptorium; *sebirin;* simile; similitude; source criticism; sources, primary and secondary; special pointing; strophe; superscription; symbol(s); synecdoche; syntax; synthetic parallelism; text; textual criticism; *tiggune sopherim;* Time Texts; Torah; translation; trope; type(s); typology; uncial(s); vellum; verbicide.

transubstantiation: a concept concerning the Eucharist that holds that while to the senses the bread and wine of the sacrament remain unaltered, the miracle of *substantia* changes the elements into the literal body and blood of Jesus. However, this change takes place only in the believer who accepts it on faith. The ministering priest then has power to forgive certain sins. The doctrine was set out by a scholarly monk named Radbert in A.D. 831. The concept is principally Roman Catholic and Eastern Orthodox in practice; they sometimes call it "the medicine of immortality." Perhaps the basic concept can be traced to Aristotle when he distinguished between *substance* and *accidents* (the form or attributes of something). Liturgical belief (championed by Aquinas) asserts that the accidents of the bread and wine remain unchanged but the substance is converted into the body and blood of Jesus. One must believe it is possible for one object to be converted into another for the doctrine to rest on the mind. Transubstantiation was strongly opposed by the Protestant Reformers, and Irenaeus called the idea "crack-brained" and demonic. *See also* Anaphora; capernaitic eating; concomitance; consubstantiation; Council of Trent (Roman Catholic); Eastern Orthodox Church; ecumenism; elevation; epiclesis; Eucharist; Eucharistic theory of the Reformers; fraction; Innocent III, Pope; invination; liturgy, Christian; Lord's Supper; Marburg Conference; monstrance; real presence; Roman Catholic Church; sacrament(s); sacring; species; theophagy; transmutation; wafer; wine.

Trappist Order: a restrictive order of monks and nuns with monasteries throughout the world. The members are a breakaway faction of the Cistercians (completed in 1892) but follow the regula of Saint Benedict. All are silent and speak in a unique sign language (though they do not take a vow of silence). They are also vegetarians and produce fine wool and a renowned beer among other industries. *See also* Assumptionist Orders; Augustinian Order; Barnabites; Benedict, Order of; Black Canons; canon(s) of the church; canons regular; clergy; Capuchin Order; Carmelites; Carthusians; Celestines; Cistercians; discalced; Dominicans; Franciscans; friar(s); house churches; Merton, Thomas; Minim; monasticism; monk(s); mysticism, mystics; orders; passalorynchite; Paulist Fathers; Premonstratensian Order; priest(s); religious organizations; Roman Catholic Church; Servite Order; Spirituals of the Franciscan Order.

traveling mercies: a Christianese expression not experienced anywhere else but in the in-house faith of believers. The phrase is a prayer plea for protection and care for one about to go on a journey by auto, airplane, or other long-distance mode. The fear is that there might be a car or plane crash, a terrorist attack, or some other danger to threaten the trip. The desire may be presented as a request for prayer from others but, generally, short trips to the grocery store or to visit grandma in the suburbs are not usually included where the accident is most likely to occur. *See also* Christianese; prayer(s).

treasury of merits: the belief declaring that the Church, or some other body, is the custodian of an excess of grace bequeathed to it from Christ and the saints. It is primarily a Roman Catholic doctrine. Since Jesus and those having undergone beatification were exceptionally worthy, there is an abundance of grace credits available from which others may "borrow" to help forgive temporal sins. Numbers of saints began to appear on the religious scene, so no longer are we forced to suffer martyrdom as a qualification. We thereby increase the treasury, particularly if appeals were directed to the Virgin Mary. Christians of the early church, both rich and poor, accepted the idea that the super-righteous could aid them, not only here on troubled earth but in heaven as well. Everyone needs a patron when struggling through life, so if there are those other than Christ who can help, they are to be welcomed and used. Some medieval monks or bishops carried about little indexes called "tariff books," which listed specific sins and the appropriate penance act for each. They were hugely popular among both commoners and noblemen. The method was convenient because monks and other pious officials could now use their prayers to carry out penances for the gentry or warriors who had no time for it themselves. Their monasteries were forts against the devil, their occupants were the soldiers, and their weapons were prayers. Also, there developed a particular mass called a "requiem," which could be said for the departed. The name comes from the opening phrase in Latin: *Requiem aeternam dona eis, Domine*—"Eternal rest grant unto them, O Lord." The requiems later inspired the great classical composers like Gabriel Faure, Maurice Durufle, and Giuseppe Verdi. At one point, such a belief was a basis for the selling of indulgences by which a ticket could be purchased to speed a dead friend or relative out of purgatory. That practice was one of the main sticking points between the Roman Church and Martin Luther on which there could be no compromise. Further, the idea had bearing on how penance was to be exercised.

Formerly, the arrangement of forgiveness consisted of contrition, confession, satisfaction, and then absolution or forgiveness by the priest. So then, satisfaction was given before absolution. The developed order was subsequently modified so that contrition and confession formed the start, absolution came after confession, and satisfaction was placed last. Thus, following confession, the priest in his authority of the keys given him by the Roman bishop could forgive the eternal sins of the petitioner but satisfaction for temporal guilt must still be assuaged, in purgatory if necessary. *See also* hyten; papal revenue; penance; purgatory; Requiem; Roman Catholic Church; saint(s); supererogation.

Treatise of the Three Imposters: an anonymous publication in 1680 that named Moses, Jesus Christ, and Mohammed as the world's greatest trio of imposters. The work completely condemned the three major Semitic faiths. It was considered too shocking to be presented publically before 1719 but nevertheless circulated freely in Europe from the Netherlands in manuscript form long before. *See also* Jesus Christ; Mohammed ibn 'Abdallah; Moses.

Treaty of Rome: the agreement that began the process of eventual European statehood. The treaty revamped the already existing European Economic Community (six-member European Atomic Energy Community (EAEC) in 1958 and signed by its member nations: Italy, Germany, France, Belgium, Luxembourg, and Holland and laid the base for the Common Market. In 1967, the European Community (EU) was formed, and Denmark and Britain joined. Fundamental prophecy buffs were interested because soon Greece enlisted in 1981, whereby they suspected that the organization may have matched the ten toes of Nebuchadnezzar's dream. Their faith was shaken when Spain and Portugal joined in 1986 and ruined the requisite numbers. *See also* Benelux Conference of 1948; conspiracy theorists; European Union, the; Maastricht Treaty; Visegrad Group (V4).

Treaty of Verdun: the formal agreement that secured peace and unity to the Holy Roman Empire in A.D. 846 by dividing the kingdom among Charlemagne's heirs. The consequences were not good, however, for it ushered in a phase of decline marked by terrifying incursions by the Hungarians, Normans, and Saracens. *See also* Charlemagne; Holy Roman Empire.

tree(s): woodland growths of many sizes and varieties. In ancient times, trees were important as economic aids, fuel, and building material, as they are today. Moreover, they were common objects of worship, especially in the days when luxuriant and huge plots of Asia and Europe were covered in forests. They are a frequent symbol of nations; Babylon, Assyria, and Israel are so named. God and his prophets continually chastised Israel for pagan worship "under every spreading tree." A kingdom is planted, it grows, it produces, and often is cut down, uprooted, or diseased. Green trees and leafy oaks symbolized the role of the fertility goddess (*e.g.,* Asherah in Canaanite religion). Moreover, they were a "big deal" for the ancients and were often symbols of greatness (as in Nebuchadnezzar's dream of the great tree in Daniel 4) or the shade of refreshment from the sun's heat and signs of peace, vigor, beauty, and prosperity. For the ancients, an ideal king could be pictured as a tree growing upside down from heaven to earth, with its branches providing such needed qualities as virtue, wisdom, strength, integrity, etc. Several species were considered sacred— the cedar, laurel, myrtle, cypress, and oak. In Revelation 7:1 the trees are a kind of barometer for monitoring the tempest being held in abeyance while the 144,000 are sealed because the leaves would be the first to quiver if a storm approaches. Trees can be a similitude for wisdom, namely when *Ecclesiasticus* speaks of the cedars of Lebanon, the cypress of Mount Harmon, and the date palm at Engedi. Others are mentioned, including the olive trees in the vale and the cassia (camel thorn), redolent with spices and the fragrance of myrrh. The galbanum, aromatic shell, and gum resin are also notable. The tenebinth, with spreading branches laden with honor and grace and the blossoms of wealth and honor, were expressive. Other tree species in Israel include the acacia, almond, balsam, box, cypress, fig, juniper, and palm. The palm, which has taste but no scent, refers to those versed in torah but lack acts of kindness; the myrtle, which has fragrance but no taste, refers to those who have good deeds but little understanding of torah. Symbolically, the palm signifies victory, the olive stands for peace, and the willow portrays blessings; each should be used as branches in the tabernacle booth of *Sukkot. See also* almond tree branch; Bile; Bodhi Tree; cedars of Lebanon; Christmas tree; citron wood; cosmic tree; Daniel's interpretation of Nebuchadnezzar's tree dream; Diviner's Tree; fig(s); fig tree(s); flora, fruit, and grain, symbology of; forest of the south; Four Species, the; fruit; juniper; laurel; lotus; May Day; mustard seed; myrtle; oak; olive(s); palm; palm branches; shittim; sound of marching in the trees; Sephiroth tree; tamarisk tree; tree of life, the; tree of the knowledge of good and evil, the; tree of Zaqqum; trees and the thornbush, fable of the; two olive trees and a lampstand; Valley of Baca; vine and the fig tree, the; willow; wisdom; Yggdrasil; Yule; Zechariah's vision of the man among the myrtle trees.

Tree of Jesse: or seen correctly as the Jesse Tree, an artistic depiction of the ancestors of Jesus, much like the modern family tree drawings. The rendering attempts to display the lineage of Jesus starting at Bethlehem with the patriarch Jesse, the father of David. The art form may be stained glass, an illustrated manuscript, a painting, tapestry, wood, bronze, tiles; mosaic, plaster, or other media in many styles. The Tree of Jesse may also be a general verbal or written reference to the family line of Jesus without illustrations. *See also* Branch from (of) Jesse, the; genealogy of Jesus; Jesse; Root and Offspring of David; Root and Offspring of Jesse; Root of Jesse.

tree dream of Nebuchadnezzar. See Daniel's interpretation of Nebuchadnezzar's tree dream.

tree of life, the: one of two trees in the Garden of Eden, this one ordained to grant eternal life and health to mankind (Gen. 2:9). Adam and Eve were forbidden to eat from it. The tree, or several of its species, reappears in the New Jerusalem (Rev. 22:2), at this point no longer forbidden but available for the healing of the nations. *Second Esdras* states that Revelation 22:5 means there are twelve trees in New Jerusalem (a concept from *Enoch*) and that they bear different fruit. The imagery is improved by the mention of twelve mountains covered in lilies and roses and twelve fountains flowing with milk and honey. The tree of life image was common in ancient culture where it may be seen as the navel of the earth, giving it sustenance and productivity. Mention is made of it in such diverse religions as Gnosticism and Buddhism and the worship of Krishna, Attis, Dionysus, and Wotan. If the tree is absent from the ancient records it may be substituted with a mountain. See *also* Bile; Bodhi Tree; cosmic tree; Eden; flora, fruit, and grain, symbology of; healing of the nations; mountain(s); New Jerusalem; Sephiroth; Sephiroth tree; tree(s); tree of the knowledge of good and evil, the; tree of Zaqqum; Yggdrasil.

tree of the knowledge of good and evil, the: one of a pair of trees in the Garden of Eden. This particular tree could awaken mankind to the sting of sin (Gen. 2:9, 16–17). Adam and Eve were forbidden to eat from it on penalty of death. They succumbed, however, and subjected the world to sin and bereavement. Fortunately, they were driven from the garden before they touched the tree of life, which presumably would have permanently embroiled them in their sin. *See also* Bodhi Tree; cosmic tree; Eden; flora, fruit, and grain, symbology of; forbidden fruit; tree(s); tree of life, the; tree of Zaqqum; Yggdrasil.

tree of Zaqqum: the "cursed tree" growing from the bottom of the Muslim hell (Jahannam). *See also* Bile; Bodhi Tree; cosmic tree; flora, fruit, and grain, symbology of; Islam; Jahannam; tree(s); tree of life, the; tree of the knowledge of good and evil, the; Yggdrasil.

trees and the thornbush, fable of the: a fable spoken by Jotham (Jud. 9:7–20), the only surviving son of Gideon after his seventy brothers were murdered by the usurper Abimelech. The tale speaks of the woodlands who wanted the olive and fig trees, or even the grapevine, to rule over them. Instead, the thistle was chosen as a last resort, out of which fire emanated and destroyed the surrounding area. The fable predicts the death of Abimelech and the fall of the city of Shechem, which had aided in the massacre of Gideon's family. *See also* Abimelech, fable(s); Jotham.

tremendum: an overwhelming emotional experience of awe brought on by a personal religious incidence. *See also* baptism of the Holy Spirit; charismatic movement; ecstasy; glossolalia; inspiration; intoxication; numinous; orans; revivalism; theolepsy.

trental: commemoration for the departed, in most liturgical churches, performed thirty days after burial. *See also* prayer(s); prayers for the dead.

trespass: a sin. Fault can be found in the religious ritual or one's moral actions as they are performed or lived. If an error is made in the sanctifying process of sacrifice or an ethical lapse, the Law deems those acts a trespass and restitution or repentance, or both, may be required. Even civil law responds to the idea when you find yourself roaming on somebody's real estate where you should not be. *See also* after one's own lusts; antinomianism; blasphemy; carnal; debauchery; demimondaines; depravity; desecrate; dissipation; harmartiology; hedonism; immorality; iniquity; orgies; Phibionites; profane; ritual defilement; sacrilege; sin(s); unclean; worldly.

Triads: criminal organizations of expatriate Chinese societies called Tongs (when found in their meeting halls in America). Triads were originally formed in secret to sponsor armed protestors dedicated to the overthrow of one emperor or another. Later they grew into regional gangs that resident Chinese called *hei she hui*—meaning "black" or sinister. The official logo of the Triads consists of a pyramid shape with each side representing Heaven, Earth, and Man which they termed the *Hung Mun.* The Tongs were involved in the usual criminal enterprises normally identified with gangs and illegal cartels everywhere and are just as secretive. In the beginning, however, Tongs were sort of aid societies for Chinese immigrants ("Coolies") to help them survive prejudice common on America's west coast. The word designates a "meeting house" where the oppressed could find a measure of protection and succor. The criminal element largely took over after 1900. Some of the more infamous Triad/Tong groups could be listed as the Red (carnation-painted) Eyebrows Society, the Copper Horses, Iron Shins, Yellow Turbans, White Lotus Society, the Green Gang/Three Harmonious Society, the 14k (named for its Hong Kong address at No. 14 Po Wah Road, Canton), Three Incense Sticks, and the White Feathers. The Fist for Righteous Harmony Society sparked the Boxer Rebellion of 1900 and set the organizations on the permanent path to criminality tied to the opium trade. *See also ghetto;* Hongmen; Kwan Ti; Mafia; secret societies; Thugs; underworld; Yakuza; *yubizeum.*

trial: 1. an inquiry by a court of law. In Israel, the Sanhedrin assumed most of the important jurisdictional procedures. Before then, Moses and the selected elders dispensed justice. 2. an affliction or persecution either from God or from our own indiscretions or inherent cruelty that must be endured (Deut. 7:19). 3. a test, either as an experiment or to settle some dispute by some disciplined action. *See also* bread of affliction; bread of despair; messenger of Satan; tear(s); thorn in the flesh; trial by combat; vale of tears; water of affliction.

trial by combat: an ancient method considered to be a judicial means of settling a dispute, especially between armies and nations. Each adversary was to choose a champion to fight each other, trusting the outcome would surely identify the party in the right as the will of God or the gods. The advantage was that lives were spared; the disadvantage was that the loser lost everything in one throw. *See also* Goliath; ordeal(s); trial.

triangle: a small three-cornered percussion instrument useful in some instances of Eastern Orthodox worship. *See also* Eastern Orthodox Church; musical instruments.

tribes of Israel, the: the various ethnic or family groups of Israel, each identified through its progenitor patriarch, Jacob (or Israel), and their assigned land grants in Israel. Always, the tribes are referred to as being twelve in number, but the various listings in the Old and New Testaments differ in some instances. If we named all we could, there would be: Judah, Reuben, Gad, Asher, Napthali, Manasseh, Simeon, Levi, Issachar, Zebulun, Joseph, Benjamin, Dan, and Ephraim. Perhaps Josephus explained the best counting method. He named Manasseh as a substitute for Levi since the latter was not eligible for warfare conscription, specific land distribution in Canaan, and certain other common societal functions. He then designated Ephraim as a substitute for Joseph since Jacob named that patron's sons as legally numbered with the twelve. Jacob's blessing of his sons and grandsons on his deathbed holds significant eschatological importance since those leaders destined the conduct and fidelity of the tribes to a large extent (Gen. 49). Moses also blessed the tribes prior to his death (Deut. 33). In the all-important listing of the tribes in Revelation 7:1–8, the ones missing are Dan and Ephraim. The latter exclusion may be necessitated by the inclusion of Joseph, the father of Ephraim and Manasseh. Legend purports that Dan is excluded because it is destined to be the tribe of the Antichrist, or more reasonably, the False Prophet. Any tribe in Israel was traditionally further delineated into clans and families.

The tribal allotment of settlements in Canaan was based on population, the fertility quality of the land (not quantity or acreage), and confirmed by lot administered by Joshua. *See also* Asher; Benjamin; Dan; division of Israel; Ephraim; Gad as tribe; Issachar; Jacob's prophecies and blessings to the tribes; Joseph; Judaism; Levi; lost tribes, the ten; Manasseh; Moses' prophecies and blessings to the tribes; Naphtali; 144,000, the; Reuben; Simeon as tribe; twelve tribes; Zebulun.

tribes, the twelve. See lost tribes, the ten; 144,000, the; tribes of Israel, the; twelve tribes.

Tribulation: a time of severe trouble, formed from the Latin *tribulum*, which names a piece of agricultural equipment used in the ancient world to separate wheat from chaff by violent shaking. The term takes on theological significance when associated with end time events. Revelation and other prophetic sources, both biblical and extrabiblical, describe a period of harsh persecution and hardship in association with God's judgment of the world near the end of the age. Isaiah called the period "the great indignation" [or "wrath"], but it goes by a number of other terms as well. The Greek word for tribulation comes from *thlipsis*, carrying a meaning of "pressure." Often, this period is defined as seven years in duration, then sometimes further divided into halves—the first period of three and one half called "the Tribulation" and the second three and a half labeled the "Great Tribulation." Usually, the violence and immorality of the time are said to be promoted and directed by the Satan-inspired Antichrist and the False Prophet as they lead a defiant world population in rebellion against God and propagating severe persecution on His people. More precisely, however, it may be presented that God Himself is allowing the wrath of the age to promote His ultimate will. The book of Daniel calls the period "the seventieth week" or equivalent terms (Dan. 9:24–27), and other sources identify it as "the time of Jacob's trouble" (Jer. 30:7) or "the day of the Lord" (Amos 5:18; 2 Pe. 3:10). Apocalyptists will recognize other names in the New Testament for tribulation (or the equivalent): the great tribulation or "great distress" (Mt. 24:21; Rev. 2:22; 7:14); the tribulation or "the distress," (Mt. 24:29); the coming wrath (1 Th. 1:10); day of the Lord (1 Th. 5:2); wrath or "your wrath" (1 Th. 5:9; Rev. 11:18); hour of trial (Rev. 3:10); wrath of the

Lamb and great day of their wrath (Rev. 6:16–17); hour of his judgment (Rev. 14:7); God's wrath (Rev. 14:10, 19; 15:1, 7; 16:1). Premillennial advocates assert that the Second Coming of Christ will end the Tribulation in complete triumph over his enemies, both human and celestial (Ps. 2:9; Rev. 11:15–18; 19:11–21). *See also* bowl(s); Daniel's vision of the seventy sevens; Days of Awe; forty-two months; four horsemen of the Apocalypse; Great Tribulation; "hard times"; hour of testing; hour of trial; prayers of Revelation; Sermon on the Mount, the; seventy weeks, prophecy of the; seal(s); time of Jacob's trouble; trumpet(s).

Tribulation prophets (two witnesses). See witnesses, the two great.

Tribulation saints. See saint(s).

Tribulation Temple: the temple of the Tribulation, supposedly to be built under the auspices of the Antichrist, then desecrated by him. *See also* rebuilding the Temple; Temple(s).

Tribunal: an official Vatican department or one in a local diocese. The local version deals with such matters as marriages, annulments, and the like. *See also* dicastry; Roman Catholic Church.

tribune: a Roman officer in command of a cohort (about 600 men). The title expanded to include very high-ranking officers and civil administrators as well. *See also* centurion(s); Cornelius; Imperial Regiment, the; Italian Regiment, the; Julius; legion; Praetorian Guard; Roman Empire; Sebastenians.

trichotomist theology: the idea that humans are of three elements: the physical (animal), the soul (psychological, reason, emotion), and the spirit (the impetus for humans to react to spiritual stimuli). The belief is a prominent Protestant understanding of the nature of humanity. *See also* trichotomy.

trichotomy: the idea that all persons consist of body, soul, and spirit. The prophets would likely resonate to this idea since they understood the creation and sustenance of the human person by the Creator. The New Testament writers would also agree based on the theology of the era. *See also* dichotomy; trichotomist theology.

Trickster: a Native American mystical hero, the Kokopelli, who teaches tribal culture, proper behavior, and generally provides for the needs of the tribe. The term should not be limited to that group, however, as Tricksters are a common feature familiar to all folklorists, anthropologists, and historians in the field. The name was coined by Daniel Brinton in 1868 to coverall pesky and mischievous entities of most ancient populations. *See also* bogle; brownie; clurichauns; devils; dryad(s); elemental(s); fairy, fairies; Fomorians; Furies; ghost(s); gnome(s); Green Man, the; hobgoblins; homunculus; huldufolk; Kokopelli; leprechaun(s); Loki; nereid; nisse; nymph(s); nyx; Norse and Old Germanic pantheon; para; Robin Goodfellow; satyr; Seelie Court, Unseelie Court; selkie; Sidhe; sirens; spiritual warfare; sprite(s); Tuatha de Danann; tutelary; undine; wight(s).

Tridentine: an ecclesiastical term meaning "of Trent," referring to the Council of Trent affairs conducted from 1545–1563. *See also* Council of Trent (Roman Catholic); Roman Catholic Church.

Tridentine Mass: the Latin Mass as authorized by the Council of Trent back in the 16th century. It was in general use until 1969 when Pope Paul VI authorized a revised ritual to be said in the vernacular. Still, nostalgia in some quarters persists for the old rite even though only a tiny fraction of attendees can understand even a portion of the process. *See also* Council of Trent (Roman Catholic); *Deo gratias;* hocus-pocus; liturgical year; Mass; Roman Catholic Church.

triduum: the "three days" constituting Maundy Thursday, Good Friday, and Holy Saturday in the Easter vigil. *See also* feasts and special days of high liturgy faiths; feasts and special days of Protestantism; Good Friday; Holy Saturday; Holy Week; Lent; liturgical year; liturgy, Christian; Maundy Thursday.

trilemma, the: a sort of puzzle posed by C. S. Lewis in his attempt to prove the divinity of Christ. He proposed that for Jesus to be or not to be God, he would either be a lunatic, a liar, or Lord. Some have substituted the results to mad, bad, or God. *See also* Lewis, Clive Staples.

Trimurti: the Hindu collection of gods as a ruling triumvirate responsible for order and devastation in the universe. These three represent different aspects of reality: Brahma is the creator (not to be confused with Brahman); Vishnu is the protector of humanity; Shiva the destroyer balances the forces of creation and destruction. *See also* Brahma; Hinduism; Shiva; Trinity; Vishnu.

Trinity: a principal doctrine of Christianity that declares that the One God can be experienced in three "persons" or personalities, sometimes called the "Godhead." The dogma is a complex one and has always held an unsettling debate or struggle to Articulate the belief. The early church proposed several understandings: 1. the *alogia* ("not the word") proposed that Christ was not the *Logos* announced in John 1:1. 2. Adoptionism postulated that Jesus was not God but that the Father "adopted" him for earthly ministry. 3. Subordinationism sets out that Jesus was indeed divine but somehow subordinate to the Father. 4. modalism states that Christ was just another name for God. So then, heaven could be emptied or occupied as Jesus or the Holy Spirit left or arrived there in his office. 5. the orthodox view triumphed at last, at least in most of the West, which asserts that the Father, Son, and Holy Spirit are of one essence and incapable of separation, yet wholly monotheistic. The tri-partite body may act individually but never without application of the whole. The idea has been expressed in that although all three persons of the Trinity share all of God's attributes, God the Father exemplifies the holiness of the Godhead, Jesus demonstrates the personality of God, and the Holy Spirit manifests the mighty power of God. Patrick of Ireland used the three-leafed clover to illustrate. One scientific example that attempts the analogy involves water—when it is natural, it is liquid; when it is frozen, it is ice; when heated, it is steam. In any form then, it remains the same element but serving different functions. Augustine tried to compare the Godhead as the human mind, knowledge, and love. These three are one and of a single substance. More philosophically, Augustine said that the Father, Son, and Holy Spirit are three aspects of the mind itself that is,—memory, understanding, and will. The influence of Neoplatonism never left Augustine's thought so much so that he hinted that the Platonists were near-Christians. Such pronouncements degraded Augustine's reputation in the East and in modern theology. All such formulas, including many more examples from the physical laws, have often been advanced, but none seem emphatic or precise enough to truly explain the mystery of the tri-union of the Godhead. It is almost certain there never will be one. *See also* Adoptionism; appropriation; Anomoeans; Arianism; Arius; binitarianism; complementarian view of the Trinity; dance; Donatism; dualism;

Dynamic Monarchianism; dynamism; eternal subordination of the Son; dyophysitism; eternal subordination of the Son; "four fences of Chalcedon"; Hilary of Poitiers; *homoiousios; homoousios;* hypostatic union; incarnation; Jesus Only Movement; *kenosis;* kenotic view of Christ; liturgical year; miaphysitism; modalism; monarchianism; monoenergism; monophysitism; monotheism; names (titles) for God; names (titles) for Jesus; names (titles) for the Holy Spirit; Nestorianism; Nestorius; *ousia;* patripassianism; Pelagianism; *perichoresis;* psilanthropism; Sabellianism; Socianism, Socinians; subordinationism; theanthroposophy; *Theophorus;* three; Trimurti; Trinity Sunday; Trisagion, the; two natures, doctrine of the; unipersonality; *Vesica Piscis.*

Trinity Sunday: the observance on the church calendar to commemorate the doctrine and meaning of the divine God as Father, Son, and Holy Spirit. In the Roman Church, the celebratory date is the first Sunday after Pentecost; in the Eastern rite, it is Pentecost Sunday itself. Some Protestant denominations also recognize the day including Anglicans, Lutherans, Presbyterians, Methodists, and some Baptists. *See also* Eastern Orthodox Church; feasts and special days of high liturgy faiths; feasts and special days of Protestantism; liturgical year; *perichoresis;* three; Roman Catholic Church; Trinity; Trisagion, the; *Vesica Piscis.*

Triodion: a Greek Orthodox liturgy book containing hymns suitable for use prior to the observance of the Great Lent. *See also* Eastern Orthodox Church; Great Lent; liturgical year; music.

tripartite division of the law: the common Jewish or theological exercise of dividing the Law of Moses into three divisions—the moral, the ceremonial, and the civil (judicial). *See also* Mosaic Law.

triple crown: the headdress of the Roman pontiff (the *triregnum*) that resembles three tiers topped by a cross in the shape of a cone or beehive. The popes have long worn headgear of some description, but the present design (or nearly so) likely dates from the 16th century and is intended to identify the bishop of Rome as ruler of the papal states, the Holy See, and Vatican City. The original meaning also included the pope's authority overall civil governments and rulers. Since Vatican II, the triple crown has been subdued in its use in the interest of ecumenicity. *See also* Roman Catholic Church.

Tripoli Prophecy: a.k.a. the Cedars of Lebanon Prophecy, a 13th century English chronicle presented as a reading of astrological signs. To modern readers, the text is nigh incomprehensible but much of the Middle Ages population came to view it as an eerie but accurate account of the Mongol armies that crossed into Russia from the Steppes of Central Asia in 1237 A.D., and as a fulfillment of the biblical prophecy recorded in Revelation 6:12–14. *See also* zodiac.

triregnum, **the.** See triple crown.

Trisagion, the: "Holy, Holy, Holy," the tri-praise words of Revelation 4:8 in which the four living creatures extol glory to God as the Lord God Almighty and He who was, is, and is to come. The phrase has become a familiar and stirring paean of worship for the Christian Church throughout much of her history. The Trisagion was said to have been devised by a boy in the mid-fifth century in the East. His variation on the penitential psalm he was chanting in procession appeared to stop the earthquakes, which became a motivation for the march. Obviously, however, the prime source is Revelation 4:8. *See also* four living creatures of Revelation; liturgical year; liturgy, Christian; music; *Sanctus, the;* Trinity.

Trismegistus, Hermes. See Hermes Trismegistus.

Trito-Isaiah: the term used to name those portions of Isaiah that were allegedly composed by a third writer. *See also* Deutero-Isaiah; Isaiah as Old Testament prophecy.

Trito-Zechariah: the term used to name that portion of Zechariah that some believe is by a third author.

Triumphal Entry: the depiction of Jesus' entry into Jerusalem just before the last Passover before his crucifixion (Mk. 11:1–11, *et al.*). On that occasion, the people of the city welcomed him with shouts of Hosanna, the waving of palm branches, and by spreading their clothing on the road as he rode into the city on a borrowed donkey. His appearance fulfilled the prophecy of Zechariah (Zech. 9:9), and some see the incident as pertaining to a part of Daniel's seventy weeks calculation.

Triumph of the Cross, Feast of the: liturgical celebration and emphasis on the victory of Jesus wrought at the time of his crucifixion. Some form of the Cross feast is observed in many high church persuasions including Russian, Roman, Syrian, Ethiopian, Anglican, Armenian, Lutheran, and others. Alternate names for the occasion include Exaltation of the Cross, Elevation of the Cross, Feasts of the Cross; Holy Rood Day, Holy Cross Day, and Roodmas. *See also* cross; Cross, Feasts of the; Church of England; crucifixion; Eastern Orthodox Church; feasts and special days of high liturgy faiths; liturgical year; Lutheran Church; Roman Catholic Church; Syrian Orthodox Church; veneration of the cross.

troparion: a Byzantine Paschal hymn sung as a refrain between verses of a Psalm. Or it can stand alone as an Easter rendition musical offering. *See also* Eastern Orthodox Church; liturgical year; music; Paschal; Paschal greeting.

trope: 1. literally, a *turn* in the language. A trope is figurative language by which one thing is said under the form of another thing. The "two nations" in Rebekah's womb are actually the fetuses of Jacob and Esau (Gen. 25:23); a "lampstand" (Rev. 2:5) is a church congregation. 2. a short phrase sung by a choir to "back up" the spoken word. *See also* accideme; alliteration; apostrophe; apothegm; assonance; autograph; Bible; Bible manuscripts; Bible translations; biblical criticism; chiasmus; conflict story; *constructio ad sensum;* context; contextualization; dittography; double sense fulfillment; doublets; doubling; edification; eisegesis; epanadiplosis; epigrammatic statements; etymology; exegesis; figure of speech; folio; form criticism; gattung; gloss; gnomic sayings; grammatical-historical interpretation; *hapax legomena;* haplography; hermeneutic(s); higher criticism; homographs; homonyms; homophones; *homoteleuton;* hyperbole; idiom; *inclusio;* interpolation; interpretation; inverted nun; irony; isagogics; *itture sopherim;* jot and tittle; kere; *kethib;* "L"; liberalists interpretation; literal interpretation; litotes; liturgical year; loan words; lower criticism; "M"; Masoretic Text; minuscule(s); music; mystery of God; omission; onomastica; onomatopoeia; palimpsest; papyrus; paradigm; parallelism; parchment; *paroimia; paronomasia;* pericope; personification; Peshitta; pointing; point of view; polyglot; principles of interpretation; proof texting; pun(s); "Q"; redaction; revelation, theological; rhetorical criticism; rhetorical devices; riddle; satire; *scripto continua;* scriptorium; *sebirin;* simile; similitude; source criticism; sources, primary and secondary; special points; strophe; superscription; symbol(s); synecdoche; syntax; synthetic parallelism; text; textual criticism; *tiggune sopherim;* Time Texts; Torah; translation; transposition; type(s); typology; uncial(s); vellum; verbicide.

Trophimus: a traveling companion and fellow missionary with Paul who hailed from Ephesus (Acts 20:4). In Jerusalem, the Jews spotted Trophimus in the city with Paul and assumed he had been sponsored by Paul in the forbidden areas of the Temple, a serious violation caused by any Gentile discovered in the holy precincts (Acts 21:27–33). The enraged Jews seized Paul and tried to kill him for his alleged desecration. Paul noted that he left Trophimus sick in Miletus at one point (2 Tim. 4:20). *See also* missions, missionaries; Tychicus.

tropology. See allegorical interpretation.

Truce of God: an attempt by the popes of Rome around the 12th century to end or misdirect the frequent martial outbursts of rival nobles and their knights against each other. These sectional armies preferred fighting internally to sustain their premier status as warriors of God and their various noble patrons. There is little use for an expensive and trained army of restless knights if it isn't used. Eventually, around the time of the early Crusades, their energies were substantially redirected toward fighting for the Holy Land under church prerogatives. *See also* Roman Catholic Church.

trumpet(s): a horn or bugle instrument used to announce, warn, or signal in warfare. Sometimes the spectacular voice of God is compared to the blare of a trumpet (Rev. 4:1). It is generally believed that the sound of a trumpet will call forth the dead at the point of the rapture. Ceremonial trumpets were usually made from precious metals. Soundings made from ram's horns (the *shofar)* were common to the Hebrews. Revelation consists of three main sections of Tribulation woes of seven independent sets of events: the seals, trumpets, and bowls. The trumpets listed consist of hail and fire mixed with blood, the blazing mountain thrown into the sea, Wormwood (a blazing object or "star") falling on freshwaters, a third of the sun struck to darkness, the release of the demonic horde from the Abyss (some postulate the smoke reveals the swarm of Islamic armies bent on destroying Christianity and Judaism), and the attack of the two hundred million invaders. Trumpets five and six are singled out and classed as "woes" or harsh events occurring in an already terrible experience. *See also* bowl(s); eschatology, eschatological; last trumpet, the; musical instrument(s); *Rosh Hashanah;* seal(s); *shofar;* sounds of the rapture; thunder revelations; Tribulation; trumpet call of the elect; Trumpets, Feast of; woe(s).

trumpet call of the elect: the sound of the trumpet, along with the voice of the archangel and the loud command of Christ, that will call the believers of the Church (both dead and living) heavenward at the rapture event. Such a sounding is mentioned in Matthew 24:31, 1 Corinthians 15:52, and Isaiah 27:13. *See also* elect, the; eschatology, eschatological; last trumpet, the; loud command, a; rapture; shout; sounds of the rapture; trumpet(s); Trumpets, Feast of; voice of God; voice of the archangel, the; voice out of heaven.

Trumpets, Feast of: known today as *Rosh Hashanah*, the Jewish New Year, but originally called *Zikhron Teruah*. The new moon of the seventh month inaugurated the festival, causing the *shofar* (ram's horn) to sound announcing the arrival of the civil new year (Lev. 23:23–25; Num. 29:1–6). The *shofar* is blown one hundred times. Three sounds are made with shorter blasts: *Tekiah* is one long, straight note; *Shevarim* is three shorter soundings; *Teruah* is nine quick blasts in short succession. The 100th sound is known as "the last trump." Appropriate prayers and rituals were performed in anticipation of the Day of Atonement. Both *Rosh Hashanah* (the New Year) and *Yom Kippur* (Day of Atonement) are considered the two "high holy days" of Judaism. The New Year festival consists of several aspects, each with meaning in its own right. 1. The Day of the Awakening Blast (*Yom Turah*) is the sounding of the *shofar* to awaken the people to the celebration. 2. The Opening of the Gates is a shout from the people that they may welcome the righteous nations. 3. The Day of Concealment (*Yom HaKeseh*) pertains to the New Moon as being concealed from the full moon, a sort of disguised righteousness. 4. The First and Last Trumps review the incomplete ritual of Abraham's sacrifice of his son Isaac. The ram sacrificed by Abraham in place of Isaac is the First Trump; the Last Trump announces the arrival of the Messiah. 5. The Book of

Remembrance is opened to expose the occurrence of the *Natzal,* a kind of rapture for the righteous to new life. The Greek New Testament equivalent of this kind of "snatching away" is *harpazo.* 6. The Day of the King (*Yom HaMelek*) represents the coronation of the Messiah. 7. The Day of Remembrance *(Yom Hazikkaron)* speaks of rewards for the righteous. 8. The Day of Judgment *(Yom HaDin)* anticipates God's judgment of the unrighteous of the entire world. The New Year's date is also considered the birthday of the world. The daily prayer ensures that people's names will be inscribed in the Book of Life for the coming year. *See also* Atonement, Day of; feasts and special days of Judaism; Judaism; last trumpet, the; *Rosh Hashanah; shofar;* sounds of the rapture; trumpet(s); trumpet call of the elect; voice of God; voice out of heaven.

trumpet, the last. See last trumpet, the.

truth: the principle of honesty in all of one's actions and dealings. For the prophets, truth was not only truth-telling but a lifestyle of integrity toward God and one's fellow man. Truth was close to the heart of the prophet and was closely associated with justice and fidelity. Jesus had much to say about truth (Jn. 8:12-58, 14:6) including his strong assertions that he, himself, was the Truth of God and that knowing that would set us free from sin and doubt. As a counter to falsehood, truth is essential to pure religion and foundational to moral integrity in all areas of life. Fidelity in word and deed, however, is often insubstantial, fleeting, and abused. It has even been said that "a lie runs half way around the world before the truth can think to get its boots on and chase after it." *See also* Ten Commandments, the.

Tryphena: a female convert whom Paul praised as a diligent worker for Christ (Rom. 16:12).

Trypho: a Jewish literary character (and possibly a real person) in Justin Martyr's *Dialogue with Trypho the Jew.* The writing reflects Jewish beliefs and attitudes toward early Christianity and extols the doctrines of the Church. *See also* Jew(s); Justin Martyr.

Tryphosa: a female convert whom Paul praised as a hard worker (Rom. 16:12).

Tuath: a community ruled by a king or lord in early Christian Ireland.

Tuatha de Danann: the "folk of the god whose mother is Danu" or "the Fair Folk"—legendary people of ancient Ireland (some identify them as belligerent leprechauns) who wrested the land from its previous inhabitants, the Fir Bolg. They have been reported to have been in Ireland since 1897 B.C. and possessed magic talismans and great intelligence. The leaders of the race assumed godlike qualities and came to be worshiped as "people of Danu (male) and Anu (female)." There appear to be associations with Brigit, the beloved goddess of ancient Ireland, with spillovers as late as the Roman Catholic legend of Saint Bridget centuries later. The Tuatha de Danann were conquered by the Milesians. Associations with the Tuatha de Danann are common among neo-paganism, New Age, and Wicca advocates. *See also* Beltane; banshee; bogle; Bridget of Kildare; Bridget's Cross; bugbears; brownies; Celtic folklore and religion; clurichauns; Dagda; Danu; elemental(s); fairy, fairies; fidhe; Fir Bolg; Fomorians; giant(s); Green Man, the; hobgoblins; huldufolk; leprechaun(s); Lugh; mythological beasties, elementals, monsters, and spirit animals; nisse; para; Robin Goodfellow; Samhain; Seelie Court, Unseelie Court; selkie; Sidhe; Tir na nOg; Trickster; tutelary; undine; Wicca; wight(s); witch(es).

Tubal: a land of Cappadocia in Asia Minor somehow associated with Gog and Magog (Ezk. 38:2–3). Some interpretations claim the area was ruled by its governor called Gog. The name is often paired with Meshech. In Genesis, Tubal is the fifth son of Japheth; those descendants have been variously identified as the Scythians, Iberians, or Hittites but we do know they were traders with Tyre (Ezk. 27:13). Modern prophecy teachers who attempt to relate them to Russia are probably incorrect. *See also* Beth Togarmah; Cush, Cushites; Gog and (of) Magog; Gomer; Meshech; Persia, Persians; Put; Rosh, Prince of.

Tubingen School: the philosophy of German theologian Ferdinand Christian Baur (1792–1860). Baur ascribed to the technique and reasoning of Friedrich Hegel and the dialectic approach to theology. The authenticity of most Scripture was rejected as were the most common doctrines of the times. *See also* biblical criticism; dialectic theology; Hegel, Georg Wilhelm Friedrich; higher criticism ; religious organizations; sociology of religion.

TULIP: John Calvin's teaching popularly summarized in the famous TULIP acrostic: Total depravity of man; Unconditional election; Limited atonement; Irresistible grace; Perseverance of the saints. Calvin's theology is most marked by the idea of "double predestination," which asserts that eternal salvation is divinely decreed to some but denied to others. Such doctrine is controversial; some denominations favor the dichotomy while others reject it. *See* also Arminianism; atonement; Arminian, Jacobus; BACON; Calvinism; Calvin, John; canons of Dort; conditional election; double predestination; election; elect, the; eternal security; fall from grace; Five-Point Calvinism; free will; grace; hyper-Calvinism; limited atonement; "once saved, always saved"; perseverance of the saints; predestination; Remonstrants; *Remonstrants,* the; reprobation; Synod of Dort; total depravity; Westminster Confession.

turban. See miter.

Turkistan Islamic Party: Chinese Islamic jihadists. Most recently they have been observed fighting the Syrian government as rebels and in some other locales. *See also Alluha Akbar;* al-Qaeda; al-Shabab; anti-Semitic; beast(s); Boko Haram; Daesh; Fatah; Hamas; Hezbollah; Islam; Islamic State in Iraq and Syrian (ISIS or ISIL); *jihad;* Muslim Brotherhood; Nusra Front; Palestinian Islamic Jihad (PIJ); Palestinian Liberation Organization (PLO); radicalized; Salafi; Taliban; terrorism; terrorist(s); Velayat Sinai; wild animals (beasts) of the earth.

turned to fables (myths): a mental attitude that bends the mind toward unsound doctrine, myth, or false precepts outside the orthodox faith. The New Testament says (2 Tim. 4:3–4) that such a psyche of disbelief and legend will be present in ever-increasing intensity and frequency as the end of days approaches. *See also* apostasy; Christian mythology; deep secrets, so-called; fable(s); folklore; godless myths; heresy; heretic; heterodoxy; miscreance; old wives' tales; Satan's so-called deep secrets; unsound doctrine.

Turner, Nat: African-American slave born in Southampton County, Virginia, in 1800 and given a rudimentary education by his master. Later, he was sold to an illiterate farmer and after 1820 became a religious fanatic believing himself to be ordained

519

to God to emancipate blacks by force. Turner claimed to see visions of white and black spirits in combat with streams of flowing blood. He also claimed a solar eclipse in 1831 was a sign from God that he was inspired to punish slave owners of the American South. On August 21, 1831, he and sixty supporters went on a killing spree. Some fifty-five whites (twenty-four of them children) were slaughtered. The rebellion terrorized the country, particularly the South, and brought on added repressive measures. Turner and sixteen of his companions were hanged. And, just to cement the movement firmly into the terrorism mold, Turner was not only executed but his body was skinned and boiled down to grease. Others suspected of cooperation were tortured, shot, or burned. Turner's adventure was partly financed by Geritt Smith (1797–1874), a recognized devout Presbyterian reformer. He was so appalled by the violence unleashed that he became temporarily deranged. *See also* slave, slavery; terrorism; terrorist(s).

Turning Point, The: a New Age book by Fritjof Capra. The so-called "Turning Point" was humanity's fall into ignorance beginning our gradual move up to enlightenment. The work is a parody of the Christian doctrine regarding humanity's fall into sin and God's subsequent saving acts.

"turn or burn": one of the **more** draconian phrases of hard-sell evangelism that holds the threat of hell to those resisting salvation. The expression carries a tinge of intimidation, despite its dramatic effect, and risks the opposite intent of drawing others to the grace of Christ's salvation. *See also* Christianese; fire insurance.

"turn your life [heart] over to Jesus": (or words to that effect) a popular appeal used in evangelical and fundamentalist circles as a directive or plea for one to accept the salvation of Christ because of the Lord's sacrificial death and resurrection. *See also* accept Christ, to; altar call; "asking Jesus into my heart"; birth from above; blood of Christ; blood of the Lamb; born again; Christianese; evangelist(s), evangelism; fishers of men; gospel; lost; "nail-scarred hands, the"; "plead the blood"; profession of faith; regeneration; "saved"; soul-winning; spreading the gospel; "walking the aisle"; "washed in the blood"; witness(es).

tutelary: a guardian or protector. In legend, the tutelary may be an ancestral god, a spirit, or the prophecy that is brought by the defender. *See also agathodaimon;* angel(s); attending spirit(s); clurichauns; daemons; deceiving spirits; Dee, John; daemons; demon(s), demonic; devils; disa; elemental(s); evil (unclean) spirit(s); familiar spirits; frog(s); guardian angel(s); medium; meonenim; mythological beasties, elementals, monsters, and spirit animals; Oniropompi; Orisha; para; paredri; séance; spirit guide(s); spiritual warfare; sprite(s); territorial spirits; things taught by demons; Third Man, the; Trickster.

Twelfth Imam, the: the anticipated twelfth imam, the final *Mahdi,* awaited by Shi'ite Muslims who will usher in the age of warfare followed by prosperity and peace for the world. Muslim belief records that he disappeared in A.D. 878 by falling into a deep well, by being lifted from the streets, or by some other mysterious means. Sometimes this avatar is called the Hidden Imam and his advocates are dubbed "twelvers." *See also* Ali Muhammad; Bab; imam; Islam; *jihad; Mahdi;* Shi'ite Islam.

Twelfth Night: January 5—marking the end of the Christmas season on Epiphany Eve. The day is one of festival, often with masquerading and partying. *See also* Christmas; Epiphany; feasts and special days of Protestantism; liturgical year; liturgy, Christian; *Mardi Gras.*

twelve: the number for a dozen that may or may not have symbolic value, depending on its particular context and usage. It is the count for the number of tribes in Israel and the original New Testament disciples. Apocalyptic languages make frequent use of the number. *See also* numbers, symbology of; twelve eagles prediction.

twelve eagles prediction: a random arithmetic system concocted by the Romans around 634 B.C. Each eagle of the omen represented ten years, implying that the Roman Empire would end 120 years after its founding. *See also* apocalyptic calculation; eagle(s); Hilary of Poitiers; numbers, symbology of; Romans as nationality; Rome; twelve.

"twelvers." See Shi'ite Islam.

twelve stars. See twelve-starred crown.

Bernie L. Calaway

twelve-starred crown: the tiara worn by the woman Israel in Revelation 12:1. The circlet helps us identify her as a sign for Israel because the stars represent the twelve tribes. *See also* moon; sun; woman clothed in (with) the sun, the.

Twelve Tribes: a religious cult founded by Elbert Eugene Spriggs (called "Yoneq") in 1971. Spriggs was a high school counselor and carnival barker before he discovered his more lucrative talent. The sect is reclusive and moves its thirty or so compounds about the country. Child abuse, financial fraud, and other violations are almost certainly extant in the organizations. *See also* cult(s).

twelve tribes: the number of tribes produced from the progeny of Abraham the patriarch and resident in its assigned territory in ancient Israel. The Old Testament names the Jewish tribes to number a dozen, even though the enumeration of their names must be fitted at times to make the count consistent; sometimes Levi (the appointed priestly tribe) is dropped and the two sons of Joseph appear as either combined or separate. They are named, as a full reckoning, as: Reuben, Simeon, Levi, Judah, Issachar, Zebulun, Gad, Benjamin, Joseph, Asher, Naphtali, Dan, Manasseh, and Ephraim. It should be noted that God also provided the descendants of Ishmael, the first son of Abraham, certain blessings (excluding the favored Jewish covenants). These also were classed into twelve tribes which Josephus named according to the sons of Ishmael: Nabaioth, Kedar, Abdeel, Mabsam, Idumas, Masmaos, Masaos, Chodad, Theman, Jetur, Naphesus, and Cadmas. *See also* Hagar and Sarah; Judaism; lost tribes, the ten; 144,000, the; tribes of Israel, the.

twenty-four elders, the: a group of two dozen worshipers gathered about the throne of God in Revelation 4:4. They are called "elders," meaning "leaders" or "wise ones." Each has a throne and a crown, the latter article they regularly cast before the seat of God in reverent worship and respect. Some identify these two dozen as representatives of Israel (for the twelve tribes) and of the Church (for the twelve apostles). Others see them as angelic beings. If their crowns are symbolic of victory, they are most likely humans; if the crowns represent authority, they are more probably angels. Perhaps the strongest argument that they are angelic is seen in Revelation 7:13–14, where one of them

522

explained to John the identity of the Great Multitude (who are definitely human), thereby indicating that the elder himself is not one of that number. One interpretation, hardly plausible even though it was exposed by Jerome in his *Gallican Psalter,* is that the twenty-four represent the books of the Old Testament. To do that, the system must combine the twelve minor prophets as a single volume, then count Ezra through Nehemiah, 1 and 2 Kings, 1 and 2 Samuel, and 1 and 2 Chronicles as a single book. *See also* angel(s); elder(s); four living creatures of Revelation.

24/7 Prayer Movement: contemporary association spanning denominational lines that seeks the pursuit of God as the focus of one's life. Continuous prayer (*laus perennis*) is offered without ceasing, a periodical practice that dates to the early church. At least one group, the Moravian Brethren, claims to have practiced uninterrupted prayer beginning in 1727 for 100 years; they renewed the effort in 1957. The International House of Prayer in Kansas City, Missouri, is a prime example of the movement and perhaps to be considered its figurative headquarters. *See also* religious organizations; sect(s).

2012 prophecy, advocates of: those persons who believe the Mayan prophecy that the world would end its age cycle or change dramatically on December 21, 2012. However, true believers hold to the idea that the specified time marks not the end of an earth cycle but the end of the world as we know it at some point as a result of that fateful day in 2012. They might be considered 2012 gurus, or as sometimes named, 2012ologists. There are many modern promoters of the theory, but some of the more prominent include: 1. Jose Arguelles, who predicted a mass disappearance of populations from the earth who are not spiritual enough to make the 2012 transition. He now calls himself Valum Votan since he received a prophecy concerning the matter, especially when the vanished people are to be taken away on "silver ships"; 2. Patrick Geryl, who quit his job with a French oil company and formed a "survival group" of like-minded men and women; 3. John Major Jenkins promotes New Age metaphysics by stating that the world will evolve into a new age of enlightenment and human growth; 4. Hwee-Jong Jang, a business professor in South Korea predicts that the "Great Change"—to which he has become aware through dreams, visions, channeling, and energy readings—will surely bring about a perfect age after 2012; 5. Lawrence Joseph says that the infamous date was to produce untold catastrophes because the sun would eclipse the view from Earth. The core of change can be sighted in the center of the Milky Way (considered by the ancients to be the "womb of the world"); 6. James O'Dea sees the date as a cosmic judgment for man's sins and a day of global cleansing; 7. Daniel Pinchbeck claims that the new day will bring in a state of human consciousness similar to the Mayan belief in the return of Quetzalcoatl; 8. Eckhart Tolle (often promoted by Oprah Winfrey) is an author who uses New Age Mayan theories to base his ideas of the new world coming after 2012. *See also* Arguelles, Jose; Aztecs; Blue Star prophecy; calendar; Chilam-Balam; cosmic cross; cosmology; crystal skull(s); Dark Rift; Day of Purification; *Dresden Codex;* eagle and the condor, the; Eagle Bowl; eclipse(s); Fifth World, the; five stages of earth, the; galactic alignment; Great Change, Prophecy of the; Great Shaking, the; impact event; Inca; Itza-Maya; *Jupiter Effect, The;* Maya; Mictlan; Pahana; *Popul Unh;* precession of the equinoxes; Quetzalcoatl; Rattlesnake Prophecy; Sun Stone, Toltecs; "transition of consciousness"; 2012, prophecy of; Votan, Pacal; Wheel of Time, the; Xibala; Xolotl; zero state; zodiac.

2012, prophecy of: the calculation of the ancient Mayans and Aztecs who predicted the end of days on December 21, 2012 (sometimes written as a shorthand 12.21.12). As a culture, the Mayans viewed history as linear, not circular, so time marches on in a precise pattern of epochs. Although they maintained some twenty calendars, the three most important are: 1. the solar (called the *Haab'*) that records a year as 365 plus days split into eighteen months of twenty days each with one five-day period or leftover month, which was considered to be malevolent. 2. the sacred or ceremonial calendar (the *Tzolk'in*) connected to the cycle of Venus containing 260 days known as the "sacred cycle." Most likely it was based on the human gestation period of nine months and has been dubbed the oldest and most widely used calendar of Mesoamerica. 3. third is the Long Count that documents the age cycles of the world. It is this calculation that produced the date of December 21, 2012. The timing starts with the emergence of the Mayas, which they believed to be August 11, 3114 B.C., represented on the Long Count as 0.0.0.0.1 (Day One). The fifth cycle ended on December 21, 2012 or 13.0.0.0.0 (Last Day). In between were one *baktun* of 144,000 days, thirteen *baktuns* representing a great cycle of 5,125 years, and five great sequences called a precessional cycle of 25,625 years. On the indicated date (when the winter solstice of the northern hemisphere manifests) the earth was predicted to line up with the galactic center of the Milky Way, an alignment occurring only once every 26,000 years. What happened then, if anything, is unknown to science, but certainly no globe-killing astronomical event transpired. Certain scientific theories predicted a massive coronal mass ejection of the sun expected between 2012-2014 and a total of four lunar eclipses between 2014-2015. The first day after the end would be 0.0.0.0.1 again, but many believe, in defiance of science, that the earth as we know it will never survive. Either the world will end in catastrophic destruction or the earth will evolve into a new human program of cultural and human enlightenment never before experienced. The more esoteric features of the belief are mainly New Age in its concepts that trend to the radical. In summation, the advent of December 21, 2012, is under review, and the world still waits for its renewal or disaster, or remains to enjoy the natural consequences of time. It is just possible that the Mayan prediction produced some effect unrecognized by us or we have miscalculated its intent. Later studies of the great Mayan calendar suggest that the correct date for the world transition may actually be December 21, 2050. *See also* Aztecs; Blue Star prophecy; calendar; Chilam-Balam; cosmic cross; cosmology; crystal skull(s); Dark Rift; Day of Purification; *Dresden Codex;* eagle and the condor, the; Eagle Bowl; eclipse(s); Fifth World, the; five stages of earth, the; galactic alignment; Great Shaking, the; impact event; Inca; *Jupiter Effect, The;* Katun Prophecies; Maya; Mictlan; Mesoamerica; omega point; ouroboros; Pahana; *Popul Unh;* precession of the equinoxes; Quetzalcoatl; Rattlesnake Prophecy; Sun Stone, "transition of consciousness"; 2012 prophecy, advocates of; Votan, Pacal; Wheel of Time, the; Xibala; Xolotl; zero state; zodiac.

Twi: the Norse god responsible for guarding the sky pole of Norse legend. He forfeited his right arm to Fenris the wolf in that animal's attempt to destroy the pole but managed to bind him giving temporary relief to the world. *See also* Norse and old Germanic pantheon; sky pole; wolf.

"twilight of the gods": a rather poetic expression to indicate the end of paganism and atheism—a total healing of the nations that can only be by divine action. The world will simply repudiate its idols and acknowledge its shame. Isaiah was convinced of this advent (Isa. 41:2, 42:17), although he did not use this elegiac phrase. The expression is also the title of a book by von Daniken supporting extraterrestrials on Earth. *See also* von Daniken, Eric.

twinkling of an eye: a description of the speed in which believers will be transformed at the rapture (1 Cor. 15:51–52). The term conveys the thought of fantastic speed, essentially instantaneous movement. Some physicists have calculated a twinkling as a quantum Planck with speeds of ten to the minus forty-third power. *See also* eschatology, eschatological; rapture.

two baskets of figs: a vision of the prophet Jeremiah (Jer. 24). In the presentation, the prophet is shown a basket of good figs and another of fully ripe or putrid fruit set before the Temple. The former represented those going into exile in Babylonia who would be faithful to God despite their hardships. The rotten figs classed those who would remain in Judah or flee to Egypt as unworthy servants. The spoiled figs had special reference to King Zedekiah, who was particularly abhorrent toward God during the pre-exilic crisis. *See also* fig(s); flora, fruit, and grain, symbology of; fruit; fruit, basket of ripe (summer).

two-horned ram, the: Daniel's interpretation of a dream for Medo-Persia, an oppressor of Israel (Dan. 8:1–4). One of the horns is more pronounced in appearance than the other, which likely denotes that the Persians were a bit more politically prominent than their allies, the Medes. The land beast from Revelation 7 is also a ram with two horns representing the False Prophet. *See also* beast from the land; chest and arms of silver; False Prophet, the; horn(s); hunched bear, the; Medo-Persia.

200,000,000 invaders: the number of attackers, possibly demonic, unleashed by the four formerly bound angels at the River Euphrates as presented in the book of Revelation. That invasion with such incredible numbers is signaled by the sounding of the sixth trumpet (Rev. 9:13–21) and the hordes released proceed to slay a third of mankind. The raiders could be human, but if so, their numbers are incredible. *See also* angel(s); eschatology, eschatological.

two natures, doctrine of the: 1. the belief that Jesus was both human and divine. 2. the idea that humans are born with dual natures—one good and one evil. A sect called the Two Seed in the Spirit Predestination Baptists is a prime example of this credence. Dualism was an early and rather common doctrine of the ancients used to explain why there is good and bad in the world and what is to be done about the situation. Jewish thinking tends to start from "tendencies" when considering one's susceptibility to sin. *See also* Adoptionism; appropriation; Anomoeans; Arianism; Arius; complementarian view of the Trinity; Councils of Ephesus; diphysitism; Donatism; dualism; Dynamic Monarchianism; dynamism; dyophysitism; eternal subordination of the Son; "four fences of Chalcedon"; *homoiousios; homoousios;* hypostatic union; incarnation; *kenosis;* kenotic view of Christ; modalism; Monarchianism; monophysitism; Mandaeanism; Manicheanism; Mithraism; monotheism; Nestorianism; Nestorius; Nicene Creed; *ousia;* patripassianism; Pelagianism; Pelagius; *perichoresis;* psilanthropism; Sabellianism; serpent seed doctrine, the; Socianism, Socinian; subordinationism; theanthroposophy; *Theophorus;* three; Trinity; Trisagion, the; union; *Vesica Piscis;* unipersonality; Zoroaster, Zoroastrianism.

two olive trees and a lampstand: another name for the two great heavenly witnesses appearing in Revelation 11. The scene springs from Zechariah 4 where two olive trees are fueling oil to a golden lampstand. The figures named there are almost certainly Joshua the high priest and Zerubbabel, the governor of restored Judah. Some claim that these two are also to be literally identified with the two witnesses of Revelation 11. *See also* flora, fruit, and grain, symbology of; Joshua; Zechariah's vision of the gold lampstand and two olive trees, the; witnesses, the two great; Zerubbabel.

Two-penny Act: the description applied to the stipend law passed by the American colonial assembly of Virginia. In those days, clergy and public officials were paid in tobacco. There was a "prodigious diminution" of that commodity in 1758, however, so money was substituted. Assembly acts in 1755 and 1758 provoked clergy to protest as they perceived their wages too severely decreased.

two shepherd's staffs. See Zechariah's oracle of two shepherds and two shepherd's staffs.

two sons and the avenger of blood, the: a parable presented to King David by the "wise woman" of Tekoa to prompt him to leave off his grief for the death of his son Absalom (2 Sam. 14) and resume paying attention to Israel's needs. The story was told at the instigation of Joab in an attempt to allay the king's despondent thoughts and feelings and to refocus his attention toward the good of all the land. *See also* parable(s); parables of the Old Testament; wise woman, a.

two states of the Church. See Church Triumphant, Church Militant.

two sticks becoming one. See Ezekiel's demonstration of the folded boards.

2,300 evenings and mornings: a prophecy of Daniel that seems to indicate that the traditional morning and evening sacrifices so important to Jewish worship would be suspended or frozen for about 1,150 days (Dan. 8:14). The hiatus of sacrifice was no doubt a literal stoppage during the oppression of Antiochus Epiphanes but will most likely occur again in the Tribulation years under the Antichrist. *See also* corban; Daniel as Old Testament prophecy; evenings and mornings, prophecy of the; morning and evening sacrifices; sacrifice; sacrifice, the daily.

two witnesses, my. See witnesses, the two great.

Tyche: goddess of ancient Syrian Antioch on the Orantes River. She was the patron of that prosperous and influential center (present-day Antakya in Turkey) and worshiped as the provider of fortune and fertility. Her city was called "the Queen of the East" but nothing remains today but rubble. *See also* Antioch of Syria; Levant pantheon.

Tychicus: a traveling companion and fellow missionary with Paul who, accompanied by Trophimus, was sent ahead to Troas to prepare for the work anticipated there (Acts. 20:4). Tychicus was a faithful servant, possibly an evangelist, pastor, or prophet who was designated to be Paul's personal spokesman to the church at Ephesus (Eph. 6:21–22; Col. 4:7; Tit. 3:12). Tychicus, along with Onesimus, Mark, Aristarchus, and Justus, were the only fellow Jews supporting Paul who was imprisoned when he wrote the Christians of Colossae (Col. 4:7). *See also* missions, missionaries; prophet(s); Trophimus.

Tyconius: a North African churchman (d. A.D. 400), one of the earliest exponents of what we today call amillennialism and one who influenced Augustine of Hippo. He was also the most active leader in the movement called Donatism, a faction which condemned the betrayal of Christians who submitted Scripture to be destroyed by the Romans and who were opposed to the rule of the church bishops. Tyconius believed that the Millennium was not future but active in the world today. His views were taken up and expanded by Augustine. He authored the *Book of Rules* as an aid to pious living. The amillennialist view of Tyconius and Augustine was quickly assumed by Roman and Greek Catholicism and were even supported by Luther and Calvin. According to Tyconius, the Millennium is a parallel development of good (God's kingdom) and evil (Satan's kingdom) and will finally conclude with the Second Coming, a general resurrection for all, global judgment for all, and eternity. *See also* Augustine, Aurelius; amillennial, amillennialism; Donatism; Roman Catholic Church.

Tyndale, William: the first to print the New Testament in English (ca. 1494–1536). He has been called the "architect of the English language," even more so than William Shakespeare. Tyndale was a true Reformer and helped Henry VIII pave the way for the breakaway Church of England but was betrayed and burned at the stake for his theological stance and work of translation. *See also* Bible translations.

type(s): an Old Testament institution, event, person, ceremony, or object that has meaning at the time of its existence but also foreshadows some prophecy yet to be revealed, usually in the New Testament. Thus, a "type" (meaning to pattern, stamp, or model) can be an example of one early event prefiguring another later one. Types can be easily viewed as anticipatory patterns or symbols that presage a significant future event. The Old Testament system of animal sacrifice, to illustrate, is a type of the redemptive sacrifice of Jesus, as is Abraham's intended sacrifice of his son Isaac (Gen. 22). Surely, the construct and equipment of the tabernacle represent the person and mission of the Messiah. Any identified type should flow reasonably to the antitype (the fulfillment) and always bear relevance to the intended prophecy. The procedure is easily abused and must be utilized with care. There are types in the New Testament as well (*e.g.*, the Lord's Supper observance may type the coming feast of the Millennium). A passage from Paul (1 Corinthians 10:1–13) is actually named by him as a type. Here, Paul recounted the unfaithfulness of the Exodus Hebrews (the forefathers of the Jews) as an example, warning his generation not to fall into the same sin. Estimates are that Christological typology includes about fifty types for Christ— about half the total number in the entire study of typology. *See also* antitype; "fingerprint of God, the"; prefiguration; semiotics; sign(s); symbol(s); typology.

Typhon: the Greek god-giant called "the father of all monsters." His wife, Echidna, was "the mother of all monsters." He was birthed by Gaia and Tartarus and stood higher than the heavens. His head was human-shaped, but he had dragons for fingers; his lower half was huge coiled vipers. He was covered with wings, and fire sprang from his eyes. At the instigation of Gaia, he warred against Zeus for imprisoning the Titans. Sometimes he was victorious but eventually Zeus confined him under Mount Etna. Seth or Apophis was an Egyptian equivalent. *See also* Apophis; Egyptian pantheon; giant(s); mythological beasties, elementals, monsters, and spirit animals; Olympian pantheon; Seth.

Typicon: a liturgical book for the Byzantine order containing instructions in ritual. *See also* Eastern Orthodox Church; liturgical year.

typology: the academic and prophetic practice of identifying and illuminating biblical types. *See also* accideme; alliteration; antitype; apostrophe; apothegm; assonance; autograph; Bible; Bible manuscripts; Bible translations; biblical criticism; chiasmus; conflict story; *constructio ad sensum;* context; contextualization; dittography; double sense fulfillment; doublets; doubling; edification; eisegesis; epanadiplosis; epigrammatic statements; etymology; exegesis; figure of speech; fingerprint of God, the; folio; form criticism; gattung; gloss; gnomic sayings; grammatical-historical interpretation; *hapax legomena;* haplography; hermeneutic(s); higher criticism; homographs; homonyms; homophones; *homoteleuton;* hyperbole;

idiom; *inclusio;* interpolation; interpretation; inverted nun; irony; isagogics; *itture sopherim;* jot and tittle; kere; *kethib;* "L"; liberalists interpretation; literal interpretation; litotes; loan words; lower criticism; "M"; Masoretic Text; minuscule(s); mystery of God; omission; onomastica; onomatopoeia; palimpsest; papyrus; paradigm; parallelism; parchment; *paroimia; paronomasia;* pericope; personification; Peshitta; pointing; point of view; polyglot; prefiguration; principles of interpretation; proof texting; pun(s); "Q"; redaction; revelation, theological; rhetorical criticism; rhetorical devices; riddle; satire; *scripto continua;* scriptorium; *sebirin;* simile; similitude; source criticism; sources, primary and secondary; special points; strophe; superscription; symbol(s); synecdoche; syntax; synthetic parallelism; text; textual criticism; *tiggune sopherim;* Time Texts; Torah; translation; transposition; trope; type(s); uncial(s); vellum; verbicide.

Tyrannus: a lecture hall in Ephesus, possibly named for a teacher or philosopher of that name (Acts 19:9). Paul used the place for successful teaching for about two years. *See also* philosophy of religion; Titus Justus.

Tyre, Tyrenians: a town mentioned by Jesus in Matthew 11:21–24 as a pagan populace who would fare better on the day of judgment than the Jewish cities of Bethsaida and Korazin because of their willingness to repent more readily than their Jewish counterparts. The actual site of Tyre was an ancient Phoenician city-state on the Mediterranean coast between Acre and Sidon. *See also* king of Tyre; Phoenicia, Phoenicians.

Tyropoeon Valley: site of the city dump of Jerusalem and a symbol of great idolatry. The site was called "the valley of the cheese makers." *See also* death; Gehenna; grave; Hades; Kidron Valley; lake of fire; *Sheol;* Tophet; Valley of Decision; Valley of Hinnom; Valley of Jehoshaphat; Valley of Slaughter.

tzitzit: knotted cords containing blue or blue-violet threads worn by observant Jews and Samaritans. The tassels are attached to the four corners of the *tallit* (prayer shawl) or *tallit katan* (undergarment) for males and are an obligation in honor of the Exodus and as a reminder to be obedient. *See also* Judaism; Vidui; *yarmulke.*

Tzotzil religion: a blend of Catholicism and indigenous Maya peoples in the highlands of Southern Mexico. The people maintain that everyone has two souls—a *wayjel* and a *ch'uel.* The latter is an inner soul situated in the heart and blood, placed there by the gods in the unborn embryo. At death, this spirit travels to *Katibak,* the land of the dead in the center of the earth. There it resides for as long as the person had lived, but moving in reverse from death to birth to become a new baby of the opposite sex. The second soul is an animal spirit companion shared with a wild beast (a *chanul*) kept by the ancestral gods. Humans and animals have a shared fate so that whatever befalls one affects the other. Animal spirits may be jungle cats or land animals like squirrels and opossums. *See also* jaguar; Maya; Mesoamerica.

U

UAP: an acronym for "unidentified aerial phenomena," a designation used by the U.S. Navy and some scientists to name flying objects in the sky they cannot identify, *viz.* UFOs. In other words, they might be Chinese, Russian, some other nation, or even alien spacecraft but, whatever they are, they are real, they aren't ours, and they continually violate U.S. airspace with impunity. Videos, eyewitnesses by pilots, and other evidence has been procured but not highly publicized. The objects duplicate what is normally used to describe the actions of a UFO—unbelievable maneuverability, rapid speed change, and other impossible aeronautical behavior, etc. *See also* Alien Disclosure Event; Area 51; Black Vault; Jason Society; Project Blue Book; UFO; Vimanas; zero-point energy.

ubiquitarianism: the belief that God is everywhere. *See also* immanency; omnipresence.

Ucal: a term found in Proverbs 30:1, paired with another written as "Ithiel." If Ucal is a noun, it must name one of two persons or contemporaries to whom Agur addresses his proverbs. Most scholars agree, however, that Ucal and Ithiel are not proper names. Another rendering with a different Hebrew word structure frames the phrase (using the Masoretic text) with the meaning of "I am weary, O God; I am weary, O God, and faint." Whether one or both of these names identifies a writing prophet is purely speculative. *See also* Ithiel; Lemuel; Proverbs as Old Testament book.

UFO: Unidentified Flying Object. UFOs are what they imply by the acronym—unidentified flying objects—or space vehicles of varying descriptions (the implication being that they are extraterrestrial). Their existence in our galaxy is a much debated issue, but many New Age, cultic, and esoteric sects have adopted their reality as a focal point of their eschatological ideas. It has been promoted that the reports of UFOs may be a means by which the Antichrist will disguise the true nature of the rapture of the Church. Thereby, the people living at that time will be deceived by the propaganda that all the Christians were kidnapped or taken away to remove their negative (to him) influence. It is assumed that any manned vehicles from outer space are piloted by an intellectually superior species that are far more technically developed than the humanity of Earth. Whether the mysterious visitors are beneficent or malevolent is debated. *See also* alien abduction; Alien Disclosure Event; alien Jesus; Anunnaki; Ancient Astronaut Theory; Area 51; Black Vault; chariot(s); *Chariots of the Gods?;* Columbus, Christopher; cosmic consciousness; cult(s); demi-god(s); egregores; Fermi paradox; Findhorn Foundation; Human Enhancement Revolution (HER); Igigi; inter-dimensional corridor; Jason Society; livestock mutilations; lulu; Merkabah; Missler, Chuck; names, symbology of; New Age religion; Nibiru; Nidle, Sheldon; panspermia theory; Parutia; Project Blue Book; Raelism; *Regatta Morte;* sect(s); Sitchin, Zechariah; UAP; Vimanas; von Daniken, Erich; Vorilhorn, Claude; zero-point energy.

Ugarit: an ancient kingdom north of Palestine but a separate political entity from the Canaanites. It was a distinctly pagan culture where Baal, Dagon, and the related pantheon were worshiped. Yahweh's battle with Leviathan and the dragon (Rahab) are drawn from some of the writings found there (Job 41:1; Ps. 74:13–14; Isa. 27:1; 51:9). The culture was an early contributor to the ancient alphabets, which may be its main claim to notoriety (ca. 1450–1200 b.c.). The sea people destroyed its major city in the 12th century, and it was never rebuilt. *See also* alphabet; Dan'el; Levant; Mesopotamia.

Ugbaru: a Persian official who was possibly associated with Cyrus the Great. There is some dispute as to his true identity, but he was likely the general who took Babylon for Cyrus. It is possible that he became governor, but if so, he ruled only briefly because the Nabonidus Chronicle says he died three weeks after the battle. *See also* Darius the Mede; Gobryas; Gubaru; Nabonidus Chronicle.

Uighur: or the Uyghurs, the largest Muslim minority ethnic group in China. *See also* Hui; Islam.

Ulai: the river, or more accurately, a canal in Elam, where Daniel received some of his prophetic visions (Dan. 8:2, 16).

Ulam: the Jewish designate on (*'ulam*) for the portico at the entrance to the Temple structure. The location was similar to a porch or modern church narthex. *See also Devir;* Heikhal; Temple(s).

Ulfilas: a Cappadocian missionary to the Goths (c. 311–383) known as the "Little Wolf." He invented a Gothic alphabet so he could translate the Bible into that language and was active in the Arian controversy of the time. He was ordained a bishop by Eusebius himself. *See also* Eastern Orthodox Church; missions, missionaries.

ultradispensationalism: a form of theological dispute as to when the Church of Christ began historically. Traditional dispensationalists believe that the Church had its start at Pentecost with the appearance of the Holy Spirit. Ultradispensationalists claim it started with the ministry of Paul. The movement had its origin with Ethelbert W. Bullinger (1837–1913), an Anglican minister and linguist with unorthodox doctrine. He held the extinction of the soul between death and resurrection but was silent on the fate of the lost. He placed the Gospels and Acts under the Law and dated the church to the time of Paul. The prison epistles (Ephesians, Philippians, Colossians) only pertained to the church age. Two baptisms are practiced, one "with" the Spirit and one "by" the Spirit as somehow drawn from Acts 1:5 and 1 Corinthians 12:13. Baptism and the Lord's Supper do not apply to this age. This concept has pushed the more extreme group (ultradispensationalism) into the position that the Great Commission (Mt. 28:19–20) is for Jews, not for the Church. They further believe that the apostles were a continuation of Christ's earthly ministry only, that water baptism does not belong as a Church ordinance, and that there is a difference between Paul's earlier and later messages. Today, ultradispensationalism is represented by Grace Mission, Grace Gospel Fellowship, and Berean Bible Society. Finally, ultradispensationalism forwards the assertion that Israel alone, not the Church, is the bride of Christ. *See also* dispensational theology; progressive dispensationalism.

ultramontanism: to "rule beyond the mountains," a technical term denoting the instances when the Church establishment has dominance, or undue influence, over the state. The identification springs from Roman Catholic supremacy in both geography and spirituality, which reached its height under Pope Pius IX (1846–1878). *See also* Abington School District vs. Schempp; Allegheny County vs. ACLU; antidisestablishmentarianism; apotheosis; caesaropapacy; collegialism; disestablishmentarianism; Edict of Milan; Emerson vs. Board of Education; Establishment Clause and Free Exercise Clause; *instrumentum regni;* Lemon vs. Kurtzman; *Pontifex Maximus; princeps; principis;* public square; Roman Catholic Church; Shubert vs. Verner; state church.

ultramundane: the realms outside the earth or beyond the solar system.

Ultraquists: a relatively moderate faction of the Hussite dissenters from the Roman Catholic dominance of the 15th century. The name means "in two kinds" from the Latin *sub utraque specie* because one of their major doctrines was that Communion should be served with both bread and wine for the worshipers. They were also known as Calixtines (meaning "chalice") for the same reason; or were simply called the "Prague Party." They finally made peace with the Roman Church and signed the *Compactata* as a treaty of reconciliation. *See also Compactata;* Hus, John; Hussites; sect(s); Taborites.

Uluru: the great spiritual mountain in the Northwest Territory of Australia, sacred to the Aborigine peoples. The hill is a sandstone rock formation containing the *djang,* the navel of the living body of Australia. It is said to hold the heart of the ancestral beings (their "Songlines" or "dreaming tracks") which can still be seen in the formation's features. Aborigines consider the land to be both their inheritance and their responsibility.

Umayyad Caliphate: the third caliphate after Mohammed beginning in the year 637 and headquartered in Baghdad. *See also* Abbasid Caliphate; Ayyubid dynasty; caliph; caliphate; Fatimid Caliphate; Islam; Rashidun Caliphate.

Umbanda: a Brazilian religion blending African traditions and Catholicism with spiritism. The leading figure of the movement was Zello Fermandinao de Moraes from the early 1900s, but the leadership has never been able to quantify the sect into a whole as there remain many and varied diversities of practice. The Creator God is Olodumare (or Zambi) and holds certain similarities to Candomble. Other lesser deities are called *orixas.* Cardinal beliefs conclude that the dead can offer counsel and guidance to the living, along with reincarnation. Umbanda beliefs can be fairly stated as less invasive than its more baleful sister religion, Quimbanda. *See also* animism; Brujeria; Candomble;

Creole (Caribbean) religions; cult(s); Kumina; Macumba; magic, magick; Obeah; Orisha; Quimbanda; Rastafarianism; Santeria; shaman, shamanism; Shango; spiritism; Spiritual Baptists; Voodoo; Voudou; Yoruba.

Unam Sanctum: the declaration that the Roman Catholic Church is one, holy, and apostolic and that outside of the institution there is no salvation or remission of sins. Within is also the directive that the church carries "two swords"—the temporal and the ecclesiastical (or spiritual), but that the temporal power is subservient to the spiritual. Furthermore, none but God may judge the pope and his actions, nor that of church polity. The announcement manifested under Boniface III in 1302 and was a major impetus to the Protestant Reformation that resented such "papist ideals." *See also* apostolic succession, Protestant Reformation, the; Roman Catholic Church.

uncial(s): the upper case print for Greek documents, also known as majuscules. Some Bible manuscripts are written in uncials entirely. *See also* accideme; alliteration; apostrophe; apothegm; assonance; autograph; Bible; Bible manuscripts; Bible translations; biblical criticism; chiasmus; conflict story; *constructio ad sensum;* context; contextualization; dittography; double sense fulfillment; doublets; doubling; edification; eisegesis; epanadiplosis; epigrammatic statements; etymology; exegesis; figure of speech; folio; form criticism; gattung; gloss; gnomic sayings; grammatical-historical interpretation; *hapax legomena;* haplography; hermeneutic(s); higher criticism; homographs; homonyms; homophones; *homoteleuton;* hyperbole; idiom; *inclusio;* interpolation; interpretation; inverted nun; irony; isagogics; *itture sopherim;* jot and tittle; kere; *kethib;* "L"; liberalists interpretation; literal interpretation; litotes; loan words; lower criticism; "M"; Masoretic Text; minuscule(s); mystery of God; omission; onomastica; onomatopoeia; palimpsest; papyrus; paradigm; parallelism; parchment; *paroimia; paronomasia;* pericope; personification; Peshitta; pointing; point of view; polyglot; principles of interpretation; proof texting; pun(s); "Q"; redaction; revelation, theological; rhetorical criticism; rhetorical devices; riddle; satire; *scripto continua;* scriptorium; *sebirin;* simile; similitude; source criticism; sources, primary and secondary;

special points; strophe; superscription; symbol(s); synecdoche; syntax; synthetic parallelism; text; textual criticism; *tiggune sopherim;* Time Texts; Torah; translation; transposition; trope; type(s); typology; vellum; verbicide.

uncircumcised: a male who has not undergone the ritual operation of circumcision. In Israel, the term was one of contempt, usually for a foreigner (1 Sam. 17:26) because circumcision was the most pointed identification for the Jewish race. In the New Testament, Paul declared that in Christ there is no prejudice or favor for either the circumcised or the uncircumcised (Col. 3:11). *See also* circumcision.

unclean: an animal, object, or person designated as ritually impure according to the Mosaic Law. Such unfortunates were deemed unlawful to share in sacrifice or to initiate any religious rite. Such labels could be either temporary (capable of being cured) or permanent (closed by the Mosaic Law). Lepers (commonly named for people with most any incurable skin disease) in Jesus' time were required by law to cry out "unclean!" when in the presence of people not afflicted with the disease. To be classed as "Unclean!" was to suffer social and legal isolation and almost always extreme poverty. The term is also common enough to denote moral turpitude in both a religious and legal context. *See also* after one's own lusts; antinomianism; blasphemy; body; carnal; concupiscence; crawling creatures on the wall; curse(s); debauchery; demimondaines; depravity; desecrate; dissipation; evil (unclean) spirits; flesh; harmartiology; haunt (prison) for every unclean and detestable bird; hedonism; human condition, the; human nature, the; immorality; "monthly uncleanliness"; moral uncleanliness; Nehushtan; owl; profane; raven; ritual defilement; sacrilege; sin(s); sinful nature, the; trespass; unclean animals, Peter's vision of the; vulture(s); wicked, wickedness; worldly.

unclean animals, Peter's vision of the: a vision or trance experienced by Peter as described in Acts 10:9–23. A tarpaulin, sailcloth, or other spread of fabric was seen descending from heaven. Inside were many varieties of animals, each one unsuitable for *kosher* consumption by a Jew nor for sacrifice. The command to Peter was nevertheless to rise, kill some, and eat them. Peter was repelled because he knew the injunction forbidding the consumption of unclean animals. Subsequent understanding, however, allowed the apostle to comprehend that the core message of the sheet vision was that he should welcome Gentiles into the new Christian faith, along with any professing Jews. Peter then arose and journeyed to the house of Cornelius the centurion where the gospel first reached Gentile ears. *See also* animals, birds, and insects, symbology of; Caesarea; Cornelius; desecrate; Peter as apostle; ritual defilement; profane; sacrilege; trespass; unclean.

unclean spirit(s). See evil (unclean) spirit(s); fallen angel(s).

unconditional covenant(s): an agreement or treaty in which the benefits of a contract will be honored despite the failure of one party to comply with the stipulations. All of God's covenants are considered unconditional, with the possible exception of the Mosaic and the Adamic. *See also* conditional covenant(s); covenant(s), biblical; covenant theology; eternal covenant; everlasting covenant, a (the); New Covenant, the; suzerainty treaty.

unction: anointing with balm or oil as a religious act. In Catholicism, "extreme unction" is the sacrament of pending death. The formal administration of the extreme unction is called "anele." *See also* anointing; liturgy, Christian; gestures; Roman Catholic Church; sacrament(s).

underground Christian Church, the: the remains of a supposedly Christian place of worship located underground in the Temple Mount. Archeologists claim that the structure was built in the second century, then rebuilt by the Crusaders using stones from the destroyed Temple of A.D. 70. The design was in the shape of a cross measuring sixty feet in height, twenty-two feet in length, and fifty feet wide. *See also* church.

underground church: not troglodytes but people of religious faith who because of persecution are forced to operate in secrecy. The term "underground" also applies to any organization that exists as far away as possible from public scrutiny. The Christian Church has been, may be, or perhaps will be, banned and therefore operating in a secret or clandestine mode as a signal event at the end of days. *See also* Church.

undershepherd. See pastor(s).

under the altar: a place of refuge and safety, poetically speaking. Revelation 6:9 portrays righteous saints awaiting the judgment of God. A similar concept is present in *2 Esdras*, which pictures the souls of the saints in storehouses. *See also* eschatology, eschatological; storehouse(s).

underworld: 1. in Old Testament terminology and most ancient writing, a name for the foreboding afterlife, usually in some dark and forbidding underground region. The Jews called it several names including *Sheol*, Dudael, Gehenna, Abaddon, Tehom, Azazel, Tophet, Abaddon, Tzoah, Rotachat, or the Abyss. Ancient mythologies defined such a death-place by various terms: Albanian (Ferri), Aztec (Mictlan), Babylonian (Aralu), Buddhism (Naraka, Niraya), Chinese (Diyu), Christianity (hell, lake of fire, Hades, outer darkness, Tartarus), Egyptian (Duat, Aaru Amente, Neter-Kitertet), Estonian (Toonela), Finnish (Tuonela), Etruscan (Charun, Culsa, Februus, Minia, Mantus, Nethuns, Tuchulcah, Vanth), German and Norse (Hel, Niflheim, Niflhel, Nastrond, Gimle, Vingolf), Greek and Roman (Elysium, Ashphodel Meadows, Erebus, Fortunate Isles, Hades, Orcus, Tartarus, Inferno, Avernus), Guanche (Echeide, Guayota), Hinduism (Patala, Naraka), Hopi (Maski), Inca Uku Pacha), Hungarian (Aluilag), Inuit (Adlivun), Irish (Tir na nOg, Tech, Duinn), Islam (Jahannam, Barzakh, Naar, Araf), Jainism (Naraka, Adho Loka), Korean (Ji-Ok), Latvian (Aizsaule), Maori (Hawaiki, Rarohenga), Mapuche (Pellumawida, Degin, Wenuleufu, Ngullchenmaiwe), Maya (Xibala, Metnal), Melanesian (Bulu, Burutu, Murimuria, Nabagatai, Tuma), Mesopotamia/Sumerian (Irkalla, Dilmun, Kur, Hubur), Oromo (Ekera), Persian (Duzakh), Philippian (Kasanaan), Polynesian (Auaiki, Bulotu, Iva, Lua-o-milu, Nag-Atua, Pulotu, Rangi Tuarea, Te Toipo-nga-Ranga, Uranga-o-Te-Ra), Pueblo (Shipap), Romanian (Taramul, Celalalt), Shinto (Yomi, Ne-no-Kuni), Slavic (Iriy, Podsvetie, Peklo, Nav, Jigoku), Turkic/Mongolian (Erlik), Vodou (Guinee), Wagawaga (Hiyoyoa), Welsh/Celtic (Annwn, Mag Mell). 2. organized criminal cartels or the generic nomenclature of those elements outside the law. *See also* Abaddon; Abraham's bosom; Abyss, the; Acheron; afterlife; Amen; Amente; Annwn; Anubis; Aralu; Azazel; black lamb; Bolos; *Book of the Dead;* cosmic tree; death; deep, the; Demeter; demon(s), demonic; Dionysus the god; Dis; Duat; Egyptian pantheon; Eriskegal; eschatology, eschatological;

eternal life; future life, doctrine of the; gargoyle(s); gates of hell; Gehenna; grave; Hadadrimmon; Hades; happy hunting ground; Hecate; Hel; Helheim; hell; hound(s) of hell; intermediate state; Jahannam; lake of fire; Levant pantheon; life after death; limbo; *Limbus Puerorum;* Mafia; Mictlan; Mot; nature cult(s); Nergal; Norse and Old Germanic pantheon; Olympian pantheon; Orpheus; Osiris; Otherworld; Perdition; Persephone; pit; Pluto; primeval ocean; purgatory; "resurrection gods"; secret societies; *Sheol;* spirits in prison; Styx; Sumerian and Babylonian pantheon; Tammuz; Tartarus; Thugs; Tiki; Tophet; Triads; world to come, the; Xibala; Yakuza.

undine: or ondine, a mythological water nymph who becomes human if she falls in love with a mortal. She will die, however, if she is unfaithful in the relationship. *See also* attending spirit(s); banshee; bogle; brownies; bugbears; clurichauns; daemons; deceiving spirits; demon(s), demonic; disa; Dogon Nommos; dryad(s); elemental(s); fairy, fairies; Furies; ghost(s); ghoul; gnome(s); Green Man, the; Gregori; hobgoblins; homunculus; household deities; huldafolk; Lares; leprechaun(s); Loa Loas; Manes; mythological beasties, elementals, monsters, and spirit animals; nereid; nisse; nymph(s); nyx; Olympian pantheon; Oniropompi; Orisha; Oya; para; paredri; penates; Robin Goodfellow; satyr; Seely Court, Unseelie Court; selkie; Sidhe; sirens; sylph(s); sprite(s); teraphim; territorial spirits; Trickster; Tuatha de Danann; tutelary; wight(s).

unfaithful Jerusalem, allegory of. See Ezekiel's allegory of unfaithful Jerusalem.

Uniat Church: an Eastern church persuasion, specifically from Poland and Southwest Russia. The church has an affiliation with Roman Catholicism but remains independent from some of its doctrines, including the issue of married clergy. The Catholics call them "Ruthenian." *See also* Byzantine Church; Melkite; Roman Catholic Church; Union of Brest.

Unification Church: the common name for the Holy Spirit Association for the Unification of World Christianity, a cult founded by the Korean Sun Myung Moon in 1954. Followers are known as "Moonies" and have been recruited by the thousands, mostly in South Korea and Japan. The group is better known as the "Unification Movement" in English-speaking countries. The

Moons (husband and wife) teach universal salvation and other non-biblical concepts gained primarily from their text called *Divine Principles* and Moon's belief that he is the incarnate Christ. Moon was convicted of tax fraud in 1982, and the Unification Church has been classed as a movement seeking a single worldwide government. The group is famous for its so-called "mass weddings" in which hundreds of couples are married *en masse* by Moon and his wife. The marriages are not legal but are believed to free the couple's offspring from original sin. *See also* cult(s); Moon, Sun Myung.

uniformitarianism: an evolutionist theory that the construct procedure from earth's beginning (its geological processes) has continued at the same rate of speed and in the same manner until this time. Such thinking is a philosophical idea that posits processes acting in the same manner as they do presently or over long periods are sufficient to account for all current features in the universe and all past changes. The thinking contradicts both scientific evolution and creationism (2 Pe. 2:4). *See also* analogical day theory; big bang theory; big crunch theory; chaos theory; cosmogony; cosmology; *creatio ex nihilo;* creation; creationism; creation science; Creator; day-age theory; evolution; evolution, theistic; framework hypothesis; intelligent design; involution; Omphalos Hypothesis; progressive creationism; "six-day theory, the"; theistic evolution; Young-Earth Creationist Movement.

Union. See Beauty; Zechariah's oracle of two shepherds and two shepherd's staffs.

Union College: America's oldest interdenominational college for men. Founded in 1795, the campus is located at Schenectady, New York. The school was the first to create a truly comprehensive campus plan and in 1825 became the first to charter Greek-letter fraternities. Presbyterian clergyman Eliphalet Nott was president for sixty-two years (1804–1866) and Chester A. Arthur, the twenty-first president of the United States, was an alumnus. *See also* religious education; religious organizations.

Union of Brest: the treaty of 1596 that placed the Ruthenium Church of the Polish-Lithuanian Commonwealth of Russia under the pope of Rome as opposed to their former status under the Eastern Orthodoxy of Constantinople. *See also* Uniat Church.

unipersonality: the conviction that Jesus possessed both divine and human natures in his personality during his earthly ministry. *See also* Adoptionism; appropriation; Anomoeans; Arianism; Arius; complementarian view of the Trinity; Donatism; dualism; Dynamic Monarchianism; dynamism; dyophysitism; eternal subordination of the Son; "four fences of Chalcedon"; *homoiousios; homoousios;* hypostatic union; incarnation; *kenosis;* kenotic view of Christ; modalism; monarchianism; monophysitism; monotheism; Nestorianism; Nestorius; *ousia;* Patripassianism; Pelagianism; psilanthropism; *perichoresis;* psilanthropism; Sabellianism; Socianism, Socinian; subordinationism; theanthroposophy; *Theophorus;* Trinity; two natures, doctrine of the.

Unitarian Universalists: a brand of religion (if it qualifies as a religion) that denies the Trinity and holds no solid religious dogma. Unitarian Universalists (formerly called a church but now the Universalist Association) affirm collective redemption for all no matter what theology or practice is set forth or discounted. The institution was formed from a combination of participants in early Universalist associations and Unitarians, both of which sprang from the chafing restrictions of Congregationalism. The first Universalist church was formed by the itinerate English preacher John Murray in Gloucester, Massachusetts, in 1779. Three colleges were born under the group's sponsorship. Unitarianism's beginnings can be traced to a time even before the American Revolution, mostly staged by the heretical sermons of Rev. Jonathan Mayhew. Thomas Payne's *Age of Reason* also helped to stimulate the movement. The first Unitarian church started as the Berry Street Conference of liberal ministers in 1820 under the leadership of the former Congregationalist Ellery Channing (1780–1842). It was he who constructed the beliefs of the sect toward moral living rather than any scheme of salvation—a decidedly humanistic approach. Christ was a man of uncommon genius, the Bible was not the codified Word of God, and God has not revealed Himself to mankind. Unitarians received a large boost in membership from disenfranchised Congregationalists after the American Revolution. The movement remained centered in New England for many years but eventually began slow expansion. The Universalist Church of America and American Unitarian Association merged in 1961 even though most Universalists were blue-collar and Unitarians attracted white-collar supporters. Ralph Waldo Emerson expanded many of its tenets to transcendentalism. Universalists name the sources of their principles from: 1. direct experience of transcending mystery, 2. words and deeds of prophetic men and women, 3. wisdom from the world's religions that inspire people in our ethical and spiritual lives, 4. Jewish and Christian teachings, 5. humanist teachings that counsel people to heed the guidance of reason and the results of science and, 6. spiritual teachings of earth-centered traditions that celebrate the sacred circle of life. Great respect is held for the "Seven Principles": the inherent dignity of every person, justice and compassion for all, acceptance and encouragement of others, a free and responsible search for truth, the right of conscience and use of the democratic process in congregations and the world at large, the goal of world community, and respect for the interdependent web of all existence. Each service opens with the lighting of the chalice of light (intellect) and closes with its extinguishment. The flaming chalice is also the national symbol of the interest groups. The movement grew under subsequent astute exponents including Andrews Norton (1786–1853), Orville Dewey (1795–1882), Thomas Whittenmore (1871–1950), Theodore Parker (1810–1860), Horace Bushnell (1802–1876), Jones Very (1813–1880), Hosea Balleu (1771–1852), James Freeman Clarke (1810–1888), Olympia Brown (1835–1926), Joseph Fletcher Jordan (1863–1929), Benjamin Rush (1746–1813), John Murray (1898–1975), Gerard Winstanly (1648), Richard Coppin (1652), Jane Leade (1697), George T. Knight (1911), Joshua Westly Hamon (1899), and Henry James Sr. (1811–1882). Other famous personalities involved in the process included John Weiss, Mark Hopkins, John Fiske, and W.T. Harris. In the United States, Unitarian Universalists make up less than 0.5% of the population. *See also* Anthropocentric and Anti-Trinitarian Churches; *apocatastasis;* Ballou, Hosea; Brownson, Owen Augustus; Bushnell, Horace; Channing, William Ellery; Chauncy, Charles; church bodies in America (typed); denomination(s), denominationalism; Everett, Edward; Hale, Edward Everett; Higginson, Thomas Wentworth; Emerson, Ralph Waldo; Hopedale Community; Kneeland, Abner; liberalism, liberalist(s); Lincoln, Abraham; Mayhew, Jonathan; Palfrey, John Graham; Parker, Theodore;

Priestly, Joseph; Ripley, George; sect(s); Socianism, Socinians; Sparks, Jared; transcendentalism; universalism; Ware, Henry; Whitby, Daniel; Winchester Platform of 1803.

Unitas Fratrum. See Moravian Brethren.

United Brethren. See Church of the United Brethren.

United Churches: those religious bodies that either intensely or blandly seek unity among believers from many denominations. They emphasize acceptance of all and personal piety within their ecumenicalism. Many of the groups were formed during the Great Awakening Crusades in frontier America. Interestingly, popular exposition of the movement has often centered on the understanding that some United congregations use musical instruments and some do not. The list of denominations might include Plymouth Brethren, Moravians (those who prompted the conversion of John Wesley), United Church of Christ, Disciples of Christ, Christian Churches (not the same as Churches of Christ), Congregationalists, some Evangelical Reformed bodies, and great numbers of interdenominational fellowships. The groups' doctrines of eschatology are almost exclusively amillennial, or postmillennial in some instances, since the Reformation. Most could be classed as favorable to realized eschatology. American Congregationalists settled in Massachusetts in 1620 and were influential in America's War of Independence. However, they lost steam after the Revolution when they saw their privileged culture and status diminished and no longer supported by the state. They did share a bit in the benefits of the Great Awakenings, but eventually, most clergy steered their people into Unitarianism or divisive Social Gospel themes like the abolition of slavery or prohibition. *See also* Congregationalists; church bodies in America (typed); Christian Church (denomination); Churches of Christ; denomination(s), denominationalism; Disciples of Christ; Great Awakenings, the; Moravian Church; Plymouth Brethren; realized eschatology.

United Church of Christ. See Churches of Christ.

United Methodists. See Methodists.

United Society of Believers: the full title being the "United Society of Believers in Christ's Second Appearing," but the short name is the "Shakers." The Shakers is a communal and socialist sect fully active around the late 1800s that stressed intense religious emotion and bodily movement (the "Shaking Quakers") and a celibate lifestyle. Growth came about via recruitment and the adoption of orphans. They also stressed pacifism, practiced uncontrolled barking and frenzied dance, glossolalia, and healing. They demanded total separation of the sexes since coitus was the root of all evil. Their eschatology was inherent in a belief in the impending destruction of the world, specifically in the year 1792. The founder and greatest leader was the visionary Ann Lee, who migrated to America in 1776, bringing with her elements of English Shakerism. Female leadership in the sect has always been prominent, including the dynamic preaching of Jane Wardley and the later administration of Lucy White. At one point, the sect may have reached 6,000 members, but today the tiny residue from a village in Maine saw the last of the sect. The Shakers were known popularly for their strong work ethic, producing fine furniture, architecture, music, (the hauntingly beautiful tune "Simple Gifts" is the most admired), herb-growing, liturgical dance, and weaving. They were industrious and inventive people being credited with such innovations as the clothespin, the flat-bottom broom, and the circular saw. The group expected that the present age would soon end (most believed 1792 or 1794), thus procreation was not only undesirable but also unnecessary. Ann Lee even predicted the demise of her community as God's will. *See also* communal communities; dance; Lee, Ann.

Unity Church: a spiritual/philosophical group within the New Thought movement also known as the Unity School of Christianity. The organization claims to promote happiness, health, prosperity, and peace of mind. Most recognition for organization should belong to Mary "Myrtle" Caroline Page Fillmore (1845–1931) and her husband, Charles. The group publishes a devotional guide called *Daily Word. See also* Fillmore, Myrtle and Charles; mind science; New Thought Movement; Psychiana; sect(s).

universal Church: 1. the catholic (worldwide and multi-aged) believers who constitute the body of believers. Such a designation usually sees the word "Church" as capitalized. 2. a universal church of some description can express the idea, fear, or prediction that a worldwide synergistic and false organization will be paramount in the Tribulation. Such an institution will be headed by the False Prophet and manipulated to benefit the Antichrist and to lead the Tribulation world in the worship of Antichrist and his master, Satan. The universal (catholic) church is not mentioned in Revelation or Daniel; instead, the believers of that age are normally called "saints." *See also* branch theory; catholic church; Church; False Prophet, the; visible and invisible church, the; New World Order; revived Roman Empire.

universalism: 1. a belief that all persons, regardless of their status before God, will be redeemed or "saved" at or near the time of the end. Even Satan may be forgiven in some of its interpretations. It is a frequent error of many sects and cults to operate outside of orthodox biblical interpretation as displayed in the Essenes, Rosicrucians, Mormons, and other sectarian beliefs. 2. the Universalist belief can define the prophet's concern for the nations outside of his own—a notion that gives the belief a more positive spin. *See also apocatastasis;* Ballou, Hosea; biblical universalism; New World Order, the (NWO); pantelism; Unitarian Universalists.

Universalists. See Unitarian Universalists.

Universal Life Church: a religious organization formed in 1962 by Kirby Hensley. To call the organization a "church" is a bit of a stretch since they have no set doctrine, no ritual, no discipline, and no belief except that, in the end, the ULC will crush Satan's head; all other denominations are "snakes." Their motto is "Do that which [you think] is right (with the bracket inserted arbitrarily by outsiders). Their main mission, however, is mail order ordination. Send a dollar and you are licensed as a minister; send twenty dollars and get your doctorate. All privileges are, surely, square with the IRS and other agencies. Truthfully, most states do not recognize the legitimacy of the certifications. *See also* sect(s).

unknown god, an: an inscription on a pagan altar in the Parthenon (Acts 17:23) spotted by Paul during his visit to Athens. Perhaps the title was the Greek attempt to assign a "catch-all" deity just in case they missed one. Paul used the object to launch his sermon by declaring that this "unknown" god can now be identified in Jesus Christ. The apostle's mission to Athens met with minimal discernible success. The Gnostics also conceived of an unknown god who dwelt in the highest heaven, the Ogdoad. *See also* Areopagus; Gnosticism, Gnostics; Ogdoad; *Sophia*.

Unkulunkulu: the creator god of the Zulu. Legend claims he came to earth from a swamp of reeds. He brought cattle with him as a livelihood for his people and is named as the first man.

unleavened bread. See bread, unleavened.

Unleavened Bread, Feast of: a vital part of the Jewish festival recognizing the Exodus from Egyptian slavery. The observance was part of the celebration of Passover during which bread without yeast (since leaven was symbolic of sin) was prepared and eaten. Celebrations were in order because the barley harvest was starting. The holiday holds eschatological significance since Jesus called himself "the bread of life" and symbolizes a holy walk with God for Christians (1 Cor. 5:7–8). Jesus was buried on the feast day after only six hours of torture instead of the usual three days on a Roman cross. *See also* barley; bread; bread, unleavened; feasts and special days of Judaism; flora, fruit, and grain, symbology of; Judaism; Passover; *Seder*.

Unmoved Mover: Aristotle's basic description of the Power that moves the universe—all of its motion and secondary causation. The phrase is still in use today by some theologians as a designation for God. *See also* evolution; Five Ways, the; names (titles) for God; philosophy of the Greeks; prime mover.

unnamed prophet(s). See man of God, a (the).

unpardonable sin, the. See sin unto death.

unsound doctrine: the mental process by which the mind discards the truth of God's Word and manufactures false doctrine, myths, or fables in its place. Many New Testament prophesies predict that the world will increasingly turn to unsound doctrine and the teachings of demons as the end of the age approaches. *See also* apostasy; Christian mythology; deep secrets, so-called; fable(s); godless myths; heresy; heretic; heterodoxy; miscreance; old wives' tales; Satan's so-called deep secrets; turned to fables (myths).

"until he comes": a phrase that seems to adjure all believers to wait for the Second Coming of Christ with patience and watchfulness (*i.e.*, Hosea 10:12). The quote from Hosea reads, "[I]t is time to seek the Lord, until he comes and showers righteousness on you." *See also* eschatology, eschatological; righteous sovereign, the; Second Coming; watch.

unwritten prophecies: oracles, especially from the Old Testament prophets, that are not recorded in the Scripture and sometimes not in any historical accounts. Some scholars and historians insist that any number of them exist, even as many actions of Jesus are not transcribed (Jn. 21:25). Oftentimes, the more general phrase "oral tradition" is substituted, especially if more than prophecy is to be expounded. *See also* Agrapha; Gospel(s); "L"; *logia;* "M"; oral tradition; "Q"; source criticism.

Upanishads: some 200 or more philosophical texts considered to be an early source of the Hindu religion. The name means "to sit up-close," as one would pay close attention to one's guru teacher because the lessons are restricted to those who are accepted for religious study. The works are a collection of treatises on the nature of man and the universe forming part of the Vedic writings. *See also Bhagwan Gita;* Brahmanism; Hinduism.

Upper Gehenna: an old Jewish belief that after a person died he or she had a period of one year to walk the earth unseen and visit familiar places and people in his former life. Some Christians believed the same and saw it as a chance to resolve any "unfinished business" before passing to eternity. *See also* Abraham's bosom; afterlife; Aralu; Arcadia; Asgard; Avalon; Dis; Duat; eternal life; future life, doctrine of the; Elysium; Gehenna; Hades; happy hunting ground; heaven; hell; Hy-Breasail; Hyperborea; intermediate state; Jade Empire, the; Jahannam; Janna; Judaism; lake of fire; life after death; limbo; *Limbus Puerorum;* Mictlan; Nirvana; Otherworld; Paradise; paradise of God; paraeschatology; Pardes; Perdition; Promised Land, the; Pure Land, the; purgatory; Shambhala legends; *Sheol;* soul sleep; space doctrine; Summerland; Thule, land of; Tir na nOg; underworld; Utopia; Valhalla; world to come, the; Xibala.

Upper Room Discourse, the: a compelling lecture given by Jesus to comfort his disciples prior to his ascension. His words are centered in the fourteenth chapter of John but continue into the fifteenth and sixteenth in some form. As such, it ranks with the Olivet Discourse as a major eschatological teaching. In his address, Jesus began with a pronouncement of comfort: "Do not let your hearts be troubled…" He then proceeded to speak of himself and them as being firm in the Father, to promise the Holy Spirit to replace his physical self, to pray for them, and to warn them of coming persecution. *See also* Cenacle; Olivet Discourse, the; Upper Room, the.

Upper Room, the: the place (the Cenacle) specified by Jesus as the site for his last celebration of the Jewish Passover, also referred to as the Lord's Supper. The disciples found the place by following a man carrying a water jar, a sign also predicted by Jesus. Many speculate that the Upper Room was in the home of Mary, the mother of John Mark, who housed the disciples before and after the resurrection of Jesus. It is possible that Mark himself was the water bearer. *See also* Cenacle; Jerusalem, landmarks of; man with a water jar; Upper Room discourse, the.

upright One: a name for God used by Isaiah (Isa. 26:7). *See also* Lord our Righteousness, the; Righteous One; names (titles) for God.

Ur: the homeland of Abraham (Gen. 11:27–31). The site is generally considered to be a point about 220 miles southeast of present-day Baghdad and is acknowledged as an important and vigorous Amorite civilization in its prime time. The area holds one of the most preserved ziggurats in existence.

Urantia Foundation: a non-profit organization primarily formed to preserve, study, and promulgate the philosophical study called *The Urantia Book.* This work, also called the "Urantia Papers" or *The Fifth Epochal Revelation,* was published somewhere between 1924 and 1955. The authorship is equally obscure but is usually agreed to have had more than one writer. The volume discusses the Trinity, cosmology, religion, destiny, and like subjects in a kind of philosophical medium that may be considered a modern twist on eschatology and the fate of the planet. The term "Urantia" is coined by the authors as a substitute name for Earth. *See also* sect(s).

Uranus: the Greek sky god, husband to the earth goddess Gaia, who begat Cronus and Rhea; also a planet. *See also* Atlas; Cronus; Gaia (Gaea); Helios; Hyperion; Olympian pantheon; planets as gods, the; Rhea; Zeus.

Urartu: a kingdom north of Assyria that was considered a threat to that empire. The presence of such a people within their sphere of influence motivated the Assyrians to be active in Syria-Palestine to build up the empire's military, economic, and political base in their own interests. The same could be said of Egypt, which stayed involved in the Middle East as a counterweight to Assyrian oppression. Unfortunately but routinely, Israel and Judah were caught in the pincer time after time.

Urban II, Pope: the pope of Rome (ca. 1042–1099) most responsible for launching the Crusades (the first occurred 1096–1099). Urban journeyed from Rome to the cathedral at Clermont to address the clergy there, along with the nobles and interested civilians who attended. He intended to redirect the martial energy of the rival nobilities from fighting among themselves to fighting Muslims in the East. He had received an urgent appeal for help from Constantinople. Records of Urban's speech are too sparse and contradictory for us to know exactly what he said, but the outcome went far beyond what he expected. Immediately, thousands pledged themselves for service in the Middle East under cries of *Deus le volt!* (God wills it!). Rich and poor, knight and peasant, clergy and civilians, lurched off to war led by Adhemar, the bishop of Le Puy, chosen by Urban who was first to join the enterprise. *See also* Crusades; *Deus le volt!*; liturgical year; pope; Roman Catholic Church.

Urbanus: a disciple in Rome praised by Paul (Rom. 16:9).

Uriah: 1. also spelled Urijah. Uriah was a prophet of Kiriath-Jearim (Jer. 26:20–23) who, along with Jeremiah, faithfully proclaimed the Word of God despite opposition directed at both men. King Jehoiakim centered his wrath on Uriah. The prophet fled to Egypt but was returned, arrested, then finally executed. 2. the husband of Bathsheba and a loyal officer in David's army. He was slain by order of the king, and Bathsheba became David's wife. From that union, Solomon was born. 3. a priest in the reign of Ahaz. It was he who was forced to copy an altar-like the one seen by Ahaz in the court of Tiglath-pileser, king of Assyria (2 Ki. 16:10). *See also* lamb, the pet ewe; martyr(s); prophet(s); Shemaiah.

Uriel: an archangel named in interbiblical sources (not in the Scripture) as governing the world and Tartarus. According to the pseudepigraphal *2 Esdras*, he was sent to the great scribe Ezra to enlighten him concerning the Law. Uriel is the most often mentioned angel in Jewish lore which claims he was one of the Cherubim who guarded the Garden of Eden after the expulsion of Adam and Eve. He is also identified as the angel who warned Noah of the coming flood, the one who wrestled with Jacob, and as the death angel who destroyed 185,000 men of the Assyrian army. Uriel, as he speaks in *4 Esdras,* predicted that women of the apocalyptic period would give birth to monsters as they did in Genesis 6. He even used the term "beginning of sorrows" to further define the time before Jesus did. In Milton's *Paradise Lost* he is noted as "the sharpest-sighted spirit in all of heaven." *See also* angel(s); archangel(s).

Urijah. See Uriah.

Urim and Thummin: 1. sacred objects associated with the ephod of the high priest's uniform, particularly the breastplate that held a logo gem representing each Hebrew tribe. The terms mean "lights" and "perfection." Interestingly, the word for Urim begins with the letter *aleph* and Thummin begins with *tau,* the first and last letters of the Hebrew alphabet. The names can then perhaps take on a New Testament symbology familiar in Revelation as Jesus Christ—"the first and the last" in all creation. From time to time, those items that made up the Urim and Thummin could convey crucial civic or religious answers asked of God by the king or priest by lot or illumination. Exactly how the process worked is conjecture. Some scholars suggest that the pocket of the ephod held a pair of thin stones colored black and white. When tossed and two whites came up, the answer was "yes"; if two blacks showed, the answer was "no"; if mixed colors were displayed, no answer from God was to be received that day. Others speculate that one or more of the dozen gems of the breastplate would glow in response to the question posed, but this idea is unlikely since the twelve breastplate gems bear no hint that they manifested any more-than-usual radiance. Yet another speculation is that the high priest repeated the words he heard from between the Cherubim on the mercy seat. Again, this understanding seems unlikely since the high priest went into the Holy of Holies only once per year, unless he could hear the voice from behind the heavy curtain aft of the Holy Place. After David's reign, there is no mention of the Urim and Thummin; they seem to have disappeared from history much as the ark of the covenant did. The Talmud states that following the destruction of Herod's Temple, the Urim and Thummin ceased to be used and could not be employed again until "the dead are raised and the Messiah ben David will come." The books of Nehemiah and Ezra, along with the apocryphal book of *1 Esdras*, state that their prophetic usage should cease until a priest who could use them appeared in Israel once more. The book of Proverbs (Pro. 16:33) speaks of the lot being cast in the lap with assurance that the decision will be from God. *First Enoch* calls one oracle object "Revelation" and the other "Truth" from a Greek rendition. 2. those articles claimed by Joseph Smith with which he was enabled to translate the Book of Mormon from "Reformed Egyptian" into English. The devices consisted of magical glasses (by most accounts) or a seeing stone atop a top hat. *See also* angel(s); black stones; Book of Mormon; breastplate of the high priest; Church of Jesus Christ of Latter-Day Saints, the; divination; ephod; furniture and furnishings of the tabernacle, temples, and modern synagogue; gem(s); lot(s); miter; onyx; oracle(s); sacred stones; sapphire; scrying; white stones.

Ursula: legendary fourth century saint. She was a British princess who was the supposed leader of some 11,000 virgin companions, all of whom were massacred by the Huns near Cologne. She and her associates were pure fiction but taken literally by some, including the "Ursulines" of the 16th century. That confraternity of women at that time, formed by Angela Merici, took Ursula's name and patronage for their charitable and Roman Church reformation efforts. The Catholic Church holds October 21 as Ursula's feast day even though it is suspect that a person with the name ever existed at all. *See also* liturgical year; Roman Catholic Church.

useless vine, a: God's description (Ezk. 15) of Jerusalem as worthless and destined for the fires of destruction. Jesus also announced that those unfaithful and cut off from the true "vine" (himself) are valueless and suited only for burning (Jn. 15:6). God's examination of rebellious Jerusalem at the time of the exile affirms that His people are as useless as the stems of grapevines because that wood is unsuitable for building anything and even more ineffectual after burning. *See also* flora, fruit, and grain, symbology of; Jerusalem as city; vine; vine (the) and the fig tree.

usher: a person who conducts people to their seats in a church, cinema, or other public auditorium. The function derives from ancient usage as a porter or doorman. In a church setting, however, an usher is more than an escort. He or she is often charged with other duties like collecting the public offering, assuring general order, welcoming or assisting guests, materials distribution, and other "housekeeping" tasks as needed. The position is usually voluntary. An usher is also a male escort at a wedding. *See also* beadle; sexton; verger.

Ussher, James: Irish archbishop (1581–1656). Ussher refined the "six-day theory" in which the age of the earth could be determined by calculations from Genesis. According to Ussher's formula, and those who adopted his methods, the six days of creation were thousand years each (*cf.* Psalm 90:4; 2 Peter 3:9). The seventh 1,000 is to be the Millennium—God's resting day. According to Ussher's theory (which was considered accurate for many years), not only the age of the world could be accurately calculated but its end as well. According to Ussher, creation occurred on Sunday, October 23, 4004 B.C., and other Old Testament events, such as Adam and Eve's expulsion from Eden and the grounding of Noah's ark, could be dated to the day. If Ussher's reckoning was deciphered according to the old Julian calendar he was using, the end would be calculated to be on October 23, 1997 (or November 1, 1996, by some calculations). Only a few ultraconservative sects still adhere to Ussher's theories because it is impossible to calculate the earth's age, its history, or its inhabitants with any sense of accuracy. *See also* archbishop(s); calendar (Hebrew); calendar (Gregorian); calendar (Julian); Hippolytus; Irenaeus; Lactantius; Roman Catholic Church; Sabbatical millennialism; septa-millennial; "six-day theory, the."

usus loquindi: the usual mode of speaking in one's own language. When applied to biblical interpretation, the phrase can take on a special scriptural meaning or theological discussion, sometimes called "Bible talk." *See also* Christianese.

Utas: the octave (eighth day) after a church feast day. *See also* liturgy, Christian.

utensils of the tabernacle and Temple. See furniture and furnishings of the tabernacle, temples, and modern synagogue.

utilitarianism: the doctrine or philosophy stating that the distinctions between right and wrong are grounded in experience—the right being identical with what is useful or that which ends well. Wrong is that which turns out badly. *See also* philosophy of religion.

Utnapishtim: a consultant of the legendary Gilgamesh whose escape from the waters of the universal flood was recorded in *The Epic of Gilgamesh*. His exploits earned him immortality from the gods as a survivor of the deluge, saved from the waters in his self-made coracle. Utnapishtim then is the Sumerian man rescued by the god Enlil from the universal flood of Sumerian lore. Legends abound about the figure who is known as *Noah* in the Bible, *Cox* to the Aztecs, *Powaco* to the Delaware Indians, *Manu Yaiasata* in Hinduism, *Dwytach* to Celts, *Sze Kha* in Patagonia, *Noa* to natives of the Amazon, *Nu-u* in Hawaii, and *Nuwah* in China. As the hero of the Babylonian flood story, the cuneiform records also call him Atrahasis or Ziusudra in its various renditions. Historians have labeled him the Babylonian Noah even though the Sumerian version predates the Genesis account by a thousand years. As Ziusudra, he is portrayed among the Sumerian dynastic lists as a mystical wise king of prediluvian times in the Sumerian cities of the gods that predate even those of the age of Gilgamesh. *See also* Ararat; atrahasis; *Epic of Gilgamesh, The;* flood; Gilgamesh; Mount Ararat; Mount Nisin; myths universally depicted in the Bible; Nachidshevan; Noah; Noah's ark; Sumerian and Babylonian pantheon.

Utopia: a term indicating the fantasy of the perfect world or even a pristine place within the world. The name was coined by the English humanist Thomas More from the corrupted Greek in the spoof of the Piagnoni cult publication called *Apocalypsis Nova*. His book, entitled *Utopia*, centers about a fictional island somewhere in the Atlantic by that name. Utopia means "nowhere," as coined by using *ou* (meaning "no") and *topos* (meaning "place"). *See also* Abraham's bosom; afterlife; Annwn; *Apocalypsis Nova;* Aralu; Arcadia; Asgard; Avalon; Dis; Duat; Dystopia; Elysium; eschatology, eschatological; eternal life; future life, doctrine of the; Gehenna; Golden Age; Hades; happy hunting ground; heaven; hell; Hy-Breasail; Hyperborea; intermediate state; Jade Empire, the; Jahannam; Janna; lake of fire; life after death; limbo; *Limbus Puerorum;* Malthus, Thomas Robert; Mictlan;

More, Thomas; Nirvana; Otherworld; Paradise; paradise of God; Pardes; Perdition; Promised Land, the; Pure Land, the; purgatory; Savonarola, Girolamo; Shambhala legends; *Sheol;* soul sleep; space doctrine; Summerland; Thule, land of; Tir na nOg; underworld; Upper Gehenna; Valhalla; world to come, the; Xibala.

Utu: a Sumerian sun god known in Babylon as Shamash. The god's function dealt with law, justice, and truth. He was depicted wearing a helmet and carrying a saw-like serrated weapon. *See also* Shamash; Sumerian and Babylonian pantheon.

Uz: thought to be the homeland of Job. The exact location is uncertain but was likely somewhere in the Arabian desert regions, perhaps Edom or Arabia (Lam. 4:21). *See also* Arabia; Job as afflicted wise man.

Uzal: possibly the city of Sana in Yemen.

Uzzah: a son of Abinadab the priest. When the ark of the covenant was being conveyed by David to Jerusalem, the oxen pulling its wagon stumbled (2 Sam. 6:3–11; 1 Chr. 13:7–14). Uzzah reached to steady the load and was immediately struck dead. The place was then called Perez-uzzah, "the breach of Uzzah." Not only did Uzzah defame the ark, but the process itself was also careless because the people tried to convey it in the manner not prescribed by Levite instructions from God.

Uzziah: the tenth king of Judah (792–740 B.C.), also known as Azariah. As ruler, Uzziah (as Isaiah called him) was godly and his realm prosperous for the most part. Uzziah was actually made king by popular consent after the disaster of Amaziah's reign, even though he was co-regent with him for a time. Uzziah had been educated by the prophet Zechariah, son of Jehoiada, before his mentor was killed by Joash. He rebuilt the army and defeated the Philistines; he was a progressive builder as well. Unfortunately, his pride proved to be his downfall. In arrogance, he assumed the duties of high priest in total disregard of the privileges and obligations of the Aaronic brotherhood. The priest Azariah ordered him out of the sacred precincts. Uzziah refused to leave and was then struck down by Yahweh with a horrid skin disease from which he never recovered. The king was then exiled as a leper and relinquished the leadership of the kingdom to his son

Jotham to prevent an interregnum. Josephus laid great emphasis on this breach of conduct by Uzziah. He stated that, at the time, there was an earthquake which damaged the Temple and "moved" the nearby mountains. There is no collaborating reference to this disturbance found in Scripture but there is a recounting of one shaking (perhaps the very same) in Uzziah's day (Zech. 14:4–5). That entry also mentions mountains. Part of Zechariah's prophecy is eschatological, but the fraction just mentioned is historical. Uzziah was even refused burial among the kings of Judah. To modern readers, this punishment of the king seems odd or even heavy-handed. In Uzziah's days, however, and in all the past history of the Jews, such ritual defamations were a grievous sin. *See also* Azariah as priest; earthquake; Jehoahaz of Judah; Jotham; king(s); kings of Israel and Judah; kings of Israel and Judah in foreign relations.

V

Vacation Bible School: a children's mission emphasis and Bible learning event. Many Protestant denominations reserve from one to two weeks each summer to interact with children to that end with volunteer teachers and aides. Child evangelism, memorization, craft activities, patriotic themes, Bible stories, recreation, snacks, and the like are common features of the curriculum. *See also* missions, missionaries; religious education; religious organizations.

Valentine: or Valentinus, the name for several saints of the Christian era. Three, in particular, have liturgical interest. The first, called Valentine of Rome, was a prisoner and martyr (A.D. 269); the second was Bishop Valentine of Torni who was martyred in A.D. 273; the third was another Valentine of Africa martyred at an unknown date. All have a tenuous connection to February 14, a partially recognized religious and secular holiday called Valentine's Day. *See also* liturgical year; Roman Catholic Church; martyr(s); Valentine's Day.

Valentine's Day: February 14, a holiday with a quasi-religious following in some denominations. The day is mostly a cultural, commercial, and unofficial celebration associated with romance and love, an occasion for lovers to exchange affectionate cards, candy, flowers, and the like. Most of its present emphasis was probably due to Geoffrey Chaucer of the 14th century who romanticized the period to some extent and to an accidental connection to Cupid, the Roman god of love. The date is an official Anglican and Lutheran feast day and is recognized by the Orthodox Church on July 6 and 30. *See also* Cupid; liturgical year; Valentine.

Valentinus, Valentinians: a foremost Gnostic teacher of the second century who constructed an elaborate cosmology of male-female Aeons who supposedly govern the universe. The Valentinians believed that a perfect pre-existent Aeon, which they called Proarche, Propater, and Bythus, exists somewhere. It is described as being invisible and incomprehensible. Valentinus was the object of much dispute among the pre-Nicene Fathers. *See also* Gnosticism, Gnostic(s); Nag Hammadi library.

vale of tears: a colloquial expression in some Christian circles that encompasses the trials and tribulations of everyday Christian living. Certainly, there are hardships encountered and so the struggle is named. The wording is also found in the liturgical song "*Salve Regina*" and in the Lutheran hymn "Be Still, My Soul." *See also* bread of affliction; bread of despair; tear(s); thorn in the flesh; trial(s); vale of tears; water of affliction.

Valerian: Roman emperor (ca. A.D. 200–260) who issued several edicts against Christians. These orders caused a short but intense persecution against the early church. Valerian was captured by the Persians in 260, bringing the disruption to an abrupt end. *See also* Christianity in the Roman Empire; king(s); Roman Empire.

Valhalla: sometimes Walhalla, a place of Viking myth, the destiny of dwelling in the afterlife. It was termed Odin's holiest mead hall where he and the hero warriors gathered to drink, eat, and seduce the prettiest maidens. It was said to have 540 doorways with room for 1,000 revelers. The walls were made of shiny spearheads with a roof of golden shields. A giant eagle was perched on top, watching and reporting the affairs of earth. Some historians believe that the Viking raids to Europe in the ninth and tenth centuries were launched to find their sacred site of destiny. There are theories that they found their destination in Gaul (France). A suburb of Valhalla was called Asgard, where slain warriors reside. *See also* Abraham's bosom; afterlife; Annwn; Aralu; Arcadia; Asatru; Asgard; Asker and Embla; Avalon; Dis; Duat; Elysium; eschatology, eschatological; eternal life; Freyr; Frigg; frost giants; future life, doctrine of the; Gehenna; Hades; happy hunting ground; heaven; hell; Hy-Breasail; Hyperborea; intermediate state; Jade Empire, the; Jahannam; Janna; lake of fire; life after death; limbo; *Limbus Puerorum;* Mictlan; Nirvana; Norse and Old Germanic pantheon; Odin; Otherworld; Paradise; paradise of God; Pardes; Perdition; Promised Land, the; Pure Land, the; purgatory; Shambhala legends; *Sheol;* soul sleep; space doctrine; Summerland; Thor; Thule, land of; Tir na nOg; underworld; Upper Gehenna; Utopia; Vikings; world to come, the; Wotanism; Xibala.

Valkyries: nine (some accounts name three or a dozen or more) dazzling but fierce female goddesses of Norse mythology who determine who will live or die in battle. During or after combat, they policed the battlefield or sinking dragon ships to gather the dead warriors of their choosing, selecting only the bravest, to present to Odin in Valhalla. These were then entertained by the maidens and set to be used as allies of the god at Ragnarok. Earlier accounts of the Valkyries name them as elderly hags and almost all versions somehow identify them with the Norns of fate. Most modern readers who prefer to remain ignorant of the multipart details of Norse mythology will still recognize the stirring strains of Wagner's opera, "The Ride of the Valkyries." *See also* Asatru; Asgard; disa; *Edda,* the; Furies; Keres; mythological beasties, elementals, monsters, and spirit animals; Norns; Norse and Old Germanic pantheon; Odin; Ragnarok; Thor; Valhalla.

valley of acacias. See valley of decision; valley of Shittim.

Valley of Achor: the "place of disaster" or "trouble" near Jericho where Achan and his family were executed (Josh. 7:26). We might type the Valley of Achor as a prefigurement to the millennial Valley of Jehoshaphat, the place of final judgment. In the Millennium, however, Isaiah (Isa. 65:10) predicted that the area will become a pleasant pasturage for herds, and in Hosea (Hos. 2:15), the place is used as a sign of hope. *See also* Achan; Sharon; Valley of Decision; Valley of Jehoshaphat; Valley of Shittim.

Valley of Aven: a poetic reference to Damascus—then ruled by Hazael—described by Amos (Amos 1:5). The prophet predicted the fall of Syria as punishment from God. *Aven* means "wickedness." *See also* Damascus.

Valley of Baca: a poetic reference (Ps. 84:6) relating to a place of trouble and fear. "*Baca*" is Hebrew for "a balsam tree" but can be punned to the word for "weep." The language in the Psalm then can also mean "valley of misery" or "valley of weeping." The term can further derive its description from the extrusion of the gum trees native to that area. The entire Psalm is a reference intended to convey a period of weeping turned to joy.

Valley of Ben Hinnom. See Valley of Hinnom.

Valley of Beracah: a place name meaning "valley of praise" or "valley of blessing." The site fixes the location where Jehoshaphat and his army celebrated God's victory over Israel's massed enemies of Mount Seir, Moab, and Ammon (2 Chr. 20:26).

Valley of Decision: a reference identical to the Valley of Jehoshaphat but not likely a physical location. The name means "valley of judgment" (Joel 3:14). Isaiah (Isa. 10:22–23; 28:22) implied it is a place of destruction for people who have been pronounced as rebellious toward God. As such, it has been figuratively named as the place where God will someday judge the nations of the world. Some scholars conjecture that the true location of the apocalyptic judgment site is the Kidron Valley. *See also* Abaddon; death; grave; eschatology, eschatological; Gehenna; Hades; hell; Jerusalem, landmarks of; Kidron Valley; lake of fire; *Sheol*; Shittim; Tophet; Tyropoeon Valley; Valley of Achor; valley of decision; Valley of Shittim; Valley of Hinnom; Valley of Jehoshaphat; Valley of Slaughter.

valley of decision: a less-than-literal naming of the Valley of Decision or Valley of Jehoshaphat. The prophet Joel used the name in a somewhat figurative sense calling it the valley of decision (not capitalized) and the valley of acacias (Joel 3:18). *See also* Abaddon; death; grave; Gehenna; Hades; hell; Kidron Valley; lake of fire; *Sheol*; Shittim; Tophet; Tyropoeon Valley; Valley of Achor; Valley of Decision; Valley of Shittim; Valley of Hinnom; Valley of Jehoshaphat; Valley of Slaughter.

valley of dry bones, vision of the. See Ezekiel's vision of the valley of dry bones.

Valley of Hamon-Gog. See Hamon-Gog.

Valley of Hinnom: a gorge alongside the west and south sides of Jerusalem and adjoining the valley of the Kidron near the southeast corner. The place is also called Tophet and Jeremiah called it the Valley of Slaughter. Hinnom was a horrid place where child sacrifice and other abominable idolatry was performed in the midst of the city garbage dump where the depression was located. The place took on the name *Gehenna*, the place of eternal torment of the wicked. *See also* child, children; death; Gehenna; grave; Hades; hell; Jerusalem, landmarks of; Kidron Valley; lake of fire; Law of the Twelve Tablets; "pass through the fire"; Tophet; Tyropoeon Valley; Valley of Decision; Valley of Jehoshaphat; Valley of Slaughter; Valley of Vision.

Valley of Jehoshaphat: an area east of Jerusalem near the Mount of Olives. It is often mentioned as a central venue for the last battle of Armageddon and a scene of great slaughter (Joel 3:2, 12). It was a favored place of burial so a legend has emerged that it may be the site for the sounding of the last trumpet of the Second Coming to raise the dead. Although that location is certainly possible, it is equally possible that the Valley of Jehoshaphat identifies the battlefield that saw the destruction of the Meunites, the Moabites, and the Ammonites during the time of King Jehoshaphat. In this contest, Israel played no part in the conflict, except as witnesses to the slaughter as each army destroyed the others. It was a totally divine victory prophesied by the Levite Jahaziel (2 Chr. 20:1–30). Jehoshaphat carries a meaning of "the Lord Judges," which is altogether appropriate. *See also* death; eschatology, eschatological; Gehenna; grave; Hades; hell; Jerusalem, landmarks of; Kidron Valley; lake of fire; *Sheol;* Tophet; Tyropoeon Valley; Valley of Achor; Valley of Decision; valley of decision; Valley of Hinnom; Valley of Jezreel; Valley of Shittim; Valley of Slaughter.

Valley of Jezreel: a place name meaning "God plants." The land is an extension of the Plain of Esdraelon. It is here, according to apocalyptic texts, where the final battle of Armageddon will be waged, at least in part. *See also* Armageddon, plain of Esdraelon; eschatology, eschatological; Valley of Jehoshaphat; Valley of Taanach.

Valley of Shittim: a barren depression near the Dead Sea, possibly the terminus of the Kidron Valley. Joel (Joel 3:18) offered it as a poetic reference, calling it the "valley of acacias." The place relates, in some manner, to the great apocalyptic judgment of the Lord in the last days. *See also* Valley of Achor; Shittim; Valley of Decision; valley of decision; Valley of Jehoshaphat.

Valley of Slaughter: a name for Tophet that Jeremiah (Jer. 32:35) announced would become its new identity as a place of massacre he called the Valley of Ben Hinnom. The place held the reputation as a center of cultic murder and is anticipated as the site of great judgment decreed by God to transpire there in the future. *See also* death; eschatology, eschatological; Gehenna; grave; Hades; hell; Jerusalem, landmarks of; Kidron Valley; lake of fire; *Sheol;* Tophet; Tyropoeon Valley; Valley of Decision; valley of decision; Valley of Hinnom; Valley of Jehoshaphat.

Valley of Taanach: An important position on the plain of Esdraelon that guarded the passage to Megiddo. The site originally belonged to the tribe of Issachar but was transferred to Manasseh when the former had difficultly dislodging the early inhabitants. *See also* Megiddo; plain of Esdraelon; Valley of Jezreel.

Valley of the Arabah: an arid place, the Great Rift Valley extending south from the Sea of Galilee through the Dead Sea and on to the Gulf of Aqabah. At its point near the Dead Sea, the geological features constitute the lowest place on the Earth's surface (averaging about 1,275 feet below sea level). Amos named it as marking the southern boundary of the kingdom of Jeroboam II (Amos 6:14), implying prophetically that the Jews there would be harassed to the extremity of the land. *See also* Hamath.

Valley of the Rephaim: or "valley of the giants" near Jerusalem. The place was a constant reminder of the giant race who occupied the site in times past and was such a dread to the Hebrews of Canaan. *See also* giant(s); Goliath; Nephilim; Og.

Valley of the Travelers. See King's Highway.

Valley of Vision: an obscure phrase but likely a reference to Zion (Isa. 22:1). As now named, however, the emphasis is on the Valley of Hinnom, the place of idolatry. The prophet Isaiah described Jerusalem as a place of hopelessness and false gaiety. The occasion was likely the relief of the city from the invasion of Sennacherib in 701 B.C. when King Hezekiah ignominiously accepted defeat, even with the loss of many Jewish captives who were killed. The population went into a state of frenzied joy when they should have been self-abasing. Isaiah had now lost hope for his people and voiced his most despondent message in the Valley of Vision oracle—all is lost despite the temporary reprieve. Perhaps it was the Valley of Vision scene that prompted the poignant Puritan prayer of the same name: "Thou hast brought me to the Valley of Vision..., hemmed in by mountains of sin I behold Thy glory." The poem continues, "Stars can be seen from the deepest wells, and the deeper the wells the brighter Thy stars shine..." Then the prayer ends: "Let me find Thy light in my darkness... Thy glory in my valley." *See also* Jerusalem, landmarks of; Valley of Hinnom.

Valuspa: a Nordic seer and storyteller and the name of the first and best-known *Poetic Edda. See also* Aesir; Armanenschafft; Asa; Asatru; blyt; *Edda,* the; filidh; Norse and Old Germanic pantheon; seior; skald(s); storyteller, a good; volva.

Vandals: one of the Germanic tribes helping to destroy the ancient Roman Empire. They swept up by way of North Africa and sacked Rome. Their barbaric methods and destructive acts gave rise to our modern word "vandal." Some see these people as one of the ten horns on the beast of Revelation 13. *See also* Goths; Heruli; Ostrogoths; Roman Empire.

van der Hoeven, Jan William: a Dutch minister (b. 1944) who was moved to establish what he called the International Christian Embassy in Jerusalem after Israel became a state. No other countries were inclined to set up an official national embassy in the new land for fear of offending the Palestinians until President Donald Trump did so in 2018. Van der Hoeven's effort was mostly a public relations gesture with no real political power but it was praised by Benjamin Netanyahu and Yitzhak Rabin.

Vane, Henry: governor of Massachusetts (1613–1662) at the young age of twenty-three, elected less than eight months after he arrived in the colony and even though he was a recent convert to Puritanism. He was a controversial leader because he aided both Roger Williams and Anne Hutchinson in their escape to religious toleration away from Massachusetts. He lost the governorship to John Winthrop in 1637 and returned to England, where he had been knighted by Charles I. When Charles II became king after the failure of the English Commonwealth, Vane was convicted of treason in 1860, imprisoned, then executed on Tower Hill in 1662. *See also* Hutchinson, Anne; Puritanism, Puritan(s); Williams, Roger.

Vanga. See Baba Vanga.

Van Impe, Jack: Baptist televangelist who predicted the return of Christ several times, then revised them. One forecast suited the Mayan calendar for 2012 and tried to explain how black holes could be hell because they swallow burning stars. *See also* revivalism; televangelism, televangelists.

Vanir. See Aesir.

vanity: an undue preoccupation with one's appearance, intellect, position, or posture. Further, vanity may be a perception that some ideal or circumstance is worthless and false. The writer of Ecclesiastes claimed that all of life is vanity and senseless striving (Ecc. 1:2). Although seemingly a bit odd for a biblical philosophy, it fits perfectly describing many a human endeavor minus God's guidance. *See also* Narcissus.

variorum: differing renditions of the same written text by various editors.

Varus: a Syrian governor who suppressed a local Jewish uprising in 4 B.C. *The Testament of Moses* calls him the "powerful king of the West" who would conquer the Jews and burn part of their Temple. He is treated here and there in the histories of Josephus as well. *See also* anti-Semitic; king(s); Syria.

Vashni. See Joel.

Vashti, Queen: the Persian queen before Esther (Esth. 1:9–2:4), the wife of Ahasuerus (Xerxes). Because Vashti refused to exhibit herself to the king's drunken guests, she was deposed. Jewish legend says she was commanded to appear in the nude. If this is so, her refusal is understandable, even heroic. There is some historical speculation that she was later restored to favor, but this eventuality is not recorded in Scripture. *See also* queen(s); Xerxes I.

vassal treaty: a covenant or agreement, usually arranged by a ruling monarch whereby the king's subjects pledged their fealty and support in exchange for certain royal concessions, such as protection and economic stability. *See also* covenant(s), biblical; covenant theology; suzerainty treaty.

vaticination. See prophesy.

Vatican I and Vatican II: modern Vatican Councils, the results of Roman Catholic conclaves that claimed to modernize or liberalize the anathemas imposed by an earlier Council of Trent. Vatican I occurred 1869–1870, and Vatican II was held in 1962–1965. The second process began under Pope John XXIII and ended with Pope Paul VI. Each conference affirmed that neither irrational commitment nor rationalism of the human mind can fashion faith without authority. In truth, both conclaves affirmed the same basic doctrines in different dress since the infallibility of the Roman pontiff disallows any change of existing rules so any changes were mostly cosmetic. *See also* aggiomamento; Council of Trent (Roman Catholic); Counter-Reformation; Roman Catholic Church.

Vatican, the: or Vatican City, the seat of the Roman Catholic see located in Rome. The area covers about 110 acres and is ruled by the bishop of Rome—the pope—and recognized as the smallest independent state in the world. *See also* camerlengo; dicastry; Lateran Treaty; papal states; Pontifical Council; pope; Roman Catholic Church; see; Vatican Secret Archives.

Vatican Secret Archives: a sacrosanct section of the Vatican library, the repository of countless secret or classified documents identified by church authorities through the centuries. Access is by permission only and for specific inquiry. *See also* Roman Catholic Church; Vatican, the.

Vaudois. See Waldenses.

Vedas: the religious writings of Hinduism, its most holy book. The collection, perhaps one of the oldest writings in existence, is in four texts—the *Rig-Vida* (Book of Mantra), *the Yajurveda* (Book of Ritual), *the Samaveda* (Book of Song), and the *Atharvaveda* (Book of Spell)—all in Sanskrit (a language-older than Latin). Most surmise the *Rig-Vida* is basic and most important. The collected text comes from no certain author or authors, prompting devotees to speak of the content as simply the "language of the gods." Most concur they appeared in India from the Aryans, the "noble ones" who migrated from the north and passing their religion by word of mouth. Perhaps the writings emerged sometime from 1500–500 B.C. but some say the content dates as far back as 12,000 B.C. Certainly, that makes them, and the Hindu religion, one of or, more likely, the oldest ritual in history. The book is a collection of hymns and other material dedicated to the gods, particularly Agni, Voruna, Indra, and Mitra. Most Indian historians believe that the text was already in its finished form by 3800 B.C. The term means "knowledge" and has always been the basic beliefs and rituals of the Hindu religion. It is interesting, even surprising, that many of the Irish and Welsh myths show remarkable resemblances to the themes, stories, and even place names of the Indian *Vedas. See also* Advaita Vedanta; *Bhagwan Gila;* Brahma; Brahmanism; Celtic folklore and religion; Hinduism; Indra; *Upanishads.*

veil(s): a cloth covering the face, or curtains used as partitions within rooms of a building. Women often wore veils for protection from the sun or as part of their wedding ensemble. Such articles of clothing could also be cloaks or shawls about the shoulders. Moses routinely covered his face to hide its shining glory (or its progressive fading) after being in intimate contact with Yahweh. A veil with Christ's image imprinted upon it is called a *vernicle*. Ornate tapestries in the tabernacle and Temples separated the holy spaces. The one between the Holy Place and the Holy of Holies was ripped from top to bottom at the moment of Christ's death on the cross (Mt. 27:51; Mk. 15:38; Lk. 23:45), and the author of Hebrews (Heb. 6:19-20) declared that Christ has penetrated the curtain of separation as our high priest after the order of Melchizedek. Paul admonished Christian women not to pray or prophesy with their head uncovered (1 Cor. 11:5). Likely, this injunction was to distinguish them from pagan females who sacrificed or worshiped with the hair disheveled and unbound. Some claim that the prescribed covering was performed in deference to the angels who continually observe the prayer participant, or the reference could be to the woman's hair which was not to be worn short. At one point (Ezk. 13:17–23), the veil was a token for women who testify falsely in order to deceive (*i.e.,* false prophetesses). The prophet Ezekiel (Ezk. 13:19–21) warns that such garments will be ripped from the wearer. To "veil the heart" was to screen off knowledge or wholesome emotion which was sometimes viewed as a punishment from God (*i.e.,* Lamentations 3:65 and 2 Corinthians 3:12–18). The symbology of veils could represent a separation of the holy from the profane, privacy, disguise, secrecy, or an attempt to shadow or heighten the ambiance of a mystical setting. In a more practical sense, Paul asserts there is a veil (spiritually speaking) over many Jewish hearts that separates them from God (an obstacle that must be cured by the "unveiling" of the word of God.) He also says that we are being transformed from this dim worldly view into a mirror image more face to face as if our faces are unveiled (2 Cor. 3:18). *See also* charm(s); curtain(s); curtain of the Temple; hair; prophetess(es); purdah; tabernacle, the; Temple(s); veil of Veronica.

veil of Veronica: (a vernicle), a supposed Roman Catholic relic said to be the sweat cloth used by Veronica, a compassionate bystander or disciple, to dab the face of Jesus on his route to Calvary. According to legend, Christ's facial image was retained on the fabric. The Gospels make no reference to this episode in the life of Jesus if it did, indeed, happen. Veronica reportedly took the material to Emperor Tiberius in Rome. The object became legendary as it was thought to possess miraculous powers, including quenching thirst, curing blindness, and even raising the dead. There is a depiction of it in Rosslyn Chapel near Edinburgh. *See also* cross; Mandylion, the Holy; relic(s); Roman Catholic Church; shrine(s); Shroud of Turin; Spear of Destiny; veil(s); vernicle; Veronica; *Via Dolorosa.*

Velayat Sinai: an Islamic jihadist group operating in Egypt. *See also Alluha Akbar;* al-Qaeda; al-Shabab; anti-Semitic; Boko Haram; Daesh; Fatah; Hamas; Hezbollah; Islam; Islamic State in Iraq and Syria (ISIS or ISIL); *jihad;* Muslim Brotherhood; Nusra Front; Palestinian Islamic Jihad (PIJ); Palestinian Liberation Organization (PLO); Salafi; Taliban; terrorism; terrorist(s); Turkistan Islamic Party.

Veleda: a deified woman worshiped in ancient Germany. The word is both a title ("priestess" or "power") and a name (the female who either led or encouraged the Batavian revolt against the Romans In 69 A.D.). In legend, she has been endorsed as a prophetess who could predict the future for her people. *See also* pagan, paganism.

vellum: an ancient writing material (not modern-day vellum paper) made from animal skins carefully prepared. The word springs from the Latin *vitulimun,* meaning "made from calf," which the French turned into *vellum.* Due to its relative expense and beauty, normally only precious manuscripts of scrolls or codices were produced on the product, including the finest Bible copies and illustrations. Quality skins of calves or antelope were acceptable for vellum material (also called parchment in the cheaper variety from sheep or goats) and were in use for Bible binding from about 300–1400 A.D. Two of the oldest vellum copies of the Bible (A.D. 325–350) in existence today are the Vatican Codex and the Sinaitic Codex. *See also* book(s); clay; folio; lower criticism; palimpsest; papyrus; parchment; scroll(s); stone(s).

Vendanta Society: essentially, the term that represents Hinduism in America. *See also* Hinduism; sect(s).

Venerable Society. See Society for the Propagation of the Gospel in Foreign Parts.

veneration of the cross: part of the solemn litany of Good Friday (usually in liturgical churches) in which the entire congregation may come forward to venerate or contemplate the meaning of the church's crucifix. *See also* Cross, Feasts of the; liturgical year; liturgy, Christian; gestures; statuary; Triumph of the Cross, Feast of the.

veneration of the saints: a doctrine or practice, primarily Roman Catholic and Eastern Orthodoxy, that promotes prayers and petitions to pronounced saints of the church. Catholic theologians would deny that the ritual is "worship" but would grant that the super good in heaven have sufficient influence there to aid or promote some cause for an earthly solicitor. *See also* Angelology; beatification; Day of the Dead; *dulia;* Eastern Orthodox Church; feasts and special days of high liturgy faiths; hyten; liturgical year; liturgy, Christian; Mariolatry; Roman Catholic Church; supererogation; treasury of merits; saint(s).

vengeance: revenge—an act of recompense or retribution, often violent, for alleged wrongs done to one's person or family. Revelation 6:9–11 records the slain martyrs under the altar of God (in the fifth seal) as crying out for vengeance against the inhabitants of the earth who had murdered them. The emphasis here, however, is not personal vendetta but a call for the true and righteous justice of God to be done on Tribulation earth. The Mosaic Law featured "the avenger of blood" as legitimate justice in certain instances but the Christian concept delineated by Jesus is not so favorable. New Testament morality tends to radically alter the law of *lex talionis*—"eye for eye and tooth for tooth" (Lev. 24:17–21; Mt. 5:38–42). Whether Jesus abrogated the Old Testament law or merely upgraded it is a matter of theological debate. In any case, apocalypticism is heavily interested in the integrity and vengeance of God, with Whom alone true justice resides. *See also* angels of vengeance; avenger of blood, the; blood feud; cities of refuge; comminate; *jus talionis; lex talionis*; social issues.

venial sin: a sinful act that, as determined by Roman Catholic definition, is one of lesser gravity than a mortal sin. The former does not result in complete separation and condemnation whereas the

Bernie L. Calaway

latter may do so if not repented. Such fine distinctions are seldom presented by reformed denominations because all sin is accounted an affront to God and causing a need for forgiveness. *See also* mortal sin; seven deadly sins; sin(s).

Venite, the: a liturgical version of Psalm 95:1–7 suitable for morning worship or its musical setting. *See also* liturgical year; liturgy, Christian; music.

Venus: 1. the ancient deity of gardens and springs, identified by the Romans as Aphrodite, the goddess of love and beauty. Some of the Roman emperors claimed to be the progeny of the goddess Venus. 2. the planet second from the sun and the most brilliant to our eyes. The celestial body was of particular importance to many ancient cultures and religions, including Judaism, which harbored an understanding that it held messianic implications (Num. 24:17–19). The planet gains particular significance in many of the 2012 prophecy details. *See also* Aphrodite; Ashtoreth(s), Ashtaroth; Dark Rift, the; Day Star; eclipse(s); Golden Bough, the; Levant pantheon; Morning Star; Olympian pantheon; planets as gods, the; Rattlesnake Prophecy, the; son of the morning, son of the dawn; Tammuz.

verbal inspiration: the belief that the Word of God (Scripture) was "verbally" transcribed to a writer who had little or no input as to the tenor or wording of his writing. The theory is mostly discredited by the majority of reasonable scholars because it presupposes a sort of holy dictation with no application from the writer's insight, feelings, or talents. The Scriptures convey a distinct "human" touch along with the grand vision of God. *See also* Bible; inerrancy; *norma normans non normata*; plenary inspiration.

verbicide: the deliberate distortion of the original meaning of a word. Such practice is an abomination to scriptural lower criticism and intellectual integrity. *See also* accideme; alliteration; apostrophe; apothegm; assonance; autograph; Bible; Bible manuscripts; Bible translations; biblical criticism; chiasmus; conflict story; *constructio ad sensum*; context; contextualization; dittography; double sense fulfillment; doublets; doubling; edification; eisegesis; epanadiplosis; epigrammatic statements; etymology; exegesis; figure of speech; folio; form criticism; gattung; gloss;

570

gnomic sayings; grammatical-historical interpretation; *hapax legomena;* haplography; hermeneutic(s); higher criticism; homographs; homonyms; homophones; *homoteleuton;* hyperbole; idiom; *inclusio;* interpolation; interpretation; inverted nun; irony; isagogics; *itture sopherim;* jot and tittle; kere; *kethib;* "L"; liberalists interpretation; literal interpretation; litotes; loan words; lower criticism; "M"; Masoretic Text; minuscule(s); mystery of God; omission; onomastica; onomatopoeia; palimpsest; papyrus; paradigm; parallelism; parchment; *paroimia; paronomasia;* pericope; personification; Peshitta; pointing; point of view; polyglot; principles of interpretation; proof texting; pun(s); "Q"; redaction; revelation, theological; rhetorical criticism; rhetorical devices; riddle; satire; *scripto continua;* scriptorium; *sebirin;* simile; similitude; source criticism; sources, primary and secondary; special points; strophe; superscription; symbol(s); synecdoche; syntax; synthetic parallelism; text; textual criticism; *tiggune sopherim;* Time Texts; Torah; translation; transposition; trope; type(s); typology; uncial(s); vellum.

verger: or virger, a church official (usually a lay person) with duties to assist ecclesiastical authority, especially in the Anglican Church. The name comes from his staff of office, the virge, which is really a mace with more than symbolic value. One of his most important duties was to bludgeon a clear path through animals or unruly crowds during religious processionals. *See also* beadle; sexton; usher.

veritas in caritate: the Latin phrase recited as "truth in love," lifted from Paul's comment on the matter in Ephesians 4:15. The quote attempts to capture the fundamental tenet of Christianity and its most distinguishing characteristic—to speak and act in love toward all others. Doctrinal arguments or sociopolitical issues must not be allowed to crowd or overwhelm the primary task of the Church to promote and evangelize the gospel of Christ to the world.

vernicle: a cloth with the image of Christ printed or somehow radiated on it. *See also* Mandylion, the Holy; relic(s); Shroud of Turin; veil of Veronica.

Veronica: a woman whom Roman Catholic legend says wiped the face of Jesus on his way to the cross. In the *Via Dolorosa* enactment, she is said to have performed her act of kindness at the site of the Sixth Station. A certain cloth is treasured by the church—said to be the imprint of Jesus' features pressed into it when Veronica cleaned the sweat from his face. There is no mention of a Veronica in the Gospels, and she and her compassionate action are purely a Roman Catholic tradition, true or not. *See also* liturgical year; Roman Catholic Church; veil of Veronica; *Via Dolorosa.*

verse: 1. a Bible text sung prior to the Gospel reading in some liturgical settings, rendered at any time except Lent. The text is normally preceded and followed by alleluias of praise. 2. a numbered portion of Scripture within each chapter. 3. a stanza of a hymn when speaking informally. *See also* liturgical year; liturgy, Christian; versicle.

versicle: a "little verse" of a psalm to be read responsively on special occasions of worship in some liturgies. *See also* antiphon; liturgical year; liturgy, Christian; psalm; responsive reading; verse.

Vesey, Denmark: leader of an abortive slave uprising in Charleston, South Carolina, in 1822. Vesey was born in 1767 but sold as a young boy to a ship's captain where he remained until 1800. In that year, he won a lottery, part of which he used to buy his freedom. He expended the rest of his winnings to start a prosperous carpentry business in Charleston. Vesey became leader of the local African Methodist Episcopal Church but stayed grounded in his fundamental hatred of slavery. While pretending to conduct religious classes for the slaves, he traveled among the plantations organizing secret cabals to murder slave owners and capture the city. Weapons were stockpiled and an army of indeterminate size was recruited. The rebellion was set to start in June of 1822, but at the last moment, he was betrayed and Charleston was able to defend itself. As repercussion, 130 blacks and 4 whites were brought to trial. Thirty-five, including Vesey, were hanged on July 2, 1822. *See also* African Methodist Episcopal Church; slave, slavery; terrorism; terrorist(s).

Vesica Piscis: "the measure of the fish." To Pythagoreans and most Gnostic-types, certain numbers had extra significance. Using the story of Jesus helping the disciples catch fish (John 21:1–14), an esoteric meaning was typically assigned because the number of fish snared, 153, was special to them. When two circles are drawn so that the perimeter of one passes the epicenter of the other, the result is a geometric design resembling a fish, an early symbol of Christianity. Further, there are within that same diagram, two equilateral triangles. Measurement of this internal figure proves to be 153 from the dorsal to the belly of the fish. The principle of *Vesica Piscis* portrays this drawing as representing the Trinity— Father, Son, and Holy Spirit—with its three resulting circles. Furthermore, Jesus was crucified at the time the zodiac was fading from the constellation Taurus to Pisces, the fish. All was thought to be significant. *See also* 888; Gnosticism, Gnostic(s); *icthus;* numbers, symbology of; Pythagoras; Pythagorean Theorem; theomatic number(s).

Vespasian: Roman general and father of Titus, also a Roman general. Vespasian began the conquest of Judah in the Jewish War of A.D. 66–70 and Titus finished it. Both became emperors of Rome. According to Josephus, Vespasian considered himself a Messiah figure. Also, Josephus further hinted that there may have been some divine manipulation in Nero's appointment of this veteran to be the Roman general against the rebellion. *See also* Christianity in the Roman Empire; Jewish War; king(s); Roman Empire; Titus.

vespers: the final prayer of the Divine Office recited in the nighttime before bed. *See also* Agpeya; canonical hours; complain, lauds; liturgical year; liturgy; liturgy, Christian; matins; nones; novena; prayer(s); prime; sext; terce.

Vesta: virgin goddess of ancient Rome responsible for home, hearth, and family. Her worship consisted mainly of the sacred fire burning continuously in her temple. *See also* diva; Olympian pantheon.

vestments. See furniture and furnishings of the modern church; vestry.

vestry: 1. a closet or storage room for church vestments and a convenient place for the priest to ready himself for worship leadership. 2. the rector, wardens, and certain members of an Anglican parish acting as a board of governors. *See also* Anglicanism; furniture and furnishings of the modern church; rector; warden.

veve: a magical pentagram used by Voodoo priests or priestesses to invoke ancestral spirits or demons or to manipulate the elements of nature. The ritual includes dance and song to stimulate the intervention. The common design style of a veve is drawn in cornmeal, flour, bark, red brick powder, gunpowder, or similar substance resulting in rather complex but beautiful work. It will act as a beacon or focus for the Loa Loas. *See also* Creole (Caribbean) religions; gris-gris; Ifa; juju; Legba; Loa Loas; magic square; mojo; pentagram; poppets; Voodoo; Voudou; wanga.

Via Dolorosa: the imagined route of Jesus from his judgment before Pilate to the cross. "The Way of Sorrows" (in Latin "sorrowful way") cannot be assuredly reproduced as to exact locations, but thousands of pilgrims in Jerusalem walk a selected prescribed route in piety each pre-Easter and try to reenact or contemplate the Lord's suffering as he carried his cross to Golgotha. There are up to fourteen "stations of the cross" to be encountered that have been designated by the Roman Catholic Church as an aid to devotion. Those who favor the modern nine stations on Jesus' path to the cross include his trial and scourging before Pilate (Stations 1 and 2), three falls (Stations 3, 7, and 9), encounter with his mother Mary (Station 4), encounter with Simon of Cyrene (Station 5), encounter with Veronica (Station 6), and encounter with the pious women (Station 8). Those who honor fourteen stations add Jesus stripped of his clothing (Station 10), nailing to the cross (Station 11), the death of Jesus (Station 12), removal from the cross (Station 13), and burial (Station 14). Of importance is the thought that each incident—from Jesus' Triumphal Entry into Jerusalem to his resurrection—has its place in fulfilling the prophecies of his advent and passion. *See also* Church of the Holy Sepulcher; crucifixion; *ecce homo;* Gabbatha; Holy Week; Jerusalem, landmarks of; Lithostrotos; Passion, the; Praetorium; stations of the cross; Tower of David; veil of Veronica; Veronica.

vial(s): a tube-like container usually envisioned as made of glass. The term is substituted for "bowls" in some earlier translations of Revelation. *See also* bowls.

viaticum: 1. the Latin designation for sacraments in the High Church Eucharistic observance, especially for a dying person. 2. a monetary advance or stipend for a journey. *See also* liturgical year; sacrament(s).

vicar-general: a Roman Catholic or Anglican ecclesiastical officer appointed by his bishop or deputy bishop to oversee administrative and jurisprudence matters. *See also* auxiliary ministries; Church of England; coadjutor; ecclesiastic(s); Roman Catholic Church.

vicarious atonement: the doctrine stating that Christ's death was "legal" in that it involved sacrificial blood and satisfied the righteous justice of God. *See also* atonement; recapitulation theory of atonement; reconciliation; satisfaction theory of atonement; vicarious suffering.

vicarious suffering: the doctrine affirming that Jesus suffered the cross on man's behalf, an act motivated by pure love without a meaning of substitution. *See also* vicarious atonement.

vicarious faith: the implied faith of the parents of baptized infants that is said to be imparted to the baby at the time of baptism and after. Basically, it was Martin Luther's explanation of the effectiveness of pedobaptism. *See also* baptism; credo-baptism; faith; pedobaptism; sin of the innocents.

vicar of Christ: a title for the pope of the Roman Catholic Church—*vicarious filial Dei*, vicar of the Son of God—a name derived from the Latin *vicarius Christi*. The term *vicar* means "a substitute," which identifies the role taken on by the popes as Christ's "stand-in." The designation emphasizes his alleged primacy over the Church, both in personal honor and jurisdiction. After Gregory VII (ruled 1073–1085), his successors abandoned the old title of "vicar of Peter" and moved to the more comprehensive "vicar of Christ." A host of appellations followed: universal bishop, sovereign pontiff, Christ's vicar, prince of the apostles, God on earth, Lord God the pope, his holiness, King of kings and Lord of lords, prince over all nations and kingdoms, most holy and most blessed, master of the universal world, father of kings, light of the world, most high and sovereign bishop, etc. Many would claim the assumed titles arrogant if not blasphemous. The new choice was a more potent title reflecting the imposed power of the papacy. The title, and others like it, exhibit great power from the pope of Rome, legitimate or not. The papal claim is disputed, often severely, by other Catholic entities and certainly by Protestantism. The proper name for the Church at Rome should be "the Western Church of the Latin Rite," but it is seldom used because it recognizes the equal historical status of the various faiths elsewhere—in Eastern Europe, in the Middle East, and those of America, Asia, and Africa. *See also* clergy; ecclesiastic(s); Innocent III, Pope; papacy; *Pontifex Maximus;* pope; priest(s); *princeps; principis;* Roman Catholic Church; ultramontanism; vice god.

vice god: a derogatory term for the Roman Catholic Church by those who oppose the pope's claim to be the regent of Peter and singular spokesman for God. *See also* Christianese; Roman Catholic Church; vicar of Christ.

viceroy: ecclesiastical rank below a patriarch in the Eastern Orthodox hierarchy. *See also* clergy; divine; Eastern Orthodox Church; ecclesiastic(s); priest(s).

Victorinus: writer of the earliest extant commentary on Revelation (died ca. A.D. 304), a bishop in Slovenia. In his writings, the chief of which is *Commentary on the Apocalypse,* Victorinus asserted that Revelation was written by John from Patmos under the Emperor Domitian, by whom he was martyred. He subscribed to the millennial doctrine and preferred the repetitive approach when viewing the seals, trumpets, and bowls. He chastised Rome as Revelation's Babylon for his day and age. Victorinus is honored by both Greek and Roman church factions. *See also* Eastern Orthodox Church; martyr(s); Roman Catholic Church.

victor motif: or dramatic atonement—the belief that Jesus' death brought about salvation by means of its spectacular victory over sin, death, and evil dominance. *See also* atonement; conquest motif; deliverance motif; endurance motif; exchange motif; exemplar motif; rector motif; salvation.

Victor of Hugo (Victor Hugo): French poet of the Romantic movement (1802–1885). It was he who pronounced what is perhaps the most clever spoof of allegorism: "First learn what you are to believe, and then go to the Scriptures to find it there." *See also* allegorism.

Vidui: the Jewish prayer of confession to be recited at one's near-pending death. When possible the hand-washing ritual is to be performed while males wear the traditional *yarmulke* and pair of *tzitzit.* The prayer invokes God's mercy and brings about atonement. *See also* Judaism; prayer(s); *yarmulke; tzitzit.*

vigil: a wake or watching. At times, *e.g.* during periods of mourning, some living persons remain with the body of the deceased at all times as a show of respect). On other occasions, the faithful may gather for extended periods of prayer for specific reasons, either as a group or in relays. Any waiting period with a worship or ritualistic purpose can be termed a vigil. *See also* burial; chant; death; dirge; exequy; funeral; jeremiad; kontakion; *kinah;* lament; liturgical year; liturgy, Christian; obit; obsequy; Pannychis; pernoctate; Requiem; requiescat; threnody; wake; watch.

Vikings: any of the several Scandinavian sea peoples, rovers, explorers, and pirates during the eighth, ninth, and tenth centuries. They routinely ravaged Europe looting and pillaging—especially Christian churches and monasteries which were particularly lucrative targets. They ranged their longboats as far as the Mediterranean and the North American continent. *See also* Armanenschafft; Asa; Asatru; Asgard; blyt; disa; *Edda,* the; Helm of Awe; Norse and Old Germanic pantheon; Ragnarok; rune(s); Valhalla; Valupsa; Wotanism.

vile person, a. See contemptible person, a.

Villa Baviera: formerly *Colonia Dignidad,* a brutal cult founded by the German expatriate Paul Schafer in 1961. Schafer was a former Nazi who relocated several of his German immigrant followers to the south of Chile, where it became a haven for torture, child molestation, and other violent behavior. The totalitarian regime at that time, through the Chilean police, used the cult's commune as a site for interrogation and torture of dissidents. The victims were also subjected to mind control and abuse by the cult's own leaders, particularly Schafer. The site was a haven for former Nazis and a cache for weapons (even including a tank). The institutions of world justice have been slow to curtail the sect. But although the compound still exists, most of the leaders have been removed or prosecuted. *See also* cult(s); Schafer, Paul.

Vimanas: Hindu names for certain flying craft found in the Vedic scriptures. Their description has caused some believers to claim the ancient Indians were familiar with alien space vehicles or "chariots." The concept may be linked to the Hindu god Vimana, the fifth avatar of Vishnu, who grew from a dwarf to a giant who could stride the earth and heavens in three steps. *See also* Alien Disclosure Event; Black Vault; chariot(s); Hinduism; Merkabah; UAP; UFO; zero-point energy.

Vincent, John Heyl: (1832–1920), ordained Methodist minister at age eighteen. He orchestrated the appeal and supply for comprehensive Protestant religious education. Vincent developed the enormously popular technique of Sunday school teaching called the "Chautauqua Movement," which he started in 1874. He was a major force in adult religious and secular education of that time, and his system is still considered important today. *See also* Chautauqua Movement, the; Methodists; religious education.

vine: the plant of the grape. In prophetic literature, however, the vine is a favorite allegory to show health or disease of the spirit, depending on the thrust of the illustration. Ezekiel (Ezk. 15:1–8) described the total devastation of the people of Jerusalem because they are worthless and unproductive; unfaithful Jerusalem is named as useless. Jesus' parable of the vine promotes the idea that he is allegorically the nourishing vine and we are the productive branches (Jn. 15:1–8). As such, we cannot survive without him. The vine plant is a frequent symbol for Israel (Isa. 5:1–7; Hos. 14:7; Ps. 80:8). Other prophets held a similar intent including Isaiah (Isa. 5:1–7), Jeremiah (Jer. 2:21), and Jesus (Mk. 12:1–9). *See also* Ezekiel's eagles, vine, and cedar allegory; flora, fruit, and grain, symbology of; parable(s); parables of the New Testament; parables of the Old Testament; useless vine, a; vine and the fig tree, the; vine, the true.

vine and the fig tree, the: a biblical wisdom saying used to imply prosperity, contentment, or happiness. To "sit under one's own fig tree" (Mic. 4:4) was considered to be peaceful contentment and a fulfilling joy or blessing. When the vine or fig fail as crops, both the causes and the results are considered a disaster. Unfaithful Jerusalem is named a useless vine in Ezekiel 15. Jeremiah cited spoiled or rotten figs as representing those reviled and left in the land after the Babylonian Captivity (Jer. 24). *See also* fig(s); fig tree(s); flora, fruit, and grain, symbology of; two baskets of figs; useless vine, a; vine; vine, the true.

vine, a useless. See Ezekiel's lioness and vine allegory.

vinegar: a sour liquid made from the fermentation of wine, cider, beer, ale, etc. Biblical metaphors for vinegar include bitterness of spirit or annoyance (Pro. 10:26; Ps. 69:21). Jesus was given vinegar wine (perhaps gall) to drink at his crucifixion (Mt. 27:48). It appears to have been common practice to equate vinegar with gall or to mix the two concoctions. *See also* gall.

vine of Sodom: a plant growing near Sodom that produced clusters of bitter fruit of some description (Deut. 32:32). Perhaps the produce was used to concoct gall or another acidic drink. Josephus mentioned a similar fruit growing in the area (or perhaps the same variety) that produced what appeared to be edible fruit but when plucked turned to ashes and powder. Such a plant would serve as figurative language for something deceptive, insubstantial, or perishable. *See also* flora, fruit, and grain, symbology of; gall.

vine out of Egypt: a parable or illustration from Psalm 80 that discusses the birth and care of God's chosen people. The story showcases the nation's origin in Egypt and her subsequent development under God's provision. *See also* Egypt, Egyptians; Hebrews as a people; Israel; Jew(s); parable(s); parables of the Old Testament.

vine, the true: Jesus' description of himself as the source of all faith (Jn. 15:1) who acts for the Father to produce an abundance of good works and fidelity. We are the branches, not the stock, and therefore unable to live without the necessary sustenance from God. *See also* flora, fruit, and grain, symbology of; names (titles) for Jesus; vine; vine and the fig tree, the.

Vineyard Ministries International: a charismatic church begun in 1974 from a single congregation; in 1982 Calvary Chapel was instituted headed by John Wimber with a ministry of praying for signs and wonders. The group became Vineyard Ministries in 1983 and now numbers about 1500 churches worldwide.

violate: 1. to render something unholy. 2. to rape. 3. to fail to obey just laws or restrictions. *See also* social issues.

Violent Age: a contrived name for the period A.D. 1328–1648 according to dispensational theology. The time is representative of the church at Sardis (Rev. 3:1–6) covering a dead age absent of spiritual vitality but filled with internecine warfare and persecution of nonconformists to the then dominant Roman Church authority. *See also* dispensation(s); dispensational theology; Sardis.

Bernie L. Calaway

"violent who storm the kingdom of heaven, the": a reference to Matthew 11:12 when Christ said that from the days of John the Baptist until now the kingdom of heaven suffers violence, and the aggressive take it by force. The unusual pronouncement from Jesus is definitely apocalyptic in force, but what is its probable meaning? By "the violent," Jesus did not allude to vicious or sadistic individuals, but those believers who by their strength and earnest striving are on the watch to clasp the kingdom for themselves when it arrives in perfection and for eternity. The Christian life is a struggle at times—in fact, much of the time—so our extraordinary efforts of prayer and diligence in our faith is essential to fully find the best of the kingdom of heaven. Jesus also said that we must "strive" to enter through the narrow gate, for many will seek to enter and will not be able (Lk. 13:24).

virger. See verger.

Virgil: *nee* Publius Vergilius Maro (70–19 B.C.) one of ancient Rome's most celebrated poet/historians. There is speculation he may have been a Celt. Virgil's most famous work includes the *Ecloges, Aeneid,* and *Georgics.* His work, along with the lesser known works of the female poets Faltonia Bertitia Probo and Prudentius (A.D. 348–ca. 413), were revered for generations after their appearance. One of Virgil's epic poems in his *Ecloges* speaks of a prophecy that a virgin would give birth to a son (believed by Constantine and the church fathers to be Jesus). Refutation of that particular text has been strong. The apostle Paul was said to have visited Virgil's tomb in the Bay of Naples and praised his greatness. So great was Virgil's reputation that Dante chose him as his guide to the underworld in his allegory *Inferno. See also* Alighieri, Dante; Celtic folklore and religion; *Divine Comedy,* the; Golden Bough, the; Roman Empire.

virgin birth: the common, though not unanimous, Christian belief that Jesus was born of the Virgin Mary via miraculous action of the Holy Spirit and not by human procreation. The virginal conception and birth of Jesus seem to have been prophesied in Isaiah 7:14. Those who question the virgin birth doctrine do so by asserting that the Isaiah passage speaks of a "young woman," not necessarily a virgin. Roman Catholicism would go further and declare that Mary herself was conceived in the same manner, a doctrine known as "immaculate conception." The technical name for Jesus' virgin birth is *parthenogenesis. See also almah;*

580

Ebionites(s); Ebionitism; Evangelical Alliance; immaculate conception; virgin(s), virginity.

Virgin Daughter of Zion (Judah): a tender name for Jerusalem as idealized in her past innocence before the subjugation by Babylon (Lam. 1:15). *See also* Daughter of Zion; Jerusalem as city; Jerusalem, landmarks of; virgin(s), virginity; Virgin Israel.

Virginia's Religious Disestablishment law: a statute promoted by Thomas Jefferson in 1786 with officially removed the Anglican Church as the official religion of the state. Secular involvement and sponsorship of the denomination ceased. Virginia was not the first to enact such legislation as North Carolina had done so as early as 1776 but Virginia's size, prestige, and population ignited the principle of church and state separation nationwide. *See also* Abington School District vs. Schempp; Allegheny County vs. ACLU; antidisestablishmentarianism; *Booke of the General Lawes and Libertyes;* Caesar cult; caesaropapacy; civil religion; collegialism; disestablishmentarianism; Emerson vs. Board of Education; Establishment Clause and Free Exercise Clause; Geghan Bill; Government Regulation Index (GRI); Johnson Amendment; Lemon vs. Kurtzman; public square; Shubert vs. Verner; state church; ultramontanism.

Virgin Israel: a name for the Jewish nation harking to the days when the land was pure in faith and innocent in virtue but now, according to Jeremiah, has made a mockery of the title (Jer. 18:13; 31:4, 21). *See also* Virgin Daughter of Zion (Judah); virgin(s), virginity.

virgin(s), virginity: a sexually inexperienced person, usually female, or something unspoiled. However, the King James Version names the 144,000 of Revelation 14:1–5 as "virgins," but the reference is unclear if they are all men, all women, or mixed sexes. The Greek word used is suitable for both sexes. In any case, the term is probably intended to denote the moral purity of the group, not their sexual inexperience. A better translation is perhaps "witnesses" or "servants" who have little spare time or peace for the comforts and responsibilities of family life. In the ancient world, virginity was an important moral and religious virtue in many cultures, particularly for Jewish girls. *See also almah;* born again virgin; 144,000, the; rose; virgin birth; Virgin Daughter of Zion (Judah); Virgin Israel.

Bernie L. Calaway

virgins' house: an outdated name for monasteries, especially of the Coptic varieties. *See also* Coptic Church; monastery; monasticism; nun(s).

Virgo: the second-largest constellation in the heavens. Her position seems to imply she is being escorted past the deadly Hydra by Leo, a scene which many of the ancients accepted as worthy of worship. Virgo represents the female aspects of the gods and humans promoting prosperity and growth. Virgo, along with Leo, Hydra, and Draco were among the most important astrological or formations to the ancients. *See also* astrology, astrologists; astronomy, astronomists; planets as gods, the; zodiac.

Virtues: ("excellences") those angelic entities in their divisions that guard Paradise both before and after the fall of Adam according to *The Life of Adam and Eve*. *See also* angel(s); archangel(s); authorities; Bene Elohim; Chashmallim; Chayoth; Cherub, Cherubim; dominions; *elohim*; Erelim; Galgallim; Hashmallim; Hayyot; Husk(s); Ishim; *mal'ak*; Ophanim; powers; principalities; Seraphim; thrones.

virtue(s): moral excellence or goodness. The prophets cherished virtue as a social and religious theme worthy of all acceptance. Roman Catholic doctrine defines three sacred virtues (faith, hope, and love) as the revealed or "theological" honors. They also name four cardinal virtues: justice, prudence, temperance, and fortitude. Protestants do not normally technically distinguish between virtuous acts or deeds except, of course, by recognizing that certain wrong acts are more harmful to human society but others less so, and certain benevolent actions are of heavier benefit to the receiver. *See also* aretology; cardinal virtues; seven heavenly virtues; temperance.

Visegrad Group (V4): an alliance of four-nations—the Czech Republic, Slovakia, Hungary, and Poland—(originally Bohemia, Poland, and Hungary) meeting in Visegrad, Hungary, in 1991 to make cultural and commercial arrangements that fortuitously managed closer ties to Israel. It also strengthened favor for the European Union. The action is important because it was a small signal of recognition for the Jewish nation; President Donald Trump's establishment of Jerusalem as America's embassy was another of even greater significance. *See also* Benelux Conference of 1948; conspiracy theorists; European Union, the; Maastricht Treaty; Treaty of Rome.

Vishnu: 1. a Hindu deity believed to have descended from heaven to earth in several incarnations (an avatar), the most important of which was Krisha of the *Bhagavad Gita*. Kalki avatar will be the final incarnation of Vishnu. 2. in later Hinduism, the second member of a trinity called "the Preserver," one of a triad consisting of Brahma the Creator and Siva the Destroyer. Vishnu is featured as the supreme god of Vaishnavite Hinduism, one of the five primary forms of God. He is pictured as a handsome being with four arms and described as the supreme soul and preserver of the universe. 3. one of a half dozen solar deities of the East, called "the Pervader," who treads across the sky three times a day in three strides. *See also Bhagwan Gita;* Hinduism; Kali; Krishna.

visible and invisible church, the: the distinction, perhaps coined by John Wycliffe, that the Church of God is really of two parts. The visible is that which is perceptible in an earthly organ, ruled by bishops, bodies, and popes and populated by both faithful and insincere Christians; the invisible Church is heavenly and to be considered the only true congregation of believers throughout the ages. Sometimes the phrase "invisible Church" is meant to equate with the Church universal, all of Christ's flock, but it does not truly portray the living Church of Christ as an active and observable entity. The intent of most who use the term "invisible" is to try to distinguish between the church form and its function. However, the New Testament knows nothing of a general church organization—only a local one known as a congregation. That is not to say, even so, that there is no "universal" and ageless collection of believers for there certainly is such a body, someday to be gathered as one. *See also* branch theory; Church; church; congregation; One, Holy, Catholic, and Apostolic Church; universal Church.

"Visible Saints," the: first-generation Puritans and dominant families in New England. They distrusted the younger colonists who had not endured the arduous sea voyage and struggle for survival in the New World. But for the Congregationalists to prosper, the younger generation was needed. Thus, the "Visible Saints" provided the Half-Way Covenant that allowed church attendance but no access to the ordinances nor the vote until fidelity could be demonstrated. *See also* Half-Way Covenant; Puritanism; Puritan(s).

vision(s): a prophetic exercise in which the seer experiences an image or mystical portrayal initiated by God and intended to instruct or motivate the observer (*i.e.*, Hosea 12:10). The term springs from the Latin *visio*, meaning "to see." A vision is distinguished from a dream with the same intent because the vision is evidently expressed in real-time consciousness, whereas the dream occurs when the dreamer is asleep. The book of Revelation is filled with John's reporting mantra of his vision experiences by repeating "I saw" and its equivalents. *See also* allegorical vision(s); almond tree branch; Amos as Old Testament prophecy; *Apocalypse of Baruch;* apocalyptic journey; apparition; *Ascension of Isaiah;* audition; beatific vision; boiling pot, vision of the; burnished man, the; celestial court, the; chariot of God; Daniel's decipher of the hand writing on the wall; Daniel's vision from the revealing angel; Daniel's vision of end time; Daniel's vision of the destroying monster; Daniel's vision of the four beasts; Daniel's vision of the mighty kingdom; Daniel's vision of the seventy "sevens"; divination; dream(s); dreams and visions; ecstasy; edible scrolls, the; *epiphaneia;* Ezekiel's call and vision of the Cherubim; Ezekiel's four visions of Israel's demise; Ezekiel's report of the scribe clothed in linen; Ezekiel's vision of the Cherubim and the departed glory; Ezekiel's vision of the fiery man and the wicked Temple; Ezekiel's vision of the man with a measuring line and rod; Ezekiel's vision of the new Temple and new land; Ezekiel's vision of the restored theocracy; Ezekiel's vision of the valley of dry bones; Fatima, Our Lady of; filidh; *4 Esdras;* fruit, basket of ripe (summer); Garabandal visions; generational prophecy; ghost(s); Guadalupe, Our Lady of; heavenly court; heavenly dwelling; Heliodorus; Herod the Great; hieraphony; illumination; *In hoc signo vinces;* inspiration; interior locution; Jacob's ladder; La Salette, vision of; Lord's shirt; Lourdes, Our Lady of; mandala; man from Macedonia; man of sorrows; Mariolatry; Medjugorje; *Mene, Mene, Tekel; Parsin* (or *Uparsin); mysticism*, mystics; Native American Church; near-death experience(s) (NDEs); *nephesh;* prince of (in) Jerusalem; "Prophecy of the Popes"; Rattlesnake Prophecy, the; remote viewing; Revelation as New Testament prophecy; Revelation, content of; revelation, theological; seal up vision and prophecy; Seraph, Seraphim; Sergius and Bacchus; seven shepherds and eight princes; shepherdless flock, the; *Shepherd of Hermes, The;* "song of the sword"; sun worshipers;

Tenrikyo; theophany; transporting angel of Ezekiel, the; tremendum; 2012 prophecy, advocates of; two baskets of figs; unclean animals, Peter's vision of the; vision quest; visitation; visualization; water, the rising; witch of Endor; woman clothed in (with) the sun, the; Zechariah's vision of a Zechariah's vision of a crown for Joshua; Zechariah's vision of garments for the high priest; Zechariah's vision of the flying scroll; Zechariah's vision of the four chariots; Zechariah's vision of four horns and four craftsmen; Zechariah's vision of the gold lampstand and two olive trees; Zechariah's vision of the man among the myrtle trees; Zechariah's vision of the man with a measuring line; Zechariah's vision of the seven-eyed stone; Zechariah's vision of the woman in a basket; Zionites.

visionary journey. See apocalyptic journey.

vision quest: a deliberate seeking of supernatural power. Often the searcher will subject himself or herself to physical and psychological punishments of varying degrees until the spirit within reveals the needed information. The process has long been a history of worldwide primitive tribes and Native Americans. It has been suggested (not totally proven) that a vision quest may be the ability of some to contact the "grey" areas of our higher and lower consciousness while remaining awake. The theory involves utilization of one or more of the measured electrical frequencies of the brain. The mind is said to operate at 15–30 Hz in the *beta* brainwave state, 9–14 Hz in the *alpha* stage, 4–8 Hz in the *theta* state, and 1–3 Hz in the *delta* stage. By deliberately tapping via various control methods into the lowest pattern still allowing consciousness (the *delta*) a person may be subject to flashes of insight or visions. It has even been suggested that it was this very process that allowed Jesus to encounter and overcome Satan in his wilderness temptation experience after prolonged fasting. *See also* New Age religion; rite of passage; vision(s); visualization.

visitation: 1. in normal understanding, the social interaction of guest and host in one's home or another's. Theologically, however, the term commonly means punishment or discipline upon part of God's creation. Nature often serves as a simile for such acts— lightning, rain, floods, windstorms, etc., (*i.e.,* Judges 5:20).

Disease, hardship, or some other malady may be chosen to project God's harsh intent. The proper response to those actions is to view them as a warning or a vehicle for learning. Certain official ecclesiastical inspections conducted internally from higher authority to lower may also be considered visitations when contemplating or administering discipline. 2. the ecclesiastical name for the visit paid by Mary before her birth of Jesus to her cousin Elizabeth who was pregnant with John the Baptist. The Catholic Church celebrates the calling on July 2. 3. a dream or vision that is particularly vivid so that, upon awakening, the dreamer may be weeping or emotionally moved far beyond the normal. *See also* liturgical year; liturgy, Christian; dream(s); Roman Catholic Church; vision (s); Visitation, Canonical.

Visitation, Canonical: acts of a Roman Catholic ecclesiastical superior who is charged to visit peoples and places looking for poor administration, church abuse, malfeasance, and the like and seeking to correct disruptions to faith and order. *See also* Roman Catholic Church; visitation.

Vissarion: *nee* Sergey Anatolyevich Torop, born January 14, 1961, a.k.a. "the Jesus of Siberia." Vissarion is a mystic and claims to be the reincarnation of Jesus. His followers are said to number about 10,000, mostly in Russia and Germany. He and some of his disciples have erected a communal retreat in Siberia called Tiberkul built on ecological principles. The town is based on three tiers—the *Abode of Dawn,* the *Heavenly Abode,* and the *Temple Peak*—said to be the headquarters of their movement known as the Church of the Last Testament. *See also* Church of the Last Testament; cult(s).

visualization: that deliberate process of the mind that uses concentration and directed imagery for some purpose conceived in the brain but anticipated in the real world. Some call the practice "seeing with the mind's eye." There are four classifications of mental imagery study but each one frequently laps over into the others. Even so, we can look for academic (teaching or scientific) projection, popular (entertainment), occult, and Christian. Excluding the first two, except as they have application, religious visualization has consequences to thinking and behavior. An occultic approach seeks to alter one's consciousness in order to pursue some goal, a destiny that may be countercultural or to obtain secret knowledge or power. Christian visualization tends more to contemplation, meditation, and prayer imagery. One type may easily slide into another and the process can be notoriously difficult to control as to method and purpose. *See also* centering prayer; cone of power; contemplative prayer movement; cult(s); divination; dream(s); dreams and visions; ecstasy; Emergent Church; Fourth Way, the; Human Potential Movement; hylomorphism; Inner Light; labyrinth walk; mantra; meditation; mind; mind control; mind science; New Age religion; New Thought Movement; occult, occultic; out-of-body experiences (OBEs); parapsychology; peace pole(s); Religious Science; remote viewing; Silva Mind Control; Transcendental Meditation; vision(s); yoga; Zen.

vital union with Christ: the understanding that the life of Christ flows into our own, renewing our inner nature (Rom. 12:2; 2 Cor. 4:16) and imparting spiritual strength. Jesus used the metaphor of the vine and the branches to explain so essential a theology as he compared himself to the vine as the source of spiritual vitality and the branches as the believers who draw sustenance from the vine (Jn. 15:4).

Vivekenanda. See Sri Ramakrishna.

vizier: high-ranking Muslim minister or political advisor. *See also* Islam.

Vladimir the Great: a.k.a. Saint Vladimir of Kiev and Prince of Novgorod (c. 958–1015). He was responsible for uniting Baltic Russian to Christianity after his conversion in 988 following a long and active life as a pagan. *See also* Russian Orthodoxy.

vocare: Latin for "to call," a weekend of spiritual retreat and renewal observed in some liturgical denominations. The purpose of the assembly is to promote "hearing God's call" for youth ages nineteen through thirty. *See also* call(ing).

vodun. See Voodoo; Voudou.

voice from the throne: the voice of God speaking to John from the heavens or from His throne (Rev. 4:1 and elsewhere). *See also* eschatology, eschatological; heaven; lightning; sounds of the rapture; thunder; voice of God; voice of rushing waters; voice out of heaven; voices of Revelation.

voice of God: God's theophanic speech that in apocalyptic style is often perceived as thunder. John, Daniel, Paul, Moses, and others all heard from God in this manner. In most instances, the primary receiver perceived discernible voices, but those nearby heard only rumbling. The voice of God is central to the theology of resurrection since that is what ignites the renewal of life at the end of earthly days: "a time is coming when all who are in their graves will hear his voice and come out—those who have done good will rise to live, and those who have done evil will rise to be condemned" (Jn. 5:24–30). *See also* "Come up here"; eschatology, eschatological; last trumpet, the; lightning; loud command, a; rapture; shout; sounds of the rapture; thunder; trumpet(s); trumpet call of the elect; voice from the throne; voice of rushing waters; voice of the archangel, the; voice out of heaven; voices of Revelation.

voice of rushing waters: the depiction of the sound of Christ's dynamic speech in Revelation 1:15. *See also* eschatology, eschatological; voice from the throne; voice of God; voice out of heaven; voices of Revelation.

voice of the archangel, the: the call of the archangel, along with the loud command of Christ and the trumpet call of God, that will call forth the living and the dead in Christ at the rapture event. *See also* angel(s); archangel(s); eschatology, eschatological; Gabriel; last trumpet, the; loud command, a; rapture; shout; sounds of the rapture; trumpet call of the elect; voice of God; voice out of heaven; voices of Revelation.

voice out of heaven: God's speech in apocalyptic language (*i.e.,* Revelation 4:1). *See also* angel(s); "Come up here"; eschatology, eschatological; heaven; lightning; last trumpet, the; loud command, a; rapture; shout; sounds of the rapture; thunder; trumpet call of the elect; voice from the throne; voice of God; voice of rushing waters; voice of the archangel, the; voices of Revelation.

voices of Revelation: those spoken commands and comments noted in the book of Revelation, some of which seem disembodied and others identified, which help carry the narrative forward. Within the prophecy, we note the voice like a trumpet (Rev. 1:10), a repeating voice calling John to the open door of heaven

(Rev. 4:1), voices of all living beings in praise (Rev. 5:3), a voice from among the four living creatures (Rev. 6:6), the cries of the multitude in white robes (Rev. 7:10), a voice from the horns of the altar (Rev. 9:13), the voice of the seven thunders (Rev. 10:4a), the voice sealing the seven thunder revelations (Rev. 10:4b), the repeated voice ordering the taking of the little scroll (Rev. 10:8), the voice commanding John to continue his prophecy (Rev. 10:11), the voice ordering the Temple measurement (Rev. 11:1), the voice calling the two faithful witnesses heavenward (Rev. 11:12), loud voices in heaven praising God (Rev. 11:15), voices celebrating Michael's victory over Satan (Rev. 12:10), a voice demanding attention to further announcements (Rev. 13:9), sounds from heaven like rushing water, harps, and thunder peals (Rev. 14:2), a voice commanding John to write further revelations (Rev. 14:13), a voice from the Temple (Rev. 16:1), a voice warning of Christ's coming (Rev. 16:5), the voice from the Temple saying, "It is done!" (Rev. 16:17), the voice from heaven ordering the faithful to evacuate Babylon (Rev. 18:4), the roar of a praising multitude in heaven (Rev. 19:1), a voice of praise from the throne of God and the Lamb (Rev. 19:5), other voices of multitudes like thunder and rushing water (Rev. 18:6), the voice announcing Christ's rule of iron (Rev. 19:15). *See also* "Come up here"; eschatology, eschatological; Gabriel; loud command, a; rapture; shout; sounds of the rapture; trumpet call of the elect; voice from the throne; voice of God; voice of rushing waters; voice of the archangel, the; voice out of heaven.

Voltaire: penname for the French Enlightenment philosopher Francois-Marie Arouet (1712–1778). By the time of his death, he was probably the most famous man in Europe. His stance against monarchies and Roman Catholicism was fanatical, and he wrote of it prolifically from the safety of Switzerland, even though he was educated by the Jesuits. In fact, Voltaire was dismissive of faith in general, sneered at the story of Christ, and considered religion as suitable only for the *canaille*—the "rabble." He was quoted as saying that he would be satisfied when the last king is strangled with the entrails of the last priest. Nevertheless, most scholars do not class him as an atheist. *See also* devil's missionary; philosophy of religion.

voluntarism: the idea that belief is simply a matter of will.

voluntary: any instrumental music of any style, but particularly the organ, used in the service of worship. *See also* liturgical year; liturgy, Christian; music.

Voluntary Human Extinction Movement: advocates of non-reproduction of the human race. The supporters do not necessarily promote murder or suicide but do believe Planet Earth can survive and thrive only if humans are not present. So far, the movement has failed to capture the strong support of the general population for some reason. *See also* eugenics; genocide; Malthus, Thomas Robert; religious organizations.

volva: the singular form of the name for a Nordic seeress; the plural being valur. The designation means "wand" or "wand wielder" as she practiced her sorcery known as *seior*. *See also See also* Aesir; Armanenschafft; Asa; Asatru; blyt; *Edda,* the; Norse and Old Germanic pantheon; seior; skald(s); storyteller, a good; Valuspa.

vomit: virulent emptying of the stomach's content through the throat and mouth. The word has a bad connotation in Scripture (as it does almost everywhere) since it imagines illness, extreme folly, or sinful behavior (2 Pe. 2:22). One of the Proverbs (Pro. 26:11) speaks of a fool repeating his folly as a dog returns to its vomit. In some Bible versions, Jonah was "vomited" from the fish's belly onto dry ground. Jesus threatened to "vomit" or "spit out" the church of Laodicea for its lukewarm spirit (Rev. 3:16). Leviticus 18:28 holds particular apocalyptic meaning: "And if you defile the land, it will vomit you out as it vomited the nations that were before you." *See also* spit.

von Daniken, Erich: a German autodidact who asserted in his variously published books in the 1970s that many miraculous terrestrial visits described in Scripture were actually landings by extraterrestrials in spaceships. He asserted that there was numerous historical, cultural, and biblical evidence that we were seeded as a race, or at least assisted in our development, by aliens. *See also* Ancient Astronaut Theory; Anunnaki; *Chariots of the Gods?*; Igigi; lulu; panspermia theory; Sitchin, Zecharia, transhumanism; "twilight of the gods"; UFO.

von Schiller, Friedrich: poet, playwright, philosopher, historian, uncertified physician (1759–1805). Schiller was reared in a religious family and he aspired to be a minister. Instead, he became a gifted man of the arts and letters, called the greatest playwright after Shakespeare. His drama *The Robbers* launched his career to overnight success and was followed by *The Ghost Seer* (a drama concerning secret societies). He and Wolfgang von Goethe (a Freemason and an Illuminati) formed a somewhat turbulent friendship but there is speculation he was influenced and sponsored by the Illuminati from the year 1784. This he denied, as well as being a Freemason. In any case, he appeared to betray the ideals of the dictatorial politics and social aims of the secret societies of the day. Napoleon and Hitler banned his work for its anti-tyrannical themes. He reputedly died of ill health but rumor persists he was poisoned by the Illuminati and secretly buried. Schiller's poem "Ode to Joy" celebrates the brotherhood of man, a work that was later set to music by Beethoven for his Ninth Symphony. It is now the anthem of the European Union reflecting the elitist view of utopian Europe and possibly the most admired composition ever produced. Schiller also wrote *Don Carlos* (an inspiration for George Lucas's *Star Wars*), *Wilhelm Tell* (inspiration for *The Lone Ranger* theme and a radical political play at the time), *Mary Stuart* (about Mary, Queen of Scots), and *The Maid of Orleans* (the story of Joan of Arc). See *also* Illuminati; music; philosophy of religion.

Voodoo: a.k.a. Voudou and other renditions, a nature religion and its practices combining pagan Native African beliefs and Roman Catholicism found mostly in the Caribbean and parts of North America. Some classify the various cults as Creole religions. Some groups are typed according to location—Louisiana Voodoo [or New Orleans Voodoo], Haitian, West African, or Dominican). Practices in each form vary slightly. Its beginnings can be traced initially to French Haiti with roots in West Africa. Interestingly, the patron saint of Ireland, Patrick, is a prominent role model. Worship centers on the supreme god *Bondye,* from the French words for "good god." Since the deity is unapproachable, Voodoo relies on manipulation of the lesser entities or spirits to alter reality through sympathetic magic. The religion involves manipulations of certain jujus or gris-gris and the practice of necromancy in some cases. Among the many variations are *Regla de Palo,* the Alakua (Abakua) Secret Society, Espiritism, Myral, and Quimbois. *See also* animism; Ayida Wedo; black arts; Bondye; bongo; Brujeria;

Candomble; caplata; conjure; conjure man; Creole (Caribbean) religions; cult(s); Dambala; execration; Ghede; gris-gris; hex; hungan; Ifa; juju; Kumina; Legba; Loa Loas; lwa; Macumba; magic, magick; mambo; *mana*; Mass of Secaire; mojo; Obeah; occult, occultic; Orisha; Oya; poppets; Quimbanda; Rastafarianism; Santeria; Shango; Spiritual Baptists; Umbanda; veve; Voudou; Waldenses; wanga; Wells, Orson; Yoruba.

Vorilhorn, Claud: a former race car driver and journalist (b. 1946) who founded the Rael Movement of 1972 and goes by the name Rael. The Raelians claim that life was seeded on the Earth by extraterrestrials. He was ordained to messiahship in 1973 after actually meeting with one of the alien overseers. *See also* Ancient Astronaut Theory; cult(s); Raelism; UFO.

Votan, Pacal: a.k.a. K'inich Janaab' Pakal (A.D. 603–683), an extraordinary seer, mathematician, and magician who was said to possess supernatural powers and divine wisdom. He was the greatest leader of the Mayan civilization who taught his people a form of meditation based on the chakras similar to the methods of Hindu mysticism. He was credited as being able to communicate with beings in the afterlife through an earth-speaking tube in his tomb called a telektonon. Votan preached about a future "transition of consciousness," which he said would occur near December 21, 2012, a time of closing for our present world-age cycle. Some have called him "Time's Special Witness" because of his emphasis on the return to living in natural time that involves more than just marking the days of our lives. *See also* Chilam-Balam; eagle and the condor, the; Inca; Itza-Maya; Katun Prophecies; Maya; Mesoamerica; *Popul Unh;* "transition of consciousness"; 2012, prophecy of; zodiac.

votive: 1. a small image or candle placed in a sacred area to honor a deceased loved one as a thanksgiving offering (a common pagan gesture), or an informal memorial using lights. Votive candles are often lighted to underscore a particular prayer or concern for another or for important emotional needs. 2. a Eucharistic celebration tied to a particular devotion. The Episcopalian tradition, for example, recites twenty-five Propers for special occasions suitable for saying an elective Mass for a specific reason. *See also* Candlemas; Eucharist; gestures; liturgical year; Propers; wake.

Voudou: [Voudoun, vodun, Vodou, and a number of alternate spellings] the name for the Voodoo pantheon of ancestral spirits elevated to contact status. The core belief is that a family head will become deified after death but continues to watch over the living. Hoodoo is similar but is classed as folk magic that makes frequent use of roots, herbs, minerals, body fluids, and the like to manipulate the supernatural. *See also* animism; Ayida Wedo; black arts; Bondye; bongo; Brujeria; Candomble; caplata; conjure; conjure man; Creole (Caribbean) religions; cult(s); Dambala; execration; Ghede; gris-gris; hex; hungan; Ifa; juju; Kumina; Legba; Loa Loas; Macumba; magic, magick; mambo; *mana*; mojo; Obeah; occult, occultic; Orisha; Oya; poppets; Quimbanda; Rastafarianism; Santeria; Shango; Spiritual Baptists; Umbanda; veve; Voodoo; wanga; Wells, Orson; Yoruba.

vouivre: a.k.a. *guivres* or *wyverns,* a winged serpent, reported by the Latin writer Pliny, known in ancient Gallic myth. It was said the snake could secrete a kind of egg that could be turned into a talisman which contained a conglomeration of all the magical creatures of the Otherworld. The creature is usually illustrated as a dragon with a gem in its head (for sight) or in its tail. She can be seen at times streaking across the sky in fiery glory. *See also* Draco; dragon; Otherworld; reptilian theory.

vow. See oath(s).

Vulcan: the Roman god of fire and blacksmithing. The Greek equivalent to Vulcan was Hephaestus. *See also* Olympian pantheon.

Vulgate: the Latin translation of the Bible completed by Jerome in A.D. 404. It contains all the modern books in the Scripture that are acceptable for the canon, along with a few Apocryphal writings deemed suitable for study. The latter section is called "deuterocanonical." The name is implied from the translation into the common, or "vulgar," tongue. *See also* Bible manuscripts; Bible translations; deuterocanonical books; Jerome; Wycliffe Bible.

vulture(s): a carrion fowl. Apocalyptic imagery sometimes portrays a vulture as part of the aftermath of a disaster. In other instances, the term is a substitute for "eagle," another carrion fowl but also a bird of prey. In the Olivet Discourse (Mt. 24:28), Jesus used the bird as an illustration of his Second Coming notoriety. As surprising as it may seem, many ancient peoples saw vultures as "soul carriers" of the deceased to the gods. *See also* animals, birds, and insects, symbology of; eagle(s); mythological beasties, elementals, monsters, and spirit animals; *psychopomps;* vultures to a carcass.

vultures to a carcass: an illustration from Jesus that draws attention to his Second Coming much as hungry vultures are drawn to a dead animal (Mt. 24:28). *See also* animals, birds, and insects, symbology of; eschatology, eschatological; lightning from east to west; vulture(s).

W

wafer: the bread for distribution and consumption during the Eucharist or Communion observance, commonly called the "host." The piece may appear as a small white and thin disk, a pill-like form, or any suitable offering. Often the bread is unleavened. *See also* Anaphora; bread; bread, unleavened; "breaking the bread"; Divine Liturgy; element(s); elevation; elugia; Eucharist; fermentum; fraction; liturgical year; liturgy, Christian; Lord's Supper; Mass; sacring; species; wine.

Wahhabism: an austere and radical doctrine of fundamentalist Islamic education centered mostly in the madrassas of Saudi Arabia. Wahhabis follow the fundamentalist teaching of Muhammad ibn Abdul Wahhab (1703–1791), who demanded a very literal interpretation of the *Qur'an*, and are excessively critical of less legalistic sects. Wahhabism is promoted by the wealth and royalty of Saudi Arabia and some 80 percent of the imams in the 3,000 mosques of the country are zealous for their extremist doctrine. The focus of learning generally emphasizes rigid Islam with heavy doses of hatred for the "infidels" of other religions, democracy, and pro-Israeli states. Terrorism is too often its most virulent product. *See also* Abode of Learning; Ahmadinejad, Mahmoud; Arabia; bin Laden, Osama; Muhammad ibn Abdul Wahhab; Islam; *jihad;* Khomeini, Grand Ayatollah Musavi; madrassa(s); *Mahdi; Qur'an;* radicalized; Rahman, Sheikh Omar; religious education; Salafi; terrorism; terrorist(s); Twelfth Imam, the.

Wailing Wall: the *Kotel* or Western Wall, the last remains of Herod's Temple. It is frequently visited by pious Jews to pray or poignantly plead for Jerusalem and for the return of the Temple, thus a "wailing" wall. Jewish lore asserts that the Kotel is never without worshipers, even in the dead of winter. Some believers affirm God dwells atop the wall as He did over the former Temples. *See also* Jerusalem, landmarks of; *Kotel;* wall(s); walls of Jerusalem.

"waiting for the Lord": an occupation of the mind and attitude that holds a godly expectancy for the return of Christ. The expression is not intended to honor a passive "ho-hum" approach to prophecy and eschatology but a proactive, exciting tension of work and meditation until the great day of his coming. Such believers are surely subjected to be recipients of the crown of righteousness. *See also* apocalyptic fervor; apocalyptic time; Christianese; crown of righteousness; eschatology, eschatological; eschaton; "soon but not yet"; things that must soon take place, the; time is near, the; timeline, eschatological; time of the Gentiles; times and the seasons, the; times of fulfillment; time, understanding (knowing) the; "which must soon (shortly) take place."

wake: a less technical term for a vigil or respectful watch in the presence of a dead body prior to burial. The term can also be extended to any commemorative or celebration of life following any observed memorial ritual or funeral. *See also* vigil; votive; watch.

Waldenses: a.k.a. Waldensians or Vaudois, dissenters of Italy and France who also influenced the Germanic states. Their most effective leader was Peter Waldo. The Waldensians had rejected some ninety-two Roman Catholic points of papal doctrine by 1389, and the movement became thoroughly evangelical. They were systematically persecuted and nearly annihilated in the 17th century by Roman Catholic authority. There are, to be sure, active Waldensian congregations in existence today. Unfortunately, the name *Vaudois* somehow became connected to Voodoo since the Waldenses were falsely accused of occultic practice. *See also* church bodies in America (typed); denomination(s), denominationalism; martyr(s); martyrdom; Voodoo; Waldo, Peter.

Waldo, Peter: a wealthy merchant from Lyons (ca. 1140–1218) credited with starting the Waldensian Christian movement in Europe. In 1177, Waldo sold all his goods (after providing for his wife) and began a following known as the "Poor Men of Lyons" who were itinerate preachers, colporteurs, given to charity, and critics of the Roman Catholic hierarchy, especially their favor for the doctrines of purgatory and transubstantiation. Waldo is also cited as the first to translate the Bible into a native tongue other than Latin. *See also* Waldenses.

"walking the aisle": an evangelical expression to describe the act of presenting oneself publically after accepting Christ's forgiveness of sin and his salvation. The penitent literally "walks the aisle" of a church or similar worship gathering, usually in response to the worship leader's invitation to do so when sensing the prompting of the Holy Spirit. Some denominations (many associated with Baptist persuasions) hold the gesture as a necessary process for church membership and is a common practice of fundamentalist revivalism. Some find the act intimidating or unnecessary, but it does tend to restrict "church hopping" and generally cements a strong bond of loyalty to the faith and the denomination. *See also* accept Christ, to; altar call; "asking Jesus into my heart"; blood of Christ; blood of the Lamb; birth from above; born again; Christianese; confession(s) of faith; conversion; gestures; "plead the blood"; profession of faith; regeneration; revivalism; "saved"; "sawdust trail, the"; turn your life [heart] over to Jesus; "washed in the blood."

walk with God: a non-theological but common expression from one who is trying to expound a personal commitment and any progress in the believer's daily association with Christ. The Christian is supposedly striving to be closer in the Holy Spirit to Jesus and to his or her fellow believers that may cause an outcry (verbally or internally) for a more comfortable yet challenging experience with the divine. It is an opportunity to explore the desire with others and an attempt to learn more about the Christian mode and manner of living in our present bodies and environment. *See also* authenticity; Christianese; "in this place"; on mission; story; will; will of God.

wall(s): the sides of a structure that provide support for the roof and shelter for the occupants. In ancient times, a wall surrounding a city was of prime importance for security. To breach a wall, or for one to bulge and crack, was a disaster (Isa. 30:13). *See also* Wailing Wall; walls of Jerusalem; walls of New Jerusalem.

Wallace, Lew: storied American lawyer, Freemason, diplomat to the Ottoman Empire, a major general of the Union Army, and governor of the New Mexico territory (1827–1905). Wallace was an accomplished writer and dedicated Christian (though not a member of any denomination), his most famous legacy being the authorship of the novel *Ben Hur: A Tale of the Christ* (published 1880). The book became a best-seller and subsequently made into movies. Wallace returned to his native Indiana upon retirement where he continued his writing of biographies, novels, and other works.

Bernie L. Calaway

wall of partition. See middle (dividing) wall of partition.

walls of Jerusalem: the protective barrier surrounding ancient Jerusalem. When walls were absent, safety for the city was lost, which prompted Nehemiah and other leaders to quickly erect or mend them. The phrase is often a metaphor for security and refuge. Both usages amplify the urgency of the Jews to erect and improve the walls of their capital whenever it was possible for them to do so. Suleiman the Magnificent expended extensive work (1537–1541) on them. *See also* Jerusalem, landmarks of; *Kotel;* wall(s); Wailing Wall; walls of New Jerusalem.

walls of New Jerusalem: an account of the walls surrounding New Jerusalem as recorded in Revelation 21:15–21. They are described there as being 144 cubits (200 feet) thick, made of jasper, and supported by twelve foundations on which were written the names of the twelve apostles. The walls contain twelve gates of pearl on which were inscribed the names of the twelve tribes of Israel. Actually, the perspectives of the walls of New Jerusalem are often distorted; the city is 1,500 miles high but the wall is only 216 feet in height. The description may be more like a decorative fence than a defensive barrier. *See also* eschatology, eschatological; foundation of New Jerusalem; gates of New Jerusalem; New Jerusalem; wall(s); walls of Jerusalem.

Walpurgis Night: a ritual witches' Sabbat, according to German tradition, held on the night before May 1. The rite is observed on the Brocken, the highest peak of the Harz Mountains. There, the witches consort with Satan and his demons. *See also* Beltane; Beltane's Eve; Church of Satan; "drawing down the moon"; esbat; Imbolc; Litha; Lughnasadh; Lummas; Mabon; Ostara; Sabbat; Samhain; Satanism; wheel of the year; Wicca; witch(es); witchcraft; Yule.

Walroff, Helena: an 18th century predictor who foresaw the last of the Roman Catholic popes fleeing Rome at the end of days, with four cardinals seeking refuge in the city of Cologne. It is unclear if the four cardinal associates are pursuing the pope or accompanying him. *See also* psychic(s).

Walvoord, John: arguably the most authoritative proponent of the dispensational views concerning the Middle East, Islam, and related eschatological concerns. He predicted an alliance of

European/Middle Eastern populations in opposition to Christ that he called the "Mediterranean Confederacy." Walvoord's book *Armageddon, Oil, and the Middle East Crisis* was important as were his prolific writings from his base at Dallas Theological Seminary. *See also* Baptists; Dallas Theological Seminary; dispensational theology; religious education.

Wandering Jew: a Christian parody with anti-Semitic basics. The term represents a rootless, confused, and indolent Jew who is doomed to wander the earth until the Second Coming judgment. One reason given for anti-Semitism is that the Jew has no permanent home and little incentive to show loyalty to the place of residence at any point. Perhaps the name arises from the fact that the Jews spent seventy years in Babylonian subjugation and some 2,000 years (A.D. 70–1948) as "wanderers among the nations." The accusation no longer applies, if it ever did, since Israel is now a nation and welcomes all Jews to settlement. See also anti-Semitic; Law of Return; slurs, religious.

wandering stars: an odd description from the brief book of Jude in the New Testament. When the writer speaks of false teachers as "wandering stars" he may be referring to the *Book of Enoch* which describes such entities as fallen angels, destined for eternal punishment. *See also Book(s) of Enoch;* devils; fallen angel(s); Jude as New Testament epistle; spirits in prison; Tartarus.

wanga: (oanga or warga), a magical charm package of silk used in Caribbean conjuring. *See also* Creole (Caribbean) religions; gris-gris; Ifa; juju; Legba; mojo; poppets; veve; Voodoo; Voudou.

Waqf: the Muslim authority in place on the Temple Mount responsible for every detail of Islamic administration and rule taking place in the area. The council is extremely antagonistic and uncompromising to Jewish concerns regarding the sacred ground and is not above inciting riots when a threat, real or perceived, is suspected. They have effectively stopped archeological digs, denied Jewish history concerning the Temple, and defiled Jewish holy places with impunity. Non-Muslims know the body more familiarly as the Supreme Muslim Religious Council. Most even deny that historical Jewish Temples once stood on the mount. *See also* anti-Semitic; Islam; religious organizations; terrorism.

ward: 1. a locally established congregation of the Church of Jesus Christ of Latter-Day Saints (Mormons). 2. a magical spell of invisibility or protection. 3. a youth or minor, normally female, under the protection of a guardian sponsor but not necessarily blood-related. *See also* apotropaic magic; cantrip; charm(s); curse(s); Church of Jesus Christ of Latter-Day Saints, the; enchantment; evil eye; execration; *geis;* hex; imprecation; magic, magick; New Age religion; occult, occultic; *pharmakeia;* psychonautics; pow-wow; skull of an ass; spell; spell names; sorcery, sorceries; stake; taboo; Voodoo; Voudou; warlock(s); Wicca; witch(es); witchcraft; wizard(s).

warden: a pair of officers in an Anglican parish council. One warden is senior and chosen by the priest; the second is junior and chosen by the congregation. Outside ecclesiology, a warden is a prison administrator, park ranger, conservation officer, college official, or other position as a community overseer. *See also* Anglicanism; vestry.

Ward, Nathaniel: (1578–1652) author of colonial New England's first legal code: the *Massachusetts Body of Liberties*. Ward was a pious Puritan, and despite the statute of freedom with his name, he ironically claimed that people such as Anabaptists, Antinomians, and others were indeed also free and that secular authorities should—"stay away from us." He also wrote the lively *The Simple Cobler of Aggawam in America*, which further chastised religious dissent. This small prophetic work, published in England in 1647, was written under Ward's pen name Theodore de la Guard. *See also* Puritanism, Puritans.

Ware, Henry: Unitarian clergyman (1764–1845), a centrist figure helping separate his sect from the Congregationalists. Ware was elected to the Harvard theological faculty, causing a split and withdrawal of conservatives who then formed Andover Theological Seminary in 1808. He fathered nineteen children, two of whom became Unitarian ministers. *See also* Unitarian Universalists.

war in heaven: the epic combat between fallen Satan and his demons in opposition to Michael and his mighty angels as reviewed in Revelation 12. The result of the clash sees Satan cast to earth where he wreaks havoc among the Tribulation population.

Although the sources of Revelation's first two "woes" are named (the fifth and sixth trumpet), the third is not mentioned. This celestial conflict could perhaps be arbitrarily termed the focus of the unnamed third woe. Celestial conflict between righteous and evil angels is also reported in Daniel (Dan. 10:12–14) and is a common eschatological theme. Consequently, most religious thought admits that celestial warfare is now raging in the heavens of which we are but minimally aware (*cf.* Daniel 10:4–14). *See also* eschatology, eschatological; heaven; Michael; war on earth.

warlock(s): a male practitioner of magic or sorcery—a wizard or male witch. The name may derive from Old English with a meaning of "deceiver." *See also* apotropaic magic; Balaam; cantrip; charm(s); curse(s); enchantment; evil eye; execration; *geis;* hex; imprecation; magic; magick; New Age religion; occult, occultic; *pharmakeia;* pow-wow; psychonautics; sorcery, sorceries; spell; spell names; taboo; Voodoo; Voudou; ward; witch(es); witchcraft; wizard(s).

Warnke, Alfred "Mike": evangelist and writer (born 1946) whose notorious publication *The Satan Seller* caused a sensation upon publication. It was not until 1991 that Warnke was exposed and debunked as a total fraud. Not only was he not a Satanist high priest, as claimed in his book, but he exaggerated his accomplishments and almost every aspect of his life and career. *See also* Church of Satan; Satanism.

War of Jewish Independence: the conflict that allowed the Jews to establish the modern state of Israel in 1948 in concert with United Nations resolutions. After bitter struggle, the independent nation has undergone many tests for its survival but has improved the land and its populations manifold. Many conservative prophecy scholars date 1948 as the beginning of Daniel's seventy weeks, thus making our generation the one to see the end of the age. *See also* Haganah; Independence Day (Jewish); seventy weeks, prophecy of, the.

War of the Sons of Light Against the Sons of Darkness: a rather officious title, also known as the *War Scroll,* the *War Rule,* or "The Rule for the Final War." The manuscript was found among the Dead Sea Scrolls and describes the ultimate apocalyptic battle between good and evil, various arrangements for the future Temple, rules for the army and weapons that will be needed, and those hymns of thanksgiving that will be sung by the victors. *See also* Copper Scroll; Dead Sea Scrolls; eschatology, eschatological; Essenes; Holy War; Isaiah Scroll; Manual of Discipline; Qumran; Shrine of the Book; Sons of Darkness; Sons of Light; War Scroll; World War III.

"War of the Worlds": a Halloween radio broadcast on October 30, 1938, produced by Orson Welles. The transmission hoax caused widespread Apocalypse-like panic among listeners at the time because some people were convinced that the planet was being invaded by aliens. *See also* Welles, Orson.

war on earth: conflict on earth in the form of battle and combat. Such conditions have always been humanity's legacy, and hostilities are predicted by Christ to increase as the end of time nears. From 1500 B.C. to 1861 A.D., there have been about 3,130 years of war but only 227 of peace. In the same period, the European nations forged more than 8,000 peace treaties that lasted, on average, about two years. In the 20th century, over 37 million people died in World War I and more than 45 million in World War II plus countless hundreds of thousands in regional conflicts. The 21st century will likely be no different. There is to be an increase in wars and rumors of war. Conflicts are graphically expressed in some of the plagues of Revelation, beginning with the red horse from the second seal named War. *See also* Holy War; war in heaven; wars of religion; World War III.

warrant of faith: the command of God that everyone everywhere is to repent of sin and believe the gospel. *See also* duty faith.

War Scroll: also called "The Rule for the Final War" or *The War of the Sons of Light Against the Sons of Darkness.* The item was a document of the Essene sect that outlined the order of the apocalyptic battle between the Sons of Light (the righteous) and the Sons of Darkness (evil persons or demons) which would come to blows in the eschatological future. *See also* Angel of Darkness; Angel of Light; Author of Mighty Deeds; Copper Scroll; Dead Sea Scrolls; eschatology, eschatological; Essenes; Holy War; Manual of Discipline; Qumran; Shrine of the Book; Sons of darkness; Sons of light; *War of the Sons of Light Against the Sons of Darkness;* Wicked Priest; World War III.

wars of religion: a kind of catch-all term for armed strife of the 16th and 17th centuries involving religious persuasions of the period. Specifically, various Protestant sects were attempting to break away from Roman Catholic domination. Rebels included the Anglicans under Henry VIII in England, the Church of Scotland led by John Knox, the Scottish Episcopal Church, French Protestants (Huguenots), Germany and Scandinavia led by Martin Luther, the Swiss under Zwingli and Calvin, various Bohemian groups, and others. *See also* Holy War; Protestant Reformation, the; war on earth.

"washed in the blood": a common expression among evangelicals or fundamentalists describing one who has accepted the personal salvation in Christ brought about by his death and resurrection. Sin has been not only covered but swept away in the sacrificial blood of the cross. *See also* accept Christ, to; altar call; "asking Jesus into my heart"; birth from above; blood of Christ; blood of the Lamb; born again; Christianese; confession(s) of faith; conversion; evangelist(s), evangelism; fishers of men; gospel; lost; "nail-scarred hands, the"; "plead the blood"; profession of faith; regeneration; "saved"; soul-winning; "turn your life [heart] over to Jesus"; "walking the aisle."

washings, ceremonial: the ritual of cleansing before an act of worship is performed. The Hebrew priests were scrupulous about hygiene and modesty before and after their ministrations before the altar. *See also* ablution; altar, washing of the; foot washing(s); *lavabo;* liturgy, Christian; Maundy Thursday.

Washington, George: America's founding father, commander-in-chief of the Continental Army, and first president. One story regarding his career claims he received an extensive revelation from a bright female angel who came to him at Valley Forge. Most of the vision revolved around the successes and failures of the newly forming United States of America and certain established countries in Europe. Throughout the experience, the angel repeatedly instructed him: "Son of the republic, look and learn." One of the few sources for this story is a republished article in the *National Tribune* (later to become *The Stars and Stripes*) in December of 1880. The writer, Wesley Bradshaw, reportedly learned the account from an old soldier in 1859 and published it. There is no definitive proof that the story is real. *See also* Founding Fathers; Lincoln, Abraham.

WASP: acronym for White Anglo-Saxon Protestant. Often the phrase is prejudicial and intended to isolate what is commonly or popularly known in some circles to be the majority class in American society. *See also* Christianese; Protestantism, Protestants; slurs, religious.

watch: 1. a period of time marking off the night whereby the on-time duties of guards or sentries could be regulated. 2. a function or tradition of waiting reverently in the presence of a deceased person until burial procedures can be completed. **3.** a maxim for the coming of Jesus by which we are admonished to diligently anticipate or "watch" the signs of the times so as not to be surprised or ashamed at Christ's coming. Greek words in Scripture urge us to heed *blepete* as *Watch!* and *gregoreite* as *Be Vigilant! See also* eschatology, eschatological; *gregoreo*; "until he comes"; vigil; wake; watchmen.

watchblogger(s): or podcaster, one who uses Internet blogging to advance some particular religious or political agenda. Many are primarily designed to discredit, smear, or otherwise defame one or another religious persuasion.

watcher of men: a name for the punishing God voiced by Job amid his physical and mental anguish (Job 7:20). *See also* Judge, the; Judge, the righteous; Lawgiver and Judge; names (titles) for God.

Watchers, the: 1. holy ones (angels) in Daniel. 2. in pseudepigraphal literature, the Watchers are usually considered to be evil angels or Ben Elohim, most often referring to those "sons of God" who introduced giants on the land by having sexual intercourse with mortal women (Gen. 6:1–4). Some of the Aramaic texts (designated there as the *Irin*) even name their leaders and report there were no less than three races of the beings. "The Book of the Watcher" in *1 Enoch* 6–16 seems to be an elaboration of that story. The pseudepigraphal *Secrets of Enoch* call them "Gorigori." Gibborim also names "The Mighty or Majestic Ones" as traitorous angels who descended from heaven to mate with human women. Some copies of such expositions were found among the Essene scrolls, but we do not know if the Qumran residents were believers or merely readers or composers of the accounts of the Watchers. *See also* Amalek, Amalekites; Anak; angel(s); *Animal Apocalypse, The;* Anunnaki; Azazel; Bene Elohim; *Book(s) of Enoch;* Book of Giants;

Chashmallim; Chayoth; Cherub, Cherubim; Cyclopes; demon(s), demonic; devils; divine council; *elohim;* fallen angel(s); Fir Bolg; "Five Satans, the"; flood; Fomorians; frost giants; Gadreel; Galgallim; *Genesis Apocryphon;* giant(s); *Gobekli Tepe;* Gregori; Guardians; Haran; holy ones; Igigi; Ishim; *Jubilees, Book of;* Laestrygonians; lulu; Molech; Mount Hermon; Naamah; Nephilim; Noah; Oannes and the Seven Sages; Ophanim; Orpah; panspermia theory; Peri; Semyaza; Seraph, Seraphim; Shinar; Sibyl(s); sin (rebellion) of the angels; thrones; Titans; transhumanism.

watchman: a sentinel, one who stands guard. More pointedly to eschatology, the watchman is a common Old Testament name for a prophet (*i.e.* Hosea 9:8, Isaiah 21:8, Habakkuk 2:1, Ezekiel 33:1–9, and Jeremiah 6:17–19). Ezekiel was particularly charged to be a watchman who was responsible for warning his nation of God's pending wrath (Ezk. 33) around the time of the Babylonian invasion. God applied the injunction that a watchman is to unfailingly report danger. If the people heeded his warning, all would be well with both the responsible guard and the people. If the populace refused to heed the warning, however, those so careless would be destroyed but the prophet held guiltless. *See also Chozeh;* Ezekiel as prophet; interpreter; *Kohen; Lewi;* man of God; man of the Spirit; messenger of Yahweh; *Nabhi'; Ro'eh;* servant of Yahweh; servants, my; *Shamar;* watch.

Watchnight: a New Year's Eve service of worship in a large number of denominations and faith practices. The celebrations began in 1864 and (according to legend) accommodated the slaves who stayed up all night to hear the Emancipation Proclamation. *See also* feasts and special days of Protestantism; liturgical year; liturgy, Christian.

Watch Tower Bible and Tract Society (WTBTS): the publishing and propaganda arm of the Jehovah's Witnesses sect. The organization was, and sometimes is, substituted as a name for the organization itself because it consists of the powerful governing body as well as its prodigious printing agency. *See also* Jehovah's Witnesses; New World Translation; religious organizations; Russell, Charles Taze; Rutherford, J. F.; sect(s).

watchtower of the flock: a millennial name for Jerusalem (*e.g.,* Micah 4:8). *See also* Jerusalem as city; millennial worship.

water(s): the liquid substance so necessary to life and civilization. In apocalyptic language, waters (or seas) frequently represent peoples, multitudes, nations, or languages (as in Revelation 17:15). The great harlot of Revelation is said to be "sitting on many waters," which, in this case, probably symbolizes the extensive and lucrative trade, commerce, and corrupted moral imports from the world over. The apostle Peter once admonished his readers (2 Pe. 3:5–6) to be faithful in their belief and conduct because the earth was created from water and was once destroyed by it; the next devastation, he added, would be by fire. Both salt and freshwater are depicted in Revelation as being fouled on occasion as punishment from God. In other instances, water in flood stage can indicate disaster or a barrier to travel (as in Revelation 9:13–14; 12:15). In a more positive aspect, water represented refreshment and fruitfulness, cleansing (both hygienic bathing and ritual action), and life itself (Jn. 4:14 Isa. 8:6), and was even a symbol for the Holy Spirit. The writer of Hebrews used pure water as a metaphor for believers who are cleansed from a guilty conscience, a clear reference to ancient Judaism's ritual sacrificial system. *See also* angel of the waters; blood; fire; fountain; Holy Spirit; names (titles) for the Holy Spirit; sea(s); spirit; Spirit, the water, and the blood, the; water, living; water, the rising; waves, raging.

water, cup of cold: a minor but worthy gift one offers to another in need of relief to the body or spirit. Jesus noted that the least of all kindnesses does not go unnoticed by the Father. To offer a cup of water to a thirsty traveler or guest was the minimum mark of hospitality but no less important than any other good work. *See also* hospitality.

water, living: Jesus' term for the refreshing or sustaining power of the believer's life in him (Jn. 4:10–11; Rev. 7:17). *See also* fountain; spring of living water; water(s); water of life; water, the rising.

water of affliction: a metaphor for suffering, sometimes introduced by God Himself (Jer. 30:21), and logically associated with the "bread of affliction." *See also* bread of affliction; bread of despair; tear(s); thorn in the flesh; trial(s); vale of tears; water, the rising; waves, raging.

water of jealousy: an ordeal recorded as a Law of Moses (Num. 5:11–25) in which a woman suspected of infidelity was forced to drink water mixed with dust from the tabernacle floor. If she did not become ill, she was pronounced innocent. *See also* ordeal(s).

water of life: a metaphor for the gospel—the refreshing good news of salvation. Revelation 21:6 offers an appeal from God to any who thirst to partake of the water of life without cost. Jesus told the woman of Sychar that he himself was the "living water" that leads to eternal life (Jn. 4:1–26). *See also* fountain; names (titles) for Jesus; river of life, the; spring of living water; water, living; water, the rising; woman at the well.

water of purification: a concoction made from the ashes of the red heifer that was needed to sanctify priests, holy utensils, and the Temples or tabernacle (Num. 19). The ashes were mixed with water, scarlet thread, cedar, and hyssop, then sprinkled on the object to be ritually cleansed. If another Jewish Temple is to be erected in Jerusalem, the water of purification will be necessary. A pure-bred heifer is the only item not readily available. *See also* ashes of the red heifer.

waters of separation: or "waters of impurity" (Num. 19:11-16)—a rite of ceremonial cleansing. The ritual purified an Israelite after touching a dead body and has implications for the Christian cleansing in Christ. *See also* ordeal(s).

water, the rising: Ezekiel's vision (Ezk. 47:1–12) of water emanating from the threshold of the Temple and gradually rising until it enters the sea. Along the way, the river produces abundant flora and fauna. The sight is a millennial portrait of splendor and bounty and one of the more pleasant aspects of the New Jerusalem (Rev. 22:1–2). Floods could also be a sign of danger or calamity (Hab. 3:8–10). *See also* New Jerusalem; water, living; water(s); water of life.

water witch: unscientific name for a person (of either sex) who possesses a dowsing ability. Those individuals use diving rods or a forked stick to find underground water or valuable minerals. *See also* divination; diving stick; rhabdomancy.

Watson, John Broadus: American psychologist (1878–1958) and a strong advocate of the philosophy known as Behaviorism. He was subjected to intense Baptist training by his mother but rejected religion completely and his youth was decidedly misspent. He even entered an adulterous affair with one of his undergraduates as a teacher. It may not be surprising, then, that his philosophy centered on emotions and outward behaviors. *See also* Behaviorism.

Watts, Isaac: English nonconformist minister (from a non-conformist stance), hymnwriter, and theologian called the "Father of English Hymnology" (1674–1748). Finding the music in his church decidedly lacking, he was challenged by his father to do better. This he did by producing over 750 hymns, many translated into other languages. His beloved "When I Survey the Wondrous Cross" has been called the greatest in the English language by the Poetry Foundation and the Christmas carol "Joy to the World" is a premier favorite, one in which the author intended to honor the Second Coming of Christ—not his nativity. *See also* carol(s); hymn; music.

Wat Tyler's Rebellion: a bloody revolt in 1381 by English workers and farmers against the oppressive gentry and clergy of the day. The outbreak was essentially the extension of the Peasants' Revolt from continental Europe into England. The rebels marched in protest of a poll tax imposed upon them and demanded economic reform. Their leader, Wat Tyler, was killed by King Richard II's soldiers during peace negotiations. *See also* Peasants' Revolt.

waves, raging: turmoil of the seas. Jude 13 calls insubstantial disciples as being shiftless as the rolling sea. *See also* sea(s); water(s).

wax: an impressionable substance used for candle making, sealing letters, and other uses. In the Old Testament, the implication can be a metaphor for God's power as He is capable of melting mountains like wax (Ps. 97:5). The symbol is fitting wherever it is used because wax is so insubstantial to heat.

way: a route to travel (Ex. 13:21) or a manner in which to live one's life (1 Sam. 12:23; Ps. 18:30). *See also* Way, the; Way of the Cross.

Way International, The. See The Way International.

Way of Holiness, the: Isaiah's description of the promised millennial highway through the former desert, terminating in restored Jerusalem (Isa. 35:8). The reference not only shows the flourishing of the deserted land but emphasizes the safety and sanctity of travelers on their joyful journey to the city of God. The road may be more figurative than literal. Later, the verse calls it "that" way. *See also* way to heaven.

Way of Sorrows. See *Via Dolorosa*.

Way of the Cross: a common phrase for the manner of life of some struggling, persecuted, or troubled Christians in their attempt to please God with their efforts and behavior. See *also* stations of the cross; Way, the; *Via Dolorosa*; way.

wayside pulpit: slang term for an outdoor church bulletin board. The structure presents useful information about the church and often carries some clever or teasing comment to encourage attendance.

Way, the: an early name for the Christian movement as represented in Acts 9:2. At the time, the movement was seen as a cult by most of the Roman population. *See also* Christian(s); Church; cult(s); *koinonia;* Way of the Cross.

way, the truth, and the life, the: one of Christ's names for himself and his personal summary of the Christian life and how it should be displayed (Jn. 14:6). Though it has many facets of understanding, at least part of the core meaning tells us the life of a believer should emphasize exceptional behavior, theological veracity, and the facility to enjoy the very uniqueness of the Christian faith. *See also* names (titles) for Jesus.

way to heaven: how one arrives in heaven by eternal decisions made. The phrase may also represent a person's lifestyle and behavior as the attempt is made to follow the demands of Christianity. Job declared that ultimately the way is via death (Job 16:22) as is common to us all. *See also* cardinal virtues; conscience; deontology; ethics; scruples; Way of Holiness, the.

wealth: great riches. Revelation 18 and elsewhere declare that excessive wealth, if used indulgently or selfishly, can be a cause of divine destruction. Some translations of Revelation 18:14 read Secular (Commercial) Babylon's ignominy as "the wealth of her sensuality," implying indolent luxury or gluttony. Paul insisted (1 Tim. 6:10) that the love of money is the root of evil. Even so, much of the ancient world looked upon an individual's collection of luxury items as a sign of divine favor usually measured in animals, rich clothing, excess food, jewels, gold, and the like. *See also* amber; bronze; electrum; fat, fatness; gem(s); gold; gold, frankincense, and myrrh; incense; ivory; *lapis lazuli;* mammon; onyx; pearl(s); prosperity religions; sapphire; silver; spices; stones, fiery.

"wearable tech": a term used by some apocalypticists, religionists, and scientists for microchips, biochips, nano-chips, and the like which might be worn with clothes, personal articles, or in our bodies. Such devices could trace our habits and movements and useful to the New World Order. Already we know of finger imaging, voice identification, facial recognition, iris scans, and VeriChips. Some have advanced that this same technology will be so despised as personally invasive in the latter days that it will speed the advance of the populations to revert to paganism and uncivilized idolatry. However, given society's fascination with social media and all forms of high technology, that turn of events seems unlikely. *See also* Christianese; eschatology, eschatological; New World Order, the (NWO); soul catcher; Web-Bot.

Web-Bot: a present-day sophisticated computer program said to isolate a significant number of prophetic events. The design was originally intended as a tool for forecasting favorable stock market opportunities but has since evolved into a complex system of prediction. The software utilizes specified "spiders" or "agents" designed to capture keywords or phrases on the World Wide Web and project them into data form that can be interpreted as oracular in some manner with a far-reaching scope and blazing speed. The inventor of the system is anonymous and simply called himself "Cliff." Whether the process has validity is open to question at this point but is generally rejected by most investigators; others say that the electronic predictions are similar to the predictions of the Hopi, Mayans, and Nostradamus but may have value. *See also* Bible Code; Blue Star prophecy; eschatology, eschatological; Maya; Nostradamus; PC; sect(s); "wearable tech"; Wiener, Norbert.

wedding supper of the Lamb. See marriage supper of the Lamb.

weed(s): noxious or wild plants that hinder the growth of crops. The parable of the sower (Mk. 4:1–20) and the parable of the weeds (Mt. 13:24–30, 36–43) illustrate the perils of presenting and living the gospel. The King James Version calls the plants "tares." *See also* flora, fruit, and grain, symbology of; parable(s); parables of Matthew 13; parables of the New Testament.

Wee Free: members of the Free Church of Scotland who refused to merge with the United Presbyterians. They formed the Free Church of Scotland in 1900. *See also* Presbyterians.

Week of Prayer for Christian Unity: an international ecumenical plea for Christian unity of fellowship worldwide. In the West, the observance is January 18–25, making it an octave observance for the churches. *See also* ecumenism; feasts and special days of high liturgy faiths; feasts and special days of Protestantism; National Council of Churches; National Day of Prayer; World Council of Churches.

Weeks, Festival of. See Pentecost.

weeks of years. See seventy weeks, the.

Weems, Mason Locke: an Anglican clergyman (1759–1825) who was far left of the usual politics of the Church of England, both in its administration and beliefs. Weems was a businessman keen to make a sale and used curious antics to make it so. He was a puppeteer, peddler, fiddle player, and was known for his preaching and performances from a wagon. He is also well-known for his semi-orthodox biography of George Washington called *Life and Memorable Actions of George Washington* (1800). It was here that he invented the fictional story of George Washington chopping down his father's cherry tree. By the time of his death, his writings were best-sellers, with the Washington novel alone running through fifty-nine editions. *See also* Church of England; evangelist(s), evangelism.

Weinland, Ronald: a Church of God minister who claimed to have been made a prophet by an act of God in 1997. His two main writings, *The Prophesied End time* and *2008: God's Final Witness,* set out his program of the end of days. Weinland's doctrine is convoluted as it interprets the book of Revelation but can be summarized by the following assertions: 1. the end of the world would happen on May 27, 2011, (changed to May 27, 2012), 2. the final of the seven seals was broken in 2008, 3. Weinland himself is to be one of the two great witnesses of Revelation 11. (He does not know, or has not revealed, his partner of that time.), 4. he has knowledge of the contents of the secret seven thunder revelations (Rev. 10:4), 5. the originator of the Worldwide Church of God, Herbert W. Armstrong, was the second prophet to come among us in the spirit of Elijah. (John the Baptist was the first.), 6. the perversions of all mainline churches are pervasive and incurable, 7. the proper day of worship is the Saturday Sabbath (in compliance with Seventh-Day Adventism). Even a brief perusal of Weinland's writings will likely lead the reader to suggest that his commentary could be a bit more palatable with a spoonful of humility and another of compassion. *See also* Armstrong, Herbert W.; Church of God.

Weishaupt, Adam: founder of the Illuminati society in the year 1776. Many occult and cultic experts view Weishaupt (probably correctly) as a rather late emanation in a series of mystery schools and secret societies present in our world from ancient times. *See also* Illuminati; Order of Perfectibilists.

welcome, a rich: the promise to believers shaping the solid maxim that those who practice the earned essence of love will be rewarded in heaven (2 Pe. 1:10–11). *See also bema;* crown(s); crown of glory; crown of incorruption; crown of life; crown of rejoicing; crown of rejoicing; crown of righteousness; judgment seat of Christ; reward(s) in heaven; robe, crown, and throne.

Weld, Theodore Dwight: clergyman and leading abolitionist (1803–1895), the consummate orator, protest organizer, and pamphleteer. Weld's admirers called him "eloquent as an angel and powerful as thunder." In doing so, they recognized a modest man who spoke effectively until he lost his voice (but only to rural audiences), used pseudonyms for his tracts, and sought no public acclaim. One of his works, *American Slavery as It Is: Testimony of a Thousand Witnesses,* was credited to have influenced Harriet Beecher Stowe's *Uncle Tom's Cabin.* Weld was a member of Charles G. Finney's "holy band" of Presbyterian revivalists and traveled throughout eastern New York preaching salvation, temperance, moral reform, the nobility of manual labor, and emancipation. *See also* Beecher, Lyman; Congregationalists; evangelist(s), evangelism; Finney, Charles Grandison; revivalism; slave, slavery.

welkin: olde English word for the vault of the firmament, the sky, or more specifically, heaven. *See also* heaven; Shamash.

Welles, Orson: accomplished filmmaker, actor, screenwriter, and movie director (May 6, 1915-October 10, 1985). Welles is perhaps remembered best for his innovative theatrical approach to acting and directing. His adaptation of H. G. Wells's novel *War of the Worlds* was broadcast, without caveat attached to the transmission, on Halloween of 1938, causing widespread panic among much of his radio audience who were convinced the Earth was being invaded by aliens or by Nazi Germany at that time. Welles was an unabashed believer in the powers of the occult, especially witchcraft and the Voodoo-type rituals typically found in the Caribbean and Brazilian regions. He claimed that the failure of his last documentary, entitled "It's All True," was caused by an evil spell cast by a Brazilian witch doctor. He felt the same for the collapse of his movie fortunes soon after. *See also* Voodoo; "War of the Worlds."

Wellhausen, Julius: German scholar (May 17, 1844–January 7, 1918) who originated the so-called "documentary hypothesis." Other terms for the same formula are named the J.E.P.D. hypothesis or the Graf-Wellhausen theory, which, according to the system, can reveal various sources for the roots of the writings of the Old Testament Pentateuch. The structure and language of the various paradigms will reveal themselves as written early or late and are modified by a scribe. Those appearing with "J" name Jehovah somewhere in the text; "E" represents the name Elohim; a priestly code shows under "P", and "D" surveys the Deuternonomist style. *See also* documentary hypothesis; Lutheran Church; redaction.

Well of Souls: a cave beneath and just east of the Dome of the Rock shrine. There, Muslims believe, lie some hairs from Mohammed's beard and a "place of prayer" where the dead meet twice a week to pray. *See also* Islam; Jerusalem, landmarks of; shrine(s).

Well of Zam-Zam: a spring or fountain of water located in Arabia near Mecca, said to be the spot where God provided water for the exiled Hagar and her son Ishmael. Taking it as a sign, mother and son settled there where Ishmael later became the father of the great Northern Arabian tribes. Muslims visit the site, usually in conjunction with the *Hajj* pilgrimage. *See also* Arabia; Islam; *Ka'bah*; Mecca; pilgrimage; Pillars of Mina, the Sacred; shrine(s).

Wells, H. G.: British novelist and writer (1866–1946) centered on political and social problems, and even some literature with apocalyptic overtones. He believed that God is powerless (finite) so He and man must work together to combat evil. Success by any standard like that is problematic at best. Wells was a strong supporter of the League of Nations, and a number of his eschatological writings pertain to the intellectual basics of that organization. Such works include: *Anticipations* (1900), *The Shape of Things to Come* (1933 and adapted to the screen in 1936), and *In the Fourth Year* (1918).

Wells's most apocalyptic work may be *The New World Order* published in 1940. His novel *War of the Worlds* was later tailored by Orson Welles and broadcast on radio in 1938. Wells expected that the human race will experience apocalyptic war if modern trends continue. According to his so-called guiding spirit, World War III will spring from an incident erupting in Basra, Iraq. *See also* "War of the Words"; New World Order, the (NWO).

Wenceslaus I, King: or Vaclav the Good to the Czechs, the patron saint of Bohemia (c. 903–935). As a ruler of his German duchy and a man, he was noted for his piety, generosity, virginity, and his love for the Latin rite of his church. He was murdered by his brother Boleslaw and the body was hacked to pieces. Later, his bones were removed to the Church of Saint Vitas in Prague as relics. Most know of him from the famous Christmas carol, "Good King Wenceslaus," written by Englishmen John Mason Neale and Thomas Helmore in 1853. The famous Wenceslaus Bible is from his era but sponsored by Wenceslaus IV, one of the most beautiful Scripture texts ever produced because of its good German translation and magnificent illuminations. *See also* king(s); liturgical year; martyr(s); Roman Catholic Church.

Weor, Samael Aun: *nee* Victor Manuel Gomez Rodriquez (1917–1977). Weor formed the Universal Christian Gnostic Movement, which he claimed was "the most powerful movement ever founded." Being a false Messiah, he claimed that he would be resurrected by the year 1978, and that the earth will be destroyed by the giant planet Hercolubus. *See also* cult(s); Hercolubus.

Werdin, Otranto: a 13th century abbot (d. 1279) who predicted that a great monarch and a great pope will arise in the last days and are to precede the advent of the Antichrist. Whether the two positions are separate individuals or both offices are combined in one person is not clear. Such dual descriptions of the secular and ecclesiastical are a sort of running theme in many papal prophecies. *See also* abbot; Roman Catholic Church.

Wesleyan Church: a Protestant denomination in the holiness Methodist tradition. The movement was officially organized in 1843 growing from the doctrinal roots of John and Charles Wesley. *See also* church bodies in America (typed); Draper, John Williams; Wesley, Charles and John.

Wesleyan Quadrilateral: John Wesley's understanding that scriptural authority—acting in accord with church history, critical thinking, and relevant experience—must be interdependent in order to form a good theology. For Wesley, religious authority was more complex than simple acceptance or mental agreement. To be authentic, doctrinal development must spring from four components: scripture itself and its truth, tradition (church history), reason, and Christian experience—the personal element. *See also* confession(s) of faith; Credo; creed(s); Methodists; Wesley, Charles and John.

Wesley, Charles and John: evangelists and church organizers active in England and America in the early 1800s. John (1703–1791) was famous as one who described himself as reborn in repentance and understanding of the gospel and as one who perfected the art of revivalism. In this, he could have only been outdone by his solid, but not entirely trouble-free, friendship with George Whitefield. John attributed his most profound spiritual experience, however, to the influence of courageous Moravians he encountered during a storm at sea while crossing to the Georgia colony. He and Charles (four years his junior) organized systematic Bible studies, formed and facilitated the famous Holy Club at Oxford, and developed itinerate preaching styles that quickly came to be known as "Methodism." John's biography reveals he was one of nineteen children born to Samuel Wesley and his indomitable wife, Susanna, who secured for their children a strong religious upbringing. He was converted, or "born again," at an outdoor preaching fest on Aldersgate Street in London where, he relates, he found his heart "strangely warmed," and offered his most famous sermon, "Free Grace," near Bristol on April 29, 1739. It was then he castigated the doctrine of predestination. Wesley's preaching style was more direct and personal than what was prevalent in the coolness and sterility of the Church of England and thus appealed to the masses. He finished his career having addressed over 40,000 sermons (about fifteen per day) and traveling horseback over 220,000 miles. His eschatological stance shows through in his book *Antichrist and His Ten Kingdoms*, which names the pope as an Antichrist, although he leaves room for a future one as well. John's brother Charles (1707–1788) was a prolific hymn writer (over 6,000 are credited to him) including

"O For a Thousand Tongues," "Love Divine, All Loves Excelling," and many other evangelical favorites. Both men could be said to represent the modern prophetic calling as few others could. Charles was said to have predicted the end of the age in1794, and John saw the Millennium beginning in 1836. *See also* circuit riders; evangelist(s), evangelism; Great Awakenings, the; Holy Club, the; Methodists; missions, missionaries; Moravian Church; music; Restoration Movement in America; revivalism; Sunday school(s); Wesleyan Church; Wesleyan Quadrilateral; Whitefield, George.

West Bank: old Samaria and Judea—the present-day territorial state of Israel occupied mostly by Palestinians. The site is on the west bank of the Jordan River and not the east, now known as Transjordan. The settlements there are a near-constant center of Israeli/Palestinian conflict. *See also* division of Israel; forest of the south; Galilee; Gilead; Idumean, Idumean(s); Israel; Judah; Judea; Kinneret; Palestine; Palestinians; *nakba*; provinces of Palestine; Samaria; Transjordan.

Westboro Baptist Church: perhaps the most notorious of America's radical fundamentalist Christians located in Topeka, Kansas. Numbering around 100 members, the group is convinced they alone will inherit heaven while the remaining seven billion of us are hell-bound. They are prone to civil demonstrations, even disrupting burials in veteran's cemeteries. Westboro's controversial founder, Fred Phelps (infamous for his "God Hates Fags" rallies), died in 2014 at the age of eighty-four. *See also* Baptists; denomination(s), denominationalism; sect(s).

Western Gate: an entrance to the Temple complex discovered by archeologists whom many believe once led to the Holy of Holies. Arabs demolished the opening and sealed it with concrete, forcing the excavations to cease. *See also* Beautiful Gate; Eastern Gate; gates of Jerusalem and the Temple; Golden Gate; Jerusalem, landmarks of.

western sea, the: the Mediterranean (*i.e.,* Zechariah 14:8).

Western Wall, the. See *Kotel;* Wailing Wall.

Westminster Abbey: the magnificent London church established by Edward the Confessor in A.D. 1065. The structure was completed only one week before the death of the king and is still the largest church in northern Europe. It has been the witness to the coronation of every English monarch since its construction. Most label it "the church of the English people." *See also* church; Edward the Confessor.

Westminster Confession: the documented explanation of Protestant Calvinist church doctrine written in 1643. There, the book of Revelation was rejected as part of the canon, according to Article 3, but the document did finger the Roman pope as the Antichrist. The "Larger Catechism" of that document expresses hope for the triumph of righteousness and pressed the surety of the crushing of Satan's kingdom. The "Shorter Catechism" of the same source clearly summarizes the true nature and purpose of prophecy: "Man's chief end is to glorify God, and to enjoy him forever." *See also* Calvinism; Calvin, John; confession(s) of faith; Confessions of 1560; Credo; creed(s); Five-Point Calvinism; Law, the; Presbyterians; Reformed Churches; "stews."

West, Samuel: colonial preacher and patriot (1730–1807), known affectionately as "Pater West." He was a sort of "absent-minded professor" instead of a busy New England pastor but a brilliant theologian and missionary to the Mashpee Indians near his home in Yarmouth, Massachusetts. He often challenged Jonathan Edwards from his more liberal theological viewpoint. West joined the Continental Army as a chaplain where he served, not only as a patriot minister, but a capable decoder of classified documents. Perhaps his equally valuable talents were used in the Massachusetts Constitutional Convention after the war. *See also* chaplain(s); clergy patriots.

What would Jesus do?: a popular phrase of the 1990s, often abbreviated as WWJD, as a moral reminder for some Christians to follow the precepts of Christ in their behavior as closely as possible. The logo appeared everywhere—on tie bars, bumper stickers, jewelry, and many other advertising outlets. The expression lost permanence, perhaps because such a question is often imponderable. The expression is reportedly a watchword for the Mormon faithful. *See also* Christianese.

Wheatley, Phillis: Afro-American poet (ca. 1755–1784), the first female of her race to gain real recognition in America. Wheatley was sold as a slave to John Wheatley of Boston where her intellectual and writing skills were encouraged by Wheatley's wife. Her first compositions included odes to Harvard College, George III, and the revivalist George Whitefield. Later in London, more success was evident, even in court. Her work, *Poems on Various Subjects, Religious and Moral* (1773) is typical of her straightforward, conventional style. *See also* Afro-American theology; Whitefield, George.

Wheelock, Eleazar: a Congregational minister (1711–1779) and master revivalist in the 1730s. Wheelock was equally interested in education and tutored young men for the ministry, including Samson Occom (Native American preacher). He established Dartmouth College in honor of his patron, the Earl of Dartmouth. Wheelock continued to guide the new school through the Revolutionary War, then passed its leadership to his son John. *See also* Congregationalists; evangelists, evangelism; Occom, Samson; religious education; revivalism.

Wheel of Existence: the process of earthly life (an Eastern concept) that results in continued reincarnation for those who choose it. Escape from the wheel was difficult but desirable to some. The Orphic called it the Circle of Necessity, while others read it as the Wheel of Rebirth. *See also* Wheel of Life; Wheel of Time, the.

Wheel of Life: a somewhat complex Buddhist explanation of the universe and the endless cycle of death and rebirth in which humans are trapped unless they follow the precepts of Buddha (the Middle Way). Buddhism insists that everything arises because of preexisting conditions and causes (called "interconnectedness"). The aim is to create conditions that replace angst and suffering with contentment and happiness. The theory is that if we could find links and change them we could alter our lives. The wheel explores those possibilities in the form of an icon or pictograph. The picture looks like a wheel with the traditional hub, spokes, and rim but being held in the jaws of a fierce demon representing death. The center of the wheel pictures a rooster, a snake, and a pig which equate to greed, hatred, and ignorance and are the root of our misery. Surrounding the hub is a circle filled with humans either ascending or descending through the realms as they try to escape to a better place. The outer rim is important because it holds the "links" called *nidanas* (there are twelve). The link between the seventh and eighth realm is crucial because it can be a breaking point to spring away from spiritual ignorance into suffering—between pain and pleasure. If we follow the Eightfold Noble Path it will lead to Nirvana. Not to break free is to continue the frustrating cycle of life, death, and rebirth. *See also* Buddhism; Wheel of Existence; Wheel of Time, the.

wheel of the year: the Wiccan designation of sacred days celebrating its naturalistic roots. The special dates are based on beliefs and customs of the cycles of life, the moon, and especially the seasons, marking them with eight "sabbats." The primary sabbats fall on or near traditional equinoxes of the sun; the others occur on "cross-quarter" days near the first of February, May, August, and November. *See also* Beltane; Beltane's Eve; Imbolc; Lammas; Litha; Lughnasadh; Mabon; Ostara; Sabbat; Samhain; Walpurgis Night; Wicca; Yule.

Wheel of Time, the: or the Wheel of Life, a Buddhist concept involving a "Wheel of Time" (the *Kalachakra*), which cycles through the ages like the yugas of Hinduism. The belief is that the Buddha will become incarnate as Lord Maitreya ("the Buddha who returns") at the end of the present cycle. The phrase also occurs in references to some other Eastern religions and certain Cherokee eschatological predictions. *See also* Buddhism; Gautama Buddha; Rattlesnake Prophecy, the; Wheel of Existence; Wheel of Life.

when Jesus Christ is revealed: a description from Peter naming the Second Appearing of the savior (1 Pe. 1:7). *See also* eschatology, eschatological; *Parousia;* Second Coming.

"where angels fear to tread": a contraction of the saying: "Fools rush in where angels fear to tread," a poetic way of saying that persons lacking wisdom or discretion are prone to attempt acts that the wise person would logically avoid. Contrary to the popular belief that the quote is from Shakespeare, it actually derives from Alexander Pope in his *Essay on Criticism. See also* fool; Raca.

where Satan has his throne: an address to the church at Pergamum (Rev. 2:13) that commends the fellowship for not succumbing to the evil in their midst. The congregation remained true to Christ even though Pergamum was a wicked city—even a headquarters of a sort for Satanic infiltration. *See also* Pergamum; Satan's throne; Sebasterion.

"which must soon (shortly) take place": the phrase in Revelation 1:1 promising the Lord's soon return. It is unclear, wherever the phrase is found, whether the meaning implies the return of the Lord will be soon in time or will proceed quickly once the process begins. If the Greek identifier is *en tachi*, the context may favor the latter. If the word is *kairos*, it may suggest the former. *See also* due time, in; *en takhei;* eschatology, eschatological; eschaton; "I am coming soon"; *kairos; kronos;* "soon but not yet"; *telos;* things that must soon take place, the.

whip: a flexible length of leather or other material used for prodding, punishment, or purgation. God describes Himself at one point (Isa. 10:26–34) as the "whip" of nations antagonistic to Israel on the day of deliverance. Jesus even used a handmade one to chase away the thieving money changers in the Temple (Mt. 21:12–13). Midian at the rock of Oreb, with Aiath, Migron, Micmash, Geba, Ramah, Gibeah, Gallim, Laishah, Gebim, Nob, and Lebanon are named as locales that will offer no relief or sanctuary for the inhabitants of Jerusalem when the remnant of Israel is restored. Instead, they will be thrashed with the rod or whip of God as He had done previously to Egypt. Jesus was whipped repeatedly before his crucifixion as were Paul and many of the apostles and believers under the auspices of the Roman Empire. *See also* cross; curses of Isaiah; flagrum; rod.

Whirling Dervishes: an order of Sufi Muslims called the Mevlevi, noted for their Sama ceremony of the spinning dance. The fast and continuing whirling is said to praise Allah (*dhikr*). The sect began in Turkey under the leadership of Jalal ad-din Muhammad Balkhi-Rumi in the 13th century. The practice today is considered a humanitarian cultural treasure, as well as a religion. *See also* dance; Islam; Sufi.

Whisenant, Edgar: former NASA engineer and author of *88 Reasons Why the Rapture Will Be in 1988*. Whisenant's idea was that the Tribulation would commence on October 3, 1988, which was *Rosh Hashanah*, the first day of the Jewish new year and that the battle of Armageddon would erupt seven years later. His prediction of the end was on September 11 and 13, but he revised his prediction by one year to September 30, 1989, after the earlier dates failed.

Whitby, Daniel: a strong supporter of the doctrine of postmillennialism (1638–1726). He was a Unitarian minister and is attributed to be the scholar who formulated the basic principles of the theory. All Reconstructionists, theonomists, and believers in dominion theology are postmillennialists and derive much of their beliefs from Whitby. *See also* dominion theology; postmillennial, postmillennialism; Reconstructionism; replacement theology; theonomy; Unitarian Universalists.

white: color without visible hue. White may be the most unique of the metaphorical colors in religious imagery—the opposite of dark. White light is actually a mixture of the primary colors— red, yellow, and blue, along with the secondary ones—orange, green, and purple. Objects appear as the colors they reflect while all the others are absorbed. Shades and variations are almost endless. Usually, we think of white as representing something wholesome—a bridal dress and veil, white hair of old age, ermine in a judge's robe, the alb (from the Latin *alba* for white) of the priest, the white table or altar cloth, the martyrs' robes, and the Second Coming Christ in Revelation 6 and 19. As such, the color is a positive one, or at least benign. But white can take on more sinister aspects as well—the polar bear (most ferocious of the species), the albatross (consult Coleridge's epic poem of that bird as an omen), the Albino man, a corpse, a shroud, a ghost, the albescent horses carrying both the Antichrist and Death in Revelation 6. *See also* colors, liturgical; colors, symbology of; white hair; white horse; white raiment; white stones; whitewash.

White Brotherhood. See Therapeutae.

White Buffalo Calf Woman: a Lakota prophetess who predicted Jesus' return in a spaceship in the year 2000. An Ogallala belief posits that she will be reborn and return the world to balance after floods, fires, earthquakes, and such disasters have overcome us. Some say the period of her influence began in 1994 when a white buffalo was born in the land. *See also* prophetess(es); sect(s).

White, Ellen G. (Harmon): the leading figure (1827–1877) in the establishment and growth of Seventh-Day Adventism and the furtherance of William Miller's failed experiment in date-setting. White's followers consider her a prophetess because most of the tenets of their sect came from her purported visions (some estimates number about 2,000 separate revelations). The majority of her oracles concerned the keeping of the Jewish Sabbath as central to the sect's being. Dr. John H. Kellogg, of boxed cereal fame, was her main support and vegetarian guide to the membership and she was assisted by her husband, James Springer White (1821–1881). *See also* date-setting; investigative judgment; prophetess(es); sect(s); Seventh-Day Adventism.

Whitefield, George: one of many dynamic evangelists (1714–1770) who helped establish Methodism, a labor certainly shared with John and Charles Wesley. Though trained for the Anglican priesthood and a pioneer of Methodism, he never considered himself (like his good friend Ben Franklin) part of any denomination. Whitefield and his comrade John Wesley were estranged for a time over the doctrine of predestination but were eventually reconciled, though both continued to agree that the Roman pope was the Antichrist. Whitefield preached extensively in England, Ireland, and America. He preached over 18,000 sermons between 1736 and 1770. It is reported that his powerful voice could carry on the wind for a mile or more. Most historians agree that such ministry as practiced by the Wesleys, Whitefield, and other revivalist-style preachers of the time saved England from the bloody revolution that later overtook France at the end of the century and boosted America during the Great Awakenings. *See also* circuit riders; clergy patriots; "Devil's Footprint, The"; evangelist(s), evangelism; Great Awakenings, the; Holy Club, the; Methodists; missions, missionaries; Reformation Movement in America; revivalism; Wesley, Charles and John; Wheatley, Phillis.

White, Gilbert: Anglican curate and much admired "parson-naturalist" (1720–1793). White was a bachelor curate, environmentalist, and ornithologist who studied over 400 species of plant and animal life in and around his beloved estate in Selborne, England, specializing in the lowly earthworm and harvest mouse. His publication, *The Natural History and Antiquities of Selborne,* has remained in continuous print since 1789. *See also* Church of England; clergy scientists.

white hair: a symbol of wisdom or greatness, as commonly associated with one (such as an elder) who is worthy of honor. Jesus is depicted in Revelation 1:14 with glowing head and hair. *See also* bald, baldness, hair; Nazirite(s); white.

white horse: or pale horse, a common apocalyptic symbol of victory, either by the righteous, such as seen in Revelation 19:11–21, or for the Antichrist, as in Revelation 6:1-2. The imagery is likely taken from ancient Roman protocol when triumphant Roman generals often rode white steeds in a grand hero's parade. The latter description has led some to identify the white horse among the four to be Christ himself; the theory is highly unlikely, however. *See also* animals, birds, and insects, symbology of; black horse; eschatology, eschatological; four horsemen of the Apocalypse; horse; pale horse; red horse; white.

white horse prophecy: a prediction (prophecy) supposedly uttered by Joseph Smith, Jr., founder of the Mormon faith, in 1843 but published late. The name of the pronouncement is taken from Revelation 6 and declares that the Mormons would immigrate to the Rockies and become a great people. Some interpret the message to mean that the United States will someday become a Mormon theocracy. Others believe that the United States Constitution will become a sham in later politics and must be rescued by the LDS. In any case, the authenticity of the white horse prophecy is debated and remains one of many possible predictions made by Smith. *See also* Church of Jesus Christ of Latter-Day Saints, the; Smith, Joseph, Jr.

White Mountain, battle of: the conclusive conflict in 1620 between Roman Catholic armies and the Bohemian dissidents (the Taborites), which saw the Tabors thoroughly crushed. The Tabors were ably led by their blind general, Ziska. *See also* Inquisition, the; Roman Catholic Church; Taborites; Ziska.

white raiment: the Bible's name for the conduct of righteous believers who are said to be "clothed in righteousness." Apocalyptic language uses the phrase in such a manner but also describes the conquering Christ as dressed in white. The righteous under the altar in the fifth seal of Revelation (Rev. 6:9–11) are clothed in white. Revelation 3:18 admonishes the church at Laodicea to adorn herself in white clothes to cover the shameful nakedness of her sin. The symbolism can then be of purity or victory. *See also* great heavenly multitude, the; heavenly multitude, the; linen; multitude in white, the; raiment; righteousness; white; wool.

white stones: pebbles sometimes used by the ancients to indicate deliverance for a condemned person (white for innocence and black for guilt). A fascinating suggestion is that the ephod of the high priest held two stones or disks within its pouch colored black and white. By the process of drawing or casting the objects, the will of God could be discerned. If two whites came up, the answer was yes; if two blacks turned, the answer was no; if one of each was revealed, there was to be no answer from God that day. *See also* black stones; ephod; white stone secretly written on; Urim and Thummin; white.

white stone secretly written on: a gift promised to the church at Pergamum (Rev. 2:17). The implication is that believers are to receive a personal gemstone engraved with a name known only to Christ and the recipient, thus making the present quite personal and precious. Any deeper meaning runs to speculation, but we do know that the white stone represents something unique and intimate for the perfected believer. *See also* gem(s); new name, my; signet ring; token; white; white stones.

white throne judgment. See great white throne judgment.

whitewash: a porous compound (white in appearance, of course) used to paint walls or other structures. Often enough, it was used to cover construction faults, as well as to protect and enhance the beauty of the edifice to which it was applied. That usage is examined in Ezekiel 13:15, which deals with the castigation of false prophets. Jesus also used the analogy in Matthew 23:27 to reprimand the scribes and Pharisees for their hypocrisy; he compared them to tombs that are whitewashed and attractive on the outside but inside are full of dead men's bones and corruption. In one instance, Paul unwittingly spoke harshly to Ananias the high priest during his trial before the Sanhedrin by calling him a "whitewashed wall" (Acts 23:2–3). As a verb, then, to whitewash is to disguise a fault or failure by covering the action with false piety or lies.

Whitman, Marcus: a medical missionary and minister without portfolio (1802–1847) to the Nez Perce Indians of the Northwest Territory. He and his wife Narcissi, along with the Presbyterian missionary Reverend H. H. Spalding and his spouse Eliza, traveled to the Northwest. The two women were the first females to traverse the

Oregon Trail. Dr. Whitman established a mission at Walla Walla, Washington, and Spalding did the same further north. In 1847 a plague of measles struck the Whitman camp that killed more Indians than whites. The tribes accused Whitman of murdering their own to make more space for Anglo settlers. The residents and whites of the post were massacred by raiders of the Cayuse tribe. Early on, many of the Northwest Territory tribes had asked for missionaries to be sent because they believed the white man's power must rest with his religion and wanted to be shown the way to heaven. Soon, however, the diversity and complexity of doctrines the advocates of the various denominations brought with them confused and angered the local populace. *See also* martyr(s); missions, missionaries.

Whitsunday. See Pentecost.

Whittenberg Chapel: the chapel at the university of Whittenberg in Germany. To its door, Martin Luther tacked his defiant list of certain Roman Catholic doctrines of the time. Such was common educational practice in the day because it invited debate and discussion among the faculty and students. No doubt he did not envision the furor his action would engender. *See also* chapel; church; Luther, Martin; "Ninety-Five Theses, The."

Whittenberg prophets, the: a radical German group (operating around 1521) that arrived at the university town of Whittenberg from neighboring Zwickau. They insisted that God had spoken to them directly and declared the Bible as unnecessary. Further, they urged that the kingdom of God was at hand and the ungodly would soon be destroyed. *See also* cult(s).

whore of Babylon. See Babylon the Great; cup of adulteries; desolate and naked; filth of her adulteries; "glorified herself"; Great Prostitute, the; Mystery Babylon the Great the Mother of Prostitutes and Abominations of the Earth; prostitute, prostitution; Religious Babylon; Secular Babylon; song of the harlot; wine of her adulteries.

Wicca: the informal but most common designation for a loose organization encompassing the various forms of witchcraft (a word originally spelled with only one "c"). Wicca is a neo-pagan, nature-based religion (sort of reconstructed paganism or neo-paganism) usually practiced by male and female witches, either singularly or in covens. Worship of the ancient fertility goddesses is prominent, along with the horned god said to be either Satan or the polytheistic godhead expressed in something akin to animism. A motto of the group sometimes appears as "we don't tell your future, we change it." Group rituals are sometimes practiced in the nude ("skyclad" is their preferred term) with chants, sacrifices (either real or staged), dancing, magic, and revelry, especially in celebration of the seasonal festivals. Covens are said to multiply and can create a "thoughtform" of psychic energy, a practice they call "drawing down the moon." Participants may advance through three degrees (in the United States) of the craft, the third being the most adept. Upon achieving the third degree, the witch may take her magical name and be recognized as qualified to cast circles and is obligated to take an oath affirming witchcraft as the highest of religions. According to doctrine (which is hardly consistent), there are five elements of life: fire, air, water, and earth, (the "elementals") plus *aether* (spirit), which incorporates the other four. They also use tools of the trade, including charms (either amulets for protection or talismans for good omens) and ceremonial knives (an athame—a black-handled one for black magic and a white for white magic). There are four mid-season days of *Sabbat*, but the lesser days (equinoxes and solstices) are *esbats*. Each coven keeps its own set of rituals and rules since there is no standard text. What records do exist are outlined in the *Book of* Shadows; the text comes closest to being an official guide for ritual ceremony, chants, incantations, and the like. The name Wicca appears to have been derived from an Old English word, which was both a noun and a verb, referring to witchcraft and those who practiced it in earlier times. Old English named the term *wicce* and Middle English preferred *wicche*. The feminine form, *wice*, evolved into "witch," with a similar designation for "wizard." Gerald Gardner perhaps had the most influence on the modern ritualism and organization of the current societies. *See also* animism; apotropaic magic; athame; Baphomet; Beltane; Beltane's Eve; besom; bitheist; black arts; black lamb; "Blessed Be"; boline; *Book of Shadows;* Burning Times; cantrip; charm(s); church abuse; Clutterbuck, Dorothy; "coming out of the broom closet"; cone of power; coven(s); curse(s); "drawing down the moon"; elemental(s); enchantment; esbat; evil eye; execration; Fortune, Dion; familiar; familiar spirit; Gardner,

Gerald Brosseau; *geis;* Gowdie, Isobel; Great Goddess; Great Rite, the; handfasting; hex; Horned God; Imbolc; imprecation; Inquisition, the; Law of the Three; Leek, Sybil; left-hand path and right-hand path; Litha; Lughnasadh; Lummas; Mabon; magic, magick; Magickal Circle, The; *Malleus Malefiracum;* Midsummer Day; Morrigan; New Age religion; occult, occultic; Ostara; *pharmakeia;* psychonautics; Sabbat; Salem witch trials; Samhain; Satanism; sorcery, sorceries; spell; spell names; taboo; thoughtform; Tuatha de Danann; Voodoo; Voudou; Walpurgis Night; ward; warlock(s); Walpurgis Night; wheel of the year; Wiccan Rede; witch(es); witch cake; witchcraft; wight(s); "witches of New Forest, the;" wizard(s); Yule.

Wiccan Rede: the first imperative of Wicca quoted as: "A 'in it harm nun, do what you wilt." In other words, "As long as it harms none, do what you want." Certainly, not all who practice witchcraft abide by the rules. *See also Book of Shadows;* Law of the Three; rede; Wicca; witch(es); witchcraft.

Wicked Bible, the: a.k.a. the Adulteress or Sinners' Bible, an early Bible (1631) printed in England which inadvertently omitted the word *not* from the Seventh Commandment. The translation then appeared as "Thou shalt commit adultery." For the error, the king's printers were fined £300 (a hefty amount at the time), all 1,000 copies were burned (except eleven that were rescued), and the printer's license was revoked. *See also* Bible translations.

Wicked Land, the: God's disparaging name for Edom (Mal. 1:4). *See also* Edom, Edomites.

Wickedness: the name of the visionary woman in the basket experienced by Zechariah (Zech. 5:5–11). She likely represents an idol or the personification of evil. *See also* Zechariah's vision of a woman in a basket.

Wicked Priest: a name for the adversary of the Teacher of Righteousness (used by the Essene sect), possibly representing Satan or one of their number who is to become a traitor. Other terms for the same figure include Lion of Wrath, the Liar or Spreader of Lies, and the Man of Scoffing. *See also* Angel of Darkness; Angel of Light; Essenes; Qumran; Renewal, the; Sons of Darkness; Sons of Light; Teacher of Righteousness; *War of the Sons of Light Against the Sons of Darkness;* War Scroll.

wicked prince, the: a figure introduced in Ezekiel 21:27 who probably represents King Zedekiah of Judah, the leader who betrayed his oath to Babylon and attempted a revolt.

wicked, wickedness: amoral behavior. Any evil action contrary to the righteousness of God may be considered as wicked, but it is a particularly harsh word in any context. Ezekiel and many of the prophets report on the wickedness of Israel (Ezk. 5:6). *See also* after one's own lusts; antinomianism; body; carnal; concupiscence; darkness; debauchery; demimondaines; depravity; dissipation; evil; flesh; harmartiology; hedonism; human condition, the; human nature, the; immorality; iniquity; moral uncleanliness; orgies; Phibionites; sin(s); sinful nature, the; social issues; total depravity; trespass; unclean; worldly; "world, the".

wider context: the practice of examining a passage or paradigm of Scripture beyond its immediate context of book, chapter, and verse. The effort to gain insight into the message under analysis often yields better results when the broader perimeters of biblical study and salvation history are researched. *See also* open question; open theism.

widdershins: a contra-deosil direction—that is, counter-clockwise. The term is sometimes used to help describe neo-pagan rituals of varying descriptions. Many of the Earth Mother devotees on the foothills of Parnassus, Olympus, and Helicon, for instance, danced around the goddess' altars, herms, and baetyls in that direction during their lunar festivals. *See also* deosil; pagan practice; prayer wheel.

widow: a female who has lost her husband to death. The term is often figurative language for desolation or want. The arrogance of Babylon the Great (Rev. 18:7) is displayed by bragging that the city is a queen, not a widow, and would never be in mourning or in need. Actual widows were often in dire straits and were a benevolent concern for both the Israelite community and the early church when believers were open to prescribed charity. In Roman times, a woman who lived a chaste life and remained unmarried after the death of her husband was considered virtuous. The tradition was seconded by the Jews and was a prominent feature of the early Christian church (*cf.* 1 Timothy 5:1–15 and 1 Corinthians 7:8–9). Remarriage in widowhood later became acceptable and was declared to be so (Rom. 7:2–3). *See also* woman (women).

"widow's mite". See widow with the meager offering.

widow's son, the. See Hiram Abiff.

widow with the meager offering: a poor woman who gave her paltry tithe of two copper coins in the Temple treasury (Lk. 21:1–4). The unselfish and sacrificial act caught the attention of Jesus who commented favorably on the woman who was giving out of her poverty in contrast to those who gave out of their wealth. Her small gift was accounted of more worth than any riches presented and had laid up treasure for her in heaven. Destitution and need were often the conditions of the prophets who nevertheless gave their best. *See also* kondrantes; lepta.

Wiener, Norbert: a powerful mathematician and computer developer (1894–1964). Wiener was the father of *cybernetics,* a term he coined from the Greek word for "steersman"—*kybernetes.* The discipline is essentially a comparative examination of the automatic control systems found in life, the biological nervous system, machinery, and information-processing devices. A child prodigy, Wiener later improved fire-control radar systems in World War II. His several books include *God and Golem, Inc.* (1964), a work of interest to theologians because it deals with the influence of cybernetics on religion. Wiener himself was Jewish and supposedly related to Moses Maimonides. *See also* Jews; Maimonides, Moses; Web-Bot.

wife of Christ. See bridegroom of Christ; bride (wife) of Christ.

wife of your youth: or wife of your marriage covenant. The phrase is a description for Judah used by God as He yearns for the affectionate association with the nation previously experienced in the best of the times past (Mal. 2:14–16). The nation is enjoined to favor its first loved legitimate spouse and desist from pandering after other gods.

Wigglesworth, Michael: a cleric of Puritan New England (1631–1705) who delved deeply into apocalyptic matters and dates. He composed a 224-stanza poem entitled "The Day of Doom" (published 1662), which quickly became quite popular in his era. It is classed as America's first best-seller. The work extols the Puritans, even in their bigotry, and describes with bloodthirsty zest the terrors of the Last Judgment. Wigglesworth was called the Laureate of Puritanism, though he was painfully introverted and self-deprecating in character. Though of ill health, he survived two wives and produced eight children. *See also* Puritanism, Puritans.

wight(s): a living being, a creature. In old English folklore, however, a wight was a supernatural elemental sometimes described as one of the undead, a witch, or a sprite. Among the famous writers using the characterizations were J. R. R. Tolkien, Shakespeare, Edmund Spenser, Lord Byron, *et al. See also* banshee; bogle; brownies; bugbears; Celtic folklore and religion; clurichauns; daemons; devils; disa; dryad(s); elemental(s); evil (unclean) spirit(s); fairy, fairies; familiar spirits; Fomorians; ghoul; gnome(s); Green Man, the; hobgoblins; homunculus; household deities; huldufolk; leprechaun(s); mythological beasties, elementals, monsters, and spirit animals; nereid; nisse; nymph(s); nyx; Oniropompi; Orisha; Oya; paredri; para; Robin Goodfellow; satyr; Seelie Court, Unseelie Court; selkie; Sidhe; sirens; sprite(s); sylph(s); teraphim; territorial spirits; Trickster; Tuatha de Danann; tutelary; undine; Wicca; witch(es).

Wilberforce, William: perhaps the most dynamic and effective abolitionist in English history (1729–1833). Wilberforce saw the importance of religion and used its principles to further many humanitarian causes ranging from the end of slave trading to starting the Society for the Prevention of Cruelty to Animals. He was a politician and philanthropist, continuing his long campaign to end slavery until finally accomplished by the Slavery Abolition Act of 1833. *See also* African Methodist Episcopal Church; Clapham sect; missions, missionaries; slave, slavery.

wild beasts (animals) of the earth: beasts of the Tribulation said to be enemies of mankind (Rev. 6:8). Those named could be actual animals that attack humans or, given that Revelation refers to beasts as evil persons, more likely they are terrorists or brigands. Wild animals were often set to fight one another and to destroy Christians in several Roman arenas before the time of Constantine. To the ancients, wild animals were a food source, for sport, and a metaphor for fear. Even then, they could be pictured as human agents bent on violence toward the innocent. *See also* animals, birds, and insects, symbology of; bear; beast(s); Daniel's vision of the destroying monster; eagle; eagle and the condor; Ezekiel's eagles, vine, and cedar allegory; Ezekiel's lioness and a vine vision; hunched bear; jackal; jaguar; leopard; lion; serpent; terrorism; terrorist(s); tiger; winged leopard; winged lion; wolf.

wilderness: an uninhabited, uncultivated, and desolate place—a desert or harsh environment. In apocalyptic imagery, the wilderness was a metaphor for the area to which someone might flee from danger or in the despondency of hope. It symbolized either safety (as in Revelation 17:3) and sanctuary (for the outlaw David) or despair (as in Jeremiah 12:10–13). Jesus wandered and suffered there early in his ministry where he faced down the deadly temptations of Satan. The fleeing Israelites from Egyptian slavery roamed the wilderness for forty years before being allowed into the Promised Land.

wildfire: a disorder of some description in a church setting. Usually, the term refers to disruptive or sinful outbursts that are not ignited by the Holy Spirit. *See also* Christianese; ritual defilement; slurs, religious.

Wild Hunt: the favorite sport of the inhabitants of the Otherworld who rode and marched a prescribed trail close to the borders of the real world. It was a boisterous outing but full of danger too. What they were hunting, other than diversion, is unclear but perhaps the prey was unwary human souls or corpses who could be mutilated, teased, harmed, or even captured. Their leader, Hellequin, corralled the hoard but revenants were prone to sneak over the invisible border intent on mischief. *See also* bugbears; Celtic folklore and religion; folklore; Mesnie Hellequin; Otherworld; Wild Man.

Wild Man: in mythology, any unhinged man or demon who is, or could become, an uncontrollable beast. Depending on where he is found, he may bear the name "the uncle," the furry man, the plantigrade, the swollen foot, the licker, the honeyed one, the old man of the mountain, the master of the forest, or something else. He may or may not bear a personal name. In different cultures, he may take on differing characteristics and, on occasion, a Wild Woman may also be active. At Candlemas (May 1) the Wild One appears in the guise of the Green Man exuding sensuality. On Saint John's Day he may show up as a green wolf (including one of the eight annual days of his appearance) but in the form of a cat, wolf, bear, or something else. In Russia, he is a bear in evidence on Saint Michael's Day. A Wild Man may manifest as a giant, and does so in a number of cultures. Sometimes, even Merlin the magician is called a Wild Man. *See also* beast(s); bugbears; mythological beasties, elementals, monsters, and spirit animals; giant(s); Green Man, the; May Day; Merlin; Mesnie Hellequin; Wild Hunt.

Wilkerson, David: (1931–2011) pastor of the nondenominational Times Square Church of New York City and author of the influential *The Cross and the Switchblade* in 1972. Wilkerson was noted for his work among the street gangs of New York and drug rehabilitation ministries. He believed America was the end times Babylon depicted in Revelation 17–18 and suspected the terrorist attacks of September 11, 2001, were the start of national collapse. His book *The Vision* predicts a great calamity of some description soon to occur in America. Most of his visions or angelic warnings he related involved fire and rioting. He was killed in an automobile crash in Texas in April of 2011.

Wilkinson, Jemima: charismatic American Quaker evangelist (1752–1819). Wilkinson preached sexual abstinence and strict adherence to the Ten Commandments, and against the odds, she obtained a large and dedicated following. After being stricken with typhoid, she revived in what she claimed was a near resurrection. Thereafter, she called herself the "Publick Universal Friend" and never again used her birth name. The larger Quaker body disowned her, but she and several siblings continued preaching in Rhode Island, Connecticut, and Pennsylvania. Later, Wilkinson and some followers migrated to New York, where they established the city of Jerusalem, later called Penn Yan, New York, where they lived as the first whites among the local tribes. *See also* evangelist(s), evangelism; revivalism; Society of Friends.

will: self-determination. The will is a core ingredient of faith and its daily practice and an important consideration in many aspects of philosophy. We, as free individuals unhampered by those who would use force, are at liberty to determine if we will have faith, pursue it, and honor God with our minds and hearts. Will is, therefore, the theological seat of both a living faith and one that does not exist by conscious effort. *See also* authenticity; decretive will; free will; *historia salutis;* "in this place"; plan of salvation; priesthood of the believer; soul freedom; story; walk with God; will of God.

Willard, Francis: one of America's most dynamic and effective activists in the temperance, labor, and suffrage efforts (1839–1898). Willard was an educator deeply involved with women's rights, family unity, prison reform, labor rights, and the temperance movement. She became president of the Woman's Christian Temperance Movement in 1879 and held the position until her death. Her work had a marked influence on the later Social Gospel Movement and Christian Socialism in the country. *See also* Social Gospel; suffragan; temperance; Woman's Christian Temperance Union.

willful king, the: a name cited in the book of Daniel to identify Antiochus Epiphanes as an oppressor of the Jews. As such, Antiochus is a precursor of the Antichrist. *See also* Antichrist; Antiochus IV Epiphanes; anti-Semitic; contemptible person, a; king(s); little horn, the; stern-faced king, the.

William of Ockham: an English Franciscan philosopher-theologian and friar (ca. 1288–1348). Although he is famous for producing the ultra-fine blade sharpener called "Occam's razor," he was a prolific and outspoken defender of the faith and early advocate of the philosophy called "nominalism." His criticism of the Catholic Church (he called Pope John XXII a heretic) brought about his excommunication and exile where he continued his writings on philosophy, physics, and theology. His feast day in the Church of England is April 10. *See also* clergy scientists; Franciscans; nominalism, nominalist(s); Occam's razor; philosophy of religion; Roman Catholic Church.

William and Mary: (William III 1650–1702) and Mary II (daughter of James II and Anne Hyde 1662–1694), king and queen of England, Scotland, and Ireland who ruled jointly for thirty-eight years. William was Dutch descended and indoctrinated early from Reformed Calvinist tutors who convinced him he was divinely destined to rule and advance the fortunes of the House of Orange. He reigned with his wife Mary (eleven years his junior) after his position was secured in 1688 when he successfully invaded England in the so-called "Glorious

Revolution" to dethrone the unpopular Catholic King James II. He was a popular monarch known to those subjects as "King Billy." The English Bill of Rights was adopted during their time. Not all supported them, however. The Jacobites continually opposed William's position and numbers of the Anglican and Scottish clergy (and some laypersons) declined to offer him fealty. Much of William's rule was focused on England's war with the French Catholic king Louis XIV but Mary was an able ruler in his absence. Mary died first (at the young age of thirty-two), much to her husband's sorrow, and William's popularity plummeted despite his conversion to Anglicanism. The king died in 1702 from complications of a fall from his horse Sorrel. The accident was caused by a misstep into a mole hole, causing his enemies to appreciate the terminal contribution of "the little gentleman in the black velvet waistcoat." *See also* Anglicanism; Church of England; "Glorious Revolution, the"; Jacobites; king(s); nonjurors; Reformed Churches.

Williams, John: Congregationalist minister (1664–1729) and pastor at Deerfield, Connecticut. He was captured in 1704 by hostile Indians and carried away to Canada. His wife was murdered in the episode. Williams chronicled his ordeal in his book *The Redeemed Church Returning to Zion* in 1707. *See also* Congregationalists.

Williams, Roger: a separatist Calvinist minister in colonial New England (1603?–1683) often cited as "America's first pastor." He began the colony called Rhode Island as a refuge for dissidents of all descriptions in 1636. His state embraced total religious toleration, even for Jews and "Turks" (everybody else), but claimed that the pope of Rome was the Antichrist. There was a shortage of *Turks* in America, but in Williams' words, "All men may walk as their consciences persuade them, every one in the name of his God." He, like many of his contemporaries, was an unabashed apocalypticist. *See also* anti-Semitic; Baptists; Clarke, John; Coddington, William; Cotton, John; Hutchinson, Anne; Providence; Vane, Henry.

William the Conqueror: king of England and Duke of Normandy (c. 1028–1087). William was an illegitimate son descended from Vikings but prospered as an exceptional leader. He initiated religious reforms and was active in church politics. He seized England at the Battle of Hastings in 1066. *See also* king(s).

will of God: a.k.a. decretive will of God, the doctrine stating that God decrees all that will happen and causes it to happen either by His personal causality or by permitting it through His creation. God's sovereignty is an attribute of self-consciousness and His authoritative determination to manage it in the way He alone determines. We know certain aspects of God's nature (his will) in that He loves us, desires our worship, provides for all of creation, and other theological descriptions that do not change. Neither humans nor circumstances of history can alter God's being or his decisions but faith allows us to trust them. We are free, however, to live life in our personal will with the same determination of destiny. The phrase has become prime Christianese as many conscientious believers seek strenuously to act in accord with God's will. *See also* Christianese; decretive will; free will; *historia salutis; Inshallah;* "in this place"; little scroll, the; on mission; plan of salvation; plan of the ages; providence; walk with God; will.

willow: a.k.a. sallows and osiers, of the genus *salix* found in 400 species. The tree or shrub is deciduous with pointed leaves. The ancients used it to relieve aches and fever but is preferential today for making charcoal for drawing. Religious association is also rich and favored by Judaism, Buddhism, Christianity, and Wicca. Jews name it as one of the great "Four Species" utilized at Sukkot and Christians may see it on Palm Sunday. Lore says the willow can "weep." *See also* flora, fruit, and grain, symbology of; Four Species, the; fruit; Ingathering, Feast of; Judaism; myrtle, palm; Tabernacles, Feast of; tree(s).

wimple: a nun's head covering. It does, however, name other similar articles of female apparel. *See also* furniture and furnishings of the modern church; guimpe; nun(s).

Winchester Platform of 1803: the official document stating that the generic man is perfectible and all will eventually be saved. It became the standard doctrine of Universalism which began in America in the 1700s, then merged (under the same Winchester Platform) with the Unitarians in 1961. *See also apocatastasis;* Ballou, Hosea; universalism; Unitarian Universalists.

wind(s): the movement of air across the Earth's surface in the lower atmosphere. In apocalyptic language, the wind often indicates either freedom or uncontrolled movement. It can demonstrate the power of God: "Who has gathered up the winds in the hollow of his hands?" (Pro. 30:4) or it may even describe the breath of God. The word can also refer to spirit or breath. Zechariah 7:14 speaks of a windstorm (a tornado?), and Jesus told a parable about a strong wind blowing down a house; so, blustery weather can have a destructive connotation as well as a positive one. Revelation 7:1 shows four angels holding back the winds of Earth in preparation for the sealing of the 144,000. Hosea predicted (Hos. 8) that Israel had sown a wind of sin and would reap a whirlwind (a cyclone?) of retribution. This dual meaning of the word "wind" may perhaps be best seen in the episode of Elijah's sojourn in the cave of Horeb, where he was hiding from the wrath of Jezebel. The prophet perceived a fierce wind outside his hidey-hole, then an earthquake, then fire. But God was not to be found in any of those; rather, God was heard in the still, small breath of a whisper (1 Ki. 19:1–18). Thus, wind, fire, earthquake, and a still, small voice are sometimes grouped as signs from God. We learn from Scripture that wind can be controlled by Christ (Mt. 8:26) but that it is naturally directionless—a metaphor for the instability of false doctrine (Eph. 4:14; Jas. 1:6). Job said that despairing words can be as useless as wind (Job 6:26), and certain proverbs declare it is a precursor of trouble (Pro. 11:29). We are told not to be blown about by every wind of doctrine and schemes by deceitful men (Eph. 4:14). Wind is a frequent symbol for the Holy Spirit in that the air moves, but none can determine whence it came or where it is going (Jn. 3:8). During Pentecost, the early church experienced the sound of a mighty wind (Acts 2:2), a disturbance that could only represent the Holy Spirit in action. The book of *3 Enoch* claims the winds kept the Cherubim aloft and reveals that the "winds of God" are a choice method for divine miracles (*e.g.,* Genesis 1:2, Exodus 10:13 and 14:21). Sometimes the winds are beneficial (Isa. 11:2) but destructive in other instances (Num. 5:14; 1 Ki. 19:11; 1 Sam. 14:23). *See also* angel(s); angels of the winds; breath; earthquake; fire; four winds of earth; four winds of heaven; Holy Spirit; names (titles) for the Holy Spirit; parable(s); parables of the New Testament; Pentecost; *pneuma; ruach;* spirit.

wine: the fermented fruit of the vine. Wine was the principal beverage in the ancient world (along with milk) and was sometimes used medicinally (1 Tim. 5:23). Often, the term is used in conjunction with oil. The drink is often figurative for pleasantness, pleasure, or satisfaction. Josephus wrote a charming description of wine used in its amiable use: "God bestows the fruit of the vine upon men for good; which wine is poured out to him, and is a pledge of fidelity and mutual confidence among men; and puts an end to their quarreling, takes away passion and grief out of the minds of them that use it, and makes them cheerful." To be "drunk with wine," on the other hand, is ignoble and a precursor to ridicule or cruelty. Jesus' first recorded miracle was to change water into wine to save embarrassment to his wedding hosts (Jn. 2:1–11). For the Church, wine in the ordinance or sacrament of the Lord's Supper is of vital importance since it represents the blood of Christ and holds deep eschatological significance. *See also* blood; Divine Liturgy; element(s); Eucharist; "four cups, the"; grapes; libation; liturgical year; liturgy, Christian; liturgy, Jewish; Lord's Supper; Mass; olive oil; parable(s); parables of the New Testament; sacred drink; *Seder;* species; wafer; wine of her adulteries; wine of wrath; winepress; wineskin(s).

wine of her adulteries: the drink of the Great Prostitute (Rev. 17:2) who sits astride the scarlet beast (Satan). The mucky contents of her gilded cup represent the evil associations she had formed with the peoples of earth. In a related description, the metaphor is expanded to "maddening wine," again representing the delusion of the Great Harlot. She has duped the world into the drunkenness from her evil because the populations are sated on her adulteries according to the Revelation report (Rev. 18:3). *See also* Babylon the Great; cup of adulteries; filth of her adulteries; "glorified herself"; Great Prostitute, the; Mystery Babylon the Great the Mother of Prostitutes and of the Abominations of the Earth; prostitute; prostitution; Religious Babylon; Secular Babylon; smoke of her burning; whore of Babylon; wine; wine of wrath; winepress.

wine of wrath: the apocalyptic drink of chaos and anger. Revelation 14:8 and 18:3 speak of the maddening wine of the adulteries of Babylon the Great. In other instances, Scripture states that the unrepentant may be forced to drink of God's wrath, even to the dregs. *See also* Babylon the Great; cup of adulteries; cup of fury (wrath); harvest of the earth; wine; wine of her adulteries; winepress.

winepress: a construct for pressing the juice from grapes, either mechanically or by stomping with the feet, in preparation for making wine. Revelation 14:17–20 describes God's punishment as the stomping in the great winepress of God's anger. Such juice extraction was usually done by the stomping of human feet within a vat. The "blood" ensuing from the crushing of the grapes displayed in the pageant crests to a distance of 1,600 stadia (about 180 miles or 300 kilometers). *See also* blood overflowing; eschatology, eschatological; grain; grapes; grapes of wrath; harvest; harvest of the earth; sickle; threshing; threshing floor; threshing sledge; wine; wine of wrath.

Wines, Enoch Cobb: Congregationalist minister and penologist (1806–1879). Wines was a pioneer in national and international prison reform measures. He introduced the concept of correction versus punishment, segregation of juvenile and adult offenders, and other advancements in the field of incarceration management of the prison system. Oddly enough, he did not begin his prison reform efforts until he was fifty-six years of age. *See also* Congregationalists; social issues.

wineskin(s): animal skins or intestines designed to hold unfermented juice or fermented wine. The bursting of a wineskin was considered a great loss and an event to be guarded against. Jeremiah 13:12–14 discusses God's threat to fill the residents of Israel with drunkenness, then smashing them against one another. Jesus warned his listeners that new wine should not be poured into old skins (Mk. 2:22) in response to the query as to why his disciples did not fast like those of John the Baptist and the Pharisees. *See also* parable(s); parables of the New Testament; wine; wine of wrath.

wing(s): 1. those appendages that allow birds to fly. Scriptural symbols for the wing suggest flight, rescue, or protection—as a hen or eagle would comfort her young under her wing. Revelation 12:14 reports that the woman of the sun is to be rescued on the wings of a great eagle. Sometimes angels are presented as having wings, but we are uncertain if they are optional equipment for them; certainly, they are just as often pictured without them. Most likely, then, angels' wings are an artistic fabrication with the possible exceptions of angelic associations by Ezekiel and John. Isaiah 40:31 promises that those who hope in the Lord will soar on wings like eagles. 2. additions to buildings that are attached to the main structure. Some eschatological references indicate the Antichrist will set up his blasphemous throne on the "wing" of the reconstructed Jewish Temple and not in the main edifice. *See also* wing of (in) the Temple.

winged leopard, the: Daniel's symbol of Greece as an oppressor of Israel (Dan. 7:6). *See also* animals, birds, and insects, symbology of; belly and thighs of bronze, the; Daniel's vision of the four beasts; mushrishu; flying goat, the; Greece.

winged lion, the: Daniel's depiction of King Nebuchadnezzar of Babylon, one of Israel's adversaries (Dan. 7:4). The lion scene was a prominent decoration for Babylonian structures as well. *See also* animals, birds, and insects, symbology of; mushrishu; mythological beasties, elementals, monsters, and spirit animals; Nebuchadnezzar II.

wing of (in) the Temple: an architectural attachment to the Tribulation Temple absent from the normal Temple blueprint. The most common interpretation sees the wing of the Temple as an addition to be supposedly built onto the main Tribulation Temple, or erected within it (Dan. 9:27). Even today, a "wing" is a common expression for a building modification. Otherwise, the wing could be referencing a foreign god or idol or the props of the Antichrist as he desecrates the Tribulation Temple. It is here, as some indicators suggest, that the abomination of desolation will be erected. If not, the abomination will likely be in the Inner Court or Holy of Holies while some other similar desecration takes place on the wing, whatever and wherever it is. Nevertheless, an indisputable description and purpose of the predicted "wing" have always been a puzzle to theologians and prophecy experts. The abomination of desolation noted in Daniel and in the Olivet Discourse from Jesus indicates the idol, whatever or whoever it is, is to be placed on a "wing" of the Tribulation Temple. We are uncertain if this wing is an architectural construct indigenous to the Temple design (as previously noted), an addition to the main structure, the pinnacle, or something else entirely. An intriguing idea suggests that the wing is a subtle method of saying the message and the image of the Antichrist is "spreading out" to speed up and broadcast his worldwide idolatry. *See also* wing(s).

winnowing fork: or fan, a harvesting implement designed to move the air above the grain or tossing it into the air to help remove the chaff from the kernels. The term is a common apocalyptic expression for a sign of God's wrath, the One Who stands ready to disturb and separate out the disobedient (Jer. 15:7; Mt. 3:12). *See also* eschatology, eschatological; grain; harvest; harvest of the earth; pruning hooks; sickle; threshing; threshing floor; threshing sledge.

Winthrop, John: first governor of the Massachusetts Bay Company for its established colony in the New World (1588–1649). He was a strict Puritan but of genteel birth. It was he who first expressed the hope that the godly purposes of the early colonists could construct a society and a governmental system that he called a "city upon a hill" for all the world to witness. The New England Winthrop family produced many notable leaders from his lineage. The second John (1606–1676) became governor of Connecticut; John (Fitz-John) (1638–1707) was also governor of Connecticut; another John (1714–1779) was a scientist and educator; Robert Charles (1809–1894) was a United States congressman and senator; Theodore (1828–1861) was a soldier and writer. *See also Booke of the General Lawes and Libertyes;* clergy scientists; Puritanism, Puritans.

wisdom: sage intelligence—the capacity to be wise and discerning in one's thinking and actions. In Scripture, wisdom encompasses more than mere intellect; it implies acumen, patience, knowledge, and most of all, reliance upon the Holy Spirit to conduct one's life and affairs (Ps. 111:10). It may be defined as "intelligent purpose," and is considered a special creation of God in some interpretations. There is a close association with the law of God and reverence for the Lord, and an inner discipline is required before humans may acquire it. So then, "a wise man is a religious man." To that we may add that wisdom exudes understanding, fair dealing, shrewdness, prudence, learning, discernment, the "fear of the Lord" (respect), practical skill, harmonious living, experience, and even charisma. Solomon's prayer to receive wisdom above all other gifts was blessed by the Lord, and it multiplied the king's effectiveness (2 Chr. 1). Perhaps the most appealing poetic description of the word is found in Job 28, which can be read as an essay on the nature of wisdom. We might surmise that the term is the fear (esteem) for the Lord. Perhaps the fullest understanding of the concept in a biblical sense is from Paul found in 1 Corinthians 2:6-16, which describes the mystery of God as "secret wisdom." In Jesus' play on words, reciting the children's tune of Luke 7:32, he lamented that the people would not respond to the teachings of John the Baptist nor his own unless they became "children of wisdom" (Lk. 7:35). His comment regarding the subject is impressive: "Wisdom is justified by all her children" (Lk. 7:35). Revelation and other apocalyptic material insist wisdom is necessary to decipher the mysteries of eschatology. In the Song of Songs and other places, wisdom is personified as a female lover ever in search of a person worthy of her esteem. The Greek is *Sophia*, a notion that seems to take on the "essence of being" when used by the Gnostics and some Greek philosophers. Wisdom (still personified) is fruit, sweet syrup, and honey dripping from the comb. Wisdom as a female is not of the Godhead but poetic of the law and fear of the Lord. The concept of Greek wisdom did not always square with that of the Hebrews or Christians (1 Cor. 1:30–31). The letter of James (James 3:13–18) explains that "worldly wisdom," is selfish but godly wisdom is pure. Wisdom is, after all, what allows us to make smart decisions and helps us understand our world. *See also* apothegm; atrahasis; children's ditty; Dame Folly; knowledge of God; Lady Wisdom; mystery; *nous;* philosophy of religion; Proverbs as Old Testament book; secret wisdom; *Sophia;* theology; tree(s); wise, the.

Wisdom of Ahikar, The. See *Story of Ahikar, The.*

Wisdom of Sirach. See Ecclesiasticus.

Wisdom of Solomon, The: in Hebrew, *Chokmah,* an example of wisdom literature not considered canonical by most church authority; it is deuterocanonical in Catholic circles but fits logically into the Apocryphal listings. The writer, said to be King Solomon himself, is most certainly a false ascription. A later writer during the Hellenistic period attempted to present Hebrew theology in a counterculture environment—namely, Hellenism—when it appeared. He used a common literary style which helped bring the Bible into everyday life, then applied it to well-couched philosophical arguments. The author spoke skillfully for the continuing validity of Jewish faith in a strange setting. In the book, the writer claims that Wisdom holds twenty-one precious attributes. He listed those qualities as: spirit, holiness, uniqueness in its kind but made of many parts, subtlety, free-moving, lucid, spotlessness, clarity, invulnerability, loving what is good, kind in disposition toward men, holding the power of God, active in the power of God, effluent, goodly, and orderly in its composition. God is all-powerful, all-surveying, permeating all, glorious, and everlasting. The writer submitted that wisdom enters into the holy soul and makes it God's friend and prophet. He finally admitted that Wisdom (personified) is of God but not within the Trinity; otherwise, its particulars remain elusive.

wisdom psalm: any Old Testament psalm relating to religious or folk advice for a more respectable or practical living, similar to the renditions found in the book of Proverbs. Psalms 111 and 112 [which should actually be classed as one] are prime examples of wisdom psalms. *See also* creation psalm; enthronement psalm; historical psalm; imprecatory psalm; messianic psalm; penitential psalm; Proverbs as Old Testament book; psalm; psalm of judgment; psalm of lament; Psalms as Old Testament book; royal psalm; supplication psalm; thanksgiving psalm; worship psalm.

wisdom writings. See Hagiographa.

Wise, Isaac Mayer: a Reformed rabbi (1819–1900) considered to be the premier originator of Reformed Judaism in America. He founded the Hebrew Union College in 1875, along with the Union of American Hebrew Congregations (1873), and the Central Conference of American rabbis (1889). Isaac Wise was somewhat unique among his class in that he disfavored Zionism. *See also* Jew(s).

Wise, John: a Puritan clergyman (1652–1725) who fought against British taxation in the colonies. Wise was the Congregationalist pastor in Ipswich, Massachusetts, and a strong advocate for democracy in the Puritan faith. He was called "the first great American democrat." Among his writings are *The Church's Quarrel Espoused* (1710) and *A Vindication of the Government of New England Churches* (1717). He was an opponent of the policies of Increase and Cotton Mather. *See also* Congregationalists; Puritanism, Puritans; Mather, Cotton; Mather, Increase.

Wise Men. See Magi.

Wise, Stephen Samuel: a Reformed rabbi (1874–1949) who fostered democratic ideals from a Jewish standpoint. He was an ardent Zionist, founded the American Jewish Congress in 1917, and was a delegate to the Versailles conference in 1919 to solicit aid for a Jewish homeland. He started the Free Synagogue in New York City in 1907 and served there for forty-two years. Next came the World Jewish Congress that Wise helped to shape in 1936 and served as its president for the rest of his life. Wise remained active in social and political reform, education, and as an anti-Nazi activist. *See also* Jew(s); Orlinsky, Harry.

wise, the: those who strive for and achieve some excelling measure of wisdom and piety. Daniel 12:3 promises that those persons who are "wise" will shine like the brightness of heaven and its stars, and will lead many to righteousness. The name also serves as the translation of the Hebrew term *maskilim* (or *Hasidim)*, the "little helpers" referenced in Daniel 11:34. *See also* amora; Assemblies of the Wise; atrahasis; elder(s); ensi; *Hasidim; maskilim;* prophet(s); prophetess(es); wisdom; Witenagemot.

wise woman, a: an unnamed woman of Tekoa sent by Joab to subtlety prompt King David to mollify his distracting grief for his exiled and deceased son Absalom (2 Sam. 14:1–21). She may or may not have been a prophetess. *See also* Joab; prophet(s); prophetess(es); Tekoa; two sons and the avenger of blood, the; woman (women).

Wissenschaft des Judentums: a scientific study of Judaism begun after the European Enlightenment of the 19th century. Jewish scholars sought to write, or rewrite, the history of Judaism in light of research done on all available Jewish documents respecting Jewish life. The movement led to developments of Reform, Conservative, and Orthodox branches of the faith. *See also* Judaism; progressive Judaism.

witch(es): a female (or more rarely a male) necromancer or Wiccan. New Age religion frequently differentiates between "white" (good) witches and "black" (evil) witches, but the entire concept of witchcraft is an abomination according to Hebrew and Christian ethics. Strangely enough, the word originally meant "prisoner." Witches were a prime target of Catholic Inquisitions (under which thousands perished), and the New England taint of it—centered at Salem, Massachusetts—saw some 150 prosecutions and nineteen executions. Wiccan ritual revolves around the magic circle (alone or in a coven) and centers on the natural pagan holidays in community observance. Legend has it that witches are prone to recite the Lord's Prayer backwards, beginning with "Give us this day our daily bread" and ending with "Hallowed be thy name." That version, of course, puts the self first and God last, placing priorities where the users want them. *See also* apotropaic magic; athame; *auto-de-fe;* Baphomet; Beltane; Beltane's Eve; *besom;* "Blessed Be"; *Book of Shadows;* bugbears; Burning Times; cantrip; charm(s); church abuse; Clutterbuck, Dorothy; "coming out of the broom closet"; cone of power; coven(s);curse(s); "drawing down the moon"; elemental(s); enchantment; esbat; evil eye; execration; familiar; familiar spirit; Fortune, Dion; Gardner, Gerald Brosseau; *geis;* Gowdie, Halloween; Imbolc; Isobel; Great Goddess; Great Rite, the; hex; Horned God; imprecation; Inquisition, the; kulam; Lammas; Law of Three; Leek, Litha; Lughnasadh; Mabon; Ostara; Sabbat; Sybil; magic, magick; Magickal Circle, The; *Malleus Malefiracum;* Morrigan; New Age religion; occult, occultic; persecution(s); *pharmakeia;* pow-wow; psychonautics; Sabbat; Salem witch trials; Samhain; Sangoma(s); sorcery, sorceries; spell; spell names; taboo; thoughtform; Tuatha de Danann; Voodoo; Voudou; Walpurgis Night; ward; warlock(s); Wheel of the Year; Wicca; Wiccan Rede; wight(s); "witches of New Forest, the"; witch cake; witchcraft; witch of Endor; wizard(s); woman (women); Yule.

witch cake: a recipe concocted by Mary Sibley, a member of the Salem, Massachusetts, colony involved in the Salem witch trials of 1692–1693. The loaf consisted of rye bread baked with the urine of the victim, then fed to a dog, which would supposedly aid the devil-possessed and help her identify her adversaries. *See also* athame; *besom;* ordeal(s); raisin cakes, the sacred; Salem witch trials; witch(es); witchcraft.

witchcraft: the practice of the arts and rituals of witchery, considered an evil and forbidden exercise (Deut. 18:10; Gal. 5:20). Both biblical and civil legislation has long tried to suppress the arcane craft. A statute from the time of King James I (1603), for example, reads, "If any person or persons shall…consult, covenant with, entertain, employ, feed or reward any evil or wicked spirit for any intent or purpose, or take up any dead man, woman or child out of their grave or any other place where the dead body resteth, to be employed or used in any manner of witchcraft, sorcery, charm or enchantment whereby any person shall be killed, destroyed, wasted, consumed, pined or lamed in his or her body, every such offender...shall suffer death." The Bible's injunction is more succinct: "Thou shalt not suffer a witch to live (Ex. 22:18)." Galatians 5:20 mentions witchcraft in the same paradigm as idolatry. It is commonly regarded that normal legal safeguards for accused witches did not apply. Furthermore, certain classes of citizens were particularly marked for suspicion: those with odd or disfiguring physical characteristics, the neurotic or feeble-minded, the elderly or solitary woman, scientifically-minded students, or those doubting current superstitions. *See also* adept; apotropaic magic; athame; *auto-de-fe;* Baphomet; Beltane; Beltane's Eve; *besom;* "Blessed Be"; *Book of Shadows;* Brujeria; Burning Times; cantrip; charm(s); church abuse; "coming out of the broom closet"; cone of power; coven(s); curse(s); devils of Loudon, the; "drawing down the moon"; elementals; enchantment; esbat; evil eye; execration; familiar; five sins of Revelation; Gardner, Gerald Brosseau; *geis;* Great Goddess; Great Rite, the; Halloween; hex; Horned God; Imbolc; imprecation; James I, King; kulam; Lammas; Law of Three; left-hand path and right-hand path; Litha; Lughnasadh; Mabon; Macumba; magic, magick; Magickal Circle, The; *Malleus Malefiracum;* mandrake(s); New Age religion; occult, occultic; Ostara; persecution(s); *pharmakeia;* pow-wow; psychonautics; Sabbat; Salem witch trials; Samhain; Sangoma(s); social issues; sorcery, sorceries; spell; spell names; taboo; thoughtform; Voodoo; Voudou; Walpurgis Night; ward; warlock(s); Wicca; Wiccan Rede; witch cake; witch(es); wizard(s); Yule.

witch doctor. See shaman, shamanism.

witch of Endor: a female necromancer from the region of Endor. She was consulted by King Saul (1 Sam. 28:3, 5–25), in violation of his own law, and was perhaps able to conjure the spirit of the prophet Samuel. If such an apparition did appear (and all indications seem to affirm that it did), the experience was of God and not superstitious magic. The witch seemed as surprised to see Samuel as Saul was. *See also* apparition; familiar spirit; ghost(s); meonenim; necromancy; séance; soothsayer(s); spirit; spiritism; vision(s); witch(es).

"witches of New Forest, the": a large coven of witches who assembled themselves in the New Forest of England during World War II. Their task, overseen by Gerald Gardner, was to protect England from Nazi invasion. Such a rite is rare in the British Isles, having only been formed on three emergency occasions: once to repel the threat of the Spanish Armada (1558), another to stave off a pending assault by Napoleon (1800s), and the third to stop the Germans. In the latter instance, a cone of psychic power was raised and directed toward the shores of France with the command, "You cannot cross the sea, you cannot cross the sea, you cannot come." According to Gardner, the life force this power generated cost the lives of several of the elderly witches due to exertion and stress. The ritual was repeated four times in each session until forced to stop by exhaustion. *See also* Clutterbuck, Dorothy; Fortune, Dion; Gardner, Gerald Brosseau; witch(es).

Witenagemot: or the Witan, an Anglo-Saxon meeting of the highest nobility and ecclesiastical authority similar to a German folkmoot. The purpose was to advise the king regarding civil and ecclesiastical matters. The term literally translates as "meeting of wise men." *See also* religious organizations; wise, the.

Witherspoon, John: a Scottish Presbyterian minister and member of the Continental Congress (1723–1794), the only preacher to sign the Declaration of Independence, representing the colony of New Jersey. He was the sixth president of Princeton and an early member of the colonial Committee of Correspondence and Safety. Witherspoon was a man of tremendous energy who served over 100 committees under the Articles of Confederation and Constitution as a member of Congress. *See also* clergy patriots; Founding Fathers; Presbyterians.

witness(es): 1. a proclaimer of the truth contained in the Word of God. 2. a favorite term for a martyr to the faith. 3. one who seeks to present the message of salvation to another. Such personal contact with such a purpose is commonly termed "witnessing." Personal action and expression with that goal in mind are favored in Scripture: "Let the redeemed of the Lord tell their story" (Ps. 107:2). *See also* Christianese; confession; drive-by evangelism; evangelist(s), evangelism; fishers of men; lost; martyr(s); martyrdom; missional; missions, missionaries;

plan of salvation; "Roman Road, the"; soul-winning; spreading the gospel; testimony; soul-winning; testimony; tract(s); "turn your life [heart] over to Jesus"; "washed in the blood"; witnesses, great cloud of; witnesses, the two great; worldwide preaching of the gospel.

witnesses, great cloud of: those of the *nephos marturon,* those saints and martyrs throughout history who have boldly stood for God (Heb.12:1). A number of them are identified by name in the previous chapter of Hebrews (chapter 11) and each is commended as faithful, preserving in persecution, and bastions of faith. Despite maltreatment, they ran the race of faith as types of Christ who died for the sins of creation. The presence of these special testifiers could even be the exoneration of the Old Testament promise of vindication promised to Israel by God Himself (Ps. 94:2, 16-23). *See also* remnant; souls under the altar; witness(es).

witnesses, the two great: a pair of mysterious figures from heaven who are to appear in Jerusalem during the Tribulation (Rev. 11:1–14). Their identity is disputed, even unknown with certainty, but their task is to testify for the Lamb, to condemn wickedness, and to (perhaps) train the 144,000 servants and/or cause the rebuilding of the Temple of the Tribulation. They are to have great power, including the ability to control the rainfall, turn water into blood, and even slay those who would oppose them. Nevertheless, the Antichrist will manage to murder them and leave their bodies unburied in the streets of Jerusalem for three and a half days. Afterward, they are resurrected and returned to heaven to the astonishment of their enemies who had been gloating over their demise. They are also called "the two olive trees and the two lampstands that stand before the Lord of the earth." If that description suggests they are not human, perhaps they are (as put forward by some) the Law and the Prophets, The Old and New Testaments, the Word of God and the blood of Christ, or even a pair of volcanoes. Or they could be the Church, Christian martyrs, the Western and Eastern divisions of the church, Israel and the Church, or Arabs and Israelites (the two nations descended from Abraham). Those theories hold serious drawbacks, however. How can any of them act out, be killed, lie dead in the streets, be ridiculed, come to life, and ascend to heaven? The *Apocalypse of Peter* suggests that the two witnesses are Enoch and Elijah. The most cited identification for the pair are Moses and Elijah, Elijah and Melchizedek, Joshua (the priest) and Zerubbabel (the governor) of Judah, Elijah and John the Baptist, Elijah and John of Revelation (Mal. 4:5–6; Rev. 10:11), Elijah and an unnamed associate, Jeremiah and Elijah, Anna and Simeon, or simply any two persons God may select for the task. They could even be two who have never lived before but will receive a unique call upon their lives. An earlier popular suggestion was that they were the martyred Peter and Paul. The suggestion that they are Moses and Elijah is a strong one boosted by several similarities. Both prophets were present at the mount of transfiguration (Mk. 9:2–13), both specialized in those supernatural powers described in Revelation, both have some mystery attached to their passing to heaven (Jude 9; 2 Ki. 2:11–12), and both "saw" God in unique circumstances (Gen. 33:12–23; 1 Ki. 19). Elijah is prophesied to be a forerunner of the Messiah (Mal. 4:5–6), but when does, or did, he operate? John the Baptist said he was not Elijah but came in that prophet's spirit. Is then the prophecy satisfied in John? The true identity of the two witnesses will remain a mystery until they manifest themselves. *See also* Elijah; Enoch; eschatology, eschatological; fire from the mouth; great and dreadful day, that; Joshua as priest; martyr(s); martyrdom; Moses; witness(es); Zerubbabel.

"witness of the stars." See zodiac.

witness, three who. See Spirit, the water, and the blood, the.

wizard(s): one who is adept in the arts of sorcery, enchantments, conjure techniques, and the like—a warlock. Such a one is commonly called a magician, but in biblical usage, he is a dabbler in the occult. Pagan cultures commonly kept them on the payroll, and King Manasseh of Judah hired them on a regular basis. Some descriptions name a wizard as a male witch. *See also* apotropaic magic; cantrip; charm(s); curse(s); enchantment; evil eye; execration; *geis;* hex; imprecation; magic, magick; meonenim; Merlin; New Age religion; occult, occultic; *pharmakeia;* psychonautics; pow-wow; sorcery, sorceries; spell; spell names; taboo; Voodoo; Voudou; ward; warlock(s); Wicca; witch(es); witchcraft.

Woden. See Odin; Wotanism.

woe(s): in apocalyptic thought, a disaster added to one already in progress, the Greek word being *hoy*. Jesus pronounced terrible woes or curses when he spoke severely against the scribes and Pharisees; their end will be terrible in the eschaton (Mt. 23). Those calamities specifically delineated in Matthew include: 1. slamming the door to the kingdom of heaven in men's faces so that they themselves do not enter nor allow anyone else to go in, 2. traveling over land and sea to make a single convert, only to make the respondent even more of a son of hell than they, personally are, 3. holding inverse priorities in that they believe that the altar of God is less important than the gifts on it (*i.e.,* the works of the Law are more important than God Himself), 4. scrupulous tithing as a petty act of service while neglecting weightier matters of the law like justice, mercy, and faithfulness, 5. looking good on the outside (cleaning the surface of the cup or dish) while inside there is only greed and self-indulgence, 6. appearing righteous to others but inside are full of hypocrisy and wickedness, 7. showing reverence for religious tradition and honoring the prophets while smugly insisting that they would have been more righteous had they lived in those past days. Revelation also speaks of woes: from the angel for the earth when Satan invades (Rev. 12:12) and from the angel (or eagle) speaking to the Tribulation peoples who will experience the final three trumpets (Rev. 8:13). There are three "woes" in the Revelation account indicating that number of particularly severe disasters— one ending after the fifth trumpet and the second after the sixth. The book does not cite the third, so we might arbitrarily pick the casting of Satan to earth (Rev. 12) or some other Revelation catastrophe as the final woe. Periodically, a loud voice in heaven also pronounces trials. Because the devil has descended to earth, woes are also reserved for the earth and sea, the trees, the sky, and the freshwaters (Rev.7:1–3; 10:2, 5–6; 14:7). Finally, the earthly authorities lament the fall of Secular Babylon (Rev. 18:10, 16, 19) with cries of "woe," sometimes translated as "alas." Some interpreters see the woes as grief and lament only, not curses. This reading does not seem to grant the word sufficient impact from the issue of sin as it appears in Scripture. *See also* eagle(s); (angel) of woe; trumpet(s); war in heaven.

woke: slang language originally brokered by an expression in so-called African-American Vernacular English (AAVE) with a basic meaning of "being aware" (awake). The expression was meant to stir attention to social justice and race issues. The Black Lives Matter movement, however, hijacked the term and turned the emphasis to activist causes and rebellion against traditional American values. Although "woke" is merely the past tense of "wake," it is now circulated on social media and the political arena to promote (usually with intimidation and violence) and to boost the far-left political agenda. Advocates are urged to be" woke" and "stay woke" until the desired radical societal changes are complete. *See also* cultural relativism; culture war; "hate crimes"; Militant Domestic Organizations; racists; social issues.

wolf: a ferocious carnivorous animal, a pack hunter. Wolves often symbolize vicious attack and mayhem (Acts 20:29; Mt. 7:15). Their favorite prey was innocent and defenseless sheep which frequently characterized the faithful continually at the mercy of the oppressor. The breed was a common animal of worship in the ancient world as well, particularly as a destructive force in the universe. Fenris the wolf (Loki's child) figures prominently in the Norse legend of Ragnarok as the devourer of worlds. *See also* alukah; animals, birds, and insects, symbology of; fox; leopard; lion and the yearling (calf), the; Loki; mythological beasties, elementals, monsters, and spirit animals; names, symbology of; *nagual;* Norse and old Germanic pantheon; Ragnarok; therianthropy; Twi; wolf will live with the lamb, the.

Wolff, Joseph: a Jew converted to Christianity (1795–1862) who predicted the end of the world in 1847. Wolff was widely traveled and preached an odd message that earned him the title of "the eccentric missionary." *See also* missions, missionaries.

wolf will live with the lamb, the: a literary picture of the millennial reign of peace and the time after on the earth as described by Isaiah (Isa. 11:6). Interestingly, it is a common error for many people to repeat the sentence found in the passage as "the lion will lie down with the lamb" when the actual quote is "the wolf will live (dwell) with the lamb." The word picture continues by portraying the coexistence of the leopard with the goat, the lion with the calf, the cow and the bear, and the young (of all species) lying together. A little child shall lead them (play with them?), and the toddler will be safe near the cobra's nest (Isa. 11:6–9). *See also* animals, birds, and insects, symbology of; lion and the yearling (calf), the; wolf.

Wolsey, Thomas: a cardinal in the Church of England (ca. 1472–1530) who was as much a statesman as clergy. He was determined to make England predominant in Western Europe and helped King Henry VIII obtain dispensations for his divorces. *See also* Church of England.

woman (women): a female. Apocalyptic language often uses the feminine as a symbol of either good (as in Revelation 12:1–2) or evil (as in Revelation 17). In a positive realm, most competent thinkers may readily admit that such subliminal talents as intuition, pious insight, and the like (what some might choose to call the eternal "feminine mystique"), may more readily arise naturally in women than in men. What women offer is difficult to define but the gifts seem to originate and grow from some unique spiritual acumen that differs somehow from the purely deeply cerebral intellect. There is little doubt that Christianity, and Jesus himself, gave a giant boost to female acceptance and honor as compared with the society around the early church and before. However, equality of the sexes has never been fully achieved. Paul was ambiguous in his discussion of the issue of women's status in the church. At times he seemed to denounce their efforts, then praise them exuberantly elsewhere. No doubt his attitude was influenced by his belief that the Second Coming was near. Because of the urgency, he even urged all to remain as they are—as married or single, as slave or free, or in your station of society where and who you now are. The popes of Roman Catholicism and fundamentalist–type Protestantism have striven to set back women's contributions and status remarkably. The Talmud even instructs Jewish men to thank God three times a day that they were not born a woman. Islam is particularly harsh in its treatment of women. In Hebrew, the word for *woman* sounds like the one for *man.* No doubt, the term was deliberate since according to the Genesis record, the woman was made from the man (Gen. 2:23). Perhaps it is expected to attempt a list of the most famous women of the Bible. Forcibly shortened, the following inventory of names should certainly appear: Abigail,

Anna the prophetess; Deborah, Delilah, Dinah, Dorcas (Tabitha), Elizabeth, Esther, Eunice, Euodia, Eve, Gomer, Hagar, Hannah, Huldah the prophetess, Jael, Jezebel, Joanna, Jochebed, Keturah, Leah, Lois, Lydia of Thyatira, Martha, Mary the mother of Jesus, Mary the sister of Martha, Mary the mother of James and Joses, Mary the wife of Cleophas, Mary Magdalene, Michal, Miriam, Naomi, Noadiah the prophetess, Phoebe, Rachel, Rebekah, Ruth, Salome, Sarah, Susanna, Tamar, and Zilpah. Many other women are unnamed in the Bible but were exceedingly accomplished. *See also* abbess; Abigail; Abishag; adulteress; Aisha; Alexandra; *almah;* Ammia; Amram and Jochebed; Amytis; Ananias and Sapphira; ancress; Anna; Anne, Queen of de la Palude; Anthony, Susan Brownell; Apollonia; Apphia; Arsinoe; Apphia; Asenath; Athaliah; Baba Vanga; Bailey, Alice A.; Bakker, Jim and Tammy Faye; Bathsheba; Beguines; Belkis; Berenice; Bernice; Besant, Annie; Bilhah; Blavatsky, Madame Helena Petrovna; Booth, Evangeline Cory; Bridget of Kildare; Bridget of Sweden; Browne, Sylvia; Cabrini, Frances Xavier; Candace; Carey, William and Dorothy; Cassandra; Cassiopeia; Catherine of Siena; Cecilia; Chloe; chosen lady and her children; chosen sister, your; *Christotokos;* Claudia; Cleopatra of Egypt; Cleopatra of Syria; Clutterbuck, Dorothy; complementarianism; concubine; convent; co-redemptrix; Crosby, Frances Jane Van Alstyne; Crystal, Ellie; Damaris; Dame Folly; daughter of Jerusalem; daughter of Zion; Daughters of Jerusalem; daughters (four) of Philip; David's wives; deacon(s), deaconess(es); *deakonos;* Deborah; Delilah; Delphi, Oracle of; demimondaines; Dinah; Dixon, Jeanne; Drusilla; Dyer, Mary; Eddy, Mary Baker; egalitarian view of authority; elect lady, the; elect sister, your; Elizabeth; Elizabeth I, Queen; Emmerich, Anna Katherine; Esther as Hebrew heroine; Eudoxia; Eunice; Euodia; Eve; Fatima; female genital mutilation; feminist theology; Fillmore, Myrtle and Charles; Fortune, Dion; Fox sisters; Fry, Elizabeth "Betsy"; Galgani, Gemma; generational prophecy; Gerberga; Gertrude; Glaphyra; godparents; Gomer; Gowdie, Isobel; Great Prostitute, the; Hagar; Hagar and Sarah; Hamutal; Hannah; hegumene; Helena; hen; Hephzibah; Herodias; Hildegard of Bingen; *houris;* Houteff, Florence; Howe, Julia Ward; Huldah; Hutchison, Anne; Hypatia; Irene; Jael; Jehosheba; Jezebel; Joanna; Joan of Arc; Judith; Judson, Adoniram and Ann; Julia;

Julian of Norwich; Junias; Kamehameha, King and Emma; Keturah; Khadija; Kuhlman, Kathryn; Lady Wisdom; Laodice; Leah; lectrice; Lee, Ann; Leek, Sybil; leman; le Royer, Jeanne; Lois; Lot's wife; Louis VII, King and Eleanor; Lydia as covert; MacDonald, Margaret; Makeda; Mama Omida; mambo; man (men); Martha; Martin, Dorothy; Mary; Mary, Queen of Scots; Mary Magdalene; Maximilla; McPherson, Aimee Semple; Meir, Golda; Michal; Miriam; "monthly uncleanness"; Moon, Lottie; Mother Shipton; mother superior; Mott, Lucretia Coffin; muti; Mystery Babylon the Great the Mother of Prostitutes and of the Abominations of the Earth; Naomi; na Prous Boneta; Nereus; Nettles, Bonnie; Nightingale, Florence; Nitocris; Noadiah; nun(s); nymph(s); Nympha; O'Hair, Madelyn Murray; Olympas; Orpah; Pandora; Pankhurst, Christabel; Perpetua and Felicity; Persis; Phoebe; Pilate's wife; Poor Clare Sisters; Pope Joan; Porete, Marguerite; prior, prioress; Priscilla; Prophet, Elizabeth Clare; prophetess(es); prostitute, prostitution; Pudens; Python, python; queen(s); queen of heaven; Queen of Sheba; Queen of the South; Rachel; Rahab; Rebekah; Regina the Seeress; Religious Babylon; Rhoda; Rizpah; Rowling, J. K.; Royall, Anne; Ruth as Old Testament heroine; Sangomas; Salome; Sanger, Margaret Higgins; Sarah; Second Eve, the; Semiramis; Seton, Elizabeth Ann; Shaw, Anna Howard; shepherd/shepherdess; she who is in Babylon; Shunammite; Sibyl(s); Sibyl of Tivoli; sister(s); slave girl of Philippi; snowflake(s); son(s) of man (men); *Sophia*; Southcott, Joanna; Stachys; Stanton, Elizabeth Cady; Susanna; sylph(s); Syntyche; Syrophoenician woman; Tabitha; Tamar; ten Boom, Corrie; Teresa of Avilla; Teresa of Calcutta; Tharbis; Thecla; Theodora; *Theotokos;* Thiota; Tryphena; Tryphosa; undine; Ursula; Vashti, Queen; Veleda; Veronica; virgin(s), virginity; Walroff, Helen; ward; Wheatley, Phillis; White Buffalo Calf Woman; White, Ellen G. (Harmon); whore of Babylon; widow; widow with the meager offering; wife of your youth; Wilkerson, Jemima; Willard, Francis; William and Mary; wise woman, a; witch(es); "witches of New Forest, the"; witch of Endor; woman at the well; woman clothed in (with) the sun, the; woman of Canaan; woman taken in adultery; woman with a blessing; woman with a jar of ointment; woman with an issue of blood; Woodward-Etta, Maria; Zeresh; Zilpah; Zipporah.

woman at the well: a common description of the Samaritan woman who encountered Jesus at Jacob's Well in Samaria (the well of Sychar). Jesus asked her for a drink, which precipitated a theological discussion between the two. Jesus explained that he was the true "water of life" and the source of salvation. The woman urgently desired this blessing when she fully understood the meaning (Jn. 4:4–26). *See also* Samaritan(s); water of life.

woman clothed in (with) the sun, the: the Revelation vision of Israel portrayed as a woman clothed in the sun, with the moon under her feet and a tiara of twelve stars in her hair (Rev. 12:1–13a). She is threatened by the great red dragon (Satan) but is rescued after she gives birth to a male child, whom we interpret to be the savior Jesus. Her adventure probably envisions the persecution of her "children"—the Jews and righteous saints of the Tribulation from which only a few will survive in the physical body. Having failed to destroy the woman's offspring (Jesus), the dragon of Revelation 12 attempts to annihilate his adversary by pursuing her into the wilderness and vomiting a torrent of water to consume her. The bright woman is rescued, however, by being given wings of an eagle (reminiscent of Exodus 19:4 and Isaiah 40:31) and causing the earth to swallow the dragon's flood (recalling Pharaoh's attempt to drown all the Hebrew boys of Exodus 1:22 in the Nile and the inundation of Pharaoh's army at the Red Sea). The woman is then given sanctuary for a time, times, and half a time (three and a half years) in the wilderness (similar to the Exodus escape into the desert under the leadership of Moses). There is confusion among theologians as to whether the confrontation between the woman and the dragon portrays the death and resurrection of Jesus or to his birth and ascension. According to one theory, the "snatching up" to rescue event within the narrative may be the Church in rapture because it, and Christ, can be viewed at this juncture; to grasp one is to claim the other. To illustrate, Paul's conversion experience (Acts 26:12–20) affirmed that he (then known as Saul) was persecuting Jesus. How could this be since the two had never met? Saul was, however, persecuting the infant church and therefore Christ himself was subject to harm. Some, on the other hand, see no reference whatsoever to the Christ in the entire paradigm. Some claim she represents the martyred Church saints or the mother church at Jerusalem. Many individuals and institutions have claimed to be the earthly representation of the woman, including the Roman Catholic Church and Mary Baker Eddy, but the Revelation pageant with its context clearly favors a Jewish setting. Others see her as representing the people of Israel, the physical descendants of Abraham, Isaac, and Jacob. The sun, moon, and stars must then be read as part of the dream experienced by Joseph in Genesis 37. There the heavenly bodies are picturing Joseph's parents, Jacob and Rachel, and the other sons who became the twelve tribes of Israel. Some even go so far as to say the image sprang from pagan myth. In the end, it is best to see the paradigm as a flashback to Satan's original rebellion against God in the early days after creation, as most scholars note. There is nothing to demand, however, that the vision cannot be, at least partially, futuristic. Rebellion of either angels or humans is not limited in time nor circumstance. *See also* dragon; Eddy, Mary Baker; eschatology, eschatological; infanticide; Judaism; Mariolatry; moon; nourishment in the wilderness; rapture; Roman Catholic Church; Southcott, Joanna; star(s); sun; twelve-starred crown; woman clothed in (with) the sun; Woman in the Wilderness.

woman in a basket. See Wickedness; Zechariah's vision of the woman in a basket.

Woman in the Wilderness: an apocalyptic cult formed by Johann Jacob Zimmerman and Johannes Kelpius, who believed the Second Coming would occur in the fall of 1694. Kelpius led a group of pilgrims to America to await the great event. The phrase may also represent the woman in conflict with the dragon covered in Revelation 12. *See also* Behmenism; cult(s); woman clothed in (with) the sun, the; Zimmerman, Johann Jacob.

woman of Canaan: a Canaanite (therefore considered a pagan) who found Jesus and pleaded loudly for the Lord to heal her daughter who was possessed by a demon (Mt. 15-21-28; Mk. 7:24–30). Her prayer was graciously answered. Neither ethnicity nor nationality is an issue with Christ and his heavenly candidates. *See also* demon(s), demonic; Sceva; slave girl of Philippi; Syrophoenician woman.

woman of the sun and moon. See woman clothed in (with) the sun, the.

Woman's Christian Temperance Union: an organization of women activists formed in 1874 with a goal of abolishing the liquor traffic. Their aims were successful with the ratification of the Eighteenth Amendment. Other issues soon emerged for the group, including women's suffrage, prostitution, drug abuse, and other reform movements of interest to women. The organization prospered under their long-serving (1879–1898) president, Frances E. Willard. The group also fostered physiology and hygiene in public education. *See also* American Society for the Promotion of Temperance; Anti-Saloon League; social issues; religious organizations; temperance; Willard, Francis.

woman taken in adultery: the *Pericope Adulterae,* a Gospel incident relating the accusation and condemnation of a woman involved in an adulterous relationship as related in John and Luke. Despite her guilt, and to shame the accusers for their hypocrisy, Jesus dismissed the crowd and proclaimed forgiveness for the victim. Some early manuscripts do not contain the story but most scholars agree it was a genuine action of Jesus. *See also* adulteress.

woman with a blessing: a spontaneous response of a woman in the crowd after hearing Jesus preach (Lk. 11:27–28). She shouted, "Blessed is the mother who gave you birth and nursed you." Jesus' response was a counter comment—that those who hear God's word and obey are the ones who are truly blessed. Christ seemed to deflect the beatitude from Mary, himself, or any other and redirected it instead to God the Father.

woman with a jar of ointment: the New Testament account (Mk. 14:1–11) of a woman in Bethany (with varying accounts in the other Gospels) who anointed the head of Jesus with expensive ointment from an alabaster jar. Some present criticized her hypocritically for such a waste but Jesus defended her motives. He announced the act had been done in love in prophetic preparation for his burial. *See also* alabaster; anointing; Mary; Mary's anointing; oil of anointing; perfumes, ointments, and spices; sacrifice.

woman with an issue of blood: an infirmed woman who ostensibly suffered from prolonged menstruation or a similar malady (Mk. 5:25–34). She had suffered for twelve years and desired to approach Jesus for healing. The incident occurred when the Lord was on his way to heal the centurion's son. The woman surreptitiously grasped Jesus' robe, thinking not to draw attention to herself. The Lord perceived her touch, however, and performed a healing, then commended her for her simple faith. Unobtrusive trust is a high-quality posture for the future heaven.

Wonderful Counselor: one of Isaiah's quartet of titles for the Messiah Jesus (Isa. 9:6). The appellation seems to mimic the advocacy powers of the Holy Spirit. *See also* Everlasting Father; Mighty God; names (titles) for Jesus; Prince of Peace.

"wonders in the heavens and in the earth": an apocalyptic expression used in Scripture to figuratively express divine judgments and revolutions. *See also* eschatology, eschatological; miracle(s); prodigy; sign(s); signs and wonders; signs in heaven.

wooden sticks, prophecy of the. See Ezekiel's demonstration of the folded boards.

Woods, Robert Archey: social reformer and Presbyterian graduate of Andover Seminary (1865–1925). Woods was passionate about poverty issues and became the director of the South End House of Boston, a settlement house concentrating on social issues and care of the urban poor. *See also* Presbyterians; settlement houses; social issues.

Woodworth-Etta, Maria: female charismatic evangelist (1844–1924) known for her public display of mental trance which she could impose upon herself or others. She evolved from a strong Quaker background and exhibited much of that sect's acted-out spirit inducements but was expelled from the Church of God of the General Eldership in 1904. *See also* Church of God; evangelist(s), evangelism.

wool: the product of the sheep producing fabric and garments. In apocalyptic language, the whiteness of wool is often a symbol of righteousness. *See also* linen; raiment; white raiment.

Woolman, John: an itinerate Quaker preacher (1720–1772), one of the earliest spokesmen to formulate meaningful anti-slavery doctrines. He was recognized as highly influential to the growing abolitionist movement in America. Woolman died in England trying to aid the poor there. *See also* slave, slavery; Society of Friends.

Word-Faith Movement: or Word of Faith Movement, a prosperity religion founded by E. W. Kenyon (1867–1948) but made famous by a Pentecostal faith healer named Kenneth Hagin. According to doctrine, God made us humans as "little gods" capable of speaking words of creation just as He did to make the world. The Fall of Adam transferred our planet to Satan. Jesus restored our godhead status by dying on the cross spiritually as well as physically. He subsequently suffered in hell but became the first "born again" while still there. Jesus then escaped hell and restored the world empowerment and can now grant us prosperity and health. The Word-Faith sect is a serious deviation from established Christianity. *See also* cult(s); prosperity religions.

Word of Faith Fellowship: a 750 member (as of 2017) sect based in Spindale, North Carolina, plus another 2000 in Brazil and Ghana. The cult has been charged a number of times for beatings and other types of abuse/coercion against non-conformist congregants but charges were dropped each time because of insider intervention in the local judiciary. Victims were also threatened and coached as to how to circumvent court evidence. *See also* cult(s).

Word of Faith Movement. See prosperity religion(s); Word-Faith Movement.

Word of God: 1. the Bible. 2. the revelation of God as He expresses Himself in various and sundry ways, as in Colossians 1:17 and Revelation 19:13, which denote him as the Son of God. 3. Jesus Christ as the Word incarnate (Jn. 1:1; Heb. 1:3). To the Gospel writer John, the Word of God (*Spermaticos Logos*) seemed to name the creative force (Jn. 1:1–5) by which the universe came into being, has eternally resided with God, and has descended to man. The Stoics and some Gnostic thought favor something akin to that concept, in that humans carry the divine spark. *See also* Bible; Bible manuscripts; Gnosticism, Gnostic(s); Logos; *logos;* means of grace; names (titles) for Jesus; names (titles) for God; revelation, theological; Stoicism, Stoics.

words of institution: the recited liturgical formula for officially introducing the observance of Communion. The words are spoken at the beginning of the Eucharist rite to invite the Holy Spirit and the participants to celebrate the Lord's Supper by acknowledging its beginning and to somewhat establish its exigency. The words of 1 Corinthians 11:23-26 or others found in the New Testament are acceptable as introductory speech for the occasion though the high liturgical recitation is probably more formal. *See also* Anamnesis; Anaphora; concomitance; consecrate; enduement; epiccesis; epiclesis; epidesis; Eucharist; Holy Spirit; invination; liturgy, Christian; liturgical year; Lord's Supper.

works: those pious or ministerial efforts put forth in the name of Jesus. While they are essential to the Christian life (1 Cor. 3:13), it must be remembered that salvation does not issue from them, but only from the voluntary sacrifice of Christ (Eph. 2:8-9). Works are our reasonable service or expected worship (Rom. 12:1) because we are called and chosen of Christ. *See also* autosoterism; covenant of works; works, salvation by.

works, salvation by: the concept, in the minds of many uninformed persons, that human effort and the accomplishment of good deeds will ensure one's entry into heaven and God's present favor. The belief is insubstantial at best and meaningless at the worse because salvation comes through the profession of Christ and his saving grace, not good works, no matter how numerous or sincere. Our human efforts can never measure God's holiness, nor alone merit His favor. *See also* Adam; Adamic Covenant; autosoterism; Cocceius, Johannes; condign merit; congruent merit; covenant of grace; covenant of works; Didache, the; monergism; salvation; solifidianism; stone of stumbling; synergism; works.

World Church of Peace: a centerpiece church in Hiroshima, Japan, built in place of one destroyed by the atomic bomb in World War II. Funds for its construction came from donors worldwide. Of note, there are many so-called Buddhist Peace Pagodas abounding worldwide dedicated to the victims and survivors of the destruction. *See also* church; religious organizations.

World Council of Churches: an international organization based in Geneva, Switzerland dedicated to promoting worldwide religious unity. The organization began in 1948 and is sponsored by a variety of ecclesiastical groups, but many Protestant denominations are not members and the Roman Catholic Church is absent from its rolls as well. *See also* ecumenism; National Council of Churches; Parliament of the World's Religions; religious organizations; Schaff, Philip; Week of Prayer for Christian Unity.

worldly: love for the false pleasures of life usually characterized by a poor attitude and immoral behavior opposed to sound religious precepts. *See also* after one's own lusts; antinomianism; body; carnal; concupiscence; debauchery; demimondaines; depravity; dissipation; flesh; harmartiology; hedonism; human condition, the; human nature, the; immorality; iniquity; kingdom of this world; moral uncleanliness; orgies; Phibionites; sin(s); sinful nature, the; social issues; trespass; unclean; wicked, wickedness; "world, the."

World Pantheist Movement: the world's largest organization of pantheism espousing the belief that spirituality is to be centered on nature. *See also* Emergent Church; nature cult(s); panentheism; pantheism; religious organizations; sect(s).

world ruler: one of many titles for Antichrist. *See also* Antichrist.

World Teacher, the: one who claims to be the Buddhist Maitreya now reported to be living in London since 1977. He is promoted by New Age enthusiast Benjamin Crème and his Share International organization. *See also* Crème, Benjamin; Exalted One, the; rescuers of the Church.

"world, the": in reality, the planet on which we live. In eschatological and ethical thinking, however, the phrase is a common contemporary idiom, and a New Testament expression, referring mainly to the corruption and evil influence of the age, which is ever trying to disparage God, promote evil, and tempt to sin. Such a "world" does not refer to the material creation but to the system of degraded values and corrupt desires that are in opposition to God and His eternal plan of righteousness. The writer of James (James 4:4) related that any man who is a friend of "the world" is an enemy of God. John urged believers not to love the world, for it and all in it are transient (1 Jn. 2:15–17). Christians are urged to be *in* the world but not *of* it, and are assured that Christ has overcome the world (Jn. 16:33). In the eschaton, Jesus will judge the world (Rev. 14:7). So then, when believers read or hear the negative phrase "the world" (and it *is* a negative thought), he or she should always remember that our earth is being described as it now is, under the curse, but will not always be so. In a more positive sense, the present world (*kosmos*) is our home, and it holds its many marks of beauty and provision. So close is our affinity that the gospel sometimes equates "world" with people (Jn. 3:16; 2 Cor. 22, 45). This world, and the people of the world, is in need of rescue, however, from this flawed planet and evil age. So, according to the truth of eschatology, this world will be renewed and refurbished as part of God's total redemptive plan (Rev. 21:1). An important part of Jesus' Model Prayer, after all, was "on earth as it is in heaven." *See also* kingdom of this world; *kosmos*; social issues; spirit of the age; worldly.

world to come, the: a reference to the Millennium (Heb. 2:5) and/ or the afterlife. The term in Hebrew is *Olam Haba. See also* Abraham's bosom; afterlife; Annwn; Aralu; Arcadia; Asgard; Avalon; destruction of heaven and earth; Dis; Duat; Elysium; eschatology, eschatological; eternal life; future; future life, doctrine of the; Gehenna; Hades; happy hunting ground; heaven; heaven and earth destroyed by fire; hell; Hy-Breasail; Hyperborea; intermediate state; Jade Empire, the; Jahannam; Janna; lake of fire; life after death; limbo; *Limbus Puerorum;* Mictlan; new heaven and new earth; Nirvana; Otherworld; Paradise; paradise of God; paraeschatology; Pardes; Perdition; Promised Land, the; Pure Land, the; purgatory; Shambhala legends; *Sheol;* soul sleep; space doctrine; Summerland; Thule, land of; Tir na nOg; underworld; Upper Gehenna; Utopia; Valhalla; Xibala.

world tree. See cosmic tree.

worldview: or worldview and worldview, a person's understanding, thoughts, and actions that manifest in her manner of life. One's cosmology, theology, futurology, morality, and many other disciplines determine an individual worldview and thereby guide the personal and public life. Considering this application, any individual or public worldview becomes vital to the study of prophecy and eschatology. The scientific term may be more familiar to some under the German name *weltanschauung. See also* Judeo-Christian ethic; Protestant ethic; "Protestant Principle, the."

World War III: the anticipated worldwide confrontation that could be the earth's final conflict. As a prelude to such eschatological thinking, some sixty million people perished in World War II and, when combined with the first World War, account for more deaths and suffering than all conflicts combined. The third promises to be much worse. Modern weapons (especially nuclear, biological, chemical, and scalar (electromagnetic) warfare, global tactics, and economic manipulation are so potently devastating as to destroy civilization. Such an eventuality would likely be an asymmetric conflict and could easily devastate civilization as we know it. Many astute individuals and any number of religious persuasions subscribe to the idea that World War III is synchronous with the battle of Armageddon. At the least, some report, the final war will bring on the New World Order headed by the Antichrist. *See also* Day of Purification; Doomsday Clock, the; end of all things, the; end of the age, the; end of the world, the; eschatology, eschatological; Great Change, Prophecy of the; Great Shaking, the; *War of the Sons of Light Against the Sons of Darkness;* war on earth; War Scroll.

Worldwide Church of God: an eccentric group akin to or part of the Anglo-Israelism sect formerly promoted by Herbert W. Armstrong. The particular branch led by David C. Pack is called the Reformed Church of God. The eschatology of the groups is flawed, even bizarre at many points, namely, that the saved do not go to heaven, that the unsaved have more than one chance at salvation after the great white throne judgment, and that those finally condemned are annihilated, not existing as undying souls. Some few commentators have suggested a more contemporary meaning for the Revelation listing of the 144,000 who are posited as Jews who have embraced Christianity since these can be counted because they are relatively few in number. Gentile converts, on the other hand, are innumerable. Revelation's mentions of the multitude of mourners are Gentile converts during the 1500 years of papal supremacy, singled out from fierce persecution from the Roman Church. At least one additional radical view of the great multitude sees them as the firstfruits made up of converts to Christianity after A.D. 66 (including the apostles). The theory further extends to the point where Mohammed is named as the Antichrist and any other of that description in the Tribulation era is mythical. The False Prophet of Revelation represents the medieval popes holding supremacy over Rome, then the Holy Roman Empire. The harvest spectacle of Revelation 14 represents the success of evangelism in the Reformation era led by men like Zinzendorf, the Wesleys, Asbury, Whitefield, Judson, Moody, etc. The predictions of Matthew 24 are already fulfilled, except the single prophecy of the Second Coming. The book of Revelation concerns the Church only with no true reference to the Jews. Armageddon is a coming end time battle, to be called World War III, and has no association with Palestine. Jesus and his followers, according to Reverend Pack, will arrive on spaceships amid the final war, which will be fought with missiles and nuclear weapons. The Second Coming will occur shortly after the rapture of believers with only enough elapsed time for the great Supper of the Lamb to transpire. All Old Testament covenants are conditional, according to men like Pack and Robert Finley, and of no effect presently since the Jewish people could not, or would not, conform to their requirements. So then, the Jewish failures have lost them their designation as the "chosen people," and any blessings of the covenants have eased into the province of the Christian Church. Contrary to most common Bible expertise, the Church *is* mentioned in the Old Testament where it is called "many nations." The book of Zechariah has no mention of the Messiah's Second Coming but only his first. *See also* Anglo-Israelism; Armstrong, Herbert W.; Finley, Robert; lions, the young; Pack, David C.; sect(s).

worldwide preaching of the gospel: the spread of the gospel throughout the world. Jesus spoke of this action as a prerequisite (though not necessarily to worldwide repentance) prior to his Second Coming (Mt. 24:14). Preterists and others view the *world* as that populated area before the Jewish War only, but many others view it as a missionary obligation that will foreshadow the Second Coming. Almost all languages of the world have access to verbal or written Scripture. Gospel preaching has reached epic proportions in our advancing age of technology. The evangelistic movie, *The Jesus Film*, as one example, has been viewed over six billion times and has been instrumental in conversion experiences for over 200 million people. *See also* eschatology, eschatological; evangelist(s), evangelism; gospel; Great Commission, the; homiletics; *kerygma;* missionary eschatology; missions, missionaries; Olivet Discourse, the; preach(ing); Second Coming; soul-winning; spreading the gospel; witness(es).

worm: bilateral invertebrates living mostly underground. The metaphorical meaning in the Bible (and still today) comprises a symbol for worthlessness (Ps. 22:6; Job 25:6) or the corruption of the grave (Isa. 14:11). The worm could be a pest (Jon. 4:7) and even cause death to the living (Acts 12:23). Hell is said to be a place where the fire never goes out and their worm never dies (Mk. 9:47–48). The text in Mark reads *their* worm and not *the* worm as we might expect because the subject is not a creepy and slimy natural worm but a metaphor of unremitting vice of the damned whose sin maggots never stop breeding and who never cease suffering for it. The Gospel quote is from the last verse of Isaiah (Isa. 66:24) which, if standing alone, appears to leave an emotion of despair at the book's closure. Fortunately, however, the context shows victory for the righteous over our natural corruption as we contemplate and prepare for life in the new and perfect age to come. But such is not so for the condemned. *See also* animals, birds, and insects, symbology of.

Wormwood: the name of the blazing star falling from the sky in the third trumpet of Revelation. The name means "bitterness," and its crash into the freshwaters of earth causes a third of them to become non-potable. The name derives from the wormwood plant, the *artemisia absinthium*, from which a gall or hallucinogen has been compounded for millennia and used by some cultures to communicate with the gods. Some assert Wormwood is not a celestial body as such but either a demon or an assisting godly angel. The description as a godly messenger does not seem to fit well with the generalized description, however. *See also* blazing star; Chernobyl.

worship: adoration and praise. Apocalyptic literature can show evil or pagan worship or its opposite, good and godly worship, in a variety of ways. Revelation 4 and 5 are magnificent representations of the grand heavenly adulation of God and the Lamb. The term is derived from an Old English word meaning "worthy." Among the major world religions, the Hindu traditional day of worship is Thursday, the Muslim on Friday, Judaism on Saturday (beginning at sundown on Friday), and Christian on Sunday. Worship of God, however, may be at no specific time or encompasses all of time. The acts of worship are sometimes classified as *lateria*—God alone, *hyperdualism*—veneration of the Virgin Mary, or *dulia*—commissioning saints, angels, and relics. In the acceptable context, real worship is a meeting with mystery, an encounter that is neither wholly controlled by nor fully perceptive to the worshiper.

The experience is uplifting or disturbing, intense or soothing, quiet or vocal, but always profound in its exchange between God and devotee. A persistent and legitimate question might be raised: "Why do people worship?" The answer is probably as varied as the individuals who do it. Nevertheless, it is likely that they do so simply because we are created to be involved as worshipers, whether that paradigm is individually or collectively recognized and practiced or whether it is denied. We cannot be otherwise, even if our worship is that of our selves, our materials, our idols, or our pleasures. Christians worship in true form because we are steeped and marinated in the love and blessing of the God we see as personal, because we celebrate an eternal future of perfection and promise, and because we allow ourselves to be challenged and prompted to evangelize such joy and urgency toward others. What of formal worship, as in a church setting? Many and varied are the methods and styles common to most congregations but the typical formula normally consists of several basic expressions. Praise to God in such a setting will likely feature music (sacred, gospel, or contemporary with or without instrumental or vocal accompaniment and individually or congregationally produced), prayers (recited spontaneously or scripted), a sermon or homily, Scripture readings for edification and enlightenment, sacramental or ordinance type acts such as the Eucharist (Communion), baptism, a marriage, a profession of faith, or the like, and certain unique rituals or ceremonies peculiar to a given denomination or congregation. The theme may be sacramental (high church), reformed (a middle ground of formality), or evangelical (low church). Incidentally, "low" church does not imply substandard or crude nor does "high" church suggest something more elegant or profound. Rather, the adjectives refer to style, not sophistication. *See also* alternative worship; arts, the; *axceyous;* blended worship; broad church; church; church models; contemporary worship; devotion, devotional; dialogical principles of worship; elements of worship; dialogical principles of worship; divine services; *dulia;* elements of worship; entheogen; epiccesis; exaltation; faith; form of worship; High Church, Low Church; Holiness Code; hymn(s); *latria;* liturgical year; liturgy; liturgy, Christian; liturgy, Jewish; means of grace; music; normative principles of worship; order of service; praise; prayer(s); regulative principles of worship; religion; rite; ritual.

worship psalm: any biblical Psalm written with the primary purpose of praise or adoration to God, of which there are many. *See also* creation psalm; Doxology, doxology; enthronement psalm; historical psalm; imprecatory psalm; messianic psalm; *Old 100;* penitential psalm; psalm; psalm of judgment; psalm of lament; Psalms as Old Testament book; royal psalm; supplication psalm; thanksgiving psalm; wisdom psalm.

worthless (wicked) shepherd, the: an allegory from the prophet Zechariah (Zech. 11:15–17) in which God promises a cruel leader to someday present himself to the Jews. The story is closely linked to the previous verses that describe the hired worthless shepherds and two staffs and is supplemented by Ezekiel's equally devastating condemnation of wicked leaders (Ezk. 34:7-10). Now, the Lord said He will raise up an even more heartless ruler [shepherd] who cares nothing for the sheep [the common people]. Rather, this brutal newcomer will abuse the citizens and use them for his own selfish ends. The Bible even describes this wicked ruler as being injured by the sword in his arm and right eye, much like the wounded head of the beast in Revelation 13:14. The recitation ends with a curse on the worthless shepherd in which he may be struck down, blinded, or made to suffer with a withered arm. Perhaps the worthless shepherd anticipates the Antichrist or one of his associates, notably the False Prophet. Jesus may have been speaking of the false shepherd in John 5:43 when he said, "I have come in my Father's name, and you do not accept me; but if someone else comes in his own name, you will accept him." *See also* Antichrist; Ezekiel's curse of the neglectful shepherds; False Prophet, the; third eye, the.

worthy is the Lamb: a central praise theme of Revelation (Rev. 5:9, *et al.*). It is the reigning Christ who is worthy of worship, to receive and open the great seals of Revelation 6, and to receive the prayers of the saints. "Worthy" also appears in Revelation 4:8–11 where it is particularly suitable because of the word's close connection to *worship*; here are the four living creatures engaged in that very act. *See also* Lamb, the.

Wotan. See Norse and Old Germanic pantheon; Odin; Wotanism.

Wotanism: a bizarre religion founded by Guido von List, a 20th century racial philosopher dealing favorably with the Aryan race.

List claimed that the ancient Tetons practiced an early Gnostic-type religion that dominated prehistoric Germany and served as a medium between humanity's modern existence and a coming initiation into the nature religions of the ancient past. He named his belief Wotanism after the great Nordic god Wotan. *See also* Armanenschafft; Asatru; cult(s); Gefjon; Irminism; Ermines; Norse and Old Germanic pantheon; Odin; Odinism; sect(s); Vikings.

wounded head of the beast: part of the description of the beast from the sea in Revelation 13:1–10. The beast (Antichrist) is pictured in verse 3 as having a head wound that should have been fatal but is now healed to a scar, allowing him continued domination of Tribulation earth for some time longer. Many theologians are certain the Antichrist is to be killed because of the critical wounding, only to rise again in resurrection. The idea is a radical one because basic doctrine holds that none but God has the power to create and grant life. Anyway, why would He resurrect His enemy? Death cannot be healed but by divine authority, but wounds can, given enough skill and modern technology. Possibly, there could have been an assassination attempt that failed, only to bring the Antichrist back with even more cruelty and punishment. The injury is assumed to be from a sword slash, but in any case, the Tribulation population is astonished because the beast has recovered, and offers worship to him. Some theologians see the imagery as the emperor Nero reborn as Domitian. *See also* eighth king, the.

Wovoka: *nee* Jack Wilson, a northern Paiute leader who predicted the Millennium in 1874 or 1890 when he received a vision while in a trace during a solar eclipse the year before. He was a member of the ghost dance cult. *See also* cult(s); dance; ghost dance cult.

wrath of the Lamb. See day of the Lamb's wrath, the.

wrath, the coming: the *dies viae,* God's warning of His violent eschatological actions in the future time of His choosing (1 Th. 1:9–10). The most pronounced description of God's wrath is perhaps located in Revelation 16 in its depiction of the bowls poured out on the unrepentant which is often identified with judgment. Oddly enough, the chapter before (Rev. 15) begins by announcing that those actions will complete, or finish, God's anger. Does that mean God has thoroughly vented His anger and is emotionally drained? Does it mean God has now gained the desired vengeance on His enemies and is now done with retribution? A correct answer for the end of divine wrath means that God has accomplished total victory over evil and there is no need for further anger and opposition. It is past the time for our culture to stop exalting God as tepid and oblivious Who is too kind to be mad at people or evil entities. Righteous indignation belongs to God whether it is perceived as eternal wrath (hell), end time wrath (eschatology), catastrophic wrath (cataclysmic judgments), the "harvest" wrath of condemnation this side of eternity, or abandonment wrath (when God repudiates evil persons and nations categorically). Divine displeasure of what is harmful to His creation and people is just as inclusive as His love for them. *See also* angelic miracles; Appointed time, the; cup of fury (wrath); day of the Lamb's Wrath, the; day of the Lord; day of vengeance of our God; eschatology, eschatological; "fall on us"; "rescue from the coming wrath."

wreath: a garland or crowning of the head as an adornment or trophy of victory. The prophetic metaphor of the word may mimic the victory crown of the ancient Olympic athletes who received a fragile and perishable crown of leaves as a winning tribute, then contrasted with the crown of glory that never fades in Christ (1 Cor. 9:24–27). In Isaiah, the wreath is presented as trampled and destroyed when discussing Israel's unfaithfulness but glorying in beauty when placed on the righteous remnant (Isa. 28:3–5). The device was utilized in some pagan practices as well (Acts 14:11–13). The garland may also represent good parental guidance (Pro. 1:9) and wisdom as it graces the head in splendor (Pro. 4:9). The ancients were known to drape garlands on themselves or their beasts as a sign of festivity or pagan worship procedure (Acts 14:13). *See also* Advent wreath; chaplet; crown(s); flora, fruit, and grain, symbology of; laurel; wisdom.

writing prophets. See canonical prophets.

Writings, the. See Hagiographa.

Written Torah and Oral Torah: Jewish scholarship and daily religion are governed by what is contained in the Hebrew Bible, the Tanakh, but authority is also derived from oral tradition. Both have value and it is believed that the oral teachings were delivered to Moses at the same time as the Commandments on Mount Sinai. From there, they were passed down verbally through the generations. By extension, the entire Jewish Bible was given to Moses (both written and oral), because, in a real sense, all the people of all generations were present at Sinai. Voluminous writings have been compiled as commentary, but commentary with essential meaning. The writings that comprise the oral traditions are vast, and Torah cannot be studied properly without investigating it all. The Talmud alone fills more than twenty oversized volumes consisting of more than sixty tractates and at least 500 chapters. Rabbis and other students consider a lifetime as insufficient to grasp it. The Mishna, Talmud, Targums and other writings are also to be consulted. A Jewish proverb says that God Himself spends three hours a day studying the Torah. *See also* Book of the Covenant; Book of the Law; Law, the; Mishna; Pentateuch; Talmud; Tanakh; Targum(s); Torah; torah; Torah Scrolls.

Wroe, John: one of the more atypical sectarian radicals of the modern age in England (1782–1863). One biographer described him as "a man of peculiar appearance who inspired uneducated and wonder-loving people with a strange fascination." Wroe was a follower of the prophetess Susana Southcott but founded his own sect, called the Christian Israelite Church, which is still active today. Wroe predicted that the Millennium would begin in 1863 and the world's end would be in 1877. He tried and failed to walk on water (or wading through it on dry land), then underwent a public baptism and circumcision reportedly viewed by some 30,000 spectators. At one point, he even stated his vision that seven virgins should be given to him for his comfort and solace—the girls were duly provided of whom some (or all by some accounts) became pregnant. *See also* Christian Israelite Church; sect(s); Southcott, Joanna.

Wyatt, Ronald Eldon: an amateur digger, explorer, and adventurer (1933–1999) who claimed to have discovered a rather large number of biblical sites and artifacts. With no background in archeology, he and his two sons declare to have located Noah's ark, the ark of the tabernacle, and other significant artifacts, having been directed to their locations by God Himself. His announcements have produced no tangible proofs and are almost universally doubted by professionals and even those of his own church, the Seventh-Day Adventists. Some of the media have dubbed him "Raider Ron" for his exploits. *See also* archeology, archeologists; ark of the covenant; Seventh-Day Adventism; pseudo-archeology.

Wycliffe Bible: the first hand-written manuscripts of the Bible in English. The translations were made from the Vulgate and were faithfully preserved and expanded by the loyal followers of John Wycliffe known as the Lollards. The Wycliffe Bible was the first book printed on Gutenberg's press appearing in 1455. Before, Wycliffe Bibles were inscribed and illustrated by hand on vellum, could take up to two years to produce, and cost a year's wage. *See also* Bible; Bible translations; Gutenberg, Johann; Lollards; vellum; Vulgate; Wycliffe, John.

Wycliffe, John: an influential church scholar and radical reformer of the 1380s who produced the first hand-written manuscripts of the Bible in English. The works and person of Wycliffe were so hated by the papacy, even though he was a Catholic priest, that the pope, some forty-four years later, ordered his bones dug up, crushed, and scattered in the river. *See also* Bible translations; Council of Constance; Hus, John; Lollards; Roman Catholic Church; Wycliffe Bible.

Wye River Agreement: an attempt at peacemaking between the Israelis and Palestinians conducted near Wye River, Maryland, in 1995. The meeting was brokered by President Bill Clinton with the help of King Hussein of Jordan. An agreement was finally signed in 1998 between Benjamin Netanyahu and Yasser Arafat in which Israel agreed to tender certain conquered lands to the Palestinians. The treaty was never implemented, however, because Arafat would not act in good faith. Some prophecy advocates see the Wye River document as a betrayal of Israel. *See also* anti-Semitic; Oslo Accords.

X

Xavier, Francis. See Francis Xavier.

xenoglossy: or xenoglossia, the ability to speak or write in a language the speaker could not have previously known. One biblical example may be the multi-language Pentecost event in Acts 2. The phenomenon is common enough as related by some foreign missionaries in third world countries, recovering victims of stroke, claims by mediums, or some under hypnosis. Sometimes glossolalia is classed as a form of xenoglossy despite its true origin from the Holy Spirit. *See also* baptism of the Holy Spirit; charisms; ecstasy; enduement; glossolalia; initial evidence; missions, missionaries; Pentecost; Pentecostalism; "river, the"; theolepsy; tongues, gift of; tongues, interpretation of; tremendum.

xenophobia: an unwarranted fear or loathing for those of another race or culture. Whether gathered from Bible or secular history, the xenophobic attitude has been the cause of many wasteful wars, personal disputes, and untold hubris throughout the ages. *See also* Columbine; enmity; "hate crimes"; militant domestic organizations; misanthropy; persecution(s); racism; social issues.

Xenophon: Greek general and historian (ca. 434–355 B.C.). He carries some interest to prophecy in that his writing seems to confirm the fall of Babylon at the exact time the book of Daniel states it happened.

xerophagy: eating dry food. Some enthusiasts practice the ritual for the week preceding Easter. The process may be punishment, such as subsisting on bread and water as a self-castigation in search of a receptive spirit. See also Lent; liturgy, Christian; mortification of the flesh.

Xerxes I: the Greek name for the ruler of a vast Persian Empire around 486–465 B.C. The Jews called him Ahasuerus, depicted in the book of Esther (who was his queen) as a vain and indecisive monarch. It is also mentioned in Ezra (Ezr. 4:6–24) that he associated with the opposition to the rebuilding of Jerusalem and its walls, even forcing a work stoppage at the instigation of the Samaritans until the labor could resume under Darius

(Ezr. 4:23–24). In Daniel 11:2, this Xerxes is probably the fourth Persian king after Cyrus who managed to crush an Egyptian revolt but lost the decisive naval engagement at Salamis with the Greeks in 480 B.C. The Persians were denied a strong victory by the heroic stand of the Spartans and Thespians at Thermopylae a year earlier, then were decisively defeated on land at the battle of Plataea in Boeotia (479 B.C.). It was this Xerxes, or his son Artaxerxes I Longimanus, who permitted the rebuilding of the walls of Jerusalem. The Ahasuerus of Daniel 9:1 has not been identified with certainty. *See also* Artaxerxes I Longimanus; Esther as Hebrew heroine; Esther as Old Testament book; king(s); Mordecai; Vashti, Queen.

Xibala: also Mitnal or Mictlan, the Mayan underworld consisting of nine levels. Quetzalcoatl and his companion Xolotl descended there to view the bones of humans. The *Popul Unh* contains a prominent discussion of the place. *See also* Abraham's bosom; afterlife; Annwn; Aralu; Arcadia; Asgard; Avalon; Bolos; Dis; Duat; Elysium; eschatology, eschatological; eternal life; future life, doctrine of the; Gehenna; Hades; happy hunting ground; heaven; hell; Hy-Breasail; Hyperborea; intermediate state; Jade Empire, the; Jahannam; Janna; lake of fire; life after death; limbo; *Limbus Puerorum;* Maya; Mesoamerica; Mictlan; Nirvana; Otherworld; Paradise; paradise of God; Pardes; Perdition; *Popul Unh;* Promised Land, the; Pure Land, the; purgatory; Quetzalcoatl; Shambhala legends; *Sheol;* soul sleep; space doctrine; Summerland; Tartarus; Thule, land of; Tir na nOg; Tophet; underworld; Upper Gehenna; Utopia; Valhalla; world to come, the; Xolotl.

Xiuquan, Hong: the most recognized leader of the so-called Taiping Rebellion in the China of 1850. In a state of nervous breakdown after failing the Chinese civil service exam for the fourth time, he began to read Christian literature and listen to certain foreign missionaries in China. He became convinced that he was chosen by God to be a preacher and perhaps restore the Ming dynasty and achieve social equality in his country. Xiuquan received numbers of ongoing visions concerning this ideology with healthy doses of apocalypticism. *Taiping* means "great peace" but the rebellion was one of the most costly in lives and fortunes than any uprising of history. Xiuquan's leadership faded, however, due to his fragile mental condition, and he was reduced to immobility toward his end and preferred only to read the Chinese translation of John Bunyan's *Pilgrims Progress* until he died in 1864. His cousin, Hong Rengan, tried to salvage what he could of the movement, but the rebellion failed and outside influences on China became greater, not less.

Xolotl: the companion of Quetzalcoatl when the pair was exploring the Mayan underworld, Xibala. *See also* Aztecs; Maya; Mesoamerica; Mictlan; *Popul Unh;* Quetzalcoatl; Xibala.

XPTO: an old abbreviation or acrostic of the Greek letters chi, rho, taw, and omicron, which form part of the word *Christos* (Christ). The same letters in Latin can be sounded as *ex-pee-tee-o*, with an understanding that something good is being, or is about to be, experienced.

xylolaters: literally, "wood worshipers." The name is a derogatory tag for those who revere icons and images, particularly those of Eastern Orthodox persuasion. *See also* icon, iconoclasts; Iconoclasts, War of the; shrine(s); slurs, religious.

xylophone: a musical instrument played by striking tone-producing strips of wood or metal with a rod or small hammer. Some legends insist xylophones are played by the angels when their harps are in for repair. *See also* musical instruments.

Xylophoria: a Hebrew festival in which wood for the Temple was collected and stocked. The observance is considered a minor festival in Judaism and of course not practiced today. *See also* feasts and special days of Judaism.

xystus: Hellenistic open-air but covered porticoed plazas with polished flagstones used for public gatherings. They typically consisted of a pleasant garden, the entrance to a gymnasium, and the like. Their existence outside of Greece was one more attempt to impose Greek culture on conquered territories, including Judah. *See also* Hellenism, Hellenization.

Y

Yahud: a non-Jewish spelling of Judah. Archeologists have found an inscription (dating from 595–570 B.C.) beneath the Ishtar Gate from Nebuchadnezzar's Babylon that reads, "Yahud, king of the land of Yahud." The reference is to Jehoiachin, king of Judah (2 Ki. 25: 27–30). *See also* Jeshurun; Judah.

Yahweh: the most significant name for God found in the Old Testament in that it is the most sacred and proper title in use by the Israelites. The term is sometimes called the Covenant Name for God. In fact, it was the name the Almighty gave Himself. After the return from the exile, *Yahweh* came to be considered so holy that it must never be written or spoken, so the compromise title "Adonai" was usually substituted. Only by one person (the high priest of Israel) on only one day (the Day of Atonement) could the Holy Name of God be spoken aloud. When he did so of necessity, it was the duty of the Temple associates to shout so as to drown out the utterance. The Masoretic scribes combined the vowels of Adonai with the consonants YHWH (called the Tetragrammaton) to remind the reader to pronounce the name as Adonai. Most recent English Bible translations render YHWH as LORD (in capital letters) to distinguish it from *Adonai*, another Hebrew name for God written with small letters. When the terms are joined it is usually rendered "Sovereign Lord." The term *tetragrammaton* is taken from "tetra" (four) and "gramma" (letter), a quartet of Hebrew words or letters for God combined with *Yod, He, Waw, and He,* which has been transliterated into YHWH. An alert reader will always speak the Name as *Adonai* ("the Lord") or *Hashem* ("the Name"). That effort produced the name Jehovah, thus leaving that term with certain questionable parentage. Since the original Hebrew contained no vowels, except as provided by memory or context, the name "Yahweh" can only approximate the sound intended. Perhaps the best rendition of the most holy name was spoken by God to Moses as "I Am"—a similar reference was used by Jesus in John 8:58, the employment of which made himself equal with God. The prophets used a variety of names and titles for God, and perhaps no other groups were on a more personal and intimate basis with Him than they. *See also* Adonai; El; Elohim; *'Emeth; hadavar; Ha Shem;* Heaven; I AM WHO I AM; Jah; Jahbulon; Jehovah; Jesus Christ; Ketef Hinnom amulets; Lord; Lord God Almighty; Messiah; name known only to Christ; Name, my; Name of the Lord, the; names, symbology of; names (titles) for God; name that is above every name, the; name that no one knows, the; Name, the; Name, your; omnific word; *Sabaoth Adonai;* Sabbatarianism; Sacred Name movement; Shemhamforesh; Sovereign Lord; *Yeshua.*

Yahweh ben Yahweh: doomsday cult started by Hulon Mitchell Jr. (1935–2007), a black nationalist who created the Nation of Yahweh and call themselves "Hebrew Israelites." Mitchell allegedly arranged the murder of dozens and was eventually imprisoned. The group operates from the Temple of Love in Miami. *See also* cult(s); Hulon, Mitchell Jr.

Yakuza: a secret crime syndicate originating and based in Japan. The organization dates from the day of the Samurai, when it existed to combat the sectarian government assassins, but morphed into the Mafia-style institution it is today. Before, they were a sort of citizen militia known as the *machi-yokko.* "Yakuza" derives from the organizations' fondness for gambling, combined with a fascination with the numbers three and eight. *See also* secret societies; Triads; underworld; *yubizeum.*

Yam: a Canaanite god of the raging sea and chaos. He was defeated by Baal-Zaphon as master of the sea. The Ugaritic texts call him "Judge River." *See also* Baal-Zaphon; Canaan, Canaanites; Levant pantheon; Leviathan.

Yama: the name given the great judge according to Hindu belief. The term is also found in Chinese, Japanese, and other doctrines or myths of the Eastern religions. Yama is responsible for assignments to the various purgatories and hells encountered in many Eastern religious cultures. In some of the Eastern religions, he is described as a green demon king with red eyes and fangs accompanied by two monster dogs. Sometimes he wears a necklace of human skulls and delights in sending souls to one or more of his hells, or back to earth to start again. *See also* demon(s), demonic; Hinduism.

Yarikh: the moon god of the ancient Canaanites. He was the source of the precious "moon dew" or "night dew," a welcome gift for desert lands. *See also* Canaan, Canaanites; Levant pantheon.

yarmulke: a skullcap, also called the *kippa*, to cover the head of Jewish males in synagogue (and sometimes at home). The practice obeys the Deuternonomist obligation to keep the head covered in worship. *See also* Judaism; *tallit; tefillin; tzitzit;* Vidui.

Yaroslav Statute: a Russian legal code concerning regulations between the Russian state and the Russian Orthodox Church. The laws cover such subjects as court jurisdictions, family law, and punishment for moral violations. Yaroslav I was Grand Prince of Rus when he ruled 1019–1054 and had something to do with the statute's institution. *See also* Russia; Russian Orthodoxy.

ya sang: a form of black magic practiced in Thailand involving poisonous plants. *See also* black arts; magic, magick; sect(s).

Yaum-al-Arafah: Islamic day of prayer (August 20) for pilgrims beginning the *Hajj* journey to Mecca. *See also* Islam.

Yazidis: a.k.a. the Cult of the Angels, a small non-violent Kurdish minority living in the mountains of Iraq but resistant to Islam throughout their long history. Their religion (Yezidism) was central to their being—a strange mix of Zoroastrianism, Christianity, Manichean, Jewish, and Muslim tenets said to be the oldest living religion on earth. The group was a particular enemy of Saddam Hussein and even the Kurds, their neighbors and relatives, are antagonistic. ISIS massacred 5,000 of them in 2014 alone. *See also* metempsychosis; reincarnation; Yezidism.

Yggdrasil: the giant ash tree (according to Norse legend) that supports the universe and nurtures the people and many animals of earth. Its common name is "Horse of Odin" or "gallows" because the god Odin sacrificed himself there to gain the knowledge to read the runes. Yggdrasil is a key element of the *Edda. See also* cosmic tree; *Edda*, the; Midgard-serpent; Norse and old Germanic pantheon; Norns; Odin; pillar(s); pillars of the universe; rune(s); sky pole; tree(s).

Year of Jubilee. See Jubilee Year.

year of the Lord. See year of the Lord's favor.

year of the Lord's favor: God's great millennial promise as recorded in Isaiah 61, the year (or season) of the Lord's favor upon Israel according to the prophet Isaiah. The chapter discussing the year of the Lord has deep messianic implications and certainly refers, at least in part, to the ministry of Jesus before it is consummated in the Millennium. Early in his earthly tenure, Jesus read Isaiah 61:1 in the synagogue but neglected its following rendition (our verse 2); that second phase of the Lord's favor (the day of vengeance written there) is reserved for his Second Coming. It will then be that Jesus will execute the second phase of his appearing—that of judgment and renewal. *See also* crown of beauty; day of vengeance of our God; garment of praise; oaks of righteousness; oil of gladness.

yeast: the condiment compound that causes bread to rise. In most instances of scriptural use, it symbolizes sin (Ex. 12:15; Mt. 16:6) that can be "caught" from others or inflicted on us—as when the Pharisees scrambled the Word of God and tried to inflict their renditions on the people. As human creations, we have a proclivity to sin and have no remedy for it within ourselves; the atonement of Christ is the only hope for salvation. Temptation and indulgence appear to be our "yeast," which promotes our rebellion. *See also* bread, unleavened; leaven; ritual defilement; sin(s).

Yeats, William Butler: Irish writer (1865–1939) considered to be among the most eminent English-speaking poets and dramatists of the 20th century. Yeats, like so many other intellectuals at the start of the new decade, was heavily into theosophical doctrine. He joined "The Ghost Club" in 1921 and was a member of Aleister Crowley's secret society called the "Hermetic Order of the Golden Dawn." Magic, by his own admission, served a vital part of his literary creativity. Perhaps his most famous poem is "The Second Coming," which touches on disturbing themes wherein he might have envisioned an Antichrist emerging from the spirit world. The publication is from 1919 and ponders his fear that society would become unhinged following the horrors of World War I. The most quoted lines seem to illumine such a possibility, or a similar disquieting theme: "Things fall apart; the center cannot hold; /Mere anarchy is loosed upon the world./ That twenty centuries of stony sleep/Were vexed to nightmare by a rocking cradle,/And what rough beast, its hour come round at last/Slouches towards Bethlehem to be born." *See also* Crowley, Aleister; Akashic Records; magic, magick; Theosophy.

Yehosua. See Jesus Christ; Joshua; Yahweh; *Yeshua*.

Yeshua: Hebrew for "Yahweh is my salvation," which is translated into Joshua or Jesus in English. Jews consider the name Jesus to be manufactured and view it as a distorted transliteralization of the original Greek into Latin. The result was a Europeanized variation of the word in the English language. *See also* Jeshua; Jesus Christ; Joshua; names (titles) for Jesus; Yahweh.

Yezidism: (or Izedism) a monotheistic Levant religion (in northeast Syria and Iraq) which avers that the care of the world was undertaken by seven holy angels, the chief of whom is Maluk Taus ("the peacock"). Belief in the concepts of hell, a devil of evil, and sin are foreign to the Yazidis. Redemption and contentment, rather, are drawn from metempsychosis—the transmigration of souls. The Yazidis were tagged early as devil-worshipers, a true-enough label, except they see Satan as a fallen angel who had repented and was restored to his position of chief of angels. The sect is linked to Zoroastrianism and ancient Mesopotamian religions with heavy doses of Sufism. There are even marks of Christianity, Judaism, and Islam in the mix. Some experts claim it is the oldest living religion on earth. Since Maluk Taus is as likely to cause hardship as blessing, he has taken on a sinister personality. The governments of Iraq persecuted the Yezidis as devil worshipers because of their strange pagan practices, their belief that evil powers dominate the world, and their rites to ward off malevolent spirits. The terrorist group ISIS destroyed 5,000 of their number in 2014 in an act of unforgivable genocide. *See also* Levant pantheon; metempsychosis; reincarnation; sect(s); Yazidis.

YHWH. See Yahweh.

Yiddish: a European (Germanic) language of the Ashkenazi Jews written in the Hebrew alphabet. *See also* Ashkenazi; Judaism; Khazaria.

Yiguandao: an ancient Chinese religion ("the consistent way') also popular in Japan and Korea—one of the many mother-goddess sects. *See also* sect(s).

yin and *yang.* See Taoism.

yoga: a physical, spiritual, and mental discipline from ancient India. The rituals and exercises constituting the yoga practice are intended to develop peace of mind and calm order of life, even to the point of achieving "a union with the divine." The training, in its various techniques, is common in Buddhism, Hinduism, and Jainism. Yoga requires no belief in an external deity but is a process of quieting the mind and clearing away the entanglements of physical experience. *See also* ayurvedic medicine; Buddhism; Hinduism; Jainism; Nirvana; Samkhya; sect(s); Shiva; three poisons of Yoga Sutra; Transcendental Meditation (TM); yogi; Yogi, Maharishi Mahesh; Zen.

yogi: a master or teacher of yoga. *See also* yoga.

Yogi, Maharishi Mahesh: founder of the mind training system known as Transcendental Meditation (TM) (1918–2008). The master was a mentor to a large segment of many societies and was influential toward celebrities like the Beatles and Rolling Stones in the 1960s and 70s. *See also* Beatles, the; Transcendental Meditation (TM); yoga.

yoke: tack for horses or oxen allowing them to pull loads, or an implement designed for human use to carry heavy burdens via a wooden or iron beam across the shoulders. Figuratively, the word often denotes slavery, harshness, or oppression (*e.g.,* Nahum 1:13). At one point, Jeremiah was urged to construct a yoke and wear it to symbolize Israel's harsh captivity by the Babylonians (Jer. 27–28). By contrast, Jesus urged his followers to "Take my yoke upon you and learn from me, for I am gentle and humble in heart, and you will find rest for your souls. For my yoke is easy and my burden is light" (Mt. 11:28–30). The prophet Hosea indicated something similar when he referenced lifting off the yoke of oppression (Hos. 11:4). With this declaration, the Lord's intent is to assure believers that fellowship with Him is not burdensome but restful, even though discipleship is sometimes difficult. Paul urged believers (2 Cor. 6:14) not to become unequally yoked (married or closely associated) to unbelievers. In a more technical sense, a "yoke" is the amount of ground a team of oxen could plow in one day, or the yoked teams themselves that are used to pull loads. *See also* shackles; slave, slavery; Syzygus.

yokefellow. See Syzygus.

Yom HaShoah. See Holocaust Remembrance Day.

Yom Kippur. See Atonement, Day of.

Yom Kippur War: a hard-won struggle of the state of Israel against a surprise attack by Muslim neighbors on the *Yom Kippur* holy day of 1973.

Yoruba: the ancient religion of Yorubaland (Southwest Nigeria, Benin, and Tago). The cult has influenced Orisha, Santeria, Umbanda, Shango, and Candomble of the Western hemisphere. Belief centers on the conviction that all humans have *Ayanmo* (fate, destiny) and believers are expected to act as one with *Olorun,* the divine creator and source of cosmic energy. *See also* animism; Brujeria; Candomble; Creole (Caribbean) religions; cult(s); Kumina; Macumba; Obeah; Orisha; Quimbanda; Rastafarianism; Santeria; shaman, shamanism; Shango; spiritism; Spiritual Baptists; Umbanda; Voodoo; Voudou.

Young, Brigham: the leader (1801–1877) of the Mormon movement (Church of Jesus Christ of Latter-Day Saints) from the Midwest to Utah in 1847. He was the strongest candidate in the estimation of the majority to replace Joseph Smith, the founder of Mormonism. Young was a Freemason like his predecessor, Joseph Smith. There were later dissensions that formed alternate Mormon sects. *See also* Church of Jesus Christ of Latter-Day Saints, the; sect(s); Smith, Joseph, Jr.

Young-Earth Creationist Movement: a religious faction holding the staunch belief that the world was created in seven literal days less than 10,000 years ago. Their stance is in opposition to most scientific views that set the date for Earth's beginning at about 4.5 million years and life at 2.5 billion. Constricted by the literal view of the Genesis chronology, the movement is persistent in its proclamation with various support groups like Creation Ministries International and the Seven Wonders Museum in Castle Rock, Washington. One radio program even stated that dinosaurs were present on Noah's ark. Young Earth's most noted founder is Henry Morris, who helped start the group in 1966. Most geologists and other experts consider it, along with its sister belief creation science, to be pseudoscience. *See also* analogical day theory; big bang theory; big crunch theory; chaos theory; cosmogony; cosmology; *creatio ex nihilo;* creation; creationism; creation science; Creator; day-age theory; evolution; evolution, theistic; framework hypothesis; gap theory of creation; intelligent design; involution; naturalism; Omphalos Hypothesis; "post-secularists"; progressive creationism; Scopes Trial; sect(s); "six-day theory, the"; uniformitarianism.

Young Men's and Young Women's Hebrew Associations: Jewish youth organizations that began in 1854 as a young men's literary society in Baltimore, Maryland; women were incorporated into the group in 1888 in New York City as an auxiliary, then reorganized in 1913 as the National Council of Young Men's Hebrew and Kindred Associations. In 1921 that group merged with the Jewish Welfare Board, then began to serve Jews of all ages, more universally known as Jewish Community Centers. They feature arts and crafts, drama, concerts, lectures, forums, camping, and clubs for the elderly. *See also* religious education; religious organizations; Young Men's Christian Association; Young Women's Christian Association; youth religious organizations.

Young Men's Christian Association (YMCA): the familiar YMCA, or "the Y." The first organization was formed in the United States in 1851 in Boston, modeled on the British experiment. By 1858 there were branches at the universities of Michigan and Virginia. Although Christian in its outlook, the Y is non-sectarian and women are accepted (although most females prefer the Young Women's Christian Association). The YMCA is a member agency of the United Services Organization (USO) that services United States military members. The game of basketball originated with a staff member named Dr. James Naismith in 1891. *See also* religious education; religious organizations; Young Men's and Young Women's Hebrew Associations; Young Women's Christian Association; youth religious organizations.

young messenger from Elisha, the: a young unnamed prophet who was numbered among the company of the prophets. It was he who anointed Jehu as king of Israel on behalf of Elisha (2 Ki. 9:1–13). Little is known about the man, except that he was wild-looking in appearance and that he tried to do his mission in secrecy. In accordance with Elisha's explicit directions, he anointed Jehu, gave instructions that the house of Ahab was to be eliminated, and then ran quickly out the door. The secret was short-lived, however, and Jehu's purge began in short order. *See also* prophet(s).

Young Women's Christian Association (YWCA): the YWCA, an organization for young women began in the United States after a merger of the Prayer Union and the General Female Training Institute in 1855. The organization was chartered under its present name in 1866 at Boston. Although Christian in its outlook, the group is nondenominational. Its prime objective, in the beginning, was to provide wholesome residences for young women but has since expanded its program to education, athletics, and cultural activities. It is also the parent body of the Business and Professional Women's Clubs, the National Traveler's Aid Association, and the Camp Fire Girls. *See also* religious education; religious organizations; Young Men's and Young Women's Hebrew Associations; Young Men's Christian Association; youth religious organizations.

your glorious name: an address to God from the Levites who returned from exile with Nehemiah when they praised God within the Temple (Neh. 9:5). *See also* Name of the Lord, the; names, symbology of; names (titles) for God; name that is above every name, the; Name, your.

your holy servant: the name for Jesus used in the prayer of the believers in Jerusalem after the Sanhedrin had arrested Peter and John and tried them for healing a crippled man on the Sabbath (Acts 4:27). *See also* names (titles) for Jesus.

"your own traditions": Jesus' indictment of the Pharisees who too often represented their own interpretation, or rather corruption, of the Law of Moses—homemade traditions and rules not addressed by Mosaic stipulations. We are prone to call their supernumerations on the Law "oral traditions." Their multitudinous regulations and prohibitions had nothing to do with authentic religious life, prophecy, nor piety in Israel. In fact, they were a hindrance. *See also* Karaites; Law, the; Pharisees; Sadducees; traditions of the elders.

your prince. See prince, your.

youth religious organizations: any association with the legal and moral intent to educate and guide youth into a deeper and more committed religious life through study, recreation, and fellowship. There exists a number of such organizations but perhaps the most prominent in America, and most often recognized, are the Young Men's and Young Women's Hebrew Association (1854), the Young Men's Christian Association (YMCA in 1844), and the Young Women's Christian Association (YWCA in 1855). *See also* Campus Crusade for Christ; InterVarsity Christian Fellowship; Navigators; religious education; religious organizations; social issues; Student Volunteer Movement; Sunday school(s); Young Men's and Young Women's Hebrew Associations; Young Men's Christian Association; Young Women's Christian Association.

Y2K: a quasi-apocalyptic phenomenon occurring near the turn of the last century expressing fear that computers would not recognize the new century and crash the data to economic and political disaster. The generation at that time also called the issue "the millennium bug." Y2K is an acronym taken from "Y" as the new millennial year, "2" as the second millennium, and "K" as the shorthand for thousand. The concern was merely an urban legend but illustrates the fuzzy eschatological thinking in the minds of some. *See also* Super-Shemitah; survivalist(s).

yubizeum: the act of cutting off one's little finger, or part of it, as punishment for offending a Yakuza master. The amputation is done voluntarily by the aberrant gang member and the body part is presented to the leader as proof of his discipline. Furthermore, members are required to ink distinctive tattoos over the entire body where not exposed by outer clothing. *See also* ordeal(s); Triads; Yakuza.

yugas: the vast cycles of creation and re-creation continually in process according to Hindu cosmology. These seasons are to function from creation to the destruction of the world devolving from light to darkness. The cycle started with the Satya yuga and proceeded to the Treta and the Dvapara; we are now in the Kali yoga, the last and most destructive, which will last 432,000 years. *See also* Hinduism; Rudra.

Yule: a designation for the Christmas season (Yuletide)—a twelve-day festival, perhaps with more of an Old World and secular intent as preferred over the religious "Christ's-mass" designation. Yule must be first considered for its occult connotations which the ancients formerly celebrated on the winter solstice, the shortest day of the year (December 21.) Some Yuletide traditions, including the burning of the huge Yule log each season, are of undiluted pagan origin. The time is an important Wiccan expression as well. For the witches, the gods must be reborn in order to bring light and warmth back into the world. *See also* Beltane; Beltane's Eve; carol(s); Christmas; Christmas tree; Druidism; Imbolc; Lammas; Litha; Lughnasadh; Mabon; Noel; occult, occultic; Ostara; pagan practice; Sabbat; Samhain; Walpurgis Night; wheel of the year; Wicca; witchcraft; Yule boar.

Yule boar: the old tradition in Sweden and Denmark of baking a loaf in the form of a boar pig using the corn of the last sheaf harvested. It was to be saved and planted with the following year's crop. Many cultures even today roast a pig as a festive main course at Christmas. Of course, the honored guest must sport an apple in his mouth. Often outlandish ceremonies accompany the feast. *See also* Christmas; Yule.

Z

Zabur: a book (possibly the Psalms) that Muslims believe was delivered to King David (Dawud) around the tenth to ninth century B.C. They view the gift as a second holy book but naturally the Jewish deny any such presentation. *See also* book(s); Islam.

Zacchaeus: a Jewish tax collector, reputedly small in stature, who climbed a fig tree in order to catch a glimpse of Jesus as he passed below in a crowd of followers. The Lord called to Zacchaeus and declared he would be a guest in his home that day (Lk. 19:1–10). Jesus used the occasion during the visit to relate the eschatological parable of the ten minas (Lk. 19:11–27). *See also* publican(s).

Zacharias. See Zechariah as priest.

zaddik: "righteous," a God-loving person. In medieval times, a zaddik was considered to be a morally perfect person and usually a charismatic leader as well. In Hasidic Judaism, such a man is a spiritual leader skilled in enthusiastic worship that may include distinctive dress drawn from early styles of Eastern European clothing and ecstatic dancing. *See also* amora; Assemblies of the Wise; atrahasis; elder(s); Eliezer, Rabbi Yisroel ben; ensi; Hasidic; *Hasidim; maskilim;* wisdom; wise, the.

Zadok: a co-priest with Abiathar and a descendant of Aaron. He served under David's reign. Both he and Abiathar supported David during Absalom's rebellion, and again Zadok was loyal to the king when Adonijah subsequently tried to seize the throne. Other priests have held the name Zadok, but the one who was active with David and Solomon was especially important because his position returned the priesthood to the recognized line of Eleazar. David called him a seer—a prophet (2 Sam. 15:27). Zadok had a son named Ahimaaz, who acted as a spy for David's cause during Absalom's rebellion. *See also* Aaronic Covenant; Abiathar; Ahimelech; Eleazar; Ithamar; Phinehas; priest(s); Zadokites.

Zadokites: the Qumran priestly residents. Also, the name of a priestly dynasty loyal to King David during the rebellion of his son

Absalom. Zadok and Abiathar are often paired as partners although they are differing priestly lines. The Zadokites may be considered a more pure line of priests in opposition to the more progressive and populist tendencies of the Pharisees. *See also* Aaronic Covenant; Abiathar; Karaites; Pharisees; priest(s); Qumran; Sadducees; Zadok.

Zadokite Document. See Damascus Document.

Zalmon: called Salmon in early versions, a wooded mountain near Sechem, evidently a place of beauty since David praised it in one of his songs (Ps. 68:14). Abimelech used its wood to set fire to the town of Sechem (Jud. 9:48).

Zaphenath-Paneah. See Joseph.

Zaphon: often spelled Zephon, 1. the psalmist's name for Mount Zion, the sacred mountain, Jerusalem, or the northerly direction when considered as a sanctified orientation (Ps. 48:2). 2. In mythology, Zaphon is a holy and sacred mountain where the weather god (Baal) of the ancient Near East was enthroned. *See also* Baal; Baal-Zaphon; Jerusalem as city; Mount Zaphon; Mount Zion; Sumerian and Babylonian pantheon.

Zarall. See Jael and Zarall.

Zarathustra. See Zoroaster, Zoroastrianism.

zeal: extreme excitement or active commitment. The emotion may be praiseworthy, as when one is zealous for the Lord, or it may be unacceptable when it is pursued for intolerance of another's view or incites to wrong causes. Certainly, it was a true mark, to one degree or another, of all the prophets (Col. 4:14; Titus 2:14).

Zealots: an extreme faction of Judaism during and after the time of Jesus. They were often no more than brigands or assassins in their zeal for patriotism, greed, cruelty, and intolerance of foreigners. They despised what they deemed to be half-hearted fidelity to strict Judaism if they harbored any religious sentiment at all. Zealot activities were highly instrumental in agitating the Jewish War of A.D. 66–70, and they bear much responsibility for the destruction that followed. They were somewhat close to the Pharisees in sympathy but not necessarily the Sadducees. It is likely that the Zealots used some of the apocalyptic writings of the time to fan the flames of nationalism, which led to the devastating war of A.D. 70. One of Jesus' disciples, Simon, may have been a Zealot, at least in sympathy or past involvement. *See also* Aram, Arameans; assassin(s); cult(s); Essenes; Hellenism, Hellenization; Herodians; Jew(s); Jewish War; Pharisees; Sadducees; Samaritan(s); scribe(s); Sicarii; Simon; Spirituals of the Franciscan Order; terrorist(s); Zelotes.

Zebedee: the family name of the disciples John and James, as well as the husband of Salome. The clan was presumably relatively wealthy and held some influence with the high priest Annas. They made their living as fishermen in the Sea of Galilee. The name is likely a Greek version of the Hebrew *Zebediah* meaning "Yahweh has endowed" or "the gift of God."

Zeboiim: one of the five cities of the plain. Its king was defeated by Chedorlaomer (Gen. 19:17–29) and was mentioned by Hosea (Hos. 11:8) as a warning since the city was destroyed earlier with Sodom and Gomorrah. *See also* Admah; cities of the plain; Gomorrah; Pentapolis; Sodom; Sodom and Gomorrah; Zoar.

Zebra Book: the 1973 edition of the Episcopalian *Book of Common Prayer.* The title was formed because the cover was striped; an earlier edition from 1970 was called the Green Book for the same reason. *See also* Alternative Service Book; *Book of Common Prayer;* Protestant Episcopal Church.

Zebulon: one of the twelve tribes of Israel descended from the patriarch Jacob and his wife Leah. Jacob's deathbed blessing of the tribe in Genesis 49:13 predicted their settlement on the seacoast where they prospered. The tribe is listed with the 144,000 servants in Revelation 7:8. *See also* lost tribes, the ten; tribes of Israel, the; twelve tribes.

Zechariah as king: the fourteenth king of Israel and the last of the house of Jehu (753 B.C.). He reigned only six months before he was assassinated by his successor, Shallum ben Jabesh. *See also* king(s); kings of Israel and Judah; kings of Israel and Judah in foreign relations.

Zechariah as Old Testament prophecy: a postexilic writing of the prophet Zechariah containing much apocalyptic material in the second half of the writing. Several of the eschatological revelations are in the form of visions. The prophet explained that the Messianic advent was a "burden" to be borne by Israel until its consummation. It is likely chapters 1–8 and 9–14 are by different authors. The first eight chapters are didactic, not particularly apocalyptic, and seem to pertain to the reign of King Uzziah around 521-518 B.C. The prophetic passages in the latter half are profound in that they are clearly Christocentric and the most descriptive of the coming Jewish Messiah (whom Christians identify as one and the same). The book speaks of the Messiah's humanity (6:12), humility (9:9), betrayal (11:12), deity (12:8), crucifixion (12:10), return (14:4), and his future reign (14:8–21). *See also* curses of Zechariah; Zechariah as true prophets.

Zechariah as priest: the father of John the Baptist. When informed by an angel of the pending birth of his son, Zechariah was disbelieving because he and his wife were senior citizens. For that attitude, he was struck dumb until the birth. At that moment his speech poured forth in praise prompted by the Holy Spirit (Lk. 1:5–23,67–79), and in obedience to the angel's instructions, he named his son John. Zechariah is considered a prophet as well as a priest. *See also Benedictus;* priest(s); prophet(s).

Zechariah as true prophets: At least thirty-two characters in the Scripture are called Zechariah, a name that means "Yahweh remembers." Three of them were prophets: 1. a younger contemporary of Haggai, assuming this preacher was the writer of the latter half of his book. If not, the original Zechariah would be an elderly man writing very late in his career from the days of King Uzziah. Zechariah's apocalyptic message in the second half of the book is a counterpoint to Haggai's rather blunt style; his approach seemed to be more exuberant and in a sort of "cheerleading" style. Like Haggai, the younger Zechariah was a repatriated exile from Babylon. 2. the son of Berakiah (as Jesus called him) or the son of the priest Jehoiada (as the historian called him). This prophet was perhaps the last to be martyred and recorded in the Old Testament as recounted by Jesus (Mt. 23:35). He was stoned to death between the altar and the sanctuary (2 Chr. 24:20–22) at the instigation, and on the orders of, Joash of Judah for upbraiding the king and nation for idolatry. The seer's last words also constitute his final prophecy: "May the Lord see this and call you to account." Fulfillment came shortly after when Joash was assassinated in retaliation for his murder of the loyal martyr. 3. a prophet who counseled Uzziah of Judah that all would be well with the kingdom as long as the king and people were faithful to Yahweh (2 Chr. 26:5). He was the king's able counselor (2 Chr. 26:5) so long as the king was faithful to God. *See also* Abel to Zechariah; martyr(s); prophet(s); Zechariah as Old Testament prophecy; Zechariah as priest.

Zechariah's oracle against Israel's enemies: a series of harsh curses against a number of nations in opposition to Israel (Zech. 9:1–8; 11; 12). *See also* curses of Zechariah.

Zechariah's oracle against the wicked shepherds. See Zechariah's oracle of the stricken shepherds and the scattered sheep.

Zechariah's oracle of Jerusalem's cleansing from sin: promises to the prophet Zechariah that Jerusalem will be forgiven the sins of its people and God's favor will be restored (Zech. 13:1–6).

Zechariah's oracle of Jerusalem's destruction: pronouncement from the prophet Zechariah that Jerusalem is to be destroyed at the hand of God (Zech. 5:5–11). *See also* curses of Zechariah; destruction of Jerusalem; flaming torch among the sheaves, a; Jerusalem, invasions of; Jerusalem, siege of (literal); Jerusalem, siege of (pantomime); remnant.

Zechariah's oracle of the stricken shepherds and the scattered sheep: a prophetic prediction that the leaders and much of the population of Judah are destined for destruction (Zech. 13:7–9). The shepherd leader will be killed in the violence, two-thirds of the population will perish, and one-third of the people will solicit God for favor during the crisis time. *See also* curses of Zechariah; Ezekiel's curse of the neglectful shepherds; Ezekiel's vision of the Cherubim and the departed glory; shepherding (cultic); shepherdless flock, the; shepherds of Israel; shepherd/shepherdess; worthless (wicked) shepherd, the.

Zechariah's oracle of two shepherds and two shepherd's staffs: a complex allegory described by the prophet Zechariah (Zech. 11:4–17). The Lord gave instructions that sheep marked for slaughter should be pastured by his shepherd [Zechariah, the king, or the Lord Himself, as the reference could be to one or both]. The prophets of the land, the leaders of the people, and all the citizens of the nation were to know that conditions in the land of Judah were like those shepherds and "mutton-butchers" who care nothing about the sheep's welfare (particularly the poor and oppressed). God was now at a point where He was weary of being the chief Shepherd of such a fickle leadership corps and was ready to reject them. Zechariah, acting in a rather ill-defined role or autobiographically, then made two shepherd's staffs—one of which he named Favor (in some translations "Grace" or "Beauty") and the other Union (in some translations "Bands" or "Bonds"). Eventually, the prophet broke the first staff, implying that the Lord's covenant with the nations was now severed; then he broke the second staff, signifying that the brotherhood between Judah and Israel was no more operable. No longer would the Lord be the God of either people. Then the shepherd suggested that he be paid his due wages, not knowing if he would receive any compensation whatsoever. The authorities did disburse him thirty pieces of silver, however (the going price of a slave). But God told the prophet to throw the money to "the potter," or "the potter's place" (which could be a reference to the Temple treasury or to a potter's guild exercising the trade near the Temple throwing inexpensive pots and littering the place with broken shards). Verse 8 of the paradigm comments that the shepherd (whoever he is) has already destroyed three other unworthy shepherds (leaders) in a single month. Likely, the land had rid itself of a trio of worthless leaders in that period of time, yet the nation could not be salvaged. It is interesting that another heartless shepherd, Judas Iscariot, was also faithless and was paid the same thirty silver pieces; these he threw back into the Temple. Now termed "blood money," they were used by the priests to purchase a potter's field (a graveyard for indigents and foreigners). *See also* curses of Zechariah; Ezekiel's curse of the neglectful shepherds; Field of Blood; Judas; Lysimachus; potter's field; shepherding (cultic); shepherding (discipleship); shepherdless flock, the; shepherds of Israel; shepherd/shepherdess; thirty pieces of silver; worthless (wicked) shepherd, the; Zechariah's oracle of the stricken shepherds and the scattered sheep.

Zechariah's oracles of Jerusalem's salvation: assurances from the prophet Zechariah (Zech. 4; 7; 8; 9:9–17; 10; 12; 13–14) that Israel and Jerusalem will have a Messiah and will survive and prosper under the wishes of God. *See also* bells on the horses;

donkey; Ezekiel's pledge to the Jewish remnant; firepot in a woodpile, a; horse; millennial sacramentalism; remnant; sacred bowls; split of the great city; Triumphal Entry.

Zechariah's predictions of the coming Messiah. See Zechariah as Old Testament prophecy.

Zechariah's vision of a crown for Joshua: the core theme of the vision of Zechariah 6:9–15. In the imagery, God instructs gold and silver to be taxed against Judah's resistors to help finance the repatriation to Judah from the Babylonian Exile. Subsequently, some of the precious metals are to be molded into a crown for the high priest Joshua. His subsequent coronation will assure everyone that ritual worship in Jerusalem will be proper and welcome to the Lord once more. Furthermore, one called "the Branch" will be allowed to reconstruct Jerusalem. The title is an obvious reference to Zerubbabel, a Persian official who had the authority to do exactly that. Use of the name "Branch" at this point denotes a proper name and should be capitalized. We then infer that the Branch identifies the Messiah; so Zerubbabel has become a sign for the coming savior. Thus, both the religious and secular aspects of the rebuilt Jerusalem will have the blessing of God, both after the exile and at the end of the age. So we may say that Joshua's new crown is a bilayer coronet representing both the priestly and secular aspects of the sanctified Jerusalem; Joshua then becomes a sign for the Messiah who will combine the priestly and kingly offices into one and forever avoid the conflict between the two that has plagued Jewish history. *See also* Branch from (of) Jesse, the; Branch of the Lord; Root and offspring of Jesse; crown(s); Joshua as priest; vision(s); Zechariah's vision of garments for the high priest; Zechariah's vision of the gold lampstand and olive trees; Zechariah's vision of the seven-eyed stone; Zerubbabel.

Zechariah's vision of garments for the high priest: Zechariah's description of the high priest Joshua being given clean clothes and God's blessing for a new era of worship in Jerusalem (Zech. 3). Such worthy administration will be more suitable for the arrival of the Messiah and would serve as a welcome comfort to the new high priest as he begins to take up his difficult duties. *See also* divine council; high priest cleansed and robed; Joshua as priest; Joshua's (the priest) associates; vision(s); Zechariah's vision of a crown for Joshua; Zechariah's vision of the gold lampstand and two olive trees.

Zechariah's vision of the flying scroll: the prophet Zechariah's explanation of a curse from God upon the land of evildoers (Zech. 5:1–4). The vision features a giant scroll (30 feet × 15 feet) on which the curses are written. Two specific sins are emphasized on the scroll—theft and perjury. No doubt these two failings were prominent in postexilic Judah. *See also* curses of Zechariah; vision(s); flying scroll, the.

Zechariah's vision of the four chariots: a vision in Zechariah 6:1–8 in which four chariots are rampaging about the earth. One chariot, pulled by black horses, heads to the north; another pulled by white horses, heads west; a third with dappled horses goes south; the chariot with red horses implicitly speeds east. They represent the spirit of God's omnipresence throughout the world. The report of the northern chariot is especially pleasing to God because it portends peace from Israel's enemies. That will certainly be the case in the new millennial world. The various chariots are said to issue from mountains of bronze. If the solid mountains have apocalyptic significance, they most likely represent military power that the charioteers could use in their mission of conquest. Compared to Zechariah's first vision of horsemen, the main difference is that the warriors of the first scene are pictured at rest among shade trees having accomplished a mission from God; the second vision of chariots shows the warriors eager to set out in active pursuit of their martial goals. *See also* animals, birds, and insects, symbology of; horse; mountains of bronze; vision(s); Zechariah's vision of a crown for Joshua; Zechariah's vision of the man among the myrtle trees.

Zechariah's vision of the four horns and four craftsmen: a vision in Zechariah 1:18–20 in which four horns and four workmen portray the destruction of the unrighteous throughout the land. The intent is to demonstrate that the horns, representing adversarial nations or empires hostile to Israel, Jerusalem, and Judah, will be removed by four carpenters or blacksmiths or the like who are agents of God. Many theologians see the four horns as oppressive Egypt, Babylon, Syria, and Rome. Or, they are said to represent

Assyria, Babylon, Egypt, and Persia. Alternately, the horns may be Nebuchadnezzar, Cyrus, Cambyses, and Alexander the Great. The four craftsmen are those named who will thwart the damage of the four horns. For the job, the name "craftsman" could denote any laborer of any occupation but a blacksmith or a lumberjack may better suit the task of dehorning about to transpire. Like the horns, some see the workers as personalities—Moses, Cyrus, Judas Maccabee, and David ben Gurion, the father of national Israel. Or, perhaps they are the more contemporary Zerubbabel, Joshua, Ezra, and Nehemiah. The horns, in any case, are to be rendered powerless. Israel's oppressors then are to be irrelevant in the new age of glory. *See also* Babylon, Babylonians; ben Gurion, David; curses of Zechariah; Cyrus the Great (Cyrus II); Egypt, Egyptians; Hasmonean dynasty; Moses; prince of the covenant (testament), a; seven shepherds and eight princes; shepherds of Israel; shepherd/shepherdess; Syria; Rome; vision(s); Zion.

Zechariah's vision of the gold lampstand and two olive trees: a reference from Zechariah 4 wherein the prophet describes a vision of a golden lampstand with a bowl ornament atop and seven lights attached. Along with the lamp are two olive trees, one on either side, to fuel the flames. Zechariah is told that the seven lights of the stand are the eyes of God sweeping to and fro on the earth and kept aglow by the Spirit of God. The two olive trees are the anointed ones appointed to serve the Lord. Most authorities agree that the two individuals represented are the civil governor of postexilic Jerusalem, Zerubbabel, and the chief priest, Joshua. More pointedly, the vision of the candlestick seems to be a particular comfort to Zerubbabel whereas the companion vision of the reclothing of Joshua is an encouragement to the priest. Sometimes Zerubbabel and Joshua are named as the two witnesses in Revelation 11, especially as noted in verse 4. *See also* eye(s); flora, fruit, and grain, symbology of; Joshua as priest; lamp, lampstand(s); two olive trees and a lampstand; vision(s); witnesses, the two great; Zechariah's vision of a crown for Joshua; Zechariah's vision of garments for the high priest; Zerubbabel.

Zechariah's vision of the man among the myrtle trees: a vision in Zechariah 1:7–17 in which a man standing amid a copse of myrtle trees introduces the prophet to riders on red, sorrel, and black horses. He states that these riders have patrolled the earth and report that all is calm—an uneventful tour of duty. By 519 B.C. Darius had managed to stabilize the Persian Empire, and there was peace in the land. This was not necessarily good news to the angel addressing Zechariah, however, because God's chosen were still captive in the land. His lament about the situation prompted a promise that God will show compassion on His people and return them to Judah. And further, He will bless them in the new age to come. *See also* animals, birds, and insects, symbology of; flora, fruit, and grain, symbology of; four chariots into the world; vision(s); Zechariah's vision of the four chariots.

Zechariah's vision of the man with a measuring line: a vision from Zechariah 2 that describes a man with a measuring line (an architectural angel) approaching the seer. The prophet inquires as to the purpose of such a disconcerting visit. The answer relates that the messenger's intent is to measure Jerusalem (figuratively, of course). Zechariah's instructor then tells a fellow angel to rush and tell "that young man" that Jerusalem is about to be joyfully rebuilt with an overflowing population and all the accouterments a city needs to be safe and prosperous. Who "that young man" references is not clear. Perhaps he is the prophet himself, or perhaps better—the man with the line himself. "Measuring" can either denote prophetic preparations to save a city (as above) or to destroy it (as in Revelation 11:1–8). *See also* angel(s); angels of measurement; Court of the Gentiles; measuring line; measuring rod; plumb line; Portion of Israel, the; reed; vision(s).

Zechariah's vision of the seven-eyed stone: an image in Zechariah 3:9 that describes a stone with seven eyes (or "facets") on its surface. The mystery of this image has many interpretations, almost enough to qualify it as an enigma. Perhaps Joshua the priest and those contemporary with him understood its symbolism more readily than we do. The intent appears to be (as derived from the context) that the all-seeing stone is to be inscribed by the Lord to represent God's blessings on the people of Israel and His omnipresent eye-sweeping inspection of His people. The land and her priest will now be made "holy" again and no longer under judgment. Perhaps it served as an emblem of forgiveness and encouragement to Joshua the high priest in particular since he is associated with the stone at close range. The decoration may not be "eyes" for seeing or sight since the stone is to be engraved—a thought that has inspired the alternation translation of "facets." As such, it could represent the diadem of the high priest's turban (though the original was gold). A more complex interpretation involves using the symbol as a quad-word inscription prophecy that is used to describe the "Branch" who will be coming as Jesus of Nazareth and his eventual reign in the Millennium. In this idea lies the naming of "my Stone," which parallels the naming of "my Branch" earlier in the vision. According to yet another interpretation, the seven inscriptions represent seven friends of Joshua the high priest at that time. Who are they? The symbol does not reveal them but Zechariah 6:9–15 names five compatriots: Heldai, Tobijah, Jedaiah, Helem, and Hen. We already know that Zerubbabel is another to make six. If we add Shealtiel as Zerubbabel's alternate or last name, we have seven. The meaning of these names (their names are all we know of most of these men) in the order they are presented form a coded Hebrew sentence: "*Yahweh has prepared* the *age* of the gospel [*good news*] of *grace*, [*Yahweh has*] *hidden* from the *foundation* of the world, that by the *pierced one*'s *salvation*, we should be cleansed [*cleanses*]from the charge God [*God's charge*] *laid up* against us and [*the Lord*] *overflows* with the Lord's [*spirit*]." (Italicized words are those translated from the Hebrew.) Some carry the symbolism further and maintain that these seven revelations also foretell the seven church ages of dispensationalism. This interpretation is speculative at best, but for that matter, the entire symbolism of the seven-sided stone is precisely that—multifaceted. Perhaps the stone represents the actual cornerstone laid for the coming Temple of Zerubbabel enacted in a ceremony at which he and Joshua were both present. Others say it is an act of "sealing" with ornamentation and inscriptions and part of the Zerubbabel Temple. For certain, the image of the witness stone is a prophetic utterance. Its full meaning will be seen in the Millennium when the land of Israel and those who serve as priests before God will be sanctified to Him. Such blessings may be imminent for Jerusalem in the days of Zechariah in some quantity, but more likely, they are reserved for the millennial age in this instance since repentance is forecasted to be "in a single day." *See also* eye(s); Joshua as priest; prophecy types; Shealtiel; stele; stone(s); vision(s); Zechariah's vision of the gold lampstand and two olive trees; Zerubbabel.

Zechariah's vision of the woman in a basket: a vision in Zechariah 5:5–11 in which an angel shows the prophet a woman (an idol?) named Wickedness who is imprisoned in an "ephah" (a basket measure). The iniquitous woman is not allowed to escape, even when the heavy lid of the prison is temporarily opened for the prophet to look inside. Instead, two more "angels" arrive and carry off the basket to the land of Shinar. These flyers who lift the basket appear quite different in appearance from the typical angelic representatives usually encountered. They are said to be "stork-like" in form and subtly ungodly in some sense. We can picture them as sisters of the wicked woman inside the basket, which the skinny angels are carrying to a place better suited for one who cheats in weights and measures. The message intended is that idolatry has no place for the people of God in the new age. The destination for the basket is Shinar, the place where Nimrod tried to establish his empire and construct the Tower of Babel. Shinar was considered a place of evil, excess, and danger, so there the basket and the evil woman incarcerated inside will be stationed forever in a state of isolation and banishment. Zechariah was written about twenty years past the fall of Babylon, so it has nothing to do with that historical city or empire but is surely apocalyptic in its setting. *See also* angels of transport; Babel; Shinar; vision(s); Wickedness.

Zedekiah as false prophets: 1. a false prophet in the court of King Ahab. In defiance of the true Word of God, Zedekiah fashioned iron horns and used them to demonstrate to Ahab and King Jehoshaphat that God would crush the Arameans. Other prophets at the time, with the exception of the true spokesman for God, Micaiah, were predicting the same. Ahab was subsequently killed and the battle lost. 2. a false prophet whose death was predicted by Jeremiah (Jer. 29:21–23) because of his lies. *See also* False Prophet, the.

Zedekiah as king: the twentieth and last ruler of Judah, a puppet king of Babylon (597 b.c.) after the attack on Jerusalem. His Hebrew name, Mattaniah, was changed to Zedekiah by his conquerors when he was appointed to rule. Zedekiah participated in a failed rebellion and tried to escape from Jerusalem. He was captured, bound, forced to watch his sons killed before him, blinded by the victorious Babylonians, and forced to join the other Jewish exiles in Babylon where he died. Thus, the prophecies of Jeremiah 34 and Ezekiel 12 concerning the fate of Judah's last king were fulfilled. The Jews do not consider him a legitimate ruler or of proper lineage. *See also* king(s); kings of Israel and Judah; kings of Israel and Judah in foreign relations.

Zelotes: the expanded name of the disciple Simon. The name means "jealous" or "zealous," as a person who is zealous for God's honor. The Gospels of Mark and Matthew transliterate the name with a simple "Simon the Cananaean." *See also* Simon; zeal; Zealots.

Zen: "meditation," a term common in India, Japan, China (where it is called Ch'an), and elsewhere in the East holding respect for the discipline of enlightenment. In the Zen process, the methods of achievement are systematized and formed into artistic expression. There are several aspects and practices that make up the movement but all center on enlightenment and life enhancement. The practice forms a resemblance to classical Buddhism but it seeks to allow enlightenment to happen naturally as a result of clearing the mind and does so without the need for rational argument or rituals. Devotees, however, consider their approach to have developed independently via a different line of transmission. Zen has no scriptures or formal teachings but is contemplative only as learned via experienced teacher to pupil. In Japan, the practice branches into two styles: Rinzai and Soto. Rinzai came in the 12th century by Eisai and reformed in the 18th century by Hakuin teaching the world is illusion. Soto bases on sitting meditation (*zazen*) with a gradual approach to enlightenment. *See also* Buddhism; meditation; yoga.

Zenas: a lawyer and a disciple on an unspecified mission for the gospel (Tit. 3:13). Paul urged Titus to provide for Zenas and Apollos when he came into contact with them.

Zend-avesta. See *Avesta.*

Zeno: a pre-Socrates Greek philosopher living in Elea of Italy (ca. 490–430 B.C.). Zeno was a student of Parmenides, and both men had visited Athens at one point. In Greece, Zeno presented his famous "paradoxes" for which he has become famous. Such problems have been described as *reduction ad absurdum* that is, "if being is many, it must be both like and unlike, and this is impossible, for neither can the like be unlike, nor the unlike, like)."

Aristotle called the puzzles "dialectical syllogism." Judaism and Christianity seem historically uninterested in Zeno's inventions. *See also* philosophy of religion; philosophy of the Greeks.

zeon: a word for "boiling" or "fervor." In Eastern Orthodox ritual, the zeon is the rite of pouring hot water into the Communion wine or the container that holds the water. Ancient usage probably intended the heat to represent the water flowing from the punctured side of Jesus at the crucifixion or the fervor of the Holy Spirit as he gives life and warmth to the body of Christ. Perhaps a more common identification of the process of combining water and wine might be the "mixed chalice" of the Eucharist, though it was rejected by Luther and Calvin. The drink was likely that used by Christ in the Lord's Supper. *See also* Eastern Orthodox Church; Eucharist; Eucharistic theories of the Reformers; gestures; liturgical year; liturgy, Christian.

Zephaniah as Old Testament prophecy: the prophetic writings of Zephaniah that holds much prophetic information. It emphasizes the "day of the Lord" and other judgment themes. Devastation in the latter days, including Tribulation descriptions, is vividly announced. Zephaniah is perhaps the most predictive book in the Bible, despite its brevity. *See also* curses of Zephaniah; Zephaniah as prophet.

Zephaniah as priest: the priest second in rank to the high priest Seraiah at the time of the fall of Jerusalem to Nebuchadnezzar. He was the one who carried messages between King Zedekiah and Jeremiah (Jer. 21:1; 37:3). Zephaniah received a letter from a false prophet in Babylon named Shemaiah who urged him to punish Jeremiah for the prophet's dire predictions concerning Judah; however, Zephaniah tendered the message to Jeremiah instead. After the fall of Jerusalem, Zephaniah was executed at Riblah along with many other high officials of Judah (Jer. 52:24–27). *See also* priest(s).

Zephaniah as prophet: God's spokesman 630–622 b.c. during the reign of Josiah. Zephaniah was an aristocrat in the kingly line of Hezekiah. When he ministered, the Scythians were threatening while Assyria was finally fading from power. The prophet indicted his people as unteachable, the rulers as predatory, the courts as merciless, the prophets as traitors, and the priests as profane. *See also* prophet(s); Zephaniah as Old Testament prophecy.

Zera: a Cushite (Ethiopian) king who invaded Judah during the reign of King Asa with a formidable army (2 Chr. 14:8–15). The Hebrews managed a great victory, though outnumbered, because of the fidelity of Asa. The court prophet at the time was Azariah son of Oded. *See also* Cush; Cushites; king(s).

Zera, Rabbi: famous amora, Talmudist, translator, and teacher in Babylon known for his exceptional piety and lofty morals. He was prone to excessive demonstrations of his character by extreme acts like fasting for 100 days and walking into a hot oven. *See also* Jew(s).

Zeresh: wife of the wicked Agagite Persian minister Haman. She assisted her husband in his cruel plot to destroy all Jews in the realm. *See also* anti-Semitic; Haman; Xerxes I.

zero-point energy: a quantum physics term to describe how a vacuum of energy that utilizes hyper-charged molecules at near-zero temperature could theoretically propel a craft through space. Some Vatican astronomers and others claim it may be the means by which UFOs are powered—a technology that aliens may want to impute to us, or deny to us. *See also* Raelism; Vimanas; UAP; UFO.

zero state: or zero hour, the end of the world (often noted by some adherents as 2012). At that time, the final days will arrive either as a great apocalypse or as a union of matter and spirit—the culmination of the human process. *See also* adjacent possible; Five Ways, the; Jumping Jesus Phenomenon; Law of Accelerating Returns, the; point of infamy; teleology; timewave, the; 2012 prophecy, advocates of; 2012, prophecy of.

"zero year" prophecies, the: or, the supposed curse of presidents of the United States who have been elected in the "zero" years. All were said to be destined to die in office at twenty-year intervals. Chief executives elected in years ending in zero held true beginning with William Henry Harrison in 1840 and continuing to Abraham Lincoln in 1860, James Garfield in 1880, William McKinley in 1900, Warren G. Harding in 1920, Franklin Roosevelt in his fourth term in 1940, and John Kennedy in 1960. The pattern would have continued but Ronald Reagan (1980) was spared death from an assassin's bullet due (most insiders agree) by prayers for his protection. Lincoln, for one, believed in omens and visions and foresaw his own death at least twice before his assassination. In the case of Harrison, the start of the so-called curse, the Native American prophet called Tenskwautawa pronounced his death because of his massacre at Tippecanoe in 1830, then to leaders every twentieth year thereafter. Now (as of this writing) we have entered the 2020 election cycle and the validity of the curse will be tested once again. The question is, however, who the target might be. The sitting president, Joe Biden, may be intended or Donald Trump who (as many claim) was denied the presidency through voter fraud. *See also* Garfield, James Abram; Kennedy, John F.; Lincoln, Abraham; Reagan, Ronald; Tenskwautawa.

Zerubbabel: a prince of Judah. Under his leadership, along with the high priest Joshua, the Jews returned to Jerusalem from the Babylonian Captivity where Zerubbabel was appointed governor and a primary builder of the new Temple there. He led the first return based on a liberation decree from Cyrus the Great and proved to be an able administrator. There is some historical confusion as to the man's identity as he is sometimes named as the same or another prince called Sheshbazzar (Ezr. 5:14). Likely, Sheshbazzar and Zerubbabel are indeed the same man or, Sheshbazzar was a relative (perhaps an uncle) of Zerubbabel who delegated the work to his nephew. He may have been the grandson of King Jehoiachin. Some legends say Zerubbabel was removed as governor of Judea by Darius and possibly executed. *See also* Artaxerxes I Longimanus; Babylonian (and Persian) restoration decrees; Babylonian Captivity, return from; Ezra as scribe; Joshua as priest; Moses; Nehemiah as governor; restoration of Israel (the Jews); Shealtiel; Sheshbazzar; signet ring; two olive trees and the two lampstands, the; witnesses, the two great; Zechariah's vision of the gold lampstand and two olive trees; Zerubbabel's Temple.

Zerubbabel's Temple: the postexilic Temple erected largely through the efforts of Zerubbabel and administered by Joshua the high priest. The construction of the postexilic Temple was considerably delayed because of the people's apathy and opposition from certain detractors in the land; it was not completed until prompted later by the prophets Haggai and Zechariah. *See also* Temple(s); Zerubbabel.

zeta: or zeter, a small room or closet in a church building. *See also* church; furniture and furnishings of the modern church.

Zeus: the high god of the Greeks. The name takes on apocalyptic interest since Antiochus Epiphanes attempted to erect a statue of Zeus in the Temple of Jerusalem, thus demonstrating a prototype for the abomination of desolation. At Lystra, the population of the city tried to name Paul as Hermes and his partner Barnabas as Zeus (Acts 14:11–20) because of the miracles and compelling preaching the pair performed there. *See also* abomination of desolation, the; Ares; Crete; Cronus; Europa; Gaia (Gaea); Hera; Hercules; Hermes; Io; Jupiter; Mercury; oak; Olympian pantheon; Roman Empire; Satan's throne; seven wonders of the ancient world; Titans; Uranus.

Zevi, Shabbatai: a messianic pretender (1626–1676), an Ottoman Jew. He was a Qabbalist and founder of the Jewish Sabbatean movement known familiarly to his followers as "Amirah." Zevi and many of his adherents were forced to convert to Islam by the Turkish sultan Mehamed IV. The movement still has followers today who call themselves Donmehs. Zevi's end of the world calculations centered on the year 1648 with himself revealed as the Messiah. He later changed the date to 1660 then 1666. *See also* Aqiba, Rabbi Joseph ben; Bible Code; Cheiro; emanations, doctrine of; *gematria;* Haggada; Halakha; *isopseplia;* Jew(s); Kaduri, Rabbi Yitzchak; Masseket Hekalot; Nathan of Gaza, rabbi; Qabbala; *Sefirot; temoorah; Zohar.*

Ziba: Mephibosheth's servant made so by King David and the one, along with his sons, who were directed to care for Saul's property on behalf of his master. Later, when David fled from Absalom, Ziba appeared with much-needed supplies. At that time, he falsely accused Saul's surviving son, Mephibosheth, of coveting the kingdom. When the deception was discovered, David's judgment was to divide the property between Mephibosheth and Ziba. *See also* Mephibosheth.

ziggurat: the stepped pyramid used in ancient pagan worship around the time of Nimrod. It most likely was the design of the structure called "the tower of Babel." The largest ziggurat in Babylon was called the *Esagil,* but there were some thirty more throughout the city. Despite what one may assume, there is little or no direct connection between the ziggurats of Mesopotamia and the pyramids of Egypt, nor those in Mesoamerica. *See also* Babel, tower of; tower; pyramid(s).

Zilpah: a maidservant of Leah given when she married Jacob (Gen. 29:24). Zilpah became Jacob's secondary wife and gave birth to Gad and Asher.

Zimmerman, Johann Jacob: a German prognosticator who determined that the world would end in the autumn of 1694 from his theological and astrological manipulations. He gathered a group of colonists and planned to take them to America to welcome Jesus. However, he died on the very date of departure. Johannes Kelpius assumed the leadership of the cult now called "Woman in the Wilderness." *See also* cult(s); Woman in the Wilderness.

Zimri: 1. the fifth king of Israel (885 B.C.), a former commander of the chariot corps. He exterminated the entire family of Baasha, including the king's son Elah. Zimri's rule lasted only seven days because he set fire to his palace and perished in the flames rather than be taken by his rival, Omri. 2. a son of Zerah (also called Zibda), grandson of Judah and Tamar (2 Chr. 2:6; Josh. 7:1, 17–18). 3. a Simonite who was executed by the priest Phinehas (Num. 25:6–18) for engaging in sexual idolatry. 4. a people of Arabia (Jer. 25:25). 5. a descendant of Jonathan, Saul's son and friend of David (1 Chr. 8:36; 9:42). *See also* Arabia; king(s); kings of Israel and Judah; kings of Israel and Judah in foreign relations.

Zin: a desert region south of Judah marking the southern edge of the Israelite territory. Sometimes the place is mentioned in connection with Kadesh.

zinnar: a sacred ribbon presented to the newly baptized or to recent grooms in the Eastern Orthodox Church. *See also* Eastern Orthodox Church.

Zinzendorf, Count Nikolaus Ludwig von: a German Pietist who established a communal-type refuge in Saxony that he called "Herrnhut" (1700–1750). Zinzendorf intended his experiment to showcase Pietism by encouraging concentrated worship in that style of religious expression and stressing an honest livelihood via craftwork and farming. His community-styled model eventually spread around Europe as far as Great Britain and Russia and even across the Atlantic. Called Moravians, many who escaped from European persecution were the cornerstone of the communities, all of whom were joyful worshipers and missionary-minded believers. Zinzendorf himself often accompanied their mission enterprises. Despite the outreach, Zinzendorf thought a great revival would only come when the Jewish people returned to the Lord. Worship consisted of seven meetings per day with more on Sundays, ample singing (with the congregation making up a full choir from time to time), and heavy use of musical instruments. Zinzendorf was particularly fond of the trombone, which was even used at funerals. The self-styled liturgy was prone to lurid descriptions and devotions concerning the bloody death of Christ on the cross, a feature that possibly limited its wider acceptance. *See also* choir; communal communities; Moravian Church; Pietism, Pietists; Tennent, Gilbert.

Zion: a name applied to Jerusalem, or portions of the city, since the reign of King David. In prophecy, it is the hill on which the Temple stood and was metaphorically extended to portray the headquarters of Yahweh. The Bible refers to Zion and Jerusalem more than 600 times. Jerusalem is considered to be both a real city and the ideal place that will exist in the messianic age. *See also* City of David; City of God; City of Truth; Daughter of Jerusalem; footstool; Hasmonean dynasty; holy mountain(s), the; Jerusalem as city; Judaism; Middle East; Mount Zion; new name, a; prince of the covenant (testament), a; seven shepherds and eight princes; shepherd/shepherdess; Zechariah's vision of the four horns and four craftsmen; Zionism.

Zionism: in modern usage, an intense fervor for the state of Israel or the culture and religion of Israel. For Muslims, the term is derogatory; for Christians and Jews who see Israel as central to the eschatological process, it is a term of hope and enthusiasm for the future of the Jewish cause. There are some particulars regarding Zionism that convey somewhat different connotations: 1. Christian Zionism—the unqualified and enthusiastic support by Christians and Christian groups for the nation of Israel. The guiding idea is that the end time scenario centers on Jerusalem, a rebuilt Temple, and other eschatological considerations, all of which are essential to the Second Coming program and must be protected and promoted at all times. 2. Messianic

Zionism (Traditional Zionism)—the yearning desire for the re-establishment or fulfillment of the Jewish Land Covenant promise from God. The result would present the world with a utopian form of society based on Messianic ideals and establish Judaism as central in the world's religious economy. 3. practical Zionism—an effort to promote peace and economic stability through dialogue and cooperation between Palestinians and Jews. Disillusionment seems to have overtaken most of the idealistic aims of the movement, undoubtedly for obvious reasons of irreconcilable animosity between the two factions. 4. secular Zionism—the ideal that the present time, not the eschaton, is the proper time for the Jews to fully occupy Palestine and live in an unthreatened Jewish state. The secularist agenda in Israel has little or nothing to do with Jewish eschatology or indeed traditional Judaism itself. What is sometimes overlooked is that Zionism in its formative stages was a political movement, not a religious one. An early instigator, Theodor Herzl, would have gladly accepted any real estate on earth for a Jewish homeland if Palestine proved unavailable. *See also* Alkalai, Rabbi Yehuda; ben Gurion, David; Blackstone, William Eugene; First Zionist Congress; Herzl, Theodore; International Fellowship of Christians and Jews; Judaism; land for peace; Law of Return; Meir, Golda; Messianic Jews; Middle East; *Neturei Karta;* New World Order, the (NWO); philo-Semitism; proselytism; sect(s); Zion; Zionism, Christian.

Zionism, Christian: the Christian understanding of Judaism in its history, modern structure, and future disposition. Christian Zionists believe that the return of the Jewish people to Israel and the establishment of the state of Israel in 1948 were fulfillment of prophecy. The International Fellowship of Christians and Jews, headed by an Orthodox rabbi named Yechiel Eckstein, has raised over a quarter-billion dollars from some 400,000 donors in support of Zionist goals, including the promotion of Jewish emigration to Israel. Each advocate may differ politically but have no doubts regarding the biblical view of Jewish destiny. The land and the people of Israel have a future in God's eschatological plan. The group bases most of its theology on Genesis 12:1–3, which ends with a promise: "I will bless those who bless you, and whoever curses you I will curse." *See also* Blackstone,

William Eugene; evangelist(s), evangelism; Gabelein, Arno C.; International Fellowship of Christians and Jews; Lindsey, Hal; Messianic Jews; philo-Semitism; proselytism; Zionism.

Zionites: a sect of visionaries active in Ronsdorf, Germany, from 1726. They sprang from the Philadelphians with Elias Eller and David Schleiermacher as leaders. In 1730, a prophetess named Anna van Bushel rose to prominence. She claimed she would bear the Messiah and turned the group into the cultic stream. Schleiermacher eventually abandoned the group with a stricken conscience. The Bushel Zionites are a different sect from the Alexander Dowie cult by the same nickname in America. *See also* Philadelphians; sect(s); vision(s).

Zipporah: a daughter of Jethro who married Moses (Ex. 2:21–22). The circumcision of one of her older sons had been neglected at some point, but when her husband's life was endangered because of this breach of the covenant, she performed the operation herself, then castigated Moses for his dangerous disregard of the covenant (Ex. 4:18–26). *See also* Hobab; Jethro; Miriam; Moses; Tharbis.

Ziska: the blind general who brilliantly led the rebellious Taborites against their Roman Catholic oppressors. *See also* White Mountain, battle of; Taborites.

Ziusudra. See Utnapishtim.

Ziz: the counterpart of the sky when compared to Behemoth on land and Leviathan in the sea. A Jewish legend says Behemoth and Leviathan will kill each other in the final days and men will eat them at the great banquet of God. That leaves, presumably, only Ziz. *See also* Behemoth; Levant pantheon; Leviathan; Rahab.

Zoan: Egyptian city also known as Ramses, Tanis, and Arius in the Delta.

Zoar: 1. one of the cities of the plain, apparently the smallest (Gen. 19:20, 22), sometimes called as Bela. At the intercession of Lot, the city was spared the destruction that enveloped the other four cities (including Sodom and Gomorrah) and was used as a sanctuary for him and his daughters when they hid themselves in nearby caves. Josephus told us that "Zoar" means "small thing," pertaining to the constricted and uncomfortable space he and his daughters were forced to inhabit after the destruction of Sodom. 2. an Egyptian city also known as Tunis, probably built by the Hyksos (see Numbers 13:22). *See also* Admah; cities of the plain; Gomorrah; Pentapolis; Sodom; Sodom and Gomorrah; Zeboiim; Zoar Society.

Zoar Society: a communal colony founded in 1817 on the Tuscarawas River in Ohio. The settlers were German Separatists led by Joseph M. Bimeler. They named their settlement from the city on the plain, which the Bible says was spared at the time of the destruction of Sodom and Gomorrah and a refuge for Lot and his daughters. The society prospered until the death of Bimeler in 1853. At its peak, the Zoar Society owned 10,000 acres of land and some 1 million dollars in assets. *See also* communal communities; Zoar.

zodiac: literally, "circle of animals," an imaginary belt in the heavens extending eight degrees on either side of the perceived path of the sun and including the movements of the moon and main planets at given times. The zodiac (often called the "witness to the stars") is divided into twelve (some say thirteen) parts, or signs, each named for a different constellation. The signs are usually presented as: 1. Aquarius, the water bearer (Jan. 20–Feb. 18), 2. Capricorn, the sea-goat (Dec. 22–Jan. 20), 3. Sagittarius, the centaur archer (Nov. 22–Dec. 22), 4. Scorpio, the scorpion (Oct. 23–Nov. 22), 5. Libra, the scales (Sept. 23–Oct. 23), 6. Virgo, the virgin (Aug. 23–Sept. 23), 7. Leo, the lion (Jul. 22–Aug. 23), 8. Cancer, the crab (Jun. 21–Jul. 22), 9. Gemini, the twins (May 21–Jun. 21), 10. Taurus, the bull (Apr. 20–May 31), 11. Aries, the ram (Mar. 20–Apr. 20), 12. Pisces, the fish (Feb. 18–Mar. 20). The zodiac is of ancient origin and was critical to early (and modern) fortune-telling, astrology, and the casting of time charts. The theory of the zodiac controlling affairs on the earth is considered superstitious by most modern interpreters of Christian theology and by even more scientists. The theory of the zodiac may also name the process of drafting an astrological forecast. Serious, but almost unnoticed, attempts have been made to equate the constellations and their luminaries to prophetic events in the reign of Christ—a wasted effort. Typically, the authors assert that the heavens display "God's invisible qualities" noted by Paul in Romans 1:20. There, it is said, is the ancient (even as remote as the creation of the universe) eternal testimony to God's omnipotence and His provisions for redemption of the earth. Around fifty of these celestial displays claim to represent some aspect of the Messiah's promise, birth, suffering, and ultimate reign. A few examples will suffice to illustrate: Virgo represents the promised seed of woman conceived in her virginity; Libra depicts the price of redemption (its chief stars denoting the Crux as the cross, the Lupus was the victim slain, the Corona as the crown bestowed); Taurus is the Messiah coming to rule; and the Lion shows the rending of the enemy (with the stars Hydra as the serpent devil, the Cup as divine wrath poured out, and the Raven as the devouring of Babylon), etc. *See also* Age of Aquarius; Ariosophy; Aries; astrology, astrologers; astronomy, astronomers; Chronos; harmonic conversion; horoscope(s); kosmokrators; mythological beasties, elementals, monsters, and spirit animals; New Age religion; Magi; *Mazzaroth;* Olympic spirits; Pisces; planetary hours; planets as gods, the; star(s); star of Bethlehem; Tripoli Prophecy.

zoe: a Greek feminine noun meaning "life" and the fullness thereof. The term is akin to "soul" that is extant in everyone and can even approximate the very essence of God. Certainly, it applies to Jesus in his incarnate being as well. To the ancient Egyptians, the soul was made up of five parts: the *ren, ba, ka, sheut,* and *ib;* the body was *ha. See also ba;* heart; heart and spirit; heart, mind, and soul; *Ka;* life; *maat;* mind; *nephesh; nous; psuche;* psyche; *qi;* soul(s); spirit; strength.

Zohar: also called *The Book of Splendor,* the most important and most holy of the Qabbalistic writings compiled by one Moses de Leon, who claimed he received it from its author, Shimon bar Yochai. Most modern scholars, however, believe that de Leon was the true composer. The legend persists, nevertheless, that Rabbi Yochai ("Rashbi") spent thirteen years in a cave during the second century studying the Torah and composing the *Zohar* material. The collection appears to be a running commentary on the Pentateuch written in medieval Aramaic. The work is an extension and Aramaic commentary on the Torah seeking to explore the mystical aspects of its stories. The doctrine claims the human soul is made up of three elements: *nefesh* (our lower, animal tendencies), *ruach* (the middle soul of moral virtues), and *neshkamah* (the highest measure of the human spirit). It is believed that the *Zohar* explains all there is about the universe and may contain secrets capable of discovering encoded passages in Scripture. At least at one point, the writing seems to predict the Messiah's coming and destruction of Rome in 2013. The same book is frequently cited as an important text for the Illuminati and a major occultic guide. Later, a new edition to the *Zohar* appeared called the *Raaya Meheimna* with more detail and expansion. *See also* Aqiba, Rabbi Joseph ben; Bible Code; Cheiro; de Leon, Moses; emanations, doctrine of; *gematria;* Haggada; Halakha; Husk(s); Illuminati; *isopseplia;* Judaism; Kaduri, Rabbi Yitzchak; Masseket Hekalot; *nephesh; notarikon;* occult, occultic; Pardes; primal light; Qabbala; *ruach; Sefirot;* Sephiroth; Sephiroth Tree; seventy-two; *temoorah;* Zevi, Shabbatai.

Zolfaghar: or Zulfiqar, an iconic sword used by an early caliph, one of Islam Shia's twelve imams named Ali. The weapon has bifurcated points, one slightly larger than the other. *See also* caliph; Excalibur; imam; Islam; Mjollnir; sword.

zombie apocalypse: the belief, or fear, possessed by some of the modern age that the end of the world will see a zombie invasion. The "dead/undead" are to rise in soul-less moldy bodies to wreak havoc on the living population. The impact of movies and pop culture is clearly in evidence here. *See also* eschatology, eschatological; Ghede; mythological beasties, elementals, monsters, and spirit animals.

zoophilia: sexual copulation between a human and an animal, also called bestiality. The practice is considered an abomination in Scripture and most countries class it as a crime against nature. *See also* Nephilim.

Zophar: one of Job's counselors whose interpretations proved neither particularly accurate nor helpful. Some consider Zophar and his friends to be prophets, but they are more accurately termed elders or philosophers. *See also* Bildad; Elihu; Eliphaz; Job as afflicted wise man.

Zoroaster, Zoroastrianism: (Mazdaism) the religion founded by Zoroaster, the ancient Persian prophet of northeastern Iran. His real name was Zarathushtra and his adherents, somewhat quasi-surviving today, are generally called Parsees. The birth date of the prophet is disputed, but the most famous designation is said to be 258 years before Alexander the Great. The history of Zoroaster's life is mostly unclear, but the strongest legend seems to be that he was born near Lake Uremia near the Turkish border, a site that has always been the center of Zoroastrian religion. Some Zoroastrian believers insist that their prophet was born around 6000 B.C., but most scholars place him in the sixth century B.C. Current reports confirm that the sacred lake is now turning to salt due to poor ecological projects in the country. Perhaps the Magi who journeyed to Bethlehem started from here. The same research claims that the prophet died there as well. More precisely, some information exists that the religion, singular in its monotheism, was first preached at Bactra [modern Balkh], in ancient Afghanistan. The tenets of the sect center on dualism—the conflict between good and evil. The great god Ahura Mazda is constantly locked in battle with the dark entity Ahriman. Ahura is assisted by his creations, the Amesha Spenta ("bounteous immortals"), six divine spirits. Humans also aid by minimizing disorder with good thoughts, good works, and good deeds (recited in ritual as *"Humata, Hukhta, Hvarshta"),* all of which support *asha,* the fundamental order of the universe, and opposing *druf* (chaos). Worship consisted of drinking the sacred liquor *haoma (soma* in India) and certain practiced rites performed before the eternal flame. The presiding fire priests are required to wear a *padan,* a facial cover, over their mouths to prevent saliva or breath from contaminating the flame. Some temple fires have been kept burning for centuries using only gifts of wood as fuel. In the fourth century, Zoroaster's teachings were compiled into the *Avesta,* including the *Gathas*—seventeen hymns believed to be the founder's own words. The most holy prayer is called Ahunavar which can cast Ahriman back into darkness. Ahura Mazda can then create human beings by forming a primal animal (a bull) which becomes a mortal called a Gayomart. Ritual practice of the religion is rather detailed. At puberty, the faithful novice was vested with a mysterious belt as a talisman against evil. Exacting and superstitious prayers, rituals, and actions were frequent, neglect of which was considered a grievous sin. Multiple genuflections, for example, were required before a man could urinate or routinely trim his nails. Zoroastrianism was sorely opposed by the Greeks and Muslims, but it nevertheless had no little influence on those religions acquainted with it, including Christianity and Judaism.

At one point, Zoroastrianism was at war with Christianity, and even precipitated the mid-fifth century massacre of ten bishops and 153,000 Christians in what is now the Iraqi city of Kirkuk. As a note of interest, the Persian word for Magus ("might" or "mighty" in English) denoted a priest or sage. They wore high hats much like our Halloween depiction of witches or ancient wizards like Merlin. These men were said to be conversant in astronomy/astrology, medicine, and magical control of wind and weather, and capable of contact with the spirit world. Zoroastrian teachings inform us that as the end of time draws near, the Saoshyant (savior) will appear to end sin and destroy the evil demon Az, raise the dead, and send fire and molten metal to purify the world. *See also* Abulfaragius; Ahriman; Ahura Mazda; Alevism; *Avesta*; bitheist; *Bundahishn*; Chinvat Bridge; *daena; dar-e-mehr;* dualism; excarnation; Fravashi; *Gathas;* Gochihr; *haoma; Khordad Sol;* Magi; magus; *Norwruz;* Parsees; people of the book; perpetual lamp; Persia, Persians; Sabians; Sassanid Empire; sect(s); Zurvan Akarana; Cave of Treasures.

zos kia cultus: a style of automatic drawing invented by Austin Osman Spare (1886–1956) that produces a magical or esoteric form centered in the *art nouveau* technique but with definitive occultic and sexual overtones. *See also* automatic writing; Oahspe Bible; sect(s); Spare, Austin Osman.

zucchetto: the round skullcap worn by Roman Catholic clergy to show rank. *See also* furniture and furnishings of the modern church; Roman Catholic Church.

Zuism: a religious sect formed in Iceland in 2010 who follow the Middle Eastern religions with Sumerian contexts, including its many gods. The Zuists Icelanders oppose state funding of religion and joining the sect can earn a tax rebate, a factor that has spurred recent growth. Already the cult has been in litigation for abuse of funds. *See also* Sumerian and Babylonian pantheon; Sumer, Sumerians.

Zurvan Akarana: the god of time in some forms of Zoroastrianism— the prime being from whom were derived Ahura Mazda and the vile Angra Mainyu. He sports the head of a lion and representing the Zoroastrian religion called Zurvanism. *See also* Zoroaster, Zoroastrianism.

Zuzim (Zuzites). See giant(s).

Zwingli, Ulrich (Huldrych): Swiss Protestant reformer of the 16th century headquartered in Zurich. He shared the country with John Calvin in Geneva. Zwingli's movement was different from Luther's, and even from Calvin's, and fits under the umbrella of "Reformed" theology and not Lutheranism. Whereas Luther's ignition for reform was the heart, it was intellectual and theological for Zwingli. Though a Reformer, he was also a humanist and admirer of Erasmus, another point of difference between him and other Protestant leaders. He and Luther held differing views of the Eucharist as well, although an attempt was made for reconciliation and alliance at the Marburg Conference. Zwingli was a parish priest, an army chaplain, and an accomplished and enthusiastic musician. The latter talent is remarkable in that he banned music in worship because it was too idolatrous; its prohibition held together until 1598 when the congregants demanded hymns and psalms in their worship like nearly every other religious persuasion. The Reformer's chief writing was *Sixty-Seven Conclusions*, a summary of his doctrines. These writings were to Zwingli what the "Ninety-Five Theses" were to Luther. As a theologian, Zwingli was disinterested in discussing the canon of Scripture but did exclude Revelation in 1522. After 1530, however, he gave it cautious acceptance. He was killed in a rebellion of five cantons allied against Zurich, then his body was quartered and burned. *See also* Calvin, John; Geneva theocracy of John Calvin; Luther, Martin; Marburg Conference; Oecolampadius, John; Protestantism, Protestants; Reformation, the.

BIBLIOGRAPHY

Abanes, Richard. *End time Visions: The Doomsday Obsession.* Nashville, TN: Broadman & Holman Publishers, 1998.

Ackroyd, P.R., A.R.C. Leaney, A.R.C., and J.W. Packer, eds. Cambridge, UK: The University Press, 1972–1974. *The Cambridge Bible Commentary on the New English Bible: The Book of Daniel;* Author: Raymond Hammer; Date: 1976; *The Cambridge Bible Commentary on the New English Bible: Ecclesiasticus;* Author: John G. Snaith Date: 1974; *The Cambridge Bible Commentary on the New English Bible: The First and Second Books of Esdras;* Author: Richard J. Coggins and M. A. Knibb Date: 1979; *The Cambridge Bible Commentary on the New English Bible: The Shorter Books of the Apocrypha;* Editor: J.C. Dancy Date: 1972; *The Cambridge Bible Commentary on the New English Bible: The Wisdom of Solomon;* Author: Ernest G. Clarke Date: 1974; *The Cambridge Bible Commentary on the New English Bible: The Book of the Prophet Ezekiel;* Author: Keith Carley Date: 1974.

Alcorn, Randy. *Heaven.* Wheaton, IL: Tyndale House Publishers, 2004.

Ali, A. Yusuf, ed. *The Holy Qur'an.* Brentwood, MD: Amana Corp., 1983.

Alighieri, Dante. *The Divine Comedy.* New York, NY: Modern Library, 1950.

Anderson, Robert A. *Signs and Wonders: A Commentary on the Book of Daniel.* Grand Rapids, MI: William B. Eerdmans Publishing Co., 1984.

_____. *The Coming Prince.* 10th ed. Grand Rapids, MI: Kregel Publications, 1977.

Ankerberg, John and Jimmy DeYoung. *Israel Under Fire: The Prophetic Chain of Events that Threatens the Middle East.* Eugene, OR: Harvest House Publishers, 2009.

Apel, Willi. *Harvard Dictionary of Music.* 14th printing. Cambridge, MA: Harvard University Press, 1962.

Archer, Gleason L., Paul D. Feinberg, Douglas J. Moo, and Richard R. Reiter. *The Rapture: Pre-, Mid-, or Post-Tribulational?* Grand Rapids, MI: Zondervan Corporation, 1984.

Armstrong, Hart. *Christ's Twofold Prophecy—The Olivet Discourse: A Topical Study of Our Lord's Great Prophetic Utterance on the Mount of Olives.* Wichita, KS: Christian Communications, Inc., 1993.

Armstrong, Karen. *A History of God: The 4,000 Year Quest of Judaism, Christianity, and Islam.* 12th printing. New York, NY: Alfred A. Knopf, Inc., 1993.

Ashley, Leonard R. N. *The Complete Book of Devils and Demons.* New York, NY: Skyhorse Publishing, 2011.

Ausubel, Nathan, ed. *A Treasury of Jewish Folklore.* New York, NY: Bantam Books, Inc., 1980.

Baker, Robert A. *A Summary of Christian History.* Nashville, TN: Broadman Press, 1959.

Ballard, H. Wayne and B. Donald Keyser. *From Jerusalem to Gaza: An Old Testament Theology.* Macon, GA: Smyth & Helwys Publishing, Inc., 2002.

Bamberger, Bernaul J. *Fallen Angels: Soldiers of Satan's Realm.* The Jewish Publication Society, Philadelphia, PA: 1952.

Barret, David V. *A Brief History of Secret Societies.* Philadelphia, PA: Running Press, 2007.

Blackstone, William E. *Jesus is Coming: God's Hope for a Restless World.* Grand Rapids, MI: Kregel Classics, 1989.

Blenkinsopp, Joseph. *A History of Prophecy in Israel.* Philadelphia, PA: The Westminster Press, 1983.

Benware, Paul N. *The Believer's Payday.* Chattanooga, TN: AMG Publishers, 2002.

_____. *Understanding End time Prophecy: A Comprehensive Approach.* Chicago, IL: Moody Publishers, 1995.

Beasley-Murray, George R. *Jesus and the Last Days: The Interpretation of the Olivet Discourse.* Vancouver, BC: Regent College Publishing, 1993.

Biltz, Mark. *Blood Moons: Decoding the Imminent Heavenly Signs.* Washington, D.C.: WND Books, 2014.

Blau, Joseph L. *Men and Movements in American Philosophy.* Englewood, NJ: Printice-Hall, Inc., 1966.

Braden, Charles Samuel. *These Also Believe.* New York, NY: The Macmillan Company, 1963.

Braswell, George W. Jr. *Islam: Its Prophet, Peoples, Politics, and Power.* Nashville, TN: Broadman and Holman Publishers, 1996.

Bright, Bill and John N. Damoose. *Red Sky in the Morning: How You Can Help Prevent America's Gathering Storms.* Orlando, FL: NewLife Publications, 1998.

Brown, William. *The Tabernacle: Its Priests and Its Services.* Peabody, MA: Hendrickson Publishers, Inc., 1996.

Bruce, F. F. *The Books and the Parchments: How We Got Our English Bible.* Westwood, NJ: Fleming H. Revell Company, 1963.

_____. Revised by David R. Payne. *Israel and the Nations: The History of Israel from the Exodus to the Fall of the Second Temple.* Downers Grove, IL: InterVarsity Press, 1997.

Bullinger, E. W. *The Witness of the Stars.* Grand Rapids, MI: Kregel Publications, 2003. Reprint of the 1894 edition.

Bush, George. *The Valley of Vision; or The Dry Bones of Israel Revived: An Attempted Proof (From Ezekiel, Chapter 37:1-14) of the Restoration and Conversion of the Jews.* New York, NY: Saxton and Miles, 1844.

Byfield, Ted, ed. *The Veil is Torn A.D. 30 to 79, Pentecost to the Destruction of Jerusalem.* Canada: National Library of Canada Cataloguing in Publication Data, 2003.

Cahn, Jonathan. *The Harbinger: The Ancient Mystery That Holds the Secret of America's Future.* Lake Mary, FL: Frontline, 2011.

_____. *The Harbinger Companion with Study Guide.* Lake Mary, FL: Frontline, 2013.

Calaway, Bernie L. *Discernment from Daniel.* Baltimore, MD: PublishAmerica, Inc., 2002.

_____. *Oracles from Olivet: The Eschatological Jesus.* Baltimore, MD: PublishAmerica, Inc., 2008.

_____. *Revealing the Revelation: A Guide to the Literature of the Apocalypse.* Bethesda, MD: International Scholars Publication (Rowman & Littlefield Publishing Group), 1998.

_____. *Revelation for Regular Readers*. Baltimore, MD: PublishAmerica, Inc., 2004.

Calaway, Bernie L. and Jan Ledford. *Operation Revelation: A Teen's Script to Earth's Final Curtain*. Baltimore, MD: PublishAmerica, Inc., 2006.

Capps, Benjamin. *Time-Life Books: The Old West—The Indians*. New York, NY: Time-Life Books, 1973.

Carson, D. A. *The God Who is There: Finding Your Place in God's Story*. Grand Rapids, MI: Baker Books, 2010.

Carter, Stephen L. *The Culture of Disbelief: How American Law and Politics Trivialize Religious Devotion*. New York, NY: Basic Books, 1993.

Charles, R. H., ed. *The Apocrypha and Pseudepigrapha of the Old Testament*. 2 vols. Oxford, England: Clarendon Press, 1979.

Charlesworth, James H., ed. *The Old Testament Pseudepigrapha*. 2 vols. Garden City, NY: Doubleday & Company, Inc., 1985.

Chitwood, Arlen L. *Mysteries of the Kingdom*. Norman, OK: The Lamp Broadcast, Inc., 2011.

Chouinard, Patrick. *Forgotten Worlds: From Atlantis to the X-Woman of Siberia and the Hobbits of Flores*. Rochester, VT: Bear & Company, 2012.

_____. *Lost Race of the Giants: the Mystery of their Culture, Influences, and Decline throughout the World*. Rochester, VT: Bear and Company, 2013.

Clouse, Robert G., Robert N. Hosack, and Richard V. Pierard. *The New Millennium Manual: A Once and Future Guide*. Grand Rapids, MI: Baker Books, 1999.

_____, ed. *The Meaning of the Millennium: Four Views*. Downers Grove, IL: InterVarsity Press, 1977.

Coleman, Robert. *Songs of Heaven*. Old Tappan, NJ: Fleming H. Revell Co., 1980.

Collins, Andrew. *Gobekli Tepe: Genesis of the Gods—The Temple of the Watchers and the Discovery of Eden*. Rochester, VT: Bear and Company, 2014.

Connelly, Douglas. *The Book of Revelation Made Clear: A User-Friendly Look at the Bible's Most Complicated Book* (formerly *The Book of Revelation for Blockheads*). Grand Rapids, MI: Zondervan, 2007.

Cornfield, Gaalyah and Daniel Noel Freedman. *Archeology of the Bible: The First Thousand years.* New York, NY: Harper and Row Publishers, Inc., 1976.

Cook, Edward M. *Solving the Mysteries of the Dead Sea Scrolls: New Light on the Bible.* Grand Rapids, MI: Zondervan Publishing House, 1994.

Couch, Mel, ed. *Dictionary of Premillennial Theology.* Grand Rapids, MI: Kregel Publications, 1996.

Couch, Paul. *The Shadow of the Apocalypse: When All Hell Breaks Loose.* Berkley Books: New York, NY, 2004.

Crim, Keith, ed. *Abingdon Dictionary of Living Religions.* Nashville, TN: Abingdon Press, 1981.

Crocket, William, ed. *Four Views of Hell.* Grand Rapids, MI: Zondervan Publishing House, 1992.

Cruden, Alexander. *Cruden's Complete Concordance.* Chicago, IL: The John C. Winston Company, 1930.

Davidson, Mark. *Daniel Revisited: Discovering the Four Mideast Signs Leading to the Antichrist.* Nashville, TN: Thomas Nelson Publishing, 2015.

Davies, J. G., ed. *The New Westminster Dictionary of Liturgy and Worship.* Philadelphia, PA: Westminster Press, 1986.

Davis, John J. *Biblical Numerology: A Basic Study of the Use of Numbers in the Bible.* Grand Rapids, MI: Baker Book House, 1968.

Day, John. *God's Conflict with the Dragon and the Sea: Echoes of a Canaanite Myth in the Old Testament.* Eugene, OR: Wipf and Stock Publishers, 1985.

Dearman, J. Andrew. *Religion and Culture in Ancient Israel.* Peabody, MA: Hendrickson Publishers, 1992.

De Haan, M. R. *Daniel the Prophet: Thirty-Five Simple Studies in the Book of Daniel.* Grand Rapids, MI: Zondervan Publishing House, 1947.

de Lange, Nicholas. *Judaism.* Oxford, England: Oxford University Press, 1986.

Dixon, Jim. *Last Things Revealed: Hope for Life and the Everafter.* Colorado Springs, CO: Biblica Publishing, 2011.

Dostoyevsky, Fyodor. *The Brothers Karamazov.* New York, NY: Sinet, 1980.

Duck, Daymond R. *Revelation: God's Word for the Biblically Inept.* Lancaster, PA: Starburst Publishers, 1998.

Efird, James M. *Left Behind? What the Bible Really Says about the End time.* Macon, GA: Smyth & Helwys Publishing, Inc., 2005.

Ellis, Peter Berresford. *A Brief History of the Celts.* London, UK: Robinson, 2003.

_____. *A Brief History of the Druids.* Philadelphia, PA: Running Press Book Publishers, 2002.

Evans, Mike. *The Final Generation.* Phoenix, AZ: Time Worthy Books, 2012.

_____. *The Temple: The Center of Gravity.* Phoenix, AZ: Time Worthy Books, 2015.

Faid, Robert W. *A Scientific Approach to Biblical Mysteries plus A Scientific Approach to More Biblical Mysteries.* Carmel, NY: Guideposts via special arrangement with New Leaf Press, 1993.

Farrar, Steve. *Get in the Ark: Finding Safety in the Coming Judgment.* Nashville, TN: Thomas Nelson Publishers, 2000.

Finegan, Jack. *Myth and Mystery: An Introduction to the Pagan Religions of the Biblical World.* Grand Rapids, MI: Baker Book House, 1989.

Finkel, Irving. *The Ark Before Noah: Decoding the Story of the Ark.* New York, NY: Doubleday, 2014.

Finley, Robert. *The Time Was at Hand.* Xulon Press, 2011.

Finto, Don. *Your People Shall Be My People: How Israel, the Jews and the Christian Church Will Come Together in the Last Days.* Bloomington, MN: Chosen Books, 2014.

Fortson, Dante. *As the Days of Noah Were: The Sons of God and the Coming Apocalypse.* USA: Impact Agenda Media, 2010.

Frazer, James G. *The Golden Bough: A Study in Religion and Magic* (abridged edition). Mineola, NY: Dover Publications, Inc., 2019.

Freund, Richard A. *Digging Through History: Archeology and Religion from Atlantis to the Holocaust.* New York, NY: Rowman and Littlefield Publishers, Inc. 2012,

Friedman, Stanton T. *Flying Saucers and Science: A Scientist Investigates the Mysteries of UFOs.* Pompton Plains, NJ: New Page Books, 2008.

Gardner, Laurence. *The Shadow of Solomon: The Lost Secret of The Freemasons Revealed.* San Francisco, CA: Weiser Books, 2005.

Garlow, James L. *The Covenant: A Bible Study.* Kansas City, MO: Beacon Hill Press of Kansas City, 1999.

Gehman, Henry Snyder, ed. *The New Westminster Dictionary of the Bible.* Wheaton, IL: Tyndale House Publishers, 1970.

Gibbon, Edward. *The Decline and Fall of the Roman Empire.* vol. 1. New York, NY: Modern Library, undated.

Glasser, William. *Reality Therapy: A New Approach to Psychiatry.* New York, NY: Harper & Row, Publishers, 1965.

Goll, Jim W. *The Seer: The Prophetic Power of Visions, Dreams, and Open Heavens.* Shippensburg, PA: Destiny Image Publishers, Inc., 2004.

Goodrich, Norma Lorre. *Ancient Myths.* New York, NY: New American Library, 1960.

Grun, Bernard. *The Timetables of History.* 3rd rev. ed. New York, NY: Simon & Schuster, 1991.

Guillermo, Jorge. *Sibyls: Prophecy and Power in the Ancient World.* New York, NY: Peter Mayer Publishers, Inc., 2013.

Haag, Michael. *The Templars: The History and the Myth.* London, UK: Harper Collins, 2009. e-books.

Hamon, Bill. *Prophetic Scriptures Yet to Be Fulfilled.* Shippensburg, PA: Destiny Image Publishers, Inc., 2010.

Hamp, Douglas. *Corrupting the Image: Angels, Aliens, and the Antichrist Revealed.* Defender Publishing, LLC, 2011.

Bernie L. Calaway

Hanegraaf, Hank. *The Apocalypse Code: Find Out What the Bible Really Says about the End times and Why It Matters Today.* Nashville, TN: Thomas Nelson Publishers, 2007.

Hancock, Graham. *The Sign and the Seal.* New York, NY: Simon & Shuster, Inc., 1992.

Heinlein, Robert A. *Job: A Comedy of Justice.* New York, NY: Ballantine Books, 1984.

_____. *The Number of the Beast.* New York, NY: Ballantine Books, 1980.

Heiser, Michael S. *Angels: What the Bible Really Says about God's Heavenly Host.* Bellingham, WA: Lexham Press, 2018.

Hester, H. I. *The Heart of the New Testament.* 10th printing. Liberty, MO: The William Jewell Press, 1950.

Hildebrand, Lloyd B. *2012: Is This the End?* Alachua, FL: Bridge Logos Foundation, 2009.

Hitchcock, Mark. *2012, the Bible, and the End of the Word.* Eugene, OR: Harvest House Publishers, 2009.

_____. *The End: A Complete Overview of Bible Prophecy and the End of Days.* Cold Stream, IL: Tyndale House Publishers, 2012.

Horn, Thomas, ed. *Pandemonium's Engine: How the End of the Church Age, the Rise of Transhumanism, and the Coming of the Ubermensch (Overman) Herald Satan's Imminent and Final Assault on the Creation of God.* Crane, Mo: Defender Press, 2011.

Horn, Thomas and Thomas Putnam. *Petrus Romanus: The Final Pope is Here.* Crane, MO: Defender Press, 2012.

Howard, Kevin and Marvin Rosenthal. *The Feasts of the Lord: God's Prophetic Calendar from Calvary to the Kingdom.* Orlando, FL: Zion's Hope, Inc., 1997.

Howard, Michael. *Secret Societies: Their Influence and Power from Antiquity to the Present-day.* Rochester, VT: Destiny Books, 2008.

Howard, W.F. *Christianity According to Saint John.* London, UK: Duckworth Printing, 1958.

Howells, Robert. *The Last Pope: Francis and the Fall of the Vatican...St. Malachy's Prophecies.* London, UK: Watkins Publishing, 2013.

Humphreys, Fisher and Philip Wise. *Fundamentalism.* Macon, GA: Smyth & Helwys Publishing, Inc., 2004.

Hutchinson, Robert J. *The Politically Incorrect Guide to the Bible.* Washington, D.C. USA: Regnery Publishing, Inc., 2007.

James, E. O. *The Ancient Gods.* Edison, NJ: Castle Books, 2004.

Jeffrey, Grant R. *The New Temple and the Second Coming: The Prophecy That Points to Christ's Return in Your Generation.* Colorado Springs, CO: Waterbrook Press, 2007.

Jeremiah, David. *The Book of Signs: 31 Undeniable Prophecies of the Apocalypse.* Nashville, TN: W Publishing Group, 2019.

_____. *Is This the End? Signs of God's Providence in a Disturbing New World.* Nashville, TN: W Publishing Group, 2016.

Jerome. *Jerome's Commentary on Daniel.* Grand Rapids, MI: Baker Book House, 1958.

Johnson, Ken. *Ancient Book of Jasher: Referenced in Joshua 10:13; 2 Samuel 1:18; and 2 Timothy 3:8.* Biblefacts Ministries, 2008.

_____. *Ancient Paganism: The Sorcery of the Fallen Angels.* 2009.

_____. *Ancient Prophecies Revealed: 500 Prophecies Listed in Order of When They Were Fulfilled.* 2010.

Jones, Gareth and Georgina Palffy (sr. editors). *The Religions Book: Big Ideas Simply Explained.* New York, NY: DK Books, 2018.

Kaufmann, Walter. *Religions in Four Dimensions: Existential, Aesthetic, Historical, Comparative.* New York, NY: Reader's Digest Press, 1976.

Kinley, Jeff. *The End of America?: Bible Prophecy and a Country in Crisis.* Eugene, OR: Harvest House Publishers, 2017.

Kirsch, Jonathan. *A History of the End of the World: How the Most Controversial Book in the Bible Changed the Course of Western Civilization.* San Francisco, CA: HarperSanFrancisco, 2006.

Klein, John and Adam Spears. *Devils and Demons and the Return of the Nephilim.* Bend, OR: Covenant Research Institute, 2005.

Knight, Christopher and Robert Lomas. *The Second Messiah: Templars, the Turin Shroud, and the Great Secret of Freemasonry.* Gloucester, MA: Fair Winds Press, 1997.

L'Engle, Madeleine. *A Wrinkle in Time.* Ariel Books: Farrar, Straus and Giroux, 1963.

LaHaye, Tim and Jerry B. Jenkins. *Left Behind.* 12 vols. Carol Stream, IL: Tyndale House Publishers, Inc., 1995.

Landay, Jerry M. *The House of David.* New York, NY: E. P. Dutton & Co., Inc., 1973.

Lang, J. Stephen. *1,001 Things You Always Wanted to Know about Angels, Demons, and the Afterlife.* Nashville, TN: Thomas Nelson, 2000.

Larson, Bob. *Larson's Book of Cults.* Wheaton, IL: Tyndale House Publishers, Inc., 1982.

Latourette, Kenneth Scott. *A History of Christianity A.D. 1500–A.D. 1975.* vol. 2 rev. ed. San Francisco, CA: Harper and Row, 1975.

Law, Terry. *The Truth About Angels.* Lake Mary, FL: Creation House, 1994.

Lehmann, Arthur C. and James E. Myers. *Magic, Witchcraft, and Religion: An Anthropological Study of the Supernatural.* Palo Alto, CA: Mayfield Publishing Company, 1985.

Leon-Dufour, Xavier. *Dictionary of Biblical Theology.* 2nd rev. ed. New York, NY: Seabury Press, 1967.

Lindsay, Dennis G. *Giants, Fallen Angels, and the Return of the Nephilim: Ancient Secrets to Prepare for the Coming Days.* Shippensburg, PA: Destiny Image Publishers, Inc., 2018.

Lindsey, Hal. *The Late Great Planet Earth.* Grand Rapids, MI: Zondervan Publishing House, 1970.

The Living Bible Encyclopedia in Story and Pictures. 16 vols. New York, NY: H. S. Struttman Co. Inc., 1968.

Lockyer, Herbert. *All the Parables of the Bible: A Study and Analysis of the More than 250 Parables in Scripture.* Grand Rapids, MI: Zondervan Publishing House, 1963.

Ludwigson, R. *A Survey of Bible Prophecy.* Grand Rapids, MI: Zondervan Publishing House, 1977.

Lumpkin, Joseph P. *The Books of Enoch: The Angels, the Watchers, and the Nephilim: (With Extensive Commentary on the Three Books of Enoch, the Fallen Angels, the Calendar of Enoch, and Daniel's Prophecy).* Blountsville, AL: Fifth Estate Publishers, 2011.

_____. *The Prophecy of Saint Malachy: The Soon Coming End of Days.* Blountsville, AL: Fifth Estate Publishers, 2012.

MacBain, Alexander. *Celtic Mythology and Religion.* Glastonbury, UK: The Lost Library, 1917.

MacCulloch, Diarmaid. *Christianity: The First Three Thousand years.* New York, NY: Penguin Books, 2009.

Martin, Walter. *The Kingdom of the Cults.* Minneapolis, MN: Bethany House Publishers, 1997.

Marshall, Debra S. *A Silent Invasion: The Truth about Aliens, Alien Abductions, and UFOs.* Atglen, PA: Schiffer Publishing, Ltd, 2014.

Matthews, Victor H. *Manners and Customs in the Bible.* rev. ed. Peabody, MA: Hendrickson Publishers, Inc., 1996.

Maus, Cynthia Pearl. *Christ and the Fine Arts: An Anthology of Pictures, Poetry, Music, and Stories Centering in the Life of Christ.* rev. ed. New York, NY: Harper & Brothers Publishers, 1959.

Mayer, F. E. *The Religious Bodies of America.* 4th ed. Saint Louis, MO: Concordia Publishing House, 1961.

McCullar, Michael. *A Christian's Guide to Islam.* Macon, GA: Smyth & Helwys Publishing, Inc., 2008.

McDowell, Josh. *The New Evidence That Demands a Verdict.* Nashville, TN: Thomas Nelson Publishers, 1999.

McGuire, Paul and Troy Anderson. *The Babylon Code: Solving the Bible's Greatest End times Mystery.* New York, NY: FaithWords (a division of Hachette Book Group), 2015.

McKay, David O., (trustee-in-trust). *The Book of Mormon.* Salt Lake City, UT: The Church of Jesus Christ of Latter-Day Saints, 1961.

McNeill, John T. *The History and Character of Calvinism.* New York, NY: Oxford University Press, 1962.

Mead, Frank S. *Handbook of Denominations in the United States.* 9th ed. Revised by Samuel S. Hill. Nashville, TN: Abingdon Press, 1990.

Merrill, Eugene H. *Kingdom of Priests: A History of Old Testament Israel.* Grand Rapids, MI: Baker Book House, 1987.

Miller, Aaron David. *The Much Too Promised Land: America's Elusive Search for Arab-Israeli Peace.* New York, NY: Bantam Books, 2008.

Miller, Stephen M. *A Visual Walk Through Genesis: Exploring the Story of How it All Began.* Eugene, OR: Harvest House Publishers, 2016.

_____. *The Complete Guide to Bible Prophecy.* Uhrichsville, OH: Barbour Publishing, Inc., 2010.

Mills, Watson E., ed. *Mercer Dictionary of the Bible.* Macon, GA: Mercer University Press, 1997.

Missler, Chuck. *Prophecy 20/20: Profiling the Future through the Lens of Scripture.* Nashville, TN: Thomas Nelson Publishers, 2006.

Mistele, Bryan P. *The Truth about Prophecy in the Bible.* Redmond, WA: Beyond Today Publishing, 2005.

Moody, Raymond A. Jr. *Life After Life* and *Reflections on Life After Life.* Carmel, NY: Guideposts, 1975.

Moore, Maree. *The Dove, the Rose, and the Sceptre: In Search of the Ark of the Covenant.* Queensland, Australia: Joshua Books, 2004.

Morgan, Giles. *Freemasonry: Its History and Mysteries Revealed.* New York, NY: Shelter Harbor Press, 2015.

Munro-Hay, Stuart. *The Quest for the Ark of the Covenant.* London, New York: I. B. Tauris, 2005.

Murphy, Derek. *Jesus Harry Potter Christ.* Portland, OR: Holy Blasphemy Press, 2011.

Needham, Matthew. *The End of the World: What You Should Know about the Last Days, the Antichrist, the Judgments of God, and the Glorious Return of Jesus Christ.* Citta San't Angelo, Italy: Evangelista Media, 2012.

Nixon, Thomas C. *The Olivet Discourse: The Mystery Revealed.* Bloomington, IN: 1st Book Library, 2003.

Noel, Ruth S. *The Mythology of Middle-Earth.* Boston, MA: Houghton Mifflin Company, 1978.

Oates, Wayne. *The Psychology of Religion.* Waco, TX: Word Books, 1973.

Odell, Margaret S., ed. *Smyth & Helwys Bible Commentary: Ezekiel.* Macon, GA: Smyth & Helwys Publishing, Inc., 2005.

Pace, Sharon. *Judaism: A Brief Guide to Faith and Practice.* Macon, GA: Smyth & Helwys Publishing, Inc., 2012.

Pack, David C. *The Bible's Greatest Prophecies Unlocked: A Voice Cries Out.* Park One Publishing, 2010.

Pagels, Elaine. *Revelations: Visions, Prophecy, and Politics in the Book of Revelation.* New York, NY: Penguin Books, 2012.

Patterson, Bob. *Discovering Revelation.* Carmel, NY: Guideposts Associates, Inc., 1987.

Payne, J. Barton. *Encyclopedia of Biblical Prophecy: The Complete Guide to Scriptural Predictions and Their Fulfillment.* 2 vols. Grand Rapids, MI: Baker Book House, 1973.

Pearson, Patricia. *Opening Heaven's Door: What the Dying May Be Trying to Tell Us About Where They're Going.* Toronto, Canada: Vintage Canada, 2015.

Pentecost, J. Dwight. *Things to Come: A Study in Biblical Eschatology.* Grand Rapids, MI: Zondervan Publishing, 1976.

Perry, Richard H. *The Complete Idiot's Guide to the Last Days: An Apocalyptic Look at the Future.* Indianapolis, IN: Alpha Books, 2006.

Petrement, Simone. *A Separate God: The Christian Origins of Gnosticism.* San Francisco, CA: Harper San Francisco, 1984.

Pfeiffer, Charles F., Howard F. Vos, and John Rea, eds. *Wycliffe Bible Encyclopedia.* vols. 1 and 2. Chicago, IL: Moody Press, 1975.

Pfeiffer, Robert H. *The Books of the Old Testament.* New York, NY: Harper & Row, Publishers, 1957.

Phillips, Graham. *The Templars and the Ark of the Covenant: The Discovery of the Treasure of Solomon.* Rochester, VT: Bear & Company, 2004.

Philpott, Kent. *A Manual of Demonology and the Occult.* Grand Rapids, MI: Zondervan Publishing House, 1976.

Piper, Don and Cecil Murphy. *90 Minutes In Heaven: A True Story of Death and Life.* Grand Rapids, MI: Revell, 2004.

Price, Isabella. *Visions of the End: The Christian Book of Revelation and Other Apocalyptic Prophecies.* Smashwords, 2014.

Price, Paula A. *The Prophet's Dictionary: The Ultimate Guide to Supernatural Wisdom.* Tulsa, OK: Whitaker House, 2006.

Price, Randall. *The Coming Last Days Temple.* Eugene, OR: Harvest House Publishers, 1999.

_____. *The Temple and Bible Prophecy: A Definitive Look at Its Past, Present, and Future.* Eugene, OR: Harvest House Publishers, 2005.

Read, Piers Paul. *The Templars: The Dramatic History of the Knights Templar, the Most Powerful Military Order of the Crusades.* Cambridge, MA: De Capo Press, 1999.

Reddish, Mitchell G., ed. *Apocalyptic Literature: A Reader.* Peabody, MA: Hendrickson Publishers, 1995.

_____. *Smyth & Helwys Bible Commentary: Revelation.* Macon, GA: Smyth & Helwys Publishing, Inc., 2001.

Reynolds, John Lawrence. *Secret Societies: Inside the Freemasons, the Yakuza, Skull and Bones, and the World's Most Notorious Secret Organizations.* New York, NY: Arcade Publishing, 2011.

Rhodes, Ron. *The End times in Chronological Order: A Complete Overview to Understanding Bible Prophecy.* Eugene, OR: Harvest House Publishers, 2012.

_____. *Unmasking the Antichrist: Dispelling the Myths, Discovering the Truth.* Eugene, OR: Harvest House Publishers, 2012.

Roberts, Scott Alan. *The Rise and Fall of the Nephilim: The Untold Story of Fallen Angels, Giants on the Earth, and Their Extraterrestrial Origins.* Pompton Plains, IL: New Page Books, 2012.

Rogerson, John. *Chronicle of the Old Testament Kings: The Reign-by-Reign Record of the Rulers of Ancient Israel.* London: Thames and Hudson, Ltd., 1999.

Rose Book of Bible Charts, Maps, and Timelines (10th anniversary edition). Peabody, MA: Rose Publishing LLC, 2005.

Rosenthal, Marvin. *The Prewrath Rapture of the Church.* Nashville, TN: Thomas Nelson Publishers, 1990.

Ross, Hugh. *Beyond the Cosmos: What Recent Discoveries in Astronomy and Physics Reveal about the Nature of God.* Colorado Springs, CO: NavPress, 1996.

Rossing, Barbara R. *The Rapture Exposed: The Message of Hope in the Book of Revelation.* New York, NY: Basic Books, 2004.

Rowling, J. K. *Harry Potter.* 7 vols. New York, NY: Scholastic Press, 1997.

Rutledge, Fleming. *The Battle for Middle Earth: Tolkien's Divine Design in The Lord of the Rings.* Grand Rapids, MI: William B. Eerdmans Publishing Co., 2004.

Ryle, James. *A Dream Come True.* Lake Mary, FL: Creation House, 1995.

Ryrie, Charles C. *Dispensationalism (Revised and Expanded).* Chicago, IL: Moody Publishers, 2007.

Sapp, David. *Sessions with Revelation: The Last Days of Evil.* Macon, GA: Smyth & Helwys Publishing Inc., 2014.

Sheets, Tim. *Angel Armies on Assignment.* Shippensburg, PA: Destiny Image Publishers, Inc., 2021.

Sims, Albert E. and Charles Dent. *Who's Who in the Bible.* New York, NY: Philosophical Society Library, Inc., 1960.

Sitchin, Zecharia. *There Were Giants on the Earth: God, Demi-gods, and Human Ancestry: The Evidence of Alien DNA.* Rochester, VT: Bear & Company, 2010.

Smith, Lee and Wes Bodin. *Religion in Human Culture: The Jewish Tradition.* Allen, TX: Argus Communications, 1978.

Smith, T.C. *Reading the Signs: A Sensible Approach to Revelation and Other Apocalyptic Writings.* Macon, GA: Smyth & Helwys Publishing, Inc., 1997.

Sora, Steven. *The Lost Treasure of the Knights Templar: Solving the Oak Island Mystery.* Rochester, VT: Destiny Books, 1999.

Sproul, R.C. *The Last Days According to Jesus.* Grand Rapids, MI: Baker Books, 1998.

Stewart, Randall. *American Literature and Christian Doctrine.* Baton Rouge, LA: Louisiana State University Press, 1958.

Stillman, William. *Under Spiritual Siege: How Ghosts and Demons Affect Us and How to Combat Them.* Atglen, PA: Schiffer Publishing, Inc., 2016.

Stone, Perry. *Deciphering End time Prophecy Codes.* Lake Mary, FL: Chrisma House, 2015.

Strong, James. *The New Strong's Concordance of the Bible.* pop. ed. Nashville, TN: Thomas Nelson Publishers, 1985.

Surburg, Raymond F. *Introduction to the Intertestamental Period.* Saint Louis, MO: Concordia Publishing House, 1975.

Swann, Eliza. *Auras: the Anatomy of the Aura.* New York, NY: St. Martin's Publishing Group, 2020.

Sweeney, Marvin A. *Reading Ezekiel: A Literary and Theological Commentary.* Macon, GA: Smyth & Helwys Publishing, Inc., 2013.

Tan, Paul Lee. *The Interpretation of Prophecy.* Rockville, MD: Assurance Publishers, 1974.

Tatford, Frederick A. *Daniel and His Prophecy: Studies in the Prophecy of Daniel.* reprint. Klock & Klock in the U. S. A., 1980.

Tenney, Merrill C., ed. *The Living Bible Encyclopedia in Story and Pictures.* New York, NY: H. S. Stuttmann Co., Inc., 1968.

Terry, Milton S. *Biblical Apocalyptics: A Study of the Most Notable Revelations of God and of Christ.* Grand Rapids, MI: Baker Book House, 1898.

Thorsen, Don. *An Exploration of Christian Theology.* Peabody, MA: Hendrickson Publishers, Inc., 2008.

Trafton, Joseph L. *Reading Revelation: A Literary and Theological Commentary.* vol. 12. Macon, GA: Smyth & Helwys, 2005.

Tsarfati, Amir. *The Day Approaching: An Israeli's Message of Warning and Hope for the Last Days.* Eugene, OR: Harvest House Publishers, 2020.

_____. *The Last Hour: An Israeli Insider Looks at the End times.* Bloomington, MN: Chosen Books, 2018.

Unger, Merrill F. *Archaeology and the Old Testament.* Grand Rapids, MI: Zondervan Publishing House, 1954.

von Daniken, Erich. *Chariots of the Gods?* New York, NY: Bantam Books, 1968.

Walter, Philippe. *Christian Mythology: Revelations of Pagan Origins.* Rochester, VT: Inner Traditions, 2003.

Walvoord, John F. *Major Bible Prophecies.* Grand Rapids, MI: Zondervan Publishers, 1991.

_____. *The Revelation of Jesus Christ.* Chicago, IL: Moody Press, 1966.

Ward, Kaari, ed. *Jesus and His Times.* Pleasantville, NY: Reader's Digest Association, 1987.

Weisburger, Bernard A., chief consultant. *Reader's Digest Family Encyclopedia of American History.* Pleasantville, NY: Reader's Digest Association, Inc., 1975.

Westminster Standards, The. Suwanee, GA: Great Commission Publications, 1978.

Whale, J.S. *Christian Doctrine.* Cambridge, UK: Cambridge University Press, 1966.

Whitson, William, trans. *The Life and Works of Flavius Josephus.* New York, NY: Holt, Rinehart, and Winston, (undated).

Willmington, H. L. *Willmington's Book of Bible Lists.* Philadelphia, PA: The Westminster Press, 1987.

Winward, Stephen. *A Guide to the Prophets.* Atlanta, GA: John Knox Press, 1976.

Wohlberg, Steve. *End Time Delusions: The Rapture, the Antichrist, Israel, and the End of the World.* Shippensburg, PA: Destiny Image Publishers, Inc., 2004.

Wood, Leon J. *A Survey of Israel's History.* Grand Rapids, MI: Academie Books, 1986.

Wright, G. Ernest, principal advisor. *Great People of the Bible and How They Lived.* Pleasantville, NY: Reader's Digest Association, 1974.

Zagami, Leo Lyon. *Confessions of an Illuminati: The Time of Revelations and Tribulation Leading Up to 2020* (Vol 2). San Francisco, CA: CCC Publications, 2016.

Other Works By The Author

Revealing the Revelation: A Guide to the Literature of the Apocalypse

Discernment from Daniel

101 Fun Fables (color illustrations by author)

Prophecy A–Z: The Complete Eschatological Dictionary

Operation Revelation: A Teen's Script to Earth's Final Curtain (with Jan Ledford)

Revelation for Regular Readers

Oracles from Olivet: The Eschatological Jesus